FamilyCircle®
All-time Favorite Recipes

FamilyCircle®
All-time
Favorite
Recipes

MORE THAN 600
DELICIOUS RECIPES
PLUS 200 PHOTOS

from the editors of
Family Circle

GRAMERCY BOOKS

New York

This 2006 edition is published by Gramercy Books, an imprint of Random House Value Publishing, by arrangement with Doubleday, divisions of Random House, Inc., New York.

Gramercy is a registered trademark and the colophon is a trademark of Random House, Inc.

Random House
New York • Toronto • London • Sydney • Auckland
www.randomhouse.com

Printed and bound in Thailand

A catalog record for this title is available from the Library of Congress.

ISBN 0-517-22825-4

10 9 8 7 6 5 4 3 2 1

For Roundtable Press:
Directors: Marsha Melnick,
Julie Merberg, Susan E. Meyer
Senior Editor: Carol Spier
Book Design: Vertigo Design
Production Editor: John Glenn
Copy Editor: Virginia Croft
Production: Bill Rose

For Family Circle Magazine:
Editor-in-chief: Susan Kelliher Ungaro
Creative director: Diane Lamphron
Executive editor: Barbara Winkler
Food director: Peggy Katalinich
Senior food editor: Diane Mogelever
Associate food editor: Julie Miltenberger
Editorial associate: Patricia Hoffman
Test kitchen assistant: Keisha Davis
Senior writer: Jonna M. Gallo
Recipe editor: David Ricketts
Nutritionist: Patty Santelli
Test kitchen: JoAnn Brett,
Lauren Huber, Michael Tyrrell,
Robert Yamarone

For G+J USA Publishing:
Books & Licensing Manager:
Tammy Palazzo
Books & Licensing Coordinator:
Eileen Lamadore

Cover photographs: front, Alan Richardson; spine, Kari Haavisto; back, Alan Richardson (top, middle, background) and Kari Haavisto (bottom); inside back flap, Ross Whitaker.
All other photography credits are found on page 512 and constitute an extension of this copyright page. The recipe for Cheesy Ziti and Meatballs, shown on page 2, appears on page 181. The recipe for Lemon Pound Cake, shown on page 3, appears on page 431.

MY FIRST COOKBOOK was a bridal shower present from Aunt Eileen. I was twenty-four and marrying a man who was a far better cook than I. It was a perfect gift. As Virginia Woolf said, "One cannot think well, love well, sleep well, if one has not dined well."

Two decades later, my first cookbook sports a noticeably tattered, worn binding. It's a sentimental favorite of mine, the one that is overstuffed with handwritten pass-along recipes, from my mother's pot roast and raisin scones to Emilie's chili and Linda's sprinkle nut cake.

Have you ever noticed how much better a friend's shared family recipe seems to taste? Perhaps it's because of the extra measure of care you put into trying to recreate that particular dish. Or perhaps it's the remembered flash of her smile when she handed you the recipe that gives it a place of honor in your cookbook file.

Those same good feelings and sense of history are what make our *Family Circle All-time Favorite Recipes* cookbook so special. From cover to cover, we share with you the magazine's most cherished and best-loved recipes. For almost seventy years, *Family Circle* has been a trusted source of creative and inspiring ideas for American women. It's my hope that the cookbook you now hold in your hands will become your personal favorite.

Susan Kelliher Ungaro, Editor-in-Chief

Contents

7

SINCE COMING to *Family Circle* in January 1994, I figure I've taken a bite out of more than 2,500 different dishes made in our test kitchen. And with each and every mouthful, I ask myself one simple question: Does it taste great? Of course, we're concerned that the instructions work, the technique is simple and the recipe makes good nutritional sense. But, the biggest issue is, does it taste great? Only when the answer is a resounding "yes" can the recipe make the grade. At the very least, it's tested three times, by three different people, to be certain the directions are clear and easy to follow.

Recipes evolve in a variety of ways. Sometimes I turn to one of our regular freelance contributors. On other occasions a hot-off-the-press cookbook provides inspiration. But most often the development takes place in our bright white test kitchen in midtown Manhattan. There Senior Food Editor Diane Mogelever hands out assignments, and Associate Food Editor Julie Miltenberger leads our crew in pursuit of excellence. Then, we present the finished dishes to the art and editorial staffs to make sure they look as good as they taste before they're ready to be photographed.

The book you have in your hands comprises the very best of the best recipes from the past five years, plus a handful of classics that have been around even longer. How to whittle all the possibilities down to a manageable number? When all was said and done, I kept coming back to those formulas and ideas that seemed to best represent what *Family*

Circle is all about—easy-on-you, family-pleasing meals and scrumptious, creative desserts. In fact, I'm getting hungry just thinking about them!

Now, for a few tips on using this cookbook. We indicate preparation and cooking times for each recipe. Prep time allows for any slicing, dicing or assembly required; cook time includes every minute devoted to boiling, simmering, sautéing, whatever. The per-serving nutritional information breaks out calories, protein, fat, sodium and cholesterol. When we thought you might enjoy using a recipe component, such as a sauce or pie crust, another way, we put that portion of the recipe into a separate paragraph and included its own nutritional analysis when relevant. In these instances the nutritional information for the main recipe also encompasses that of the subsidiary recipe.

Even as I write this, the constant flurry of activity that has accompanied putting out this book is winding down. But the job can't be considered done until you head to the supermarket, grocery list in hand, excited about the prospect of whipping up a batch of Texas Red Chili or Chocolate Strawberry Shortcake—just two of the recipes I predict will become your new favorites. But no matter which ones you and your family end up liking the most, may these pages soon show signs of frequent use and serve you well.

Peggy Katalinich, Food Director

Clockwise from top right:
Pineapple chipotle salsa *page 40,*
Salsa fresca *page 39,*
Roasted tomato salsa *page 41,*
Salsa verde *page 41,*
Black bean mango salsa *page 40*

Ravioli crisps *page 28*

THERE'S SOMETHING about appetizers that coaxes a culinary adventurer out of even the most timid of tasters. Perhaps it's the lack of commitment required; most hors d'oeuvres are only a bite or two. Or maybe it's the promise inherent in their timing—the stage is set for scrumptious food still to come.

Whether the gathering is a casual get-together or a pull-out-all-the-stops affair, the beauty of appetizers is that they can almost always be made ahead of time. For an informal party, a layered Tex-Mex dip or a Mediterranean take on always-popular deviled eggs will get things off to a great beginning. But if elegant is the order of the evening, you're

Here's where the littlest course can make the biggest impression.

destined to impress with luxe Shrimp Rémoulade or a stunning Stuffed Baby Brie. And in the end, the starters will always be remembered.

Appetizers

Curried deviled eggs

Makes 6 servings   *Prep* 15 minutes

Curry makes these special, but so would chili powder, ground cumin with a touch of cloves, or ground coriander.

Per serving
166 calories, 7 g protein, 15 g fat, 2 g carbohydrate, 182 mg sodium, 220 mg cholesterol.

6 hard-cooked eggs, shelled
⅓ cup mayonnaise
1 tablespoon curry powder
1 teaspoon grated lemon rind
1 teaspoon fresh lemon juice
½ teaspoon dry mustard
⅛ teaspoon ground red pepper (cayenne)
⅛ teaspoon salt
⅛ teaspoon black pepper

1. Halve eggs lengthwise. Remove yolks; press through a sieve into a small bowl. Stir in mayonnaise, curry powder, lemon rind, lemon juice, mustard, red pepper, salt and black pepper.

2. Spoon or pipe mixture (using a large plain tip) into egg-white halves. Place on a plate. Cover loosely with plastic wrap. Refrigerate until ready to serve.

Mediterranean deviled eggs

Makes 6 servings   *Prep* 15 minutes

The all-American picnic nibbler, with capers and olives.

Per serving
172 calories, 7 g protein, 16 g fat, 1 g carbohydrate, 250 mg sodium, 219 mg cholesterol.

6 hard-cooked eggs, shelled
⅓ cup mayonnaise
1 tablespoon finely chopped onion
1 tablespoon capers, rinsed, drained and chopped
2 teaspoons chopped pitted Kalamata olives
2 teaspoons Dijon mustard
¼ teaspoon hot-pepper sauce

1. Halve eggs lengthwise. Remove yolks; press through a sieve into a small bowl. Stir in mayonnaise, onion, capers, olives, mustard and hot-pepper sauce.

2. Spoon or pipe mixture (using a large plain tip) into egg-white halves. Place on a plate. Cover loosely with plastic wrap. Refrigerate until ready to serve.

Pear wraps

Makes 16 servings   *Prep* 15 minutes

Sweet, tangy and salty—all in one bite.

Per serving
42 calories, 3 g protein, 2 g fat, 3 g carbohydrate, 168 mg sodium, 8 mg cholesterol.

2 ripe pears
½ lemon
3 ounces blue cheese, crumbled
¼ pound thinly sliced honey-baked ham, cut into 1-inch-wide strips

Halve and core pears; cut each lengthwise into 8 equal wedges. Rub cut surfaces with lemon. Press a little cheese into cored cavity of each pear wedge. Wrap each wedge in a ham strip. Secure each with a wooden pick.

Endive cups

Makes about 24 servings   *Prep* 25 minutes   *Refrigerate* 15 minutes

For variety on your appetizer tray, pipe some of the cheese filling into split, lightly blanched snow peas.

Per serving

21 calories, 1 g protein, 2 g fat, 0 g carbohydrate, 62 mg sodium, 5 mg cholesterol.

3 ounces Port-wine cheese, at room temperature

2 ounces less-fat cream cheese, at room temperature

3 heads Belgian endive

24 sprigs fresh parsley

1. Beat together Port-wine cheese and cream cheese in a small bowl until creamy. Spoon mixture into a pastry bag fitted with the star tip.

2. Cut base from each head of endive; separate into leaves. Pipe a small amount of cheese into base of each leaf. Refrigerate 15 minutes. Garnish each "cup" with parsley.

Bruschetta

Makes 12 servings   *Prep* 25 minutes   *Bake* at 500° for 3 to 5 minutes

The suggested topping in this recipe is one of the easiest. But if you're craving a slightly more robust flavor, try adding pieces of prosciutto and small cubes of mozzarella.

Per serving

126 calories, 3 g protein, 7 g fat, 13 g carbohydrate, 211 mg sodium, 2 mg cholesterol.

Seasoning oil

⅓ cup olive oil

4 cloves garlic, crushed

6 fresh basil leaves, chopped

⅛ teaspoon crushed red-pepper flakes

Tomato topping

1½ pounds plum tomatoes, chopped

½ cup chopped fresh basil

1 tablespoon balsamic vinegar

1 tablespoon olive oil

½ teaspoon salt

¼ teaspoon black pepper

1 loaf French bread (8 ounces), split horizontally

Small fresh basil leaves for garnish

1. Prepare seasoning oil: Heat oil in a small skillet over medium-low heat. Add garlic, basil and red-pepper flakes; cook, stirring, 5 to 7 minutes or until garlic is golden. Cool the oil and strain.

2. Meanwhile, prepare tomato topping: Stir together tomatoes, basil, vinegar, oil, salt and pepper in a large bowl.

3. Heat oven to 500°.

4. Brush cut sides of split bread with about 2 tablespoons seasoning oil. Place on a baking sheet. Bake in heated 500° oven 3 to 5 minutes or until golden.

5. Slice toasted bread into 2-inch widths and arrange on a large serving platter. Spoon tomato topping over and garnish with fresh basil leaves.

Tortellini en brochette

Makes 20 servings   *Prep* 30 minutes   *Cook* 8 minutes

Actually, any creamy-style bottled salad dressing is a good starting point for the dip: Italian and blue cheese are delicious picks.

Per serving
146 calories, 5 g protein,
10 g fat, 9 g carbohydrate,
233 mg sodium,
33 mg cholesterol.

1 package (9 ounces) refrigerated spinach-cheese tortellini
1 package (9 ounces) refrigerated plain cheese tortellini

Parmesan dip
1½ cups ranch-style salad dressing

¾ cup grated Parmesan cheese
2 tablespoons chopped fresh parsley
2 cloves garlic, finely chopped
Salt (optional)
¼ teaspoon black pepper

1. Cook tortellini in a large pot of lightly salted boiling water until al dente, firm but tender. Drain; cool under cold running water.

2. Prepare Parmesan dip: Combine dressing, Parmesan cheese, parsley, garlic, salt if desired and pepper in a small bowl. Refrigerate until ready to serve.

3. Skewer tortellini on wooden picks; place on a serving plate. Serve with dip.

Cheese straws

Makes 24 servings   *Prep* 15 minutes   *Bake* at 400° for 12 to 15 minutes

Before folding the pastry over into thirds, sprinkle evenly with caraway seeds for added crunch.

Per serving
159 calories, 5 g protein,
11 g fat, 10 g carbohydrate,
275 mg sodium,
15 mg cholesterol.

2 cups grated Parmesan cheese
2 teaspoons paprika
¾ teaspoon salt
¾ teaspoon ground red pepper (cayenne)

1 package (17¼ ounces) frozen puff pastry sheets, thawed according to package directions
1 egg, lightly beaten

1. Combine Parmesan cheese, paprika, salt and red pepper in a small bowl.

2. On a lightly floured surface with a rolling pin, roll one pastry sheet into an 18 x 8-inch rectangle. Brush surface with egg. Sprinkle with ½ cup cheese mixture; press mixture into sheet with rolling pin. Turn sheet over. Repeat with egg and cheese mixture. Starting from one 8-inch end, fold one-third of dough over middle one-third; fold opposite one-third over both to make an 8 x 6-inch rectangle. Repeat with remaining sheet. Cut each sheet lengthwise into twelve ½-inch-wide strips.

3. Heat oven to 400°.

4. Place strips ½ inch apart on ungreased baking sheets, twisting each strip twice and pressing ends onto sheet to prevent strips from uncurling during baking. Bake in heated 400° oven 12 to 15 minutes or until puffed and golden. Transfer to wire racks to cool.

Cheese straws
opposite
**BBQ chicken
quesadillas**
page 27

Salmon canapés

Makes 16 servings *Prep* 15 minutes *Bake* at 400° for 8 minutes

Penny saver: If you're buying the salmon in a deli where they slice their own, ask for the trimmings, which are usually less expensive.

Per serving
80 calories, 4 g protein, 4 g fat, 8 g carbohydrate, 212 mg sodium, 8 mg cholesterol.

1 loaf Italian bread (18 inches), cut into about 32 slices ½ inch thick
2 tablespoons butter, melted
1 tablespoon honey mustard
2 tablespoons sour cream
2 heads Bibb lettuce
8 ounces smoked salmon, sliced
1 bunch fresh dill

1. Heat oven to 400°.

2. Lightly brush both sides of bread slices with melted butter. Place in a single layer on a baking sheet. Bake in heated 400° oven 8 minutes or until golden brown, turning each slice over after first 4 minutes.

3. Stir together honey mustard and sour cream in a small bowl. Brush one side of each piece of toast with mustard mixture. Arrange toast pieces, mustard side up, on a serving platter.

4. Carefully select blemish-free inner leaves from the heads of Bibb lettuce. (Reserve remainder of heads for salad.) Trim leaves so they fit neatly on top of bread slices. Place 1 leaf on each bread slice.

5. Cut salmon into 2½ x 1-inch strips. Roll up each strip loosely and shape to form a rose. Place 1 rose on each lettuce leaf. Garnish with dill.

Smoked trout canapés

Makes 16 servings *Prep* 15 minutes *Bake* at 400° for 8 minutes

Thin slices of party rye bread or focaccia and whole-wheat crackers also make tasty "little plates" for the trout.

Per serving
72 calories, 4 g protein, 2 g fat, 8 g carbohydrate, 182 mg sodium, 8 mg cholesterol.

1 loaf Italian bread (18 inches), cut into about 32 slices ½ inch thick
2 tablespoons butter, melted
3 tablespoons sour cream
1 teaspoon bottled horseradish
⅛ teaspoon salt
2 heads Bibb lettuce
6 to 8 ounces smoked trout fillet, skinned, bones removed, and cut into 1-inch pieces
¼ sweet red pepper, cored, seeded and cut into ½-inch diamonds

1. Heat oven to 400°.

2. Lightly brush both sides of bread slices with melted butter. Place in a single layer on a baking sheet. Bake in heated 400° oven 8 minutes or until golden brown, turning each slice over after first 4 minutes.

3. Stir together sour cream, horseradish and salt in a small bowl.

4. Carefully select blemish-free inner leaves from the heads of Bibb lettuce. (Reserve remainder of heads for salad.) Trim leaves so they fit neatly on top of bread slices. Place 1 leaf on each bread slice.

5. Top each with a piece of trout and a dollop of horseradish mixture. Garnish each canapé with a sweet red pepper diamond.

Shrimp with cocktail sauce

Makes 6 servings   *Prep* 10 minutes   *Cook* 2 to 4 minutes

If you're in a real pinch, doctor up prepared cocktail sauce with a squirt of lemon juice, a splash of hot-pepper sauce and a dash of Worcestershire sauce— all to taste.

Per serving
169 calories, 24 g protein, 2 g fat, 13 g carbohydrate, 725 mg sodium, 173 mg cholesterol.

1½ pounds medium shrimp, in shells
Seasoned bouillon (see box, below)

Cocktail sauce
½ cup ketchup
½ cup chili sauce

2 to 3 tablespoons bottled horseradish
1 tablespoon fresh lemon juice
½ teaspoon Worcestershire sauce
½ teaspoon hot-pepper sauce

1. Cook shrimp in seasoned bouillon. Peel and devein.

2. Prepare cocktail sauce: Stir together ketchup, chili sauce, horseradish, lemon juice, Worcestershire sauce and hot-pepper sauce.

3. Serve sauce as a dip with cooled shrimp.

Make-ahead tip: Both shrimp and sauce can be prepared a day in advance and then refrigerated, covered.

Poaching shrimp

THE BEST WAY to prepare shrimp for canapés or salads is to boil them in their shells in a seasoned bouillon. Cook up to 2 pounds shrimp using the following method, doubling the recipe as needed.

In a large saucepan, combine 3 quarts water, rind and juice of ½ lemon, 1 sprig parsley, 2 crushed cloves garlic, 1 teaspoon salt, 6 black peppercorns and 1 bay leaf. Bring to boiling. Add shrimp; return to boiling; cook 1 minute or until pink and cooked through. Drain; rinse under cold running water. Peel and devein shrimp (see page 220). Use in any recipe calling for cooked shrimp.

Shrimp rémoulade

Makes 6 servings   *Prep* 15 minutes   *Cook* 2 to 4 minutes

Make this sauce a day ahead and refrigerate so the flavors have a chance to mellow. For a switch, substitute chopped fresh cilantro for the parsley.

Per serving
187 calories, 15 g protein,
13 g fat, 3 g carbohydrate,
314 mg sodium,
135 mg cholesterol.

1½ pounds large shrimp, in shells
   Seasoned bouillon (see box, page 17)

Rémoulade sauce
2 tablespoons tarragon vinegar
2 tablespoons Dijon mustard
2 tablespoons ketchup
1 tablespoon bottled horseradish
2 teaspoons paprika

2 cloves garlic, finely chopped
½ teaspoon black pepper
¼ teaspoon coarse kosher salt
¼ teaspoon hot-pepper sauce
⅔ cup olive oil
1 cup chopped green onion
1 tablespoon chopped fresh parsley

2 lemons, thinly sliced, for garnish

1. Cook shrimp in seasoned bouillon. Peel and devein.

2. Prepare rémoulade sauce: Combine vinegar, mustard, ketchup, horseradish, paprika, garlic, pepper, salt and hot-pepper sauce in a blender or food processor. Whirl until pureed. With motor running, gradually pour in oil in a slow, steady stream. Pour into a serving bowl. Stir in green onion and parsley.

3. Place shrimp on a plate and garnish with lemon slices. Serve with sauce.

Shrimp rémoulade

Candied walnuts

Makes 4½ cups   *Prep* 5 minutes   *Bake* at 350° for 20 to 25 minutes

Store in a tightly covered container at room temperature for up to 3 weeks. The citrus flavor actually improves with time.

Per ¼ cup
185 calories, 4 g protein, 16 g fat, 11 g carbohydrate, 64 mg sodium, 0 mg cholesterol.

¾ cup firmly packed brown sugar
½ teaspoon salt
1 teaspoon grated orange rind

2 tablespoons fresh orange juice
1 pound walnut halves

1. Heat oven to 350°. Line a large jelly-roll pan with aluminum foil. Coat with nonstick cooking spray.

2. Combine brown sugar, salt, orange rind and orange juice in a large bowl. Add walnuts; toss to coat. Spread walnuts evenly over prepared pan. Bake in heated 350° oven 20 to 25 minutes or until dark brown and bubbly, stirring halfway through.

3. Meanwhile, coat a large piece of aluminum foil with nonstick cooking spray. Remove nuts from oven. Immediately spread on prepared foil, separating nuts with 2 forks. Cool completely. Store in an airtight container.

To microwave walnuts: Cook coated walnuts in a large microwave-safe dish on 100% power 8 to 10 minutes, stirring every 2 minutes, until dark brown and bubbly. Proceed with step 3, above.

Caramel popcorn mix

Makes 14 cups   *Prep* 10 minutes   *Cook* 5 minutes   *Bake* at 250° for 1 hour

Remember trail mix? This recipe turns it into a caramel treat, much improved—the ideal snack. Store in an airtight container for up to 1 week.

Per cup
246 calories, 4 g protein, 13 g fat, 32 g carbohydrate, 214 mg sodium, 18 mg cholesterol.

10 cups popped popcorn
1 cup roasted peanuts
2 cups wheat cereal squares
1 cup salted wheat crackers, broken into bite-size pieces
½ cup (1 stick) butter

1 cup firmly packed dark-brown sugar
½ cup light corn syrup
¼ teaspoon baking soda
½ teaspoon vanilla

1. Heat oven to 250°.

2. Combine popcorn, peanuts, cereal and crackers in a large roasting pan.

3. Melt butter in a medium-size saucepan over low heat. Add brown sugar and corn syrup. Bring mixture to boiling, stirring constantly. Gently boil without stirring 5 minutes. Remove from heat. Stir in baking soda and vanilla until smooth. Pour over popcorn mixture; toss to coat evenly.

4. Bake in heated 250° oven 1 hour, stirring every 15 minutes. Remove from oven and cool. Break popcorn into small clusters.

Cajun popcorn

Makes 10 cups   *Prep* 15 minutes   *Bake* at 300° for 10 minutes

Experiment with other spice mixtures, such as cumin and coriander, or cinnamon and nutmeg.

Per cup

73 calories, 1 g protein, 5 g fat, 7 g carbohydrate, 108 mg sodium, 12 mg cholesterol.

½ cup unpopped popcorn, (4 ounces)
¼ cup (½ stick) unsalted butter, melted
1 teaspoon paprika

½ teaspoon onion powder
½ teaspoon garlic powder
⅛ teaspoon ground red pepper (cayenne)
½ teaspoon salt

1. Heat oven to 300°.

2. Pop popcorn according to package directions. Melt butter in a small saucepan over low heat. Transfer hot popcorn to a large bowl and immediately pour butter over it.

3. Combine paprika, onion powder, garlic powder, red pepper and salt in a small bowl. Sprinkle paprika mixture over popcorn; toss to coat popcorn evenly. Spread popcorn in a single layer on a baking sheet.

4. Bake popcorn in heated 300° oven 10 minutes. Serve warm.

Sugar and spice nuts

Makes 5 cups   *Prep* 10 minutes   *Bake* at 375° for 20 minutes

It's always nice to arrive at a friend's house for dinner carrying a gift. Pack some of the nuts into a pretty jar, and another invitation will almost be guaranteed.

Per ¼ cup

219 calories, 7 g protein, 18 g fat, 12 g carbohydrate, 51 mg sodium, 0 mg cholesterol.

2 egg whites
1 cup whole almonds, with skins
1 cup pecan halves
1 cup walnut halves
1 cup cashews

1 cup unsalted peanuts
½ cup sugar
2 teaspoons ground cinnamon
¼ teaspoon ground allspice
⅛ teaspoon ground nutmeg

1. Heat oven to 375°. Grease a 15 x 10 x 1-inch jelly-roll pan.

2. Beat egg whites in a large bowl until very frothy. Stir in almonds, pecans, walnuts, cashews, peanuts, ¼ cup sugar, cinnamon, allspice and nutmeg; toss until nuts are evenly coated. Spread nuts in an even layer on prepared pan.

3. Bake in heated 375° oven 10 minutes or until coating is partially set. Stir in remaining ¼ cup sugar until nuts are well coated. Bake 10 minutes longer or until nuts are golden brown. Transfer pan to wire rack to cool completely. Store in an airtight container up to 1 month.

Artichoke puffs

Makes 18 servings *Prep* 15 minutes *Cook* 8 minutes

Bake at 450° for 10 minutes; at 400° for 20 minutes; then at 375° for 10 minutes

Serve hot or at room temperature—your choice. And remember, these are lower in fat than the standard version, so help yourself to an extra.

Per serving
70 calories, 4 g protein, 2 g fat, 8 g carbohydrate, 74 mg sodium, 26 mg cholesterol.

1 cup skim milk
2 tablespoons vegetable oil
¼ teaspoon salt
1 cup all-purpose flour
2 eggs
3 egg whites

Artichoke filling
1 package (9 ounces) frozen artichoke hearts
2 ounces less-fat cream cheese
½ small onion, chopped
2 teaspoons fresh lemon juice
⅛ teaspoon hot-pepper sauce

1. Heat oven to 450°. Coat baking sheets with nonstick cooking spray.

2. Heat milk, oil and salt in a medium-size heavy saucepan. As soon as mixture comes to boiling, remove from heat. Immediately stir in flour with a wooden spoon; beat until dough pulls away from sides of pan.

3. Beat in eggs and egg whites, one at a time, beating after each addition, until mixture is smooth and glossy. Place mounds of dough (about the size of a large walnut) on prepared baking sheets, leaving 1½ inches between mounds. Flatten with moistened fingertips to ½-inch thickness.

4. Bake in heated 450° oven 10 minutes. Lower oven temperature to 400°. Bake 20 minutes more or until puffed, golden and lightly crusty. Remove puffs from sheets to wire racks to cool. Lower oven temperature to 375°.

5. Meanwhile, prepare artichoke filling: Place artichoke hearts in a medium-size saucepan with 2 tablespoons water. Cover and cook over medium heat 4 minutes. Drain. Combine cream cheese, onion, lemon juice, hot-pepper sauce and drained artichoke hearts in a food processor. Whirl until smooth and blended.

6. Cut tops from puffs. Spoon in filling. Replace tops.

7. To heat, place puffs on a baking sheet. Cover lightly with aluminum foil. Bake in heated 375° oven 10 minutes.

Make-ahead tip: The baked puffs can be frozen. To reheat, place frozen on a baking sheet. Cover lightly with foil. Bake in heated 375° oven 20 minutes.

Fried zucchini sticks

Makes 8 servings   *Prep* 10 minutes   *Chill* 10 minutes   *Deep-fry* 8 to 12 minutes

Want an easy dip for the sticks? Set out little bowls of different flavored jarred pasta sauces, such as roasted sweet red pepper, mushroom, hot red pepper and simple marinara. Don't forget the napkins!

Per serving
287 calories, 6 g protein,
21 g fat, 20 g carbohydrate,
290 mg sodium,
54 mg cholesterol.

½ cup all-purpose flour
½ teaspoon salt
2 eggs
¼ cup milk
1¼ cups dry seasoned bread crumbs

1½ pounds zucchini, cut into
2½ x ½ x ½-inch sticks
Vegetable oil for frying
Jarred tomato sauce for serving
(optional)

1. Combine flour and salt on a sheet of waxed paper. Combine eggs and milk in a small bowl. Place bread crumbs on a second sheet of waxed paper. Coat zucchini with flour mixture; dip in egg mixture; coat with bread crumbs; place on a baking sheet. Place sheet in freezer 10 minutes.

2. Pour oil into an electric skillet or a regular large skillet to a depth of ½ inch. Set electric skillet at 350° or heat oil in regular skillet over medium heat until oil registers 350° on a deep-fat thermometer.

3. Working in 4 batches, add zucchini to hot oil; fry, turning with a slotted metal spoon, until golden brown, 2 to 3 minutes. Remove with slotted spoon to paper toweling to drain. Keep hot in a warm oven until all are fried. Serve with tomato sauce if you wish.

Cheese toasts

Makes 24 servings   *Prep* 10 minutes   *Bake* at 375° for 10 minutes

Try these other "bases" for the toasts: toasted pita triangles, whole-wheat crackers or Scandinavian flat crackers.

Per serving
55 calories, 2 g protein,
4 g fat, 3 g carbohydrate,
84 mg sodium,
6 mg cholesterol.

4 slices bacon, chopped, cooked
    until crisp and drained
⅓ cup chopped pitted ripe black
    olives
2 tablespoons chopped fresh chives
2 teaspoons chopped fresh parsley

¼ cup mayonnaise
1 teaspoon Worcestershire sauce
    Dash hot-pepper sauce
12 slices party rye bread
1 cup shredded Swiss cheese

1. Heat oven to 375°.

2. Mix bacon, olives, chives, parsley, mayonnaise, Worcestershire sauce, and hot-pepper sauce. Spread on bread slices; top with cheese. Place on an ungreased baking sheet.

3. Bake in heated 375° oven 10 minutes to melt cheese. Cut into triangles. Serve immediately.

Mushroom pinwheels

Makes 8 dozen   *Prep* 20 minutes   *Cook* 15 minutes   *Refrigerate* 1 hour   *Bake* at 400° for 15 minutes

Portabella, cremini and shiitake are a few tasty choices for the mushroom filling, as well as the usual white button.

Per pinwheel
37 calories, 1 g protein,
3 g fat, 3 g carbohydrate,
25 mg sodium,
4 mg cholesterol.

5 tablespoons butter
18 ounces fresh mushrooms (your choice of variety), finely chopped
1 large onion, finely chopped (2 cups)
2 tablespoons all-purpose flour
1½ teaspoons dried thyme
½ teaspoon salt
¼ teaspoon black pepper
1 teaspoon fresh lemon juice
1½ packages (17¼ ounces each) frozen puff pastry (3 sheets), thawed according to package directions
1 egg, lightly beaten
1 tablespoon water

1. Melt butter in a large skillet over medium heat. Add mushrooms and onion; cook, stirring, 13 minutes or until liquid evaporates and mushrooms are tender. Stir in flour, thyme, salt, pepper and lemon juice. Cook, stirring, 2 minutes or until thickened. Cool.

2. Unfold 1 pastry sheet on a lightly floured surface. Spread one-third of mushroom mixture over pastry; roll up from each end toward the center. Repeat with remaining pastry and mushroom mixture. Cover; chill 1 hour.

3. Heat oven to 400°.

4. Cut chilled pastry crosswise into ¼-inch-thick slices, about 32 slices per roll. Place, cut side down, 1 inch apart on ungreased baking sheets. Stir egg and water in a small bowl. Brush slices with egg wash without letting wash drip down sides.

5. Bake in heated 400° oven 15 minutes or until golden. Serve warm.

Make-ahead tip: Unbaked, uncut filled rolls can be refrigerated a day ahead; then cut and bake, steps 4 and 5 above, 15 to 18 minutes. Or unbaked rolls can be frozen up to 3 weeks; thaw in refrigerator, cut and bake as above.

Mushroom pinwheels

Chile mushroom caps

Makes 24 servings   *Prep* 30 minutes   *Cook* 15 minutes   *Bake* at 350° for 10 minutes

Monterey Jack, Colby and even Fontina are nice cheese alternatives to mix into the filling.

Per serving
111 calories, 7 g protein,
9 g fat, 2 g carbohydrate,
169 mg sodium,
27 mg cholesterol.

4 slices bacon
24 medium mushrooms
  (1½ pounds)
1 tablespoon butter
¼ cup finely chopped onion
1 clove garlic, finely chopped
⅓ cup finely chopped sweet
  red pepper
2 to 3 pickled jalapeño chiles,
  seeded and finely chopped
½ cup shredded cheddar cheese
  (2 ounces)
¼ cup chopped fresh parsley

1. Cook bacon in a skillet until almost crisp. Remove bacon from skillet; chop. Drain fat from skillet.

2. Remove stems from mushrooms. Finely chop two-thirds of stems. (Save stems from remaining mushrooms for soup making or other uses.) Cook mushroom caps in boiling water 1 minute. Drain; rinse under cold water. Drain on paper toweling.

3. Heat oven to 350°.

4. Melt butter in skillet. Add chopped mushroom stems, onion, and garlic; cook 5 minutes. Add sweet red pepper and jalapeños; cook 3 minutes. Cool. Stir in bacon, cheese and parsley. Spoon mixture into mushroom caps. Place on a baking sheet.

5. Bake in heated 350° oven 10 minutes or until cheese is melted.

Fried stuffed jalapeños

Makes 24 servings   *Prep* 25 minutes   *Deep-fry* 2 to 3 minutes per batch

For dipping, serve these with one of our homemade salsas (pages 39–41) or a jarred version.

Per serving
108 calories, 4 g protein,
6 g fat, 6 g carbohydrate,
125 mg sodium,
34 mg cholesterol.

24 fresh medium jalapeño chiles
  (1¼ pounds)
1½ cups shredded cheddar cheese
6 cups vegetable oil for frying
3 eggs, slightly beaten
2 cups dry plain bread crumbs

1. Wearing plastic gloves, cut stem end off jalapeños with a paring knife. Carefully remove seeds and white membrane.

2. Stuff chiles with cheese.

3. Fill a large saucepan with oil, making sure to leave at least 6 inches between top of oil and top of pan. Heat oil over medium heat until oil registers 375° on a deep-fat thermometer.

4. Meanwhile, place eggs in a small bowl. Place crumbs in a shallow bowl.

5. Drop 4 chiles into eggs; toss to coat. Using a fork, lift one chile at a time out of eggs, shaking off excess. Drop into crumbs; toss to coat. Place on a baking sheet. Repeat 5 more times with remaining chiles. When all chiles are coated, set aside 15 minutes to set up and dry.

6. With a slotted spoon, slip chiles, 5 or 6 at a time, into hot oil. Fry 2 to 3 minutes or until golden. Remove to a platter lined with paper toweling to drain. Keep hot in a warm oven. Repeat with remaining chiles. Serve immediately.

Layered nachos

Makes 12 servings   *Prep* 20 minutes   *Cook* 10 minutes   *Bake* at 400° for 7 to 8 minutes

Save on prep time: open a jar of chunky salsa instead of making our homemade version in the recipe.

Per serving
315 calories, 14 g protein, 15 g fat, 32 g carbohydrate, 565 mg sodium, 27 mg cholesterol.

Beef filling
1 teaspoon vegetable oil
½ pound lean ground beef
1 clove garlic, finely chopped
1½ teaspoons chili powder
¼ teaspoon ground cumin
¼ teaspoon salt

Tomato salsa
½ pound plum tomatoes, seeded and chopped
¼ cup finely chopped sweet green pepper

¼ cup finely chopped red onion
1 to 2 jalapeño chiles, seeded and chopped
¼ teaspoon salt
2 avocados
1 tablespoon fresh lemon juice

12 corn tortillas (6-inch)
2 cans (16 ounces each) refried beans
6 ounces cheddar cheese, shredded (1½ cups)

Handling hot peppers

When working with fresh chile peppers, wear rubber gloves to keep the stinging oils from touching your fingers—and avoid touching your face.

1. Prepare beef filling: Heat oil in a small skillet over medium heat. Add beef and garlic and sauté until browned, 5 minutes, breaking beef up with a wooden spoon. Stir in chili powder, cumin and salt; cook 1 to 2 minutes.

2. Prepare salsa: Mix tomatoes, green pepper, red onion, jalapeños and salt in a small bowl. Set aside.

3. Peel, pit and mash avocados. Place in a small bowl. Squeeze lemon juice over avocados but don't mix in; cover with plastic wrap and set aside.

4. Heat oven to 400°.

5. Cut tortillas into quarters. Place in a single layer on ungreased baking sheets. Spoon 1 tablespoon refried beans on each piece, then top with 2 teaspoons beef filling and 2 to 3 teaspoons cheese.

6. Bake in heated 400° oven 7 to 8 minutes or until cheese is melted and edges are slightly crisp. Place on a serving platter. Mix lemon juice into mashed avocados. Top nachos with avocado and salsa. Serve immediately.

Caramelized onion quesadillas

Makes 4 servings   *Prep* 5 minutes   *Cook* 17 minutes   *Bake* at 400° for 8 minutes

Add a tossed green salad and this appetizer becomes a delicious lunch. Speedy snack? Make ahead, refrigerate and then reheat in a microwave oven.

Per serving
448 calories, 20 g protein, 26 g fat, 35 g carbohydrate, 601 mg sodium, 55 mg cholesterol.

1 tablespoon olive oil
1 red onion, halved lengthwise and thinly sliced crosswise
4 green onions, sliced
3 cloves garlic, chopped
¾ teaspoon ground cumin
¼ teaspoon dried oregano, crumbled
1 tablespoon fresh lime juice

4 flour tortillas (10-inch)
1 cup shredded pepper-Jack cheese (4 ounces)
1 cup shredded sharp cheddar cheese (4 ounces)
Salsa Fresca (recipe, page 39) or jarred salsa (optional)
Sour cream (optional)

1. Heat oil in a skillet over medium-low heat. Add red onion, green onions and garlic; cook, covered, stirring occasionally, until softened, about 15 minutes.

2. Add cumin and oregano; cook, uncovered, 1 minute. Remove from heat. Stir in lime juice.

3. Heat oven to 400°.

4. Place 2 tortillas side by side on an ungreased baking sheet. Divide onion mixture between tortillas; spread evenly over surface. Sprinkle each with Jack cheese and cheddar cheese. Top each with a remaining tortilla.

5. Bake in heated 400° oven 8 minutes or until heated through and tortillas are golden. Let stand 5 minutes. Cut each quesadilla into 6 wedges. Garnish with salsa and sour cream if you wish. Serve immediately.

Caramelized onion quesadillas

BBQ chicken quesadillas

Makes 8 servings   *Prep* 20 minutes   *Bake* at 450° for 8 minutes

Monterey Jack cheese is an excellent substitute for the cheddar in this recipe. To make things even easier, use the jalapeño-flavored version and omit the can of chopped green chiles.

Shown on page 15.

Per serving
218 calories, 15 g protein, 9 g fat, 20 g carbohydrate, 541 mg sodium, 42 mg cholesterol.

8 flour tortillas (8-inch)
1 can (4 ounces) chopped mild green chiles
2 cups shredded ready-to-eat barbecued chicken
½ cup shredded extra-sharp cheddar cheese
½ cup bottled taco sauce
1 cup jarred salsa
¼ cup sour cream
Cilantro sprigs for garnish

1. Heat oven to 450°.

2. Place 1 tortilla on a large baking sheet. Spread with 1 tablespoon chiles. Top with one-quarter of the chicken, cheese and taco sauce. Place another tortilla on top. Repeat with remaining tortillas, chiles, chicken, cheese and sauce, to make a total of 4 quesadillas.

3. Bake in heated 450° oven 8 minutes or until tortillas are golden and cheese is melted. Let stand 5 minutes. Cut each quesadilla into quarters. Garnish with salsa, sour cream and cilantro. Serve immediately.

Tasty pizza squares

Makes 15 servings   *Prep* 30 minutes   *Bake* crust at 425° for 10 to 12 minutes; pizza at 425° for 5 to 10 minutes

Varied toppings make this quick pizza a party favorite. For an appealing presentation, arrange each topping in its own separate strip.

Per serving
122 calories, 4 g protein, 6 g fat, 11 g carbohydrate, 251 mg sodium, 12 mg cholesterol.

1 or 2 dry-pack sun-dried tomatoes
1 tube (10 ounces) refrigerated pizza dough
½ cup jarred marinara sauce or pizza sauce
⅓ cup bottled pesto sauce
1½ cups shredded mozzarella cheese (6 ounces)
¼ cup sliced canned ripe olives
¼ cup sliced green onion
1 to 2 jalapeño chiles, seeded and chopped

1. Heat oven to 425°. Grease a 15 x 10 x 1-inch jelly-roll pan.

2. Soak sun-dried tomatoes in very hot water to cover in a bowl until softened, about 5 minutes. Drain. Chop; you should have about 1½ tablespoons.

3. Roll dough onto prepared baking pan. Press dough to sides of pan. Bake in heated 425° oven 10 to 12 minutes or until golden brown.

4. Top half of the dough with marinara sauce and the other half with pesto sauce. Top with cheese, olives, green onion, sun-dried tomatoes and jalapeño. Bake in heated 425° oven 5 to 10 minutes or until cheese melts. Cut into 15 squares. Serve warm.

Focaccia florentine

Makes 12 servings   *Prep* 40 minutes   *Rise* 30 minutes   *Bake* at 400° for 20 to 25 minutes

With a glass of wine and an appetizer slice of spinach-and-bacon-topped focaccia, your party is off to a great start. A special touch: Sprinkle kosher or coarse salt over the focaccia just before baking.

Per serving
220 calories, 10 g protein,
9 g fat, 26 g carbohydrate,
440 mg sodium,
19 mg cholesterol.

3 tablespoons olive oil
2 packages (10 ounces each) frozen chopped spinach, thawed and squeezed dry
3 ounces Canadian bacon, diced
1¼ teaspoons salt
3 cups all-purpose flour
1 envelope fast-rising dry yeast
1 cup water
1½ cups shredded Fontina cheese

1. Heat 2 tablespoons oil in a skillet. Add spinach, bacon, and ¼ teaspoon salt; sauté 5 minutes. Remove from heat.

2. Combine 1 cup flour, yeast and remaining salt in a bowl.

3. Heat water and remaining oil in a saucepan until very warm (125° to 130°). Gradually beat water mixture into flour mixture. Beat in 1½ cups flour with a wooden spoon, ½ cup at a time, to make a soft dough.

4. Knead dough on a floured surface until smooth and elastic, 10 minutes, working in remaining flour as needed to prevent sticking. Shape into a ball. Cover; let rest 10 minutes.

5. Grease a 15 x 10 x 1-inch jelly-roll pan. Roll dough out on floured surface into a 15 x 10-inch rectangle. Fit into prepared pan, gently pushing dough up into corners. With a finger, make indentations all over surface of dough, pressing almost to bottom of pan. Scatter spinach mixture over top. Sprinkle with cheese. Cover with plastic wrap. Let rise in a warm place until almost doubled in bulk, 30 minutes.

6. Heat oven to 400°. Bake focaccia 20 to 25 minutes or until lightly browned. Cut into 12 pieces. Serve warm.

Ravioli crisps

Makes about 24 servings   *Prep* 5 minutes   *Deep-fry* 2 to 3 minutes per batch

Who would have thought—ravioli served as a finger food!
Shown on page 11.

Per serving
82 calories, 2 g protein,
4 g fat, 10 g carbohydrate,
158 mg sodium,
6 mg cholesterol.

4 cups vegetable oil
1 package (16 ounces), fresh or frozen small cheese ravioli (about 48), thawed and patted dry
2 cups marinara sauce, homemade (recipe, page 157) or jarred
2 tablespoons chopped fresh basil

1. Fill a large saucepan with oil, making sure there is at least 6 inches between top of oil and top of pan. Heat oil over medium heat until it registers 300° on a deep-fat thermometer. Line a baking sheet with paper toweling.

2. With a metal slotted spoon, carefully slip 8 ravioli at a time into hot oil to avoid overcrowding; fry 1 to 2 minutes or until ravioli turn light brown. Adjust heat as needed to maintain oil temperature. With slotted spoon, remove ravioli to towel-lined sheet to drain. Keep hot in a warm oven until all are deep-fried.

3. Heat together marinara sauce and basil in a small saucepan 2 to 3 minutes or until hot. Pour into a small serving dish. Serve alongside ravioli.

Make-ahead tip: Ravioli can be fried up to 2 hours ahead. To serve, place on a baking sheet and reheat in a heated 400° oven 5 to 10 minutes or until hot.

Spinach triangles

Makes 30 servings   *Prep* 25 minutes   *Cook* 3 minutes   *Bake* at 375° for 15 minutes

From the taste, you would never guess these phyllo pastries check in as a low-fat nibble. The cook's secrets? Using reduced-fat feta cheese and omitting the usual butter for layering the phyllo sheets.

Per serving
67 calories, 3 g protein, 2 g fat, 10 g carbohydrate, 187 mg sodium, 3 mg cholesterol.

1 teaspoon olive oil
1 small onion, finely chopped
1 package (10 ounces) frozen chopped spinach, thawed and squeezed dry
8 ounces reduced-fat feta cheese, crumbled
1 tablespoon chopped fresh mint
1 egg white
1 pound frozen phyllo dough, thawed according to package directions
¼ cup dry plain bread crumbs

1. Heat oil in a small skillet over medium heat. Add onion and sauté 3 minutes.

2. Combine spinach, feta and mint in a medium-size bowl. Stir in egg white and sautéed onion.

3. Carefully unroll phyllo dough on a cutting board. Cut stack lengthwise into thirds. Stack thirds into one pile. Cover dough with plastic wrap.

4. Heat oven to 375°.

5. Remove 1 strip of dough from pile and lay flat on a work surface. Lightly coat with nonstick cooking spray. Very lightly sprinkle with crumbs. Repeat with 2 more layers, stacking on first for total of 3 layers. Place a scant tablespoon of spinach mixture on one end of stack. Fold dough over to form a triangle; continue folding triangle to end of strip. Place triangle packet on an ungreased baking sheet. Repeat with remaining dough and filling.

6. Bake in heated 375° oven 15 minutes or until golden. Serve warm or at room temperature.

Mini crab cakes

Makes 24 servings *Prep* 20 minutes *Refrigerate* 30 minutes *Deep-fry* 1 to 1½ minutes per batch

Make sure to refrigerate the crab mixture as directed—this makes for a drier mixture, which results in better frying and crispier crab cakes. If you want to save money, buy crab-flavored surimi—a product made from neutral-flavored white fish that is processed and seasoned in a variety of ways.

Per serving
138 calories, 3 g protein,
11 g fat, 7 g carbohydrate,
157 mg sodium,
35 mg cholesterol.

1 sweet red pepper, cored, seeded and coarsely chopped
2 green onions, coarsely chopped
½ pound surimi, cut up, or lump crabmeat, picked over to remove bits of cartilage
1 rib celery, chopped
1 teaspoon Dijon mustard
¼ teaspoon hot-pepper sauce
6 slices thin-sliced white bread, torn into small pieces

3 eggs
½ teaspoon Worcestershire sauce
½ cup dry plain bread crumbs

Cajun mayonnaise
1 cup mayonnaise
1 tablespoon ketchup
1 teaspoon Dijon mustard
½ teaspoon hot-pepper sauce
½ teaspoon Worcestershire sauce

Vegetable oil for frying

1. Place sweet red pepper, green onions, surimi, celery, mustard, hot-pepper sauce, bread, eggs and Worcestershire sauce in a food processor. Pulse to chop. Refrigerate 15 minutes to allow bread to absorb any liquid.

2. Place bread crumbs on a piece of waxed paper.

3. Shape rounded tablespoons of surimi mixture into twenty-four 1½-inch balls. Roll each ball in bread crumbs; flatten slightly into a thick patty. Place on a baking sheet. Refrigerate 15 minutes.

4. Meanwhile, prepare Cajun mayonaise: Whisk mayonnaise, ketchup, mustard, hot-pepper sauce and Worcestershire sauce in a small bowl.

5. Pour oil into a large skillet to a depth of 1 inch. Heat over medium heat until oil registers 375° on a deep-fat thermometer.

6. Fry 6 crab cakes at a time until golden brown, 1 to 1½ minutes. Remove cakes with a slotted spoon to paper toweling to drain. Keep hot in a warm oven until all cakes are fried. Serve warm with Cajun mayonnaise.

Make-ahead tip: Crab cakes can be cooked ahead, cooled thoroughly, wrapped and frozen. To serve, thaw in refrigerator. Place in a single layer in a shallow baking pan. Bake in heated 350° oven until heated through, about 10 minutes. Cajun mayonaise can be refrigerated, covered, up to 2 days.

Mini crab cakes
opposite

Skewered sesame shrimp

Makes 8 servings   *Prep* 15 minutes   *Refrigerate* 1 hour   *Broil* 6 minutes

Fresh ginger lends a tiny bit of "sweet" heat.

Per serving
85 calories, 8 g protein, 1 g fat, 10 g carbohydrate, 340 mg sodium, 67 mg cholesterol.

1 can (20 ounces) juice-packed pineapple chunks
⅓ cup reduced-sodium soy sauce
2 tablespoons sugar
1 tablespoon rice-wine vinegar
1 tablespoon plum wine or sherry

2 quarter-size pieces peeled fresh ginger
1 green onion, finely chopped
1 teaspoon dark Asian sesame oil
1 pound large shrimp (about 24), peeled and deveined
1 pint cherry tomatoes (about 24)

1. Drain pineapple, reserving juice.

2. Combine soy sauce, sugar, vinegar, plum wine, ginger, green onion and sesame oil in a blender or food processor. Whirl until pureed. Transfer marinade to a plastic food-storage bag. Add reserved pineapple juice. Add shrimp; seal and turn bag to coat shrimp. Refrigerate 1 hour.

3. Soak eight 12-inch wooden skewers in a bowl of cold water 15 minutes.

4. Heat broiler.

5. Thread 3 shrimp, 3 cherry tomatoes and 3 pineapple chunks on each skewer, alternating pieces. Place on rack in a broiler pan; spoon some marinade over skewers. Broil 3 inches from heat about 6 minutes or until shrimp are cooked through, turning once and basting again with marinade.

Coconut peanut chicken

Makes 30 servings   *Prep* 20 minutes   *Deep-fry* 4 to 6 minutes per batch

Crazy about nuts? Substitute macadamias or pecans for the peanuts; add ¼ teaspoon salt to the flour. And why not try turkey instead of the chicken?

Per serving
131 calories, 5 g protein, 10 g fat, 7 g carbohydrate, 63 mg sodium, 23 mg cholesterol.

¾ cup cocktail peanuts
2 cups sweetened flake coconut
¼ cup all-purpose flour
2 eggs
1 pound boneless, skinless chicken breast, cut into 1-inch pieces
  Vegetable oil for frying

Dipping sauce
3 tablespoons honey
3 tablespoons orange marmalade
1 tablespoon soy sauce
½ teaspoon prepared mustard

1. Place peanuts in a food processor. Whirl until finely chopped. Combine peanuts with coconut in a medium-size bowl. Place flour in a small bowl. Lightly beat eggs in another small bowl.

2. Dip chicken pieces in flour to coat lightly, shaking off excess, then in eggs and then in peanut-coconut mixture.

3. Pour oil into an electric skillet or a regular large skillet to a depth of ½ inch. Set electric skillet at 350° or heat oil in regular skillet over medium heat until it registers 350° on deep-fat thermometer.

4. With a slotted spoon, carefully slip chicken into hot oil, 6 pieces at a time. Fry 4 to 6 minutes or until cooked through, turning once; adjust heat as needed to prevent peanut coating from overbrowning. Transfer chicken to paper toweling to drain. Keep hot in a warm oven. Repeat with remaining chicken.

5. Prepare dipping sauce: Combine honey, marmalade, soy sauce and mustard in a small bowl.

6. Place chicken on a serving plate. Serve with sauce.

Spicy chicken skewers

Makes 8 servings   *Prep* 15 minutes   *Refrigerate* 1 hour   *Broil* 6 to 8 minutes

If the party schedule allows, marinate the chicken cubes in the refrigerator overnight. Look for plum sauce in the Asian ingredient section of your supermarket.

Per serving
80 calories, 6 g protein,
2 g fat, 8 g carbohydrate,
304 mg sodium,
18 mg cholesterol.

1 can (4 ounces) green chiles, drained
1 green onion, cut into 1-inch pieces
2 cloves garlic
¼ cup jarred plum sauce or jam
1 tablespoon soy sauce
1 teaspoon dark Asian sesame oil
¼ teaspoon salt

2 boneless, skinless chicken breast halves (½ pound total), cut into 1½-inch cubes
1 sweet green pepper, cored, seeded and cut into 1-inch squares
1 medium onion, cut into 1-inch pieces
1 sweet red pepper, cored, seeded and cut into 1-inch squares

1. Combine drained chiles, green onion, garlic, plum sauce, soy sauce, sesame oil and salt in a food processor or blender. Whirl until pureed.

2. Place chicken in a medium-size bowl. Add half of the plum sauce mixture. Cover; refrigerate 1 hour to marinate. Reserve remaining plum mixture.

3. Soak 24 small wooden skewers in a bowl of cold water 15 minutes.

4. Heat broiler.

5. Thread 1 piece each of green pepper, onion, red pepper and chicken on each skewer. Place skewers on rack in a broiler pan. Spoon on remaining reserved plum mixture. Broil 6 inches from heat 6 to 8 minutes or until chicken is cooked through, turning once.

Garlicky cheese spread

Makes 1 cup *Prep* 30 minutes

For a good-for-you treat, replace the farmer cheese with less-fat cream cheese.

Per 2 tablespoons
75 calories, 9 g protein, 3 g fat, 3 g carbohydrate, 296 mg sodium, 78 mg cholesterol.

1 package farmer cheese (7 ounces)
2 tablespoons cream cheese
2 tablespoons dried sage
1 to 2 cloves garlic, finely chopped
1 teaspoon red-wine vinegar
½ teaspoon salt
⅛ teaspoon ground black pepper
Cracked black pepper
Assorted crackers for serving

Place farmer cheese, cream cheese, sage, garlic, vinegar, salt and ground black pepper in a food processor. Whirl until smooth. Scoop into a small serving bowl. Garnish with cracked black pepper. Serve at room temperature with crackers.

Sonora cheese dip

Makes about 2 cups *Prep* 15 minutes

If you like, serve with fresh vegetable crudités instead of tortilla chips.

Per 2 tablespoons
108 calories, 6 g protein, 8 g fat, 1 g carbohydrate, 280 mg sodium, 26 mg cholesterol.

2 cups shredded Monterey Jack cheese (8 ounces)
2 cups shredded American cheese (8 ounces)
6 green onions, sliced
⅔ cup finely chopped sweet red pepper
2 tablespoons finely chopped, seeded jalapeño chiles
Tortilla chips for serving

Melt together cheeses in top of a double boiler over simmering water. Stir in green onions, sweet red pepper and jalapeño. Serve hot with tortilla chips.

Pesto–red pepper cream cheese torte *opposite*

Pesto–red pepper cream cheese torte

Makes 5 cups   *Prep* 45 minutes   *Cook* 3 to 5 minutes   *Refrigerate* 2 to 3 hours

The red pepper and green basil color the spread with festive holiday appeal. If you need to move quickly, substitute prepared pesto for the homemade in the recipe—about a quarter cup should do it.

Per 2 tablespoons
54 calories, 2 g protein,
4 g fat, 2 g carbohydrate,
88 mg sodium,
14 mg cholesterol.

Roasting sweet peppers

Preparing your own roasted sweet peppers is easy. Roast each pepper on a long-handled fork over a flame, under the broiler or on the grill, turning as necessary until charred all over. Place in a paper bag, let cool, and then core, seed and peel off the blackened skin. That's it!

3 packages (8 ounces each) less-fat cream cheese, at room temperature
2 cups packed fresh basil leaves
¼ cup pine nuts
2 cloves garlic, coarsely chopped
¼ cup grated Parmesan cheese

1 jar (7 ounces) roasted red peppers, drained
2 teaspoons cornstarch
½ cup finely chopped green onion
Fresh basil leaves and tomato roses for garnish (optional)
Thin slices of party breads, crackers or pita chips for serving

1. Beat softened cream cheese in a large bowl until light and fluffy. Divide into thirds.

2. For pesto, combine basil, pine nuts and garlic in a food processor. Whirl until finely chopped.

3. Stir basil mixture and Parmesan cheese into a third of the cream cheese until well blended.

4. Place roasted red peppers in a clean food processor bowl. Whirl until pureed. Transfer to a small skillet. Whisk in cornstarch until well blended and smooth. Bring to simmering over medium heat; cook 3 to 5 minutes or until thickened. Cool 15 minutes. Whisk into another third of cream cheese until well blended.

5. Mix green onion into remaining third of cream cheese until blended.

6. Line a 6-cup bowl with plastic wrap, leaving a 2-inch overhang.

7. Turn pesto mixture into lined bowl; pack firmly. Spoon on green onion mixture; carefully spread to cover pesto layer. Top with red pepper layer, spreading to completely cover onion layer. Cover top with the plastic wrap overhang. Refrigerate 2 to 3 hours or until firm.

8. Fold back plastic wrap; unmold onto a serving plate. Garnish with fresh basil leaves and tomato roses if desired. Serve with thin slices of party bread, crackers or pita chips.

Stuffed baby Brie

Makes 8 servings   *Prep* 20 minutes

Spectacular looking, spectacular tasting! Be sure to use oil-packed sun-dried tomatoes—the dry-pack require soaking to reconstitute.

Per serving
125 calories, 7 g protein,
10 g fat, 1 g carbohydrate,
186 mg sodium,
28 mg cholesterol.

1 baby Brie (8 ounces)
6 oil-packed sun-dried tomato halves
2 tablespoons pine nuts, toasted

6 fresh basil leaves
Toast triangles or water crackers for serving

1. Slice Brie in half horizontally.

2. Combine sun-dried tomatoes and pine nuts in a food processor. Whirl until blended into a paste.

3. Spread half of the sun-dried tomato mixture over cut side of each half of the Brie. Arrange basil leaves over tomato mixture on bottom half. Top with the other half of the Brie, cut side down. Wrap Brie in plastic wrap; refrigerate several hours to blend flavors.

4. To serve, place Brie on a dish and surround with toast or crackers.

Note: Pine nuts are easily toasted in a dry skillet over medium heat for about 3 minutes.

Nutty goat cheese canapés

Makes 12 servings   *Prep* 15 minutes   *Broil* 3 minutes

The texture of goat cheese can range from rich and creamy to dry and semifirm, but the taste is always distinguishably tart. The shapes are varied too: cylinders, discs, pyramids and cones.

Per serving
116 calories, 5 g protein,
4 g fat, 18 g carbohydrate,
124 mg sodium,
2 mg cholesterol.

12 bite-size pitas, each split in half, or 24 rounds melba toast
½ cup shelled pistachios
¼ cup soft goat cheese (2 ounces)

1 teaspoon fresh lemon juice
6 cherry tomatoes
1 sprig fresh rosemary, chopped
Freshly ground black pepper

1. Heat broiler. Lightly toast pita halves under broiler, about 1 minute. Leave broiler on.

2. Finely grind pistachios in a food processor. Add goat cheese and lemon juice. Whirl until just combined.

3. Cut tomatoes into quarters or thin slices. Spread each pita half with ½ teaspoon goat cheese spread. Top with a tomato wedge or slice, a sprinkling of rosemary and a grinding of black pepper. Place on a baking sheet.

4. Broil pitas until warmed through, about 2 minutes.

Mediterranean dip

Makes 1½ cups *Prep* 10 minutes *Cook* 2 minutes

Want to cut back on the fat even more in this dip? Use low-fat or nonfat yogurt. Toss in lots of chopped parsley for color and a "fresh" taste.

per 2 tablespoons
60 calories, 4 g protein, 2 g fat, 10 g carbohydrate, 166 mg sodium, 2 mg cholesterol.

1 tablespoon olive oil
1 clove garlic, finely chopped
1 teaspoon ground cumin
1 can (19 ounces) chick-peas, drained
½ teaspoon salt
2 tablespoons fresh lemon juice
½ cup plain yogurt
   Assorted crudités or breads
   for serving

1. Heat oil in a medium-size nonstick skillet over medium heat. Add garlic; sauté until lightly golden, 1 to 2 minutes. Remove from heat; stir in cumin and chick-peas.

2. Combine chick-pea mixture, salt and lemon juice in a food processor. Whirl until pureed. Transfer to a small bowl. Stir in yogurt. Serve with raw vegetables, crispy flat bread, pita bread wedges or crackers.

Guacamole

Makes 1⅔ cups *Prep* 20 minutes

Like your guacamole smooth or chunky? It's simple to make either way. Let the food processor run continuously for a puree, or pulse with an on-and-off motion for more texture.

per 2 tablespoons
44 calories, 0 g protein, 4 g fat, 2 g carbohydrate, 88 mg sodium, 0 mg cholesterol.

2 green onions, cut into 1-inch pieces
1 tablespoon chopped fresh cilantro or parsley
2 ripe avocados
2 tablespoons fresh lime juice (2 limes)
1 tablespoon medium or medium-hot picante sauce or salsa
½ teaspoon salt
⅛ to ¼ teaspoon hot-pepper sauce
   Tortilla chips for serving

1. Place green onions and cilantro in a food processor. Whirl until evenly chopped.

2. Halve avocados. Peel and pit. Cut avocados into 2-inch pieces. Add about half of the avocado to green onion mixture in processor. Add 1 tablespoon lime juice, picante sauce, salt and hot-pepper sauce. Whirl, using on-and-off pulses, until finely chopped.

3. Add remaining avocado to mixture in processor. Whirl with on-and-off pulses until mixture is the desired consistency.

4. Scrape guacamole into a serving dish. Sprinkle remaining lime juice on top. Refrigerate, tightly covered with plastic wrap, up to 4 hours. Stir before serving. Serve with tortilla chips.

Curry dip

Makes 2 cups *Prep* 30 minutes

Make the dip a day ahead so the curry will mellow.

Per 2 tablespoons
62 calories, 1 g protein, 4 g fat, 5 g carbohydrate, 250 mg sodium, 5 mg cholesterol.

1 cup reduced-fat mayonnaise
1 cup reduced-fat sour cream
1 teaspoon curry powder
2 tablespoons bottled plum sauce
¼ cup chopped fresh parsley

½ teaspoon black pepper
¼ teaspoon salt
  Assorted crudités or potato chips for serving

Combine mayonnaise, sour cream, curry powder, plum sauce, parsley, pepper and salt in a medium-size bowl. Refrigerate, tightly covered, until ready to serve. Serve with crudités or chips.

Roasted red pepper dip

Makes 16 cups *Prep* 30 minutes

If you're a barbecue addict, roast and chop 2 grilled sweet peppers instead of using jarred ones.

Per 2 tablespoons
64 calories, 1 g protein, 4 g fat, 5 g carbohydrate, 254 mg sodium, 6 mg cholesterol.

1 jar (7 ounces) roasted red peppers, drained and chopped
2 teaspoons dried basil
½ teaspoon salt
½ teaspoon black pepper

1 cup reduced-fat sour cream
1 cup reduced-fat mayonnaise
2 tablespoons grated Parmesan cheese
  Assorted crudités or crackers for serving

Combine roasted peppers, basil, salt, black pepper, sour cream, mayonnaise, and Parmesan cheese in a medium-size bowl. Refrigerate, tightly covered, until ready to serve. Serve with crudités or crackers.

Horseradish dip

Makes 1¼ cups *Prep* 5 minutes

Spread over fish before grilling, for moisture.

Per 2 tablespoons
42 calories, 2 g protein, 4 g fat, 2 g carbohydrate, 128 mg sodium, 0 mg cholesterol.

1 cup reduced-fat sour cream
¼ cup chopped fresh dill
3 tablespoons bottled horseradish

½ teaspoon salt
  Bagel chips or pita chips for serving

Stir together sour cream, dill, horseradish and salt in a small bowl. Refrigerate, tightly covered, until ready to serve. Serve with bagel chips or pita chips.

Tex-Mex party appetizers

Makes 24 servings *Prep* 15 minutes

No cooking, no baking. In fact, even the children can help with this one—it's all assembly.

Per serving
181 calories, 5 g protein, 15 g fat, 9 g carbohydrate, 515 mg sodium, 17 mg cholesterol.

3 ripe avocados
2 tablespoons fresh lemon juice
½ teaspoon salt
¼ teaspoon black pepper
1 container (8 ounces) regular or reduced-fat sour cream
½ cup mayonnaise or salad dressing
1 envelope taco seasoning mix
1 bunch green onions

2 cans (10½ ounces each) plain or jalapeño-flavored bean dip
3 medium tomatoes, cored, seeded and diced (2 cups)
1 can (6 ounces) pitted ripe olives, drained and coarsely chopped
2 cups shredded sharp cheddar cheese (8 ounces)
Tortilla chips for serving

1. Halve, pit and peel avocados. Mash avocados with a fork in a medium-size bowl with lemon juice, salt and pepper until well blended.

2. Stir together sour cream, mayonnaise and taco seasoning in a small bowl until well blended.

3. Finely chop white portion of green onions and some of the green; you should have about 1 cup.

4. Spread bean dip over a large shallow serving platter. Top with seasoned avocado mixture, spreading nearly to edge but leaving a little bean dip showing around edge. Spread sour cream mixture in an even layer over avocado mixture. Sprinkle evenly with chopped green onions, then tomatoes and olives. Sprinkle whole top evenly with cheese.

5. If desired, cover dip and chill in refrigerator. Serve with tortilla chips.

Salsa fresca

Makes 3 cups *Prep* 15 minutes

To increase the heat, use 1 or 2 serrano chiles instead of jalapeños.
Shown on page 10.

Per ¼ cup
15 calories, 0 g protein, 0 g fat, 3 g carbohydrate, 138 mg sodium, 0 mg cholesterol.

1½ pounds tomatoes, seeded and diced
1 small onion, finely chopped
2 jalapeño chiles, seeded and finely chopped

2 tablespoons chopped fresh cilantro
2 tablespoons fresh lime juice
¾ teaspoon salt
Tortilla chips for serving

Combine tomatoes, onion, jalapeños, cilantro, lime juice and salt in a medium-size bowl. For best flavor, cover and refrigerate a few hours or overnight. Serve with tortilla chips.

Pineapple chipotle salsa

Makes 4 cups *Prep* 20 minutes

Serve as a side dish with grilled chicken, pork tenderloin or shrimp. The chipotle chile imparts a hint of smokiness.

Shown on page 10.

Per ¼ cup
20 calories, 0 g protein, 0 g fat, 5 g carbohydrate, 8 mg sodium, 0 mg cholesterol.

1 small fresh pineapple (about 3½ pounds), top removed, peeled, cored and chopped (about 6 cups)
1 sweet red pepper, cored, seeded and chopped
¾ cup chopped red onion
2 tablespoons chopped fresh cilantro
3 tablespoons fresh lime juice
1 teaspoon mashed canned chipotle chile in adobo sauce
2 teaspoons adobo sauce, from can of chipotle chiles
Tortilla chips for serving

Combine pineapple, sweet red pepper, red onion, cilantro, lime juice, chipotle chile and adobo sauce in a large bowl. For best flavor, cover and refrigerate a few hours or overnight. Serve with tortilla chips.

Black bean mango salsa

Makes 8 cups *Prep* 20 minutes

A tangy accompaniment to strong-flavored fish such as bluefish, mackerel or monkfish.

Shown on page 10.

Per ¼ cup
31 calories, 2 g protein, 0 g fat, 7 g carbohydrate, 27 mg sodium, 0 mg cholesterol.

2 cans (15¾ ounces each) black beans, drained and rinsed
2 oranges, peeled, seeded and chopped
2 mangoes, peeled, pitted and chopped
½ sweet red pepper, cored, seeded and chopped
3 serrano chiles, seeded and thinly sliced, or 1 large jalapeño chile, seeded and thinly sliced
2 tablespoons fresh lime juice
2 tablespoons chopped fresh cilantro
1 teaspoon grated fresh ginger
Tortilla chips for serving

Combine black beans, oranges, mangoes, sweet red pepper, chiles, lime juice, cilantro and ginger in a large bowl. For best flavor, cover and refrigerate a few hours or overnight. Serve with tortilla chips.

Salsa verde

Makes 2½ cups *Prep* 15 minutes

Tomatillos have a parchmentlike husk and a lemony apple flavor.

Shown on page 10.

Per ¼ cup
20 calories, 1 g protein,
0 g fat, 3 g carbohydrate,
214 mg sodium,
0 mg cholesterol.

1 pound tomatillos (9 small to medium), husked and cut in half
⅓ cup chopped red onion
⅞ cup chopped fresh cilantro

2 jalapeño chiles, seeded and chopped
2 tablespoons fresh lime juice
1 teaspoon salt
   Tortilla chips for serving

Place tomatillos, onion, cilantro, jalapeños, lime juice and salt in a blender or food processor; puree. Place in a medium-size bowl. For best flavor, cover and refrigerate a few hours or overnight. Serve with tortilla chips.

Roasted tomato salsa

Makes 2½ cups *Prep* 10 minutes *Broil* 3 minutes *Cook* 7 minutes

The roasted tomatoes can be used on their own as a topping for bruschetta, pasta or even pizza. For the simplest of salads, toss with a little balsamic vinegar and olive oil.

Shown on page 10.

Per ¼ cup
62 calories, 1 g protein,
4 g fat, 5 g carbohydrate,
119 mg sodium,
0 mg cholesterol.

3 large tomatoes (about 2 pounds), cut in half and seeded
3 tablespoons olive oil
1 cup chopped onion
2 jalapeño chiles, seeded and chopped

2 cloves garlic, crushed
2 teaspoons chili powder
2 tablespoons red-wine vinegar
1½ teaspoons hot-pepper sauce
½ teaspoon salt
   Tortilla chips for serving

1. Heat broiler.

2. Place tomatoes, cut side down, on a broiler-pan rack. Broil 3 inches from heat until blackened, about 3 minutes. Remove from heat. Coarsely chop.

3. Heat 1 tablespoon olive oil in a large nonstick skillet over medium-high heat. Add onion, jalapeños and garlic; sauté 4 minutes or until lightly browned. Add chili powder; sauté 3 minutes.

4. Transfer onion mixture and tomatoes to a food processor or blender; puree. Pour into a medium-size bowl. Add remaining 2 tablespoons oil, vinegar, hot-pepper sauce and salt. For best flavor, cover and refrigerate a few hours or overnight. Serve with tortilla chips.

Antipasto salad *page 44*

Taco salad with shrimp *page 45*

THEORY HOLDS that a whole can be greater than the sum of its parts, and salads are a perfect example. They take ingredients that might not be spectacular on their own—cooked turkey and rice, for example, or assorted beans or greens—meld them with other items, then dress them up to shape a total that's quite unexpected.

This collection offers both side salads and options substantive enough to do lunch or dinner duty on their own. Mixed Marinated Vegetables and German Potato Salad are always appropriate accompaniments; for a main dish, go

Meet candidates old and new for the ultimate best-dressed list.

Mexican with Taco Salad with Shrimp. If greens are all you want, they marry well with homemade dressing; in fact, a batch tossed with from-scratch Creamy Blue Cheese or Ranch proves a little of this and a little of that add up to a lot of great taste.

salads and dressings

Antipasto salad

Makes 6 servings   *Prep* 10 minutes   *Cook* 10 minutes

Want to use a different shaped pasta? Try penne or small shells. Use good-quality black olives—it makes a big difference in the taste.

Shown on page 42.

Per serving
466 calories, 13 g protein,
20 g fat, 59 carbohydrate,
489 mg sodium,
6 mg cholesterol.

1 pound bow-tie pasta
3 cups torn romaine lettuce
½ cup thinly sliced celery
½ cup thinly sliced red onion
1 ounce sliced ham, cut into ¼-inch-wide strips

1 ounce sliced provolone cheese, cut into ½-inch-wide strips
¼ cup pitted oil-cured black olives
½ cup Oregano Dressing (recipe below)

1. Cook pasta in a large pot of lightly salted boiling water until tender but firm. Drain, rinse with cool water to stop the cooking and drain again.

2. Place pasta in a large bowl. Add romaine, celery, onion, ham, provolone and olives. Toss gently.

3. Add dressing to pasta mixture and toss to coat. Serve at room temperature.

Greek salad

Makes 6 servings   *Prep* 15 minutes

Made from goat's or sheep's milk, Greek feta cheese is tangy because it's cured in brine. The texture is dry and crumbly.

Per serving
277 calories, 4 g protein,
27 g fat, 21 g carbohydrate,
301 mg sodium,
17 mg cholesterol.

6 cups torn pieces iceberg and/or romaine lettuce
2 small tomatoes, cored and cut into wedges
1 medium cucumber, peeled and sliced

1 sweet green pepper, cored, seeded and cut into rings
4 ounces feta cheese, crumbled
⅔ cup Oregano Dressing (recipe follows)

1. Toss together lettuce, tomatoes and cucumber in a serving bowl. Top with green pepper and feta cheese.

2. To serve, toss salad with dressing.

Oregano dressing

Per tablespoon
108 calories, 0 g protein,
12 g fat, 0 g carbohydrate,
89 mg sodium,
0 mg cholesterol.

Whisk together ⅔ cup olive oil, 3 tablespoons red-wine vinegar, 1 teaspoon dried oregano, ½ teaspoon salt and ¼ teaspoon black pepper. Makes ¾ cup.

Mexican tuna salad

Makes 4 servings   *Prep* 15 minutes   *Bake* at 350° for 10 minutes; then at 400° for 10 minutes

For a low-fat lunch or supper, pair this salad with a dessert of vanilla frozen yogurt topped with fruit. No-fat flour tortillas make even better nutrition sense.

Per serving

327 calories, 29 g protein, 5 g fat, 41 g carbohydrate, 647 mg sodium, 25 mg cholesterol.

4 flour tortillas (10-inch)
1 large can (12 ounces) water-packed tuna, drained and rinsed
1 sweet red pepper, cored, seeded and chopped
½ cup frozen corn kernels, thawed
2 green onions, chopped
⅓ cup medium-hot salsa
⅓ cup nonfat sour cream
¼ teaspoon ground cumin
2 cups shredded lettuce

1. Heat oven to 350°. Wrap tortillas in aluminum foil. Heat in oven 10 minutes. Meanwhile, coat outside of four 10-ounce custard cups with nonstick cooking spray. Invert onto a baking sheet.

2. Flake tuna and combine with sweet red pepper, corn and green onions in a small bowl. Combine salsa, sour cream and cumin in another small bowl. Gently stir salsa mixture into tuna.

3. Remove tortillas from oven. Increase oven temperature to 400°. Place one tortilla at a time (keep others wrapped) on a prepared custard cup, pressing gently to shape. Bake tortillas in heated 400° oven 10 minutes. Carefully remove baked shells to a wire rack to cool completely.

4. Line tortilla shells with lettuce. Fill each with tuna mixture.

Taco salad with shrimp

Makes 4 servings   *Prep* 20 minutes

As part of a buffet spread or light lunch, this salad is an easy do-ahead. If fresh cilantro is unavailable, substitute chopped fresh parsley and a pinch of ground coriander.

Shown on page 43.

Per serving

380 calories, 36 g protein, 11 g fat, 44 g carbohydrate, 923 mg sodium, 174 mg cholesterol.

½ cup salsa-style salad dressing
½ teaspoon ground cumin
3 tablespoons chopped fresh cilantro
1½ cups chopped tomato (2 medium)
1 sweet yellow or green pepper, cored, seeded and cut into ½-inch cubes
1 can (16 ounces) black beans, drained and rinsed
1 pound cooked shrimp, peeled and deveined (see box, page 17)
4 cups shredded iceberg lettuce
4 cups tortilla chips
Sour cream for garnish (optional)

1. Stir together dressing, cumin and cilantro in a large bowl. Stir in tomato, pepper, beans and shrimp. (The mixture can be made 3 hours ahead up to this point and then covered and refrigerated.)

2. Arrange lettuce on a shallow serving platter. Crush tortilla chips; stir into shrimp mixture. Or arrange 3 cups chips around perimeter of platter and crush remaining chips and stir into shrimp. Spoon shrimp mixture over lettuce. Garnish with sour cream if you wish.

Tropical shrimp and pasta salad

Makes 6 servings *Prep* 35 minutes *Refrigerate* 30 minutes

Purchase already cooked shrimp for the salad and the only "cooking" you'll do is bringing a pot of water to a boil to pour over the angel hair pasta— that's it!

Per serving
286 calories, 20 g protein, 16 g fat, 18 g carbohydrate, 322 mg sodium, 115 mg cholesterol.

1 pound cooked, peeled medium shrimp (see box, page 17)
½ cup fresh lime juice
½ teaspoon salt
2 cucumbers, peeled, quartered lengthwise, seeded and sliced
4 green onions, sliced
1 sweet red pepper, cored, seeded and cut into thin strips
1 cup chopped unsalted roasted cashews
½ cup unsweetened reduced-fat coconut milk
1 teaspoon hot-pepper sauce
¼ cup chutney
¼ cup chopped fresh cilantro
½ pound angel hair pasta
Additional salt to taste

1. Stir together shrimp, lime juice and ½ teaspoon salt in a medium-size bowl. Refrigerate 30 minutes.

2. Meanwhile, place cucumber slices in a sieve; let drain 15 minutes.

3. Combine green onions, red pepper, cashews and cucumbers in a bowl.

4. Mix coconut milk, hot-pepper sauce and chutney in a small bowl. Pour over cucumber mixture. Add shrimp with its marinade and cilantro. Refrigerate.

5. Pour a generous amount of boiling water over pasta in a large heatproof bowl. Add salt to taste. Let stand 3 to 4 minutes, stirring frequently to prevent clumping. Drain. Serve salad chilled or at room temperature over the pasta.

Chicken and apple salad

Makes 4 servings *Prep* 15 minutes

If you'd like to substitute fresh tarragon or thyme for the parsley, start out with a tablespoon, then add to taste.

Per serving
247 calories, 28 g protein, 10 g fat, 10 g carbohydrate, 475 mg sodium, 73 mg cholesterol.

1½ tablespoons Dijon mustard
1 clove garlic, finely chopped
2 tablespoons red-wine vinegar or balsamic vinegar
2 tablespoons vegetable oil
½ cup chopped fresh parsley
½ teaspoon salt
½ teaspoon black pepper
2½ cups cubed cooked chicken breasts (about 1¼ pounds uncooked)
2 apples, cored and diced
4 green onions (white part only), sliced

1. Combine mustard, garlic and vinegar in a medium-size bowl. Whisk in oil, a tablespoon at a time, until thickened. Stir in parsley, salt and pepper.

2. Add chicken, apples and green onions; toss to combine. Serve on a bed of lettuce or in sandwiches.

Spicy orange chicken salad

Makes 4 servings   *Prep* 10 minutes   *Cook* 27 minutes

Chock-full of Chinese vegetables—snow peas, Napa cabbage, water chestnuts—and laced with peanuts, this Asian-inspired salad gets its kick from fresh ginger and garlic.

Per serving
310 calories, 33 g protein,
9 g fat, 26 g carbohydrate,
443 mg sodium,
66 mg cholesterol.

1 cup lower-sodium chicken broth
¾ cup fresh orange juice
1 tablespoon grated fresh ginger
2 cloves garlic, crushed
4 boneless, skinless chicken breast halves (1 pound total)
4 ounces snow peas, trimmed
1 tablespoon honey
1 tablespoon creamy peanut butter
1 tablespoon rice-wine vinegar

2 teaspoons soy sauce
2 teaspoons dark Asian sesame oil
4 cups sliced Napa cabbage
4 cups sliced romaine lettuce
1 can (8 ounces) sliced water chestnuts, drained and rinsed
1 sweet red pepper, cored, seeded and cut into 2-inch-long strips
2 tablespoons chopped unsalted peanuts

1. Combine broth, orange juice, ginger and garlic in a medium-size saucepan. Bring to simmering. Add chicken breasts; cook, covered, 15 minutes or until internal temperature registers 170° on an instant-read thermometer; turn over halfway through the cooking.

2. Add snow peas. Cover and cook 2 minutes more or until crisp-tender. Remove chicken and snow peas with a slotted spoon and reserve liquid. Cool chicken and cut into cubes.

3. Meanwhile, boil cooking liquid until reduced to ¾ cup, about 10 minutes. Whisk in honey, peanut butter, vinegar, soy sauce and sesame oil to make a dressing. Serve dressing warm, or chill in freezer about 15 minutes.

4. To serve, line a platter with cabbage and romaine. Toss together chicken, snow peas, water chestnuts, sweet red pepper and half of dressing. Spoon onto platter. Sprinkle with peanuts. Serve remaining dressing on the side.

Zesty chicken salad

Makes 2 servings   *Prep* 15 minutes

Next time you serve chicken, cook up extra for this salad.

Per serving
267 calories, 24 g protein,
11 g fat, 16 g carbohydrate,
506 mg sodium,
170 mg cholesterol.

2 tablespoons reduced-fat mayonnaise
3 tablespoons chopped sweet gherkin pickles
1 tablespoon pickle liquid
1 teaspoon prepared mustard

⅛ teaspoon black pepper
1 cup cubed cooked chicken
4 leaves lettuce
1 hard-cooked egg, shelled and sliced
4 large cherry tomatoes, sliced

Combine mayonnaise, pickles, pickle liquid, mustard and pepper in a bowl; stir in chicken. Mound onto lettuce leaves. Top with egg and tomato slices.

47

Santa Fe chicken salad

Makes 6 servings *Prep* 30 minutes *Cook* 8 minutes

Use a combination of red or yellow tomatoes—the yellow are slightly less acidic than the red.

Per serving

265 calories, 21 g protein, 16 g fat, 11 g carbohydrate, 430 mg sodium, 52 mg cholesterol.

4 boneless, skinless chicken breast halves (1¼ pounds total)
3 large tomatoes (about 1¾ pounds), cut into wedges
½ cup sliced red onion

½ cup chopped fresh cilantro
1 scant cup Spicy Tex-Mex Dressing (recipe follows)
Tortilla chips
Fresh cilantro sprigs for garnish

1. Combine chicken and enough water to cover in a large skillet. Bring to boiling. Reduce heat to low; simmer chicken 8 minutes or until internal temperature registers 170° on an instant-read thermometer. Transfer chicken to a plate. When cool enough to handle, tear into long shreds.

2. Combine chicken, tomatoes, red onion and cilantro in a large bowl. Add dressing and toss to mix. Spoon onto individual serving plates. Tuck in a few tortilla chips. Garnish with cilantro sprigs.

Spicy Tex-Mex dressing

Per tablespoon

87 calories, 0 g protein, 9 g fat, 2 g carbohydrate, 264 mg sodium, 0 mg cholesterol.

Combine ⅓ cup olive oil; ¼ cup fresh lemon juice; 1 small shallot, finely chopped; 1 tablespoon finely chopped, seeded fresh jalapeño chile; 1 tablespoon Dijon mustard; 2 cloves garlic, finely chopped; ¾ teaspoon salt and ½ teaspoon pepper in a small bowl. Cover with plastic wrap and refrigerate until ready to use. Makes scant 1 cup.

Smoked turkey salad calypso

Makes 10 servings *Prep* 15 minutes *Cook* 35 to 40 minutes *Bake* coconut at 375° for 10 minutes

Converted rice has been parboiled; when cooked, it forms fluffy, separate grains—ideal for a salad. For a smaller crowd, you can easily cut this recipe in half.

Per serving

274 calories, 14 g protein, 5 g fat, 45 g carbohydrate, 390 mg sodium, 18 mg cholesterol.

¾ cup wild rice
1½ cups converted white rice
1 cup sweetened flake coconut
1 large sweet red pepper, cored, seeded and finely chopped
1 large sweet green pepper, cored, seeded and finely chopped
1 red onion, finely chopped

½ cup chopped fresh parsley
2 papayas, peeled, seeded and chopped
1 pound sliced smoked turkey, cut into matchstick strips
1¾ cups Orange Dressing (recipe follows)

1. Add water to wild rice in a saucepan to cover by 2 inches. Simmer, covered, 35 to 40 minutes or until rice is tender and starts to split open. Drain; cool under cold tap water. Drain. Meanwhile, cook white rice according to package directions. Drain; cool under cold tap water. Drain.

2. As rice is cooking, heat oven to 375°. Spread coconut evenly in a baking pan. Bake in heated 375° oven 10 minutes or until lightly browned, stirring occasionally. Cool.

3. Combine wild rice, white rice, coconut, sweet peppers, onion, parsley, papayas and turkey in a large bowl. Add dressing; mix well.

Orange dressing

per tablespoon
23 calories, 0 g protein, 2 g fat, 2 g carbohydrate, 76 mg sodium, 0 mg cholesterol.

Whisk together 1½ cups fresh orange juice, ¼ cup olive oil, 1 tablespoon balsamic vinegar, 1 teaspoon salt and ½ teaspoon freshly ground black pepper in a small bowl. Makes 1¾ cups.

Curried turkey salad

Makes 4 servings   *Prep* 15 minutes   *Refrigerate* 2 hours

Heat tortillas at 350° for 10 minutes; then at 400° for 10 minutes

Kiwi and papaya are the sweet-tangy fruits in this salad, which comes piled up in its own edible flour tortilla cup. Select papayas with richly colored golden yellow skin that gives slightly to the touch, and ripen them in a paper bag at room temperature.

per serving
418 calories, 31 g protein, 9 g fat, 53 g carbohydrate, 249 mg sodium, 68 mg cholesterol.

2½ cups shredded cooked turkey
1 cup Creamy Curried Dressing (recipe follows)
4 flour tortillas (6-inch)
1 large papaya, peeled, seeded and sliced

3 kiwi, peeled, cut lengthwise in half and sliced crosswise
¼ cup blanched slivered almonds, toasted
  Fresh spinach leaves, stemmed, washed and dried

1. Mix together turkey and dressing in a large bowl. Refrigerate 2 hours.

2. Heat oven to 350°. Wrap tortillas in aluminum foil. Heat in oven 10 minutes. Meanwhile, coat outside of four 10-ounce custard cups with nonstick cooking spray. Invert onto a baking sheet.

3. Remove tortillas from oven. Increase oven temperature to 400°. Place one tortilla at a time (keep others wrapped) on a prepared custard cup, pressing gently to shape. Bake tortillas in heated 400° oven 10 minutes. Carefully remove baked shells to a wire rack to cool completely.

4. Add papaya, kiwi and almonds to turkey mixture. Line cooled tortilla cups with spinach leaves. Fill each shell with turkey mixture and serve.

Creamy curried dressing

per tablespoon
44 calories, 1 g protein, 0 g fat, 10 g carbohydrate, 61 mg sodium, 0 mg cholesterol.

Whisk together ½ cup chutney, 1 teaspoon curry powder and ½ teaspoon ground ginger in a small saucepan. Bring to boiling over medium heat. Cook, stirring occasionally, 2 to 3 minutes. Remove from heat; cool slightly. Stir in ⅓ cup plain nonfat yogurt. Scrape into a small bowl, cover with plastic wrap and refrigerate until ready to use. Makes 1 cup.

Mexican chili-steak salad

Makes 4 servings   *Prep* 30 minutes   *Refrigerate* overnight   *Broil* 6 minutes

Create a leaner salad and a leaner you by trimming the flank steak back to 12 ounces or by increasing the servings to six.

Per serving

544 calories, 29 g protein, 37 g fat, 29 g carbohydrate, 678 mg sodium, 59 mg cholesterol.

½ cup olive oil
2 tablespoons chili powder
2 teaspoons ground cumin
2 teaspoons dried thyme
1 teaspoon salt
½ teaspoon black pepper
⅔ cup red-wine vinegar
1 flank steak (1 pound), scored

2 ears fresh corn, shucked
1 package (9 ounces) frozen cut green beans, cooked according to package directions
1 pint cherry tomatoes, halved
6 cups torn romaine leaves
½ small head radicchio, leaves torn into bite-size pieces

1. Combine oil, chili powder, cumin, thyme, salt and pepper in a small saucepan. Bring to boiling. Reduce heat; simmer 5 minutes. Add vinegar. Cool marinade slightly.

2. Place meat in a large plastic food-storage bag. Add ½ cup marinade; seal. Refrigerate overnight, turning occasionally. Refrigerate remaining ¾ cup marinade for dressing.

3. Steam corn over boiling water 7 minutes. Cool slightly. Slice kernels from cob; you should have about 1 cup.

4. Heat broiler. Broil steak 4 inches from heat or cook on a grill skillet over medium-high heat 6 minutes or to desired doneness (until an instant-read thermometer registers an internal temperature of 140° for medium-rare, 160° for well-done); turn once and baste once or twice with marinade.

5. Let steak stand 5 minutes. Cut across grain into very thin slices. Toss with corn, green beans, cherry tomatoes and reserved marinade in a large bowl. Arrange romaine and radicchio leaves on a platter. Top with salad.

Mexican
chili-steak
salad

Lettuce varieties

SOME PEOPLE like a bowlful before their main course; others prefer it after. But whenever you choose to enjoy salad, the fresher the greens, the better—and there are more choices than ever at most markets. Pick only perky leaves with no signs of wilting or decay. Tender-leaf lettuces can be stored for a few days, hardier varieties up to a week; wrap loosely in damp paper toweling and tuck into your refrigerator's crisper drawer. Mix greens as you like, then pair with one of our delicious do-ahead dressings: Ranch or Zesty Vinaigrette (see recipes, pages 64 and 65). And for a restaurant-style treat, follow our simple directions for a fabulous Caesar Salad (see recipe, page 62).

Chicory Dark green; comes in several varieties, this one with dandelion-like leaves; bitter.

Bibb Pale green; small, loose head; buttery texture, mild taste.

Radicchio Bright-hued, purplish red chicory with white stem; round or long, loose-leafed head; bitter.

Red leaf Similar to green leaf but with bronze-tipped leaves; crisp stem; tender; mild.

Romaine Dark green; crisp, loosely packed, long stemmed, sturdy leaves; pale inner leaves; mild.

Boston Medium green; large, fragile, loose leaves; tender; mild.

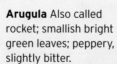

Arugula Also called rocket; smallish bright green leaves; peppery, slightly bitter.

Green leaf Also called salad bowl lettuce; tender, crinkly leaves with a crisp stem; mild.

Iceberg Pale green; tight, heavy head; crisp; neutral flavor.

Gazpacho salad

Orzo may look like rice, but it's really pasta. Against the assertive flavors of the salad, it's a perfect foil that also adds texture.

Per serving
264 calories, 7 g protein, 13 g fat, 30 g carbohydrate, 615 mg sodium, 2 mg cholesterol.

2½ cups chicken broth
1 cup orzo
5 tablespoons olive oil
2 cups diced, peeled, seeded ripe tomatoes
1 cup chopped mushrooms (about 3 ounces)
1 cup diced, peeled, seeded cucumber
1 cup diced sweet green pepper
6 green onions (both white and green parts), chopped (about ½ cup)
3 tablespoons chopped fresh parsley
2 tablespoons red-wine vinegar
2 cloves garlic, finely chopped
¼ teaspoon salt
⅛ teaspoon black pepper
½ bunch spinach (about 4 ounces), stemmed, washed and dried

1. Bring broth to boiling in a medium-size saucepan. Add orzo and cook 10 minutes or until tender. Drain excess liquid if necessary. Place orzo in a large bowl. Stir in 1 tablespoon olive oil.

2. Add tomatoes, mushrooms, cucumber, green pepper, green onions and parsley to orzo; stir until ingredients are well combined.

3. Whisk together remaining 4 tablespoons olive oil, vinegar, garlic, salt and black pepper in a small bowl. Pour over orzo mixture; toss gently until well combined. Serve salad on a bed of spinach.

Cucumber salad

Salting cucumbers and letting them stand draws out excess moisture.

Per serving
40 calories, 1 g protein, 2 g fat, 6 g carbohydrate, 430 mg sodium, 0 mg cholesterol.

3 large cucumbers, thinly sliced
2 teaspoons salt
3 tablespoons fresh lemon juice
1 tablespoon vegetable oil
1 tablespoon sugar
2 tablespoons chopped fresh dill
½ cup thinly sliced red onion

1. Toss cucumbers with salt in a large bowl. Place a plate directly on surface of cucumbers; weight down with a 1-pound can. Let stand 1 to 2 hours. Drain in a colander; rinse well.

2. Combine lemon juice, oil, sugar and dill in a medium-size bowl. Mix in onion and cucumber. Refrigerate overnight. Serve cold or at room temperature.

Tomato-bread salad

Makes 6 servings *Prep* 15 minutes

In Italian restaurants this is called panzanella. It's a no-cook meal, made even easier with a store-bought version of caponata, an Italian eggplant mixture.

Per serving
328 calories, 7 g protein, 16 g fat, 40 g carbohydrate, 980 mg sodium, 0 mg cholesterol.

6 cups torn pieces country-style round Italian bread
2½ pounds ripe beefsteak tomatoes, halved, seeded and cut into ½-inch pieces
1 can (4¾ ounces) caponata (eggplant appetizer)
2 tablespoons red-wine vinegar
1½ teaspoons salt
½ teaspoon black pepper
⅓ cup good-quality olive oil
1 tablespoon chopped fresh herbs, such as oregano, basil, rosemary or thyme
Lettuce leaves

1. Combine bread, tomatoes and caponata in a large bowl.

2. Whisk together vinegar, salt and pepper in a small bowl. Slowly whisk in oil. Pour over bread mixture; toss to coat. Toss in herbs. Serve on a bed of lettuce leaves.

Double bean and corn salad

Makes 4 servings *Prep* 15 minutes

Even though this salad is meatless, the beans along with the corn provide enough protein for a main meal. The optional ham add-in is only for those who need a meat fix.

Per serving
382 calories, 17 g protein, 20 g fat, 51 g carbohydrate, 978 mg sodium, 0 mg cholesterol.

⅓ cup olive oil
3 tablespoons fresh orange juice
1½ tablespoons red-wine vinegar
1½ teaspoons ground cumin
½ teaspoon salt
½ to ¾ teaspoon hot-pepper sauce
1 can (19 ounces) black beans, drained and rinsed
1 can (19 ounces) white kidney beans, drained and rinsed
1 can (16 ounces) corn niblets, drained
1 sweet red or green pepper, cored, seeded and cut into thin strips
4 ounces baked ham, cut into thin strips (1 cup) (optional)
1 small red onion, cut in half lengthwise, then crosswise into thin slices (¾ cup)
Lettuce leaves

1. Whisk together oil, orange juice, vinegar, cumin, salt and hot-pepper sauce in a large bowl until well blended.

2. Stir black beans, white beans, corn, sweet pepper, ham if using and onion into dressing; toss together until all ingredients are well coated. Serve immediately or refrigerate, covered, for several hours or until well chilled.

3. To serve, spoon salad over a bed of lettuce leaves.

Bean and
onion salad

Moroccan
carrot salad
opposite

Red and green salad
opposite

Bean and onion salad

Makes 8 servings   *Prep* 10 minutes   *Cook* 10 minutes   *Stand* 30 minutes

**Use a red onion
instead of the usual
yellow or white for a
touch of color.**

Per serving
162 calories, 2 g protein,
14 g fat, 9 g carbohydrate,
286 mg sodium,
0 mg cholesterol.

2 tablespoons vinegar
1 teaspoon Dijon mustard
½ cup olive oil
1 teaspoon salt
⅛ teaspoon black pepper

1 pound green beans, trimmed
1 pound yellow wax beans,
   trimmed
1 onion, thinly sliced

1. Whisk vinegar and mustard in a small bowl. Whisk in oil, salt and pepper.

2. Steam green and yellow beans 10 minutes or until crisp-tender. Dump beans in a colander and run under cold water to stop the cooking; drain.

3. Combine beans and onion in serving a bowl. Add dressing. Let stand at room temperature 30 minutes. For best flavor, refrigerate overnight; serve at room temperature.

Moroccan carrot salad

Makes 6 servings   *Prep* 10 minutes   *Refrigerate* 2 hours or overnight

Cumin is the dried fruit of a plant in the parsley family. Its slightly sweet, nutty, aromatic flavor can be detected in chili powder and curries.

Per serving
114 calories, 2 g protein,
7 g fat, 12 g carbohydrate,
143 mg sodium,
0 mg cholesterol.

6 cups shredded carrot (1½ pounds)
3 tablespoons olive oil
2 tablespoons fresh lime juice
1 teaspoon ground cumin
  Pinch ground ginger
¼ teaspoon salt
⅛ teaspoon black pepper
½ bunch spinach
  (about 4 ounces), stemmed,
  washed and torn into large pieces
  (about 2 cups)

1. Place carrots in a medium-size bowl.

2. Whisk oil, lime juice, cumin, ginger, salt and pepper in a small bowl. Add to carrots; toss to coat. Cover and refrigerate 2 hours or overnight.

3. Mound carrot salad over spinach leaves on a serving platter.

Red and green salad

Makes 6 servings   *Prep* 30 minutes

Make the dressing a day or two ahead to get a jump on things. But don't add to the salad more than 2 hours before serving.

Per serving
95 calories, 1 g protein,
7 g fat, 8 g carbohydrate,
196 mg sodium,
0 mg cholesterol.

1 sweet green pepper, cored, seeded and cut into ½-inch-wide strips
1 sweet red pepper, cored, seeded and cut into ½-inch-wide strips
1 cucumber, peeled, seeded and cut into ½-inch pieces
4 plum tomatoes, seeded and cut into ½-inch pieces
2 carrots, shredded
1 small bunch arugula, cut into 2-inch pieces
3 tablespoons olive oil
1 tablespoon balsamic vinegar
½ teaspoon salt
⅛ teaspoon black pepper

Combine sweet peppers, cucumber, tomatoes, carrots and arugula in a medium-size bowl. Whisk together oil, vinegar, salt and pepper in a small bowl. Pour dressing over vegetables, tossing to coat. Serve chilled or at room temperature.

Mixed marinated vegetables

Makes 8 servings   *Prep* 15 minutes   *Cook* 9 minutes

This easy make-ahead is at home practically anywhere: as an appetizer or as an accompaniment to grilled chicken and fish or those American favorites, hot dogs and hamburgers.

Per serving
204 calories, 4 g protein, 16 g fat, 14 g carbohydrate, 537 mg sodium, 0 mg cholesterol.

Per tablespoon
124 calories, 0 g protein, 14 g fat, 1 g carbohydrate, 432 mg sodium, 0 mg cholesterol.

1 small head cauliflower, cut into small flowerets (5 cups)
2 heads broccoli, cut into small flowerets (4 cups)
4 thin carrots, sliced diagonally
1 sweet yellow pepper, cut into ½-inch-wide strips
½ cup pitted oil-cured black olives
1 scant cup Mustard Vinaigrette (recipe follows)
¼ cup finely chopped fresh parsley
3 green onions, finely chopped

1. Cook cauliflower in boiling water 2 minutes. Add broccoli and carrots; cook 3 minutes. Add yellow pepper; cook 3 to 4 minutes or until vegetables are crisp-tender. Drain; rinse under cold running water.

2. Place vegetables and olives in a serving bowl. Add dressing, parsley and green onions; toss to mix. Serve at room temperature or chilled.

Mustard vinaigrette

Whisk ½ cup olive oil, 3 tablespoons fresh lemon juice, 2 tablespoons balsamic vinegar, 2 teaspoons Dijon mustard, 1½ teaspoons salt and ¼ teaspoon black pepper in a small bowl. Cover with plastic wrap and refrigerate until ready to use. Makes scant 1 cup.

Barbecue coleslaw

Makes 8 servings   *Prep* 15 minutes

No time to shred your cabbage and carrots? Buy packaged preshredded cabbage and carrots or a coleslaw mix.

Per serving
68 calories, 2 g protein, 2 g fat, 12 g carbohydrate, 214 mg sodium, 217 mg cholesterol.

¼ cup cider vinegar
2 tablespoons sugar
⅔ cup bottled barbecue sauce
¼ cup water
2 tablespoons mayonnaise
1 teaspoon dry mustard
  Hot-pepper sauce to taste
6 cups shredded cabbage (1½- to 2-pound head)
2 cups shredded carrot (about 3 medium carrots)

1. Combine vinegar and sugar in a small saucepan. Cook over low heat just until sugar is completely dissolved. Stir in barbecue sauce, water, mayonnaise, dry mustard and hot-pepper sauce.

2. Combine cabbage and carrots in a large bowl. Pour dressing over; toss to combine. Refrigerate, covered, until ready to serve.

Classic Missouri coleslaw

Makes 10 servings   *Prep* 15 minutes   *Stand* 1 hour

Salting the cabbage draws out excess moisture, keeping the cabbage crisp even after it's been tossed with the dressing.

Per serving
86 calories, 1 g protein,
3 g fat, 16 g carbohydrate,
554 mg sodium,
5 mg cholesterol.

1 medium head cabbage (about 2 pounds), cored and shredded (8 cups)
2½ teaspoons salt
½ cup sour cream

½ cup sugar
3 tablespoons cider vinegar
⅓ cup finely chopped onion
2 carrots, shredded

1. Combine cabbage and 2 teaspoons salt in a large bowl. Place a plate directly on surface of cabbage; weight down with a 1-pound can. Let stand 1 hour.

2. Stir sour cream, sugar, vinegar and remaining ½ teaspoon salt in a bowl.

3. Squeeze cabbage by the handful to remove extra liquid. Add to sour cream mixture along with onion and carrots. Toss to combine.

Mustard-horseradish potato salad

Makes 6 servings   *Prep* 10 minutes   *Cook* 20 minutes   *Refrigerate* 1 hour

It looks like celery, it's crunchy like celery, but it isn't celery. Fennel imparts the subtle flavor of licorice or anise to dishes in which it is used.

Per serving
198 calories, 4 g protein,
10 g fat, 23 g carbohydrate,
121 mg sodium,
2 mg cholesterol.

2 pounds red new potatoes, cut into eighths
¼ cup olive oil
¼ cup red-wine vinegar
1 clove garlic, finely chopped
2 tablespoons sour cream
1½ teaspoons spicy brown mustard
1½ teaspoons bottled horseradish

1 teaspoon sugar
¼ teaspoon salt
⅛ teaspoon black pepper
2 pounds fresh fennel or celery, trimmed and diced (about 3 cups)
½ bunch green onions (about 3), trimmed and thinly sliced

1. Cook potatoes in boiling lightly salted water until tender, about 20 minutes. Drain; refrigerate 1 hour.

2. Whisk oil, vinegar, garlic, sour cream, mustard, horseradish, sugar, salt and pepper in a large bowl.

3. When potatoes are cool, add to dressing along with fennel and green onions. Toss to combine.

German potato salad

The church supper standard by which all others are judged. There's no mayonnaise here—rather, a cidery bacon dressing, hard-cooked eggs and gherkin pickles. It's delicious either warm or at room temperature.

Per serving
169 calories, 6 g protein, 7 g fat, 21 g carbohydrate, 499 mg sodium, 59 mg cholesterol.

3 pounds new potatoes, cut into ½-inch pieces
6 slices bacon
1 large onion, chopped
3 tablespoons cider vinegar
1 teaspoon salt
¼ teaspoon freshly ground black pepper
3 hard-cooked eggs, shelled
½ cup chopped sweet gherkin pickles

Dressing
2 tablespoons all-purpose flour
2 tablespoons sugar
1 teaspoon salt
1 teaspoon dry mustard
¼ teaspoon black pepper
¾ cup water
¼ cup cider vinegar

1. Cook potatoes in boiling lightly salted water until tender, about 10 minutes. Drain.

2. Meanwhile, cook bacon in a medium-size skillet over medium heat 6 to 8 minutes or until crisp; reserve bacon fat to use in dressing (you should have 3 tablespoons). Crumble bacon.

3. Place onion, vinegar, salt and pepper in a large bowl. Add potatoes, tossing well to coat with seasonings.

4. Remove yolks from hard-cooked eggs. Place in a small bowl and mash. Coarsely chop whites; reserve separately, along with gherkins.

5. Prepare dressing: Heat reserved bacon fat in skillet over medium heat. Stir in flour; cook, stirring, 1 minute. Stir in sugar, salt, dry mustard and pepper. Stir in water and vinegar. Bring mixture to simmering; cook 1 minute, stirring constantly. Remove from heat. Stir in mashed egg yolks until smooth.

6. Add dressing to potatoes; toss to mix. Stir in chopped egg whites and gherkins. Sprinkle with bacon. Serve warm or at room temperature.

Warm red potato salad

Makes 6 servings *Prep* 10 minutes *Cook* 15 to 20 minutes

This recipe won first prize in the salad category in a contest co-sponsored by *Family Circle* magazine and the National Honey Board. See if your family can guess the secret ingredient in the dressing.

Per serving
224 calories, 7 g protein,
6 g fat, 36 g carbohydrate,
211 mg sodium,
11 mg cholesterol.

1½ pounds small red new potatoes
4 strips bacon
1 medium red onion, chopped (1 cup)
6 tablespoons honey
6 tablespoons cider vinegar
½ teaspoon cornstarch mixed with ½ teaspoon cold water
2 tablespoons chopped fresh dill or 1 tablespoon dried dillweed
1 bunch watercress

1. Cook potatoes in boiling lightly salted water until tender but firm, 15 to 20 minutes. Drain. When potatoes are cool enough to handle, cut in half or quarters, depending on size. Place potatoes in a large bowl.

2. Meanwhile, cook bacon in a medium-size skillet until slightly crisp. With a slotted spoon, transfer bacon to paper toweling to drain. Cook onion in bacon fat until softened, about 3 minutes. Add honey and vinegar; cook over medium heat 2 minutes. Stir in cornstarch mixture. Bring to boiling; cook, stirring, until thickened, about 2 minutes. Remove from heat. Crumble bacon; stir into dressing along with dill.

3. Tear watercress into bite-size pieces; add to potatoes in bowl. Pour warm dressing over; gently toss. Serve immediately.

Warm red potato salad

Mediterranean salad

Makes 4 servings   *Prep* 20 minutes

Black olives and tuna are among the classic flavors of the Mediterranean. Assemble the salad in the cool morning hours of a summer day. Then it's ready when you are.

Per serving
391 calories, 24 g protein, 11 g fat, 53 g carbohydrate, 1,125 mg sodium, 31 mg cholesterol.

1¼ cups water
½ teaspoon salt
2 cups packaged precooked brown rice
¾ cup light Italian salad dressing
1 can (12 ounces) water-packed tuna, drained and flaked

1 package (9 ounces) frozen French-cut green beans, thawed and drained
1 cup small pitted ripe olives
¼ to ½ teaspoon black pepper
Lettuce leaves
3 small tomatoes, cored and cut into thin wedges

1. Combine water and salt in a medium-size saucepan. Bring to boiling. Stir in rice; cover saucepan and set aside 10 minutes or until water is absorbed by rice. Transfer rice to a large bowl.

2. Gently stir Italian dressing into rice until rice is well coated. Gently fold in tuna, green beans, olives and pepper with a rubber spatula. Serve salad immediately at room temperature or refrigerate, covered, several hours or until well chilled.

3. To serve, arrange lettuce leaves on 4 plates. Spoon salad over lettuce leaves. Surround with tomato wedges.

Wild rice salad

Makes 12 servings   *Prep* 10 minutes   *Cook* 30 to 35 minutes   *Refrigerate* 2 hours or overnight

As an alternative, try balsamic or sherry vinegar. For extra color, toss in a little chopped sweet red pepper.

Per serving
209 calories, 4 g protein, 6 g fat, 38 g carbohydrate, 454 mg sodium, 0 mg cholesterol.

1 head broccoli
1½ cups brown rice
½ cup wild rice or brown rice
2½ teaspoons salt
¼ cup olive oil

⅓ cup red-wine vinegar
⅓ cup fresh orange juice
2 teaspoons honey
1 tablespoon grated orange rind
1 cup chopped dates

1. Divide broccoli into stems and flowerets. Peel stems; cut into ¾-inch pieces. Cut flowerets into 1-inch pieces.

2. Bring a large saucepan of water to boiling. Stir in brown rice, wild rice and 1½ teaspoons salt. Simmer 30 to 35 minutes or until rice is tender, adding broccoli to rice during last 4 minutes of cooking. Drain rice and broccoli; rinse under cold running water. Drain.

3. Whisk oil, vinegar, orange juice, honey, orange rind and remaining teaspoon of salt in a large bowl. Add rice mixture and dates. Refrigerate 2 hours or overnight. Serve cold or at room temperature.

Roasted peppers with mozzarella

Makes 8 servings *Prep* 5 minutes *Roast* peppers about 10 minutes *Refrigerate* overnight

Sliced tomatoes make another great pairing with mozzarella and basil.

Per serving
228 calories, 12 g protein, 18 g fat, 7 g carbohydrate, 280 mg sodium, 45 mg cholesterol.

2 sweet red peppers
2 sweet yellow peppers
2 sweet green peppers
3 tablespoons olive oil
1 large clove garlic, finely chopped
¼ teaspoon salt
⅛ teaspoon black pepper
10 fresh basil leaves, thinly sliced
1 pound fresh mozzarella cheese, sliced

1. Roast and peel sweet peppers (see Roasting Sweet Peppers, page 35). Cut peppers into wide strips.

2. Combine oil, garlic, salt, black pepper and basil in a small bowl.

3. Arrange mozzarella on a platter, alternating with pepper strips. Drizzle oil mixture on top. For best flavor, cover dish and refrigerate overnight.

Pistachio pear salad

Makes 6 servings *Prep* 20 minutes

When shopping for pears, select ones that are firm and unblemished. Avoid bruised, hard fruits or oddly shaped ones. Ripen at room temperature and then refrigerate for a few days as needed.

Per serving
354 calories, 14 g protein, 20 g fat, 36 g carbohydrate, 794 mg sodium, 32 mg cholesterol.

Dressing
1 ripe pear, peeled, cored and chopped
1 tablespoon white-wine vinegar
1 teaspoon Dijon mustard
1 teaspoon vegetable oil
½ teaspoon dried rosemary
¼ teaspoon salt
¼ teaspoon black pepper

Salad
⅓ cup shelled pistachios
1 tablespoon dry plain bread crumbs
1 teaspoon dried rosemary
3 red Bartlett pears
8 cups lightly packed, washed, torn red-leaf lettuce and curly endive
6 ounces Stilton or other blue cheese

1. Prepare dressing: Place pear, vinegar, mustard, oil, rosemary, salt and pepper in a small food processor or blender. Whirl until smooth and creamy. If necessary, add water to thin to desired consistency.

2. Prepare salad: In a blender or small food processor, grind pistachios, bread crumbs and rosemary. Spread mixture on a sheet of waxed paper.

3. Cut pears in half; core them and thinly slice lengthwise. Coat each pear slice on both sides with pistachio mixture.

4. Arrange lettuce and endive on 6 small plates, dividing equally. Arrange coated pear slices on top. Crumble 1 ounce Stilton over each serving. Drizzle with 1 to 2 tablespoons dressing. Serve immediately.

Avocado citrus salad

Makes 8 servings *Prep* 15 minutes

Per serving
130 calories, 2 g protein, 11 g fat, 8 g carbohydrate, 84 mg sodium, 0 mg cholesterol.

Per tablespoon
80 calories, 1 g protein, 7 g fat, 4 g carbohydrate, 143 mg sodium, 0 mg cholesterol.

1 large ruby grapefruit, peeled
1 large avocado, peeled and pitted
½ pound jicama, peeled and cubed
4 cups prepared mixed greens
½ cup Lime Dressing (recipe follows)

Cut grapefruit into ¾-inch pieces; seed. Cut avocado into ¾-inch pieces. Toss avocado, grapefruit, jicama, greens and dressing in a serving bowl.

Lime dressing

Whisk ¼ cup nonfat or reduced-fat sour cream, 2 tablespoons olive oil, 2 tablespoons fresh lime juice, 1 tablespoon fresh orange juice, 1½ teaspoons sugar, ½ teaspoon poppy seeds, ¼ teaspoon salt and 3 drops hot-pepper sauce in a small bowl. Refrigerate up to 3 days. Makes ½ cup.

Caesar salad

Makes 4 servings *Prep* 5 minutes *Cook* 15 minutes

Per serving
438 calories, 8 g protein, 39 g fat, 15 g carbohydrate, 264 mg sodium, 12 mg cholesterol.

Dressing
1 large clove garlic
2 tablespoons frozen or refrigerated cholesterol-free egg replacement
3 canned anchovy fillets (optional)
½ teaspoon Dijon mustard
2 tablespoons grated Parmesan cheese
1 tablespoon fresh lemon juice
½ cup olive oil

Croutons
2 tablespoons olive oil
1 tablespoon butter
1 large clove garlic, finely chopped
2 cups ¾-inch cubes Italian bread
1 tablespoon chopped fresh parsley
1 tablespoon grated Parmesan cheese

Salad
1 head romaine lettuce, torn into bite-size pieces

1. Prepare dressing: Cook garlic in a small saucepan of boiling water 5 minutes. Drain. Place garlic in a food processor or blender. Add egg replacement, anchovies if desired, mustard, Parmesan and lemon juice. Puree 1 minute. With machine running, add oil in a stream until blended.

2. Prepare croutons: Heat oil and butter in a large nonstick skillet over medium-low heat. Add garlic; cook 2 minutes. Add bread cubes. Increase heat to medium-high; cook, stirring frequently, until croutons are evenly browned, 7 to 8 minutes. Stir in parsley and Parmesan; toss to coat.

3. To assemble: Toss romaine, croutons and dressing in a large bowl.

Avocado citrus salad *opposite*

Green herbed dressing

Makes ¾ **cup** *Prep* **5 minutes**

Per 2 tablespoons
80 calories, 2 g protein,
8 g fat, 2 g carbohydrate,
66 mg sodium,
6 mg cholesterol

½ cup plain low-fat yogurt
¼ cup mayonnaise
¼ cup finely chopped fresh parsley
1 tablespoon white-wine vinegar
1 tablespoon grated onion

1 tablespoon drained capers, finely chopped (optional)
1 tablespoon chopped fresh chives
½ teaspoon dried tarragon, crumbled

Whisk together yogurt, mayonnaise, parsley, vinegar, onion, capers if using, chives and tarragon in a small bowl. Cover and refrigerate until ready to serve.

Thousand Island dressing

Makes 1½ **cups** *Prep* **5 minutes**

Per 2 tablespoons
79 calories, 1 g protein,
8 g fat, 3 g carbohydrate,
116 mg sodium,
6 mg cholesterol.

½ cup mayonnaise
½ cup plain low-fat yogurt
2 tablespoons chili sauce

2 tablespoons pickle relish
2 tablespoons chopped sweet red pepper

Whisk together mayonnaise, yogurt, chili sauce, relish and sweet red pepper in a small bowl. Cover and refrigerate until ready to serve.

Ranch dressing

Makes 1½ **cups** *Prep* **5 minutes**

Per 2 tablespoons
54 calories, 1 g protein,
5 g fat, 1 g carbohydrate,
135 mg sodium,
6 mg cholesterol.

¾ cup buttermilk
¼ cup mayonnaise
⅓ cup sour cream
1 tablespoon fresh lime juice
1 tablespoon chopped fresh parsley

1 small clove garlic
½ teaspoon salt
⅛ teaspoon black pepper
1 tablespoon chopped fresh chives

Place buttermilk, mayonnaise, sour cream, lime juice, parsley, garlic, salt and pepper in a food processor or blender. Whirl 1 minute or until dressing is creamy and smooth. Pour into a small bowl. Stir in chives. Cover and refrigerate up to 1 week.

Creamy blue cheese dressing

Makes 1¾ cups   *Prep* 5 minutes

1 container (8 ounces) sour cream
5 ounces blue cheese

3 tablespoons milk
1 tablespoon red-wine vinegar

Combine sour cream, blue cheese, milk and vinegar in a food processor or blender. Whirl until well blended. Cover and refrigerate until ready to serve.

Zesty vinaigrette

Makes 1¼ cups   *Prep* 5 minutes

⅔ cup olive oil
2 tablespoons balsamic vinegar
2 tablespoons chopped onion
½ cup loosely packed fresh parsley
1 tablespoon Dijon mustard

1 small clove garlic
7 cornichons (tiny French pickles)
1 teaspoon Worcestershire sauce
⅛ teaspoon black pepper

Place oil, vinegar, onion, parsley, mustard, garlic, cornichons, Worcestershire sauce and pepper in a food processor or blender. Whirl until well blended. Cover and refrigerate up to 1 week.

Creamy Dijon Parmesan dressing

Makes 1½ cups   *Prep* 5 minutes

1 cup buttermilk
1 container (8 ounces) sour cream
⅓ cup grated Parmesan cheese

1 tablespoon Dijon mustard
1 teaspoon fresh lemon juice
¼ teaspoon black pepper

Place buttermilk, sour cream, Parmesan, mustard, lemon juice and pepper in a food processor or blender. Whirl until well blended. Cover and refrigerate until ready to serve.

Corn and
crab chowder
page 81

Mexican corn
soup
page 73

Cranberry turkey stew *page 88*

Soups and stews

WHY DO WE so love soups and stews? Perhaps it's the heady aroma that fills the house as they simmer atop the stove, or the sense of serenity once you start to eat. Even thick, chunky versions go down easy and soothe from head to toe.

No collection in this category would be complete without chicken soup, and offered here is a richly flavored classic broth with four variations, including a velvety cream-laced one and an old-fashioned version thickened with orzo. For equally tempting but not-so-traditional options, you can spoon into a bowlful of

Spoonful by spoonful, a brimming bowl means instant comfort.

Asian Beef-Noodle, Barbecue Chili or Stewed Coconut Shrimp. And if cool is what you need, you won't be disappointed by Super-Simple Gazpacho or Chilled Tomato Soup accented with vinegar. Hot or not, one thing is certain: These tasty liquids never fail to please.

Winter vegetable chowder

Makes 4 servings   *Prep* 30 minutes   *Cook* 12 minutes

The low-fat tricks in this not-as-rich-as-it-tastes soup are part-skim ricotta cheese and low-fat milk instead of heavy cream. Instant potato flakes thicken the soup, adding to the illusion.

Per serving
298 calories, 15 g protein,
7 g fat, 49 g carbohydrate,
602 mg sodium,
24 mg cholesterol.

1 pound parsnips
1 large sweet potato (½ pound)
1 small head broccoli (½ pound)
1 small onion, finely chopped
  (¼ cup)
3 cups water
¾ teaspoon salt

1 cup part-skim ricotta cheese
2 cups low-fat (1%) milk
½ cup instant potato flakes
¼ teaspoon black pepper
⅛ teaspoon ground nutmeg
2 tablespoons grated Parmesan
  cheese

1. Peel parsnips; halve lengthwise and cut crosswise into ½-inch-thick slices. Peel sweet potato; cut into ½-inch cubes. Cut broccoli head from stem and separate into small flowerets. Peel stem and cut into ½-inch cubes.

2. Bring water and salt to boiling in a large saucepan. Add parsnips, sweet potato, broccoli stem and onion. Lower heat and simmer 6 minutes. Add broccoli flowerets; simmer 3 minutes or until all the vegetables are tender.

3. Meanwhile, combine ricotta cheese, milk, potato flakes, pepper and nutmeg in a blender. Whirl until pureed. Stir ricotta mixture into soup until well blended. Gently heat through. Ladle into soup bowls and sprinkle with Parmesan cheese.

Classic onion soup

Makes 6 servings   *Prep* 15 minutes   *Cook* 50 minutes   *Broil* 1 to 2 minutes

Our version of the French bistro classic is made with beef broth, but for a lighter flavor, use half chicken and half beef broth.

Per serving
313 calories, 14 g protein,
14 g fat, 32 g carbohydrate,
616 mg sodium,
32 mg cholesterol.

1 tablespoon olive oil
1 tablespoon butter
6 Spanish onions, sliced
3 tablespoons all-purpose flour
3 cans (14¾ ounces each) lower-
  sodium beef broth

¼ cup dry sherry (optional)
6 thick slices Italian bread
6 slices low-sodium
  Swiss cheese

1. Heat oil and butter in a large saucepan over medium heat. Add onions and cook, stirring frequently, 30 minutes or until softened and caramelized. Stir in flour to coat onions. Cook 1 minute. Slowly stir in broth. Cover; cook over low heat 20 minutes. Add sherry if you wish.

2. Heat broiler.

3. Spoon soup into 6 individual ovenproof bowls. Top each with a slice of bread and a slice of cheese. Broil briefly to melt cheese.

Butternut squash soup with ginger cream

Makes 4 servings   *Prep* 30 minutes   *Cook* 30 minutes

Here's a double hit of ginger—grated fresh ginger in the soup and finely chopped candied ginger folded into the whipped-cream garnish.

Per serving
212 calories, 7 g protein,
10 g fat, 26 g carbohydrate,
968 mg sodium,
28 mg cholesterol.

1 tablespoon butter
3 carrots, sliced (1¼ cups)
1 small onion, chopped (¼ cup)
1 tablespoon grated fresh ginger
1 small butternut or acorn squash (1 pound), peeled, seeded and cut into large chunks
3 to 4 cups chicken broth
½ teaspoon dried thyme, crumbled
¼ teaspoon salt
⅛ teaspoon ground nutmeg
⅛ teaspoon black pepper
1 tablespoon finely chopped candied ginger
¼ cup heavy cream, whipped

1. Melt butter in a medium-size saucepan over medium-low heat. Add carrots, onion and fresh ginger; sauté about 5 minutes or until carrots are tender. Add squash, broth, thyme, salt, nutmeg and pepper to saucepan. Simmer 20 to 30 minutes or until squash is tender. Drain solids, reserving liquid. Working in batches, puree squash solids in a food processor. Return to saucepan with reserved liquid. Heat.

2. Fold candied ginger into whipped cream. Swirl into each serving.

Curried yellow split-pea soup

Makes 6 servings   *Prep* 15 minutes   *Cook* 65 minutes

Dried split peas cook up quicker than other dried beans, and they require no presoaking. You may wish to substitute good-quality canned vegetable broth for the bouillon granules and water.

Per serving
345 calories, 20 g protein,
6 g fat, 56 g carbohydrate,
282 mg sodium,
0 mg cholesterol.

2 tablespoons vegetable oil
2 medium onions, chopped
3 cloves garlic, finely chopped
1 tablespoon curry powder
6 cups water
1 tablespoon vegetable-flavor bouillon granules
1 pound dried yellow split peas
2 carrots, sliced
2 large ribs celery, sliced
⅛ teaspoon ground cloves
⅛ teaspoon black pepper
1 tablespoon fresh lemon juice
¼ teaspoon salt
Plain yogurt and pumpernickel croutons for serving (optional)

1. Heat oil in a medium-size saucepan over medium heat. Add onions and sauté until softened but not browned, about 3 minutes. Add garlic and curry powder; cook 1 minute. Stir in water and bouillon granules.

2. Wash and pick over split peas. Add to pan along with carrots, celery, cloves and pepper. Bring to boiling. Lower heat; cover and simmer 1 hour.

3. Cool soup slightly. Working in batches, spoon soup into a food processor. Whirl until smooth; return to pan. Stir in lemon juice and salt. Heat to serving temperature. Garnish with yogurt and pumpernickel croutons if you wish.

Harvest gumbo

Okra is the traditional thickener in gumbo. If you get a hankering for this fresh vegetable soup in the dead of winter, don't fret. You can replace the fresh okra, peas, lima beans and corn with frozen versions. For best flavor, cook gumbo a day ahead.

Per serving
182 calories, 7 g protein, 8 g fat, 22 g carbohydrate, 585 mg sodium, 13 mg cholesterol.

2 tablespoons olive oil
2 tablespoons all-purpose flour
1 onion, chopped
2 ribs celery, chopped
1 fresh jalapeño chile, seeded and chopped
2 sweet red peppers, cored, seeded and chopped
2 cups thinly sliced fresh okra
1 teaspoon dried oregano
1 teaspoon paprika
½ teaspoon dried thyme

3 cups vegetable broth
3 cups water
2 medium tomatoes, seeded and chopped
½ pound kielbasa, sliced lengthwise and cut crosswise into half moons
1½ cups fresh black-eyed peas
1½ cups fresh lima beans
3 ears fresh corn, shucked
¼ pound fresh green beans, trimmed and cut into 2-inch pieces

1. Heat oil in a large heavy saucepan over medium-low heat. Stir in flour; cook, stirring with a wooden spoon, 5 minutes. Add onion, celery, jalapeño, sweet red peppers, okra, oregano, paprika and thyme; cook 6 minutes, stirring frequently.

2. Add broth, water, tomatoes and kielbasa. Simmer 15 minutes. Add black-eyed peas and lima beans; cook 15 minutes. Slice corn kernels from cob; you should have about 1½ cups. Add corn and green beans to pan; cook 10 minutes or until all the vegetables are tender.

Harvest gumbo

Leek and potato soup *opposite*

Broccoli-potato chowder

Makes 4 servings   *Prep* 10 minutes   *Cook* 15 minutes

For a thicker chowder, try this: Before whisking in the mashed potatoes, puree about 2 cups of the soup in a food processor and then stir the puree back into the pot. Now add the potatoes.

Per serving
210 calories, 11 g protein, 5 g fat, 34 g carbohydrate, 1,047 mg sodium, 7 mg cholesterol.

3 slices bacon, cut into pieces
1 onion, chopped
1 carrot, shredded
2 cans (13¾ ounces each) lower-sodium chicken broth
½ teaspoon dried thyme
¼ teaspoon caraway seeds
1 package (10 ounces) frozen chopped broccoli, thawed
2½ cups mashed potatoes
  Salt and black pepper (optional)

1. Cook bacon in a large saucepan over medium heat until crisp, 3 to 5 minutes. Remove with a slotted spoon to paper toweling to drain.

2. Pour off all but 1 tablespoon bacon fat from saucepan. Add onion and carrot; cook over medium heat, stirring, until soft but not browned, about 3 minutes. Add broth, thyme and caraway seeds. Bring to boiling. Add broccoli; bring to boiling. Lower heat, cover and simmer 5 minutes.

3. Whisk in potatoes. Cover and gently heat through. Stir in bacon. Add salt and pepper if needed.

Leek and potato soup

Makes 6 servings   *Prep* 40 minutes   *Cook* 45 minutes

Yukon gold potatoes instead of the all-purpose will create a soup with an almost buttery flavor.

Per serving
153 calories, 3 g protein, 7 g fat, 20 g carbohydrate, 856 mg sodium, 3 mg cholesterol.

2 tablespoons vegetable oil
2 large leeks, trimmed and well washed, white and light green parts diced (about 2½ cups)
1 large onion, diced
1 pound all-purpose potatoes, peeled and thinly sliced
1 carrot
1 sprig fresh parsley
1 sprig fresh dill
½ teaspoon salt
¼ teaspoon black pepper
4 cups chicken broth or water
1 tablespoon finely chopped fresh chives for garnish
1 tablespoon finely chopped fresh parsley for garnish

1. Heat oil in a large saucepan over medium heat. Add leeks and onion; sauté 5 minutes or until softened but not browned.

2. Add potatoes, carrot, parsley, dill, salt, pepper and broth. Bring to boiling. Lower heat; cover and simmer 35 to 40 minutes or until vegetables are tender.

3. Working in batches if necessary, puree soup in a blender or food processor. Serve immediately, garnished with chopped chives and parsley.

Cheesy cauliflower soup

Makes 4 servings *Prep* 10 minutes *Cook* 15 minutes

Using prepackaged cauliflowerets makes this soup practically effortless. If your taste runs to less spicy foods, try regular Monterey Jack cheese instead of the pepper variety.

Per serving

294 calories, 15 g protein, 21 g fat, 14 g carbohydrate, 1,265 mg sodium, 43 mg cholesterol.

1 tablespoon olive oil
1 cup chopped green onion
4 cups chicken broth
2 packages (8 ounces each) fresh cauliflowerets
¼ cup all-purpose flour
1½ cups shredded pepper-Jack cheese (6 ounces)
¼ cup roasted red peppers
½ teaspoon salt (optional)
¼ teaspoon hot-pepper sauce

1. Heat oil in a large saucepan over medium heat. Add green onions and sauté about 3 minutes or until tender. Add 3 cups broth; bring to boiling. Add cauliflowerets; return to boiling. Reduce heat to medium-low; cook about 6 minutes or until cauliflower is almost tender.

2. Whisk together flour and remaining 1 cup chicken broth in a small bowl. Stir into saucepan. Bring to boiling; cook, stirring occasionally, 2 to 3 minutes or until soup is thickened.

3. Remove soup from heat. Add cheese, stirring until melted. Stir in roasted red peppers, salt if using and hot-pepper sauce, breaking up red peppers with a wooden spoon.

Hearty mushroom soup

Makes 6 servings *Prep* 10 minutes *Cook* 30 minutes

Take advantage of the wide range of mushrooms now available in your supermarket. Skip over the familiar white button mushrooms—although they're delicious in this soup—and opt for the cremini, portabella, shiitake or oyster varieties.

Per serving

222 calories, 6 g protein, 12 g fat, 22 g carbohydrate, 818 mg sodium, 30 mg cholesterol.

½ cup chopped onion
3 strips bacon, diced
1 pound mushrooms, thinly sliced
⅓ cup all-purpose flour
1 large can (46 ounces) chicken broth (5¾ cups)
1 cup water
1 small packet lower-sodium chicken bouillon granules
1¼ pounds all-purpose potatoes, peeled and cubed
2 tablespoons dry sherry
½ cup heavy cream
1 tablespoon chopped fresh parsley

1. Cook onion and bacon in a Dutch oven over medium heat until onion is golden, 2 to 3 minutes. Add mushrooms; cook until liquid evaporates, about 8 minutes. Add flour; cook, stirring, about 1 minute.

2. Stir broth, water and bouillon granules into saucepan. Add potatoes and sherry; simmer 15 minutes or until potatoes are tender. Transfer 4 cups of soup mixture to a food processor. Puree and return to pot. Stir in cream. Gently reheat, stirring occasionally.

3. Ladle into soup bowls. Garnish with parsley.

Wisconsin beer-cheese soup

Makes 12 servings *Prep* 15 minutes *Cook* 30 minutes

There's no better way to warm up a cold winter afternoon than with steaming mugs of this rich soup.

Per serving

208 calories, 7 g protein, 16 g fat, 11 g carbohydrate, 751 mg sodium, 36 mg cholesterol.

3 tablespoons olive oil
½ cup chopped onion
1 small carrot, chopped
1 rib celery, finely chopped
¼ cup all-purpose flour
1 pound baking potatoes, peeled and cubed
6 cups chicken broth
1 bottle (12 ounces) beer
½ cup heavy cream
1 tablespoon Dijon mustard
½ teaspoon salt
½ teaspoon hot-pepper sauce
¼ teaspoon Worcestershire sauce
2 cups shredded extra-sharp cheddar cheese

1. Heat oil in a Dutch oven over medium heat. Add onion, carrot and celery; cook until very tender, about 10 minutes. Stir in flour; cook 1 minute. Add potatoes, broth and beer. Bring to boiling; cook 10 to 15 minutes or until potatoes are tender.

2. Combine cream, mustard, salt, hot-pepper sauce and Worcestershire sauce in a small bowl. Stir into soup. Remove from heat. Add cheese, stirring until melted and smooth. Transfer 2 cups of soup to a food processor. Puree and return to pot. Serve immediately.

Mexican corn soup

Makes 4 servings *Prep* 20 minutes *Cook* 45 minutes

To turn this into a main course, add small pieces of deli barbecued chicken or ribs.

Shown on page 66.

Per serving

198 calories, 5 g protein, 5 g fat, 38 g carbohydrate, 691 mg sodium, 0 mg cholesterol.

1 tablespoon vegetable oil
1 large onion, finely chopped
2 small sweet red peppers, cored, seeded and chopped
1 jalapeño chile
2 cloves garlic, finely chopped
6 large ears fresh corn, shucked
2 small tomatoes, seeded and chopped
2 to 3 drops hot-pepper sauce
3 cups water
1¼ teaspoons salt
1 lime, cut in wedges, for garnish
8 tortilla chips, broken, for garnish

1. Heat oil in a Dutch oven over medium heat. Add onion, sweet red peppers and jalapeño; sauté 4 minutes. Add garlic; sauté until softened, 30 seconds. Slice corn kernels from cob into pot, making sure to scrape milky white substance from cob. Add tomatoes; sauté 1 minute.

2. Add hot-pepper sauce, water and salt. Simmer 30 minutes or until vegetables are tender. Cool to room temperature.

3. Transfer half of soup to a food processor. Puree and return to pot. Reheat gently. Garnish bowls of soup with lime wedges and tortilla chips.

Super-simple gazpacho

Makes 4 servings   *Prep* 20 minutes   *Refrigerate* several hours or overnight

For a smooth soup, set aside some of the vegetables to use as a garnish along with the lemon slices, then puree the remaining vegetable mixture in a food processor.

Per serving
89 calories, 4 g protein,
1 g fat, 21 g carbohydrate,
735 mg sodium,
0 mg cholesterol.

1 cucumber, peeled, seeded and diced
2 small red onion, finely chopped
2 cloves garlic, finely chopped
3 large tomatoes, peeled, seeded and diced
1 small sweet green pepper, cored, seeded and diced
2 cups thick tomato juice

1½ cups lower-sodium chicken broth
¼ cup red-wine vinegar
1 tablespoon finely chopped fresh oregano or 1 teaspoon dried
1 tablespoon finely chopped fresh basil or 1 teaspoon dried
½ teaspoon salt
¼ teaspoon black pepper
¼ teaspoon hot-pepper sauce

Combine cucumber, onion, garlic, tomatoes and green pepper in a large bowl. Stir together juice, broth, vinegar, oregano, basil, salt, black pepper and hot-pepper sauce. Pour over vegetables. Cover and refrigerate several hours or overnight.

Super-simple gazpacho

Chilled tomato soup

Makes 4 servings *Prep* 15 minutes

Next to a sliced tomato salad, this is the easiest way to showcase the best of the summer's vine-ripened tomatoes. Red-wine vinegar or sherry vinegar works just as well as balsamic.

Per serving
143 calories, 3 g protein, 8 g fat, 19 g carbohydrate, 1,098 mg sodium, 0 mg cholesterol.

¾ cup finely diced, seeded, unpeeled cucumber
½ cup chopped fresh basil
¼ cup finely chopped red onion
2 tablespoons extra-virgin olive oil
3 pounds tomatoes, chopped
3 tablespoons balsamic vinegar
2 teaspoons salt
½ teaspoon black pepper

1. Combine ¼ cup cucumber, 2 tablespoons basil, 2 tablespoons onion and 2 teaspoons oil in a small bowl.

2. Working in batches, puree tomatoes, vinegar, salt, pepper and remaining cucumber, basil and onion in a food processor or blender. Serve immediately or refrigerate. Garnish with diced cucumber-onion mixture. Drizzle each serving with 1 teaspoon olive oil.

Cold beet soup

Makes 6 servings *Prep* 15 minutes *Refrigerate* 1 hour

Serve this colorful soup as a summer lunch or pack into a chilled thermos and take to a picnic as a cooling first course.

Per serving
179 calories, 4 g protein, 9 g fat, 21 g carbohydrate, 784 mg sodium, 29 mg cholesterol.

1½ tablespoons grated orange rind
2 cups loosely packed fresh mint leaves
2 jars (16 ounces each) cooked beets
1½ cups fresh orange juice
1 container (16 ounces) reduced-fat sour cream
¾ cup water
1 teaspoon salt

1. Combine orange rind and mint leaves in a food processor or blender. Whirl until mint is finely chopped. Add beets with their liquid to processor or blender. Whirl until beets are thoroughly pureed.

2. Add orange juice, sour cream, water and salt. Whirl until well blended. Refrigerate 1 hour.

Classic chicken broth

Makes about 16 cups broth; about 5½ cups shredded chicken   *Prep* 15 minutes   *Cook* 3¼ hours

Having a pot of chicken broth bubbling on the stove leaves the kitchen smelling great and the cook ahead of the curve. Use the broth in any of these four soups straightaway or freeze to pull out at a later date. Either way, it's comfort in a bowl.

Per serving
114 calories, 15 g protein, 6 g fat, 0 g carbohydrate, 45 mg sodium, 40 mg cholesterol.

3 large carrots
4 ribs celery
2 small onions or 1 large
6 sprigs fresh parsley
3 cloves garlic, crushed
¼ bunch fresh thyme, with stems

16 whole black peppercorns
1 bay leaf
1 whole chicken (5 pounds), gizzards and liver removed
16 cups cold water or as needed

1. Cut carrots and celery crosswise into quarters. Cut each onion into 8 wedges.

2. Place carrots, celery, onions, parsley, garlic, thyme, peppercorns, bay leaf and chicken in a stockpot. Add enough cold water to cover. Bring to boiling over high heat. Boil 3 to 5 minutes, skimming off foam from surface as it appears. Lower heat; simmer, uncovered, 3 hours, skimming fat as needed. Add water as necessary to keep chicken covered.

3. Strain broth through a colander lined with a double thickness of cheesecloth into a large bowl; reserve. Discard vegetables and bay leaf. Let chicken stand until cool enough to handle. When cool, remove skin. Remove chicken from bones; tear into shreds and reserve.

Make-ahead tip: Refrigerate broth overnight; remove solidified fat from surface. Freeze broth in 8-cup batches up to 3 months.

Chicken soup with tortellini

Per serving
494 calories, 49 g protein, 25 g fat, 17 g carbohydrate, 596 mg sodium, 167 mg cholesterol.

Heat 2 tablespoons olive oil over medium-high heat in a large saucepan. Add 2 cloves garlic, finely chopped, and 1 large onion, diced, and cook over medium-high heat until softened, about 8 minutes. Add 8 cups Classic Chicken Broth and bring to boiling. Lower heat to simmering. Add 2 tomatoes, peeled, seeded and chopped, and a 9-ounce package fresh or frozen tortellini; simmer 6 minutes. Add 3 cups thinly sliced fresh spinach, 1 teaspoon salt, ½ teaspoon freshly ground black pepper and reserved chicken shreds. Simmer another 4 minutes. Serve with grated Parmesan cheese. Makes 6 servings.

Springtime vegetable chicken soup

Per serving

413 calories, 43 g protein,
20 g fat, 14 g carbohydrate,
433 mg sodium,
118 mg cholesterol.

Bring 8 cups Classic Chicken Broth to boiling. Dice and add 2 ribs celery, 3 carrots and 1 onion. Lower heat and simmer 20 minutes or until vegetables are tender. Add 2 cups diced cabbage and 1 package (10 ounces) frozen peas; simmer 10 minutes or until tender. Add reserved chicken shreds, 1 teaspoon salt, ½ teaspoon freshly ground black pepper and 2 tablespoons butter. Makes 6 servings.

Old-fashioned chicken soup with orzo

Per serving

465 calories, 47 g protein,
18 g fat, 26 g carbohydrate,
508 mg sodium,
112 mg cholesterol.

Bring 8 cups Classic Chicken Broth to boiling. Add 1 large carrot, diced; 2 ribs celery, diced; 1 large tomato, peeled, seeded and chopped, and 1 cup orzo. Boil 5 minutes, skimming any fat. Add reserved chicken shreds, 1 teaspoon salt, ½ teaspoon Italian seasoning and ¼ teaspoon freshly ground black pepper. Cook 5 minutes more or until orzo and vegetables are tender. Makes 6 servings.

Cream of chicken soup

Per serving

525 calories, 47 g protein,
32 g fat, 13 g carbohydrate,
578 mg sodium,
160 mg cholesterol.

Bring 8 cups Classic Chicken Broth to boiling. Add ½ cup heavy cream and 1 bag (16 ounces) frozen mixed vegetables. Lower heat to simmering and cook 10 minutes or until vegetables are tender. Stir in 1 teaspoon salt, ¼ teaspoon dried tarragon, ½ cup cream cheese and reserved chicken shreds. Heat through. Makes 6 servings.

garnishes with flair

ADD a crisp flourish to soups and salads with homemade croutons. All you need is a few slices of bread—pumpernickel, rye, whole wheat, French or Italian are all good choices—a little oil, and 5 minutes. Use a ratio of 1 tablespoon oil to 3 slices of bread. Cut the bread into cubes or thin strips and place in a single layer in a large nonstick skillet. Sprinkle with vegetable oil. Heat skillet over medium heat, stirring, until bread is crisped. Remove from heat.

TOP a spicy soup with a dollop of plain yogurt blended with shredded cucumber.

DRIZZLE a puree of roasted red peppers or pesto-flavored whipped cream cheese over smooth, creamy soups.

FLOAT thin slices of wild mushrooms or scallions on clear soups; melted cheese on toasted bread on onion or vegetable soups.

Asian beef-noodle soup

Makes 6 servings *Prep* 10 minutes *Cook* 10 minutes

Chinese cabbage comes in long heads with crisp, veiny leaves that are creamy white with green-tipped ends. Its flavor is more delicate than that of the familiar round cabbage.

Per serving
314 calories, 16 g protein, 5 g fat, 53 g carbohydrate, 1,591 mg sodium, 24 mg cholesterol.

6 cups water
2 tablespoons soy sauce
2 tablespoons chili sauce or ketchup
1 teaspoon ground ginger
⅛ teaspoon ground red pepper (cayenne)
2 packages (3 ounces each) low-fat ramen instant noodle soup
2½ cups thinly sliced Chinese cabbage or green cabbage
3 carrots, cut into slivers
1 cup sliced small mushrooms
½ cup frozen corn kernels
½ pound cooked top round steak, thinly sliced
4 green onions, cut into slivers
2 teaspoons dark Asian sesame oil

1. Mix water, soy sauce, chili sauce, ginger, red pepper and 1 seasoning packet from noodles in a large saucepan (reserve other packet for another use). Bring to simmering. Add cabbage and carrots; cook 5 minutes.

2. Add mushrooms, corn and ramen noodles; simmer 3 minutes. Add beef and green onions; heat through. Stir in sesame oil.

Hearty Portuguese soup

Makes 6 servings *Prep* 15 minutes *Cook* 40 minutes

To create a more traditional version, use linguiça—a spicy Portuguese sausage—or pork-based kielbasa. Serve the soup with Portuguese bread for soaking up the broth; the bread's sweetness contrasts nicely with the spiciness of the sausage.

Per serving
168 calories, 11 g protein, 6 g fat, 30 g carbohydrate, 762 mg sodium, 23 mg cholesterol.

1 teaspoon olive oil
6 ounces turkey kielbasa, sliced
1 large onion, chopped
1 large clove garlic, chopped
1 pound fresh kale, washed, or 1 package (10 ounces) frozen chopped kale, thawed and drained
4 cups water
2 cans (13¾ ounces each) lower-sodium chicken broth
2 carrots, sliced
1 teaspoon dried marjoram, crumbled
½ teaspoon salt
⅛ teaspoon black pepper
½ cup long-grain white rice

1. Heat oil in a large saucepan over medium-low heat. Add kielbasa, onion and garlic and sauté until onion is tender, about 10 minutes.

2. If using fresh kale, cut off and slice stems into ½-inch pieces. Keep stem pieces separate. Coarsely chop fresh leaves.

3. Add water, broth, carrots, marjoram, salt, pepper and sliced kale stems or frozen kale to saucepan. Bring to boiling. Lower heat; cover and simmer 15 minutes.

4. If using fresh kale, add leaves to pan. Add rice; bring to boiling. Lower heat; cover and simmer 15 minutes or until rice is tender.

Asian beef-noodle soup
opposite

79

Ukrainian borscht

Makes 6 servings (about 12 cups)   *Prep* 20 minutes   *Cook* 1½ hours

Cubed beef, beets, potatoes and cabbage make this hearty winter soup a one-dish meal. Serve with pumpernickel or rye bread.

Per serving
213 calories, 14 g protein, 8 g fat, 25 g carbohydrate, 477 mg sodium, 23 mg cholesterol.

1 tablespoon vegetable oil
½ pound beef top round, cut into ¾-inch cubes
2 cans (13¾ ounces each) lower-sodium beef broth
3 cups water
1 bay leaf
2 beets (about 8 ounces total)
2 all-purpose potatoes, peeled and cubed
1 large onion, chopped
1 large rib celery, sliced
1 carrot, sliced
1 white turnip, peeled and cubed

¾ cup tomato juice
¾ teaspoon salt
½ teaspoon dried basil
½ teaspoon dried thyme
¼ teaspoon black pepper
1 small head cabbage, chopped (4 cups)
¼ cup fresh lemon juice
¼ cup chopped fresh dill
1 tablespoon sugar
    Few drops hot-pepper sauce
    Sour cream and fresh dill sprigs for garnish (optional)

1. Heat oil in a large saucepan. Add beef and brown 6 minutes. Add broth, water and bay leaf. Simmer, covered, 1 hour. Meanwhile, cook beets in water to cover in a small saucepan until tender, 30 minutes. Drain.

2. Remove bay leaf from beef broth and discard. Skim off foam. Add potatoes, onion, celery, carrot, turnip, tomato juice, salt, basil, thyme and pepper. Simmer, covered, 20 minutes.

3. Peel and coarsely shred beets. Add to soup along with cabbage. Cover and cook 10 minutes more. Stir in lemon juice, chopped dill, sugar and hot-pepper sauce. Garnish servings with sour cream and dill sprigs if you wish.

Perfect onion chopping

1. Cut peeled onion in half lengthwise. Place, flat side down, on cutting board. Starting near root end, cut vertically into even slices.

2. Steady onion at uncut end. Hold knife parallel to cutting surface and make 2 horizontal cuts across onion. Do not cut all the way through.

3. Hold onion by uncut end; cut straight down, making evenly spaced slices across first series of cuts. Chop uncut end.

Corn and crab chowder

Makes 6 servings Prep 35 minutes Cook 45 minutes

After you've removed the kernels from the cobs with a sharp knife, scrape down the cob with the back of the knife to "squeeze" out the sweet milk.

Shown on page 66.

Per serving
227 calories, 14 g protein, 7 g fat, 29 g carbohydrate, 432 mg sodium, 50 mg cholesterol.

1 tablespoon olive oil
2 all-purpose potatoes (¾ pound total), peeled and cut into ½-inch cubes
1 small onion, finely chopped
2 small shallots, finely chopped
1 can (13¾ ounces) chicken broth
¼ cup water
4 large ears fresh corn, shucked
4 to 5 drops hot-pepper sauce
½ pound lump crabmeat or firm white fish, cut into chunks
Few sprigs fresh thyme (optional)
¼ teaspoon black pepper
2 cups milk

1. Heat oil in a large saucepan over medium heat. Add potatoes, toss in oil and sauté about 3 minutes. Add onion and shallots; sauté 3 minutes. Add broth and water; bring to boiling. Lower heat; simmer, covered, 15 minutes or until potatoes are just tender. Transfer about 1 cup soup to a blender or food processor. Whirl until pureed. Stir back into saucepan.

2. Slice corn kernels from cobs into pan, making sure to scrape milky white substance from cob. Add hot-pepper sauce; cook 5 to 7 minutes or until corn is tender. Add crabmeat or fish, thyme sprigs if desired, and pepper; simmer gently, uncovered, until crab is opaque, about 5 minutes; do not boil.

3. Remove thyme sprigs. Stir in milk; heat soup gently and let thicken slightly. Do not boil.

Codfish chowder

Makes 4 servings Prep 20 minutes Cook 20 minutes

Dinner in a hurry? This six-ingredient recipe will put you on the fast track.

Per serving
346 calories, 13 g protein, 6 g fat, 64 g carbohydrate, 690 mg sodium, 25 mg cholesterol.

3 cups milk
3 cups water
1 onion, chopped
1 pound new potatoes, cubed
1 tablespoon fish bouillon granules
1 package (10 ounces) frozen corn kernels
1 pound cod fillets, cut into 1-inch chunks
Black pepper to taste

1. Bring milk and water to simmering in a large saucepan. Add onion, potatoes and bouillon granules. Simmer 12 minutes or until potatoes are tender. (If you prefer a thickened chowder, remove 1 cup potatoes and puree in a blender. Stir back into chowder.)

2. Add corn. Return to simmering. Add cod; barely simmer 3 minutes or until fish is opaque. Stir in pepper and serve.

Mediterranean fish chowder

Makes 4 servings   *Prep* 15 minutes   *Cook* 25 to 30 minutes

FAMILY CIRCLE ALL-TIME FAVORITE RECIPES

Grouper, red snapper or monkfish can substitute for the cod. Fennel seed, a classic Mediterranean seasoning, adds a distinctive licorice tang.

Per serving
310 calories, 26 g protein,
13 g fat, 23 g carbohydrate,
865 mg sodium,
66 mg cholesterol.

Freezing soups
Most soups freeze well, but some ingredients should be omitted when you first cook the soup and added while reheating.
• Cheese, cream and other dairy products may separate and curdle when thawed and reheated.
• Some vegetable pieces and pasta become soft when frozen and reheated.

1 tablespoon vegetable oil
2 large onions, coarsely chopped
1 can (13¾ ounces) lower-sodium chicken broth
1 can (14½ ounces) no-salt-added stewed tomatoes
1 bottle (8 ounces) clam juice
1 teaspoon dried basil, crumbled
½ teaspoon salt
¼ teaspoon fennel seeds
⅛ teaspoon black pepper
⅛ teaspoon red-pepper flakes
1 cup water
2 tablespoons unsalted butter
¼ cup flour
1 pound cod fillets, cut into bite-size pieces
1 tablespoon fresh lemon juice
8 oil-cured black olives, pitted and sliced
2 tablespoons chopped fresh parsley for garnish (optional)

1. Heat oil in a large saucepan over medium-low heat. Add onions and sauté until softened, about 3 minutes. Add broth, tomatoes, clam juice, basil, salt, fennel seeds, black pepper, red-pepper flakes and water. Bring to boiling. Lower heat; cover and simmer about 15 minutes.

2. Meanwhile, melt butter in a small skillet. Stir in flour until smooth. Cook over low heat, stirring, until flour is browned, about 5 minutes. Cool slightly. Add about 1 cup soup to flour mixture, stirring until smooth.

3. Stir flour mixture into soup in pot. Bring to boiling, stirring constantly. Add cod, lemon juice and olives. Cook gently, uncovered, 5 to 10 minutes or until fish is cooked through. Garnish with parsley if you wish.

Mediterranean fish chowder

Beef stew
with roasted
vegetables

Beef stew with roasted vegetables

Makes 4 servings　*Prep* 15 minutes　*Cook* 1 hour 10 minutes　*Roast* at 450° for 25 to 35 minutes

When roasting the
vegetables, keep the
pieces uniform to
ensure they all cook in
the same amount of
time. And spread all the
vegetables evenly in a
single layer in the
baking pan without
overlapping so they
roast uniformly. For a
special treat, serve the
stew over mashed
potatoes or creamy
polenta.

Per serving
544 calories, 38 g protein,
17 g fat, 58 g carbohydrate,
789 mg sodium,
48 mg cholesterol.

3　teaspoons olive oil
1　pound beef chuck, cut into
　　½-inch cubes
3　cloves garlic, peeled, left whole
1½ teaspoons dried thyme
½　teaspoon salt
¼　teaspoon black pepper
1　can (13¾ ounces) lower-sodium
　　beef broth
2　large sweet potatoes (1 pound),
　　peeled and cut into ½-inch cubes

½　pound mushrooms, sliced
1　Spanish onion, cut into chunks
2　sweet red peppers, cut into ½-inch
　　pieces
1　tablespoon plus 1 teaspoon
　　balsamic vinegar
4　teaspoons cornstarch dissolved in
　　2 tablespoons water
　　Savory Biscuit Wedges for serving
　　(recipe, page 348)

1. Heat 1 teaspoon oil in a Dutch oven over medium heat. Add beef and garlic and brown about 5 minutes. Drain fat. Stir in thyme, salt, pepper and broth. Lower heat; cover and simmer 1 hour or until tender.

2. Meanwhile, heat oven to 450°.

3. Toss sweet potatoes, mushrooms, onion and peppers in 2 teaspoons oil and 1 tablespoon vinegar until coated. Spread in a baking pan in one layer; do not overlap. Roast in heated 450° oven 25 to 35 minutes or until sweet potatoes are tender, tossing once or twice during cooking.

4. When ready to serve, bring stew to boiling. Stir in cornstarch mixture; cook, stirring, 2 minutes to thicken slightly. Stir in roasted vegetables and remaining 1 teaspoon vinegar. Serve with Savory Biscuit Wedges.

Lamb stew

Makes 6 servings   *Prep* 15 minutes   *Cook* 50 minutes

Like many stews, this one is even tastier the day after it's made. You can substitute veal shoulder for the lamb.

Per serving

370 calories, 28 g protein, 11 g fat, 36 g carbohydrate, 574 mg sodium, 73 mg cholesterol.

1½ pounds boneless leg of lamb, cut into 1-inch cubes
2 tablespoons all-purpose flour
2 tablespoons olive oil
1 onion, thinly sliced
3 cloves garlic, chopped
1 cup dry red wine
1 cup beef broth
¼ cup ketchup

2 large all-purpose potatoes, peeled and diced
3 large carrots, thinly sliced
2 ribs celery, sliced
1 cup fresh or frozen peas
1 bay leaf
½ teaspoon salt
⅛ teaspoon black pepper
½ teaspoon dried thyme

1. Combine lamb and flour in a plastic food-storage bag; shake to coat. Remove meat; tap off excess flour.

2. Heat oil in a large skillet over medium heat. Add lamb; cook until browned all over, about 6 minutes. Add onion and garlic; cook, stirring, 3 minutes. Add wine, broth, ketchup, potatoes, carrots, celery, peas, bay leaf, salt, pepper and thyme. Simmer, covered, 40 minutes or until lamb and potatoes are cooked through. Discard bay leaf before serving.

U.S.A. pork stew

Makes 4 servings   *Prep* 15 minutes   *Cook* about 13 minutes   *Bake* at 375° for 50 minutes

Sautéing the pork chops first for this easy-bake stew with a vinegar-spiked sauce gives the chops an appetizing color as well as flavor.

Per serving

461 calories, 40 g protein, 17 g fat, 37 g carbohydrate, 548 mg sodium, 97 mg cholesterol.

4 center-cut pork chops (about 2 pounds total)
½ teaspoon salt
½ teaspoon black pepper
2 tablespoons all-purpose flour
2 tablespoons peanut oil
⅔ cup chicken broth
½ teaspoon dried marjoram
2 bay leaves

4 small sweet potatoes (about 1¼ pounds total), peeled and cut into 2-inch pieces
2 medium turnips (about ½ pound), peeled and quartered
2 small Golden Delicious apples, peeled, cored and quartered
2 tablespoons cider vinegar

1. Heat oven to 375°.

2. Season pork chops with salt and pepper. Coat chops with half of flour.

3. Heat oil in a large flameproof casserole or Dutch oven over medium heat. Working in batches if necessary, add pork chops and brown well on both sides, 6 to 8 minutes. Pour off fat from pan.

4. Add broth, marjoram, bay leaves, sweet potatoes and turnips to casserole. Bring to simmering. Cover.

5. Bake in heated 375° oven 30 minutes. Add apples. Cover and bake 20 minutes or until pork and potatoes are tender.

6. With a slotted spoon, remove pork, potatoes, turnips and apples from casserole to a serving dish; keep warm. Discard bay leaves.

7. Stir together vinegar and remaining flour in a small bowl. Stir into juices in pan. Bring to boiling. Reduce heat; simmer, whisking occasionally, about 5 minutes or until thickened. Pour over pork and vegetables.

Veal stew with onions

Makes 8 servings   *Prep* 20 minutes   *Cook* 1½ hours

After adding all the vegetables and liquid to the pot, be sure to scrape up any flavor-laden browned bits from the bottom.

Per serving
529 calories, 41 g protein, 20 g fat, 45 g carbohydrate, 910 mg sodium, 170 mg cholesterol.

Peeling pearl onions
Slice off the root ends. Place the onions in a pot, cover with water, bring to boiling, and boil for 1 minute or until the skins begin to loosen. Drain and run under cool water. Now just pull away the outer skin.

2 pounds boneless veal shoulder, cut into 1-inch cubes
¼ cup plus 2 tablespoons all-purpose flour
2 tablespoons vegetable oil
5 ribs celery, cut into 1-inch pieces
1 pound baby carrots
2 pounds all-purpose potatoes, peeled and cut into ¾-inch cubes
2 turnips, peeled and cut into ¾-inch cubes
1¼ pounds pearl onions, peeled

2 cloves garlic, finely chopped
1 bay leaf
1 tablespoon tomato paste
2 cans (13¾ ounces each) beef broth
1¾ cups water
¾ cup dry red wine
½ teaspoon dried rosemary
½ teaspoon salt
½ teaspoon black pepper
¼ teaspoon dried thyme
1 cup heavy cream

1. Combine veal and ¼ cup flour in a plastic food-storage bag; shake to coat.

2. Heat 1 tablespoon oil in a large Dutch oven. Brown half of veal, about 5 minutes. Remove browned veal and repeat with remaining oil and veal. Return all meat to pot. Add celery, carrots, potatoes, turnips, onions, garlic, bay leaf, tomato paste, broth, 1½ cups water, wine, rosemary, salt, pepper and thyme. Simmer 1¼ hours or until meat is tender.

3. Mix remaining ¼ cup water and 2 tablespoons flour in a small bowl. Add to pot; cook 2 minutes. Combine cream and 1 cup stew in a small bowl, then stir into pot. Remove bay leaf before serving.

Choucroute Alsatian

Makes 8 servings *Prep* 10 minutes *Cook* 1¼ hours

Choucroute literally
means sauerkraut
cooked with meat.
Smoked sausage and
pork chops are
simmered in the
"stew" with carrots,
red potatoes—and
sauerkraut, of course.

Per serving
416 calories, 22 g protein,
25 g fat, 17 g carbohydrate,
1,858 mg sodium,
68 mg cholesterol.

3 refrigerated bags (1 pound each) sauerkraut, well drained
1½ pounds red new potatoes, scrubbed and halved
6 carrots, cut into ½-inch-thick diagonal slices
¼ teaspoon cracked black pepper

2 smoked pork chops (about ¾ pound total)
2 regular pork chops (about ¾ pound total)
1 cup dry white wine
1 pound smoked sausage, such as knockwurst or kielbasa, sliced
Salt to taste (optional)

1. Combine sauerkraut, potatoes, carrots and pepper in a large flameproof casserole or Dutch oven. Arrange pork chops over sauerkraut. Add wine. Cover tightly. Bring to simmering. Cook gently about 1 hour or until potatoes are tender.

2. Add sausage. Cook 15 minutes or until sausage is heated through. Add salt to taste if desired.

Choucroute
Alsatian

Mexican-style beef
and sausage stew

Mexican-style beef and sausage stew

Makes 8 servings   *Prep* 10 minutes   *Cook* 1¼ hours

Beef chuck is a good choice for stews. Although chuck tends to be tougher than other cuts, slow cooking in a simmering liquid helps tenderize it.

Per serving
360 calories, 23 g protein,
17 g fat, 48 g carbohydrate,
687 mg sodium,
89 mg cholesterol.

2 teaspoons oil
1 pound lean beef chuck for stew, cut into 1½-inch chunks
4 turkey sausages (1 pound total), cut into 1-inch pieces
1 onion, chopped
1 sweet green pepper, cored, seeded and chopped
1 clove garlic, finely chopped
1 tablespoon chili powder

1 can (16 ounces) stewed tomatoes
2 cups plus 2 tablespoons water
1½ pounds sweet potatoes, peeled and cut into 1½-inch chunks
1 tablespoon all-purpose flour
½ cup shredded cheddar cheese
3 tablespoons chopped, seeded, pickled jalapeño chiles

1. Heat oil in a large Dutch oven. Working in batches, add beef and sausages; sauté until browned. Remove beef and sausages to a plate.

2. Add onion, green pepper and garlic to drippings in pot; cook, stirring occasionally, until tender, about 8 minutes. Stir in chili powder; cook 1 minute. Stir in tomatoes and 2 cups water. Bring to boiling. Return beef and sausages to pot. Lower heat; cover and simmer 40 minutes. Stir in sweet potatoes; cook until potatoes are tender, 10 to 15 minutes.

3. Whisk flour and remaining 2 tablespoons water in a small bowl until smooth. Stir into stew; cook, stirring, until thickened, about 5 minutes.

4. To serve, ladle stew into bowls. Top each serving with cheese and jalapeño, dividing equally.

87

Cranberry turkey stew

Makes 8 servings *Prep* 20 minutes *Cook* 45 minutes *Bake* at 400° for 30 minutes

Delicious corn bread

This cranberry corn bread topping can also be baked as bread.
• Prepare the batter as directed. Heat oven to 375°. Coat an 8 x 8 x 2-inch metal baking pan with nonstick cooking spray. Scrape batter into pan and bake in heated 375° oven 18 to 20 minutes. Cool completely before serving.

4 strips bacon
½ cup all-purpose flour
1 teaspoon garlic salt
1 teaspoon lemon pepper
1 boneless, skinless turkey breast (3 pounds), cut into 1-inch pieces
Vegetable oil as needed
1 medium onion, cut into eighths
3 large leeks, trimmed and well washed, white and light green parts cut into ½-inch slices (5 cups)
2 ribs celery, cut into ½-inch slices (1½ cups)
2 cloves garlic, finely chopped

1 teaspoon dried rosemary
½ cup dry white wine
1 can (14½ ounces) chicken broth, plus water to equal 2 cups
1 tablespoon soy sauce
1 tablespoon finely chopped lemon rind
1 tablespoon fresh lemon juice
½ cup sweetened dried cranberries, softened in hot water 30 minutes and drained
1 teaspoon salt
¼ teaspoon black pepper
Cranberry Corn Bread Topping (recipe follows)

1. Cook bacon in a large skillet over medium heat until crisp and fat is rendered, about 4 minutes. Remove bacon to paper toweling to drain; crumble and reserve. Reserve fat in skillet.

2. Reserve 1 tablespoon flour; mix remaining flour, garlic salt and lemon pepper in a large bowl. Lightly coat turkey pieces in flour mixture, shaking off excess.

3. Heat bacon fat in skillet over medium-high heat. Working in batches, brown turkey, adding vegetable oil if needed. Transfer to a plate. Add onion, leeks and celery to remaining fat in skillet, adding more oil if needed; sauté over medium heat until tender and lightly browned, 10 to 12 minutes.

4. Add garlic, rosemary and reserved 1 tablespoon flour; cook, stirring, until flour browns, 2 to 3 minutes. Add wine; bring to boiling, stirring up any browned bits from bottom of skillet. Add chicken broth mixture; bring to simmering.

5. Return turkey to skillet, along with any juices that have collected. Add crumbled bacon and simmer 15 minutes. Stir in soy sauce, lemon rind, lemon juice, cranberries, salt and pepper. Turn into a 3-quart casserole.

6. Heat oven to 400°.

7. Prepare Cranberry Corn Bread Topping. Spread topping over stew. Bake in heated 400° oven 30 minutes or until corn bread is browned and crisp and filling is hot.

Make-ahead tip: The casserole can be prepared without the topping up to 1 day ahead. Cover and refrigerate until ready to bake, then prepare and add the topping.

Cranberry corn bread topping

Cook 2 tablespoons finely chopped onion and ½ cup sweetened dried cranberries in 2 tablespoons oil in a medium-size skillet 5 minutes. Stir together ¾ cup yellow cornmeal, ⅓ cup all-purpose flour, 2 tablespoons sugar, 1 teaspoon baking powder and ½ teaspoon salt in a medium-size bowl. Mix in onion mixture. Stir in 1 egg and ½ cup milk.

Moroccan chicken stew

Makes 6 servings *Prep* 10 minutes *Cook* 40 minutes

One spoonful takes you on a tour of popular Moroccan ingredients: almonds, raisins and sweet spices, such as cinnamon, ginger and cumin. Using skinless chicken thighs cuts back on the fat, and the dark meat stays flavorfully moist.

Per serving
475 calories, 26 g protein, 12 g fat, 69 g carbohydrate, 679 mg sodium, 47 mg cholesterol.

6 chicken thighs (1½ pounds total)
2 tablespoons all-purpose flour
1 tablespoon olive oil
2 red onions, quartered lengthwise, then sliced crosswise
2 cloves garlic, finely chopped
1 teaspoon ground cinnamon
1 teaspoon ground ginger
1 teaspoon ground cumin
¼ teaspoon ground red pepper (cayenne)
1 can (16 ounces) reduced-sodium tomato puree

¼ cup honey
1½ teaspoon salt
2 sweet green peppers, cored, seeded and cut into ½-inch squares
⅓ cup golden raisins
1 can (15 ounces) chick-peas, rinsed and drained
¾ pound orzo
⅓ cup slivered almonds, toasted
3 tablespoons chopped fresh parsley

1. Remove skin from chicken. Place flour on a sheet of waxed paper. Lightly coat chicken in flour, shaking off excess. Heat oil in a large nonstick skillet over medium heat. Add chicken and cook 6 minutes or until browned, turning once. Transfer to a plate.

2. Cook onions in skillet 7 minutes. Add garlic, cinnamon, ginger, cumin and red pepper; cook 1 minute. Stir in tomato puree, honey and salt. Add chicken; simmer, covered, 10 minutes. Stir in green peppers, raisins and chick-peas; simmer, stirring, 15 minutes or until peppers are tender and internal temperature of chicken registers 180° on an instant-read thermometer.

3. Meanwhile, cook orzo in a large pot of lightly salted boiling water until al dente, firm but tender. Drain. Serve stew over orzo. Sprinkle with almonds and parsley.

Curried chicken 'n' rice stew

Makes 4 servings   *Prep* 10 minutes   *Cook* 25 minutes

If you prefer a spicier curry, add hot-pepper sauce while the onion is cooking.

Per serving

357 calories, 18 g protein, 16 g fat, 39 g carbohydrate, 790 mg sodium, 135 mg cholesterol.

2 tablespoons butter
1 small onion, chopped
½ sweet green pepper, cored, seeded and diced
2 teaspoons curry powder
1 box (6 ounces) rice pilaf

2 cups water
2 boneless, skinless chicken breast halves (½ pound total), cut into ½-inch cubes
½ cup raisins

1. In a medium-size saucepan, melt butter over medium heat. Add onion, green pepper and curry powder and cook 5 minutes, stirring occasionally.

2. Add rice pilaf, with seasoning packet, and water; cover and simmer over medium heat 7 minutes. Add chicken and raisins; cover and cook another 10 to 15 minutes or until rice is tender and chicken is cooked.

Stewed coconut shrimp

Makes 8 servings   *Prep* 30 minutes   *Cook* 25 minutes

Coconut milk adds a bit of the Caribbean. For a "leaner" stew, use reduced-fat coconut milk.

Per serving

357 calories, 18 g protein, 16 g fat, 39 g carbohydrate, 790 mg sodium, 135 mg cholesterol.

2 tablespoons vegetable oil
1 large onion, chopped (1 cup)
1 sweet green pepper, chopped
2 cloves garlic, finely chopped
2 tablespoons all-purpose flour
2¼ cups vegetable broth
½ cup golden raisins
1 cinnamon stick (1-inch)
⅛ teaspoon ground cloves
1¼ teaspoons salt

1 pound butternut squash, peeled and cut into small cubes (3 cups)
1 pound medium shrimp, peeled and deveined
4 tomatoes, cut into wedges
3 unripe bananas, cut into ¾-inch slices
1 cup unsweetened coconut milk
¾ cup unsweetened flake coconut, toasted

1. Heat oil in a Dutch oven over medium heat. Add onion, green pepper and garlic and sauté 5 minutes.

2. Stir flour into broth. Add to pot with raisins, cinnamon stick, cloves and salt. Boil 3 minutes. Add squash; lower heat and simmer, covered, 10 minutes. Remove cinnamon stick.

3. Add shrimp, tomatoes and bananas. Simmer, covered, 5 minutes or until shrimp is cooked. Stir in coconut milk; heat but do not boil. Sprinkle with coconut.

Texas red chili

Texas red chili

Makes 8 servings   *Prep* 15 minutes   *Cook* 2 hours

The guacamole is a cooling sidekick for the spicy jalapeño chile and ground red pepper. Brisket, a cut of beef from the breast, requires slow cooking, but the reward is a real meaty flavor.

Per serving
334 calories, 30 g protein,
17 g fat, 15 g carbohydrate,
712 mg sodium,
84 mg cholesterol.

2 tablespoons vegetable oil
1 beef brisket (about 2 pounds), cut into ¼-inch cubes
1 cup chopped onion
3 jalapeño chiles, halved, seeded and finely chopped
2 cloves garlic, finely chopped
¼ cup chili powder
1 tablespoon ground cumin
½ teaspoon salt

½ teaspoon ground red pepper (cayenne)
1 can (13¾ ounces) beef broth
2 cans (14½ ounces each) stewed tomatoes
1 bottle (12 ounces) beer
1 bay leaf
   Guacamole for serving (recipe, page 37)
   Lime wedges for garnish

1. Heat oil in a Dutch oven over medium-high heat. Working in batches, sauté brisket until browned, about 10 minutes. Transfer to a plate.

2. Add onion, jalapeños and garlic to drippings in pot; cook over medium-low heat until onion is very tender, about 8 minutes. Stir in chili powder, cumin, salt and red pepper; cook 1 minute. Return meat to pot. Stir in broth, tomatoes, beer and bay leaf. Heat to boiling. Lower heat; simmer with cover slightly ajar until meat is tender, about 1½ hours. For last 20 minutes, uncover to thicken chili.

3. To serve, ladle chili into bowls. Top each serving with some guacamole. Garnish with lime wedges.

Vegetarian chili

Makes 10 servings *Prep* 15 minutes *Cook* 35 minutes

In this meatless chili, the beans and corn combine to make a complete protein with the nine essential amino acids.

Per serving
194 calories, 11 g protein, 4 g fat, 37 g carbohydrate, 679 mg sodium, 0 mg cholesterol.

- 2 tablespoons vegetable oil
- 1 sweet green pepper, cored, seeded and chopped
- 1 onion, chopped
- 2 medium tomatoes, peeled and chopped, or 1 can (14½ ounces) stewed tomatoes, drained
- 2 zucchini, diced
- 2 yellow squash, diced
- 3 jalapeño chiles, halved, seeded and chopped
- 2 tablespoons chili powder
- 1 tablespoon ground cumin
- 2 teaspoons sugar
- ½ teaspoon salt
- 2 cans (13¾ ounces each) vegetable broth
- 2 cans (19 ounces each) black beans, drained and rinsed
- 2 packages (10 ounces each) frozen corn kernels, thawed
- 1 can (15 ounces) pinto beans, drained and rinsed
- ¼ cup chopped fresh cilantro (optional)

1. Heat oil in a large Dutch oven over medium heat. Add green pepper and onion; cook until vegetables are tender, about 8 minutes. Stir in tomatoes; cook, stirring occasionally, 5 minutes.

2. Add zucchini, yellow squash, jalapeños, chili powder, cumin, sugar and salt; cook 1 minute. Add broth, black beans, corn and pinto beans. Simmer, uncovered, 20 minutes.

3. To serve, ladle chili into bowls. Sprinkle with cilantro if desired.

Chili nachos

HERE'S another way to use your favorite chili recipe. In addition to 1½ cups of chili, you need 6 ounces tortilla chips, 1½ cups shredded cheddar cheese, ½ cup prepared salsa, ¼ cup prepared guacamole, 2 tablespoons sour cream and some pickled jalapeño chiles, sliced and seeded.

Heat oven to 400°. Heat chili in a small saucepan over medium heat, stirring often. Spread half of tortilla chips over bottom of a 10-inch glass pie plate. Spoon half of chili over tortilla chips. Sprinkle with half of cheese. Repeat with remaining chips, chili and cheese. Bake in heated 400° oven until cheese is melted, 6 to 8 minutes. Top with salsa, guacamole, sour cream and jalapeño slices. Serve immediately.

Chili blanco

Makes 4 servings   *Prep* 15 minutes   *Cook* 20 minutes

What makes this a white chili? White cannellini beans, turkey and the sour cream stirred in at the end.

Per serving
467 calories, 34 g protein, 24 g fat, 32 g carbohydrate, 1,088 mg sodium, 95 mg cholesterol.

1 tablespoon olive oil
1 large onion, chopped
2 ribs celery, diced
1 cup sliced mushrooms
2 cloves garlic, finely chopped
1 pound ground turkey
1 can (16 ounces) cannellini beans
1 can (11 ounces) corn kernels
1 teaspoon ground cumin
1 teaspoon dried oregano
½ teaspoon salt
½ teaspoon hot-pepper sauce
1 can (4 ounces) diced green chiles
½ cup reduced-fat sour cream
½ cup shredded Monterey Jack cheese
2 tablespoons chopped fresh cilantro

1. Heat oil in a large skillet over medium heat. Add onion, celery, mushrooms and garlic and sauté until tender, about 5 minutes. Push vegetables to edge of skillet.

2. Add turkey to skillet; cook, breaking it up, until no longer pink, about 5 minutes. Drain and rinse beans and corn; stir into pan with cumin, oregano, salt, hot-pepper sauce and chiles. Simmer, covered, 10 minutes.

3. Stir in sour cream; gently heat through. Do not let boil. Sprinkle servings with cheese and cilantro.

Barbecue chili

Makes 12 servings   *Prep* 15 minutes   *Cook* 1 hour

This chili could also be labeled three-bean chili since it contains red kidney, pinto and cannellini beans. The tangy barbecue flavor? It's the combination of molasses, brown sugar, Worcestershire sauce and ketchup.

Per serving
270 calories, 17 g protein, 8 g fat, 41 g carbohydrate, 644 mg sodium, 25 mg cholesterol.

1 tablespoon vegetable oil
1 pound ground beef
1 cup chopped onion
2 cloves garlic, finely chopped
¼ cup chili powder
1 tablespoon ground cumin
1 can (16 ounces) stewed tomatoes
1 cup ketchup
⅓ cup packed brown sugar
¼ cup molasses
¼ cup Worcestershire sauce
1 tablespoon dry mustard
2 cans (15¼ ounces each) dark red kidney beans, drained
2 cans (15 ounces each) pinto beans, drained
1 can (15 ounces) cannellini beans, drained

1. Heat oil in a large Dutch oven over medium-high heat. Add meat, onion, garlic, chili powder and cumin; cook, stirring to break up meat, until meat is no longer pink and onion is tender, about 10 minutes.

2. Stir in tomatoes, ketchup, brown sugar, molasses, Worcestershire sauce and dry mustard; cover and simmer 20 minutes, stirring occasionally. Stir in kidney, pinto and cannellini beans; cover and simmer, stirring occasionally, 30 minutes to blend flavors. To serve, ladle chili into bowls.

Grilled vegetables *page 145*

Artichoke cheese salad
page 96

Vegetables

WHETHER THEY hail from a plot in your own yard, a nearby farm stand or the supermarket produce aisle, vegetables pack much more than health benefits. They're chock-full of flavor, easy to cook and can be transformed into anything from slaws to stews, tarts to timbales.

Though scouting what's in season and turning it into something tasty is extra rewarding, today's technology means most familiar picks are available year-round. Find out how to turn two dozen different vegetables, from artichokes to zucchini, into delicious dishes that flaunt their main ingredient. Creative options run the gamut. Choose from impressive main courses—some vegetarian,

Proof that good-for-you and good-tasting aren't mutually exclusive.

some not—such as a stunning Tomato Tart and crusty Scalloped Corn with Ham. Or try intriguing side dishes such as Roasted Turnips with Ginger or Artichoke Cheese Salad. Just a taste guarantees no one will have to remind you to eat your vegetables ever again.

Artichoke cheese salad

Makes 12 servings   *Prep* 15 minutes

Fewer people than you expected for dinner? Halve or quarter the recipe as needed.
Shown on page 95.

Per serving
181 calories, 9 g protein, 13 g fat, 9 g carbohydrate, 522 mg sodium, 30 mg cholesterol.

1 pound fresh mozzarella cheese, cut into ½-inch cubes
2 jars (7 ounces each) roasted red peppers, drained and diced
1 medium red onion, diced
2 ribs celery, diced (about ¾ cup)
5 jars (6 ounces each) marinated artichoke hearts, drained
2 tablespoons balsamic vinegar
¼ teaspoon black pepper
1 cup loosely packed fresh parsley leaves

Combine cheese, roasted peppers, onion, celery, artichoke hearts, vinegar, black pepper and parsley in a large bowl; toss to mix. Refrigerate until ready to serve. Let come to room temperature.

Asparagus with orange saffron sauce

Makes 8 servings   *Prep* 15 minutes   *Cook* 8 minutes   *Refrigerate* 2 hours

Saffron adds a distinctive color and taste to the sauce, but it is expensive—over 14,000 tiny flower stigmas of a crocus are used to make 1 ounce. Want a low-cost alternative? Substitute ¼ teaspoon curry powder or turmeric.

Per serving
71 calories, 3 g protein, 3 g fat, 8 g carbohydrate, 284 mg sodium, 1 mg cholesterol.

2 bunches large asparagus (about 2 pounds total), tough ends trimmed and stems peeled
¼ cup chicken broth
5 threads saffron
⅛ teaspoon dried tarragon
1 teaspoon grated orange rind
2 tablespoons fresh orange juice
¼ teaspoon salt
½ cup low-fat mayonnaise

1. Cook asparagus in ½ inch lightly salted boiling water in a large skillet 5 to 7 minutes or until tender. Drain and cool asparagus in an ice-water bath. When cooled, drain and place on a serving dish. Cover and refrigerate.

2. Bring broth to boiling in a small saucepan. Turn off heat; add saffron and tarragon. Cover and let stand 4 minutes. Pour into a medium-size bowl to cool. Add orange rind, orange juice, salt and mayonnaise. Whisk sauce and refrigerate, covered, 2 hours.

3. To serve, pour sauce over asparagus.

Make-ahead tip: Sauce can be made a day ahead and kept, covered, in refrigerator.

Asparagus omelets

Makes 6 servings   *Prep* 15 minutes   *Cook* 30 minutes

If you're a fast cook, make individual omelets—otherwise, whip up two larger ones for your brunch crowd.

Per serving
276 calories, 20 g protein,
20 g fat, 4 g carbohydrate,
816 mg sodium,
461 mg cholesterol.

Picking the best
Look for asparagus with dry, tightly closed tips, slightly purplish in hue. The ends should be moist, with no dried-out or woody parts.

Filling
½ cup milk
1½ teaspoons flour
½ cup shredded Fontina cheese
⅛ teaspoon salt
⅛ teaspoon black pepper
   Pinch ground nutmeg
½ bunch large asparagus
   (about ½ pound), tough ends
   trimmed and stems peeled
¼ pound cooked ham

1½ teaspoons butter
1 small sweet green pepper, cored,
   seeded and diced (about ⅓ cup)
2 tablespoons dry white wine
2 tablespoons chicken broth

Omelets
12 eggs
¾ cup water
¾ teaspoon salt
   Pinch black pepper
2 tablespoons butter

1. Prepare filling: Stir together milk and flour in a small saucepan over medium heat; cook, whisking occasionally, until mixture thickens and begins to boil, 7 to 10 minutes. Boil 2 minutes; remove from heat. Whisk in cheese, salt, pepper and nutmeg. Cover and set aside.

2. Cut asparagus into 1-inch pieces. Dice ham. Melt butter in a large skillet over medium-high heat. Add ham, asparagus and green pepper; sauté 5 minutes. Add wine and broth; cook until reduced by half, 5 to 7 minutes. Remove from heat. Stir in cheese sauce. Cool slightly.

3. Meanwhile, prepare omelets: Whisk together eggs, water, salt and pepper until frothy.

4. Melt 1 tablespoon butter in each of 2 large nonstick skillets; add half of egg mixture to each. Cook briefly. Lift an edge to let egg flow under. Cook until egg is no longer runny. Divide asparagus filling between omelets. Once egg is completely set, fold each omelet in half, divide into thirds and serve.

Preparing fresh asparagus

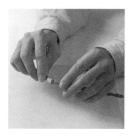

Thin spears: Grasp bottom and midpoint of stalk. Snap; stalk should break above the tough white part.

Thick spears: Lay stalk flat and hold steady with fingertips. Using a sharp knife, cut 1 to 1½ inches off the bottom.

Peel: If any tough white fiber remains, use a vegetable peeler to shave it from the area where white meets green.

Asparagus gratin

Try flavorful Black Forest ham instead of the prosciutto, and for the Gruyère, shredded Jarlsberg or crumbled Gorgonzola.

Per serving

228 calories, 9 g protein, 12 g fat, 21 g carbohydrate, 392 mg sodium, 27 mg cholesterol.

1 bunch large asparagus (about 1 pound), tough ends trimmed and stems peeled
6 slices prosciutto or thin-sliced deli ham

3 tablespoons butter
½ cup fresh bread crumbs
½ cup shredded Gruyère cheese

1. Cook asparagus in ½ inch lightly salted boiling water in a large skillet 5 to 7 minutes or until tender. Drain.

2. Divide asparagus into 6 equal bundles. Wrap each bundle with a slice of prosciutto; place in a shallow flameproof baking dish.

3. Melt butter in a small saucepan over medium-low heat. Add bread crumbs; cook, stirring, 1 minute. Pour mixture over asparagus bundles. Top with cheese.

4. Heat broiler. Run bundles under broiler until cheese lightly browns, about 1 minute.

Asparagus gratin

Asparagus with garlic vinaigrette

Makes 8 servings   *Prep* 10 minutes   *Cook* 15 minutes

Asparagus on its own is low in calories—about 30 in an eight-stalk serving—and high in both folic acid and vitamin C. Use the dressing sparingly to avoid too many extra calories from fat.

Per serving
96 calories, 2 g protein, 9 g fat, 3 g carbohydrate, 95 mg sodium, 0 mg cholesterol.

2 bunches large asparagus (about 2 pounds total), tough ends trimmed and stems peeled
¼ cup olive oil
3 cloves garlic, sliced
1 tablespoon fresh lemon juice
1 tablespoon balsamic vinegar
¼ teaspoon salt
⅛ teaspoon black pepper
⅛ teaspoon dried rosemary, crumbled

1. Cook asparagus in ½ inch lightly salted boiling water in a large skillet 5 to 7 minutes or until tender. Drain; keep warm on a serving platter.

2. Meanwhile, heat oil and garlic in a small saucepan over low heat; cook, stirring occasionally, until garlic is tender and golden, about 8 minutes; be careful garlic doesn't burn. Pour into a small bowl.

3. Add lemon juice, vinegar, salt, pepper and rosemary to garlic mixture; mix well. Pour over warm asparagus. Serve.

Dry-cooked green beans with pork

Makes 4 servings   *Prep* 20 minutes   *Cook* 20 minutes

Need a tasty vegetarian side dish? Here it is. Just omit the pork in this recipe and substitute vegetable broth for the chicken broth.

Per serving
231 calories, 14 g protein, 12 g fat, 19 g carbohydrate, 730 mg sodium, 0 mg cholesterol.

½ cup lower-sodium chicken broth
¼ cup reduced-sodium soy sauce
1 tablespoon dry sherry
1 teaspoon cornstarch
1 teaspoon sugar
⅛ teaspoon red-pepper flakes
2 teaspoons vegetable oil
1 pound green beans, cut into 2-inch lengths
½ pound lean ground pork
2 cloves garlic, finely chopped
1 tablespoon chopped fresh ginger
½ can (8-ounce can) sliced water chestnuts, drained

1. Combine broth, soy sauce, sherry, cornstarch, sugar and red-pepper flakes in a small bowl.

2. Heat a wok or large skillet over medium-high heat. Add oil; swirl to coat wok. Add beans; stir-fry 4 minutes or until beans are spotted black.

3. Add pork; stir-fry 2 minutes, breaking up meat. Add garlic and ginger; stir-fry 1 minute longer.

4. Add broth mixture. Cover and cook 5 minutes. Uncover; stir in water chestnuts and cook over high heat 5 to 8 minutes or until mixture is practically dry. Serve at once.

Smoky green beans

Imagine German potato salad seasoned with bacon and vinegar, but made with green beans rather than potatoes.

Per serving
87 calories, 4 g protein, 3 g fat, 12 g carbohydrate, 109 mg sodium, 5 mg cholesterol.

8 slices thick-cut bacon
1 large onion, chopped (1 cup)
⅓ cup cider vinegar or distilled white vinegar
1 tablespoon sugar
½ teaspoon black pepper
2 pounds green beans, trimmed, cooked and drained, or 3 packages (9 ounces each) frozen whole green beans, cooked and drained

1. Cook bacon in a large skillet over medium heat until crisp. Remove to paper toweling to drain. Pour off all but 1 tablespoon fat.

2. Add onion to skillet; sauté 3 to 5 minutes or until tender. Crumble bacon; add to skillet along with vinegar, sugar and pepper. Cook, stirring, until sugar is dissolved and mixture is hot and bubbly. Add cooked beans; toss to coat and heat through. Serve immediately.

Green beans with tomato and honey

Try this menu suggestion: Broiled pork chops accented with cumin, coriander and cayenne, served with these beans and parsleyed rice.

Per serving
146 calories, 3 g protein, 7 g fat, 20 g carbohydrate, 722 mg sodium, 0 mg cholesterol.

1 pound green beans, trimmed and cut crosswise in half
2 tablespoons olive oil
½ cup finely chopped onion
2 cloves garlic, finely chopped
½ teaspoon ground cinnamon
½ teaspoon ground cumin
½ teaspoon black pepper
Pinch ground red pepper (cayenne)
1 can (16 ounces) plum tomatoes, drained and coarsely chopped
1 teaspoon salt
3 teaspoons honey
1 tablespoon fresh lemon juice

1. Place beans in a vegetable steamer with water. Steam until they turn very bright green but are still crunchy, about 5 minutes. Rinse in steamer basket under cold running water. Drain.

2. Heat oil in a wide, shallow saucepan. Add onion and garlic; sauté until softened, about 5 minutes. Add cinnamon, cumin, black pepper and red pepper; sauté 1 minute. Add tomatoes and ½ teaspoon salt. Bring to boiling, stirring frequently to prevent sticking, 8 to 10 minutes or until mixture has a thick, jamlike consistency.

3. Stir in honey. Add beans; lower heat. Cook, covered, at a slow simmer, stirring occasionally, until beans are tender, about 15 minutes. Stir in lemon juice. Season with remaining salt if needed.

Orange-flavored beans with tofu

Makes 4 servings *Prep* 10 minutes *Refrigerate* 20 minutes *Cook* about 40 minutes

Since the flavor of protein-rich tofu is neutral, it takes well to marinades, such as the orange mixture in this recipe.

Per serving
513 calories, 26 g protein, 18 g fat, 69 g carbohydrate, 437 mg sodium, 0 mg cholesterol.

Tofu tips
• Tofu comes in four consistencies: soft, with a custard-like texture that blends into dips; medium, for steaming or adding to soups; firm and extra-firm, for stir-frying or marinating and broiling.
• Refrigerate tofu in a dish of fresh water, covered, for up to 1 week; change water daily to prevent souring.

1 cup brown rice
½ cup fresh orange juice
½ teaspoon red-pepper flakes
¼ teaspoon ground ginger
2 tablespoons honey
2 tablespoons soy sauce
1 clove garlic, finely chopped
2 tablespoons rice vinegar
1 pound extra-firm tofu

½ pound green beans, trimmed
½ pound yellow wax beans, trimmed
1 orange
2 tablespoons vegetable oil
1 sweet red pepper, cored, seeded and cut into thin slices
1¼ teaspoons cornstarch
1 green onion, thinly sliced

1. Prepare brown rice according to package directions; keep warm.

2. While rice is cooking, mix orange juice, red-pepper flakes, ginger, honey, soy sauce, garlic and rice vinegar in a glass measuring cup.

3. Drain tofu; press gently with paper toweling to remove any excess moisture. Cut into ½-inch cubes and place in an 8 x 8 x 2-inch glass or plastic dish. Pour half of orange juice mixture over tofu; cover with plastic wrap. Refrigerate 20 minutes to marinate.

4. Meanwhile, bring a large saucepan of water to boiling. Add green and yellow wax beans; cook 3 to 4 minutes or until crisp-tender. Drain.

5. Using a knife, remove rind and bitter white pith from orange. Section, removing membranes and seeds. Cut sections into pieces.

6. Heat oil in a large skillet over medium-high heat. Add beans and sweet red pepper; sauté 5 minutes. Add remaining orange juice mixture; cook another 3 minutes. Remove tofu with a slotted spoon from marinade and add to skillet; reserve marinade left in dish. Stir orange pieces into skillet.

7. Whisk cornstarch into reserved marinade until smooth. Stir into skillet; cook, stirring occasionally, until sauce thickens and clears, about 3 minutes. Serve with brown rice. Sprinkle with green onion.

Summer beet salad

Makes 6 servings   *Prep* 15 minutes   *Cook* 18 to 24 minutes

If fresh beets are unavailable, use canned whole beets—they'll make your prep time faster too.

Per serving
226 calories, 7 g protein,
13 g fat, 24 g carbohydrate,
872 mg sodium,
150 mg cholesterol.

Picking the best
• **Choose beets with bright greens and firm, smooth skin. Small beets are generally better than larger ones, which run a greater chance of having a woody texture.**
• **If you stain your fingers while you're peeling beets, just rub with a cut lemon and wash.**

2 teaspoons salt
¼ cup fresh lemon juice
2 bunches beets (about 8 beets), trimmed
¼ cup honey
2 tablespoons red-wine vinegar
2 to 3 Kirby cucumbers, peeled or scored
¼ cup chicken broth
2 tablespoons finely chopped fresh parsley
1 tablespoon finely chopped fresh dill
1 tablespoon finely chopped fresh thyme
2 tablespoons olive oil
6 cups assorted salad greens
4 hard-cooked eggs, shelled and cut into wedges
½ cup sour cream

1. Bring 2 quarts water to boiling in a large saucepan. Add ½ teaspoon salt and 1 tablespoon lemon juice. Add beets; cover and simmer 15 to 20 minutes. Drain; reserve broth for beet soup if desired (see pages 75 and 80).

2. Meanwhile, combine honey, vinegar, remaining 1½ teaspoons salt and remaining 3 tablespoons lemon juice in a large bowl; remove half of mixture and reserve for dressing the greens. Cut cucumbers into slices. Add to honey mixture in bowl; let stand to marinate.

3. When beets are cool enough to handle but still warm, remove skins. Slice in half lengthwise; cut crosswise into ¼-inch-thick slices. Place in a large bowl; cover and set aside.

4. Remove cucumbers from marinade with a slotted spoon and place in a small saucepan. Add broth; gently cook until broth evaporates, 3 to 4 minutes. Remove from heat.

5. Add parsley, dill and thyme to beets in bowl and mix.

6. Whisk oil into reserved honey mixture along with any marinade left over from cucumbers. Add greens; toss to coat. Divide greens equally among 6 plates. Arrange beets, cucumbers and egg wedges on plates. Serve warm or at room temperature with sour cream.

Oven-
roasted
beets

Garlicky
broccoli rabe
with pasta
page 104

Oven-roasted beets

Makes 4 servings   *Prep* 5 minutes   *Roast* at 425° for 1 hour

No balsamic in the cupboard? Then reach for cider vinegar—it's a super flavor partner with both the beets and the walnuts.

Per serving
149 calories, 5 g protein,
11 g fat, 10 g carbohydrate,
191 mg sodium,
0 mg cholesterol.

6 medium beets, trimmed
1 tablespoon balsamic vinegar
2 teaspoons olive oil
¼ teaspoon salt

¼ teaspoon black pepper
½ cup coarsely chopped walnuts, toasted

1. Heat oven to 425°. Wrap each beet individually in aluminum foil.

2. Roast beets in heated 425° oven 1 hour or until fork-tender.

3. Remove beets from oven; let stand until cool enough to handle. Remove foil. Using a paring knife, slip skin off beets. Cut beets into quarters or eighths, depending on size of beets. Toss with vinegar, oil, salt, pepper and walnuts in a large bowl. Serve slightly warm or at room temperature.

Broccoli and yellow squash

Makes 6 servings   *Prep* 10 minutes   *Cook* 10 minutes

Serve hot as a side dish or at room temperature as a salad. For livelier flavor, squirt on a little lemon juice.

Per serving
53 calories, 1 g protein,
5 g fat, 3 g carbohydrate,
275 mg sodium,
0 mg cholesterol.

1 head broccoli (1½ pounds), tough ends trimmed and stems peeled
1 medium yellow squash
2 tablespoons olive oil
1 clove garlic, pressed
½ teaspoon dried oregano
¾ teaspoon salt

1. Cut broccoli into spears. Halve squash lengthwise, then cut crosswise into ¼-inch-thick slices. Steam broccoli and squash in a steamer basket in a covered large pot over gently boiling water until crisp-tender, about 10 minutes. Drain.

2. Whisk together oil, garlic, oregano and salt in a serving bowl. Add vegetables to bowl. Toss and serve.

Garlicky broccoli rabe with pasta

Makes 6 servings   *Prep* 10 minutes   *Cook* 30 minutes

Related to both the cabbage and the turnip families, broccoli rabe has long, green leafy stalks with tiny buds similar to broccoli. The pungent flavor marries well with garlic.
Shown on page 103.

Per serving
634 calories, 24 g protein,
30 g fat, 69 g carbohydrate,
705 mg sodium,
84 mg cholesterol.

1 pound fettuccine
2 to 4 cloves garlic, sliced
1 cup heavy cream
1 cup chicken broth
½ teaspoon red-pepper flakes
2 tablespoons olive oil
3 bunches broccoli rabe (2 pounds total), washed and trimmed
½ teaspoon salt
¼ teaspoon black pepper
½ cup grated Parmesan cheese
¼ pound Fontina or mozzarella cheese, cut into thin strips

1. Cook fettuccine in a large pot of lightly salted boiling water until al dente, firm but tender.

2. Meanwhile, simmer garlic, cream, broth and red-pepper flakes in a small saucepan 20 minutes or until garlic is softened. Mash garlic into cream to blend.

3. Heat oil in a large skillet. Add broccoli rabe; sauté 3 minutes. Add ¼ cup water; cook until water evaporates, about 5 minutes. Add salt and black pepper. Remove from heat.

4. Drain pasta; return to pot. Add broccoli rabe; spoon garlic mixture over top. Sprinkle with Parmesan and Fontina cheeses; toss to mix.

Note: A large head of broccoli can be used in place of broccoli rabe. Cut off tough ends and peel stems, then cut stems into 1-inch pieces and heads into flowerets. Add to pasta pot during last 5 minutes of cooking.

Broccoli with pine nuts and Parmesan

Makes 6 servings   *Prep* 20 minutes   *Cook* 8 minutes

Per serving
138 calories, 5 g protein, 11 g fat, 9 g carbohydrate, 263 mg sodium, 0 mg cholesterol.

picking the best
Perfect broccoli is darkish green with tightly closed buds.

1 large head broccoli (about 2 pounds), tough ends trimmed and stems peeled
3 tablespoons olive oil
2 cloves garlic, finely chopped
¼ cup chicken broth
½ teaspoon salt
¼ cup pine nuts, toasted
Shaved Parmesan cheese for garnish

1. Cut broccoli stems into coins; cut heads into flowerets.

2. Heat oil in a large skillet over medium-high heat. Add garlic; cook, stirring constantly, 45 seconds. Add broccoli; cook, stirring constantly, until broccoli is bright green, 2 to 3 minutes. Add broth; cover and cook until broccoli is crisp-tender, about 3 minutes. Sprinkle with salt and toss.

3. If serving warm, add pine nuts; toss and serve. If serving cold, cool slightly, place in a tightly sealed container and refrigerate. Just before serving, add pine nuts and toss.

4. Garnish with thin shavings of Parmesan cheese.

Holiday brussels sprouts

Makes 8 servings   *Prep* 5 minutes   *Cook* 10 minutes   *Bake* at 350° for 20 minutes

Brussels sprouts are best in late fall—perfect for Thanksgiving. If you're a mustard lover, stir a little Dijon into the cheese sauce.

Per serving
91 calories, 5 g protein, 5 g fat, 11 g carbohydrate, 245 mg sodium, 21 mg cholesterol.

1 pound brussels sprouts, trimmed
1 tablespoon fresh lemon juice
2 tablespoons butter
2 tablespoons all-purpose flour
1 cup milk, warmed
¼ cup shredded cheddar cheese
½ teaspoon salt
¼ teaspoon black pepper
¼ teaspoon ground nutmeg
Pinch ground red pepper (cayenne)

1. Heat oven to 350°.

2. Place brussels sprouts in a medium-size saucepan with enough water to cover. Add lemon juice. Simmer, uncovered, 8 to 10 minutes or until tender. Drain.

3. Meanwhile, melt butter in a small saucepan. Stir in flour; cook 1 to 2 minutes. Gradually whisk in milk; cook, whisking, until sauce thickens, about 2 minutes. Stir in cheese, salt, pepper, nutmeg and red pepper.

4. Transfer brussels sprouts to a 1-quart casserole. Pour sauce over top.

5. Bake in heated 350° oven 20 minutes or until heated through.

Cabbage, Italian style

Makes 6 servings *Prep* 10 minutes *Cook* 20 minutes

Surprisingly, olives seem made for cabbage.

Per serving
104 calories, 2 g protein,
8 g fat, 8 g carbohydrate,
366 mg sodium,
0 mg cholesterol.

2 tablespoons olive oil
  Pinch red-pepper flakes
1 small head cabbage (1½ pounds),
  cored and coarsely chopped

½ teaspoon salt
½ cup oil-cured black olives,
  pitted and coarsely chopped

1. Heat oil and red-pepper flakes in a heavy Dutch oven or large saucepan with a tight-fitting lid over medium heat 1 minute. Add cabbage and salt; toss to coat cabbage with oil. Cover pot; cook, stirring occasionally, 12 minutes or until cabbage is crisp-tender.

2. Add olives. Cook, covered, 3 to 5 minutes longer or until cabbage is tender. Serve.

Cranberry-carrot slaw

Makes 6 servings *Prep* 10 minutes *Refrigerate* 1 hour

Not your usual coleslaw—colorfully bright and brightly flavored with dried cranberries, pineapple juice, lime juice and crystallized ginger.

Per serving
131 calories, 2 g protein,
0 g fat, 33 g carbohydrate,
223 mg sodium,
0 mg cholesterol.

½ cup pineapple juice
  Juice of 1 lime (1 tablespoon)
1 teaspoon cider vinegar
½ teaspoon salt
⅛ teaspoon black pepper

2 tablespoons honey
½ cup dried cranberries
2 tablespoons finely chopped
  crystallized ginger
2 pounds carrots, shredded

1. Stir pineapple juice, lime juice, vinegar, salt, pepper and honey in a bowl until honey dissolves.

2. Add cranberries, ginger and carrots and toss to combine. Refrigerate at least 1 hour. Toss again before serving.

Cauliflower and broccoli crepes

Makes 8 servings *Prep* 10 minutes *Cook* 8 minutes

A vegetarian dish that fills the bill any time of day: breakfast, brunch, lunch or supper.

Per serving
269 calories, 11 g protein, 14 g fat, 26 g carbohydrate, 431 mg sodium, 165 mg cholesterol.

Picking the best
Select tight, heavy heads of cauliflower. They should be creamy white, not yellowing.

1 medium head cauliflower (about 2 pounds)
1 head broccoli (1½ pounds), tough ends trimmed and stems peeled
1 can (10¾ ounces) condensed cheddar cheese soup
¼ teaspoon black pepper
Pinch ground red pepper (cayenne)
1 tablespoon chopped fresh chives
16 prepared crepes (homemade, see page 131, or purchased)

1. Chop the cauliflower and broccoli; you should have 3 cups of each.

2. Bring a large saucepan of water to boiling. Add cauliflower and broccoli; cook 4 minutes. Drain; return vegetables to pan.

3. Add condensed soup (undiluted), black pepper and red pepper. Heat over medium-high heat until bubbly, 3 to 4 minutes. Remove from heat. Stir in chives.

4. If desired, heat crepes in a microwave oven. Divide vegetable-cheese mixture among crepes. Fold over. Serve immediately, 2 crepes per serving.

Cauliflower and broccoli crepes

Cauliflower and broccoli with cheese sauce

Makes 8 servings *Prep* 10 minutes *Cook* 15 minutes

While cheddar is the first choice for the sauce, other good bets include Monterey Jack, Fontina, Swiss and blue cheese.

Per serving
220 calories, 12 g protein, 16 g fat, 10 g carbohydrate, 806 mg sodium, 48 mg cholesterol.

1 large head cauliflower (about 3 pounds)
1 large head broccoli (about 2 pounds), tough ends trimmed and stems peeled
2 teaspoons salt

Cheese sauce
3 tablespoons butter
3 tablespoons all-purpose flour
1 teaspoon dry mustard
1½ cups milk
½ pound sharp cheddar cheese, shredded (about 2 cups)
¼ teaspoon hot-pepper sauce

1. Bring 6 cups water to boiling in a large saucepan. Cut cauliflower into flowerets. Cut broccoli stems into coins; cut heads into flowerets. Add cauliflower, broccoli and salt to saucepan. Return to boiling; cook, stirring occasionally, until vegetables are crisp-tender, about 8 minutes. Drain.

2. Meanwhile, prepare cheese sauce: Melt butter in a 2-quart saucepan over medium heat. Whisk in flour and dry mustard until smooth; cook 1 minute. Gradually stir in milk until smooth. Bring to boiling. Remove saucepan from heat. Stir in cheese and hot-pepper sauce, stirring until cheese is melted. Spoon sauce over vegetables.

Curried cauliflower

Makes 6 servings *Prep* 15 minutes *Cook* 40 minutes

Rich coconut milk softens the strong spice flavors in this curry dish.

Per serving
237 calories, 4 g protein, 18 g fat, 15 g carbohydrate, 414 mg sodium, 0 mg cholesterol.

2 tablespoons vegetable oil
2 medium onions, finely chopped
1 teaspoon curry powder
½ teaspoon ground turmeric
½ teaspoon ground cardamom
Pinch ground cloves
Pinch ground red pepper (cayenne)

1 can (15 ounces) unsweetened coconut milk
1 large head cauliflower (2½ pounds), cut into flowerets
1 teaspoon salt or to taste
2 tablespoons chopped fresh cilantro

1. Heat oil in a large shallow saucepan over medium heat. Add onions; sauté until golden and softened, 8 to 10 minutes.

2. Stir in curry powder, turmeric, cardamom, cloves and red pepper; cook 1 minute. Add coconut milk, cauliflower and salt. Cook, uncovered, stirring occasionally, until cauliflower is very tender, about 30 minutes. Stir in cilantro. Add more salt if needed.

Scalloped corn with ham

Makes 6 servings   *Prep* 15 minutes   *Cook* 10 minutes   *Bake* at 350° for 50 minutes

In the winter when fresh corn is not around, substitute frozen whole kernels. One ear of corn yields about ⅔ cup kernels.

Per serving
176 calories, 8 g protein,
11 g fat, 14 g carbohydrate,
385 mg sodium,
50 mg cholesterol.

3 slices bacon, chopped
10 saltines, finely crumbled
1 small onion, finely chopped
1 small sweet red pepper, cored, seeded and chopped
6 large ears fresh corn, shucked
¾ cup shredded cheddar cheese
2 green onions, chopped
1 cup ham strips
1 egg
½ cup heavy cream
½ cup milk
¼ teaspoon salt
    Pinch black pepper

1. Cook bacon in a medium-size skillet over medium heat until crisp. Remove to paper toweling to drain. Transfer 2 tablespoons bacon fat to a small bowl; leave remaining fat in skillet. Add ½ cup cracker crumbs to fat in bowl.

2. Heat fat in skillet. Add onion, sweet red pepper and remaining crumbs; sauté 3 to 5 minutes or until softened. Remove from heat. Stir in bacon.

3. Heat oven to 350°. Butter a 1-quart casserole.

4. Slice corn kernels from cobs; you should have about 4½ cups. In several layers, place corn, bacon mixture, cheese, green onions and ham in casserole.

5. Beat egg, cream, milk, salt and pepper in a small bowl. Pour over casserole. Top with reserved crumbs in bacon fat. Bake in heated 350° oven 50 minutes or until golden brown.

V E G E T A B L E S

Storing vegetables

MAXIMIZE FLAVOR by storing fresh vegetables properly.

Asparagus: Remove rubber band; stand in 1 inch of water in a sturdy glass; refrigerate up to 2 days.

Beans, broccoli, cauliflower, lima beans, okra: Refrigerate in perforated plastic food storage bags up to 2 days.

Beets, cabbage, carrots: Refrigerate in nonperforated plastic bags up to 1 week for beets, 2 weeks for cabbage and carrots.

Corn, sweet and hot peppers, zucchini: Refrigerate, unwrapped, in crisper drawer, up to 2 days for corn, 5 days for peppers and zucchini.

Eggplant: Refrigerate, unwrapped, up to 2 days.

Potatoes, onions, winter squash: Store in a cool dry spot up to 1 week for acorn squash, several weeks for others.

Corn stew

Brimming with the best of summer, this vegetarian stew is a meal all by itself. Just add a tossed green salad and crusty bread.

Per serving
393 calories, 12 g protein,
26 g fat, 34 g carbohydrate,
366 mg sodium,
79 mg cholesterol.

8 ears fresh corn, shucked
2 tablespoons butter
1 onion, chopped
½ cup chopped sweet green pepper
½ cup chopped sweet red pepper
1 cup light cream
2 tablespoons chopped fresh parsley
½ teaspoon salt
¼ teaspoon black pepper
1¼ cups shredded cheddar cheese
½ teaspoon hot-pepper sauce

1. Slice corn kernels from cobs; you should have about 6 cups.

2. Melt butter in a medium-size saucepan over medium-high heat. Add onion; cook, stirring, until golden and glazed, about 5 minutes. Add green and red peppers; cook, stirring, 2 to 3 minutes. Add corn kernels.

3. Increase heat; cook, stirring, 2 minutes. Add cream, parsley, salt and pepper. Cover and simmer 45 minutes.

4. Stir in 1 cup cheese and hot-pepper sauce until cheese is melted. Ladle into bowls. Sprinkle with remaining ¼ cup cheese. Serve warm.

Flavored butters

A pat of any of these butters is delicious not only on fresh corn but also stirred into rice, tucked into a baked potato or spread on a slice of freshly baked bread.

TO PREPARE a flavored butter, begin with ½ cup (1 stick) of softened unsalted butter. Cut butter into small pieces and place in a small food processor or a small mixer bowl. Add the other ingredients for your chosen butter. Process or beat with mixer or mash with wooden spoon until butter is smooth and all ingredients are well blended. Scrape butter onto a piece of waxed paper. Shape into a log 6 to 8 inches long, rolling up paper; twist ends of paper to seal. Wrap tightly in aluminum foil. Refrigerate for 1 day for flavors to develop, or freeze for longer storage. When ready to use, slice off pats as needed. Each recipe makes about ½ cup.

Chive butter: 2 tablespoons chopped fresh chives or green onions, green part only

Coriander butter: ¼ teaspoon ground coriander and ¼ teaspoon turmeric

Lime butter: 1 tablespoon fresh lime juice and ½ teaspoon grated lime rind

Sweet red pepper butter: 2 tablespoons finely chopped roasted red peppers

Corn fritters

Corn fritters

Makes 8 servings (about twenty 3-inch fritters)   *Prep* 15 minutes   *Fry* 2 to 4 minutes per batch

Fry up ahead and then rewarm the fritters in a 350° oven until heated through, 10 to 15 minutes.

Per serving
261 calories, 4 g protein,
18 g fat, 23 g carbohydrate,
460 mg sodium,
35 mg cholesterol.

4 large ears fresh corn, shucked
½ cup fine-ground yellow cornmeal
½ cup all-purpose flour
1½ teaspoons baking soda
¾ teaspoon salt
½ teaspoon black pepper

1 egg yolk, lightly beaten
2 tablespoons butter, melted
½ teaspoon ground nutmeg (optional)
½ cup buttermilk
½ cup vegetable oil

1. Slice corn kernels from cobs; you should have about 3 cups.

2. Combine cornmeal, flour, baking soda, salt and pepper in a large bowl. Make a well in center; add egg yolk, corn kernels, melted butter, nutmeg if using and buttermilk. Stir wet ingredients into dry to moisten.

3. Heat ¼ cup oil in a large heavy skillet. Spoon dollops of dough into skillet; flatten with spatula. Fry until golden brown, 1 to 2 minutes each side, using remaining oil as needed. Drain on paper toweling. Serve warm.

Variation: For savory fritters to serve with meats, omit nutmeg. Add a few drops hot-pepper sauce and 1 finely chopped green onion.

Corn timbales with tomato-lime salsa

Makes 4 servings   *Prep* 20 minutes   *Cook* 30 to 35 minutes

FAMILY CIRCLE ALL-TIME FAVORITE RECIPES

These corn custards, served either hot or cold, are nutritionally more sensible than might be expected because egg substitute is used in place of whole eggs.

Per serving
157 calories, 8 g protein, 5 g fat, 22 g carbohydrate, 577 mg sodium, 32 mg cholesterol.

Picking the best
The husks of fresh corn should be green, the silks golden and moist and the stem ends pale green.

2 ears fresh corn, shucked
¾ cup milk
¼ cup all-purpose flour
½ teaspoon baking powder
½ teaspoon salt
⅛ teaspoon ground red pepper (cayenne)
½ cup cholesterol-free egg replacement (not frozen)
¼ cup chopped green onion
1 tablespoon chopped fresh cilantro
  Tomato-Lime Salsa (recipe follows)

1. Coat four 6-ounce custard cups with nonstick cooking spray. Fold a 12 x 11-inch sheet of aluminum foil into quarters, forming a small rectangle. Using a custard cup as guide, trace top of cup onto folded foil. Cut out round ½ inch larger than tracing. Separate into 4 foil rounds.

2. Slice corn kernels from cobs; you should have 1½ cups. Combine ½ cup corn kernels and ¼ cup milk in a food processor or blender. Whirl until coarsely pureed.

3. Combine flour, baking powder, salt and ground red pepper in a medium-size bowl.

4. Slowly whisk remaining ½ cup milk and egg replacement into flour mixture until well blended and smooth. Stir in pureed corn mixture, remaining 1 cup corn kernels, green onion and cilantro. Pour equal amounts of mixture into prepared custard cups. Lay a cut foil round on top of each cup; press tightly around edge of cup. Place cups in a large skillet. Pour in enough boiling water to come halfway up sides of cups.

5. Cook over medium heat (water should be simmering) 30 to 35 minutes or until a knife inserted near center of a timbale comes out clean. Remove cups to a wire rack and cool 10 minutes. If serving immediately, loosen around edge of each custard cup with a thin metal spatula. Invert onto a serving platter and serve immediately with Tomato-Lime Salsa. Or refrigerate timbales until thoroughly chilled. Unmold and serve.

Tomato-lime salsa

Per tablespoon
5 calories, 0 g protein, 0 g fat, 1 g carbohydrate, 38 mg sodium, 0 mg cholesterol.

Combine 2 large ripe tomatoes, peeled, seeded and chopped; ¼ teaspoon grated lime rind; 1 teaspoon fresh lime juice; ¼ teaspoon salt and ⅛ teaspoon black pepper in a small bowl. Refrigerate until ready to use.

Fried corn

Makes 8 servings *Prep* 15 minutes *Cook* 10 to 15 minutes

This recipe is terrific with grilled meats or any egg dish.

Per serving
97 calories, 2 g protein, 3 g fat, 17 g carbohydrate, 137 mg sodium, 8 mg cholesterol.

6 ears fresh corn, shucked
2 tablespoons butter
1 tablespoon heavy cream (optional)

½ teaspoon salt
¼ to ½ teaspoon black pepper

1. Slice corn kernels from cobs into a bowl, making sure to scrape milky white substance from cobs. You should have about 4 cups.

2. Melt butter in a large skillet. Add corn, cream if using, salt and pepper. Cook over medium-high heat, stirring occasionally, 10 to 15 minutes or until corn is tender.

Braised endive

Makes 8 servings *Prep* 10 minutes *Cook* 35 minutes *Bake* at 350° for 45 minutes

A nice accompaniment to grilled chicken or roast pork tenderloin, this side dish is special enough for a dinner party.

Per serving
164 calories, 7 g protein, 12 g fat, 9 g carbohydrate, 509 mg sodium, 17 mg cholesterol.

8 strips bacon
8 large heads Belgian endive
1 large onion, finely chopped
1 tablespoon olive oil
½ cup cider vinegar
3 tablespoons sugar

½ cup dry white wine
½ cup chicken broth
½ teaspoon salt
¼ teaspoon black pepper
2 tablespoons chopped fresh parsley

1. Heat oven to 350°.

2. Cook bacon in a large deep skillet until crisp, about 10 minutes. Remove to paper toweling to drain. Leave fat in skillet. Crumble bacon.

3. Trim hard white bases and any wilted leaves from endive. Halve each lengthwise. Heat bacon fat. Working in batches, brown endive on both sides, about 5 minutes per side. Place, cut side up, in a 13 x 9 x 2-inch baking dish.

4. Add onion and oil to bacon fat in skillet; sauté until onion browns slightly, 4 minutes. Add vinegar, sugar, wine, broth, salt and pepper. Bring to boiling. Pour over endive.

5. Cover dish with aluminum foil and bake in heated 350° oven 45 minutes or until endive is fork-tender. Sprinkle with parsley and reserved bacon.

Make-ahead tip: Casserole can be baked ahead and refrigerated up to 10 hours. (Sprinkle with parsley and bacon when ready to serve.) Let stand at room temperature 30 minutes, then reheat in heated 350° oven 20 minutes.

Layered eggplant

Makes 6 servings   *Prep* 20 minutes   *Cook* 15 minutes   *Bake* at 400° for 10 minutes

A spectacular vegetarian entrée. Each diner gets an individual tower of eggplant slices layered with cheese.

Per serving
456 calories, 17 g protein, 35 g fat, 21 g carbohydrate, 706 mg sodium, 31 mg cholesterol.

Picking the best
Eggplant is extremely perishable. No matter which variety you are buying, be sure it has a green cap and firm, shiny skin.

1 large eggplant (about 2 pounds), trimmed
½ cup all-purpose flour
½ teaspoon salt
½ teaspoon black pepper
¾ to 1 cup vegetable oil
1 container (16 ounces) cottage cheese or ricotta cheese
¼ pound sharp cheddar cheese, shredded (about 1 cup)
1 tablespoon finely chopped fresh parsley
1 teaspoon finely chopped fresh marjoram
1 tablespoon dry plain bread crumbs
   Fresh Tomato Sauce (recipe follows)

1. Heat oven to 400°.

2. Cut eggplant crosswise into 18 slices. Pat dry with paper toweling. Spread out more paper toweling for blotting. Mix together flour, salt and ¼ teaspoon pepper in a shallow dish or on waxed paper.

3. Heat ¼ cup oil in each of 2 large skillets over medium-high heat. Coat each eggplant slice in flour, shaking off excess.

4. Fry 2 or 3 slices of eggplant per skillet until browned on both sides, about 4 minutes total. Transfer to paper toweling to drain. Repeat until all slices are fried, adding more oil as needed.

5. Mix cottage cheese, cheddar cheese, parsley, marjoram and remaining ¼ teaspoon pepper in a bowl.

6. Place 1 eggplant slice in a large baking dish. Spread with 3 tablespoons cottage cheese mixture; top with another eggplant slice, 3 more tablespoons cottage cheese mixture and a final slice of eggplant. Repeat with remaining eggplant and cottage cheese mixture to make 6 stacks. Sprinkle with bread crumbs.

7. Bake, uncovered, in heated 400° oven 10 minutes. Serve immediately with Fresh Tomato Sauce.

Fresh tomato sauce

Per tablespoon
17 calories, 1 g protein, 2 g fat, 1 g carbohydrate, 23 mg sodium, 0 mg cholesterol.

Mix together in a bowl 1 large tomato, seeded and diced; 3 tablespoons sliced fresh basil; 3 tablespoons balsamic vinegar; 3 tablespoons olive oil; ¼ teaspoon salt and ⅛ teaspoon freshly ground black pepper. Makes about 1½ cups sauce.

Layered eggplant
opposite

115

Mushroom tart

Makes 12 servings   *Prep* 30 minutes   *Cook* 14 minutes

Bake crust at 400° for 15 minutes; pie at 400° for 20 to 25 minutes

Use all one kind of mushroom or a combination: white button, cremini, oyster, shiitake or portabella.

Per serving

198 calories, 7 g protein, 14 g fat, 12 g carbohydrate, 337 mg sodium, 72 mg cholesterol.

Mushroom tips

• To clean mushrooms, gently wipe with a damp cloth or soft brush. You can also rinse them, but do so quickly under cold water and pat dry immediately so they don't become mushy.
• Sliced white mushrooms cook down by half: 1 pound, sliced, yields about 4 cups raw, 2 cups cooked. Other types lose less moisture, so their yield is greater.

1 Single-Crust Pie Pastry (recipe, page 384)

Filling
2 tablespoons olive oil
2 onions, thinly sliced
3 cups sliced mushrooms
½ teaspoon dried thyme
½ teaspoon salt
½ teaspoon black pepper
3 eggs
1 cup milk
⅛ teaspoon ground nutmeg
1 tablespoon Dijon mustard
1½ cups shredded Fontina cheese
   Fresh thyme sprigs for garnish

1. Position oven rack in lower third of oven. Heat oven to 400°.

2. Roll out dough into a 12-inch round. Ease dough into a 10-inch tart pan with removable bottom; do not stretch. Trim edge; prick bottom all over with a fork. Line dough with aluminum foil, gently pushing foil against sides. Fill foil with dried beans or pie weights.

3. Bake crust in heated 400° oven 15 minutes. Remove from oven. Carefully remove foil and beans. Cool on a wire rack. Leave oven temperature at 400°.

4. Meanwhile, prepare filling: Heat oil in a large nonstick skillet over medium heat. Add onions and cook until softened slightly, about 10 minutes. Add mushrooms, thyme, salt and pepper; cook over high heat until vegetables are tender and any liquid has evaporated, 3 to 4 minutes.

5. Combine eggs, milk and nutmeg in a bowl. Stir in mushroom mixture.

6. Brush bottom of pastry shell with mustard. Sprinkle with cheese. Scrape mushroom mixture into shell.

7. Bake in lower third of heated 400° oven 20 to 25 minutes or until center is just set and top is golden. Transfer to a rack to cool slightly. Garnish with thyme sprigs.

Stuffed portabella mushrooms

Makes 6 servings   *Prep* 10 minutes   *Cook* 10 minutes   *Bake* at 425° for 15 minutes

Serve these alongside grilled steak or chicken. Or for a light lunch, present two to each person along with a green salad.

Per serving
136 calories, 7 g protein, 7 g fat, 13 g carbohydrate, 372 mg sodium, 13 mg cholesterol.

6 portabella mushrooms, cleaned
⅓ cup beef or vegetable broth
1 tablespoon olive oil
1 onion, chopped
1 clove garlic, finely chopped
1 tomato, cored, seeded and chopped
1 teaspoon dried oregano
⅓ cup dry seasoned bread crumbs
2 tablespoons grated Parmesan cheese
¾ cup shredded mozzarella cheese (3 ounces)

1. Heat oven to 425°.

2. Remove stems from mushrooms; chop stems. Place mushroom caps, tops down, in a large baking dish. Pour broth over mushrooms. Cover dish with aluminum foil.

3. Bake in heated 425° oven 15 minutes or until mushrooms are tender. Remove mushrooms from baking dish. Turn oven to broil.

4. Meanwhile, heat oil in a large nonstick skillet. Add onion and garlic; sauté 5 minutes. Add chopped mushroom stems, tomato and oregano; cook 5 minutes. Stir in bread crumbs and Parmesan cheese. Set aside and keep warm.

5. Coat a baking sheet with nonstick cooking spray. Stuff mushrooms with tomato mixture. Sprinkle with mozzarella. Broil until cheese melts. Serve hot or at room temperature.

VEGETABLES

Mushroom varieties

THE DISTINCTIVE FLAVORS of different mushrooms lend pizzazz to all manner of dishes.

Cremini: Meaty, earthy flavor. Use in place of white mushrooms (a relative) when you want a more intense taste.

Oyster: Delicate, briny nuances, velvety texture and creamy color. Subtly enhances sauces, soups, sautés, pasta and seafood.

Portabella: Very rich, almost beefy flavor. Good on its own, grilled, baked or deep-fried. Try stuffed (see above) as a side dish or appetizer or use in stir-fries and sauces.

Shiitake: Rich, smoky flavor; meaty texture. Sauté or grill on its own; also good in stir-fries, pastas and soups.

White, or button: Woodsy taste when raw—excellent in salads and with dips. Milder when cooked; nice in casseroles, stir-fries, soups and stuffings.

Glazed pearl onions with cranberries

Makes 8 servings   *Prep* 20 minutes   *Cook* 15 minutes   *Bake* at 400° for 30 minutes

Equally delicious straight out of the oven or at room temperature. The perfect companion to roast turkey or chicken or a pork roast.

Per serving
82 calories, 1 g protein,
3 g fat, 14 g carbohydrate,
263 mg sodium,
8 mg cholesterol.

2 containers (10 ounces each) pearl onions
2 tablespoons butter
¼ cup sugar

2 cups fresh or frozen cranberries (about 8 ounces)
⅛ teaspoon salt
⅛ teaspoon black pepper
⅓ cup chicken broth

1. Slice off root ends of onions. Place onions in a pot, cover with water, bring to boiling and boil 1 minute or until skins begin to loosen. Drain and run under cool water. Pull away outer skin.

2. Heat oven to 400°.

3. Melt butter in a large skillet. Add onions and cook over medium-high heat, stirring occasionally, until lightly browned, about 10 minutes.

4. Add sugar; toss to coat. Add cranberries, salt and pepper. Stir in broth, scraping up any browned bits from bottom of skillet. Transfer onion mixture to an 11 x 7 x 2-inch nonaluminum baking pan.

5. Bake in heated 400° oven until onions and cranberries are tender and glazed, about 30 minutes.

Fried onion rings
opposite

Fried onion rings

Makes 6 servings *Prep* 15 minutes *Stand* 30 minutes *Deep-fry* 2 to 3 minutes per batch

The key to making great-tasting onion rings at home is to fry only three or four at a time—each one will remain light and crispy.

Per serving
384 calories, 8 g protein, 17 g fat, 46 g carbohydrate, 309 mg sodium, 99 mg cholesterol.

Batter
2 eggs, separated
1 bottle (12 ounces) beer
⅓ cup butter, melted
2 cups all-purpose flour

Onion rings
6 cups vegetable oil
3 medium onions (1¼ pounds), cut into ½-inch-thick slices and separated into rings
¼ cup all-purpose flour
½ teaspoon salt

1. Prepare batter: Beat egg yolks in a medium-size bowl 3 minutes or until light colored. Stir in beer and butter. Stir in flour. Let stand 30 minutes.

2. Beat egg whites with clean beaters in a small bowl until stiff but not dry peaks form. Fold whites into batter.

3. Prepare onion rings: Heat oil in a large saucepan until temperature reaches 375° on a deep-fat thermometer. Adjust heat as needed to maintain temperature. Line a baking sheet with paper toweling.

4. Toss onion rings in flour to coat; shake off excess flour.

5. Dip onion rings, one at a time, in batter; let excess batter drain back into bowl. Place rings in hot oil, several at a time; do not overcrowd. Cook 2 to 3 minutes or until golden brown. Remove with a slotted spoon, letting excess oil drain back into pan; place rings on lined baking sheet. Repeat with remaining rings and batter. Sprinkle with salt.

Peas and new potatoes in cream

Makes 8 servings *Prep* 15 minutes *Cook* 25 to 30 minutes

Fresh peas are best, but when they are out of season, use frozen and reduce the cooking time by 2 to 3 minutes.

Per serving
329 calories, 8 g protein, 13 g fat, 48 g carbohydrate, 559 mg sodium, 41 mg cholesterol.

2 pounds red new potatoes
4 cups shelled green peas
2 teaspoons salt
1 teaspoon sugar

2 tablespoons butter
3 green onions, chopped
½ teaspoon black pepper
1 cup light cream

1. Steam new potatoes about 20 minutes or until fork-tender.

2. Combine peas, salt and sugar in a saucepan and add water to cover. Cook, uncovered, 5 to 8 minutes or until tender. Drain; return peas to pan.

3. Add butter and green onions to peas. Heat until butter is melted. Add potatoes, pepper and cream. Heat through but do not cook.

Garlicky snow peas

Makes 8 servings   *Prep* 10 minutes   *Cook* 6 minutes

The whole snow pea is edible—pod and pea. If buying fresh, choose brightly colored green, crisp pods with small peas inside.

Per serving
73 calories, 3 g protein, 4 g fat, 8 g carbohydrate, 138 mg sodium, 0 mg cholesterol.

2 tablespoons olive oil
3 green onions (both green and white parts), chopped (about ⅔ cup)
2 cloves garlic, chopped
1 large sweet red pepper, cored, seeded and chopped
1½ pounds fresh or frozen snow peas, trimmed
½ teaspoon salt
¼ teaspoon black pepper
2 tablespoons fresh lemon juice

1. Heat oil in a large skillet over high heat. Add green onions and garlic; sauté until fragrant, 30 seconds. Add sweet red pepper; sauté until slightly softened, about 2 minutes. Add snow peas; sauté until heated through but still crisp-tender, about 3 minutes. Add oil if necessary to prevent sticking.

2. Season with salt, pepper and lemon juice. If not serving immediately, cover the skillet.

Rosemary-minted sugar snap peas

Makes 8 servings   *Prep* 15 minutes   *Cook* 15 minutes

A cross between a snow pea and an English pea, the sugar snap, like the snow pea, is entirely edible. Make sure the pods are crisp, not limp. The rosemary-mint combination is good with other green vegetables.

Per serving
85 calories, 4 g protein, 4 g fat, 9 g carbohydrate, 138 mg sodium, 4 mg cholesterol.

2 sprigs fresh rosemary or 2 teaspoons dried
1 cup water
½ teaspoon salt
2 pounds sugar snap peas, trimmed
1 tablespoon butter or margarine
¼ cup blanched slivered almonds
¼ cup chopped fresh mint or 2 teaspoons dried
⅛ teaspoon black pepper

1. Place rosemary in a piece of cheesecloth; tie closed with string.

2. Bring water, salt and rosemary to boiling in a large skillet or Dutch oven over high heat. Add peas; return to boiling. Cover, lower heat to medium and cook 8 to 10 minutes or until peas are tender as desired.

3. Meanwhile, melt butter in a small skillet over medium heat. Add almonds and mint; sauté until almonds are golden, 2 minutes.

4. Drain peas. Remove cheesecloth bag. Toss peas with butter mixture and pepper until well coated. Serve immediately.

Mediterranean stuffed peppers

Makes 6 servings *Prep* 15 minutes *Cook* 18 minutes *Bake* at 350° for 40 minutes

Pepper prep is a breeze with the hints below. To make halves just right for stuffing, see step 1. For no-mess strips, continue with steps 2 through 4.

Per serving
403 calories, 22 g protein, 16 g fat, 46 g carbohydrate, 522 mg sodium, 55 mg cholesterol.

6 sweet peppers (red, yellow and green)
1 package (6 ounces) wheat pilaf mix
1 tablespoon olive oil
1 onion, chopped
2 cloves garlic, chopped
½ teaspoon curry powder
½ pound ground beef
¼ cup raisins
2 tablespoons chopped fresh parsley
2 cups shredded mozzarella cheese (8 ounces)

1. Cut off one side of each pepper. Core and seed peppers. Chop cut-off sides and reserve.

2. Heat oven to 350°. Prepare pilaf according to package directions.

3. Meanwhile, cook hollowed peppers in a large pot of simmering water 8 minutes. Cool under running cold water. Drain upside down on paper toweling.

4. Heat oil in a large skillet over medium heat. Add onion, reserved chopped pepper, garlic and curry powder and sauté 5 minutes or until onion is softened. Add beef, breaking it up with a wooden spoon; cook 5 minutes. Transfer to a large bowl to cool slightly.

5. Stir in pilaf. Fold in raisins, parsley and 1½ cups cheese. Spoon mixture into peppers. Top each with remaining cheese. Place peppers in a 9 x 9 x 2-inch baking pan. Cover with aluminium foil.

6. Bake in heated 350° oven 30 minutes. Remove foil; bake another 10 minutes.

VEGETABLES

How to core and seed sweet peppers

1. Hold pepper by stem and cut downward, following inside curve of pepper.

2. Rotate pepper slightly and slice again, cutting away another section.

3. Continue cutting—four sections for a large pepper, three for a slender one.

4. After final cut, simply discard the stem with seeds attached for easy cleanup.

Cheese-topped peppers

Makes 4 servings   *Prep* 40 minutes   *Cook* 26 minutes   *Bake* at 350° for 35 to 40 minutes

The classic meat-stuffed favorite, with a touch of horseradish for extra zip.

Per serving
416 calories, 22 g protein,
21 g fat, 37 g carbohydrate,
752 mg sodium,
67 mg cholesterol.

Picking the best
Sweet peppers of any color should be plump and firm, with glossy, unblemished skins.

4 sweet peppers (any color), tops cut off, seeded and hollowed out
1 tablespoon olive oil
1 onion, chopped
2 cloves garlic, finely chopped
½ teaspoon ground cumin
½ pound ground beef
1 can (8 ounces) tomato sauce
2 tablespoons Worcestershire sauce
¼ teaspoon black pepper
2 tablespoons ketchup
½ teaspoon bottled horseradish
½ teaspoon salt (optional)
1½ cups cooked white rice
1 cup shredded cheddar cheese (about 4 ounces)
2 tablespoons chopped fresh parsley

1. Heat oven to 350°.

2. Cook peppers in a large pot of simmering water 8 minutes. Cool under running cold water. Drain upside down on paper toweling.

3. Heat oil in a large skillet over medium heat. Add onion and garlic; sauté 5 minutes or until onion is softened. Stir in cumin; cook 2 minutes. Add beef, breaking it up with a wooden spoon; cook 5 minutes. Add tomato sauce, Worcestershire sauce, black pepper, ketchup, horseradish and salt if using. Cook 6 minutes. Remove from heat. Stir in rice and cheese.

4. Spoon mixture into pepper shells. Top with parsley. Place peppers in a 9 x 9 x 2-inch baking pan. Bake in heated 350° oven 35 to 40 minutes.

Cheese-topped peppers

Peppers and eggs

Makes 6 servings   *Prep* 15 minutes   *Cook* 15 minutes

Although the recipe calls for green frying peppers, there's no reason not to use sweet peppers—green, red, orange and/or purple.

Per serving
157 calories, 9 g protein, 9 g fat, 11 g carbohydrate, 173 mg sodium, 223 mg cholesterol.

2 tablespoons butter
1 small onion, diced
3 green frying peppers, diced
1 potato, cooked, peeled and diced

6 eggs
2 egg whites
½ teaspoon salt
⅛ teaspoon black pepper

1. Melt 1 tablespoon butter in a large nonstick skillet. Add onion and peppers and sauté 8 minutes. Add potato; cook 5 minutes. Transfer to a small bowl.

2. Whisk eggs, egg whites, salt and pepper in a medium-size bowl. Melt remaining butter in skillet. Add eggs; cook until almost set, stirring occasionally, 2 minutes. Stir in sautéed vegetables.

Scalloped potatoes and leeks

Makes 8 servings   *Prep* 30 minutes   *Cook* 15 minutes   *Bake* at 350° for 1 hour   *Broil* 2 to 3 minutes

Leeks are notorious for the sand and dirt hidden in their leaves. Wash well! After trimming off the tough green ends, slice lengthwise through the stalks toward the stem end. Rinse thoroughly under running water.

Per serving
197 calories, 5 g protein, 4 g fat, 37 g carbohydrate, 354 mg sodium, 10 mg cholesterol.

2 tablespoons butter or margarine
3 leeks, trimmed and well washed, white and light green parts thinly sliced
2 cloves garlic, chopped
1 teaspoon dried thyme
2 pounds all-purpose potatoes, peeled and thinly sliced

2 tablespoons all-purpose flour
1 teaspoon salt
¼ teaspoon black pepper
1 cup skim milk
¼ cup dry plain bread crumbs
2 tablespoons grated Parmesan cheese

1. Melt 1 tablespoon butter in a large skillet. Add leeks and sauté 8 to 10 minutes or until just tender. Remove half of leeks. Add garlic and thyme; sauté 2 minutes.

2. Heat oven to 350°. Coat a 2-quart shallow baking dish with nonstick cooking spray. Arrange half of potatoes in a layer in prepared dish.

3. Whisk together flour, salt, pepper and milk in a small bowl. Gradually stir into leeks in skillet; cook, stirring, 3 to 5 minutes or until thickened and bubbly. Spread mixture over potatoes. Top with remaining potatoes. Cover with foil. Bake in heated 350° oven 1 hour or until potatoes are tender.

4. Melt remaining 1 tablespoon butter in a small saucepan over low heat. Stir in bread crumbs and Parmesan.

5. Remove potatoes from oven. Remove foil. Sprinkle reserved leeks around outside edge. Sprinkle top with crumb mixture. Increase oven temperature to broil. Broil potatoes 2 to 3 minutes or until golden.

Rosemary-roasted potato sticks

Makes 8 servings *Prep* 30 minutes *Grill* 30 minutes, or *bake* at 450° for 30 minutes

Grilled or baked, these are an awesome accent for grilled foods, including hamburgers.

Per serving
205 calories, 4 g protein, 2 g fat, 43 g carbohydrate, 292 mg sodium, 0 mg cholesterol.

2 tablespoons lower-sodium chicken broth
2 tablespoons chopped fresh rosemary or 1 teaspoon dried, crumbled
1 tablespoon olive oil
1 teaspoon salt
¼ teaspoon black pepper
3 pounds red boiling potatoes, cut into matchstick strips
1 cup chopped green onion

1. Prepare a charcoal grill with medium-hot coals, or heat a gas grill to medium-high, or heat oven to 450°. Position grill rack 6 inches from heat. Cut out eight 8 x 8-inch squares of heavy-duty aluminum foil.

2. Combine broth, rosemary, oil, salt and pepper in a large bowl. Add potatoes and green onion; toss to mix. Place about 1⅓ cups potatoes on each square of foil. For each packet, fold 2 opposite sides of foil over; fold edges together 3 times to seal. Fold open ends over 3 times.

3. Grill packets over medium-hot coals on covered grill 30 minutes or until potatoes are fork-tender, or bake in heated 450° oven 30 minutes.

Cheese and bacon stuffed potatoes

Makes 4 servings *Prep* 20 minutes *Cook* 10 minutes *Bake* at 375° for 1¼ to 1¾ hours

A luxurious version of the American favorite— bacon, mushrooms, cheddar, butter and sour cream. Not something to have every day but when you crave a treat.

Per serving
539 calories, 20 g protein, 27 g fat, 58 g carbohydrate, 946 mg sodium, 78 mg cholesterol.

4 large baking potatoes (about 3 pounds total)
3 slices bacon, chopped
½ pound mushrooms, cut into ½-inch pieces
4 green onions, sliced
1½ cups shredded cheddar cheese (6 ounces)
1 tablespoon butter
1 teaspoon black pepper
½ teaspoon salt
1 container (8 ounces) reduced-fat sour cream

1. Heat oven to 375°. Bake potatoes 1 to 1½ hours or until fork-tender. Leave oven on.

2. Meanwhile, cook bacon in a medium-size skillet over low heat until almost crisp. Add mushrooms and green onions; cook 4 to 5 minutes or until mushrooms are lightly cooked. Transfer mixture to a medium-size bowl.

3. Cut potatoes in half; scoop out pulp, leaving ½ inch on the skin. Put potato pulp in a large bowl; mash until smooth. Stir in mushroom mixture, cheese, butter, pepper and salt. Spoon into potato shells. Place on a baking sheet. Bake in heated 375° oven 15 minutes or until potato is piping hot. Top each potato with sour cream and serve.

Potatoes au gratin

Makes 6 servings   *Prep* 15 minutes   *Cook* 15 minutes   *Bake* at 350° for 45 minutes

The baking, or russet, potato, with its low moisture content, makes the perfect choice for a gratin. The slices hold their shape during baking, and rather than watering down the sauce, they actually help thicken it.

Per serving
264 calories, 8 g protein,
11 g fat, 33 g carbohydrate,
279 mg sodium,
15 mg cholesterol.

2 pounds baking potatoes, peeled and thinly sliced
1 can (13¾ ounces) reduced-sodium chicken broth
3 tablespoons plus 2 teaspoons olive oil
3 tablespoons all-purpose flour
1½ cups low-fat (1%) milk
1 cup shredded Gruyère cheese
2 green onions, chopped
¼ teaspoon salt
⅛ teaspoon black pepper
3 tablespoons dry plain bread crumbs

1. Heat oven to 350°. Butter a 2-quart shallow casserole dish.

2. Place potatoes and broth in a large saucepan. Add water if needed to cover potatoes. Bring to boiling. Lower heat; simmer 5 minutes. Drain. Save broth for a soup. Transfer potatoes to a large bowl.

3. Heat 3 tablespoons oil in a small saucepan over low heat. Whisk in flour; cook 1 minute. Add milk. Cook, stirring, to thicken. Remove from heat. Stir in cheese, green onions, salt and pepper. Add to potatoes; stir gently. Pour into casserole.

4. Bake in heated 350° oven 30 minutes.

5. Stir together bread crumbs and remaining 2 teaspoons oil. Sprinkle over casserole and bake another 15 minutes or until potatoes are tender.

Oven-fried potatoes

Makes 5 servings   *Prep* 10 minutes   *Roast* at 425° for 30 to 40 minutes

For a slightly different take on the onion, substitute 1 cup chopped green onion for the diced white or yellow onion.

Per serving
236 calories, 4 g protein,
7 g fat, 41 g carbohydrate,
186 mg sodium,
0 mg cholesterol.

3 pounds red new potatoes, cut in half
1 medium onion, diced
3 tablespoons olive oil
1 teaspoon dried rosemary, crumbled
½ teaspoon salt
¼ teaspoon black pepper

1. Heat oven to 425°. Lightly oil a roasting pan.

2. Place potatoes, onion, oil, rosemary, salt and pepper in pan; toss to coat.

3. Roast potatoes in heated 425° oven until tender, 30 to 40 minutes, stirring about halfway through.

Note: When new potatoes—young potatoes of any variety—are large, cutting them into quarters will reduce their cooking time.

Baked garlic potatoes

Makes 8 servings   *Prep* 20 minutes   *Bake* at 425° for 1 hour

Twice-baked potatoes are always a favorite. The flavor secret is roasting whole heads of garlic—not cloves but whole heads—and then squeezing the sweetly flavored pulp into the potato filling.

Per serving
297 calories, 7 g protein, 6 g fat, 55 g carbohydrate, 337 mg sodium, 2 mg cholesterol.

2 whole heads garlic
3 tablespoons plus ½ teaspoon olive oil
6 large baking potatoes (about 3 pounds total), scrubbed
⅔ cup chicken broth
¾ teaspoon salt
½ teaspoon white pepper
3 tablespoons grated Parmesan cheese
Paprika

1. Heat oven to 425°.

2. Rub garlic heads with ½ teaspoon olive oil. Wrap each head loosely in aluminum foil. Pierce each potato in several places with a fork.

3. Bake potatoes and garlic in heated 425° oven 50 minutes or until potatoes are knife-tender and garlic is soft to the touch. Leave oven on.

4. Halve each potato lengthwise. Scoop out pulp into a large bowl. Reserve 8 potato shells (use other 4 shells for potato skins). Unwrap garlic; cut heads of garlic in half horizontally. Squeeze garlic pulp from papery skins into bowl with potatoes; discard garlic skins. Add broth, remaining 3 tablespoons oil, salt and pepper to potato mixture. Mash with potato masher until smooth and creamy. Spoon back into 8 reserved potato shells. Sprinkle with Parmesan and paprika.

5. Bake in 425° oven 10 minutes or until tops are golden brown.

Sesame steak fries

Makes 4 servings   *Prep* 10 minutes   *Bake* at 425° for 40 to 45 minutes

For more of a sesame punch, toss the potatoes with a teaspoon of dark Asian sesame oil, made from roasted sesame seeds.

Per serving
275 calories, 5 g protein, 5 g fat, 55 g carbohydrate, 546 mg sodium, 0 mg cholesterol.

4 large baking potatoes (about 2 pounds total), scrubbed
1 tablespoon olive oil
1 tablespoon sesame seeds
1 teaspoon salt
½ teaspoon black pepper

1. Heat oven to 425°. Grease a large shallow roasting pan.

2. Peel potatoes. Cut lengthwise into ¾-inch-thick wedges.

3. Toss potatoes, oil, sesame seeds, salt and pepper in a large bowl until well coated. Place in prepared roasting pan.

4. Bake in heated 425° oven 40 to 45 minutes or until potatoes are tender and golden brown. For extra crispness, broil potatoes for last 5 minutes of cooking.

Foolproof fries

As all serious French-fry lovers know, the key to really terrific fries is double frying—first at a lower temperature to cook through, and then at a higher temperature for extra crispness. High starch baking (russet) potatoes are the potato of choice because they hold their shape well.

Per serving
183 calories, 2 g protein,
12 g fat, 18 g carbohydrate,
93 mg sodium,
0 mg cholesterol.

6 cups (approximately) vegetable oil
3 large baking potatoes (about 1½ pounds total), cut into 3 x ¾ x ¾-inch sticks

¼ teaspoon salt

1. Pour oil into a deep saucepan to a depth of 5 to 6 inches. Heat to 325° on a deep-fat thermometer.

2. With a slotted metal spoon, add 10 potato sticks to oil; fry 2 minutes or until very lightly colored. Remove to a baking sheet lined with paper toweling. Repeat, letting oil return to 325° before adding each batch of sticks.

3. Second frying: Heat oil to 375°. Working in 2 or 3 batches, add potato sticks to oil; fry 1½ to 2 minutes or until golden brown. Transfer to paper toweling to drain. Sprinkle with salt.

Foolproof fries

Spicy smashed potatoes

Makes 8 servings   *Prep* 20 minutes   *Cook* 15 minutes

Feeling wicked? Add a finely chopped, seeded jalapeño chile, a grinding of black pepper and ¼ cup shredded pepper-Jack cheese.

Per serving
182 calories, 3 g protein,
9 g fat, 23 g carbohydrate,
213 mg sodium,
25 mg cholesterol.

5 large baking potatoes (about 2½ pounds total), peeled and cut into chunks
2 cloves garlic, peeled
6 tablespoons butter

½ cup milk
¾ teaspoon salt
1 teaspoon hot-pepper sauce (optional)

1. Bring 6 cups water to boiling in a large saucepan. Add potatoes and garlic. Simmer, covered, until potatoes are fork-tender, about 15 minutes; drain.

2. Return potatoes and garlic to saucepan. Add butter, milk and salt. Mash potato mixture with a potato masher. Sprinkle with a little hot-pepper sauce if desired.

Mashed potatoes

Makes 12 servings   *Prep* 10 minutes   *Cook* 20 minutes

For those who dare to cross over the edge, use half-and-half or heavy cream instead of milk. On the other hand, you could use skim milk.

Per serving
233 calories, 4 g protein,
7 g fat, 39 g carbohydrate,
382 mg sodium,
39 mg cholesterol.

10 large baking potatoes (about 5 pounds total)
2 teaspoons salt
1½ cups milk

6 tablespoons butter
¼ teaspoon black pepper
¼ teaspoon ground nutmeg
½ cup chopped fresh parsley

1. Peel potatoes. Cut into 1½-inch chunks, dropping into a large saucepan half filled with cold water. Add ½ teaspoon salt. Bring to boiling and boil, partially covered, until potatoes are tender, 15 minutes. Drain and set potatoes aside.

2. In same saucepan, bring 1 cup milk and butter to simmering. Turn off heat. Return potatoes to pan.

3. Add pepper, nutmeg, and remaining 1½ teaspoons salt. Mash. Stir in parsley and remaining ½ cup milk.

Potato pancakes

Makes 20 mini pancakes   Prep 10 minutes   Cook 3 minutes per batch

Shredded carrot provides a touch of sweetness and color in these tasty fritters.

Per pancake
70 calories, 1 g protein,
5 g fat, 7 g carbohydrate,
60 mg sodium,
11 mg cholesterol.

1 pound all-purpose potatoes,
   peeled and shredded
1 medium onion, shredded
1 medium carrot, shredded
½ teaspoon fresh lemon juice
1 egg, lightly beaten

1 tablespoon all-purpose flour
½ teaspoon salt
⅛ teaspoon black pepper
½ cup vegetable oil
   Applesauce or sour cream
   (optional)

1. Combine potatoes, onion, carrot, lemon juice, egg, flour, salt and pepper in a large bowl.

2. Heat oil in a large nonstick skillet. Spoon 5 pancakes into oil, using 1 heaping tablespoon potato mixture for each; cook 1½ minutes on each side. Remove to paper toweling to drain. Repeat with remaining mixture. Serve with applesauce or sour cream if desired.

Buttery spaghetti squash

Makes 6 servings   Prep 5 minutes   Microwave 25 to 30 minutes

Since the cooked strands of this particular squash look like spaghetti, that's how the squash got its name. For a quick dinner, toss store-bought pasta sauce with the cooked strands.

Per serving
95 calories, 1 g protein,
5 g fat, 13 g carbohydrate,
168 mg sodium,
11 mg cholesterol.

1 spaghetti squash (3 pounds),
   halved lengthwise and seeded
2 tablespoons butter, melted
¼ cup chicken broth

2 tablespoons chopped fresh parsley
¼ teaspoon salt
⅛ teaspoon black pepper

1. Place squash, cut side down, in a microwave-safe dish. Add 2 tablespoons water. Cover dish tightly with plastic wrap. Microwave on 100% power 25 to 30 minutes or until squash is tender. Let stand 5 minutes.

2. Carefully remove plastic wrap. Pull out squash strands with a fork; place in a large bowl.

3. Mix butter, broth, parsley, salt and pepper; add to squash. Serve.

Mini spinach tarts

Makes 6 servings *Prep* 12 minutes *Bake* at 425° for 10 minutes; then at 350° for 10 to 15 minutes

Arrange the tarts on a party platter and watch them disappear. They're a cinch to make when you use store-bought tartlet shells.

Per serving
284 calories, 16 g protein,
20 g fat, 14 g carbohydrate,
533 mg sodium,
139 mg cholesterol.

1 package frozen mini pastry tart shells (12 per package)
1 pound fresh spinach, stemmed, washed and chopped
4 ounces Gruyère or other favorite cheese, such as cheddar, Swiss or feta, grated (1 cup)

1¾ cups milk
3 eggs
1 tablespoon Dijon mustard
½ teaspoon salt
¼ teaspoon black pepper
2 tablespoons grated Parmesan cheese

1. Heat oven to 425°. Arrange tart shells on a baking sheet.

2. Bring ½ cup water to boiling in a large skillet. Add spinach; cook 1½ minutes. Drain and rinse under cold running water to stop the cooking. Squeeze out excess liquid.

3. Mix together spinach and Gruyère cheese in a medium-size bowl. Divide equally among tart shells.

4. Whisk together milk, eggs, mustard, salt and pepper in a large measuring cup until well blended. Pour into tart shells, dividing equally. Sprinkle each with ½ teaspoon Parmesan cheese.

5. Bake tarts in heated 425° oven 10 minutes. Lower oven temperature to 350°. Bake tarts 30 minutes more or until golden and set. Cool slightly on a wire rack. Remove tarts from tins and serve.

Spinach layered crepes *opposite*

Spinach layered crepes

Makes 4 servings   *Prep* 15 minutes   *Cook* 15 minutes   *Bake* at 400° for 15 minutes

Attention, all cheese lovers: This stacked crepe pie, its colors reminiscent of the Italian flag, is a showstopper for breakfast, brunch or Sunday supper.

Per serving
666 calories, 27 g protein, 45 g fat, 40 g carbohydrate, 1,033 mg sodium, 202 mg cholesterol.

1 tablespoon olive oil
1 large onion, chopped
2 cloves garlic, finely chopped
2 ounces fresh mushrooms, chopped (1 cup)
1 package (10 ounces) frozen chopped spinach, thawed and drained
¼ teaspoon salt
⅛ teaspoon black pepper
1 container (10 ounces) light Alfredo sauce
12 Crepes (recipe follows)
1¼ cups shredded mozzarella cheese
¼ cup grated Parmesan cheese

1. Place oven rack in upper third of oven. Heat oven to 400°.

2. Heat oil in a large nonstick skillet. Add onion; sauté 4 minutes. Add garlic; sauté 2 minutes. Add mushrooms; sauté 3 minutes. Stir in spinach, salt and pepper; cook 5 minutes or until spinach is tender. Stir in 2 tablespoons Alfredo sauce.

3. Place largest crepe on a 9-inch pie plate. Brush with 1 tablespoon Alfredo sauce. Spread with 2 tablespoons spinach filling. Sprinkle with 1½ tablespoons mozzarella and ½ teaspoon Parmesan. Repeat until all crepes and filling are used; leave top crepe plain. Pour rest of Alfredo sauce over; top with remaining Parmesan.

4. Bake in upper third of heated 400° oven 15 minutes. Let stand 15 minutes before cutting into wedges.

Crepes

Per serving
80 calories, 3 g protein, 4 g fat, 9 g carbohydrate, 69 mg sodium, 43 mg cholesterol.

Beat 2 eggs and 1 cup milk in a bowl until blended. Beat in 1 cup flour and ¼ teaspoon salt. Stir in 2 tablespoons melted butter. Refrigerate at least 30 minutes. Batter should be like heavy cream; if too thick, thin with milk. Heat an 8-inch crepe pan or skillet; coat with nonstick cooking spray. Pour in 2 tablespoons batter, swirling pan to cover bottom. Cook crepe 2 to 3 minutes or until bottom is lightly browned and top is dry. Remove from pan. Repeat with rest of batter, stacking crepes between pieces of waxed paper. Makes 12 crepes.

Sweet potato chips

Makes 4 servings   *Prep* 15 minutes   *Bake* at 400° for 30 minutes

Sweet and crispy, these homemade chips are irresistible.

Per serving
146 calories, 2 g protein, 4 g fat, 34 g carbohydrate, 143 mg sodium, 0 mg cholesterol.

2 large sweet potatoes (about 1½ pounds total)

1 tablespoon olive oil
¼ teaspoon salt

1. Heat oven to 400°.

2. Scrub sweet potatoes but do not peel. Cut into very thin slices, then toss with oil and salt until potatoes are evenly coated.

3. Spread in a single layer on a wire rack on a large baking sheet. Bake in heated 400° oven 30 minutes or until crisp and edges are curled. Serve immediately.

Sweet potatoes with apricots

Makes 8 servings   *Prep* 30 minutes   *Bake* at 350° for 30 minutes

If you've never tried the combo of tart apricots with sweet potatoes, you'll be deliciously surprised.

Per serving
351 calories, 4 g protein, 12 g fat, 60 g carbohydrate, 80 mg sodium, 8 mg cholesterol.

Sweet potato or yam?
Sweet potatoes have orange skins, true yams off-white or brown skins. Of the two, yams have more natural sugar and a higher moisture content, but you can interchange them.

6 medium sweet potatoes (about 3 pounds total), cooked and peeled, or 3 cans (16 ounces each) sweet potatoes, drained
¼ cup plus 2 tablespoons packed light-brown sugar
1 tablespoon all-purpose flour
½ teaspoon ground cinnamon
⅛ teaspoon salt

1½ cups fresh orange juice
2 tablespoons butter
1 tablespoon orange liqueur (optional)
2 to 3 teaspoons grated orange rind
1 cup dried apricots, halved or quartered
¼ cup golden raisins
1 cup pecans, chopped

1. Heat oven to 350°.

2. Cut sweet potatoes in half lengthwise; place in a single layer in a 2-quart shallow baking dish.

3. Combine ¼ cup brown sugar, flour, cinnamon and salt in a medium-size saucepan; stir to mix well. Gradually stir in orange juice until mixture is well blended and smooth. Bring mixture to boiling over medium heat; cook, stirring constantly, 1 minute.

4. Remove from heat; stir in butter until melted. Add orange liqueur if using, orange rind, apricots and raisins. Pour mixture over potatoes in baking dish. Sprinkle with pecans and remaining 2 tablespoons brown sugar.

5. Bake in heated 350° oven 30 minutes or until hot and bubbly. Serve.

Sweet potato salad

Makes 6 servings   *Prep* 15 minutes   *Cook* 8 to 10 minutes

Substitute walnuts, pecans or almonds for the hazelnuts—or for a real splurge, try macadamias.

Per serving
289 calories, 4 g protein,
11 g fat, 46 g carbohydrate,
499 mg sodium,
0 mg cholesterol.

3 large sweet potatoes (2 pounds total), peeled and cut into ½-inch cubes
1 to 2 tablespoons fruit vinegar or sherry vinegar
2 tablespoons vegetable oil
½ teaspoon salt
½ cup chopped hazelnuts
⅓ cup chopped, pitted dates

1. Place sweet potatoes in a medium-size saucepan and cover with water. Bring to boiling and boil 8 to 10 minutes or until tender. Drain.

2. Whisk vinegar, oil and salt in a medium-size bowl. Add cooked potatoes, hazelnuts and dates. Toss gently. Serve warm.

Candied sweets

Makes 12 servings   *Prep* 5 minutes   *Bake* at 400° for 50 to 55 minutes   *Cook* 18 minutes

Bake the sweet potatoes ahead of time and then refrigerate. Just let them return to room temperature and toss in the skillet with the glaze to heat through.

Per serving
203 calories, 2 g protein,
8 g fat, 31 g carbohydrate,
101 mg sodium,
13 mg cholesterol.

8 medium sweet potatoes (about 4 pounds total)
½ cup pecans, chopped
5 tablespoons butter
½ cup packed dark-brown sugar
2 teaspoons grated orange rind
¾ cup blended citrus juice
¼ teaspoon ground nutmeg
½ teaspoon salt
2 teaspoons vanilla

1. Place oven rack in top third of oven. Heat oven to 400°.

2. Place potatoes in a shallow baking pan. Bake in top third of heated 400°oven until tender, 50 to 55 minutes. Cool; peel.

3. Toast pecans in a dry small skillet over medium heat until lightly browned, 6 minutes.

4. Slice potatoes ¾ inch thick. Melt butter in a large skillet. Add brown sugar; increase heat, stirring, until foamy, 3 minutes. Add orange rind, juice, nutmeg and salt; cook to thicken, 4 minutes. Add potatoes; toss until glazed, 4 minutes. Remove from heat. Add vanilla and toss. Top with pecans. Serve.

VEGETABLES

Tomato tart

Makes 12 servings   *Prep* 30 minutes   *Refrigerate* 40 minutes

Bake crust at 400° for 25 minutes; tart for 20 to 25 minutes

The fennel is an ideal match with the tomatoes and Kalamata olives. Other herbs that can be used in the crust are fresh basil, oregano, thyme or rosemary.

Shown on back cover and page 135.

Per serving
263 calories, 7 g protein, 18 g fat, 19 g carbohydrate, 440 mg sodium, 47 mg cholesterol.

Fresh or dried

If good-quality fresh herbs are not available, substitute the dried leaf variety. Rule of thumb: 1 tablespoon finely chopped fresh equals 1 teaspoon dried: Try not to keep your dried herbs longer than 6 months, and store them in a cool dark place to help maintain their freshness.

Fennel crust
2 cups all-purpose flour
1 tablespoon fennel seeds, crushed
¾ teaspoon salt
¾ cup (1½ sticks) butter, cut into small pieces
3 tablespoons ice water
1 egg white, lightly beaten

Tomato filling
10 Kalamata olives, pitted and chopped
2 tablespoons chopped shallots
1 tablespoon chopped fresh thyme or 1 teaspoon dried
1 tablespoon olive oil
1½ cups shredded Fontina cheese
3 large tomatoes (about 1½ pounds total), cored, cut into ⅛-inch-thick slices and well drained on paper toweling
¾ teaspoon salt
½ teaspoon coarsely ground black pepper
Fresh thyme sprigs for garnish

1. Prepare fennel crust: Combine flour, fennel seeds and salt in a food processor. Whirl 3 seconds to mix. Add butter; pulse until mixture resembles coarse crumbs. With machine running, add water, 1 tablespoon at a time, until dough just starts to come together; do not overprocess. Gather dough into a ball; pat into an 8-inch disc. Cover with waxed paper. Refrigerate until firm, about 40 minutes.

2. Heat oven to 400°.

3. On a lightly floured surface, roll dough into a 14-inch round. Carefully lift dough into a 12-inch tart pan with removable bottom; ease dough gently into pan, being careful not to stretch it. Trim edges. Prick dough all over bottom (not sides) with a fork. Line dough with aluminum foil, gently pushing foil against sides of tart pan to prevent shrinkage. Fill foil with dried beans or pie weights.

4. Bake crust in heated 400° oven on bottom rack 15 minutes.

5. Remove crust from oven. Carefully remove foil and beans or weights. Brush bottom of crust with egg white; return to oven and bake 10 minutes more or until golden. Remove to a wire rack to cool slightly.

6. Meanwhile, prepare tomato filling: Combine olives, shallots, thyme and oil in a small bowl until blended. Sprinkle cheese over bottom of cooled fennel crust. Arrange well-drained tomato slices in concentric circles over bottom of tart. Sprinkle tomatoes evenly with salt and pepper. Spoon olive mixture on top of tomatoes.

7. Bake tart in 400° oven 20 to 25 minutes or until cheese is melted and tomatoes are golden and bubbly. Transfer tart to a wire rack to cool slightly before serving. Garnish with thyme sprigs.

Tomato tart
opposite

Sliced tomatoes Provençal

Makes 8 servings   *Prep* 10 minutes   *Bake* at 475° for 15 minutes

Why does this dish reflect the cooking of the south of France? The seasonings—garlic, oregano and parsley—plus the olive oil. The bread crumb mixture can be made ahead, refrigerated and then sprinkled over the tomato slices just before baking.

Per serving
78 calories, 3 g protein, 3 g fat, 10 g carbohydrate, 325 mg sodium, 3 mg cholesterol.

4 large tomatoes (2½ pounds total)
¾ teaspoon salt
3 slices white bread, torn into pieces
¼ cup grated Parmesan cheese
2 tablespoons chopped fresh parsley

1 tablespoon olive oil
1 clove garlic, finely chopped
½ teaspoon dried oregano, crumbled
½ teaspoon black pepper

1. Heat oven to 475°.

2. Core tomatoes and cut each into 4 equal slices about ¾ inch thick. Place slices in a single layer on a large ungreased baking sheet. Sprinkle tomatoes with a total of ½ teaspoon salt.

3. Place bread in a food processor or blender. Pulse until fine crumbs form.

4. Combine bread crumbs, Parmesan, parsley, oil, garlic, oregano, pepper and remaining ¼ teaspoon salt in a small bowl. Sprinkle evenly over tomato slices.

5. Bake tomatoes in heated 475° oven 15 minutes or until they are tender and topping is golden. Serve hot or at room temperature.

135

Tomato chutney

Makes 4 cups *Prep* 15 minutes *Cook* 1 hour 10 minutes

Chutneys are sweet condiments that go well with curries and grilled meats. Or stir into egg salad, spread on bread for sandwiches or serve with cheese.

Per 2 tablespoons
54 calories, 2 g protein,
2 g fat, 10 g carbohydrate,
72 mg sodium,
0 mg cholesterol.

Tomato savvy
Remember—never refrigerate a tomato. The cold makes the flesh mushy and ruins the taste.

1 tablespoon olive oil
1 small onion, chopped
½ sweet green pepper, cored, seeded and diced
2½ pounds tomatoes, cored, seeded and coarsely chopped
2 cups crushed pineapple, drained
1 cup golden raisins
½ cup packed light-brown sugar
⅓ cup cider vinegar
1 teaspoon salt
1 teaspoon ground ginger
¼ teaspoon ground allspice
¼ teaspoon ground red pepper (cayenne)
½ cup pine nuts, toasted (see Note, below)
¼ cup chopped fresh parsley

1. Heat oil in a large nonaluminum saucepan. Add onion and green pepper; cook over low heat until very tender, 10 minutes.

2. Add tomatoes, pineapple, raisins, brown sugar, vinegar, salt, ginger, allspice and ground red pepper to saucepan. Bring to boiling. Lower heat; simmer, stirring occasionally, until chutney is thickened, about 1 hour.

3. Remove from heat. Stir in pine nuts and parsley. Cool. Refrigerate until ready to serve. Serve at room temperature.

Note: To toast pine nuts, spread them evenly on a baking sheet, place in a heated 350° oven and bake until golden brown and aromatic, 5 to 10 minutes. A dry skillet over medium heat works just as well.

Peeling and seeding tomatoes

Parboil: Cut a shallow X on smooth end of tomato. Place on a slotted spoon and submerge in boiling water 10 seconds.

Check: Lift spoon and check to see if tomato skin comes off easily. If not, reimmerse on spoon another 10 seconds.

Peel: Catch a bit of tomato skin between your thumb and a paring knife, then pull to strip skin away.

Seed: Cut tomato in half horizontally, then hold each half over a bowl, cut side down; gently squeeze out seeds.

Fried green tomatoes

Makes 6 servings *Prep* 15 minutes *Fry* 2 to 4 minutes per batch

Although green usually means unripe, there are some tomato varieties that are green when they're ripe. For this recipe be sure to use underripe tomatoes because you want the tarter flavor.

Per serving
202 calories, 3 g protein, 15 g fat, 15 g carbohydrate, 375 mg sodium, 36 mg cholesterol.

1 egg
1 tablespoon milk
⅓ cup all-purpose flour
⅓ cup yellow cornmeal
1 teaspoon salt
¼ teaspoon paprika

⅛ teaspoon ground red pepper (cayenne)
⅛ teaspoon black pepper
3 firm green or underripe tomatoes (about 1½ pounds total)
Vegetable oil for frying

1. Beat egg and milk in a small bowl. Combine flour, cornmeal, salt, paprika, red pepper and black pepper on waxed paper.

2. Core tomatoes; cut a thin slice from top and bottom of tomatoes and discard. Cut each tomato crosswise into 4 slices. Dip tomato slices first in egg, then in cornmeal mixture to coat.

3. Heat ¼ inch oil in a large nonstick skillet over medium-high heat. In batches, brown tomatoes on both sides, turning once, 1 to 2 minutes per side. Remove with a slotted spatula to paper toweling to drain. Serve immediately.

Orzo-stuffed tomatoes

Makes 4 servings *Prep* 20 minutes *Cook* 15 minutes

Not only do these stuffed tomatoes taste great, they're even better made in advance.

Per serving
197 calories, 4 g protein, 6 g fat, 33 g carbohydrate, 327 mg sodium, 0 mg cholesterol.

4 large tomatoes
1 tablespoon olive oil
1 onion, chopped
1 cup chopped fresh fennel
¼ cup fresh orange juice
½ cup orzo

1 tablespoon grated orange rind
1 can (14½ ounces) lower-sodium chicken broth
8 pitted ripe black olives, chopped
⅓ cup raisins

1. Cut ¼ inch off top of each tomato. Hollow out each tomato. Drain tomatoes upside down on paper toweling.

2. Heat oil in a large skillet over medium heat. Add onion and fennel and sauté until softened, 5 minutes. Slowly add juice to prevent sticking. Set aside.

3. Combine orzo, orange rind and broth in a medium-size saucepan. Bring to boiling and simmer, uncovered, 5 minutes. Stir in olives and raisins; simmer 5 minutes more. Add orzo mixture to fennel. Cool.

4. Spoon filling into tomatoes. Serve at room temperature.

Potato-stuffed tomatoes

Makes 4 servings   *Prep* 20 minutes   *Cook* 15 minutes   *Bake* at 400° for 10 minutes

A glamorous way to serve mashed potatoes—spectacular, too, as a finger-food treat.

Per serving
197 calories, 6 g protein,
5 g fat, 36 g carbohydrate,
630 mg sodium,
2 mg cholesterol.

8 small tomatoes (¼ pound each)
1 teaspoon salt
1 tablespoon olive oil
1 medium onion, finely chopped

1 pound all-purpose potatoes,
   peeled and quartered
½ cup plain low-fat yogurt

1. Cut tops from tomatoes and save for another use. Hollow out tomatoes, using a grapefruit knife or spoon, leaving a generous ¼-inch-thick shell. Sprinkle a total of ½ teaspoon salt over insides of tomatoes. Place tomatoes, upside down, on paper toweling to drain for 15 minutes.

2. Heat oil in a medium-size skillet. Add onion; sauté over medium-high heat until golden, 7 to 8 minutes.

3. Meanwhile, bring a medium-size saucepan of water to boiling. Add potatoes and cook until tender, about 10 minutes. Drain water from pan.

4. Add yogurt and remaining ½ teaspoon salt to potatoes. Mash with a potato masher until smooth. Stir in sautéed onion.

5. Heat oven to 400°.

6. Spoon about ¼ cup potato mixture into each tomato and place on a roasting pan.

7. Roast in heated 400° oven 10 minutes or until heated through.

Note: You can use 4 large (½ pound each) tomatoes. Spoon about ½ cup potato mixture into each and place on a roasting pan. Roast in a heated 400° oven 15 minutes or until heated through.

About tomatoes

AT THEIR BEST in summertime, tomatoes are low calorie, fat free and vitamin rich. Keep tomatoes in the open in a cool place—but don't expect them to ripen on a windowsill. If you wish to interchange fresh and canned tomatoes, 3 pounds fresh is the equivalent of one 28-ounce can.

Round: Large, deep red, all-purpose; good for sandwiches, salads, soups and sauces.

Plum: Oblong or pear shaped with meaty pulp; ideal for long-cooking sauces and stews.

Cherry: Small, sweet and juicy; use for salads, kabobs, sautés—and for snacking.

Green: Immature; good for frying and pickling.

Yellow: Less acidic than red tomatoes; use raw or for kabobs.

Sautéed tomatoes

Makes 4 servings   *Prep* 5 minutes   *Cook* 8 minutes

The balsamic vinegar in this recipe balances the sweetness of yellow tomatoes.

Per serving
60 calories, 1 g protein,
4 g fat, 7 g carbohydrate,
541 mg sodium,
0 mg cholesterol.

1 tablespoon olive oil
1 sweet onion, sliced and separated into rings
1 pint red cherry tomatoes or a mix of yellow and red
¼ cup chopped fresh basil
1 teaspoon salt
2 teaspoons balsamic vinegar

Heat oil in a large nonstick skillet over medium heat. Add onion and sauté 5 minutes. Add tomatoes, basil and salt. Sauté until skins just begin to split, 3 minutes. Remove from heat. Sprinkle with vinegar.

Potato-stuffed tomatoes *opposite*

Fresh tomato-basil pizza

Makes 6 servings   *Prep* 20 minutes   *Stand* 20 minutes   *Bake* at 450° for 20 to 25 minutes

Fast-rising yeast gets the crust moving quickly. For a leaner pie, omit the mozzarella altogether or cut the amount in half.

Per serving
425 calories, 15 g protein, 16 g fat, 55 g carbohydrate, 681 mg sodium, 30 mg cholesterol.

3 cups all-purpose flour
1 envelope fast-rising dry yeast
2 teaspoons sugar
1½ teaspoons salt
1 cup very warm water (115° to 120°)

3 tablespoons olive oil
2 tablespoons cornmeal
2 cups shredded mozzarella cheese
2 large tomatoes, thinly sliced
¼ cup fresh basil leaves, torn
1 teaspoon dried oregano

1. Heat oven to 450°.

2. Combine flour, yeast, sugar and 1 teaspoon salt in a medium-size bowl. Stir in warm water and 2 tablespoons olive oil until mixture comes together.

3. Turn dough out onto a lightly floured surface. Knead 10 minutes. Cover and let rest 20 minutes.

4. Sprinkle a 16-inch pizza pan with cornmeal. Pat dough over bottom of pizza pan, stretching and shaping to a ½-inch-high rim at edge of pan. Sprinkle with half of cheese. Top with tomatoes and basil. Brush tomatoes and rim of dough with remaining oil. Sprinkle pizza with oregano and remaining ½ teaspoon salt. Top with remaining cheese.

5. Bake on bottom rack of heated 450° oven 20 to 25 minutes.

Roasted turnips with ginger

Makes 4 servings   *Prep* 15 minutes   *Cook* 3 minutes   *Roast* at 375° for 40 minutes

Fabulous with pork roast, broiled pork chops or roast chicken.

Per serving
52 calories, 1 g protein, 2 g fat, 7 g carbohydrate, 343 mg sodium, 0 mg cholesterol.

½ teaspoon salt
1 pound turnips, peeled and cut into 2 x ½ x ½-inch strips

2 teaspoons dark Asian sesame oil
1 teaspoon ground ginger
⅛ teaspoon black pepper

1. Heat oven to 375°.

2. Bring 2 quarts water and ¼ teaspoon salt to boiling in a large saucepan over high heat. Add turnips; return to boiling. Lower heat to medium; cover and cook 3 minutes or until turnips are just tender.

3. Drain turnips. Turn into a large roasting pan. Stir in sesame oil, ginger, pepper and remaining ¼ teaspoon salt.

4. Roast in heated 375° oven 40 minutes, stirring turnips several times with a wooden spoon.

Winter squash gratin

Makes 10 servings *Prep* 15 minutes *Cook* 30 minutes *Bake* at 350° for 35 minutes

The walnuts that top the gratin sweeten as they bake. For a southern flair, scatter with pecans.

Per serving
173 calories, 5 g protein, 10 g fat, 18 g carbohydrate, 355 mg sodium, 78 mg cholesterol.

Squash varieties
• Spaghetti squash is oval with a yellow rind and golden flesh that can be separated into long strands when cooked.
• Hubbard squash is round with a gray-green, blue-green or orange rind. Its deep orange flesh has a nutty flavor.
• Sugar pumpkin is squat and round with a ridged orange rind. Its muted orange flesh has a subtle flavor.
• Butternut squash is pear shaped with a golden rind. Its pale yellow flesh has a buttery taste.
•Acorn squash is rounded with a deeply ridged black, orange or green rind. Its yellow-orange flesh is sweet.

1 butternut or acorn squash (3 pounds), peeled, seeded and cut into cubes, or 3 packages (12 ounces each) frozen cooked winter squash, thawed and drained
6 tablespoons dark-brown sugar
2 tablespoons butter
2 tablespoons all-purpose flour
1 cup milk
1 bay leaf
1½ teaspoons salt
¼ teaspoon black pepper
½ teaspoon granulated sugar
½ teaspoon ground cinnamon
⅛ teaspoon ground nutmeg
3 eggs, lightly beaten

Topping
1½ tablespoons butter
1 tablespoon brown sugar
½ cup chopped walnuts

1. Heat oven to 350°. Coat a shallow 2-quart baking dish with nonstick cooking spray.

2. Steam fresh squash 15 minutes or until tender. Puree cooked squash in a food processor along with brown sugar. Scrape into a fine-mesh sieve; drain 15 minutes, pressing down occasionally. (If using frozen squash, combine with brown sugar.) Transfer to a bowl.

3. Melt butter in a small saucepan. Stir in flour until smooth; cook, stirring, 1 minute. Whisk in milk until smooth. Add bay leaf, salt, pepper, granulated sugar, cinnamon and nutmeg; cook, stirring, over low heat 10 minutes. Cool. Remove bay leaf.

4. Whisk eggs into squash. Whisk in cooled white sauce. Transfer squash mixture to prepared baking dish; smooth top.

5. Prepare topping: Melt butter in a small nonstick saucepan over low heat. Stir in brown sugar; cook 5 minutes. Stir in walnuts.

6. Bake in lower third of heated 350° oven 25 minutes. Sprinkle topping over baking dish and bake 10 minutes more or until set in center.

Make-ahead tip: Squash mixture can be prepared up to a day ahead and refrigerated, covered, until needed. Bring to room temperature before baking.

VEGETABLES

Glazed winter squash

The perfect cool-weather combination: acorn squash and maple syrup. For best flavor, use pure maple syrup, not the imitation.

Per serving
51 calories, 1 g protein, 0 g fat, 13 g carbohydrate, 71 mg sodium, 0 mg cholesterol.

2 acorn or butternut squash (3½ pounds total), halved and seeded
2 tablespoons brown sugar
2 tablespoons maple syrup

½ teaspoon ground cinnamon
¼ teaspoon ground ginger
¼ teaspoon salt
2 tablespoons chopped fresh parsley

1. Place squash, cut side down, in a shallow microwave-safe dish. Add 2 tablespoons water. Cover tightly with plastic wrap. Microwave on 100% power 8 to 10 minutes or until tender. Let stand 5 minutes.

2. Heat oven to 375°.

3. Carefully remove plastic wrap. Cut squash halves in half lengthwise. Place, skin side down, in a baking pan.

4. Mix brown sugar, maple syrup, cinnamon, ginger and salt in a small bowl. Spoon over squash. Bake in heated 375° oven 10 minutes or until squash is glazed. Sprinkle with parsley. Serve immediately.

Glazed winter squash

Nutty zucchini halves

Makes 4 servings *Prep* 15 minutes *Cook* 5 minutes *Bake* at 375° for 30 minutes

4 medium zucchini (1½ pounds total)
1 medium onion, finely chopped
¼ cup chopped walnuts
1 tablespoon olive oil
1 teaspoon salt
¼ teaspoon freshly ground black pepper
¼ cup dry plain bread crumbs

2 tablespoons grated Parmesan cheese
1 teaspoon chopped fresh parsley
1 teaspoon chopped fresh thyme or ½ teaspoon dried
1 teaspoon chopped fresh oregano or ½ teaspoon dried
1 tablespoon butter, melted

1. Heat oven to 375°.

2. Cut a ¼-inch-thick lengthwise slice from each zucchini and discard or save for salad. Scoop out each zucchini with a small spoon, keeping outer skin intact, to form little boats. Chop scooped-out pieces of zucchini. Mix with onion and walnuts in a medium-size bowl.

3. Heat oil in a medium-size skillet. Add zucchini mixture; sauté about 5 minutes or until onion is softened and any liquid has been cooked off. Remove skillet from heat. Stir in ¾ teaspoon salt, pepper, bread crumbs, Parmesan, parsley, thyme and oregano until well mixed. Sprinkle inside of zucchini shells with remaining ¼ teaspoon salt. Spoon zucchini stuffing into shells, dividing equally.

4. Place zucchini shells, stuffed side up and side by side, in a baking dish large enough to hold them snugly. Bake in heated 375° oven 20 minutes. Brush with melted butter; bake another 10 minutes.

VEGETABLES

Zucchini prep

LOOK FOR ZUCCHINI with shiny, unblemished, dark green skin and an inch of stem. And remember, smaller (less than 1½ pounds) is better. Large zucchini are best stuffed or grated for bread. Here are three easy ways to cut zucchini for cooking.

Coins: Slice across the squash, making each round about ¼ inch thick; you can also cut on the diagonal. Coins are a good shape for sautéing.

Sticks: Cut in half, then slice each half into sticks. Use these for fried sticks or dipping. Or add to a stir-fry at the last minute—they cook fast.

Shreds: Grate on large holes of a grater. Allow moisture to weep on paper toweling; blot with dry paper toweling. Add to bread batter or salad.

Zucchini alla cece

Makes 4 servings *Prep* 10 minutes *Cook* 15 minutes

Cece is the Italian word for chick-peas. Inspired by caponata, which is an Italian eggplant salad, this dish pairs well with our Parmesan Chicken Fingers (page 230).

Per serving
113 calories, 4 g protein,
4 g fat, 18 g carbohydrate,
349 mg sodium,
0 mg cholesterol.

2 teaspoons olive oil
1 onion, chopped
2 small zucchini (½ pound total), cut into ¼-inch-thick slices
½ teaspoon dried basil, crumbled
¼ teaspoon dried thyme, crumbled

1 can (14¾ ounces) stewed tomatoes
1 cup canned chick-peas, drained and rinsed
⅛ teaspoon black pepper

1. Heat oil in a medium-size skillet over medium heat. Add onion, zucchini, basil and thyme. Cook, covered, 8 minutes, stirring occasionally.

2. Stir in tomatoes, chick-peas and pepper; cover and simmer 5 minutes or until zucchini is just tender. Serve immediately or refrigerate, covered, up to 3 days; gently reheat before serving.

Easy sautéed zucchini

Makes 6 servings *Prep* 10 minutes *Cook* 10 minutes

Serve this in late summer when there's an abundance of zucchini. Vary the amount of red-pepper flakes to suit your taste.

Per serving
41 calories, 2 g protein,
2 g fat, 5 g carbohydrate,
182 mg sodium,
0 mg cholesterol.

1 tablespoon olive oil
6 zucchini (about 1¾ pounds total), cut into ¼-inch-thick slices
3 cloves garlic, finely chopped

½ teaspoon salt
¼ teaspoon red-pepper flakes
1 tablespoon balsamic vinegar

1. Heat oil in a large nonstick skillet over medium heat. Add zucchini and half of garlic; sauté until zucchini is softened, about 10 minutes.

2. Add remaining garlic, salt and red-pepper flakes to zucchini mixture. Cool to room temperature.

3. Before serving, sprinkle zucchini with vinegar.

Grilled vegetables

Makes 6 servings   *Prep* 15 minutes   *Grill* 15 to 25 minutes

Per serving
200 calories, 5 g protein,
8 g fat, 33 g carbohydrate,
415 mg sodium,
0 mg cholesterol.

2 yellow summer squash (about ½ pound total)
2 zucchini (about ¾ pound total)
2 sweet green peppers
2 sweet red peppers
2 sweet yellow peppers
1 small eggplant (1 pound)
1 red onion
3 ears sweet corn
¾ cup Asian Baste or Garlic Baste (recipes follow)

1. Cut yellow squash and zucchini lengthwise in half. Cut peppers lengthwise in half, discard seeds. Cut eggplant lengthwise into 1-inch-thick slices. Thickly slice onion. Shuck corn; remove silk.

2. Prepare a charcoal grill with medium-hot coals or heat a gas grill to medium-high. Place a grill rack 5 inches from source of heat. Set vegetables on rack. Brush with 3 tablespoons baste.

3. Grill vegetables 15 to 25 minutes or until cooked through, turning often and brushing with 3 more tablespoons baste. Transfer vegetables to a platter. Serve with remaining baste.

To broil vegetables: Heat broiler. Arrange vegetables in a single layer on a broiler-pan rack. Brush vegetables with baste. Broil 6 inches from source of heat 8 to 10 minutes or until cooked through, rotating broiler pan and turning vegetables as necessary to prevent overbrowning.

Asian baste

Per tablespoon
44 calories, 0 g protein,
3 g fat, 4 g carbohydrate,
203 mg sodium,
0 mg cholesterol.

In a small bowl, whisk together 2 cloves garlic, finely chopped, 1 teaspoon grated fresh ginger, 3 tablespoons red-wine vinegar, 3 tablespoons tamari or soy sauce, and 2 tablespoons honey. Whisk in 3 tablespoons dark Asian sesame oil in a slow, steady stream until blended. Stir in ¼ teaspoon red-pepper flakes. Makes ¾ cup.

Garlic baste

Per tablespoon
58 calories, 0 g protein,
6 g fat, 1 g carbohydrate,
98 mg sodium,
0 mg cholesterol.

In a small food processor or blender, combine 5 cloves garlic, ⅓ cup olive oil, 1 tablespoon Chinese oyster-flavored sauce, 1 tablespoon red-wine vinegar, 1 teaspoon prepared mustard, 1 teaspoon dried rosemary, 1 teaspoon dried thyme, 1 teaspoon black pepper and ½ teaspoon salt. Whirl until smooth. Transfer to a small saucepan; simmer 4 minutes. Cool. Makes ¾ cup.

Beer-battered vegetables with three sauces

The trick to deep-fat frying is not to overcrowd the pan—too many vegetables drops the temperature of the oil, resulting in a coating that is less than crispy. For an easy party platter, match cut-up raw veggies with the three sauces.

Per serving
154 calories, 5 g protein,
8 g fat, 15 g carbohydrate,
200 mg sodium,
43 mg cholesterol.

Per tablespoon
51 calories, 0 g protein,
5 g fat, 2 g carbohydrate,
138 mg mg sodium,
4 mg cholesterol.

Per tablespoon
5 calories, 0 g protein,
0 g fat, 1 g carbohydrate,
36 mg sodium,
0 mg cholesterol.

Per tablespoon
12 calories, 0 g protein,
0 g fat, 1 g carbohydrate,
95 mg sodium,
0 mg cholesterol.

2 eggs
1 cup flat beer (not a dark beer)
¾ teaspoon salt
1 cup all-purpose flour
   Vegetable oil for frying
1 small head broccoli (about 1 pound), cut into flowerets

1 head cauliflower (about 1½ pounds), cut into flowerets
   Garlic-Parsley Sauce, Roasted Red-Pepper Sauce and Oriental Sauce (recipes follow)

1. Beat eggs, beer and salt in a bowl. Gradually stir in flour until smooth. Cover; refrigerate 30 minutes.

2. Fill a deep, heavy saucepan, wok or deep-fryer with oil to a depth of several inches. Heat oil until it registers 375° on a deep-fat thermometer.

3. Dip vegetables in beer batter and shake off excess. Using tongs, a slotted spoon or a fry basket, slip vegetables into oil, about 5 at a time. Fry, turning once, until lightly browned, 2 to 3 minutes. Remove to paper toweling to drain. Repeat with remaining vegetables. Serve dipping sauces with vegetables.

Garlic-parsley sauce

Heat oven to 450°. Wrap 1 whole head garlic in aluminum foil. Roast in heated oven 40 minutes or until soft. Remove foil. When cool enough to handle, cut head in half horizontally. Squeeze roasted garlic pulp into a food processor. Add 1 cup fresh parsley leaves, ⅓ cup mayonnaise, ¼ cup fresh lemon juice and ½ teaspoon salt. Whirl until pureed. Scrape into a serving bowl. Makes about ⅔ cup.

Roasted red-pepper sauce

Heat broiler. Core, seed and split 2 sweet red peppers. Place on a broiling pan. Broil, skin side up, until blackened all over, 10 to 15 minutes. When cool enough to handle, peel off skins and discard. Place peppers in a food processor with ¼ cup nonfat sour cream and ¼ teaspoon salt. Whirl until pureed. Scrape into a serving bowl. Makes about 1 cup.

Asian sauce

Combine ¼ cup vegetable broth, 3 tablespoons sherry, 2 tablespoons reduced-sodium soy sauce, 1 tablespoon brown sugar and 2 teaspoons grated fresh ginger in a small serving bowl. Makes about ⅔ cup.

**Beer-battered vegetables
with three sauces** *opposite*

Scalloped vegetables

Makes 6 servings *Prep* 30 minutes *Cook* 15 minutes *Bake* at 375° for 50 to 55 minutes

Chase away the chill from a cold winter night with this richly pleasing vegetable casserole. Crumble blue cheese over the top instead of cheddar and see how your diners take to that.

Per serving
370 calories, 15 g protein,
11 g fat, 54 g carbohydrate,
631 mg sodium,
30 mg cholesterol.

Carrot savvy
Carrots are not all created equal! The farther west they're grown, the sweeter the flavor. And while all carrots are high in beta carotene (from which the body produces vitamin A), the deeper the orange color, the more beta carotene for your dollar.

3 to 4 carrots, thinly sliced (2 cups)
2 pounds all-purpose potatoes, peeled and sliced (4½ cups)
2 large onions, thinly sliced
½ teaspoon salt
4 strips bacon
½ cup water
½ cube chicken bouillon
1¼ cups milk
⅓ cup grated Parmesan cheese
½ teaspoon dried rosemary, crumbled
½ teaspoon black pepper
¼ cup all-purpose flour
½ cup fresh bread crumbs (1 slice bread)
1 cup shredded cheddar cheese (4 ounces)

1. Steam carrots, potatoes and onions, seasoned with salt, in a steamer basket over gently boiling water 15 minutes or just until tender. Drain.

2. Meanwhile, cook bacon in a skillet until crisp. Drain on paper toweling; reserve 1 tablespoon bacon fat.

3. Crumble bacon; add to vegetables.

4. Coat a shallow 2-quart baking dish with nonstick cooking spray. Spread vegetable mixture in dish.

5. Heat oven to 375°.

6. Bring water to a boiling in a small saucepan. Add bouillon cube and stir until dissolved. Stir in ¾ cup milk, all but 2 tablespoons Parmesan, rosemary and pepper. Pour over vegetable mixture.

7. Bake, loosely tented with aluminum foil, in heated 375° oven 25 minutes.

8. Whisk together flour and a little of remaining milk in a small bowl until smooth and no lumps remain. Whisk in remaining milk. Pour over casserole. Toss together bread crumbs, remaining 2 tablespoons Parmesan and reserved bacon fat in a small bowl. Sprinkle mixture evenly over casserole.

9. Bake, uncovered, 20 to 25 minutes or until hot and bubbly. Sprinkle top with cheddar cheese. Bake another 5 minutes or until cheese is melted.

Caponata

Makes 12 servings   *Prep* 10 minutes   *Cook* 30 minutes

Serve this classic eggplant appetizer spooned over grilled bread for a variation on bruschetta, or toss with cooked pasta for a simple sauce.

Per serving
59 calories, 1 g protein,
3 g fat, 8 g carbohydrate,
278 mg sodium,
0 mg cholesterol.

1 large red onion
1 large sweet yellow pepper
1 large sweet green pepper
1 eggplant (about 1¼ pounds)
2 tablespoons olive oil
3 cloves garlic, chopped
1 can (16 ounces) stewed tomatoes

1½ teaspoons dried basil
2 tablespoons tomato paste
3 tablespoons red-wine vinegar
¾ teaspoon salt
¼ teaspoon hot-pepper sauce
⅓ cup Kalamata olives, pitted and halved

1. Cut onion, peppers and eggplant into 1-inch cubes.

2. Heat oil in a large Dutch oven over medium heat. Add onion and peppers; cook 10 minutes, stirring occasionally.

3. Add eggplant, garlic, tomatoes, basil, tomato paste, vinegar and salt to Dutch oven. Cook, uncovered, 10 minutes. Stir in hot-pepper sauce and olives. Partially cover and cook 10 minutes more or until vegetables are just tender. Cool caponata and refrigerate up to 1 week. Serve cold or at room temperature.

Summery vegetable medley

Makes 4 servings   *Prep* 15 minutes   *Cook* 5 minutes

This is an excellent salad on its own with some crusty bread. Or serve it with grilled hamburgers.

Per serving
89 calories, 4 g protein,
3 g fat, 15 g carbohydrate,
472 mg sodium,
0 mg cholesterol.

2 small yellow squash, cut into matchstick strips
2 teaspoons olive oil
½ pound sugar snap peas, trimmed and halved crosswise
2 cups cherry tomatoes

¼ cup chopped fresh parsley
¾ teaspoon ground coriander
¾ teaspoon salt
⅛ teaspoon black pepper
1 lemon, cut in wedges, for garnish

1. Bring 1 inch water to simmering in a nonstick skillet. Add squash; cook 2 minutes or until tender. Drain well in a colander. Dry the skillet.

2. Heat oil in same skillet over medium heat. Add sugar snap peas, cherry tomatoes, parsley and coriander; cook, stirring, 3 minutes. Remove from heat.

3. Stir in salt, pepper and reserved squash. Serve at room temperature, garnished with lemon wedges.

Bourbon three-bean bake

Makes 8 servings *Prep* 10 minutes *Cook* 20 minutes *Bake* at 350° for 45 minutes

Don't worry about the bourbon—all the alcohol cooks off, leaving just the rich, sweet flavor.

Per serving
268 calories, 13 g protein,
2 g fat, 54 g carbohydrate,
760 mg sodium,
1 mg cholesterol.

2 strips bacon
1 large onion, chopped (1 cup)
1 large sweet green pepper, chopped
1 can (16 ounces) diced tomatoes
½ cup molasses
6 tablespoons tomato paste
⅓ cup bourbon
¼ cup firmly packed light-brown sugar

2 tablespoons Dijon mustard
½ teaspoon salt
¼ teaspoon black pepper
1 can (19 ounces) black beans, drained and rinsed
1 can (19 ounces) red kidney beans, drained and rinsed
1 can (19 ounces) white kidney beans, drained and rinsed

1. Heat oven to 350°.

2. Cook bacon in a large skillet over medium heat until crisp. Remove to paper toweling to drain. Pour off all but 2 tablespoons fat from skillet.

3. Add onion and green pepper to skillet; sauté 8 to 10 minutes or until tender. Stir in tomatoes, molasses, tomato paste, bourbon, brown sugar, mustard, salt and black pepper. Bring to boiling; cook, stirring occasionally, 3 to 5 minutes.

4. Crumble bacon. Add to sauce along with black beans, red kidney beans and white kidney beans. Pour into a shallow 2-quart baking dish.

5. Bake in heated 350° oven 45 minutes or until hot and bubbly.

Frijoles à la charra

Makes 8 servings *Prep* 10 minutes *Cook* 15 minutes

The perfect partner for these fiery beans is crispy tortilla chips or warmed flour tortillas.

Per serving
183 calories, 13 g protein,
8 g fat, 24 g carbohydrate,
570 mg sodium,
15 mg cholesterol.

4 strips bacon, chopped
1 medium onion, chopped
2 cloves garlic, chopped
3 serrano chiles, seeded and finely chopped
½ teaspoon dried cilantro

1 teaspoon dried oregano
2 cans (15 ounces each) black beans, undrained
1 tomato, seeded and diced
½ cup shredded Monterey Jack cheese

1. Cook bacon in large saucepan, stirring occasionally, over medium-high heat 4 minutes; bacon should not be crispy. Add onion, garlic, chiles, cilantro and oregano; cook, stirring, 5 minutes or until onion is softened.

2. Add beans with liquid and tomato; heat through, about 6 minutes. Remove from heat; top with cheese.

Barbecued baked beans

Makes 8 servings   *Prep* 20 minutes   *Soak* 1 hour   *Cook* 40 minutes   *Bake* at 300° for 3 hours

Rather than soaking the dried beans overnight, this recipe utilizes the quick-soak method. And dark-brown sugar, used instead of light, gives these beans a wonderful caramel taste.

Per serving
329 calories, 16 g protein, 8 g fat, 49 g carbohydrate, 714 mg sodium, 12 mg cholesterol.

1 pound small dried navy or pea beans, picked over and rinsed
¼ pound lean bacon strips
¾ cup bottled barbecue sauce
¼ cup dark molasses
¼ cup packed dark-brown sugar
2 tablespoons cider vinegar
1 tablespoon spicy brown mustard
1 teaspoon salt

1. Combine beans and 7 cups water in a large saucepan. Bring to boiling; cook 2 minutes. Remove from heat. Cover and let soak 1 hour.

2. Bring undrained beans slowly to boiling over medium-low heat; this should take about 25 minutes. Simmer until firm-tender, 15 minutes. Drain, reserving 2 cups of cooking liquid.

3. Heat oven to 300°.

4. Cook bacon between pieces of paper toweling in a microwave oven on 100% power to remove some of the fat, 3 to 4 minutes. Reserve.

5. Stir together beans, reserved cooking liquid, barbecue sauce, molasses, brown sugar, vinegar, mustard and salt in a large bowl. Scrape into a 2½-quart casserole or bean pot. Place bacon on top. Cover.

6. Bake in heated 300° oven 3 hours or until beans are tender. Add water if needed to keep beans just covered. Serve warm.

Barbecued baked beans

Old-fashioned baked beans

Makes 8 servings   *Prep* 20 minutes   *Soak* beans overnight

Cook about 1 hour   *Bake* at 325° for 3 hours

Black coffee is the surprise ingredient here. Starting with dried beans ensures the beans will retain their shape through the long, slow cooking.

Per serving
318 calories, 14 g protein, 2 g fat, 63 g carbohydrate, 441 mg sodium, 7 mg cholesterol.

1 pound dried pea beans
¾ cup molasses
1½ cups brewed black coffee
¼ cup packed dark-brown sugar
1 tablespoon cider vinegar
2 teaspoons dry mustard
1½ teaspoons salt
¼ teaspoon black pepper
1 medium onion, peeled, halved, and stuck with 4 cloves
1 smoked ham hock or 4 slices cooked bacon

1. Soak beans in water to cover by 2 inches overnight. Drain; cover with fresh water and cook in a large saucepan about 1 hour or until very tender. Drain well. Place beans in 13 x 9 x 2-inch baking dish.

2. Heat oven to 325°.

3. Stir together molasses, coffee, brown sugar, vinegar, dry mustard, salt and pepper in a small bowl. Stir into beans in baking dish. Place onion and ham hock in dish. Cover dish with aluminum foil.

4. Bake in heated 325° oven 3 hours, stirring every hour, or until beans are tender and flavored through, adding more water if beans become too dry. Remove onion and ham hock. Shred ham and stir into beans.

Creole bean burger

Makes 4 servings   *Prep* 5 minutes   *Cook* 6 minutes

No cumin on your spice rack? Sprinkle in chili powder instead. For extra heat, use a touch of cayenne pepper or hot-pepper sauce.

Per serving
344 calories, 13 g protein, 13 g fat, 48 g carbohydrate, 751 mg sodium, 57 mg cholesterol.

1 can (15 ounces) red kidney beans, drained, rinsed and mashed
1 onion, chopped
1 egg
1 tablespoon ketchup
1 teaspoon mustard
2 teaspoons Worcestershire sauce
¼ teaspoon ground cumin
3 tablespoons dry seasoned bread crumbs
1 tablespoon oil
4 hamburger buns
¼ cup Thousand Island dressing

1. In a bowl, combine beans, onion, egg, ketchup, mustard, Worcestershire sauce, cumin and bread crumbs. Shape into 4 patties.

2. Heat oil in a nonstick skillet. Cook patties 3 minutes per side over medium-low heat. Serve on buns spread with dressing.

Prairie baked beans

Makes 8 servings   *Prep* 15 minutes   *Bake* at 350° for 1 hour 20 minutes

Got a crowd to feed? This goes together in practically no time and bakes unattended while you fix the rest of the meal. The chopped sweet pepper adds a touch of color.

Per serving
124 calories, 3 g protein, 1 g fat, 27 g carbohydrate, 373 mg sodium, 0 mg cholesterol.

½ cup packed dark-brown sugar
⅓ cup prepared mustard
¼ cup molasses
3 cans (about 16 ounces each) pinto beans, drained and rinsed
1 sweet green pepper, cored, seeded and chopped
1 sweet red pepper, cored, seeded and chopped
1 medium onion, chopped

1. Heat oven to 350°.

2. Whisk together brown sugar, mustard and molasses in a medium-size bowl until smooth.

3. Place ½ cup beans in a food processor or blender. Whirl until pureed. Stir into brown sugar mixture along with remaining beans, green and red peppers and onion. Pour mixture into a 2-quart baking dish.

4. Bake, uncovered, in heated 350° oven 1 hour 20 minutes or until slightly thickened.

Black bean enchiladas

Makes 8 servings   *Prep* 15 minutes   *Cook* 12 minutes   *Bake* at 350° for 35 minutes

Assemble these in the morning and then refrigerate. If red kidney beans or pinto beans are more to your liking, stir them in instead of the black beans.

Per serving
344 calories, 18 g protein, 14 g fat, 46 g carbohydrate, 1,165 mg sodium, 22 mg cholesterol.

2 tablespoons oil
1 onion, finely chopped
2 cloves garlic, finely chopped
2 cans (16 ounces each) black beans, 1 can drained and rinsed, 1 can undrained
1 cup frozen corn kernels, thawed and drained
8 flour tortillas (8-inch)
2 cups shredded cheddar cheese (8 ounces)
2 cans (10 ounces each) enchilada sauce

1. Heat oven to 350°.

2. Heat oil in a medium-size saucepan over medium-low heat. Add onion and garlic; sauté 5 minutes or until softened. Add both cans of beans; cook 7 minutes. Slightly mash mixture with a potato masher, leaving half of beans somewhat unmashed. Stir in corn.

3. Spoon an equal amount of bean mixture in center of each tortilla. Top each with cheese, dividing equally. Tuck in sides of tortillas; roll each tortilla into an egg-roll-shaped log. Place enchiladas in a 13 x 9 x 2-inch baking dish. Pour enchilada sauce over top and around sides of enchiladas. Cover with aluminum foil.

4. Bake in heated 350° oven 35 minutes or until heated through.

Bow-ties alfresco
page 156

Tropical
couscous
page 192

IF THERE'S ONE food no cook should ever be without, it's pasta. Not only is this must-have staple inexpensive and quick to prepare, it's filling yet naturally low in fat. Even better, the mild flavor invites bold pairings with sauces and add-ins.

While many may associate pasta with Italian-style sauces—such as marinara and Alfredo—it works just as well in recipes inspired all over the world. From across the Pacific, you can sample Spicy Thai-Style Fettuccine or Sesame Chicken Soba Noodles. Closer to home, there's traditional Country Ham and Macaroni Casserole,

From old-time to new-wave, these global favorites always hit the spot.

not to mention Savory Apple Harvest Linguine and Lone Star Steak and Wagon Wheels. Grains are another smart and tasty choice when time is of the essence; sure-fire pleasers include Curried Rice Pilaf, Basic Risotto and Tropical Couscous. In other words, classic or not, pasta and grains fill the bill.

pasta and grains

Bow-ties alfresco

Makes 6 servings   *Prep* 20 minutes   *Stand* 2 hours   *Cook* 12 minutes

The easiest of pasta dishes—an uncooked sauce that needs the ripest tomatoes you can find. When the cooked pasta is tossed with the sauce, the heat releases the wonderful flavors of summer.
Shown on page 154.

Per serving
416 calories, 12 g protein, 14 g fat, 63 g carbohydrate, 361 mg sodium, 0 mg cholesterol.

¼ cup extra-virgin olive oil
2 tablespoons fresh lemon juice
2 teaspoons grated lemon rind
¾ teaspoon salt
¾ teaspoon cracked black pepper
2 pounds plum tomatoes, finely chopped

½ cup chopped fresh parsley
3 tablespoons capers (optional)
1 pound bow-tie pasta or ziti
1 red onion, finely chopped
⅓ cup pine nuts or walnuts, toasted
   Additional chopped fresh parsley for garnish (optional)

1. Whisk together oil, lemon juice, lemon rind, salt and pepper in a large serving bowl until blended. Add tomatoes, parsley and capers if using. Cover and let stand at room temperature 2 hours.

2. Cook pasta in a large pot of lightly salted boiling water until al dente, firm but tender. Add onion during last 2 minutes of cooking. Drain well. Add pasta to sauce in serving bowl; toss to mix. Scatter on pine nuts. Garnish with parsley if you wish.

Bow-tie broccoli and artichokes

Makes 6 servings   *Prep* 10 minutes   *Cook* 12 minutes

Beat the clock: Make boiling water do double duty. First, add the pasta to boiling water, then throw in the broccoli for the last 5 minutes.

Per serving
440 calories, 17 g protein, 14 g fat, 66 g carbohydrate, 744 mg sodium, 11 mg cholesterol.

1 pound bow-tie pasta
1 large head broccoli, cut into small flowerets, stems discarded
2 jars (6½ ounces each) marinated artichoke hearts, undrained
2 ounces thinly sliced pepperoni, cut into 1-inch slivers

½ cup julienned oil-packed sun-dried tomatoes
3 green onions, chopped
1 tablespoon red-wine vinegar
¼ teaspoon salt
¼ teaspoon black pepper
¼ cup grated Parmesan cheese

1. Cook pasta in a large pot of lightly salted boiling water until al dente, firm but tender. Add broccoli during last 5 minutes of cooking. Drain well.

2. Meanwhile, combine artichoke hearts, pepperoni, sun-dried tomatoes, green onions, vinegar, salt and pepper in a large bowl. Add pasta and broccoli mixture; toss to combine. Serve with Parmesan.

Spaghetti with marinara sauce

Makes 6 servings *Prep* 10 minutes *Cook* 40 minutes

The combination of grated orange rind and fresh mint adds a fresh accent to the tomato flavor. You can refrigerate this sauce up to 3 days or freeze for up to 3 months.

Per ½ cup
384 calories, 12 g protein, 6 g fat, 71 g carbohydrate, 395 mg sodium, 5 mg cholesterol.

1 tablespoon olive oil
1 tablespoon butter
1 onion, chopped
2 cloves garlic, finely chopped
2½ pounds plum tomatoes, peeled, seeded and chopped
1 teaspoon salt
1 teaspoon grated orange rind
1 bay leaf
1 tablespoon chopped fresh mint
1 pound spaghetti

1. Heat oil and butter in a large skillet. Add onion and garlic; sauté until softened, 8 minutes. Add tomatoes, salt, orange rind and bay leaf. Cook, stirring occasionally, 20 to 25 minutes or until thickened. Stir in mint; cook 5 minutes.

2. Meanwhile, cook spaghetti in a large pot of lightly salted boiling water until al dente, firm but tender. Drain well.

3. Toss sauce with the cooked pasta on a large serving platter.

Linguine with pesto and green beans

Makes 4 servings *Prep* 20 minutes *Cook* 15 minutes

The pesto here is a version made creamy with ricotta cheese. Flat-leaf parsley, more strongly flavored than the familiar curly leaf, adds a "greener" taste to traditional basil.

Per serving
487 calories, 12 g protein, 35 g fat, 35 g carbohydrate, 418 mg sodium, 10 mg cholesterol.

2 cloves garlic
1½ cups firmly packed fresh basil leaves
¾ cup firmly packed fresh flat-leaf parsley leaves
½ cup olive oil
⅓ cup pine nuts, toasted
¼ cup part-skim ricotta cheese
½ teaspoon salt
¼ cup grated Parmesan cheese
¾ pound linguine
¾ pound green beans, trimmed

1. Cook garlic in a small saucepan of boiling water 2 minutes; drain. Transfer to a food processor along with basil, parsley, oil, pine nuts, ricotta and salt. Whirl until creamy. Stir in Parmesan. Transfer to a large bowl.

2. Cook pasta in a large pot of lightly salted boiling water until al dente, firm but tender. Add green beans during last 5 minutes of cooking.

3. Drain pasta and green beans. Add to pesto in bowl; toss to coat.

Fettuccine with trio of mushrooms

Makes 4 servings *Prep* 10 minutes *Cook* 25 minutes

Thick fettuccine is a smart choice for soaking up this creamy mushroom sauce.

Per serving
534 calories, 18 g protein, 15 g fat, 79 g carbohydrate, 714 mg sodium, 17 mg cholesterol.

2 tablespoons olive oil
½ pound white mushrooms, sliced
¼ pound oyster mushrooms, sliced
¼ pound shiitake mushrooms, stemmed and sliced
2 cloves garlic, finely chopped
½ cup dry white wine

½ cup chicken broth
½ cup tomato sauce
½ cup half-and-half
½ teaspoon salt
⅛ teaspoon black pepper
¾ pound fettuccine
¼ cup grated Parmesan cheese

1. Heat oil in a large nonstick skillet over medium heat. Add mushrooms and garlic; cook, stirring occasionally, 6 minutes or until mushrooms begin to brown. Add wine; cook until evaporated, about 5 minutes.

2. Add broth, tomato sauce, half-and-half, salt and pepper. Bring to boiling. Reduce heat; simmer 10 minutes.

3. Meanwhile, cook fettuccine in a large pot of lightly salted boiling water until al dente, firm but tender. Drain well. Toss pasta with sauce in pot. Sprinkle with Parmesan and serve.

Bow-ties with spring vegetables and walnuts

Makes 6 servings *Prep* 10 minutes *Cook* 12 minutes

Asparagus out of season? Substitute an equal amount of broccoli flowerets. In this vegetarian dinner, the protein comes from the two cheeses as well as the pasta.

Per serving
303 calories, 14 g protein, 11 g fat, 38 g carbohydrate, 212 mg sodium, 16 mg cholesterol.

½ pound bow-tie, rotelle or radiatore pasta
1 small bunch asparagus, tough ends trimmed, stems peeled, cut into 1½-inch pieces
1 yellow summer squash, halved lengthwise, then thinly sliced crosswise
8 ounces part-skim ricotta cheese
¼ cup grated Parmesan cheese

¼ cup milk
1 cup packed fresh basil leaves, finely chopped
2 teaspoons fresh lemon juice
¼ teaspoon salt
¼ to ½ teaspoon black pepper
½ pint cherry tomatoes, halved
½ cup walnuts, toasted and chopped

1. Cook pasta in a large pot of lightly salted boiling water until al dente, firm but tender. Add asparagus during last 3 minutes of cooking. Add squash during last 2 minutes. Drain well in a colander.

2. Meanwhile, combine ricotta cheese, Parmesan, milk, basil, lemon juice, salt and pepper in a large shallow serving bowl. Add drained pasta and vegetables; toss gently to combine well. Scatter tomatoes and walnuts over the top. Toss lightly and serve at once.

Penne with broccoli and beans

Makes 6 servings   *Prep* 10 minutes   *Cook* 20 minutes

Italians frequently toss beans into their pasta dishes, and here the pasta tubes pair well with the other chunky ingredients.

Per serving
521 calories, 17 g protein, 21 g fat, 69 g carbohydrate, 561 mg sodium, 2 mg cholesterol.

1 pound penne
2 slices bacon, chopped
¼ cup olive oil
5 cloves, garlic, crushed
2 heads broccoli, cut into flowerets (8 cups), stems discarded
½ sweet red pepper, cored, seeded and cut into matchstick strips
1 can (16 ounces) cannellini beans, undrained
¾ teaspoon salt

1. Cook penne in a large pot of lightly salted boiling water until al dente, firm but tender. Drain well, reserving ½ cup cooking water.

2. Meanwhile, cook bacon in a small saucepan over medium-low heat 5 minutes or until cooked but not crisp. Drain on paper toweling.

3. Heat oil in a large nonstick saucepan over medium-low heat. Add garlic and cook, stirring, 3 minutes or until golden; do not let burn. Discard garlic. Add broccoli and sweet red pepper to oil in saucepan. Cover; cook over low heat 8 minutes or until broccoli is tender.

4. Add beans with their liquid, salt, bacon, reserved cooking water and pasta to broccoli in saucepan; heat through. Serve.

Penne with broccoli and beans

Spinach and cheese dumplings

Makes 6 servings *Prep* 40 minutes *Cook* 20 minutes

Wonton wrappers are a fast-fix ingredient for making dumplings, as well as homemade ravioli. Look for the wrappers in the produce section of the supermarket.

Per serving

323 calories, 13 g protein, 13 g fat, 39 g carbohydrate, 566 mg sodium, 43 mg cholesterol.

Dumplings

1 package (10 ounces) frozen chopped spinach, thawed
½ cup finely grated Swiss cheese
¼ cup part-skim ricotta cheese
¼ teaspoon ground nutmeg
¼ teaspoon salt
¼ teaspoon black pepper
36 wonton wrappers (3 x 3 inches)

Sauce

1 tablespoon butter or margarine
3 shallots, chopped
1 pound mushrooms, sliced
2 tablespoons white-wine vinegar
¼ cup chopped fresh parsley
1 ½ cups half-and-half
¼ teaspoon salt
¼ teaspoon black pepper

1. Prepare dumplings: Blanch spinach in a saucepan of boiling water 1 minute. Drain in a sieve; press to extract all moisture. Combine spinach, Swiss cheese, ricotta, nutmeg, salt and pepper in a small bowl.

2. Lay out 6 wonton wrappers on a clean, dry surface. Place a rounded teaspoonful of spinach filling in center of each, then use a pastry brush to moisten edges with water. Fold wonton in half to form a triangle; press edges to seal. Fold over longest edge of triangle to make a ridge. Fold 2 corners back until they overlap, then press together to seal.

3. Place each finished dumpling on a baking sheet. Cover with a damp cloth. Continue until you have 36 dumplings.

4. Bring a large pot of lightly salted water to boiling.

5. Meanwhile, prepare sauce: Melt butter in a large skillet over medium-high heat. Add shallots; cook 2 minutes or until softened. Add mushrooms; cook until moisture is released, 7 minutes. Add vinegar and half of parsley; cook until vinegar is almost completely evaporated, about another 3 minutes. Add half-and-half, salt and pepper to skillet with mushrooms. Lower heat; simmer until sauce is thickened, 5 minutes.

6. Cook dumplings in boiling water 2 to 3 minutes or until they rise to the surface. Remove dumplings with a slotted spoon to a platter or individual plates. Pour sauce over dumplings. Sprinkle with remaining parsley. Serve immediately.

Make-ahead tip: Shaped dumplings can be frozen, separated between layers of waxed paper, in a plastic bag or container for several weeks or refrigerated up to 12 hours. Cook, still frozen, in boiling water 5 minutes.

Making dumplings

When filled, fold over the longest edge of the triangle to make a ridge.

Fold two corners back until they overlap, then press together to seal.

Garlic-potato gnocchi

Makes 4 servings   *Prep* 15 minutes   *Cook* 20 to 25 minutes

Gnocchi is the Italian word for dumplings. Toss them with a little butter and chopped fresh parsley and serve on their own with a green salad and crusty Italian bread for a light supper or as a side dish with meat or poultry.

Per serving
137 calories, 5 g protein,
2 g fat, 24 g carbohydrate,
252 mg sodium,
5 mg cholesterol.

2 large baking potatoes (1 pound total)
3 cloves garlic
¼ cup grated Parmesan cheese
¼ teaspoon salt
¼ teaspoon black pepper
⅔ cup all-purpose flour
Butter and chopped fresh parsley or favorite pasta sauce for serving

1. Peel and quarter potatoes. Cook with garlic in a saucepan of boiling water until tender, 15 minutes. Drain.

2. Bring a large pot of water to boiling.

3. Meanwhile, beat together potatoes, garlic, Parmesan, salt and pepper in a large bowl until smooth. Mix in flour. Place dough on a lightly floured surface; knead 1 minute. Divide in half. Roll each half into a ¾-inch-thick rope. Cut into 1-inch pieces.

4. Working in batches, drop dough pieces into boiling water. Cook until gnocchi rise to surface, 2 to 3 minutes. Remove with a slotted spoon to a large serving bowl, and keep warm.

5. Add butter and parsley or sauce to bowl and toss to mix.

Roasted red-pepper tortellini

Makes 6 servings   *Prep* 10 minutes   *Cook* 10 minutes

The roasted red-pepper sauce—ready in less time than it takes to cook the pasta—is also appealing with fettuccine. Sour cream is what makes the pureed sauce creamy.

Per serving
418 calories, 19 g protein,
15 g fat, 53 g carbohydrate,
639 mg sodium,
59 mg cholesterol.

2 packages (9 ounces each) refrigerated cheese tortellini
1 package (10 ounces) frozen green peas, thawed
1 jar (12 ounces) roasted red peppers, drained
2 cloves garlic
1 container (8 ounces) reduced-fat sour cream
¼ cup grated Parmesan cheese
½ teaspoon black pepper
1 cup chopped pitted ripe black olives

1. Cook tortellini in a large pot of lightly salted boiling water until al dente, firm but tender. Add thawed peas to boiling tortellini during last 2 minutes of cooking. Drain pasta and peas.

2. Meanwhile, puree peppers and garlic in a blender or food processor. Pour into a large serving bowl. Whisk in sour cream, Parmesan and black pepper.

3. Add cooked tortellini, peas and olives to roasted-red-pepper puree; toss together until well combined. Serve immediately.

Penne primavera

Makes 4 servings   *Prep* 15 minutes   *Cook* about 12 minutes

Primavera means springtime—lots of fresh, tender vegetables. Don't feel wedded to those listed in the recipe. Select whatever looks freshest in the market, and then cook either in the pasta water, for vegetables that tend to be "woody," or in the skillet.

Per serving
536 calories, 16 g protein, 22 g fat, 71 g carbohydrate, 387 mg sodium, 28 mg cholesterol.

¾ pound penne
¼ pound baby carrots, each cut lengthwise into 8 strips
1 small bunch thin asparagus, trimmed and cut into 1-inch lengths
2 tablespoons olive oil
½ medium onion, chopped
¼ pound mushrooms, cleaned, stemmed and sliced

½ teaspoon salt
½ teaspoon black pepper
1 sweet red pepper, cut into matchstick strips
½ cup frozen peas
1 container (8 ounces) regular or reduced-fat sour cream
2 tablespoons grated Parmesan or Romano cheese

1. Cook penne in a large pot of lightly salted boiling water until al dente, firm but tender. Add carrots during last 5 minutes of cooking. Add asparagus during last 2 minutes.

2. Meanwhile, heat oil in a large, deep skillet over high heat. Add onion; cook, stirring occasionally, until just softened, 1 to 2 minutes. Add mushrooms, salt and pepper; cook, stirring occasionally, until mushrooms lose their raw look, about 3 minutes Add sweet red pepper; cook 2 minutes. Add peas; cook another 2 minutes or until everything is tender.

3. Drain pasta, carrots and asparagus, reserving ½ cup of cooking water. Toss pasta, carrots, asparagus and reserved cooking water with sautéed vegetables, sour cream and cheese in a large serving bowl. Serve immediately.

Penne primavera

Herbed fusilli

Makes 8 servings *Prep* 10 minutes *Stand* 45 minutes *Cook* about 12 minutes

This recipe belongs to the wonderful family of speedy pasta dishes— the heat of the cooked pasta releases flavors in the uncooked sauce. Instead of the Brie, you can try a soft goat cheese.

Per serving
567 calories, 17 g protein, 33 g fat, 50 g carbohydrate, 678 mg sodium, 43 mg cholesterol.

2¼ pounds yellow and red cherry tomatoes, halved, or 6 medium tomatoes, cut into ¾-inch cubes
¾ cup extra-virgin olive oil
2 cups shredded fresh basil
¾ pound Brie, rind discarded, cut into chunks
1 tablespoon chopped fresh thyme
1 tablespoon grated lemon rind
1 clove garlic, finely chopped
1 teaspoon salt
½ teaspoon coarse black pepper
1 pound fusilli
Fresh basil sprigs for garnish

1. Combine tomatoes, oil, basil, Brie, thyme, lemon rind, garlic, salt and pepper in a large bowl. Let stand at room temperature 45 minutes.

2. Cook fusilli in a large pot of lightly salted boiling water until al dente, firm but tender. Drain well. Add to tomato mixture and toss thoroughly until cheese starts to melt. Garnish with basil sprigs and serve immediately.

Fettuccine with garlic-basil cream sauce

Makes 6 servings *Prep* 10 minutes *Cook* 12 minutes

The sauce can be made several hours ahead, refrigerated and then brought to room temperature before tossing with the hot pasta.

Per serving
387 calories, 15 g protein, 11 g fat, 57 g carbohydrate, 360 mg sodium, 7 mg cholesterol.

1 pound fettuccine
1 tablespoon olive oil
4 large cloves garlic, crushed
½ cup chopped fresh basil
1 container (8 ounces) reduced-fat or nonfat sour cream
½ cup grated Parmesan cheese
½ teaspoon salt
¼ teaspoon black pepper

1. Cook fettuccine in a large pot of lightly salted boiling water until al dente, firm but tender.

2. Meanwhile, heat oil in a small skillet over low heat. Add garlic; cook until golden, turning cloves over as they color, 6 minutes. Add basil; cook 10 seconds. Transfer to a food processor. Add sour cream, Parmesan, salt and pepper. Whirl until creamy. Pour into a serving bowl.

3. Drain pasta well. Add to bowl with cream sauce; toss to mix.

Angel hair with broccoli-clam sauce

Makes 4 servings   *Prep* 15 minutes   *Cook* 6 minutes   *Stand* 5 minutes

A real bonus for this fast-prep meal: The thin pasta cooks right in the sauce—no need to use a separate pot for boiling water.

Per serving
416 calories, 27 g protein,
8 g fat, 59 g carbohydrate,
554 mg sodium,
39 mg cholesterol.

2 cans (6½ ounces each) chopped clams
1 bottle (8 ounces) clam juice
2 cups water
2 teaspoons chopped garlic
½ teaspoon dried oregano
⅛ teaspoon red-pepper flakes

4 cups fresh or frozen small broccoli flowerets (½ pound)
½ pound angel hair pasta, broken in half
1 tablespoon olive oil
⅓ cup grated Parmesan cheese

1. Drain clams over a medium-size skillet; reserve clams. Add bottled clam juice, water, garlic, oregano and red-pepper flakes to skillet. Bring to boiling. Add broccoli; cook 3 minutes. Add pasta and oil; cook 3 minutes more, stirring occasionally. Remove from heat.

2. Stir clams into skillet. Cover; let stand 5 minutes or until pasta is tender. Stir mixture. Sprinkle with Parmesan.

Fusilli puttanesca

Makes 6 servings   *Prep* 15 minutes   *Cook* 40 minutes

Several stories surround the naming of this quick dish. *Puttana* **in Italian means whore, and it is said that the dish can be speedily prepared for a gentleman caller. Others speculate that the fragrance of the simmering sauce with its garlic, olives, capers and herbs acts as a siren's call.**

Per serving
573 calories, 20 g protein,
23 g fat, 73 g carbohydrate,
998 mg sodium,
8 mg cholesterol.

¼ cup olive oil
1 medium red onion
3 large cloves garlic, chopped
2 cans (16 ounces each) diced tomatoes, drained
2 tablespoons capers, drained and rinsed
¼ cup Greek olives, pitted and chopped

¼ teaspoon dried oregano, crumbled
1 can (6⅛ ounces) water-packed tuna, drained and flaked
1 pound fusilli or other shaped pasta
¼ cup chopped fresh parsley

1. Heat oil in a medium-size saucepan over low heat. Add onion and garlic; cook, stirring occasionally, about 10 minutes or until softened. Add tomatoes, capers, olives and oregano. Increase heat to medium; cook, stirring occasionally, 30 minutes. Add tuna and heat through.

2. Meanwhile, cook pasta in a large pot of lightly salted boiling water until al dente, firm but tender. Drain well.

3. Spoon sauce over hot cooked pasta on a large serving platter. Sprinkle with parsley.

Linguine with salmon

Makes 6 servings *Prep* 15 minutes *Broil* 8 to 10 minutes *Cook* 12 minutes

Did you know?

• In 1279, years before Marco Polo returned to Italy from China, pasta was so treasured a delicacy that one man actually left his macaroni to his heirs.
• President Thomas Jefferson brought the first macaroni-making machine to the United States from France.
• In Italian, *orecchiette* means little ears; *ziti* means bridegrooms.

1 pound salmon fillet, with skin
2 tablespoons butter
½ teaspoon chopped fresh thyme or ¼ teaspoon dried
1 teaspoon finely chopped fresh dill or ¼ teaspoon dried dillweed
½ teaspoon black pepper
1⅛ teaspoons salt
½ pound green beans, trimmed
2 tablespoons olive oil
1 small onion, halved lengthwise then thinly sliced crosswise

1 large sweet orange or red pepper, cored, seeded and cut into matchstick strips
2 cloves garlic, finely chopped
2 medium ripe tomatoes, cored and coarsely chopped
1 pound linguine
¼ cup milk, heated
¼ cup plus 2 tablespoons grated Parmesan cheese
Pinch paprika

1. Heat broiler.

2. Place salmon in a baking dish. Dot with 1 tablespoon butter. Sprinkle with thyme, ½ teaspoon dill, ¼ teaspoon black pepper and ⅛ teaspoon salt.

3. Broil 5 to 6 inches from heat 8 to 10 minutes or until salmon almost flakes at touch of a fork. Remove from broiler; keep warm.

4. Cook beans in a saucepan of boiling water 5 minutes. Drain.

5. Heat oil in a large skillet. Add beans, onion, sweet pepper and garlic and sauté over high heat 5 to 7 minutes or until beans are tender. Add tomatoes and remaining 1 teaspoon salt and ¼ teaspoon pepper. Remove from heat and keep warm.

6. Meanwhile, cook linguine in a large pot of lightly salted boiling water until al dente, firm but tender. Drain well. Place in a warmed large bowl. Add remaining 1 tablespoon butter, hot milk and ¼ cup Parmesan.

7. Spoon vegetables with juices over linguine. Skin salmon; place on vegetables; flake with a fork. Sprinkle with remaining 2 tablespoons Parmesan and ½ teaspoon dill and a pinch of paprika. Toss just before serving.

Floribbean "risotto"

Makes 6 servings *Prep* 10 minutes *Cook* 16 minutes *Stand* 10 minutes

In this prizewinner, Virginia C. Anthony of Florida incorporates ingredients from her native state: orange juice and local river shrimp matched with Caribbean seasonings.

Per serving
474 calories, 34 g protein,
4 g fat, 75 g carbohydrate,
578 mg sodium,
135 mg cholesterol.

1 tablespoon olive oil
1 large onion, chopped
1 sweet red pepper, chopped
2 large cloves garlic, finely chopped
1 pound orzo
2 cans (14½ ounces each) fat-free reduced-sodium chicken broth, plus enough water to make 4 cups

2 cups orange juice
¼ cup sherry vinegar
1½ to 2 teaspoons Caribbean jerk seasoning
1½ pounds medium shrimp, peeled and deveined
1 can (15 ounces) black beans, drained and rinsed
¼ cup chopped fresh cilantro

1. Heat oil in a large saucepan over medium heat. Add onion, sweet red pepper and garlic; sauté until the vegetables are tender, about 4 minutes.

2. Stir in orzo, broth mixture, orange juice, vinegar and jerk seasoning. Bring to boiling, stirring frequently. Lower the heat to medium-low and partially cover saucepan; simmer about 10 minutes, stirring occasionally.

3. Stir in shrimp and beans; simmer 2 minutes. Remove pan from heat; cover tightly and let stand 10 minutes or until almost all the liquid is absorbed and the pasta has a creamy consistency. Stir in cilantro and serve.

Floribbean "risotto"

Angel hair with shrimp fra diavolo

Makes 4 servings *Prep* 15 minutes *Cook* 15 minutes

The "heat of the devil" here comes from red-pepper flakes. For a more substantial pasta, replace the angel hair with spaghetti or linguine.

Per serving
465 calories, 25 g protein, 6 g fat, 78 g carbohydrate, 365 mg sodium, 86 mg cholesterol.

1 tablespoon olive oil
1 large onion, chopped
1 clove garlic, finely chopped
¼ teaspoon red-pepper flakes
1 can (14½ ounces) Italian-style stewed tomatoes
1 can (8 ounces) reduced-sodium tomato sauce
½ pound shrimp, peeled, deveined and halved lengthwise
¾ pound angel hair pasta

1. Heat oil in a large saucepan over medium heat. Add onion and garlic and sauté 3 minutes. Add red-pepper flakes; sauté 1 minute. Add tomatoes and sauce; simmer 5 minutes. Add shrimp; simmer until shrimp are translucent, 5 minutes.

2. Meanwhile, cook pasta in a large pot of lightly salted boiling water until al dente, firm but tender. Drain well. Toss with sauce in a large serving bowl.

Hearty penne alla vodka

Makes 6 servings *Prep* 15 minutes *Cook* 12 minutes

Here's how to make this restaurant favorite in your own kitchen.

Per serving
582 calories, 27 g protein, 23 g fat, 60 g carbohydrate, 510 mg sodium, 83 mg cholesterol.

1 pound penne
1 pound lean ground beef
⅓ cup dry plain bread crumbs
2 cloves garlic, finely chopped
½ teaspoon salt
½ cup milk
1 tablespoon butter
½ cup heavy cream
¼ cup vodka
3 tablespoons tomato paste
¼ teaspoon red-pepper flakes
1 can (15 ounces) diced tomatoes, drained well
¼ cup grated Parmesan cheese
3 tablespoons slivered fresh basil
Additional grated Parmesan cheese (optional)

1. Cook penne in a large pot of lightly salted boiling water until al dente, firm but tender. Drain well.

2. Meanwhile, combine beef, bread crumbs, half of garlic, salt and milk in a bowl. Shape into about sixteen 1-inch balls.

3. Melt butter in a large nonstick skillet over medium heat. Add meatballs; cook 6 minutes, turning as they brown. Add cream, vodka, tomato paste, red-pepper flakes and remaining garlic to skillet. Simmer, covered, 5 minutes. Stir in tomatoes and Parmesan; cook 1 minute or until heated through.

4. Spoon meatballs and sauce over cooked pasta. Sprinkle with basil. Serve with additional Parmesan if desired.

Spaghetti with meat sauce

Makes 12 servings   *Prep* 10 minutes   *Cook* 1 hour 20 minutes

Red wine adds a depth of flavor to the meat sauce. If you'd like, substitute dried oregano for half of the basil, or use all oregano.

Per serving
429 calories, 19 g protein,
9 g fat, 68 g carbohydrate,
352 mg sodium,
26 mg cholesterol.

2 tablespoons olive oil
2 medium onions, finely chopped
2 cloves garlic, finely chopped
1 pound ground beef or ½ pound each ground beef and ground pork
½ cup dry red wine
2 cans (28 ounces each) crushed tomatoes in puree

2 tablespoons tomato paste
2 teaspoons dried basil, crumbled
½ bay leaf
2 teaspoons sugar
½ teaspoon salt
¼ teaspoon black pepper
2 pounds spaghetti

1. Heat oil in a large Dutch oven over medium-low heat. Add onions and garlic; sauté 12 minutes or until golden. Add meat; brown 5 minutes or until no longer pink, breaking up with a wooden spoon.

2. Add wine, tomatoes, tomato paste, basil, bay leaf, sugar, salt and pepper, scraping up any browned bits from bottom of pot with a wooden spoon. Bring to a bare simmer; cook 1 hour or until thickened.

3. Meanwhile, cook spaghetti in a large pot of lightly salted boiling water until al dente, firm but tender. Drain well.

4. Remove bay leaf from sauce and discard. Spoon sauce over hot cooked pasta on a large serving platter.

Make-ahead tip: Sauce can be made ahead and refrigerated, covered, up to 3 days or frozen, tightly sealed, up to 3 months.

Saucy substitutes

WHILE THERE ARE no exact rules, these suggestions should help you match pasta to sauce.

For small shapes: Interchange ruote (wagon wheels), shells, elbows, orecchiette (ear shaped) and farfalle (bow-ties). Pair with seafood, tomato or creamy sauces that will nestle in the holes and twists.

For bulky shapes: Rigatoni, fusilli, penne, ziti and radiatore (radiator shaped) can be switched around. The best sauces for these shapes contain chunky vegetables or meat; these pastas are also well suited to baked dishes.

For long, thin pasta: Swap spaghetti, fettuccine, angel hair (cappellini), linguine, perciatelle and fusilli lunghi as you like. The best sauces for these long shapes are pureed, creamy or clingy; they flow evenly over the strands.

Lone Star steak and wagon wheels

Makes 6 servings   *Prep* 20 minutes   *Cook* about 12 minutes

Per serving
558 calories, 37 g protein,
12 g fat, 79 g carbohydrate,
753 mg sodium,
62 mg cholesterol.

1 pound wagon wheel pasta
1 boneless top sirloin steak (1¼ pounds), about 1 inch thick
2 tablespoons corn oil
¼ cup fresh lime juice
1 can (about 10 ounces) diced tomatoes and green chiles, undrained
1 can (about 16 ounces) black beans, drained and rinsed
1 sweet green pepper, cored, seeded and chopped
1 cup frozen corn kernels, thawed
¼ cup sliced green onion
½ cup loosely packed fresh cilantro leaves
2 cloves garlic, finely chopped
½ teaspoon ground cumin
1 teaspoon salt
Fresh sprigs cilantro for garnish (optional)

1. Cook pasta in a large pot of lightly salted boiling water until al dente, firm but tender.

2. Meanwhile, with a knife, trim any fat from steak. Cut steak lengthwise in half and then crosswise into ⅛-inch-thick strips.

3. Heat 1 tablespoon oil in a large skillet over medium-high heat. Add half of steak; sauté 1 to 2 minutes or until meat is lightly browned. Remove steak to a platter. Repeat with remaining oil and sliced steak.

4. In same skillet, mix lime juice, tomatoes and chiles with liquid, beans, green pepper, corn, green onion, cilantro, garlic, cumin and salt; simmer over medium-low heat 6 to 8 minutes or until mixture is heated through and green onion and green pepper are slightly tender but not completely cooked.

5. Add meat to skillet along with any juices that have accumulated on the platter; cook, stirring, until heated through, 1 to 2 minutes.

6. To serve, drain pasta and place on a clean platter. Spoon meat mixture on top of pasta. Garnish with cilantro sprigs if desired.

PASTA AND GRAINS

Rigatoni with sausage

Makes 6 servings *Prep* 15 minutes *Cook* 30 minutes

Vary the taste of the sauce by using all sweet or all hot Italian sausage or a combination of both. Another pasta shape? Medium-size shells.

Per serving
382 calories, 15 g protein, 5 g fat, 70 g carbohydrate, 708 mg sodium, 9 mg cholesterol.

2 links Italian sausage (about 5 ounces total), casings removed
2 onions, chopped
1 sweet green pepper, cored, seeded and chopped
4 cloves garlic, chopped
1 can (28 ounces) crushed tomatoes in puree
1 cup water
1 package (10 ounces) frozen chopped spinach, thawed and drained
½ teaspoon salt
⅛ teaspoon red-pepper flakes
1 pound rigatoni

1. Cook sausage in a saucepan over medium heat, breaking up with a wooden spoon, 3 minutes. Add onions, green pepper and garlic; cook 8 minutes. Add tomatoes, water, spinach, salt and red-pepper flakes; cook, partially covered, 15 minutes or until heated through.

2. Meanwhile, cook rigatoni in a large pot of lightly salted boiling water until al dente, firm but tender. Drain well. Toss with sauce and serve.

Beer-brat pasta

Makes 8 servings *Prep* 5 minutes *Roast* at 425° for 25 minutes *Cook* 12 minutes

In this prize-winning recipe from Barbara Anderson of Wisconsin, a little of the pasta cooking water is reserved to stir into the sauce to make it creamier.

Per serving
404 calories, 16 g protein, 19 g fat, 42 g carbohydrate, 296 mg sodium, 40 mg cholesterol.

2 sweet red peppers, cored, seeded and cut into matchstick strips
1 medium onion, coarsely chopped
4 cloves garlic, chopped
2 tablespoons olive oil
1 pound fresh bratwurst
½ cup beer
1 pound rigatoni
½ cup torn fresh basil
1½ cups shredded cheddar cheese

1. Heat oven to 425°. Mix red peppers, onion, garlic and oil in a 13 x 9 x 2-inch baking dish. Bake in heated 425° oven 25 minutes, stirring occasionally.

2. Remove casing from bratwurst; crumble bratwurst. Cook in a skillet over medium-high heat 5 minutes. Add beer; simmer about 3 minutes.

3. Meanwhile, cook rigatoni in a large pot of lightly salted boiling water until al dente, firm but tender.

4. Drain pasta, reserving ½ cup cooking water. Place pasta in a serving bowl. Add vegetables, bratwurst with beer, basil and 1 cup cheese; toss to mix thoroughly, adding some of the reserved pasta water if sauce is too dry. Top with remaining cheese and serve.

Quick bolognese

Makes 4 servings *Prep* 10 minutes *Cook* about 12 minutes

This totally satisfying, rich-tasting pasta with meat sauce is ready in 25 minutes, not the hours required for a long-simmering Bolognese. A dried chile pepper adds an unexpected kick.

Shown on front cover.

Per serving
599 calories, 29 g protein, 19 g fat, 77 g carbohydrate, 1,086 mg sodium, 57 mg cholesterol.

¾ pound rigatoni
2 tablespoons olive oil
1 large onion, chopped
1 dried chile pepper (optional)
2 cloves garlic, finely chopped
¾ pound ground beef or turkey
2 tablespoons tomato paste

4 cups diced tomatoes, drained (about 8 tomatoes), or 1 can (28 ounces) crushed tomatoes
2 teaspoons salt (½ teaspoon if using canned tomatoes)
½ teaspoon black pepper
1 tablespoon chopped fresh parsley

1. Cook rigatoni in a large pot of lightly salted boiling water until al dente, firm but tender.

2. Meanwhile, heat oil in a large skillet over high heat. Add onion; cook until browned, about 2 minutes. Add chile pepper if using, garlic and meat; cook, breaking up meat with a wooden spoon, until it is no longer pink, about 3 minutes.

3. Add tomato paste, tomatoes, salt and pepper; bring to boiling. Lower heat; simmer 5 minutes. Stir in parsley. Remove chile pepper.

4. Drain pasta; toss with sauce in pot. Serve immediately.

Quick bolognese

Fusilli Colorado

Makes 6 servings   *Prep* 10 minutes   *Cook* 15 minutes

Since many Italian and Mexican people call Colorado home, prizewinner Jonathan Elbaum combines popular staples from both cuisines: tomatoes and chipotle chiles.

Per serving
586 calories, 40 g protein, 22 g fat, 55 g carbohydrate, 464 mg sodium, 138 mg cholesterol.

1 pound fusilli
6 boneless, skinless chicken breast halves (2 pounds total)
1 tablespoon vegetable oil
1 medium onion, diced (about 1 cup)
1 clove garlic, chopped
½ teaspoon ground cumin
2 canned chipotle chiles, seeded and finely diced
2 medium tomatoes, cored and cut into ½-inch cubes (about 2 cups)
1 cup heavy cream
1 teaspoon salt
¼ teaspoon black pepper
2 tablespoons chopped fresh cilantro

1. Cook fusilli in a large pot of lightly salted boiling water until al dente, firm but tender. Drain, reserving ½ cup pasta cooking water.

2. Meanwhile, cut chicken into 2 x ½ x ½-inch strips. Heat oil in a large skillet over medium-high heat. Add chicken; sauté 5 minutes or until it begins to brown. Add onion; cook 3 minutes. Add garlic and cumin. Reduce heat to medium; cook 1 minute.

3. Add chiles, tomatoes, cream, salt and pepper. Lower heat; simmer 5 minutes. Add cilantro.

4. Add pasta to sauce; toss. Stir in reserved pasta water as needed for a creamier consistency. Serve.

Cooking pasta

HERE'S THE FOOLPROOF method—about as easy as it gets.

Use a tall, heavy pot and pour in 4 quarts of water for each pound of pasta. Bring the water to a full rolling boil; add salt as desired. If you're cooking pasta shapes, add them all at once to the boiling water. If you're cooking long pasta, add it in 2 or 3 batches, slowly pushing each batch into the boiling water as the pasta softens (this keeps it from breaking).

Stir the pasta to separate and cover the pot so the water returns quickly to boiling; then immediately remove the lid. Stirring occasionally, cook the pasta until al dente—tender but firm; taste to be sure. Drain the pasta in a colander. Do not rinse unless you are serving it cold.

Long pasta: 2 ounces uncooked (a ½-inch-diameter bunch) yields a 1-cup serving.

Short pasta and shapes: 2 ounces uncooked (just over ½ cup) yields a 1-cup serving.

Hawaiian angel hair with kiawe-grilled chicken

Makes 6 servings *Prep* 15 minutes *Refrigerate* 30 minutes *Cook* 8 to 10 minutes

A taste of the islands: pineapple, sweet Maui onions and macadamia nuts. Janet Kruse used her state's ingredients in this winning submission to a *Family Circle* pasta recipe contest.

Per serving

661 calories, 44 g protein, 15 g fat, 88 g carbohydrate, 1,521 mg sodium, 84 mg cholesterol.

¾ cup soy sauce
½ cup packed dark-brown sugar
1½ teaspoons grated fresh ginger
2 cloves garlic, finely chopped
2 tablespoons dark Asian sesame oil
1 can (20 ounces) juice-packed pineapple chunks, drained, ⅓ cup juice reserved
6 boneless, skinless chicken breast halves (2 pounds total), cut into 3 x 1-inch strips

2 medium Maui or other sweet onions, cut into 1-inch chunks
2 medium sweet green peppers, cored, seeded and cut into 1-inch pieces
1 tablespoon oil
1 pound angel hair pasta
¼ cup chopped macadamia nuts, toasted

1. Mix together soy sauce, brown sugar, ginger, garlic, sesame oil and reserved pineapple juice in a medium-size bowl. Reserve 1 cup sauce for pasta. Pour remaining sauce into a resealable plastic food-storage bag; add chicken, pineapple chunks, onions and green peppers. Marinate in refrigerator 30 minutes, turning once.

2. Meanwhile, prepare a charcoal grill with kiawe (mesquite) charcoal until medium-hot, or heat a gas grill or broiler.

3. Bring large pot of water (do not salt) to boiling. Add oil and pasta; cook until pasta is tender, about 3 minutes. Drain; transfer to a large serving platter; toss pasta with reserved 1 cup sauce.

4. On metal skewers or presoaked wooden skewers, alternately thread marinated chicken, pineapple chunks and vegetables.

5. Grill or broil 8 to 10 minutes or until chicken is no longer pink in center, turning once. Remove from skewers; arrange over pasta. Sprinkle with macadamia nuts and serve.

Savory apple harvest linguine

Makes 6 servings   *Prep* 15 minutes   *Cook* 30 minutes

6 slices smoked bacon
1 green apple, cored and sliced into 16 wedges
1 red apple, cored and sliced into 16 wedges
1 small onion, chopped
¼ cup frozen apple juice concentrate, thawed
1 cup chicken broth
1 cup heavy cream
¼ cup shredded sharp cheddar cheese
2 tablespoons chopped fresh chives
¾ teaspoon salt
¼ teaspoon black pepper
  Pinch ground nutmeg
1 pound linguine

1. Cook bacon in a large skillet over medium-high heat until crisp. Remove to paper toweling to drain; crumble.

2. Pour off all but 1 tablespoon fat from skillet. Add apples; cook over medium-high heat 8 minutes or until golden and softened; remove to a plate. Add onion to skillet; cook over medium heat 4 minutes. Pour apple juice concentrate, broth and cream into skillet; simmer 10 minutes or until slightly thickened. Add cheese, chives, salt, pepper and nutmeg, stirring until cheese is melted.

3. Meanwhile, cook linguine in a large pot of lightly salted boiling water until al dente, firm but tender. Drain.

4. Add pasta to sauce in skillet; toss to coat. Transfer to a large platter. Sprinkle with bacon and apples. Serve warm.

Savory apple
harvest linguine

Sesame chicken and soba noodles

Sesame chicken and soba noodles

Makes 4 servings   *Prep* 15 minutes   *Cook* 5 minutes

Dark brown Japanese soba noodles are a tasty change from traditional pasta. Cook's trick: Since garlic flavors the uncooked sauce, blanch the cloves first to soften the flavor.

Per serving
493 calories, 30 g protein, 21 g fat, 53 g carbohydrate, 766 mg sodium, 31 mg cholesterol.

1 clove garlic
1 cup fresh cilantro leaves
3 tablespoons lime juce
3 tablespoons dark Asian sesame oil
3 tablespoons reduced-sodium soy sauce
1 teaspoon hot-pepper sauce
½ cup smooth peanut butter
2 boneless, skinless chicken breast halves (½ pound total), cut into thin strips
½ pound soba noodles
2 green onions, sliced thinly on the diagonal

1. Bring a large pot of water to boiling. Add garlic and cook 1 minute. With a slotted spoon, remove garlic from water; keep water boiling.

2. Press blanched garlic through a garlic press or chop. Place in a food processor or blender with cilantro. Whirl to chop finely. Add lime juice, sesame oil, soy sauce, hot-pepper sauce and peanut butter. Whirl until smooth. Thin sauce with ¼ cup boiling water or as needed.

3. Add chicken and noodles to boiling water; cook 2 to 3 minutes or until chicken is cooked through and noodles are tender. Drain; toss chicken and noodles with sesame sauce in a serving bowl. Garnish with green onions. Serve immediately.

Spicy Thai-style fettuccine

Makes 4 servings   *Prep* 20 minutes   *Cook* 12 minutes

Experiment with different vinegars: rice wine, cider, balsamic or distilled white. You'll find mung bean sprouts in the produce section of your supermarket or in Asian or Indian food shops.

Per serving
605 calories, 28 g protein, 15 g fat, 92 g carbohydrate, 618 mg sodium, 37 mg cholesterol.

¾ pound fettuccine
1 tablespoon vegetable oil
2 cloves garlic, chopped
2 turkey cutlets (½ pound total), cut into thin strips
3 green onions, sliced
½ pound mung bean sprouts
3 tablespoons reduced-sodium soy sauce

¼ cup vinegar
6 tablespoons sugar
4 teaspoons paprika
2 anchovies, mashed
½ to ¾ teaspoon ground red pepper (cayenne)
2 tablespoons chopped fresh cilantro (optional)
¼ cup chopped peanuts

1. Cook pasta in a large pot of lightly salted boiling water until al dente, firm but tender. Drain well.

2. Meanwhile, heat oil in a large skillet over medium heat. Add garlic and turkey; stir-fry 2 minutes or until turkey is cooked. Add green onions and bean sprouts; cook, stirring, 1 minute. Add soy sauce, vinegar, sugar, paprika, anchovies, ground red pepper and cilantro if using.

3. Add pasta; toss until heated through. Top with peanuts.

Vegetable rice noodles

Makes 4 servings   *Prep* 15 minutes   *Cook* 10 minutes

A scattering of toasted sesame seeds adds a pleasant nutty note to these noodles. Simply heat a large nonstick skillet over medium heat and cook the sesame seeds, stirring frequently, until toasted.

Per serving
294 calories, 7 g protein, 5 g fat, 55 g carbohydrate, 1475 mg sodium, 0 mg cholesterol

¾ cup lower-sodium beef broth
⅓ cup soy sauce
2 tablespoons balsamic vinegar
1 tablespoon grated fresh ginger
1 tablespoon dark Asian sesame oil
2 teaspoons cornstarch
¼ teaspoon sugar

1 package (7 ounces) rice flour noodles
¼ pound mushrooms, quartered
½ pound sugar snap peas, trimmed
1 cup cherry tomatoes, halved
1 tablespoon sesame seeds, toasted

1. Combine broth, soy sauce, vinegar, ginger, 1 teaspoon sesame oil, cornstarch and sugar in small a bowl. Set aside.

2. Cook noodles in a large pot of boiling water 3 minutes; drain well.

3. In a large nonstick skillet, heat 1 teaspoon sesame oil over medium-high heat. Add mushrooms and sauté, stirring occasionally, 2 minutes. Add broth mixture and sugar snap peas and cook 4 minutes or until thickened. Stir in tomatoes and remaining 1 teaspoon sesame oil and heat through. Spoon over noodles in serving bowl; toss to coat. Sprinkle with toasted sesame seeds.

Pork stir-fry

Makes 6 servings *Prep* 30 minutes *Marinate* 20 minutes *Cook* 10 minutes

Even though all cabbages are suited for this dish, the Napa variety cooks up to great advantage because of both its delicate color and its crispness.

Per serving
271 calories, 18 g protein, 12 g fat, 23 g carbohydrate, 929 mg sodium, 44 mg cholesterol.

½ cup reduced-sodium soy sauce
½ cup lower-sodium chicken broth
2 teaspoons dark Asian sesame oil
3 tablespoons rice-wine vinegar
2 teaspoons sugar
2 teaspoons cornstarch
1 pound center-cut pork roast, cut into 2 x ½ x ¼-inch strips
1 bag (8 ounces) rice noodles

2 tablespoons vegetable oil
½ cup thinly sliced green onion
1 tablespoon finely chopped garlic
1 tablespoon finely chopped fresh ginger
3 cups thinly sliced cabbage (about ¼ head cabbage)
1 sweet red pepper, cored, seeded and cut into matchstick strips

1. Stir together soy sauce, broth, sesame oil, vinegar and sugar in a small bowl. Pour ¼ cup of the marinade into a medium-size bowl; stir in cornstarch. Add pork; toss to coat. Set aside to marinate 20 minutes. Reserve remaining marinade in the small bowl.

2. Bring 4 cups water to boiling in a saucepan. Place rice noodles in a large heatproof bowl. Pour boiling water over and let stand 5 minutes. Drain.

3. Meanwhile, heat 1 tablespoon oil in a wok or very large skillet over high heat. Add marinated pork; cook, stirring constantly, until pork is no longer pink, 2 to 3 minutes. With a slotted spoon, remove pork to a bowl.

4. Wipe any residue from wok. Heat remaining tablespoon oil in wok. Add green onion, garlic and ginger; cook, stirring, 1 to 2 minutes. Add cabbage and red pepper strips; cook 1 minute. Return pork to wok. Pour in reserved marinade. Add noodles; toss to combine and heat through.

About Asian noodles

EXPLORE THE WORLD of pasta from the Far East.

Banh trang: Thin rice papers used to wrap Vietnamese spring rolls.

Chinese cellophane noodles: Also called shining, silver or glass noodles. Made from mung beans, they're great deep-fried and crispy, as a bed for stir-fries.

Jantaboon noodles: Flat, thin, dried rice noodles often used in the Thai classic, pad Thai.

Ramen: A Japanese favorite. It's a yellow wheat noodle used in stir-fries and soup.

Rice noodles: Also known as rice vermicelli. Soak or fry these noodles before adding to a recipe.

Soba: A Japanese buckwheat noodle. Serve chilled with a spicy dipping sauce or hot in broth.

Three-cheese penne

Makes 8 servings   *Prep* 10 minutes   *Cook* 20 minutes   *Bake* at 400° for 20 to 30 minutes

How did penne get its name? The ends of the tubular pasta are cut on an angle, resembling a pen or quill. Other chunky pastas, such as radiatore or wagon wheels, are playful replacements for the penne.

Per serving
466 calories, 29 g protein, 14 g fat, 58 g carbohydrate, 516 mg sodium, 33 mg cholesterol.

Cooking with low-fat cheese
• Add flour or cornstarch to cheese sauces and cook over low heat.
• Grate cheese extra fine so it melts evenly.
• Add a small amount of acid, such as vinegar or lemon juice, to aid the melting process.

1 pound penne
2 tablespoons olive oil
1 pound mushrooms, sliced
1 large onion, chopped
2 cloves garlic, finely chopped
¼ cup all-purpose flour
4 cups low-fat (1%) milk
½ teaspoon salt
¼ teaspoon ground nutmeg

4 teaspoons fresh lemon juice
¼ teaspoon black pepper
1½ cups shredded reduced-fat cheddar cheese (6 ounces)
1¼ cups shredded reduced-fat Swiss cheese (5 ounces)
1 cup shredded reduced-fat Monterey Jack cheese (4 ounces)

1. Cook penne in a large pot of lightly salted boiling water until al dente, firm but tender. Drain well.

2. Meanwhile, heat 1 tablespoon oil in a large skillet over medium-high heat. Add mushrooms; sauté 8 minutes or until tender. Remove from skillet.

3. Heat remaining oil in skillet. Add onion; sauté 5 minutes. Add garlic; sauté 2 minutes.

4. Whisk together flour and milk in a small bowl. Add to skillet. Bring to boiling, stirring occasionally. Reduce heat to low; add salt and nutmeg and simmer 5 minutes.

5. Heat oven to 400°. Lightly grease a 13 x 9 x 2-inch shallow baking dish.

6. In same pot used to cook penne, toss penne with sauce, mushrooms, lemon juice and pepper.

7. Combine all the cheeses in a bowl; set aside ¼ cup. Add remaining cheese to penne mixture, stirring gently. Spoon into prepared baking dish. Sprinkle with reserved cheese.

8. Bake, uncovered, in heated 400° oven, 20 to 30 minutes or until browned and bubbly.

Make-ahead tip: Prepare through step 7, then refrigerate, covered, up to 3 days or freeze up to 1 month. To serve, if frozen, thaw in refrigerator overnight. Bake as directed.

Creamy primavera bake

Makes 6 servings   *Prep* 10 minutes   *Cook* 25 minutes   *Bake* at 375° for 25 minutes

A vegetarian casserole hearty enough to please the whole family. During the summer months, use all fresh vegetables; in the winter, turn to their frozen cousins.

Per serving
326 calories, 16 g protein,
8 g fat, 52 g carbohydrate,
868 mg sodium,
16 mg cholesterol.

1 tablespoon vegetable oil
2 large onions, finely chopped
2 cloves garlic, finely chopped
1 can (16 ounces) tomatoes, undrained
1 can (8 ounces) tomato sauce
1 teaspoon dried basil
½ teaspoon dried oregano
1 teaspoon salt
¼ teaspoon black pepper

½ pound rigatoni
1 package (10 ounces) frozen chopped spinach, thawed and drained
1 package (10 ounces) frozen corn kernels, thawed
1 cup fresh or frozen green peas
1 cup part-skim ricotta cheese
¼ cup grated Parmesan cheese

1. Heat oil in a large nonstick skillet over medium heat. Add onions and sauté 3 minutes. Add garlic; sauté 1 minute. Stir in tomatoes with their liquid, tomato sauce, basil, oregano, salt and pepper, breaking up tomatoes. Simmer, uncovered, 15 minutes or until slightly thickened.

2. Meanwhile, cook rigatoni in a large pot of lightly salted boiling water until al dente, firm but tender; drain and return to pot.

3. Heat oven to 375°. Coat an 11 x 7 x 2-inch baking dish with nonstick cooking spray.

4. Stir spinach, corn and peas into skillet with vegetable mixture. Cook 5 minutes. Add vegetable mixture and ricotta to drained pasta. Spoon into prepared baking dish. Sprinkle with Parmesan. Bake in heated 375° oven 25 minutes or until cheese is golden brown. Let stand 5 minutes before serving.

Creamy primavera bake

Maryland crab shells

Makes 8 servings   *Prep* 15 minutes   *Cook* 15 minutes   *Bake* at 350° for 30 minutes

1 box (12 ounces) jumbo pasta shells
¼ cup (½ stick) butter
2 tablespoons chopped sweet green pepper
1 tablespoon chopped red onion
1½ pounds lump crabmeat, picked through, or crabmeat blend
½ teaspoon black pepper
1 teaspoon Old Bay seasoning
1 egg, slightly beaten
2½ cups milk
1 cup mayonnaise
3 tablespoons all-purpose flour
½ cup grated Parmesan cheese

1. Heat oven to 350°.

2. Cook pasta shells in a large pot of lightly salted boiling water until al dente, firm but tender. Drain; rinse and cool.

3. Meanwhile, melt 1 tablespoon butter in a medium-size skillet. Add green pepper and onion and sauté until softened, 3 to 5 minutes. Remove to a medium-size bowl. Stir in crabmeat, black pepper, ½ teaspoon Old Bay seasoning, egg, ½ cup milk and mayonnaise.

4. Melt ½ tablespoon butter in each of two 11 x 7 x 2-inch baking dishes. Spoon filling into pasta shells. Arrange shells in each baking dish.

5. Melt remaining 2 tablespoons butter in a medium-size saucepan over medium-low heat. Whisk in flour. Gradually whisk in remaining 2 cups milk; cook until slightly thickened. Stir in Parmesan. Drizzle sauce evenly over shells. Sprinkle with remaining ½ teaspoon Old Bay seasoning.

6. Bake in heated 350° oven 30 minutes or until bubbly. Let cool 10 minutes.

Note: For a lighter meal, substitute reduced-fat margarine, skim milk and light mayonnaise for the full-fat varieties above. Two egg whites can be substituted for the whole egg.

Cheesy ziti and meatballs

Makes 8 servings *Prep* 15 minutes *Cook* 30 minutes *Bake* at 375° for 35 minutes

Chicken meatballs, lots of cheddar cheese and ziti—who could resist! Get a jump on the party by assembling earlier in the day and refrigerating. Monterey Jack cheese, or even pepper-Jack for a flavor wallop, substitutes nicely for the cheddar.

Shown on page 2.

Per serving
557 calories, 28 g protein, 23 g fat, 57 g carbohydrate, 1,100 mg sodium, 101 mg cholesterol.

2 slices white bread, torn into pieces
¼ cup milk
1 pound ground chicken
½ cup dry seasoned bread crumbs
3 tablespoons grated Parmesan cheese
¼ cup chopped fresh parsley
1 teaspoon salt

3 tablespoons olive oil
1 cup chopped sweet green pepper
½ cup chopped onion
¼ cup water
1 can (28 ounces) crushed tomatoes
1 pound ziti or penne
2 cups shredded sharp cheddar cheese (8 ounces)

1. Combine torn bread and milk in a large bowl. Let stand 5 minutes or until bread softens. Add ground chicken, bread crumbs, Parmesan, 2 tablespoons parsley and ¼ teaspoon salt; mix well with your hands. With hands kept wet with cold water, shape mixture into 1½-inch balls.

2. Heat oil in a large skillet over medium heat. Working in batches if necessary, add meatballs to skillet; cook, turning, until browned on all sides, about 5 minutes. Transfer meatballs to a plate.

3. In fat remaining in skillet, cook green pepper and onion over medium-high heat until just tender, about 2 minutes. Add water; continue cooking, stirring occasionally, until vegetables are very tender, about 6 minutes more.

4. Stir in meatballs, tomatoes and remaining ¾ teaspoon salt. Bring to boiling. Reduce heat; cover and simmer, stirring occasionally, 15 minutes or until meatballs are cooked through.

5. Meanwhile, cook ziti in a large pot of lightly salted boiling water until al dente, firm but tender. Drain.

6. Heat oven to 375°.

7. Toss pasta with sauce and meatballs in skillet. Spoon half of mixture into a 3-quart oval casserole. Sprinkle with half of cheddar cheese. Spoon remaining pasta mixture on top. Top with remaining cheese. Tent with aluminum foil (do not let foil touch cheese).

8. Bake in heated 375° oven 35 minutes or until hot and bubbly and cheese is melted. Remove foil. Sprinkle with remaining 2 tablespoons parsley.

Idaho baked potato 'n' shells

Makes 8 servings   *Prep* 20 minutes   *Microwave* 15 minutes   *Bake* at 425° for 45 minutes

Most likely you'll have all these ingredients on hand, making this one-dish meal a spur-of-the-moment favorite. It's a real winner from contest entrant Tammy Stapleton of Idaho.

Per serving
597 calories, 25 g protein,
24 g fat, 70 g carbohydrate,
851 mg sodium,
66 mg cholesterol.

2½ pounds red boiling potatoes, cut into ½-inch cubes (about 6 cups)
2 cups sour cream
1 can (about 10¾ ounces) condensed cream of chicken soup, plus 1 can milk
1 pound small shell pasta

2 cans (about 5 ounces each) water-packed white chunk chicken, drained
1 cup shredded cheddar, Colby or Monterey Jack cheese (4 ounces)
1 teaspoon salt
¼ teaspoon freshly ground black pepper

1. Heat oven to 425°.

2. Spread potatoes evenly in a 13 x 9 x 2-inch glass baking dish. Cover tightly with plastic wrap. Microwave on 100% power 15 minutes. Carefully uncover. Transfer to a large bowl.

3. Whisk sour cream, condensed chicken soup and milk in a small bowl. Add to potatoes. Add uncooked pasta shells, chicken, cheese, salt and pepper. Pour into baking dish. Cover dish tightly with aluminum foil.

4. Bake in heated 425° oven about 45 minutes or until the pasta and potatoes are tender. Let cool slightly and serve.

Turkey-stuffed manicotti *opposite*

Turkey-stuffed manicotti

Makes 6 servings   *Prep* 15 minutes   *Cook* 15 minutes   *Bake* at 350° for 40 minutes

Like ground chicken? Go ahead and use it. If fresh, tender kale is available, replace the spinach with it. And don't forget that manicotti is the great make-ahead. Get all that stuffing done up to a day ahead of time, through step 5.

Per serving
479 calories, 34 g protein, 19 g fat, 44 g carbohydrate, 1,070 mg sodium, 108 mg cholesterol.

12 manicotti shells
12 ounces ground turkey
4 cups coarsely chopped fresh
   spinach (8 ounces)
1 cup shredded carrot
2 cloves garlic, finely chopped
½ teaspoon salt
½ teaspoon dried sage
¼ teaspoon fennel seeds, crushed
⅛ teaspoon ground red pepper
   (cayenne)

3 cups marinara sauce
¼ cup chopped fresh basil
1 cup part-skim ricotta cheese
1 egg, lightly beaten
¼ cup grated Parmesan cheese
1½ cups shredded low-fat mozzarella
   cheese (6 ounces)
   Additional grated Parmesan
   cheese (optional)

1. Simmer manicotti in a large pot of lightly salted water until barely tender, about 7 minutes. Remove with a slotted spoon to a bowl of cold water; drain when cool.

2. Heat oven to 350°. Coat a 13 x 9 x 2-inch baking pan with nonstick cooking spray.

3. Coat a large nonstick skillet with cooking spray. Heat over medium heat. Add turkey, spinach, carrot, garlic, salt, sage, fennel seeds and red pepper; cook, breaking up meat with a wooden spoon, 8 minutes or until meat is no longer pink. Carefully drain excess liquid from skillet.

4. Combine marinara sauce and basil in a small bowl. Spread 1 cup over bottom of prepared baking dish.

5. Stir ricotta, egg, Parmesan and half of mozzarella into turkey mixture. Spoon filling into manicotti shells. Place shells in prepared dish. Spoon remaining pasta sauce over manicotti. Cover with aluminum foil.

6. Bake in heated 350° oven 30 minutes. Remove foil. Sprinkle with remaining mozzarella cheese. Bake, uncovered, 10 minutes more or until cheese is melted and golden brown. Serve with additional Parmesan if desired.

Broccoli lasagna

Makes 8 servings   *Prep* 10 minutes   *Cook* 15 minutes   *Bake* at 350° for 35 minutes

No meat here! Blanched zucchini or carrot slices or green beans are tasty alternatives to the broccoli.

Per serving
389 calories, 22 g protein,
11 g fat, 51 g carbohydrate,
467 mg sodium,
33 mg cholesterol.

1 box (1 pound) lasagna noodles
⅓ cup all-purpose flour
3½ cups low-fat (1%) milk
  Pinch ground nutmeg
1 teaspoon salt
¼ teaspoon black pepper
¼ cup grated Parmesan cheese

¼ teaspoon hot-pepper sauce
1 package (16 ounces) frozen broccoli flowerets, thawed and chopped
2 cups shredded Swiss cheese (8 ounces)

1. You should have about 18 lasagna noodles. Cook them in a large pot of lightly salted boiling water until al dente, firm but tender. Drain and cool.

2. Meanwhile, whisk flour and ½ cup milk in a saucepan until smooth. Whisk in remaining milk. Bring to boiling, whisking. Boil 1 minute or until thickened. Remove from heat.

3. Stir in nutmeg, salt, black pepper, Parmesan and hot-pepper sauce. Reserve 1 cup of mixture for topping.

4. Heat oven to 350°. Coat a 13 x 9 x 2-inch baking dish with nonstick cooking spray.

5. Place 2 layers of noodles (4 noodles per layer) in prepared baking dish. Spoon on half of broccoli, ¾ cup Swiss cheese and half of white sauce. Add another 2 layers noodles (3 noodles per layer). Spoon on remaining broccoli, ¾ cup Swiss cheese and remaining white sauce. Arrange remaining noodles on top. Spread with reserved 1 cup white sauce; sprinkle with remaining Swiss cheese.

6. Bake in heated 350° oven 35 minutes. Let stand 15 minutes before cutting.

Quick jazz-ups

SPARK EVEN the most basic pasta sauce with a few extras.

Whip up a smooth tomato sauce, then mix in cooked spinach and 1 or 2 sautéed garlic cloves.

Stir cooked broccoli flowerets and red-pepper flakes into classic marinara, or toss in a few pieces of chopped cooked prosciutto and a splash of heavy cream.

Give Alfredo an unexpected touch with fresh mozzarella, Fontina or Bel Paese.

Zip up pesto by blending in heavy cream and a few chopped black olives and toasted pine nuts.

Chili macaroni and cheese

Makes 8 servings   *Prep* 15 minutes   *Cook* 20 minutes   *Bake* at 375° for 30 minutes

Chili powder and hot-pepper sauce give this classic a southwestern spin. The key to the crunchy topping is cornflake cereal crumbs. Try this with fusilli or penne or even radiatore or wagon wheels.

Per serving
639 calories, 33 g protein, 28 g fat, 63 g carbohydrate, 1,054 mg sodium, 101 mg cholesterol.

2 tablespoons chili powder
1 tablespoon ground cumin
1 tablespoon unsalted butter
¾ cup cornflake crumbs
¼ cup all-purpose flour
4 cups milk
2 teaspoons salt

½ teaspoon hot-pepper sauce
3 cups shredded cheddar cheese
   (12 ounces)
1 pound elbow macaroni
1 pound ground beef
1 onion, finely chopped
2 tablespoons tomato paste

1. Heat oven to 375°. Coat a 13 x 9 x 2-inch baking dish with nonstick cooking spray. Mix chili powder and cumin in small bowl.

2. Melt butter in a medium-size saucepan. Add cornflake crumbs, stirring to coat. Scrape onto waxed paper; reserve for topping. (Wipe out saucepan with paper toweling.)

3. Shake flour and 1 cup milk in a covered container until blended. Combine remaining milk, salt, hot-pepper sauce and 1 tablespoon chili powder mixture in a saucepan. Bring to simmering.

4. Whisk flour-milk mixture into milk mixture in saucepan; cook, stirring, 10 minutes or until thickened and smooth. Remove from heat. Stir in 2 cups cheese. Cover.

5. Cook macaroni in a large pot of lightly salted boiling water until al dente, firm but tender. Drain.

6. Meanwhile, heat a nonstick skillet over medium-high heat. Add beef and onion; cook, breaking up meat with a wooden spoon, 6 minutes or until meat is no longer pink. Carefully drain excess liquid from skillet. Stir tomato paste and remaining chili powder mixture into meat mixture; cook, stirring, 3 minutes. Remove from heat.

7. Combine macaroni and cheese sauce in the macaroni cooking pot. Spoon half of macaroni mixture into prepared baking dish. Spoon meat mixture over top, spreading evenly. Top with remaining macaroni. Sprinkle evenly with remaining cheese and reserved cornflake crumbs.

8. Bake in heated 375° oven 30 minutes or until bubbly and golden brown.

Country ham and macaroni casserole

Makes 10 servings   *Prep* 10 minutes   *Cook* 10 minutes   *Bake* at 400° for 30 minutes

This winning recipe, from Donna A. Kidd of Tennessee, is truly a dish for ham lovers. The cooking water for the macaroni is even flavored with pieces of the country ham.

Per serving
482 calories, 24 g protein, 22 g fat, 47 g carbohydrate, 1,098 mg sodium, 57 mg cholesterol.

1 pound country ham slices or regular smoked ham in 1 piece
1 large onion, diced
1 pound elbow macaroni
2 cups shredded extra-sharp cheddar cheese (8 ounces)
1 cup sour cream
1 can (about 10¾ ounces) condensed cream of chicken soup
¼ cup (½ stick) margarine, melted
1 cup dry plain bread crumbs

1. Heat oven to 400°.

2. Bring 4 quarts water and ham to boiling in a large pot. Once water begins to boil, remove ham to a plate. Add onion and macaroni to pot. Return water to boiling; cook 8 minutes, stirring occasionally.

3. Coarsely chop ham, discarding any fat and bones.

4. Drain macaroni and onion and return to pot. Add ham, cheese, sour cream and condensed soup. Scrape into a 13 x 9 x 2-inch baking dish. Pour melted margarine over top. Sprinkle with bread crumbs.

5. Bake in heated 400° oven 30 minutes or until heated through and top is golden brown. Let stand 5 minutes before serving.

Country ham and macaroni casserole

Creamy bacon and tomato shells

Makes 6 servings *Prep* 15 minutes *Cook* 30 minutes *Bake* at 400° for 15 minutes

Try part-skim ricotta cheese for a trimmer version of this recipe.

Per serving

360 calories, 18 g protein, 14 g fat, 42 g carbohydrate, 740 mg sodium, 41 mg cholesterol.

1 tablespoon olive oil
4 ounces Canadian bacon, diced
1 medium red onion, halved and sliced
3 medium tomatoes, seeded and diced
1 can (8 ounces) tomato sauce
3 tablespoons balsamic vinegar
¾ teaspoon salt
¼ teaspoon freshly ground black pepper
1 box (12 ounces) jumbo shells
1 container (15 ounces) ricotta cheese
¼ cup grated Parmesan cheese
¼ cup chopped fresh basil

1. Heat 2 teaspoons oil in a large skillet over medium-high heat. Add bacon; sauté 3 minutes. Add onion and remaining 1 teaspoon oil; lower heat to medium. Cook, stirring frequently, 5 minutes or until onion is softened. Add tomatoes, tomato sauce, vinegar, ½ teaspoon salt and pepper. Lower heat; simmer 15 to 20 minutes or until sauce is thickened.

2. Meanwhile, cook shells in a large pot of lightly salted boiling water until al dente, firm but tender; drain. Stir together ricotta cheese, Parmesan, basil, remaining ¼ teaspoon salt and 1 cup cooked sauce in a large bowl; set aside.

3. Heat oven to 400°.

4. Divide ricotta filling among shells. Place filled shells in a 13 x 9 x 2-inch baking dish. Spoon remaining sauce on top. Bake in heated 400° oven 15 minutes or until hot.

Spaghetti pie

Makes 4 servings *Prep* 15 minutes *Bake* 40 to 45 minutes

Leftover spaghetti—or any shape pasta, for that matter—becomes a second meal. Presto!

Per serving

430 calories, 18 g protein, 12 g fat, 63 g carbohydrate, 833 mg sodium, 215 mg cholesterol.

¼ cup dry plain bread crumbs
4 cups cooked spaghetti (8 ounces uncooked spaghetti, broken into pieces)
2 cups marinara sauce
4 eggs, slightly beaten
2 tablespoons grated Parmesan cheese

1. Heat oven to 350°. Coat bottom and 1 inch up sides of a 9-inch cast-iron skillet with nonstick cooking spray. Sprinkle with bread crumbs.

2. Mix cooked spaghetti with 1½ cups sauce in a medium-size bowl. Mix in eggs. Transfer to prepared skillet. Bake in heated 350° oven 40 minutes or until eggs are set. Using a thin metal spatula, remove pie from skillet. Sprinkle top with Parmesan. Heat remaining sauce and serve alongside.

Curried rice pilaf

Makes 4 servings   *Prep* 10 minutes   *Cook* 30 minutes

A pilaf always begins with sautéing or cooking the rice in butter or oil until lightly colored, which gives a subtle nutty flavor to the finished dish.

Per serving

281 calories, 5 g protein, 8 g fat, 49 g carbohydrate, 607 mg sodium, 0 mg cholesterol.

2 tablespoons olive oil
1 onion, finely chopped
3 cloves garlic, chopped
1 tablespoon curry powder
2 teaspoons chili powder
½ teaspoon ground ginger

1 cup basmati rice
2½ cups water
½ cup chopped carrot
1 cinnamon stick
3 cardamom pods, crushed
1 teaspoon salt

1. Heat oil in a medium-size saucepan over medium heat. Add onion and garlic; sauté until golden and softened, about 5 minutes. Stir in curry powder, chili powder and ginger; sauté 30 seconds. Stir in rice to coat, 1 to 2 minutes.

2. Add water. Bring to boiling. Lower heat; stir in carrot, cinnamon stick, cardamom pods and salt. Simmer, covered, 20 minutes or until rice is tender. Remove cinnamon stick and cardamom. Serve hot.

Mushroom rice

Makes 12 servings   *Prep* 15 minutes   *Cook* 45 to 50 minutes

When soaking dried mushrooms to soften, be sure to save the broth to add to dishes for extra flavor. But first strain through a fine sieve lined with dampened paper toweling or a double thickness of dampened cheesecloth to remove any bits of grit.

Per serving

277 calories, 7 g protein, 5 g fat, 51 g carbohydrate, 507 mg sodium, 8 mg cholesterol.

½ ounce dried porcini mushrooms
¾ cup wild rice
2 tablespoons butter
1 medium onion, chopped
1 teaspoon chopped fresh rosemary or ½ teaspoon dried, crumbled

1 cup shredded carrot
3 cups long-grain white rice
3 cans (13¾ ounces each) chicken broth, plus enough water to make 6 cups
½ teaspoon black pepper
¼ cup chopped fresh parsley

1. Cover dried mushrooms with warm water in a small bowl. Let stand 10 minutes or until softened. Drain; rinse; squeeze out excess water from mushrooms. Chop finely.

2. Combine wild rice and enough water in a medium-size saucepan to keep rice well covered. Bring to boiling. Lower heat; simmer, uncovered, until rice is tender and individual grains have opened, 45 to 50 minutes. Add water as needed to keep rice covered. Drain; keep warm.

3. Meanwhile, melt butter in a large saucepan over medium heat. Add onion, rosemary, mushrooms and carrot; cook, stirring, 6 minutes or until vegetables are softened. Add white rice, broth and pepper. Bring to boiling. Lower heat; cover and simmer 20 minutes or until rice is tender. Drain.

4. Mix wild rice, white rice and parsley in a serving bowl. Serve hot.

Vegetable fried rice

Makes 6 servings *Prep* 15 minutes *Cook* 30 minutes

A key ingredient in Asian cooking, soy sauce is made by fermenting boiled soybeans with roasted wheat or barley. To reduce the sodium in your cooking, look for "lite" or reduced-sodium versions.

Per serving
303 calories, 11 g protein, 9 g fat, 43 g carbohydrate, 695 mg sodium, 148 mg cholesterol.

2½ cups water
2 tablespoons reduced-sodium soy sauce
2 cloves garlic, finely chopped
1 cube chicken bouillon
1½ cups long-grain white rice
2 tablespoons vegetable oil
1 carrot, cut into ¼-inch-thick diagonal slices (1 cup)
2 ribs celery, cut into ¼-inch-thick diagonal slices (1 cup)
1 sweet green pepper, cored, seeded and cut into thin strips (1 cup)
1 large onion, halved lengthwise then thinly sliced crosswise
4 eggs
½ cup thinly sliced baked ham
¼ teaspoon black pepper

1. Bring water, soy sauce, garlic and bouillon cube to boiling in a medium-size saucepan, stirring to dissolve cube. Add rice; return to boiling. Lower heat; cover and simmer 20 minutes or until liquid is absorbed.

2. Meanwhile, heat 1 tablespoon oil in a large nonstick skillet over medium-high heat. Add carrot, celery, green pepper and onion; stir-fry 3 to 4 minutes. Add 3 tablespoons water; cover and cook 3 to 4 minutes. Uncover; stir-fry 3 to 4 minutes or until all liquid is absorbed and vegetables are tender. Remove vegetables with a slotted spoon to a medium-size bowl.

3. Lower heat to medium. Heat remaining tablespoon oil in skillet.

4. Whisk eggs in a small bowl. Add to skillet; cook, breaking up into small pieces as eggs set. Add rice and vegetable mixture to skillet. Stir in ham and black pepper. Stir until heated through. Serve immediately.

Making pilaf and risotto

1. Sauté finely chopped onion and any desired seasonings in olive oil, butter, or margarine until golden, about 5 minutes.

2. For pilaf, add long-grain white rice; **for risotto,** add short-grain white rice. Stir over moderate heat to coat rice, 1 to 2 minutes.

For pilaf, add all broth at once. Stir gently, lower heat and simmer, covered, without stirring, 20 minutes.

For risotto, add ½ cup broth; stir over low heat until liquid is absorbed. Repeat until 1 cup broth remains. Add remaining broth ⅓ cup at a time, stirring until rice is just cooked through.

Basic risotto

Makes 4 servings *Prep* 10 minutes *Cook* 35 to 40 minutes

Traditionally made with short-grain Arborio rice, which has a high starch content that thickens the cooking liquid, risotto is a wonderfully creamy rice dish. But don't get the wrong idea—this isn't mush; the grains of rice remain separate and firm and slightly chewy.

Per serving
306 calories, 10 g protein, 14 g fat, 34 g carbohydrate, 932 mg sodium, 025 mg cholesterol.

2 tablespoons butter or margarine
1 tablespoon olive oil
1 onion, finely chopped
1 cup Arborio or other short-grain white rice
4 cups lower-sodium chicken broth
½ cup grated Parmesan cheese

1. Heat 1 tablespoon butter and oil in a medium-size heavy saucepan over medium heat. Add onion; sauté until golden and softened, about 5 minutes. Stir in rice to coat, 1 to 2 minutes.

2. Add ½ cup chicken broth; stir until liquid is absorbed. Continue adding broth, ½ cup at a time, stirring constantly until each addition is absorbed before adding next ½ cup, until there is only 1 cup broth remaining.

3. Add remaining broth, ⅓ cup at a time, stirring and cooking until rice is just cooked through. Cooking time should be about 30 minutes. Finished dish should be creamy.

4. Stir in Parmesan and remaining tablespoon butter.

Butternut risotto

Makes 6 servings *Prep* 20 minutes *Cook* 30 minutes

To vary your squash repertoire, substitute the acorn variety, or even pumpkin, for the butternut.

Per serving
326 calories, 11 g protein, 14 g fat, 40 g carbohydrate, 1,080 mg sodium, 10 mg cholesterol.

2 tablespoons oil
1 tablespoon butter
1 large onion, diced
1½ cups Arborio rice
1 butternut squash (2 pounds), peeled, diced and cut into ½-inch pieces
5 cups chicken broth, heated
½ cup dry white wine
5 tablespoons grated Parmesan cheese
1 tablespoon chopped fresh parsley
⅛ teaspoon crushed dried rosemary
⅛ teaspoon black pepper
1 piece (6 ounces) prosciutto or ham, diced

1. Heat oil and butter in a large nonstick saucepan. Add onion; cook, stirring, until softened, 5 minutes. Add rice and squash; cook 5 minutes.

2. Add 1 cup hot broth. Cook, stirring, until broth is absorbed, 1 to 2 minutes. Stir in wine; cook, stirring occasionally, until wine is absorbed. Repeat with remaining broth, 1 cup at a time. After about 20 minutes, rice should be firm yet tender, with a creamy sauce.

3. Stir in Parmesan, parsley, rosemary, pepper and prosciutto. Serve at once.

Easy risotto with ham and corn

Makes 8 servings   *Prep* 10 minutes   *Cook* 30 to 35 minutes

Our no-stir risotto gives you time to fix a salad while the rice is cooking.

Per serving
378 calories, 19 g protein, 13 g fat, 46 g carbohydrate, 1,467 mg sodium, 42 mg cholesterol.

¼ cup olive oil
1 medium onion, chopped
2 cloves garlic, chopped
2 cups Arborio rice
½ cup dry white wine
3 cans (14½ ounces each) chicken broth
½ teaspoon salt

⅛ to ¼ teaspoon ground red pepper (cayenne)
1 package (16 ounces) frozen corn kernels, thawed
1 ham steak (about 1 pound), cut into ½-inch cubes
¼ pound Fontina cheese, shredded
2 tablespoons chopped fresh parsley for garnish

1. Heat oil in a large saucepan. Add onion and garlic; cook over medium heat 5 to 7 minutes or until softened.

2. Stir in rice to coat with oil; cook 2 minutes. Add wine; cook 1 minute. Add chicken broth. Bring to boiling. Lower heat; cover and simmer 20 minutes or until liquid is absorbed.

3. Stir in salt, ground red pepper, corn, ham and cheese. Cook over low heat, stirring occasionally, 2 minutes. Garnish with parsley and serve.

Easy risotto with ham and corn

Tropical couscous

Makes 8 servings *Prep* 20 minutes

Couscous—pasta granules made from semolina wheat—is a staple in the cuisine of North Africa. It is destined to become a favorite here too, since the only preparation it requires is a 5-minute soaking in hot water. Shown on page 155.

Per serving
178 calories, 5 g protein, 7 g fat, 26 g carbohydrate, 102 mg sodium, 0 mg cholesterol.

2¼ cups fresh orange juice
1 teaspoon ground cumin
1 box (10 ounces) couscous
2 tablespoons olive oil
2 tablespoons reduced-sodium soy sauce
2 tablespoons fresh lime juice
¼ cup chopped fresh cilantro
2 tablespoons chopped fresh basil or 1 teaspoon dried
2 tablespoons chopped fresh chives
1 teaspoon grated fresh ginger
1 mango, peeled, pitted and chopped
1 orange, peeled and chopped
¼ cup pine nuts, toasted

1. Bring juice and cumin to boiling in a medium-size saucepan. Add couscous; cover. Remove from heat and let stand 5 minutes. Remove to a large bowl; cool.

2. Mix oil, soy sauce and lime juice in a small bowl. Stir into couscous. Stir in cilantro, basil, chives, ginger, mango and orange. Sprinkle with nuts.

Couscous Casablanca

Makes 6 servings *Prep* 20 minutes *Cook* 12 minutes

Grated citrus rind adds fresh, bright flavor to foods. Be sure to include only the outer colored portion of the rind, not the bitter white pith just underneath.

Per serving
267 calories, 8 g protein, 6 g fat, 48 g carbohydrate, 483 mg sodium, 0 mg cholesterol.

1½ teaspoons ground cumin
½ teaspoon ground ginger
⅛ teaspoon ground cloves
⅛ teaspoon ground red pepper (cayenne)
2 tablespoons olive oil
1 red onion, halved lengthwise, then thinly sliced crosswise
1 sweet red pepper, cored, seeded and cut into 1-inch pieces
1 medium zucchini, halved lengthwise, cut into chunks
½ cup chopped dates
1 teaspoon salt
1 teaspoon grated orange rind
1 can (19 ounces) chick-peas, drained and rinsed
2 cups water
⅓ cup fresh orange juice
1 box (10 ounces) couscous
2 tablespoons chopped fresh mint

1. Heat cumin, ginger, cloves and ground red pepper in a large saucepan over medium-low heat, stirring, until fragrant, 1 minute. Add oil and onion; cook 5 minutes or until onion is softened.

2. Add sweet red pepper and zucchini; cook 5 minutes. Add dates, salt, orange rind and chick-peas; stir to mix. Add 2 cups water and orange juice. Increase heat to high. Bring to boiling. Stir in couscous. Remove from heat; cover and let stand 5 minutes. Fluff with a fork; stir in mint. Serve warm.

Zesty barley medley

Makes 6 servings   *Prep* 20 minutes   *Cook* 1¼ hours   *Refrigerate* several hours or overnight

Pearl barley has the outer husk and bran removed; the grain is then polished, or "pearled." Found in the rice section of the supermarket, barley has a nutty flavor and slightly chewy texture.

Per serving
217 calories, 19 g protein, 9 g fat, 16 g carbohydrate, 949 mg sodium, 43 mg cholesterol.

1 cup pearl barley
3 cups water
1½ teaspoons salt
2 jars (6 ounces each) marinated artichoke hearts, undrained
1 tablespoon fresh lemon juice
2 small cloves garlic, pressed
6 green onions, thinly sliced

¾ pound roasted turkey breast, cut into thin strips
1 medium zucchini, halved lengthwise, then cut crosswise into ¼-inch-thick slices (2 cups)
1 jar (7½ ounces) roasted red peppers, drained and chopped
½ teaspoon black pepper

1. Simmer barley in water with salt in a medium-size saucepan, covered, 1¼ hours or until water is absorbed and barley is tender.

2. Combine artichoke hearts with their liquid, lemon juice, garlic and green onions in a large bowl. Add cooked barley, turkey, zucchini, roasted peppers and black pepper. Refrigerate, covered, several hours or overnight. Serve chilled or at room temperature.

Wheat berry and shrimp salad

Makes 4 servings   *Prep* 15 minutes   *Soak* overnight   *Cook* 50 minutes   *Refrigerate* several hours

Wheat berries, an excellent source of B vitamins and iron, are the whole wheat grain with the fiber-rich bran still attached. They do need to be soaked before using, so plan accordingly.

Per serving
371 calories, 22 g protein, 15 g fat, 41 g carbohydrate, 730 mg sodium, 121 mg cholesterol.

1 cup wheat berries
3½ cups water
1 teaspoon salt
1 bunch asparagus (¾ pound), trimmed and cut into 1-inch pieces
¾ pound medium shrimp, peeled and deveined

1 sweet red pepper, cored, seeded and cut into thin strips
¼ cup olive oil
3 tablespoons balsamic vinegar
1½ teaspoons Dijon mustard
½ teaspoon dried thyme
1 clove garlic, finely chopped
¼ teaspoon black pepper

1. Soak wheat berries overnight in water. Drain, reserving soaking water. Add ¾ teaspoon salt and enough cold water to soaking water to equal 3½ cups. Bring to boiling in a medium-size saucepan. Add wheat berries; simmer 50 minutes or until tender.

2. Meanwhile, cook asparagus (see page 97) and cook and shell shrimp (see pages 17 and 220).

3. Combine cooked wheat berries, asparagus, shrimp and sweet red pepper in a large bowl. Combine oil, vinegar, mustard, thyme, garlic, remaining ¼ teaspoon salt and black pepper in a jar. Shake dressing; pour over mixture and toss to mix. Refrigerate several hours before serving.

Parmesan shrimp skewers
page 220

Broiled salmon with confetti salsa *page 204*

SOME INSIST on reeling in their own; others are perfectly content to let someone else do the water work. Either way, fish is close to being nature's ideal food. Besides being low in calories and fat, it's blessedly uncomplicated to prepare: You add a topping or a marinade, then bake, grill or broil your way to a tender, mouth-watering meal.

Experiment with different accents to find those most pleasing to your palate. There's everything from a parsley-caper sauce to oregano-walnut pesto. Best of all, toppings are generally interchangeable. For instance, one recipe matches

Savor a host of divine ideas
for the catch of the day.

a corn and red pepper salsa with broiled salmon, but you could use halibut, bluefish or tuna.

In the mood for shrimp? Sample Parmesan Shrimp Skewers or any of several other options, from scampi to jambalaya. Lobster? Steam it, or go all out with Linguine with Lobster Sauce.

No matter what you choose, you'll be pleased when dinner is a deep-water delight.

Crispy cornmeal catfish

Makes 4 servings   *Prep* 5 minutes   *Cook* 10 minutes

Catfish, most of which is now "farm raised," is firm fleshed, with a mild, almost sweet flavor. It has a tough skin that should be removed before cooking.

Per serving

294 calories, 20 g protein, 16 g fat, 15 g carbohydrate, 680 mg sodium, 76 mg cholesterol.

⅓ cup yellow cornmeal
¼ cup grated Parmesan cheese
1 tablespoon all-purpose flour
1 teaspoon dried basil, crumbled
1 teaspoon salt

⅛ teaspoon ground red pepper (cayenne)
1 egg
4 catfish fillets, about ½ inch thick (1 pound total)
1 tablespoon vegetable oil

1. Combine cornmeal, Parmesan, flour, basil, salt and red pepper in a shallow dish. Beat egg in a small bowl. Dip fillets in egg, then lightly coat in cornmeal mixture, shaking off excess.

2. Heat oil in a large nonstick skillet over medium heat. Working in batches if necessary, place fish in skillet; cook 4 minutes on each side or until cooked through.

Baked catfish with vegetables

Makes 4 servings   *Prep* 15 minutes   *Bake* at 350° for 35 minutes

The technique here—*en papillote*, or cooking in parchment paper or a foil packet—is ideally suited to fish because it makes overcooking almost impossible.

Per serving

237 calories, 24 g protein, 11 g fat, 9 g carbohydrate, 496 mg sodium, 94 mg cholesterol.

1 large carrot
1 leek, trimmed and well washed
2 tablespoons butter, cut into pieces
4 catfish fillets (1½ pounds total)
12 cherry tomatoes, halved

⅓ cup Spanish olives, sliced
⅓ cup dry white wine
½ teaspoon dried thyme
¼ teaspoon salt
⅛ teaspoon black pepper
⅓ cup fresh basil leaves, sliced

1. Heat oven to 350°. Cut four 12 x 12-inch pieces of aluminum foil.

2. Cut carrot and white and light green part of leek into matchstick strips.

3. Distributing it equally, place butter in center of each piece of foil. Top with fish, carrot, leek, tomatoes and olives.

4. Mix wine, thyme, salt, pepper and basil in a bowl; spoon over fish. Fold edges of foil together in a double pleat to seal. Place on a baking sheet.

5. Bake in heated 350° oven 35 minutes or until fish is opaque.

Catfish with poblano sauce

Makes 6 servings   *Prep* 15 minutes   *Cook* 25 minutes   *Bake* at 375° for 20 minutes

Poblano chiles range in hotness from mild to snappy. Roughly triangular in shape and 4 to 5 inches long, the chile turns reddish brown from green as it ripens and becomes sweeter in flavor. Serve this over cooked yellow rice.

Per serving
282 calories, 19 g protein, 19 g fat, 8 g carbohydrate, 350 mg sodium, 83 mg cholesterol.

Poblano sauce
1 pint half-and-half
1 fresh poblano chile, cored, seeded and cut into 1-inch pieces
1 sweet red pepper, cored, seeded and cut into 1-inch pieces
1 medium onion, diced
1 clove garlic, cut in half
¼ teaspoon dried tarragon

1 tablespoon all-purpose flour
½ teaspoon salt

Fish
1 tablespoon butter
¼ cup dry white wine
6 small catfish fillets (1½ pounds total)
¼ teaspoon salt
⅛ teaspoon black pepper

1. Heat oven to 375°.

2. Prepare sauce: Combine half-and-half, poblano, sweet red pepper, onion, garlic and tarragon in a saucepan. Bring to boiling. Lower heat; simmer 25 minutes. Add flour and salt. Puree in a blender; return to pan. Keep warm.

3. Prepare fish: Rub an 11 x 7 x 2-inch baking dish with butter. Add wine and fish. Sprinkle with salt and pepper. Cover with aluminum foil. Bake in heated 375° oven 20 minutes or until fish is easily flaked with a fork. Spoon sauce over top.

Cod Provençal

Makes 4 servings   *Prep* 10 minutes   *Cook* 12 minutes   *Bake* at 450° for 10 minutes

Mild-tasting cod takes well to baking, as in this recipe, but also benefits from poaching, steaming, braising, stewing, broiling, grilling and sautéing.

Per serving
244 calories, 28 g protein, 10 g fat, 12 g carbohydrate, 615 mg sodium, 61 mg cholesterol.

4 cod fillets (1¼ pounds total)
2 tablespoons olive oil
1 medium onion, chopped
2 cloves garlic, finely chopped
1 can (28 ounces) tomatoes, drained and chopped
1 tablespoon capers

¼ cup chopped fresh basil
8 black Greek olives, pitted
1 tablespoon fresh lemon juice
1 teaspoon dried oregano, crumbled
½ teaspoon salt (optional)
¼ teaspoon black pepper

1. Heat oven to 450°. Arrange fillets in an 8 x 8 x 2-inch baking dish.

2. Heat oil in a medium-size skillet over medium heat, add onion and garlic and sauté 3 to 5 minutes or until slightly softened. Add tomatoes, capers, basil, olives, lemon juice, oregano, salt if using and pepper. Simmer, stirring occasionally, 8 minutes. Spoon sauce over fish.

3. Bake in heated 450° oven 10 minutes or until cooked through.

Cod fillets with parsley-caper sauce

Makes 4 servings   *Prep* 10 minutes   *Bake* at 400° for 25 minutes

Made with a bottled dressing, this easy sauce is a tasty garnish with most fish, whether mild like cod, halibut, haddock or tilefish, or more strongly flavored like mackerel or bluefish.

Per serving
341 calories, 38 g protein, 19 g fat, 3 g carbohydrate, 917 mg sodium, 115 mg cholesterol.

4 cod fillets or other firm-fleshed white fish fillets (1½ pounds total)
2 teaspoons olive oil
2 teaspoons finely chopped garlic
¼ teaspoon salt
⅛ teaspoon black pepper

1 tomato, sliced
¾ cup bottled Caesar salad dressing
¼ cup finely chopped fresh parsley
2 to 4 teaspoons fresh lemon juice
2 tablespoons drained capers

1. Heat oven to 400°. Arrange cod fillets in an 11 x 7 x 2-inch baking dish.

2. Stir together oil, garlic, salt and pepper in a small dish. Brush or drizzle about two-thirds of mixture over fish. Arrange tomato slices over top; brush or drizzle with remaining oil mixture.

3. Bake in heated 400° oven 25 minutes or until opaque in center and fish just begins to flake when tested with a fork.

4. Meanwhile, stir together dressing, parsley, lemon juice and capers in a small bowl. Serve with cod.

Creamy Cajun flounder
opposite

Creamy Cajun flounder

Makes 4 servings   *Prep* 10 minutes   *Cook* 5 minutes   *Bake* at 400° for 15 minutes

You can't get much leaner than flounder: only 1 gram of fat per 3-ounce cooked portion. The flat, thin fillets are ideally suited for stuffing and baking, as well as poaching, steaming and sautéing.

Per serving
263 calories, 33 g protein, 4 g fat, 29 g carbohydrate, 755 mg sodium, 68 mg cholesterol.

1 teaspoon olive oil
1 onion, chopped
1 clove garlic, finely chopped
1 sweet red pepper, cored, seeded and chopped
1 teaspoon dried thyme, crumbled
⅔ cup canned black beans, drained and rinsed
⅔ cup packaged corn-bread stuffing mix

4 flounder fillets (1¼ pounds total)
½ teaspoon paprika
1 cup vegetable broth
2 teaspoons cornstarch
2 teaspoons hot-pepper sauce
⅛ teaspoon salt
2 tablespoons nonfat sour cream
1 teaspoon fresh lemon juice

1. Heat oven to 400°. Coat an 8 x 8 x 2-inch baking dish with nonstick cooking spray.

2. Heat oil in a medium-size nonstick skillet over medium heat. Add onion, garlic, red pepper and thyme; sauté until softened, about 5 minutes.

3. Remove half of vegetable mixture to a medium-size bowl; reserve remainder in skillet. Stir beans and stuffing mix into mixture in bowl.

4. Place fillets flat on a work surface. Spoon vegetable-stuffing mixture in center of each fillet, dividing equally. Fold fillets in half over mixture. Place fillets in prepared baking dish. Sprinkle with paprika.

5. Bake fish in heated 400° oven 15 minutes or until fillets just begin to flake when tested with a fork.

6. Meanwhile, whisk together broth, cornstarch, hot-pepper sauce and salt in a small bowl. Stir into vegetable mixture remaining in skillet. Heat over medium heat, stirring, until thickened, about 2 minutes. Remove from heat. Stir in sour cream and lemon juice. Serve sauce with fish.

FISH AND SHELLFISH

Gingered flounder in parchment

A meal in a packet—and low-fat at that—with no pots or pans to wash. A loaf of bread and frozen yogurt with berries would be lovely accompaniments.

Per serving
294 calories, 20 g protein, 16 g fat, 15 g carbohydrate, 680 mg sodium, 76 mg cholesterol.

3 tablespoons reduced-sodium soy sauce
2 tablespoons olive oil
1 clove garlic, finely chopped
1 tablespoon grated fresh ginger
4 flounder fillets (1¼ pounds total)

3 ounces snow peas, trimmed
1 small sweet red pepper, cored, seeded and cut into thin strips
1 carrot, cut into thin strips
⅓ cup chopped green onion

1. Heat oven to 375°. Combine soy sauce, oil, garlic, ginger and fish in a bowl. Refrigerate 10 minutes.

2. Cut four 20-inch lengths of parchment paper or foil; fold each in half. Starting at folded edge, cut out half a heart shape. Open hearts on a flat surface. Spread one-quarter of vegetables on one side of each heart. Place a fish fillet on top of each; spoon remaining marinade over fillets. Fold paper over; seal by double-pleating edges. Place packets on a large baking sheet.

3. Bake in heated 375° oven 15 to 20 minutes or until fish flakes easily with a fork; carefully open one packet to test. If using foil packets, check fish after 12 minutes. Open packets; serve.

Mediterranean flounder roll-ups

An easy skillet dinner with a touch of the Mediterranean: black olives, tomatoes and olive oil. Thin fillets of sole or turbot can be substituted for the flounder.

Per serving
304 calories, 27 g protein, 10 g fat, 26 g carbohydrate, 819 mg sodium, 63 mg cholesterol.

6 flounder fillets (1½ pounds total)
1 package (6.8 ounces) Spanish rice mix
2 tablespoons olive oil
1 cup water

1 can (8 ounces) tomatoes, cut up
¼ cup sliced ripe black olives
½ cup shredded Monterey Jack cheese (2 ounces)

1. Beginning at narrow end, tightly roll up flounder fillets.

2. Prepare rice mix in a skillet, following package directions and using 2 tablespoons olive oil for sautéing and 1 cup water plus 1 can of tomatoes for cooking liquid.

3. When mixture begins to boil, arrange rolled-up fish, seam side down, over rice mixture. Cover; lower heat and simmer 15 minutes.

4. Sprinkle olives on top; cover and cook another 3 to 5 minutes or until rice is cooked and fish is tender. Remove from heat. Sprinkle cheese over fish; cover and let stand until cheese begins to melt.

Poached fillets with tropical salsa

Makes 4 servings *Prep* 10 minutes *Stand* 10 minutes *Microwave* 3 to 4 minutes

Although poaching works beautifully in a microwave oven, you can also poach on top of the stove. Cover the fish and liquid with a piece of buttered waxed paper, buttered side down, and simmer until the fish is cooked. Make sure there's enough liquid in the pan to almost cover the fish.

Per serving
199 calories, 32 g protein, 3 g fat, 10 g carbohydrate, 406 mg sodium, 82 mg cholesterol.

1 clove garlic, finely chopped
1 large ripe mango, peeled, pitted and finely chopped
2 green onions, white part only, finely chopped
½ teaspoon salt
⅛ teaspoon black pepper
  Pinch red-pepper flakes
½ teaspoon vegetable oil
  Juice of ½ lemon
4 flounder fillets (1½ pounds total)
½ cup fresh orange juice

1. Place garlic in a small glass dish. Cover loosely with microwave-safe plastic wrap. Microwave on 100% power 50 seconds. Remove to a medium-size bowl. Mash with a fork.

2. Add mango, green onions, ¼ teaspoon salt, black pepper, red-pepper flakes, oil and 1 teaspoon lemon juice to garlic and stir. Cover and let stand 10 minutes.

3. Meanwhile, place fish fillets in a microwave-safe baking dish just large enough to hold fish in a single layer. Season with remaining ¼ teaspoon salt. Pour orange juice and remaining lemon juice over fish.

4. Cover tightly with microwave-safe plastic wrap or with lid. Microwave at 100% power 3 to 4 minutes or until fish is opaque in center. Let stand 1 minute. Carefully pierce plastic wrap or remove lid to release steam; uncover. Remove fillets with a slotted spoon to serving plates. Serve with salsa.

The best catch

WHENEVER possible, buy fresh fish that's openly displayed on ice in refrigerator cases. Fresh ocean fish smells pleasantly briny—not fishy. When you get it home, rinse with cold water, pat dry and place in an airtight plastic bag. Refrigerate until ready to cook, for no more than 1 day.

Whole fish: Look for tiny scales, bright, clear eyes that bulge a little, and red gills (lift outer flap slightly to peak inside).

Fillets, steaks and other cuts: Choose those that are springy to the touch and have firm, translucent flesh without tears or blemishes.

Frozen fish: Check for packages that are intact and frozen solid, with no ice crystals or discoloration visible. Store in the freezer in original wrapping at 0° for up to 6 months. Thaw overnight in the refrigerator. For a hurry-up defrost, thaw in the original wrapper under cold running water. Or thaw in a microwave following the instructions in the owner's manual.

Flounder primavera

Makes 6 servings *Prep* 15 minutes *Cook* 20 minutes

Keep dinner simple: Serve with steamed sliced red potatoes with their skins left on and lemon wedges for jazzing up the flavor.

Per serving
320 calories, 30 g protein, 13 g fat, 18 g carbohydrate, 566 mg sodium, 181 mg cholesterol.

⅓ cup all-purpose flour
3 eggs
2 tablespoons butter
2 tablespoons vegetable oil
6 flounder fillets (1¾ pounds total)
1 leek, trimmed and well washed, cut into 2-inch pieces, then thinly sliced lengthwise
3 carrots, cut into 2-inch pieces, then thinly sliced lengthwise
¼ teaspoon salt
⅛ teaspoon black pepper
¾ cup chicken broth
¼ cup dry white wine
1 tablespoon fresh lemon juice
3 tablespoons capers, drained

1. Place flour on a small plate; lightly beat eggs in a small bowl.

2. Heat half of butter and oil in a large nonstick skillet. Coat 3 fillets with flour; dip in eggs. Add to skillet and cook 2½ minutes per side or until lightly golden. Remove to a platter. Repeat with remaining butter, oil and fillets.

3. Add leek, carrots, salt and pepper to skillet; sauté 4 minutes. Add broth, wine, lemon juce and capers. Cover; cook 6 minutes. Spoon over fish.

Salmon with dilled potatoes

Makes 4 servings *Prep* 15 minutes *Cook* 12 minutes *Grill or broil* 10 minutes

What could be more summery than this combo: mustard-glazed grilled salmon and creamy dilled potatoes? Want to drop the fat and calories a little more? Use reduced-fat or nonfat sour cream.

Per serving
399 calories, 31 g protein, 18 g fat, 29 g carbohydrate, 601 mg sodium, 83 mg cholesterol.

½ cup sour cream
½ cup plain low-fat yogurt
4 tablespoons Dijon mustard
1 tablespoon plus 1 teaspoon chopped fresh dill
   Salt and black pepper to taste
1½ pounds new potatoes, cut into ¼-inch-thick slices
10 ounces fresh spinach, stemmed, washed and chopped
4 salmon fillets (1 pound total)
1 teaspoon olive oil

1. Stir sour cream, yogurt, 3 tablespoons mustard, 1 tablespoon dill, salt and pepper in a large bowl. Cook potatoes in a large saucepan of boiling water 10 minutes. Add spinach. Cook another 2 minutes or until potatoes are tender. Drain. Add to sour cream mixture and stir well.

2. Meanwhile, prepare a charcoal grill with hot coals, or heat a gas grill to high, or heat broiler.

3. Spread fillets with remaining 1 tablespoon mustard. Sprinkle with salt, pepper and remaining 1 teaspoon dill. Drizzle with oil. Grill or broil salmon 4 to 6 inches from heat 10 minutes or until cooked through. Let stand off heat 5 minutes. Serve with potatoes.

Salmon with dilled potatoes, *opposite*

203

Key West grilled salmon

Makes 4 servings *Prep* 15 minutes *Refrigerate* 10 minutes *Grill* 4 minutes *or broil* 8 minutes

The citrusy marinade not only is a flavorful partner to salmon but complements most richly flavored fish, such as tuna and mackerel.

Per serving
269 calories, 28 g protein, 16 g fat, 2 g carbohydrate, 330 mg sodium, 78 mg cholesterol.

⅓ cup lime juice (2 limes)
2 tablespoons olive oil
½ teaspoon salt
½ teaspoon celery seeds
⅛ teaspoon black pepper
Few drops hot-pepper sauce

4 salmon steaks (1½ pounds total), each ¾ inch thick
¼ cup chopped green onion
1 tablespoon water
¼ teaspoon honey

1. Combine lime juice, oil, salt, celery seeds, black pepper and hot-pepper sauce in a small bowl. Place salmon in a shallow dish. Pour ¼ cup lime juice mixture over fish; turn to coat. Refrigerate 10 minutes, turning once. Reserve remaining mixture for sauce.

2. Prepare a charcoal grill with hot coals, or heat a gas grill to high, or heat broiler. Position grill rack 6 inches from coals or broiler pan 3 inches from heat.

3. Stir green onion, water and honey into reserved lime juice mixture.

4. Grease grill rack or rack of a shallow roasting pan. Place salmon on rack. Drizzle with half of lime juice mixture from marinade dish. Grill over hot coals on covered grill 2 minutes per side or until cooked through, or broil 4 minutes per side. Serve salmon with green onion sauce.

Broiled salmon with confetti salsa

Makes 4 servings *Prep* 10 minutes *Refrigerate* 30 minutes *Broil* 8 minutes

Once raw fish has been marinated, discard the marinade. Or if you wish to use it as a sauce, boil it for at least 3 minutes.
Shown on page 195.

Per serving
308 calories, 31 g protein, 10 g fat, 24 g carbohydrate, 375 mg sodium, 78 mg cholesterol.

2 tablespoons reduced-sodium soy sauce
1 tablespoon fresh lemon juice
1 clove garlic, mashed
2 teaspoons sugar
1 salmon fillet (1¼ pounds)
1 teaspoon coarse black pepper

Confetti salsa
1 package (10 ounces) frozen corn kernels, thawed
1 jar (7 ounces) water-packed roasted red peppers, drained (reserve liquid) and chopped

1. Combine soy sauce, lemon juice, garlic and sugar in a shallow baking dish. Place salmon in dish, turning to coat both sides of fish. Cover with plastic wrap and refrigerate 30 minutes. Turn the fish over in the marinade several times.

2. Heat broiler.

3. Remove salmon from marinade; sprinkle both sides with pepper. Place salmon on a rack in a roasting pan.

4. Broil 4 inches from heat, turning once, about 4 minutes per side or until fish just begins to flake when tested with a fork.

5. Meanwhile, prepare confetti salsa: Combine corn, roasted peppers and reserved roasted pepper liquid in a small saucepan. Bring to boiling; remove from heat. Serve salsa with salmon.

Chilled poached salmon

Makes 6 servings *Prep* 20 minutes *Cook* 10 minutes

For a no-fuss summer supper, serve this with a salad of mixed greens. The avocado cream will do nicely on any cold poached fish and is also terrific as a dressing for chicken salad.

Per serving
309 calories, 44 g protein, 13 g fat, 3 g carbohydrate, 248 mg sodium, 111 mg cholesterol.

3 slices onion
6 salmon steaks (3 pounds total), each ¾ inch thick
1 cup dry white wine
2 cups fresh orange juice
1 teaspoon dried thyme

Avocado-cilantro cream
½ avocado, peeled, pitted and cubed
½ cup reduced-fat sour cream

2 teaspoons fresh lime juice
1 tablespoon chopped fresh cilantro
¼ teaspoon salt
6 drops hot-pepper sauce

Fresh cilantro sprigs for garnish
Lime wedges for garnish

1. Place onion slices in bottom of a deep skillet with lid or Dutch oven large enough to just hold salmon in a single layer. Arrange salmon steaks on top. Add wine, orange juice and thyme.

2. Cover and bring just to simmering over medium-low heat. Cook 10 minutes or until salmon is firm to the touch and cooked through. Remove from heat; cool salmon in cooking liquid. Store, covered and refrigerated, up to 2 days.

3. Prepare avocado-cilantro cream: Combine avocado, sour cream, lime juice, cilantro, salt and hot-pepper sauce in a blender or food processor. Whirl until smooth.

4. Arrange salmon on plates. Dollop sauce on top. Garnish with cilantro sprigs and lime wedges.

Teriyaki salmon

If soba, Japanese buckwheat noodles, are not near at hand, substitute linguine or just plain spaghetti. If you're crazy about tuna or bluefish, they marry well with the teriyaki sauce.

Per serving
580 calories, 48 g protein,
18 g fat, 58 g carbohydrate,
870 mg sodium,
111 mg cholesterol.

2 tablespoons soy sauce
2 tablespoons dry sherry
1 tablespoon sugar
1 tablespoon rice-wine vinegar
1½ teaspoons finely chopped fresh ginger
1 clove garlic, chopped
½ teaspoon Chinese five-spice powder
4 salmon fillets (1½ pounds total)
8 ounces soba noodles, cooked and cooled
½ cup bottled peanut sauce
3 green onions, sliced

1. Combine soy sauce, sherry, sugar, vinegar, ginger, garlic and five-spice powder in a plastic food-storage bag; squeeze to mix. Remove and reserve half of marinade. Add salmon to bag; seal and refrigerate 1 hour.

2. Prepare a charcoal grill with medium-hot coals, or heat a gas grill to medium-high, or heat broiler. Oil grill or broiler-pan rack.

3. Grill salmon, skin side down, 6 to 8 minutes or until cooked. Or broil 6 inches from heat 6 minutes or until cooked.

4. Toss noodles, peanut sauce, reserved marinade and green onions in a large bowl. Divide noodles among 4 plates. Top with salmon.

Zesty snapper fillets

If juicy-ripe fresh tomatoes are in season, by all means use them instead of the canned.

Per serving
143 calories, 27 g protein,
2 g fat, 4 g carbohydrate,
605 mg sodium,
47 mg cholesterol.

1 can (8 ounces) whole tomatoes, drained and chopped
2 tablespoons finely chopped onion
1 tablespoon finely chopped fresh ginger
1 clove garlic, finely chopped
1 teaspoon finely chopped jalapeño chile
1 teaspoon salt
4 red snapper fillets (1 pound total)

1. Heat oven to 500°. Tear off four 15 x 12-inch sheets of aluminum foil. Combine tomatoes, onion, ginger, garlic, jalapeño and ½ teaspoon salt in a small bowl; set the salsa aside.

2. Sprinkle snapper fillets with remaining ½ teaspoon salt. Place 1 fillet on each piece of foil. Top each fillet with 2 tablespoons salsa. Seal packets tightly, folding the edges over twice.

3. Heat a large baking sheet in heated 500° oven about 2 minutes.

4. Place packets on heated baking sheet; bake 8 minutes or until fish is cooked through. Let each diner carefully cut open his or her own packet.

"Stuffed" sole fillets

Makes 4 servings   *Prep* 10 minutes   *Cook* 8 minutes   *Bake* at 400° for 12 to 15 minutes

Buy sole fillets of equal size so that a stack of two will simulate a small whole fish. Flounder works well too.

Per serving
204 calories, 25 g protein, 6 g fat, 11 g carbohydrate, 744 mg sodium, 67 mg cholesterol.

3 teaspoons olive oil
¼ cup diced celery
2 large shallots or 1 medium onion, finely chopped
2 cloves garlic, finely chopped
¼ cup dry plain bread crumbs
½ cup medium-hot salsa

¼ teaspoon salt
⅛ teaspoon black pepper
4 sole fillets (2 pounds total)
½ cup chicken broth
2 tablespoons dry white wine
Chopped fresh parsley for garnish

1. Heat oven to 400°.

2. Heat 1 teaspoon oil in a small nonstick skillet. Add celery, shallots and garlic; sauté 5 minutes or until glazed. Stir in bread crumbs; heat, stirring occasionally, just to toast crumbs, about 3 minutes. Remove from heat. Stir in salsa, salt and pepper.

3. Place 2 fillets side by side in a small shallow baking dish. Spread salsa mixture evenly over each. Top with remaining fillets. Drizzle remaining oil over fish. Pour broth and wine around fish. Cover fish with waxed paper.

4. Bake in heated 400° oven 12 to 15 minutes or until fish just begins to flake when pierced with a fork. Cut each fillet stack crosswise in half. Pour pan liquid over fish. Garnish with parsley.

FISH AND SHELLFISH

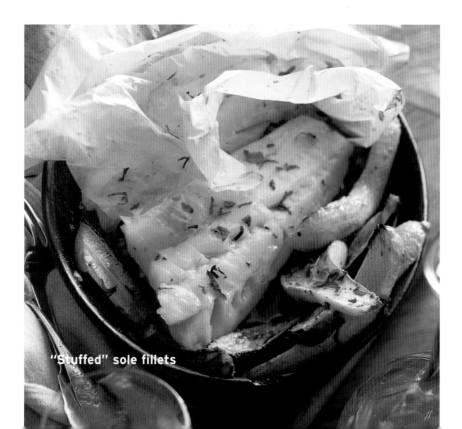
"Stuffed" sole fillets

"Fried" sole with tartar sauce

Makes 4 servings   *Prep* 15 minutes   *Broil* 8 minutes

This sole tastes like it's fried, but it's actually baked with a crunchy cornflake coating. This cooking method—as well as broiling, grilling and steaming—keeps fish lean.

Per serving
408 calories, 49 g protein,
9 g fat, 29 g carbohydrate,
1,018 mg sodium,
134 mg cholesterol.

¾ cup cornflake crumbs
1 tablespoon chili powder
1 teaspoon ground cumin
½ teaspoon onion powder
½ teaspoon ground red pepper (cayenne)

4 sole or flounder fillets (2 pounds total)
3 tablespoons reduced-fat mayonnaise
Tartar Sauce (recipe follows)
Fresh parsley sprigs for garnish
Lemon wedges for garnish

1. Heat broiler. Grease a large baking sheet.

2. Combine cornflake crumbs, chili powder, cumin, onion powder and ground red pepper on a large sheet of waxed paper. Brush each fillet with about 1 teaspoon mayonnaise per side. Dip fillets into crumb mixture, coating both sides. Spray both sides of each fillet with nonstick cooking spray. Place on prepared baking sheet.

3. Broil 5 inches from heat, without turning, 8 to 10 minutes or until fish just begins to flake and coating is golden. Serve with Tartar Sauce. Garnish with parsley sprigs and lemon wedges.

Tartar sauce

Per tablespoon
43 calories, 0 g protein,
3 g fat, 3 g carbohydrate,
168 mg sodium,
0 mg cholesterol.

Combine ½ cup reduced-fat mayonnaise, ¼ cup sweet relish, 2 tablespoons chopped fresh tarragon, 1 tablespoon chopped parsley, 1 tablespoon chopped capers, 1 tablespoon Dijon mustard, 1 tablespoon fresh lemon juice and ⅛ teaspoon ground red pepper (cayenne) in a small bowl. Cover and refrigerate until ready to use. Makes about 1 cup.

Fish substitutions

If a recipe calls for	SOLE	RED SNAPPER	BLUEFISH	COD	TUNA
You can also use	flounder, tilapia, rainbow trout, catfish, fluke	rockfish, weakfish, sea bass, grouper, orange roughy	lake trout, mackerel, shad, sturgeon	tilefish, haddock, halibut	swordfish, mahi-mahi, mako shark, salmon
Characteristics	thin, tender, lean, mild- to medium-flavored fillets	thin, firm, lean, mild- to medium-flavored fillets	thick, firm, dark-fleshed, oily, strong-flavored fillets	thick, firm, lean, mild-flavored steaks, fillets	thick, firm, slightly oily, full-flavored steaks, fillets

Baked stuffed sole

Makes 6 servings   *Prep* 20 minutes   *Bake* at 400° for 42 minutes

Elegant but easy to prepare, this recipe is perfect for parties.

Per serving
306 calories, 32 g protein, 14 g fat, 11 g carbohydrate, 552 mg sodium, 103 mg cholesterol.

3 ribs celery, cut into 2½-inch-long strips
2 carrots, peeled and cut into 2½-inch-long strips
1 large leek, trimmed and well washed, white and light green parts cut lengthwise into 2½-inch-long strips
2 tablespoons olive oil
1 tomato, seeded and diced
½ pound surimi, cut into 2½-inch-long strips
1 teaspoon salt
½ teaspoon garlic powder
½ teaspoon onion powder
¼ teaspoon black pepper
6 sole fillets (2 pounds total)
½ cup coarsely chopped fresh basil
⅓ cup dry white wine
6 sprigs fresh thyme or ½ teaspoon dried
¼ cup (½ stick) butter
2 tablespoons fresh lemon juice

1. Heat oven to 400°. Toss together celery, carrots, leek and oil in a flame-proof 13 x 9 x 2-inch baking pan.

2. Roast vegetables in heated 400° oven 20 minutes, stirring once or twice during cooking. Add tomato and surimi. Bake another 10 minutes. Remove vegetables from pan and reserve.

3. Mix salt, garlic powder, onion powder and pepper in a small cup; reserve half. Season skinned side of each fillet with remaining salt mixture. Spoon roasted vegetables over half of each fillet, dividing equally. Top vegetables with basil, dividing equally. Fold empty half of fillet over filled half; place in roasting pan. Drizzle with wine. Season with remaining salt mixture. Place a sprig of thyme on top of each fillet. Cover pan with aluminum foil.

4. Bake in heated 400° oven 12 minutes or until fish is cooked through. Remove to a serving platter; keep warm.

5. On top of stove, reduce cooking liquid in pan by half. Whisk in butter and lemon juice. Serve with fish.

Asian trout bundles

Makes 4 servings *Prep* 10 minutes *Bake* at 425° for 10 to 12 minutes

Cooking in a packet guarantees the fish will arrive at the table delectably moist.

Per serving
244 calories, 31 g protein,
9 g fat, 10 g carbohydrate,
551 mg sodium,
82 mg cholesterol.

4 green onions, cut into thin diagonal slices
1 large sweet red pepper, cored, seeded and cut into matchstick strips
2 tablespoons soy sauce
2 tablespoons red-wine vinegar
2 teaspoons dark Asian sesame oil
2 teaspoons grated fresh ginger or ½ teaspoon ground ginger
1 tablespoon sugar
4 trout fillets (1 pound total)
4 teaspoons sesame seeds

1. Heat oven to 425°. Tear off four 14 x 12-inch sheets of aluminum foil.

2. Combine green onions, red pepper strips, soy sauce, vinegar, sesame oil, ginger and sugar in a medium-size bowl. Arrange each fillet on a piece of foil. Spoon green onion mixture over top of each fillet, dividing equally. Sprinkle each fillet with 1 teaspoon sesame seeds. Fold top of foil over fish. Fold edges of foil over twice; crimp to seal tightly . Arrange packets on a baking sheet.

3. Bake in heated 425° oven 10 to 12 minutes or until foil is puffed and fish is cooked through.

Grilled tuna Niçoise

Makes 4 servings *Prep* 20 minutes *Grill* 6 to 10 minutes

This renowned French dish gets its punch from capers, the flower buds of a bush native to the Mediterranean region. Capers can be found in the condiment section of the supermarket. Just a small amount adds a lot of flavor.

Per serving
317 calories, 36 g protein,
17 g fat, 4 g carbohydrate,
809 mg sodium,
69 mg cholesterol.

4 tablespoons olive oil
1 tablespoon mashed anchovies
1 clove garlic, crushed
2 small tomatoes (about ¾ pound total), seeded and diced
¼ cup chopped, pitted Kalamata olives
3 tablespoons capers, drained and rinsed
2 tablespoons chopped fresh basil
1 tablespoon chopped fresh thyme
½ teaspoon black pepper
4 tuna steaks (1¼ pounds total), each 1 inch thick
½ teaspoon salt
Fresh thyme sprigs for garnish

1. Prepare a charcoal grill with hot coals, or heat a gas grill to high.

2. Stir together 2 tablespoons oil, anchovies and garlic in a medium-size bowl. Add tomatoes, olives, capers, basil, thyme and pepper; toss to mix.

3. Rinse tuna steaks and pat dry. Brush with the remaining 2 tablespoons olive oil. Sprinkle with salt. Grill tuna 3 minutes per side for medium-rare or until desired doneness. Place on 4 plates. Spoon tomato mixture over tuna. Garnish with thyme sprigs.

Tropical tuna

Makes 4 servings *Prep* 20 minutes *Refrigerate* up to 2 hours *Grill or broil* 10 minutes

Here's a prizewinner from a contest sponsored by *Family Circle* magazine along with the Florida Citrus Growers. The challenge was to come up with a healthy main dish using orange or grapefruit juice—this recipe from Margee Berry of Buffalo, West Virginia, uses both.

Per serving
332 calories, 33 g protein, 15 g fat, 15 g carbohydrate, 58 mg sodium, 50 mg cholesterol.

4 tuna steaks (1¼ pounds total), each 1 inch thick
3 tablespoons grapefruit juice
2 tablespoons olive oil
1 teaspoon ground cumin

Salsa
2 oranges, peeled, white pith removed, seeded and diced
¼ cup finely chopped red onion
¼ cup chopped fresh cilantro
1 jalapeño chile, seeded and finely chopped
¼ cup fresh orange juice
1 teaspoon ground cumin
1 medium avocado

1. Rinse tuna and pat dry.

2. Combine grapefruit juice, oil and cumin in a shallow glass baking dish. Add tuna; turn to coat both sides. Marinate, covered, in refrigerator at least 15 minutes or up to 2 hours.

3. Prepare salsa: Combine oranges, onion, cilantro, jalapeño, orange juice and cumin in a medium-size bowl. Cover and refrigerate.

4. Prepare a charcoal grill with hot coals, or heat a gas grill to medium-high, or heat broiler. Remove tuna from marinade. Grill or broil, turning once, 10 minutes or until just cooked through. Meanwhile, peel, pit and chop avocado. Stir into salsa. Place tuna on individual plates and top with salsa.

Grilled tuna Niçoise
opposite

Baked clams

Makes 12 servings   *Prep* 5 minutes   *Bake* at 350° for 20 minutes

If you can get good-quality fresh clams from a reliable source, use them instead of the canned.

Per serving
60 calories, 4 g protein,
1 g fat, 9 g carbohydrate,
305 mg sodium,
9 mg cholesterol.

12 mini pita rounds or 24 clam shell halves (about 2 inches)
2 cans (6½ ounces each) minced clams, undrained
1 teaspoon finely chopped garlic

⅔ cup seasoned sodium-free bread crumbs
1 ounce turkey pepperoni, diced (about ¼ cup)
Lemon wedges for garnish

1. Heat oven to 350°. If using mini pitas, split them in half, coat with nonstick cooking spray and place on a baking sheet. Bake until crisp, about 10 minutes. If using clam shell halves, place them on a baking sheet.

2. Combine undrained clams, garlic and bread crumbs in a small bowl. Spoon about 1 tablespoon clam mixture into each pita half or clam shell. Sprinkle with pepperoni.

3. Bake in heated 350° oven until heated through, about 10 minutes. Garnish with lemon wedges.

Warm clam dip

Makes 16 servings (4 cups)   *Prep* 5 minutes   *Bake* at 350° for 30 minutes

Serve with a platter of cut-up fresh vegetables, such as sweet peppers carrots and celery, and a plate of assorted crackers, toasts and bagel chips.

Per serving
78 calories, 5 g protein,
4 g fat, 6 g carbohydrate,
334 mg sodium,
17 mg cholesterol.

3 cans (6½ ounces each) minced clams
8 ounces less-fat cream cheese
3 ounces nonfat cream cheese
2 tablespoons skim milk

½ cup chopped green onion
1 tablespoon fresh lemon juice
¼ teaspoon hot-pepper sauce
24 reduced-fat buttery crackers, finely crushed (1 cup)

1. Heat oven to 350°.

2. Drain 2 cans of clams and reserve juice for another use.

3. Beat cream cheeses and milk in a large bowl until fluffy. Stir in 2 drained cans and 1 undrained can of clams. Add green onion, lemon juice and hot-pepper sauce; beat until combined. Stir in crushed crackers. Scrape clam mixture into a 9-inch glass pie plate.

4. Bake in heated 350° oven 30 minutes or until center is set. Serve warm.

Crab imperial

This classy appetizer will satisfy even your fussiest guests.

Per serving
83 calories, 2 g protein, 7 g fat, 4 g carbohydrate, 196 mg sodium, 11 mg cholesterol.

6 portabella mushrooms
  Olive oil
¼ teaspoon salt
⅛ teaspoon black pepper
1 pound crabmeat or surimi
2 tablespoons finely chopped celery
2 tablespoons finely chopped sweet red or green pepper
3 tablespoons mayonnaise
2 tablespoons fresh lemon juice

1 tablespoon dry sherry
1 teaspoon Worcestershire sauce
  Few drops hot-pepper sauce
1 tablespoon chopped fresh parsley
½ cup dry plain bread crumbs
2 tablespoons unsalted butter, melted
¼ cup grated Parmesan or Romano cheese

1. Heat broiler.

2. Lightly brush mushrooms with oil. Sprinkle with salt and pepper. Place on broiler pan and broil 5 minutes. Remove and cool slightly. Lower oven temperature to 400°.

3. Combine crabmeat, celery, sweet pepper, mayonnaise, lemon juice, sherry, Worcestershire sauce, hot-pepper sauce and parsley in a large bowl. Combine bread crumbs, butter and Parmesan in a small bowl. Divide crab mixture among mushrooms. Evenly distribute bread crumb mixture on top. Place mushrooms in baking pan. Bake in heated 400° oven 15 minutes or until golden brown.

Crabmeat pasta salad

Ready in practically no time at all, this crabmeat pasta salad can be made up to a day ahead and refrigerated.

Per serving
342 calories, 14 g protein, 18 g fat, 31 g carbohydrate, 524 mg sodium, 38 mg cholesterol.

1½ pounds fusilli
1½ bunches fresh dill
1½ cups fresh parsley leaves
3 green onions, sliced
2 tablespoons capers
2 tablespoons water

1 tablespoon fresh lemon juice
1 teaspoon salt
½ teaspoon black pepper
1 container (8 ounces) sour cream
½ cup mayonnaise
1 pound lump crabmeat or surimi

1. Cook fusilli in a large pot of lightly salted boiling water until al dente, firm but tender. Drain, cool under tap water and drain again.

2. Combine dill, parsley, green onions, capers, water, lemon juice, salt and pepper in a food processor. Puree; transfer to a large bowl. Stir in sour cream and mayonnaise. Fold in crabmeat and pasta.

FISH AND SHELLFISH

Steamed lobster

Just a little melted butter for dipping, corn on the cob and steamed new potatoes are all it takes to make this dinner a real pleaser.

Per serving
111 calories, 23 g protein, 1 g fat, 1 g carbohydrate, 431 mg sodium, 81 mg cholesterol.

2 quarts water
2 tablespoons salt
4 live Maine lobsters (about 1½ pounds each)

2 lemons, cut into wedges
  Fresh parsley sprigs for garnish
¾ cup (1½ sticks) unsalted butter, melted (optional)

1. Place a steamer rack, vegetable steamer basket or small cooling rack in a very large canning pot or stockpot (16 quarts) with lid. Add water and salt. Bring to boiling.

2. Holding a lobster by its body, near head, place head-first in pot. Repeat with others. Cover. Return water to boiling. Steam, covered, 15 minutes. Remove lobsters with tongs to a colander and rinse under cold water; let stand 5 minutes. Garnish with lemon wedges and parsley sprigs. Serve with melted butter if you wish.

New England lobster roll

This recipe creates fantastic crab rolls too—use 2 cups fresh lump crabmeat in place of the lobster.

Per roll
408 calories, 18 g protein, 28 g fat, 22 g carbohydrate, I g fiber, 1,002 mg sodium, 70 mg cholesterol.

2 lobsters (1¼ pounds each) or 3 frozen lobster tails (6 ounces each), thawed
½ cup mayonnaise
2 teaspoons fresh lemon juice
1½ teaspoons Dijon mustard
1 teaspoon olive oil

¾ teaspoon chopped fresh tarragon or ¼ teaspoon dried
¼ teaspoon hot-pepper sauce
¼ teaspoon salt
⅛ teaspoon black pepper
4 soft frankfurter rolls

1. Cook live lobsters according to directions above. Or cook lobster tails in simmering water 10 minutes. Remove lobsters from water and cool. Remove meat from shells and chop. You should have about 2 cups lobster meat.

2. Whisk mayonnaise, lemon juice, mustard, oil, tarragon, hot-pepper sauce, salt and pepper in a medium-size bowl. Mix in lobster; cover with plastic wrap; refrigerate at least 1 hour.

3. Gently open each roll; lightly toast. Fill each with lobster mixture.

Linguine with lobster sauce

Makes 12 servings   *Prep* 30 minutes   *Cook* 35 minutes

Need a show-stopper for entertaining? This is it! A luxurious pasta dish to feed 12, and the four lobster tails won't break the bank. Impressive, but quite easy.

Per serving
532 calories, 27 g protein, 14 g fat, 74 g carbohydrate, 1,324 mg sodium, 64 mg cholesterol.

4   frozen lobster tails (2 pounds total), thawed
6   tablespoons olive oil
⅓   cup chopped garlic (6 cloves)
2   cups diced onion
3   cans (14½ ounces each) ready-cut tomatoes
1½ teaspoons dried oregano
1½ teaspoon salt
¼   teaspoon ground mace
¼   to ½ teaspoon black pepper
1   bay leaf
1   can (15 ounces) tomato puree
2   pounds linguine
¼   cup heavy cream
½   cup coarsely chopped fresh parsley

1. Remove meat from lobster shells and cut into ½-inch pieces. Heat 3 tablespoons oil in a Dutch oven. Add 3 tablespoons garlic; sauté 2 minutes. Add lobster meat; sauté 5 minutes. Remove lobster to a bowl; keep covered.

2. Add remaining oil, remaining garlic and onion to Dutch oven; sauté 10 minutes. Add tomatoes, oregano, salt, mace, pepper, bay leaf and tomato puree; cook over medium-low heat 15 minutes. Remove bay leaf and discard.

3. Meanwhile, cook linguine in a large pot of lightly salted boiling water until al dente, firm but tender. Drain and keep warm.

4. Remove 2 cups tomato mixture to a blender or food processor. Whirl until pureed. Return pureed mixture to pot. Add lobster meat with any accumulated juices; cook 2 minutes or until lobster meat is cooked through. Remove from heat. Stir in cream.

5. Place hot cooked pasta in a large serving bowl. Pour sauce over; top with parsley. Toss to mix.

New England lobster roll
opposite

Mussels in broth

No mussels available? Steam littleneck clams or steamer clams in the savory wine-onion broth.

Per serving
231 calories, 22 g protein, 10 g fat, 10 g carbohydrate, 336 mg sodium, 66 mg cholesterol.

3 pounds mussels, scrubbed and debearded
3 tablespoons unsalted butter
1 cup chopped onion
1 teaspoon finely chopped garlic
¼ teaspoon black pepper
¼ cup fresh lemon juice
1 cup dry white wine
⅓ cup chopped fresh parsley, plus extra for garnish

1. Discard any open mussels that don't close when lightly touched.

2. Melt 1 tablespoon butter in a large saucepan or Dutch oven over medium heat. Add onion and garlic and sauté until softened, about 3 minutes. Stir in pepper, lemon juice and wine. Bring to boiling. Add ⅓ cup parsley.

3. Add mussels to pot. Cover and reduce heat to low; cook 8 to 10 minutes or just until shells open.

4. Remove mussels with a slotted spoon to a bowl. Discard any mussels that don't open. Swirl remaining butter into cooking liquid. Spoon over mussels. Garnish with parsley.

Note: To debeard mussels, grab any loose filaments sticking out from hinged part of shell and pull off.

Pan-fried oysters

As with most seafood, all these need is a wedge of fresh lemon on the side.

Per serving
249 calories, 8 g protein, 18 g fat, 14 g carbohydrate, 383 mg sodium, 110 mg cholesterol.

3 dozen small fresh oysters, shucked
2 eggs
⅓ cup all-purpose flour, or more
1 cup finely ground saltines (30 crackers)
6 tablespoons butter or margarine
3 tablespoons vegetable oil

1. Drain oysters. Blot oysters dry on paper toweling.

2. Beat eggs slightly in a small bowl. Place flour and cracker crumbs on separate sheets of waxed paper. Lightly coat oysters in flour, shaking off excess; dip into egg, then in crumbs, pressing crumbs to adhere. Place on a sheet of waxed paper.

3. Heat 2 tablespoons butter and 1 tablespoon oil in a large skillet over medium-high heat until butter is melted. Add one-third of oysters and sauté 2 minutes or until golden brown. Turn over and sauté another 2 minutes. Remove to a baking sheet lined with paper toweling; keep warm in low oven. Wipe skillet clean. Fry remaining oysters in 2 batches.

Scallops au gratin

One ramekin or shell makes a teasing appetizer, while two create a main course. You can use the larger sea scallops—just cut them into smaller pieces.

Per serving
151 calories, 14 g protein, 5 g fat, 11 g carbohydrate, 474 mg sodium, 27 mg cholesterol.

3 teaspoons unsalted butter
1½ pounds bay scallops
½ cup finely chopped shallots
½ teaspoon dried tarragon
½ cup evaporated nonfat milk
¼ cup dry white wine
2 teaspoons Dijon mustard
1 tablespoon cornstarch
3 tablespoons water

¼ cup shredded reduced-fat Jarlsberg cheese
¼ dry plain bread crumbs
1 tablespoon grated Parmesan cheese
¼ teaspoon salt
¼ teaspoon black pepper
Lemon wedges for serving

1. Heat oven to 400°.

2. Melt 1 teaspoon butter in a large nonstick skillet over medium heat. Add scallops, shallots and tarragon and sauté until scallops are translucent, 3 minutes. Remove with a slotted spoon to a medium-size bowl.

3. Add milk, wine and mustard to skillet. Bring to boiling. Stir together cornstarch and water in a small cup; stir into skillet. Cook, stirring, until thickened. Remove from heat. Stir in Jarlsberg until melted. Add to scallops.

4. Mix together bread crumbs, Parmesan cheese, remaining 2 teaspoons butter, salt and pepper in a small bowl. Spoon scallop mixture into six ½-cup ovenproof ramekins or scallop shells. Top with bread crumb mixture. Bake in heated 400° oven 10 to 13 minutes or until cheese is bubbly and crumbs are golden. Serve with lemon wedges.

FISH AND SHELLFISH

shellfish smarts

AS IF TERRIFIC taste weren't enough, shellfish offer essential vitamins and minerals: B-12, iodine, iron, and selenium. Plus they are low in calories and have almost no saturated fat.

Blue crab: 3 ounces have 87 calories, 1½ grams fat.

Clams: 6 small fresh clams have 42 calories, ½ gram fat.

Mussels: 6 fresh blue mussels have 84 calories, 2 grams fat.

Lobster: 4 ounces meat (the yield from a 1¼-pound lobster) has 111 calories, less than 1 gram fat.

Oysters: 12 steamed oysters (3 ounces) have 115 calories, 4 grams fat.

Scallops: 3 ounces have 90 calories, 3 grams fat.

Shrimp: 3 ounces (14 cooked large shrimp) have 83 calories, 1 gram fat.

Scallop skewers

Makes 4 servings   *Prep* 15 minutes   *Grill or broil* 6 minutes

For a nice variation, omit the tomatoes from the skewers and serve the scallops and artichoke hearts with parsleyed rice and sliced tomatoes.

Per serving
279 calories, 20 g protein, 17 g fat, 13 g carbohydrate, 851 mg sodium, 34 mg cholesterol.

2 tablespoons balsamic vinegar
¼ cup olive oil
2 cloves garlic, finely chopped
¾ teaspoon salt
⅛ teaspoon black pepper
1 pound sea scallops
1 can (16 ounces) artichoke hearts, drained and cut in half

12 red and yellow cherry tomatoes
1 head green-leaf lettuce, torn into bite-size pieces
1 small head radicchio, chopped
1 cucumber, peeled, seeded and diced
4 green onions, chopped

1. Prepare a charcoal grill with hot coals, or heat a gas grill to high, or heat broiler.

2. Whisk together vinegar, oil, garlic, ¼ teaspoon salt, and pepper in a small bowl. Set dressing aside.

3. Alternately thread scallops, artichoke hearts and tomatoes onto 4 skewers. (If using wooden skewers, soak in water 30 minutes before using.) Season with remaining ½ teaspoon salt. Brush skewers lightly with 3 tablespoons dressing.

4. Grill skewers over hot coals or broil 4 to 6 minutes, turning occasionally, until scallops are white; don't overcook.

5. Toss together leaf lettuce, radicchio, cucumber, green onions, and remaining dressing in a large bowl. Arrange salad on plates with scallop skewers on top.

Peppered scallops

Makes 6 servings   *Prep* 10 minutes   *Cook* 10 minutes

Not a moment to spare? This skillet dish gets dinner done fast.

Per serving
198 calories, 26 g protein, 5 g fat, 11 g carbohydrate, 285 mg sodium, 60 mg cholesterol.

2 tablespoons butter
2 cloves garlic, finely chopped
3 green onions, sliced
2 pounds sea scallops
1 sweet red pepper, cored, seeded and cut into thin strips

1 sweet yellow pepper, cored, seeded and cut into thin strips
1 sweet green pepper, cored, seeded and cut into thin strips
½ cup fresh orange juice

Melt butter in a large nonstick skillet over medium heat. Add garlic and green onions; sauté 2 minutes. Add scallops; sauté 3 minutes. Add sweet peppers; sauté 3 minutes. Add orange juice; cook 2 minutes or until scallops are cooked through.

**Grilled scallops
with oregano-walnut pesto**

Grilled scallops with oregano-walnut pesto

Makes 4 servings   *Prep* 15 minutes   *Grill or broil* 3 to 4 minutes

**Serve with crusty bread
and a cherry tomato
salad for a great
summer meal.**

Per serving
398 calories, 16 g protein,
35 g fat, 6 g carbohydrate,
542 mg sodium,
28 mg cholesterol.

½ cup fresh oregano leaves
½ cup fresh basil leaves
2 small cloves garlic, peeled
¼ cup walnuts
½ cup extra-virgin olive oil

1¼ pounds sea scallops
¼ teaspoon salt
⅛ teaspoon black pepper
¼ cup grated Parmesan cheese

1. Place oregano and basil leaves and garlic in a food processor. Whirl until finely chopped. Add walnuts; whirl 30 seconds. Reserve 2 tablespoons of oil. With processor running, slowly pour remaining oil through feed tube. Remove pesto to a medium-size bowl; cover and refrigerate until ready to serve.

2. Prepare a charcoal grill with hot coals, or heat a gas grill to high, or heat broiler. Place grill rack or broiler pan 4 inches from source of heat. Drizzle reserved 2 tablespoons oil over scallops in a medium-size bowl and season with salt and pepper; toss lightly to coat scallops evenly. Thread scallops onto several metal skewers.

3. Grill or broil scallops 3 to 4 minutes or until centers are opaque, turning once.

4. To serve, stir Parmesan into reserved pesto. Spoon some pesto over scallops. Serve remaining pesto in a bowl.

Parmesan shrimp skewers

Makes 4 servings *Prep* 15 minutes *Grill or broil* about 8 minutes

Shrimp are available fresh and quick-frozen, both cooked and raw, with and without the shells, and occasionally with the heads still intact. Whatever form they're in, be careful not to overcook or the shrimp will toughen. Shown on page 194.

Per serving
547 calories, 26 g protein, 18 g fat, 69 g carbohydrate, 540 mg sodium, 142 mg cholesterol.

2 anchovy fillets (optional)
4 teaspoons Dijon mustard
2 tablespoons fresh lemon juice
2 tablespoons white-wine vinegar
2 tablespoons water
1 teaspoon Worcestershire sauce
¼ cup plus 2 tablespoons grated Parmesan cheese

¼ cup olive oil
2 sweet red peppers
2 sweet yellow peppers
1 pound large shrimp (about 20), peeled and deveined
Pinch salt and black pepper
4 cups hot cooked white rice

1. Prepare a charcoal grill with hot coals, or heat a gas grill to high, or heat broiler.

2. Combine anchovies if using, mustard, lemon juice, vinegar, water, Worcestershire and ¼ cup Parmesan in a food processor or blender. Whirl until smooth. With machine running, slowly add oil. Transfer to a small cup.

3. Core and seed sweet peppers and cut into 1-inch squares; finely chop any scraps and reserve. Combine shrimp, sweet pepper squares and half of anchovy paste in a large bowl. Thread shrimp onto 4 metal skewers, alternating with pieces of pepper. Place any remaining peppers on a separate skewer. Sprinkle skewers with salt, pepper and 1 tablespoon Parmesan cheese.

4. Grill or broil skewers 5 inches from heat 4 minutes. Turn skewers; sprinkle with remaining Parmesan. Grill another 4 minutes or until opaque.

5. Stir finely chopped sweet pepper scraps into half of remaining baste; stir into prepared rice. Transfer rice to a serving platter. Brush skewers with remaining baste. Serve over rice.

Preparing shrimp in 3 steps

1. Lay a shrimp on its side. With your fingers, peel back the shell; start from the legs and leave the tail of the shell attached to the shrimp.

2. Hold the shrimp steady with your fingers. Using a sharp knife, carefully make a cut about ¼-inch deep along the outer edge to reveal the inner vein.

3. Continue to hold the shrimp steady. With the tip of the knife, simply scrape out the exposed inner vein and discard it.

Basil shrimp sauté

Makes 4 servings *Prep* 15 minutes *Refrigerate* 1 hour *Broil* 8 minutes

Re-create the taste of Italy with this combo of basil and sun-dried tomatoes.

Per serving
196 calories, 24 g protein, 9 g fat, 5 g carbohydrate, 372 mg sodium, 173 mg cholesterol.

2 cloves garlic, finely chopped
2 tablespoons olive oil
2 tablespoons fresh lemon juice
1 cup chopped fresh basil

¼ cup dry-pack sun-dried tomatoes (¾ ounce), chopped
¼ teaspoon salt
1 pound large shrimp, peeled and deveined

1. Combine garlic, oil, lemon juice, basil, sun-dried tomatoes, salt and shrimp in a plastic food-storage bag. Gently press with hands to coat shrimp. Refrigerate 1 hour, turning occasionally.

2. Heat broiler.

3. Soak 4 long wooden skewers in water 5 minutes. Thread shrimp onto each skewer. Place skewers on broiler-pan rack.

4. Broil skewers 3 inches from heat until shrimp are cooked through, about 8 minutes, turning once.

Shrimp and mango pitas

Makes 4 servings *Prep* 15 minutes

Here's a cooling choice on a hot summer's day.

Per serving
343 calories, 30 g protein, 5 g fat, 43 g carbohydrate, 698 mg sodium, 221 mg cholesterol.

1 mango, peeled, pitted and chopped
¼ cup apricot nectar
1 tablespoon olive oil
1 teaspoon grated fresh ginger
1 pound cooked shrimp (see box, page 17), peeled and deveined

¼ cup chopped green onion
¼ teaspoon fresh lemon juice
¼ teaspoon salt
⅛ teaspoon black pepper
1 package (8 ounces) small pita rounds

1. Puree 2 tablespoons chopped mango, nectar, oil and ginger in a food processor until smooth.

2. Combine shrimp, green onion, lemon juice, salt, pepper, remaining chopped mango and pureed mango mixture in a large bowl.

3. Split each pita open part way around its edge. Spoon shrimp mixture into each.

Sesame shrimp stir-fry

Makes 4 servings   *Prep* 10 minutes   *Cook* 10 minutes

The double hit of sesame oil and seeds adds nutty flavor to crisp peppers and shrimp.

Per serving
400 calories, 25 g protein, 10 g fat, 51 g carbohydrate, 1,036 mg sodium, 162 mg cholesterol.

1 pound medium shrimp, peeled and deveined
¼ teaspoon ground ginger
¼ teaspoon ground red pepper (cayenne)
1 clove garlic, finely chopped
1 tablespoon sesame seeds
¼ teaspoon black pepper
2 cups packaged precooked rice
2 tablespoons dark Asian sesame oil

1 sweet red pepper, cored, seeded and sliced into thin strips
1 sweet yellow pepper, cored, seeded and sliced into thin strips
3 green onions, sliced
3 tablespoons teriyaki sauce
½ pound sugar snap peas
1 tablespoon cornstarch
¾ cup chicken broth
¼ teaspoon salt

1. Combine shrimp, ginger, ground red pepper, garlic, sesame seeds and black pepper in a large plastic food-storage bag.

2. Place rice in a heatproof serving bowl. Bring 2½ cups water to boiling; pour over rice in bowl. Cover with foil; set aside.

3. Heat sesame oil in a large wok or skillet. Add sweet peppers and green onions; sauté 3 to 4 minutes to soften slightly. Add teriyaki sauce. Add peas and shrimp with seasoning; sauté 4 minutes or until shrimp are opaque. Stir cornstarch into broth and add to wok; cook, stirring, until mixture boils. Sprinkle with salt. Fluff rice with fork. Spoon shrimp mixture over rice.

Shrimp scampi

Makes 4 servings   *Prep* 10 minutes   *Cook* 5 minutes

For a lovely, light dinner, spoon over a little orzo and garnish with lemon wedges.

Per serving
172 calories, 15 g protein, 11 g fat, 3 g carbohydrate, 473 mg sodium, 142 mg cholesterol.

1 tablespoon butter
2 tablespoons olive oil
4 cloves garlic, finely chopped
1 pound large or medium shrimp, peeled and deveined
¼ cup dry white wine

1 tablespoon fresh lemon juice
½ teaspoon salt
⅛ teaspoon black pepper
1 tablespoon dry seasoned bread crumbs
2 tablespoons chopped fresh parsley

1. Heat butter and oil in a large nonstick skillet over high heat. When butter starts to brown, add garlic. Lower heat; cook 1 minute, stirring to prevent garlic from overbrowning.

2. Add shrimp; cook 2 minutes, stirring occasionally. Add wine, lemon juice, salt and pepper; cook 2 minutes or until shrimp are cooked through. Stir in bread crumbs and parsley. Serve immediately.

Sesame shrimp stir-fry *opposite* 223

Shrimp jambalaya

Makes 4 servings *Prep* 10 minutes *Cook* 55 minutes

The name of this Creole dish is thought to come from the French word *jambon*, meaning ham—one of the main ingredients in the dish. You can use white rice instead of brown if you prefer, which will cook in a shorter amount of time.

Per serving
432 calories, 26 g protein, 11 g fat, 51 g carbohydrate, 1,166 mg sodium, 120 mg cholesterol.

1 tablespoon olive oil
1 large onion, coarsely chopped (1 cup)
1 clove garlic, crushed
1 cup brown rice
1 can (16 ounces) whole tomatoes in juice, chopped
1½ cups chicken broth
1 teaspoon ground thyme
1 bay leaf
2 packages (8 ounces each) fresh broccoli flowerets
½ pound medium shrimp, peeled and deveined
¼ pound sliced smoked ham, torn into strips

1. Heat oil in a large skillet. Add onion and garlic; sauté over medium-high heat 3 to 5 minutes or until softened. Stir in rice; sauté 2 to 3 minutes.

2. Add tomatoes, broth, thyme and bay leaf to skillet. Cover; simmer 30 minutes.

3. Stir in broccoli. Cover; simmer 10 minutes or until just tender. Add shrimp and ham; simmer, covered, 5 minutes. Remove bay leaf.

Shrimp quesadillas

Makes 4 servings *Prep* 15 minutes *Bake* at 450° for 10 minutes

Great as an appetizer or first course, or as meal accompanied with a packaged red bean and rice mix.

Per serving
463 calories, 28 g protein, 19 g fat, 42 g carbohydrate, 800 mg sodium, 148 mg cholesterol.

8 flour tortillas (7-inch)
1½ cups shredded taco cheese
½ pound cooked shrimp (see box, page 17), chopped (or small frozen shrimp, thawed)
½ cup diced jarred roasted red peppers, drained well
3 green onions, sliced
1 tablespoon chopped canned jalapeño chile
½ teaspoon ground cumin
Sour cream for serving
Salsa for serving

1. Place rack in lowest position in oven. Heat oven to 450°. Arrange 4 tortillas on a large baking sheet lined with aluminum foil. Lightly coat tortillas with nonstick cooking spray; flip over.

2. Sprinkle half of cheese over tortillas. Sprinkle with shrimp, roasted peppers, green onions, jalapeño and cumin. Top with remaining cheese, then remaining 4 tortillas. Coat with nonstick cooking spray.

3. Bake on bottom rack in heated 450° oven about 10 minutes, flipping over halfway through cooking, or until cheese is melted and tortillas are crisped. Cut into wedges. Serve with sour cream and salsa.

Seafood paella

A little something for everybody in this festive dish: chicken, shrimp and shellfish, all seasoned with a pinch of saffron and Canadian bacon.

Per serving
393 calories, 33 g protein,
6 g fat, 50 g carbohydrate,
977 mg sodium,
97 mg cholesterol.

1 tablespoon vegetable oil
4 boneless, skinless chicken breasts (1 pound total), cut in half crosswise
1 teaspoon salt
½ teaspoon black pepper
½ pound medium shrimp, peeled and deveined
1 large onion, coarsely chopped (1 cup)
1 large sweet green pepper, cored, seeded and chopped

4 cups lower-sodium chicken broth
1 can (14½ ounces) whole tomatoes
2 cloves garlic, freshly chopped
Pinch ground saffron
2 cups converted white rice
1 package (10 ounces) frozen peas
2 ounces Canadian bacon, chopped (½ cup)
12 clams, scrubbed clean
12 mussels, scrubbed clean

1. Heat 1½ teaspoons oil in a Dutch oven or large saucepan over medium-high heat.

2. Sprinkle chicken with ¼ teaspoon salt and ¼ teaspoon pepper. Add chicken to pot; sauté until browned on all sides, 5 to 6 minutes. Remove chicken to paper toweling to drain. Add shrimp to pot; sauté until pink and curled, 2 minutes. Remove shrimp to paper toweling. Cover and keep chicken and shrimp warm.

3. Reduce heat to medium. Add remaining 1½ teaspoons oil to Dutch oven. Add onion and green pepper; sauté until softened, 3 to 5 minutes.

4. Add broth, tomatoes, garlic and saffron to pot. Bring to boiling. Add rice, chicken and remaining ¾ teaspoon salt and ¼ teaspoon pepper. Lower heat; simmer, covered, 15 minutes or until most of liquid is absorbed and rice is almost tender.

5. Stir in peas and Canadian bacon. Press clams and mussels into top of paella. Cover and steam 5 to 8 minutes or until clams and mussels open. Discard any unopened shellfish. Add shrimp. Serve immediately.

Lemon-thyme
chicken
page 238

Turkey "London broil" *page 260*

DRUMSTICKS OR breasts, wings or thighs—chances are, poultry turns up on a typical family's menu at least once a week. And why not? Our preferred birds cook up in a vast variety of ways, from crispy fried to tender baked, constantly proving they offer something for everyone.

Of course, there's the basic but beloved roast bird, even better glazed with cherry jam. Beyond that, sample an assortment of recipes that show off a bounty of cuts to best advantage. For instance, Lemon-Thyme Chicken makes the most of cut-up parts, while Spicy Skillet Chicken showcases skinless breasts. Thighs are especially appetizing prepared osso-buco style, and legs deliver

For a flock of tempting possibilities, nothing beats a bird.

dynamic taste prepared in Thai or tandoori tradition. Meanwhile, turkey fans can enjoy Turkey "London Broil" plus inventive twists on sloppy Joes or sweet-and-sour meatballs. There's even a pair of piquant game hen recipes. With some kind of poultry in your pot, there's virtually no way you can go wrong.

poultry

Confetti chicken roll-ups

Makes 4 servings *Prep* 10 minutes *Cook* 5 minutes *Bake* at 350° for 40 to 45 minutes

From Amy Dittrich of Massachusetts, this prizewinner in the *Family Circle* chicken-for-dinner contest is an easy make-ahead bursting with vegetables.

Per serving
244 calories, 28 g protein,
10 g fat, 7 g carbohydrate,
814 mg sodium,
67 mg cholesterol.

2 tablespoons olive oil
1 shallot, finely chopped, or
  1 tablespoon finely chopped
  onion
1 clove garlic, finely chopped
1 cup chopped mushrooms
¼ cup dry sherry
¼ cup matchstick strips yellow
  squash
¼ cup matchstick strips zucchini

½ cup chopped parsley
4 boneless, skinless chicken breast
  halves (1 pound total)
4 teaspoons Dijon mustard
½ teaspoon salt
¼ teaspoon black pepper
4 teaspoons grated Parmesan cheese
1 medium tomato, chopped
1 teaspoon paprika

1. Heat oven to 350°. Lightly coat a shallow 1½-quart baking dish with nonstick cooking spray.

2. Heat oil in a small skillet over medium heat. Add shallot and garlic; sauté 1 minute. Add mushrooms; sauté just until liquid is released. Add sherry; cook until about 2 tablespoons liquid remain.

3. Add yellow squash, zucchini and ¼ cup parsley; cook 1 to 2 minutes. Remove from heat.

4. Place chicken breast halves between sheets of plastic wrap. Lightly pound until ¼ inch thick.

5. Spread each breast with 1 teaspoon mustard; sprinkle with salt and pepper. Top each with one-quarter of vegetable mixture. Sprinkle each with 1 teaspoon Parmesan. Roll breasts up, jelly-roll style; secure with a wooden pick. Place rolls in prepared dish.

6. Combine tomato, remaining ¼ cup parsley and paprika in a small bowl. Sprinkle mixture over chicken rolls. Cover dish with aluminum foil. Bake in heated 350° oven 40 to 45 minutes or until internal temperature registers 170° on an instant-read thermometer. Remove picks before serving.

Brie-stuffed chicken breasts

Makes 4 servings   *Prep* 20 minutes   *Cook* 13 minutes   *Bake* at 400° for 35 minutes

A meltingly rich stuffing is spooned under the skin of the chicken breast, so when the chicken bakes, the flavors permeate the meat.

Per serving
478 calories, 46 g protein, 25 g fat, 16 g carbohydrate, 807 mg sodium, 139 mg cholesterol.

2 tablespoons olive oil
1 medium onion, chopped
1 Granny Smith apple, cored and coarsely chopped
1 teaspoon dried thyme
1 teaspoon salt
½ teaspoon black pepper
¾ cup apple cider
4 ounces Brie, rind removed, cut into chunks
4 chicken breast halves (2 pounds total)

1. Heat oil in a medium-size nonstick skillet over medium heat. Add onion; cook until very tender, about 8 minutes. Add apple, ½ teaspoon thyme, ¼ teaspoon salt, ¼ teaspoon pepper and ¼ cup cider; cook until apple is tender, about 5 minutes. Remove from heat; cool slightly. Stir in Brie. Divide stuffing into 4 equal portions.

2. Heat oven to 400°.

3. Run fingers under breast skin to separate from flesh. Dividing equally, insert stuffing under skin of each breast half. Season chicken with ½ teaspoon salt and ¼ teaspoon pepper. Place in a 13 x 9 x 2-inch baking dish.

4. Bake in heated 400° oven 35 minutes or until internal temperature registers 170° on an instant-read thermometer. Remove chicken to a platter; keep warm.

5. Skim fat from baking dish. Scrape drippings into a small saucepan. Add remaining ½ cup apple cider, ½ teaspoon thyme and ¼ teaspoon salt; cook over medium heat to reduce by half. Spoon over chicken.

POULTRY

Pick the right part

VERSATILE CHICKEN is one of the cook's best friends. Choose the right part for your recipe.

Whole: Perfect to roast or smoke on the grill. In soup, a whole bird lends intense flavor.

Breast: Low in fat. Cutlets need quick cooking, such as stir-frying, sautéing or grilling, to stay juicy.

Leg and thigh: Contain more fat than breast and thus stay juicy whether baked, broiled, grilled or fried. Cut thigh meat from the bone and use for kabobs or stir-fries. You can substitute thigh meat for breast meat in recipes, but increase the cooking time slightly.

Wing: Full of flavor and fat. Can be baked, grilled or broiled.

Ground: A mix of light and dark meat gives the best taste and texture. Ground chicken is mildly flavored, so don't be shy with seasonings.

Parmesan chicken fingers

Makes 4 servings   *Prep* 5 minutes   *Refrigerate* 30 minutes   *Bake* at 450° for 8 to 10 minutes

These may remind you of your favorite take-out food, but there's much less fat. Using buttermilk and baking rather than frying make all the difference.

Per serving
198 calories, 29 g protein, 2 g fat, 14 g carbohydrate, 555 mg sodium, 69 mg cholesterol.

⅓ cup buttermilk or ⅓ cup milk plus 2 teaspoons vinegar
1 large clove garlic, chopped
¾ teaspoon hot-pepper sauce
4 boneless, skinless chicken breast halves (1 pound total), cut lengthwise into ½-inch-wide strips

Coating
20 nonfat saltines, crushed into crumbs (¾ cup)
1 teaspoon paprika
½ teaspoon salt
2 tablespoons grated Parmesan cheese

1. Stir together buttermilk, garlic and hot-pepper sauce in a large bowl. Add chicken; toss until evenly coated. Refrigerate 30 minutes.

2. Heat oven to 450°.

3. Prepare coating: Combine cracker crumbs, paprika, salt and 1 tablespoon Parmesan in a pie plate. Line a baking sheet with aluminum foil; coat with nonstick cooking spray. Drain chicken; dip in coating, tossing to coat. Arrange on baking sheet. Sprinkle with remaining 1 tablespoon Parmesan.

4. Bake chicken in heated 450° oven 8 to 10 minutes or until cooked through.

Make-ahead tip: The chicken fingers can be prepared through step 3 and frozen up to 1 month. Freeze on a baking sheet, then place in a plastic food-storage bag and seal. To serve, place frozen chicken on a foil-lined baking sheet and bake in heated 450° oven 12 minutes or until done.

Tomato-rosemary chicken *opposite*

Tomato-rosemary chicken

Makes 12 servings   *Prep* 15 minutes   *Cook* about 30 minutes   *Bake* at 375° for 20 minutes

For a smashing party dish, serve the chicken over a bed of wild and white rice tossed with sautéed mushrooms.

Per serving
257 calories, 34 g protein, 11 g fat, 5 g carbohydrate, 377 mg sodium, 89 mg cholesterol.

12 boneless, skinless chicken breast halves (4 pounds total)
½ teaspoon salt
¼ teaspoon black pepper
¼ cup all-purpose flour
2 tablespoons vegetable oil
2 tablespoons butter
5 cloves garlic, chopped
¼ pound prosciutto, chopped
⅓ cup dry white wine
1 tablespoon chopped fresh rosemary or 1 teaspoon dried, crumbled
12 plum tomatoes, diced
½ cup chicken broth

1. Season both sides of chicken breast halves with salt and pepper. Place flour on a sheet of waxed paper. Turn chicken in flour to coat both sides; shake off any excess and place chicken on another piece of waxed paper.

2. Heat oven to 375°.

3. Heat 1 tablespoon oil and 1 tablespoon butter in a large nonstick skillet over medium-high heat. Add 6 chicken breast halves and sauté until lightly browned, about 3 minutes per side. Place chicken in a 15 x 10 x 1-inch jelly-roll pan in a single layer, filling half of pan. Repeat with remaining oil, butter and chicken.

4. Bake chicken in heated 375° oven 20 minutes or until internal temperature registers 170° on an instant-read thermometer.

5. Meanwhile, add garlic and prosciutto to skillet; cook over medium heat, stirring constantly, 3 minutes. Add wine and rosemary; cook 2 minutes, stirring up any browned bits from bottom of skillet.

6. Add tomatoes and broth. Bring to boiling. Reduce heat; simmer 10 minutes.

7. Place chicken on a serving platter; pour sauce over top. Serve immediately.

Spicy skillet chicken

Makes 4 servings   *Prep* 10 minutes   *Cook* 16 minutes

In a contest sponsored by *Family Circle* magazine and the Florida Citrus Growers, this recipe was the grand prize winner from Darol Wetzel. Serve with couscous; when following the package directions, substitute orange juice for part of the water.

Per serving
251 calories, 29 g protein, 7 g fat, 17 g carbohydrate, 291 mg sodium, 78 mg cholesterol.

1½ teaspoons citrus or lemon pepper
¼ teaspoon ground red pepper (cayenne)
½ teaspoon ground ginger
½ teaspoon garlic salt
4 boneless, skinless chicken breast halves (1¼ pounds total)

1 tablespoon olive oil
½ cup fresh orange juice
½ cup mango chutney, chopped
  Orange slices for garnish (optional)
  Chopped fresh chives for garnish (optional)

1. Combine citrus pepper, ground red pepper, ginger and garlic salt in a small bowl. Sprinkle over both sides of chicken breast halves.

2. Heat oil in a large skillet over medium heat. Add chicken; cook, turning once, 12 minutes or until internal temperature registers 170° on an instant-read thermometer. Remove chicken from skillet and keep warm.

3. Add orange juice and chutney to drippings in skillet; cook, stirring, until thickened slightly, 4 minutes. To serve, spoon some sauce onto 4 serving plates. Place chicken on sauce and top with remaining sauce. Garnish with orange slices and chives if desired.

Mexican chicken mole

Makes 4 servings   *Prep* 15 minutes   *Cook* 30 minutes

To complete the theme, spoon the chicken mole over rice with corn. Just prepare four servings of rice, adding 1 cup corn kernels.

Per serving
199 calories, 25 g protein, 6 g fat, 11 g carbohydrate, 502 mg sodium, 63 mg cholesterol.

2 teaspoons olive oil
4 boneless, skinless chicken breast halves (1 pound total)
1 carrot, thinly sliced
1 rib celery, thinly sliced
1 medium onion, slivered
1 can (8 ounces) tomato sauce

½ cup lower-sodium chicken broth
1 tablespoon chili powder
2 teaspoons breakfast cocoa mix
¼ teaspoon sugar
¼ teaspoon ground cinnamon
  Pinch black pepper
1 tablespoon chopped almonds

1. Heat oil in a large nonstick skillet over medium heat. Add chicken; brown on all sides, about 6 minutes. Remove chicken and set aside.

2. Add carrot, celery and onion to skillet; sauté until tender. Add tomato sauce, broth, chili powder, cocoa mix, sugar, cinnamon and pepper.

3. Bring to boiling. Add chicken. Lower heat and simmer, covered, 12 minutes or until internal temperature of chicken registers 170° on an instant-read thermometer. Sprinkle with almonds.

Mediterranean chicken

Makes 4 servings   *Prep* 10 minutes   *Cook* 25 minutes

Perfect for the busy cook: a skillet dinner with the crunch and licorice taste of fresh fennel.

Per serving
275 calories, 27 g protein, 11 g fat, 18 g carbohydrate, 362 mg sodium, 66 mg cholesterol.

2 teaspoons olive oil
4 boneless, skinless chicken breast halves (1 pound total)
¾ pound fennel bulb, sliced
1 onion, chopped
1 clove garlic, chopped
1 can (14½ ounces) no-salt-added stewed tomatoes
8 oil-cured black olives, pitted
¼ teaspoon salt

1. Heat oil in a large nonstick skillet over medium heat. Add chicken; brown on all sides, about 6 minutes. Remove chicken and set aside.

2. Add fennel, onion and garlic to skillet. Cook over medium heat, stirring, until the vegetables are lightly browned, about 3 minutes.

3. Add tomatoes, olives and salt to skillet. Bring to boiling. Add reserved chicken. Lower heat; cover and simmer 15 minutes or until internal temperature of chicken registers 170° on an instant-read thermometer.

Thai chicken curry

Makes 6 servings   *Prep* 15 minutes   *Cook* 15 minutes

Thanks to lemon and lime rind and chopped fresh ginger, all mixed into a coconut milk sauce, this tempting chicken meal has a subtle Asian flavor. Look for bottled fish sauce in the Asian food section of your supermarket or in Asian specialty food shops.

Per serving
269 calories, 27 g protein, 15 g fat, 5 g carbohydrate, 321 mg sodium, 64 mg cholesterol.

1½ pounds fresh spinach, stemmed and washed, but not dried
1 can (13½ ounces) unsweetened coconut milk
2 tablespoons chopped shallot
1 tablespoon chopped fresh ginger
4 teaspoons paprika
1 clove garlic, finely chopped
1 teaspoon grated lemon rind
½ teaspoon grated lime rind
½ teaspoon red-pepper flakes
6 boneless, skinless chicken breast halves (1½ pounds total), cut into 2-inch-long strips
1 to 2 tablespoons bottled fish sauce
½ cup fresh basil leaves, chopped
½ teaspoon salt

1. Place spinach in a large skillet; cover. Steam over medium-high heat until it just wilts, 3 minutes. Drain in a colander; run under cold water to cool. Squeeze spinach dry.

2. Place ½ cup coconut milk, shallot, ginger, paprika, garlic, lemon and lime rinds and red-pepper flakes in a blender; pureé.

3. Transfer coconut milk mixture to a large skillet. Cook over medium-high heat until mixture is thickened and turns brighter red, 1 to 2 minutes. Add chicken, remaining coconut milk and fish sauce. Heat to boiling. Lower heat; simmer, uncovered, until chicken is cooked through, 8 to 10 minutes. Stir in spinach and basil; heat through. Add salt and serve.

Chicken piccata

This sauté, a variation on veal piccata, uses pounded skinless chicken breasts and tops them with an easy pan sauce made with fresh lemon juice, capers and chopped parsley. Check below for two more easy-to-fix saucy finishes.

Per serving
350 calories, 30 g protein, 15 g fat, 23 g carbohydrate, 1241 mg sodium, 134 mg cholesterol.

6 boneless, skinless chicken breast halves (1½ pounds total)
3 tablespoons Dijon mustard
2 eggs
1½ cups dry seasoned bread crumbs
¼ cup olive oil
¼ cup chicken broth
2 tablespoons fresh lemon juice
2 tablespoons drained capers
¼ teaspoon salt
6 very thin lemon slices
1 tablespoon chopped fresh parsley

1. Place chicken breast halves between sheets of plastic wrap. Lightly pound.

2. In a shallow bowl, stir together mustard and eggs until well blended. Spread bread crumbs on a plate. Dip chicken into egg mixture and then coat with crumbs, patting to make crumbs adhere.

3. Heat 2 tablespoons oil in a large skillet over medium heat. Add half of chicken to skillet in a single layer and sauté 5 minutes. Using tongs, turn chicken over and cook about 5 minutes more or until internal temperature registers 170° on an instant-read thermometer. Transfer chicken to a platter; cover and keep warm. Repeat with remaining oil and chicken.

4. Drain any excess fat from skillet and add broth, lemon juice, capers and salt. Bring mixture to boiling, scraping up browned bits from bottom of skillet with a wooden spoon. Add lemon slices and parsley.

5. Remove from heat and spoon lemon sauce over chicken on platter. Serve immediately.

Chicken with raisin and pine nut sauce

Per serving
450 calories, 32 g protein, 19 g fat, 36 g carbohydrate, 657 mg sodium, 134 mg cholesterol.

Prepare Chicken Piccata through step 3. Then add 1½ cups dry white wine, ½ cup chicken broth, ½ cup raisins, ½ cup pine nuts, ½ teaspoon dried rosemary, ¼ teaspoon salt and pinch black pepper to skillet. Bring to simmering and cook 12 minutes or until syrupy. Serve over chicken. Makes 6 servings.

Chicken with tarragon cream sauce

Per serving
428 calories, 30 g protein, 23 g fat, 23 g carbohydrate, 1294 mg sodium, 162 mg cholesterol.

Prepare Chicken Piccata through step 3. Then add ⅔ cup dry white wine or chicken broth to skillet and cook over medium-high heat 4 minutes, scraping browned bits from pan. Add 1 teaspoon dried tarragon, 1 cup broth and ½ cup heavy cream. Cook over medium-high heat, stirring, 8 minutes or until reduced by half. Remove from heat. Stir in 1 tablespoon coarse-grain mustard. Serve over chicken. Makes 6 servings.

Chicken piccata *opposite*

Chicken rollatine

Makes 8 servings   *Prep* 40 minutes   *Freeze* 20 minutes   *Cook* 2 to 4 minutes per batch

Bake at 350° for 20 to 25 minutes

A pretty dish that looks more difficult to make than it really is, this is perfect for company. The chicken breasts can be stuffed, coated and refrigerated several hours ahead.

Per serving
403 calories, 24 g protein, 27 g fat, 16 g carbohydrate, 556 mg sodium, 146 mg cholesterol.

Keeping herbs fresh

To store fresh basil or parsley, stick the stem ends in water in a small glass or jar and cover the top of the bunch with a plastic food-storage bag; refrigerate. Avoid getting the leaves wet or they will soon turn black.

2½ tablespoons butter
2 large cloves garlic, chopped
1 sweet red pepper, diced
4 green onions, finely chopped
8 boneless, skinless chicken breast halves (2½ pounds total)
½ teaspoon salt
½ teaspoon black pepper
½ pound mozzarella cheese, shredded (2 cups)
¼ cup all-purpose flour
3 eggs, beaten
1 cup dry seasoned bread crumbs
⅓ cup chopped fresh parsley
½ cup oil

1. Melt butter in a small saucepan. Add garlic, sweet red pepper and green onions; sauté 5 minutes. Cool.

2. Place chicken breast halves between sheets of plastic wrap. Lightly pound until paper-thin. Season chicken with salt and pepper.

3. Combine mozzarella and red pepper mixture in a small bowl. Place 2 tablespoons mixture in center of each chicken breast half. Fold sides over to form a hockey-puck-type patty. Place patties, flap side down, in a metal baking pan. Freeze 20 minutes to hold together for frying.

4. Place flour, eggs and bread crumbs in 3 separate shallow bowls. Mix parsley into bread crumbs. Dip patties first in flour, then in eggs and crumbs to coat. (Wrap and refrigerate up to 4 hours if you wish.)

5. Heat oven to 350°.

6. Heat half of oil in a medium-size skillet. Working in batches, sauté patties in skillet 1 to 2 minutes per side or until golden brown, adding more oil as needed. Place on baking pan.

7. Bake in heated 350° oven 20 to 25 minutes or until internal temperature of chicken registers 170° on an instant read-thermometer.

Grilled chicken with tomato-basil relish

Makes 4 servings   *Prep* 20 minutes   *Refrigerate* 1 hour   *Broil or grill* 15 minutes

If you can find it, try dark opal basil instead of the common green variety. It's purple in color and has spicy-ginger overtones.

Per serving
324 calories, 33 g protein, 12 g fat, 25 g carbohydrate, 643 mg sodium, 78 mg cholesterol.

Tomato-basil relish
2 cups loosely packed fresh basil leaves, finely chopped
⅓ cup fresh orange juice
1 teaspoon balsamic vinegar
1 clove garlic, finely chopped
1 teaspoon salt

½ teaspoon black pepper
4 to 5 ripe tomatoes, cored and diced

4 boneless, skinless chicken breast halves (1¼ pounds total)
2 tablespoons extra-virgin olive oil

1. Prepare tomato-basil relish: Mix together basil, orange juice, vinegar, garlic, ½ teaspoon salt, ¼ teaspoon pepper and tomatoes in a small bowl. Refrigerate at least 1 hour.

2. Heat broiler, setting rack 4 inches from heat; or prepare a charcoal grill with hot coals, setting rack 4 inches from coals; or heat a gas grill to high.

3. Rub chicken breast halves with olive oil and remaining salt and pepper. Broil or grill chicken, turning frequently, 6 to 7 minutes per side or until internal temperature registers 170° on an instant-read thermometer. Serve each breast topped with some of the relish.

Sweet 'n' nutty chicken

Makes 4 servings   *Prep* 5 minutes   *Bake* at 350° for 20 minutes   *Broil* 1 to 2 minutes

Feel free to substitute your favorite jam for the apricot and vary the salted nuts as you wish.

Per serving
308 calories, 37 g protein, 9 g fat, 19 g carbohydrate, 387 mg sodium, 94 mg cholesterol.

3 tablespoons plus 1 teaspoon apricot jam
2 tablespoons prepared mustard
¼ cup chopped salted nuts, such as cashews or macadamias

¼ cup dry plain bread crumbs
2 tablespoons all-purpose flour
4 boneless, skinless chicken breast halves (1½ pounds total)

1. Heat oven to 350°.

2. Combine 2 tablespoons jam, mustard, nuts and bread crumbs in a small bowl to form a thick paste.

3. Place flour on a sheet of waxed paper. Dip chicken breast halves in the flour to coat lightly, shaking off excess. Spread 1 teaspoon of remaining jam on each chicken breast half, covering both sides. Place chicken in one layer in a large baking dish. Spread seasoned paste on top.

4. Bake in heated 350° oven 20 minutes or until internal temperature of chicken registers 170° on an instant-read thermometer. Increase oven temperature to broil. Place chicken under broiler to crisp, 1 to 2 minutes.

237

Buttermilk fried chicken

Makes 4 servings   *Prep* 20 minutes   *Refrigerate* 1 hour   *Cook* 7 to 9 minutes

Bake at 350° for 15 to 20 minutes

In our reduced-fat version of fried chicken, we discard the skin before breading, fry the pieces briefly, drain and then bake. Soaking the chicken first in buttermilk adds flavor without fat.

Per serving
448 calories, 38 g protein, 24 g fat, 18 g carbohydrate, 355 mg sodium, 104 mg cholesterol.

1 whole chicken (2½ pounds), quartered
⅛ teaspoon ground red pepper (cayenne)
½ teaspoon black pepper
1½ cups buttermilk
Vegetable oil for frying
¾ cup dry plain bread crumbs

1. Cut wings from breast quarters. Remove skin from chicken. Place chicken in a 10-inch pie plate. Sprinkle both sides with red and black pepper. Pour on buttermilk. Cover; refrigerate at least 1 hour, turning once.

2. Heat oven to 350°. Pour ½ inch oil into an electric skillet or a regular large skillet. Heat oil to 375°.

3. Spread bread crumbs on waxed paper. Lift chicken from buttermilk; coat chicken on all sides with bread crumbs. Carefully cook chicken in oil to brown on both sides, 7 to 9 minutes total. Drain on paper toweling. Arrange chicken in a single layer in a shallow baking pan.

4. Bake in heated 350° oven 15 to 20 minutes or until internal temperature of a thigh registers 180° on an instant-read thermometer.

Lemon-thyme chicken

Makes 4 servings   *Prep* 15 minutes   *Bake* 45 minutes at 350°   *Broil* 3 minutes

Are you a barbecue fanatic? Then grill the chicken over medium-hot coals until crisp and cooked through. The hint of smoke balances the tart-herbal flavors.
Shown on front cover and page 226.

Per serving
431 calories, 43 g protein, 27 g fat, 2 g carbohydrate, 441 mg sodium, 134 mg cholesterol.

3 tablespoons fresh lemon juice
1 tablespoon olive oil
2 cloves garlic
1 teaspoon coarse kosher salt
1 teaspoon chopped fresh thyme
1 teaspoon prepared mustard
¼ teaspoon ground red pepper (cayenne)
½ teaspoon black pepper
1 whole chicken (3 pounds), quartered

1. Heat oven to 350°.

2. Place lemon juice, oil, garlic, salt, thyme, mustard, red pepper and black pepper in a food processor or blender. Process 15 seconds. Insert fingers under chicken skin to loosen. Rub half of lemon juice mixture under skin. Rub remaining mixture on top.

3. Place chicken on a rack in a 13 x 9 x 2-inch baking pan. Bake in heated 350° oven 45 minutes or until internal temperature of a thigh registers 180° on an instant-read thermometer. Increase oven temperature to broil. Place chicken under broiler 2 to 3 minutes to crisp skin.

Crusty baked chicken

Makes 6 servings *Prep* 20 minutes *Bake* at 350° for 45 minutes *Broil* 5 to 8 minutes

Per serving
392 calories, 30 g protein,
23 g fat, 14 g carbohydrate,
326 mg sodium,
98 mg cholesterol.

½ cup dry plain bread crumbs
½ cup all-purpose flour
1 tablespoon chopped fresh parsley
1 teaspoon dried basil
½ teaspoon salt
½ teaspoon paprika
¼ teaspoon black pepper

Juice of 1 lemon
2 tablespoons butter or margarine, melted
2 tablespoons vegetable oil
1 whole chicken (3 to 4 pounds), cut into 8 serving pieces

1. Heat oven to 350°.

2. Combine bread crumbs, flour, parsley, basil, salt, paprika and pepper in a small brown paper bag; close and shake to mix.

3. Combine lemon juice, butter and oil in a large bowl. Add chicken, turning pieces to coat. Working with a few pieces at a time, shake chicken in crumb mixture in bag to coat evenly; place the pieces on a 15 x 10 x 1-inch jelly-roll pan.

4. Bake in heated 350° oven 45 minutes or until internal temperature of a thigh registers 180° on an instant-read thermometer.

5. Increase oven temperature to broil. Broil chicken until lightly golden, 5 to 8 minutes.

POULTRY

Crusty baked chicken

239

Southwestern-style chicken

Makes 10 servings *Prep* 10 minutes *Refrigerate* 6 hours or overnight *Cook* 4 minutes

Bake at 375° for 45 minutes *Broil or grill* 6 to 8 minutes

Try the spice rub over roast pork or pork chops or even strong-flavored fish such as tuna.

Per serving

343 calories, 36 g protein, 18 g fat, 7 g carbohydrate, 589 mg sodium, 114 mg cholesterol.

Nutrition know-how

As long as we cook it right, chicken is good for us. Consider these facts:

• A 3-ounce cooked serving of skinless breast has about 140 calories and 3 grams fat (only 1 gram saturated fat).

• Remove the skin from chicken thighs, and calories drop from 197 to 166 and fat from 13 grams to 8 for a 3-ounce cooked serving.

• Want to ensure that chicken stays moist? Remove the skin after cooking.

Rub

Grated rind of 2 lemons
4 cloves garlic, chopped
2 teaspoons salt
1 teaspoon black pepper
¼ cup packed dark-brown sugar
1 tablespoon dry mustard
2 teaspoons ground red pepper (cayenne)

2 whole chickens (3 pounds each), each cut into 8 serving pieces

Basting sauce

2 tablespoons dark-brown sugar
2 tablespoons fresh lemon juice
1 teaspoon dry mustard
½ teaspoon ground red pepper (cayenne)
¼ teaspoon salt
¼ cup flat beer or apple cider

1. Prepare rub: Combine lemon rind, garlic, salt and pepper in a medium-size bowl; mash together with back of a spoon. Stir in brown sugar, mustard and ground red pepper.

2. If desired, remove skin from chicken pieces. Rub mixture into chicken. Place in a single layer in 2 glass baking pans. Cover with plastic wrap; refrigerate 6 hours or overnight.

3. Prepare basting sauce: Combine brown sugar, lemon juice, mustard, ground red pepper, salt and beer in a small saucepan. Simmer 4 minutes.

4. Heat oven to 375°. Arrange chicken pieces in a single layer in 2 clean baking pans. Cover with foil.

5. Bake in heated 375° oven 45 minutes or until internal temperature of a thigh registers 180° on an instant-read thermometer.

6. Meanwhile, if desired, prepare a charcoal grill with hot coals, or heat a gas grill to high. Otherwise, when chicken is cooked, increase oven temperature to broil.

7. Brush chicken with basting sauce. Broil or grill 6 inches from heat 6 to 8 minutes, turning occasionally and brushing with basting sauce.

Garlic chicken

Makes 4 servings   *Prep* 20 minutes   *Bake* garlic at 400° for 1 hour 10 minutes

Broil pepper for 10 minutes   *Cook* 50 minutes

Vividly flavored and brightly colored with a roasted red pepper sauce, this dish successfully fills the dinner bill.

Per serving
361 calories, 43 g protein, 12 g fat, 16 g carbohydrate, 602 mg sodium, 129 mg cholesterol.

1 whole head garlic
1 sweet red pepper
1 can (16 ounces) plum tomatoes, drained and chopped (about 1 cup)
¼ cup fresh basil leaves
1 whole chicken (3 pounds), cut into 8 serving pieces

¼ cup all-purpose flour
¼ teaspoon salt
⅛ teaspoon black pepper
1 tablespoon olive oil
⅓ cup dry white wine
⅓ cup oil-cured black olives, halved and pitted (¼ cup pitted)
6 thin lemon slices, seeds removed

1. Heat oven to 400°. Wrap garlic in aluminum foil. Place on a baking pan. Bake in heated 400° oven 1 hour 10 minutes or until soft. Remove from oven. When cool enough to handle, unwrap. Cut off about ¼ inch from top (not stem) of bulb. Squeeze soft garlic into a food processor.

2. Heat broiler. Broil sweet red pepper 6 inches from heat, turning it as needed, until blackened all over, about 10 minutes.

3. Transfer pepper to a paper bag and seal. When cool enough to handle, remove from bag. Remove stem; pour any pepper juices through a strainer into food processor with garlic. Remove skin and seeds; discard. Place pepper in food processor. Add tomatoes and basil leaves. Whirl until smooth.

4. Remove skin from chicken. Mix flour, salt and pepper in a plastic bag. Add chicken and toss to coat.

5. Heat oil in a large skillet over medium-high heat. Add chicken and brown, about 4 minutes per side. Remove to a medium-size bowl.

6. Add wine to skillet; cook about 1 minute. Lower heat to medium-low. Add red pepper puree and chicken to skillet. Bring to simmering; cover and cook 20 minutes. Add olives and lemon slices, turning chicken over. Cook, covered, 15 to 20 minutes longer or until internal temperature of a thigh registers 180° on an instant-read thermometer.

Chicken cacciatore

Makes 4 servings *Prep* 10 minutes *Cook* 40 minutes

This tasty "can-do" meal takes its cue from pantry staples: canned tomatoes, mushrooms and tomato paste.

Per serving

363 calories, 31 g protein, 16 g fat, 26 g carbohydrate, 759 mg sodium, 90 mg cholesterol.

4 whole chicken legs (2 pounds total)
3 tablespoons all-purpose flour, or more as needed
2 tablespoons olive oil
5 shallots, finely chopped
3 cloves garlic, finely chopped
1 can (28 ounces) crushed tomatoes
2 tablespoons tomato paste

¼ teaspoon dried oregano
¼ teaspoon dried thyme
1 tablespoon fresh lemon juice
1 teaspoon chicken bouillon granules
1 bay leaf
2 cans (4 ounces each) sliced mushrooms, drained
Chopped fresh parsley for garnish

1. Cut chicken legs into thighs and drumsticks; remove skin. Working in batches, combine chicken pieces and flour in a plastic food-storage bag; shake to coat chicken. Remove from bag; shake off excess flour.

2. Heat oil in a large nonstick skillet over medium heat. Add pieces of chicken, working in batches if necessary, and brown on one side. Turn chicken over. Add shallots and garlic. Brown other side of chicken.

3. Add tomatoes, tomato paste, oregano, thyme, lemon juice, chicken bouillon granules and bay leaf. Lower heat; cover and simmer 30 minutes or until chicken falls loosely from the bone. Remove bay leaf and discard. Add mushrooms; gently heat through. Garnish with chopped parsley.

Tarragon chicken with mushrooms *opposite*

Tarragon chicken with mushrooms

Makes 12 servings *Prep* 20 minutes *Cook* 1 hour

Here's an easy one-pot meal that feeds a crowd. No reason why this couldn't be prepared with just chicken legs if that's your preferred chicken part.

Per serving
383 calories, 37 g protein, 19 g fat, 12 g carbohydrate, 463 mg sodium, 113 mg cholesterol.

½ cup diced bacon (about 4 strips)
2 whole chickens (3½ pounds each), each cut into 8 serving pieces
2 pounds frozen small white onions
1½ pounds large mushrooms, each cut in half
1 can (13¾ ounces) chicken broth
¾ cup dry white wine

2 tablespoons fresh lemon juice
2 teaspoons dried tarragon
1 teaspoon salt
½ teaspoon black pepper
5 tablespoons all-purpose flour
5 tablespoons cold water
   Fresh tarragon sprigs for garnish (optional)

1. Cook bacon in a Dutch oven over medium-high heat until browned, about 3 minutes. With a slotted spoon, remove to paper toweling to drain.

2. Discard all but 2 tablespoons fat in Dutch oven. Remove skin from chicken. Working in batches, add chicken to pot and brown on both sides over medium heat, about 6 minutes. Transfer chicken to a plate. Cook onions in pot until golden, about 5 minutes. Transfer to plate with chicken. Cook mushrooms in pot until golden, about 4 minutes.

3. Return chicken and onions to pot. Add broth, wine, lemon juice, tarragon, salt and pepper. Bring to boiling. Reduce heat; cover and simmer 40 minutes or until internal temperature of a thigh registers 180° on an instant-read thermometer.

4. Stir together flour and water in a small bowl until smooth. Whisk 1 cup chicken cooking liquid into flour mixture until smooth. Stir flour mixture into chicken mixture in pot. Cook until mixture boils and thickens slightly, about 5 minutes.

5. Arrange chicken on a deep, large platter. Spoon vegetables and sauce over chicken. Sprinkle with bacon. Garnish with tarragon sprigs if desired.

Chicken and parsleyed dumpling stew

Makes 6 servings *Prep* 20 minutes *Cook* 40 minutes

Some things never go out of style. This gutsy stew is a much-requested recipe that first appeared in a 1983 issue of *Family Circle*.

Per serving
495 calories, 33 g protein, 27 g fat, 30 g carbohydrate, 622 mg sodium, 95 mg cholesterol.

½ cup all-purpose flour
¾ teaspoon salt
   Black pepper
1 whole chicken (3 pounds), cut into 8 serving pieces
3 tablespoons vegetable oil
1 tablespoon butter
1 medium onion, sliced
1 clove garlic, finely chopped
1 can (13¾ ounces) chicken broth

2 cups water
1 large rib celery, sliced
1 cup all-purpose baking mix (buttermilk or regular)
1½ tablespoons chopped fresh parsley
1½ teaspoons dried rosemary
⅓ cup milk
1 package (10 ounces) frozen mixed vegetables

1. Mix flour, ¼ teaspoon salt and pinch pepper in a plastic food-storage bag. Add chicken; shake to coat.

2. Heat oil and butter in a large Dutch oven over medium heat. Add chicken; sauté until lightly browned, 10 minutes. Add onion and garlic; sauté 3 minutes or until golden brown.

3. Add broth, water, celery, remaining ½ teaspoon salt and ¼ teaspoon pepper. Simmer, covered, 15 minutes or until internal temperature of a thigh registers 180° on an instant-read thermometer.

4. Combine baking mix, parsley, rosemary and milk in a medium-size bowl.

5. Uncover stew; bring to boiling; add vegetables. Heap a wet teaspoon with dough and drop into stew; repeat, using all dough. You should have about 20 dumplings. Cook, uncovered, 5 minutes over medium heat. Cover; cook 5 minutes or until dumplings are firm. Ladle stew into bowls.

Cooking times for chicken

	BAKE OR ROAST 350° TO 400°		BROIL 6" TO 8" FROM HEAT	POACH OR BRAISE	SAUTÉ OR FRY
Breast half, skinless, boneless	25–30	minutes	5 minutes per side	15–20 minutes	10–12 minutes
Drumstick	40–45	minutes	8–10 minutes per side	25–30 minutes	15–20 minutes
Thigh	45–50	minutes	10–12 minutes per side	30–35 minutes	20–25 minutes
Wing	25–35	minutes	5–8 minutes per side	15–20 minutes	10–15 minutes
Whole fryer	1½–2¼	hours			

Chicken potpie

Makes 6 servings   *Prep* 20 minutes   *Cook* 30 minutes   *Bake* at 450° for 35 minutes

The lattice crust lets the chunks of chicken, carrots and potatoes peek through. For seasoning, sprinkle a pinch of rosemary, thyme or tarragon into the chicken mixture.

Per serving
612 calories, 28 g protein, 23 g fat, 72 g carbohydrate, 911 mg sodium, 52 mg cholesterol.

Shopping and storage smarts
• Chicken should have no smell at all or just a faint pleasant aroma. When you get home, open the package; if there is an off odor, return it.
• Avoid packages containing a lot of blood or juice, which could mean the bird was frozen, then thawed and held too long.
• Refrigerate poultry up to 2 days. To hold longer, freeze it, overwrapped with foil or plastic wrap, up to 1 year if whole, up to 9 months if in parts.
• Thaw poultry in the refrigerator, never on the counter.

1 pound small new potatoes, quartered
4 carrots, cut into ½-inch-thick slices
2 cans (13¾ ounces each) lower-sodium chicken broth
4 boneless, skinless chicken breast halves (1 pound total), cut into ½-inch pieces
1 package (10 ounces) frozen petite peas, thawed
1 cup low-fat (1%) milk
⅓ cup all-purpose flour
¼ cup grated Parmesan cheese

Biscuit topping
2 tablespoons butter
¼ cup chopped onion
2 cups sifted all-purpose flour
2 teaspoons baking powder
1 teaspoon salt
¼ teaspoon baking soda
⅓ cup solid vegetable shortening
¾ cup buttermilk

1. Simmer potatoes and carrots in broth in a large skillet 15 minutes or until tender. Add chicken; cook 5 minutes. Remove chicken and vegetables with a slotted spoon to a large bowl. Strain broth through a sieve and reserve. Stir peas into chicken and vegetables.

2. Whisk milk and flour in a small saucepan. Stir in Parmesan cheese. Cook over medium heat, stirring, until thickened, 5 minutes. Slowly stir in 1 cup reserved broth. Cook, stirring, until thickened, 3 minutes. Pour over chicken.

3. Heat oven to 450°. Coat a 13 x 9 x 2-inch baking dish with nonstick cooking spray. Spoon chicken mixture into dish.

4. Prepare topping: Melt butter in a small skillet over medium heat. Add onion and sauté 5 minutes. Sift together flour, baking powder, salt and baking soda in a bowl. Cut shortening into flour mixture until it resembles coarse meal. Make a well in center; stir in sautéed onion and buttermilk; mix with a fork until dough forms a ball.

5. Press dough out on a lightly floured surface into a 12 x 6-inch rectangle. Fold dough crosswise in half. Press out into a rectangle again. Give dough a quarter turn. Repeat folding and turning 10 times. With a lightly floured rolling pin, roll into a 14 x 5-inch rectangle. Cut lengthwise into ½-inch-wide strips. Arrange strips in crisscross pattern over casserole; trim lengths to fit; tuck ends down into side of dish.

6. Bake in lower half of heated 450° oven 35 minutes or until topping is lightly browned and filling is bubbly. Let stand 10 minutes before serving.

Barbecue wings

Makes 6 servings   *Prep* 15 minutes   *Bake* at 375° for 45 minutes   *Broil* 4 to 6 minutes

Here is the sweet-and-sour classic: honey for the sweet, red-wine vinegar for the sour and hot-pepper sauce for the zing.

Per serving

251 calories, 21 g protein, 15 g fat, 9 g carbohydrate, 592 mg sodium, 61 mg cholesterol.

2½ pounds chicken wings
¾ cup chili sauce
2 tablespoons honey
2 tablespoons soy sauce
2 teaspoons dry mustard

1 teaspoon red-wine vinegar
5 drops hot-pepper sauce
2 green onions, sliced
1 teaspoon salt

1. Heat oven to 375°. Grease a large baking pan.

2. Cut off wing tips and save tips for soup or stock. Cut trimmed wings in half at joint.

3. Combine chili sauce, honey, soy sauce, mustard, vinegar, hot-pepper sauce, green onions and salt in a large bowl. Add wings; toss to coat.

4. Place wings on prepared baking pan. Bake in heated 375° oven, turning every 15 minutes, 45 minutes or until fully cooked. Increase oven temperature to broil. Broil wings on both sides until crisp, 2 to 3 minutes per side.

Oven-fried chicken wings

Makes 6 servings   *Prep* 20 minutes   *Refrigerate* 2 hours   *Bake* at 425° for 35 minutes

A crisp coating makes these finger-licking wings especially irresistible. Put out a bowl of blue cheese dressing for dipping, and you'll be a little closer to the original recipe from Buffalo.

Per serving

278 calories, 20 g protein, 12 g fat, 21 g carbohydrate, 605 mg sodium, 50 mg cholesterol.

2 pounds chicken wings
1 cup buttermilk
  Juice of ½ lemon
2 cloves garlic, finely chopped
½ teaspoon hot-pepper sauce

½ teaspoon salt
⅛ teaspoon black pepper
½ cup yellow cornmeal
½ cup dry seasoned bread crumbs

1. Cut off wing tips and save tips for soup or stock. Cut trimmed wings in half at joint.

2. Combine buttermilk, lemon juice, garlic, hot-pepper sauce, salt and black pepper in a plastic food-storage bag. Add chicken wings and seal bag; toss to coat. Refrigerate 2 hours.

3. Heat oven to 425°. Lightly grease a large baking pan.

4. Combine cornmeal and bread crumbs in a plastic food-storage bag. Drain chicken wings well. Add to crumb mixture in plastic bag; shake several times or until wings are completely coated. Arrange wings in prepared pan. Coat chicken lightly with nonstick cooking spray. Bake in heated 425° oven 35 minutes or until tender and golden.

Barbecue wings
opposite

Sticky wings

Makes 6 servings *Prep* 15 minutes *Bake* at 450° for 25 minutes *Broil* 8 minutes

Definitely a treat for those who love Asian seasonings—these tangy pick-me-ups are made with soy sauce, chili sauce, oyster sauce, dark sesame oil and ginger. They're proof that chicken wings are fabulous in any language.

Per serving
267 calories, 17 g protein, 16 g fat, 14 g carbohydrate, 618 mg sodium, 49 mg cholesterol.

2 pounds chicken wings
½ cup chopped green onion
¼ cup honey
2 tablespoons soy sauce
2 tablespoons Asian chili sauce
2 tablespoons oyster sauce
2 tablespoons dark Asian sesame oil
1 teaspoon ground ginger
2 cloves garlic, finely chopped

1. Heat oven to 450°. Grease a large baking pan.

2. Cut off wing tips and save tips for soup or stock. Cut trimmed wings in half at joint.

3. Combine green onion, honey, soy sauce, chili sauce, oyster sauce, sesame oil, ginger and garlic in a large bowl. Add wings; toss to coat. Place wings with sauce in a single layer in prepared baking pan.

4. Bake in heated 450° oven, turning occasionally, 25 minutes or until chicken is evenly browned.

5. Increase oven temperature to broil. Broil wings 6 inches from heat, turning occasionally, 8 minutes or until sauce is thick enough to coat back of spoon. Remove wings to a platter; spoon sauce on top.

247

Crispy baked drumsticks

Makes 6 servings *Prep* 15 minutes *Bake* at 375° for 45 minutes

You'll get a crunch from the cornflakes and a kick from the red pepper. And kids will like 'em too.

Per serving

289 calories, 22 g protein, 14 g fat, 18 g carbohydrate, 718 mg sodium, 84 mg cholesterol.

6 chicken drumsticks (2 pounds total)
1¼ teaspoon salt
⅓ cup all-purpose flour
2 tablespoons milk
1 egg

¾ cup cornflake crumbs
1 tablespoon chopped fresh parsley
3 tablespoons butter or margarine
2 tablespoons fresh lemon juice
¼ teaspoon ground red pepper (cayenne)

1. Heat oven to 375°.

2. Remove skin from drumsticks. Sprinkle drumsticks evenly with 1 teaspoon salt.

3. Place flour on a sheet of waxed paper. Whisk together milk and egg in a medium-size bowl. On another sheet of waxed paper, combine cornflake crumbs and parsley. Coat each drumstick in flour, dip in egg mixture, then coat with cornflake crumbs, pressing crumbs onto chicken to adhere. Place on a small ungreased baking sheet.

4. Heat together butter, lemon juice, remaining ¼ teaspoon salt and ground red pepper in a small saucepan until butter is melted. Drizzle butter mixture over chicken.

5. Bake in heated 375° oven 45 minutes or until chicken is golden and internal temperature registers 180° on an instant-read thermometer.

Chicken thighs, osso-buco style

Makes 4 servings *Prep* 15 minutes *Cook* 50 minutes

We've replaced the usual veal shanks with chicken thighs in this Italian specialty, but we've kept the flavorful gremolata garnish— a mixture of parsley, lemon and garlic.

Per serving

630 calories, 40 g protein, 21 g fat, 70 g carbohydrate, 924 mg sodium, 169 mg cholesterol.

8 chicken thighs (2½ pounds total)
½ teaspoon salt
½ teaspoon black pepper
3 tablespoons all-purpose flour
1½ tablespoons olive oil
1 cup finely chopped celery
½ cup finely chopped carrot
½ cup finely chopped onion

1 can (14½ ounces) stewed tomatoes
1 cup chicken broth
1 bay leaf
1 package (12 ounces) wide egg noodles
1 tablespoon finely chopped parsley
1 tablespoon grated lemon rind
1 clove garlic, finely chopped

1. Remove skin from chicken thighs. Season chicken with salt and pepper. Combine chicken and flour in a medium-size bowl; toss to coat chicken.

2. Heat oil in a Dutch oven over medium-high heat. Add chicken; cook until browned on both sides, about 5 minutes. Transfer to a large plate.

3. Add celery, carrot and onion to pot; cook over medium heat until vegetables are very tender, about 10 minutes.

4. Return chicken to pot. Stir in tomatoes, broth and bay leaf. Bring to boiling. Lower heat; simmer, covered, 20 minutes. Uncover pot; simmer 15 minutes or until internal temperature of chicken registers 180° on an instant-read thermometer. Remove and discard bay leaf.

5. Meanwhile, cook noodles in a large pot of lightly salted boiling water until al dente, firm but tender. Drain.

6. Combine parsley, lemon rind and garlic in a small bowl. Arrange chicken on a large, deep platter. Spoon sauce over. Sprinkle with parsley mixture. Serve with cooked noodles on the side.

Tandoori chicken legs

Makes 6 servings *Prep* 20 minutes *Refrigerate* 4 to 24 hours

Grill over indirect heat 30 minutes *or broil* 40 minutes

The yogurt marinade borrows the seasonings of Indian tandoori cooking: cumin, turmeric, cinnamon and allspice. If you have a preference for drumsticks or thighs, use them exclusively.

Per serving
171 calories, 16 g protein, 9 g fat, 7 g carbohydrate, 430 mg sodium, 52 mg cholesterol.

1 onion, cut into 8 wedges
1 piece (2 inches) fresh ginger, peeled and quartered
4 cloves garlic
1 tablespoon olive oil
2 tablespoons fresh lemon juice
1 teaspoon ground cumin
1 teaspoon ground turmeric
½ teaspoon ground cinnamon
½ teaspoon ground allspice
1 teaspoon salt
½ teaspoon black pepper
1 container (8 ounces) plain low-fat yogurt
6 chicken legs (3½ pounds total)

1. Combine onion, ginger, garlic, oil, lemon juice, cumin, turmeric, cinnamon, allspice, salt and pepper in a blender or small food processor. Pulse until smooth. Add yogurt; pulse to combine. Transfer to a plastic food-storage bag large enough to hold chicken.

2. Remove skin from chicken legs. Cut 2 slashes down to the bone on each thigh; pierce each drumstick 4 or 5 times with tip of a knife. Add to bag with yogurt mixture; push out air; seal. Refrigerate 4 to 24 hours.

3. Prepare a charcoal grill with hot coals around sides and drip pan in center. Or heat a gas grill to high, then turn off burner directly beneath where you'll place chicken. Or heat broiler. Position grill rack or broiler shelf 6 inches from heat. Place chicken on rack in grill or broiler pan; place marinade in a small saucepan.

4. Boil marinade 5 minutes. Grill chicken, covered, 15 minutes per side, or broil 20 minutes per side. Brush chicken occasionally with marinade up to last 5 minutes. Cook until internal temperature registers 180° on an instant-read thermometer.

Spicy BBQ chicken
thighs *opposite*

Classic grilled chicken

Makes 4 servings   *Prep* 10 minutes   *Cook* 3 minutes   *Grill* 45 minutes

Mix up a double or triple batch of the BBQ sauce and refrigerate for up to a week or so to have on hand for other BBQ moments.

Per serving
493 calories, 52 g protein,
26 g fat, 11 g carbohydrate,
734 mg sodium,
166 mg cholesterol.

1 teaspoon vegetable oil
1 onion, finely chopped
2 cloves garlic, finely chopped
3 tablespoons cider vinegar
¾ cup ketchup
2 teaspoons spicy brown mustard
1 tablespoon Worcestershire sauce

1 tablespoon molasses
2 teaspoons hot-pepper sauce
1 whole chicken (3½ pounds),
   cut into 8 serving pieces
½ teaspoon salt
¼ teaspoon black pepper

1. Lightly brush a grill rack with vegetable oil. Then prepare a charcoal grill with low-heat coals, or heat a gas grill to medium-high.

2. Heat oil in a medium-size skillet over medium heat. Add onion and garlic and sauté until softened, 3 minutes. Remove to a small bowl and stir in vinegar, ketchup, mustard, Worcestershire sauce, molasses and hot-pepper sauce. Season chicken with salt and pepper.

3. Grill, uncovered, 5 minutes or until lightly browned. Turn over; spoon sauce on chicken. Grill 5 minutes. Turn over; spoon on more sauce. Cover grill. Grill 10 minutes. Spoon on sauce. Turn chicken every 5 to 10 minutes until internal temperature registers 180° on instant-read thermometer, about 25 minutes more. Do not spoon on sauce during last minutes of cooking.

Spicy BBQ chicken thighs

Makes 4 servings   *Prep* 5 minutes   *Refrigerate* 1 hour   *Grill or bake* 45 minutes

Soaking the chicken first in a brine keeps the flesh moist and flavorful during cooking. This technique works for any chicken parts or even a whole chicken or turkey. If you're not familiar with spice rubs, here's your chance to try one. They're a wonderful way to flavor foods without adding fat.

Per serving
363 calories, 41 g protein, 18 g fat, 10 g carbohydrate, 1,737 mg sodium, 144 mg cholesterol.

⅓ cup coarse salt
⅓ cup sugar
4 cups water
8 chicken thighs (2½ pounds total)
1 tablespoon brown sugar
¼ cup paprika

1 teaspoon ground cumin
⅛ teaspoon ground red pepper (cayenne)
½ teaspoon black pepper
½ teaspoon garlic powder
¼ teaspoon onion powder

1. To make a brine for soaking chicken, combine salt, sugar and water in a large nonaluminum bowl. Stir to completely dissolve salt and sugar.

2. If desired, remove skin from chicken thighs. Place chicken in brine, making sure all the pieces are submerged. Cover bowl with plastic wrap and refrigerate 1 hour.

3. Meanwhile, to make a spice rub, mix together brown sugar, paprika, cumin, red pepper, black pepper, garlic powder and onion powder in a small bowl.

4. Lightly brush a grill rack with vegetable oil or coat a rack in a baking pan with nonstick cooking spray. Then prepare a charcoal grill with low-heat coals, or heat a gas grill to medium-high, or heat oven to 375°.

5. Remove chicken from brine and pat dry. Dust chicken on both sides with spice rub, pressing gently to make sure rub adheres; if keeping skin on, spread rub evenly under skin with your fingers. Place chicken on grill rack or broiler-pan rack.

6. Grill chicken, uncovered, about 5 minutes per side or until surfaces begin to brown. Turn thighs over, cover grill and cook 5 more minutes per side. Uncover and continue grilling, turning thighs every 5 minutes, until internal temperature registers 180° on an instant-read thermometer, 25 minutes more. Chicken should be mahogany brown, and flesh should feel firm.

To bake: Bake thighs in heated 375° oven 5 minutes, then turn over and bake another 5 minutes. Turn thighs again and bake 10 minutes. Turn and bake 10 minutes more. Turn a final time and bake until internal temperature registers 180° on an instant-read thermometer, about 15 minutes more. If cooking with skin on, you may wish to run under broiler for 3 minutes to crisp skin.

Chicken burgers

Makes 6 servings   *Prep* 10 minutes   *Grill or broil* about 10 minutes

Instead of just resting a slice of cheddar on top of the burger, we mix the cheese right into the meat. Crushed garlic croutons and Worcestershire sauce are the other taste enhancers.

Per serving
380 calories, 23 g protein, 21 g fat, 24 g carbohydrate, 565 mg sodium, 138 mg cholesterol.

1½ pounds ground chicken
1 small onion, finely chopped
3 tablespoons water
¾ cup garlic croutons, finely crushed
1 tablespoon Worcestershire sauce
½ cup shredded cheddar cheese
½ teaspoon salt
¼ teaspoon black pepper
2 tablespoons chopped fresh parsley
2 tablespoons olive oil
6 hamburger buns
3 leaves romaine lettuce, cleaned and halved
1 medium tomato, cut into 6 slices

1. Lightly brush a grill rack with vegetable oil or coat a broiler-pan rack with nonstick cooking spray. Then prepare a charcoal grill with medium-hot coals, or heat a gas grill to medium-high, or heat broiler.

2. Mix together chicken, onion, water, croutons, Worcestershire sauce, cheese, salt, pepper and parsley in a large bowl. With moistened hands, form mixture into 6 burgers. Brush completely with olive oil.

3. Grill or broil burgers 3 to 4 inches from heat 4 to 5 minutes per side or until internal temperature reaches 165° on an instant-read thermometer. Serve on buns, topped with lettuce and tomato.

Chicken burritos

Makes 10 servings   *Prep* 15 minutes   *Cook* 18 minutes   *Microwave* tortillas 1 to 2 minutes

To help with party prep, cook the chicken mixture a day ahead. Then warm the tortillas and let guests roll their own burritos.

Per serving
282 calories, 20 g protein, 10 g fat, 30 g carbohydrate, 583 mg sodium, 44 mg cholesterol.

2 teaspoons olive oil
1 large onion, chopped
2 cloves garlic, finely chopped
1 sweet red pepper, chopped
1 sweet green pepper, chopped
2 jalapeño chiles, seeded, chopped
1 tablespoon chili powder
1 tablespoon ground cumin
⅛ teaspoon ground allspice
1 pound ground chicken breast
1 can (8 ounces) reduced-sodium tomato sauce
1 teaspoon sugar
¾ teaspoon salt
1 can (15 ounces) pinto beans, drained, rinsed and mashed
10 flour tortillas (10-inch)
3 tablespoons chopped fresh cilantro
2½ cups shredded jicama or romaine lettuce
1½ cups shredded cheddar cheese
Salsa, avocado and sour cream for serving (optional)

1. Heat oil in a large nonstick skillet over medium heat. Add onion, garlic, sweet peppers and jalapeños and sauté 10 minutes or until crisp-tender.

2. Add chili powder, cumin and allspice; cook 30 seconds. Add chicken, breaking up with a wooden spoon; cook 6 minutes or until no longer pink. Stir in tomato sauce, sugar, salt and beans.

3. Meanwhile, wrap tortillas in damp paper toweling. Microwave on 100% power 1 to 2 minutes or until steaming and very pliable.

4. Stir cilantro into chicken mixture. Spoon about ⅓ cup chicken mixture on each tortilla. Top each with ¼ cup jicama and 2 tablespoons cheese. Roll up, envelope style. Serve with salsa, avocado and sour cream if you wish.

Asian chicken and slaw

Makes 4 servings   *Prep* 10 minutes   *Cook* 18 minutes

Here's a quick meal with a terrific flavor blast: gingery chicken burgers paired with sesame oil-spiked coleslaw.

Per serving
344 calories, 32 g protein,
21 g fat, 5 g carbohydrate,
579 mg sodium,
99 mg cholesterol.

1¼ pounds ground chicken
3 cloves garlic, minced
2 green onions (including some green), finely chopped
1 tablespoon grated fresh ginger
1 can (8 ounces) water chestnuts, drained and chopped
2 tablespoons dark Asian sesame oil

3 tablespoons soy sauce
1 tablespoon hoisin sauce
1 teaspoon salt
¼ teaspoon black pepper
1 package (16 ounces) shredded coleslaw mix
¼ cup beef broth

1. Combine chicken, 2 cloves garlic, green onions, 2 teaspoons ginger, half of water chestnuts, 2 teaspoons sesame oil, 2 tablespoons soy sauce, hoisin sauce, ¾ teaspoon salt and pepper in a medium-size bowl. Shape into patties.

2. Heat remaining 2 teaspoons sesame oil in a large nonstick skillet over medium-high heat. Add patties and cook 4 minutes per side or until internal temperature registers 165° on an instant-read thermometer. Remove to a serving platter and keep warm.

3. Add remaining garlic, ginger, water chestnuts, soy sauce and salt to skillet, along with coleslaw mix. Cook over medium-high heat 7 minutes. Add broth, cover and cook 3 minutes or until tender. Serve slaw alongside patties.

Roast chicken with vegetables

Other root vegetables, such as cut-up parsnips or turnips, will roast nicely alongside the chicken.

Per serving
528 calories, 53 g protein, 25 g fat, 20 g carbohydrate, 523 mg sodium, 159 mg cholesterol.

1 whole chicken (5 pounds)
½ teaspoon salt
¼ teaspoon black pepper
2 sprigs fresh tarragon or ½ teaspoon dried
2 sprigs fresh thyme or ½ teaspoon dried

1 pound red boiling potatoes, cut into quarters or halves if large
1 container (10 ounces) white pearl onions, peeled
2 large carrots, cut into thick slices
12 ounces mushrooms, quartered
½ cup chicken broth or water

1. Heat oven to 450°.

2. Pat chicken dry with paper toweling. Remove excess fat. Sprinkle with salt and pepper inside and out. Place tarragon and thyme in cavity of chicken. Slip tips of chicken wings under bird. Tie legs closely together. Place chicken, breast side down, in a roasting pan large enough to hold vegetables heaped around it. Place potatoes, onions and carrots around chicken.

3. Roast in heated 450° oven 30 minutes.

4. Lower oven temperature to 350°. Turn chicken breast side up. Add mushrooms around chicken in pan. Add broth. Roast another 45 minutes or until internal temperature of a thigh registers 180° on an instant-read thermometer.

5. Remove chicken to a platter; let rest 5 to 7 minutes before cutting into portions. Return roasting pan with vegetables to oven for another 15 minutes or until potatoes are tender.

Cook to the safe degree

To minimize risk, always cook poultry thoroughly, as indicated here. Use an instant-read thermometer to ascertain the following temperatures, making sure the thermometer does not touch a bone when inserted. Never use marinade from raw poultry as a sauce unless you boil it rapidly for at least 5 minutes.

Ground	165°
Whole (measured in thigh)	180°
Thigh or drumstick	180°
Breast	170°
Stuffing (preferably cooked separately)	165°

Roast chicken
with vegetables
opposite

255

Cherry-glazed roast chicken

Makes 8 servings   *Prep* 15 minutes   *Refrigerate* 1 to 4 hours   *Roast* at 350° for 1½ hours

What's the secret ingredient here? A tea marinade.

Per serving

547 calories, 54 g protein, 26 g fat, 22 g carbohydrate, 724 mg sodium, 166 mg cholesterol.

great grilling

Ever try cooking a whole chicken on the grill? It's easy and yummy. Bank the charcoal on the sides and place a drip pan in the center. Replenish the coals as needed. For a three-burner gas grill, turn on all burners for 10 minutes. Then turn off the center burner, place drip pan on top, place the food on the grill over the pan, and turn the other burners to medium or low. For a two-burner grill, heat as above, then turn both burners to medium.

4 tea bags
1 cup boiling water
1 cup water
½ cup reduced-sodium soy sauce
2 large cloves garlic, crushed
1 whole chicken (5 pounds)

Cherry glaze
⅓ cup cherry jam
2 teaspoons reduced-sodium soy sauce

2 teaspoons grated fresh ginger
1 teaspoon dark Asian sesame oil

Gravy
6 tablespoons cherry jam
2 tablespoons honey
3 tablespoons cornstarch
¼ cup water
¾ teaspoon salt
2 tablespoons fresh lemon juice

1. Steep tea bags in 1 cup boiling water 5 minutes; discard bags. Add other 1 cup water, soy sauce and garlic to tea.

2. Loosen skin around chicken breasts and legs. Place chicken in a food-storage bag. Add tea mixture to bag; push out air; seal. Refrigerate 1 to 4 hours.

3. Heat oven to 350°.

4. Remove chicken from plastic bag; pour marinade into a large roasting pan. Place neck and gizzard in pan. Place chicken, breast side up, on rack in pan. Roast in heated 350° oven 1½ hours or until internal temperature of a thigh registers 180° on an instant-read thermometer.

5. Meanwhile, prepare cherry glaze: Combine jam, soy sauce, ginger and sesame oil in a small bowl. Brush over chicken during last hour of cooking.

6. Let chicken stand at least 20 minutes before carving.

7. Meanwhile, prepare gravy: Discard neck and gizzard from pan. Pour drippings into a 1-quart measuring cup. Skim off fat. Add water to equal 3 cups. Pour into a saucepan with jam and honey. Bring to simmering. Combine cornstarch, water and salt in a small bowl. Stir into saucepan. Simmer, stirring, 2 to 3 minutes or until gravy is thickened. Remove from heat. Stir in lemon juice. Serve with sliced chicken.

Garlicky roast chicken

Makes 8 servings   *Prep* 10 minutes   *Roast* at 400° for 1 hour 15 minutes

**Want more vegetables?
Toss in baby carrots.**

Per serving
478 calories, 40 g protein,
22 g fat, 28 g carbohydrate,
492 mg sodium,
119 mg cholesterol.

1 lemon, quartered
1 whole chicken (5 pounds)
½ bunch fresh thyme
1 tablespoon plus 2 teaspoons
  olive oil
1 teaspoon salt
¾ teaspoon coarse black pepper
2 pounds small (about 1½-inch)
  red new potatoes

1 large red onion, sliced through
  root end into 8 wedges
2 large heads garlic, cut lengthwise
  in half
15 Kalamata olives, pitted
2 plum tomatoes, cut lengthwise
  in half

1. Heat oven to 400°.

2. Place lemon inside chicken. Chop enough thyme for 2 teaspoons. Reserve remainder for garnish. Mix 1 teaspoon chopped thyme, 2 teaspoons oil, ¼ teaspoon salt and ¼ teaspoon pepper in a small bowl. Rub over chicken. Place chicken in a large roasting pan.

3. Combine potatoes, onion, garlic, olives and remaining 1 teaspoon chopped thyme, 1 tablespoon oil, ¾ teaspoon salt and ½ teaspoon pepper in a medium-size bowl. Arrange potatoes around chicken.

4. Roast in heated 400° oven 1 hour. Add tomatoes. Roast 15 minutes or until internal temperature of a thigh registers 180° on an instant-read thermometer. Arrange on a platter. Garnish with thyme sprigs.

POULTRY

garlic tips

GARLIC IS ONE OF the most versatile seasonings. The longer it cooks, the milder its flavor. Store garlic in a cool, dry place, as you do onions. Here are some tips for handling it.

To peel: Place a clove on a cutting board; press down on the clove with the flat side of a knife. The skin will loosen so you can slip it off. If not, rinse the clove in hot water and press again.

To mince: Starting near the root end, cut vertically into thin, even slices. Make one horizontal cut across the garlic parallel to the cutting surface. Then, cutting vertically again, make thin slices perpendicular to the first cuts. To chop, make larger slices.

To make paste: Sprinkle ½ teaspoon salt over 2 minced cloves; mash with the flat side of a knife.

To sauté: Garlic burns easily, so sauté only over medium heat and stir constantly.

To roast: Slice the tip off an entire unpeeled head of garlic, then brush the cut surface lightly with oil. Bake, covered, in a 350° oven for 1 hour. Squeeze the pulp from the cloves.

Turkey satay

Makes 6 servings *Prep* 20 minutes *Refrigerate* 1 to 4 hours

Cook sauce 6 minutes *Grill* over direct heat 12 minutes

The Indonesian classic on a skewer, served with a spicy peanut sauce. It's great as a main dish or pass-around appetizer.

Per serving
447 calories, 37 g protein, 23 g fat, 27 g carbohydrate, 491 mg sodium, 93 mg cholesterol.

Skewer strategies
• Metal skewers are great for main-dish portions. Look for 2-pronged versions that make turning kabobs even easier.
• To turn a main portion into an appetizer, switch to short wooden skewers. But always soak wooden skewers for at least 30 minutes; otherwise, you'll be serving your kabobs flambé.

2 turkey thighs (1½ pounds total)
1 tablespoon olive oil
1 tablespoon soy sauce
1 tablespoon red-wine vinegar
1 tablespoon honey
1 teaspoon curry powder
1 teaspoon ground ginger
1 teaspoon ground cumin
1 sweet red pepper, cored, seeded and cut into 1-inch pieces
1 sweet green pepper, cored, seeded and cut into 1-inch pieces
3 ears fresh corn, shucked, cut crosswise into 1-inch-wide pieces
2 tomatoes, cut into 6 wedges and halved

Satay sauce
1 tablespoon olive oil
1 onion, chopped
2 cloves garlic, chopped
2 teaspoons curry powder
⅛ teaspoon ground cinnamon
⅛ teaspoon ground red pepper (cayenne)
¼ cup water
¼ cup creamy peanut butter
3 tablespoons light-brown sugar
1 tablespoon soy sauce
1 tablespoon fresh lemon juice

1. Remove skin from thighs. Using a sharp knife, cut meat away from bone. Remove any tendons. Cut turkey into ¾-inch cubes.

2. Combine oil, soy sauce, vinegar, honey, curry powder, ginger and cumin in a plastic food-storage bag. Add turkey to bag; push out air; seal. Refrigerate 1 to 4 hours.

3. Prepare a charcoal grill with hot coals, or heat a gas grill to medium-high. Position a grill rack 6 inches above source of heat.

4. Thread turkey, sweet peppers, corn and tomatoes onto 6 metal skewers, alternating pieces. Grill 12 minutes or until meat is cooked through, turning occasionally.

5. Prepare satay sauce: Heat oil in a medium-size skillet over medium heat. Add onion and garlic and sauté 5 minutes to soften. Stir in curry powder, cinnamon and ground red pepper; sauté 1 minute. Transfer to a blender and add water, peanut butter, brown sugar, soy sauce and lemon juice. Whirl until smooth. Serve with the skewers.

Turkey saltimbocca

Makes 4 servings *Prep* 10 minutes *Cook* 4 minutes

You've seen this on restaurant menus made with veal, prosciutto and cheese. Our easy do-at-home version uses turkey cutlets, ham and Swiss cheese, with sage for seasoning.

Per serving
297 calories, 27 g protein, 17 g fat, 7 g carbohydrate, 683 mg sodium, 68 mg cholesterol.

4 turkey cutlets (¾ pound total)
¼ cup all-purpose flour
½ teaspoon salt
½ teaspoon dried sage
2 tablespoons vegetable oil
4 thin slices cooked ham (about 3 ounces total)
4 thin slices Swiss cheese (about 2 ounces total)
¼ cup dry white wine
¼ cup lower-sodium chicken broth
2 tablespoons chopped fresh parsley for garnish (optional)

1. Place turkey cutlets between sheets of plastic wrap. Lightly pound until paper-thin. Combine flour, salt and sage on a sheet of waxed paper. Dip cutlets into flour mixture to coat both sides; tap off excess.

2. Heat oil in large nonstick skillet over medium-high heat. Add cutlets; cook until browned on bottom, 1 to 2 minutes. Turn cutlets over; top with 1 slice each of ham and cheese. Add wine and broth; cook over high heat until cheese is melted and sauce thickens, about 2 minutes longer.

3. Transfer cutlets to a platter. Spoon sauce over. Garnish with parsley if desired. Serve immediately.

Turkey saltimbocca

Turkey "London broil"

Makes 6 servings *Prep* 15 minutes *Refrigerate* 1 hour *Broil or grill* 20 minutes

This turkey version of a fast-to-grill London broil gets its great taste from a lemon marinade.

Shown on page 227.

Per serving

297 calories, 37 g protein, 14 g fat, 2 g carbohydrate, 158 mg sodium, 102 mg cholesterol.

4 cloves garlic, finely chopped
⅓ cup olive oil
1 tablespoon grated lemon rind
2 tablespoons fresh lemon juice
¼ cup chopped fresh oregano
1 tablespoon chopped fresh parsley

¼ teaspoon salt
¼ teaspoon black pepper
½ cup dry white wine
1 boneless, skinless turkey breast (2 pounds)

1. Combine garlic, oil, lemon rind and juice, oregano, parsley, salt, pepper and wine in a 13 x 9 x 2-inch baking dish.

2. Place turkey breast, smooth side down, on a cutting board. Starting in center of thickest part on one half of the breast, cut meat horizontally in half but not all the way through. Spread meat out like an open book. Press lightly on thickest parts to make a rectangle of even thickness.

3. Place turkey in marinade in dish; turn several times to coat thoroughly. Cover and refrigerate at least 1 hour to marinate.

4. Heat broiler, or prepare a charcoal grill with hot coals, or heat a gas grill to medium-high. Place broiler pan or grill rack 4 inches from source of heat.

5. Remove turkey from marinade. Bring marinade to boiling in a small saucepan; boil 5 minutes. Broil or grill turkey 8 to 10 minutes per side or until internal temperature registers 170° on an instant-read thermometer; baste with marinade every minute until last 3 or 4 minutes. Let turkey rest about 5 minutes. Cut into ¼-inch-thick slices.

Provençal turkey cutlets

Makes 4 servings *Prep* 15 minutes *Cook* 35 minutes

For accompaniments, prepare couscous with currants and chicken broth and a side salad of crisp frisée.

Per serving

274 calories, 29 g protein, 9 g fat, 21 g carbohydrate, 534 mg sodium, 58 mg cholesterol.

2 tablespoons all-purpose flour
¼ teaspoon salt
⅛ teaspoon black pepper
4 turkey cutlets (1 pound total)
3 teaspoons olive oil
12 ounces zucchini, sliced
1 medium onion, chopped
1 clove garlic, finely chopped

1 can (14½ ounces) stewed tomatoes
1 teaspoon grated orange rind
½ cup fresh orange juice
½ teaspoon dried thyme
2 tablespoons chopped pitted oil-cured black olives

1. Combine 2 tablespoons flour, salt and pepper on a sheet of waxed paper. Coat turkey with flour mixture.

2. Heat 1 teaspoon oil in a large nonstick skillet over medium heat. Add half of cutlets; brown on both sides, about 6 minutes per side. Remove from skillet. Repeat with another teaspoon oil and remaining cutlets.

3. Sauté zucchini, onion and garlic in remaining teaspoon oil in skillet until almost tender, 2 minutes. Add tomatoes, orange rind, ¼ cup orange juice and thyme. Simmer, covered, 5 minutes or until vegetables are tender.

4. Combine remaining ¼ cup orange juice and flour. Stir into skillet along with olives; cook, stirring, until mixture thickens and boils, about 2 minutes. Return cutlets to skillet. Cook, covered, until cutlets are cooked through, 8 to 10 minutes.

Sweet-and-sour turkey meatballs

Makes 4 servings   *Prep* 25 minutes   *Cook* 25 to 30 minutes

POULTRY

Omit the rice from the recipe, and spoon the meatballs and sauce over fettuccine for a Thursday night pasta dinner.

Per serving
533 calories, 26 g protein, 12 g fat, 80 g carbohydrate, 1,937 mg sodium, 118 mg cholesterol.

1 medium onion, chopped
1 large sweet green pepper, cored, seeded and chopped
1 large carrot, chopped
1 can (14½ ounces) chicken broth
1 can (15 ounces) tomato sauce
¼ cup packed light-brown sugar
¼ cup distilled white vinegar
1 small can (8 ounces) juice-packed crushed pineapple
¼ cup ketchup

1 slice white bread
2 tablespoons milk
¾ pound ground turkey
½ medium zucchini, shredded (about ½ cup)
1 egg, lightly beaten
1 teaspoon salt
½ teaspoon garlic powder
½ teaspoon black pepper
2 cups packaged precooked rice

1. Combine onion, green pepper, carrot, broth, tomato sauce, brown sugar, vinegar, pineapple and ketchup in a large skillet. Simmer, uncovered, 10 minutes or until vegetables are tender.

2. Meanwhile, soak bread in milk in a large bowl until milk is absorbed. Add turkey, zucchini, egg, salt, garlic powder and black pepper. Shape turkey mixture into 12 meatballs, about 2 tablespoons each.

3. Drop meatballs into simmering sauce; simmer, uncovered, 15 minutes or until cooked through; turn over once during cooking.

4. Remove from heat. Stir in rice; cover; let stand 5 minutes. Fluff rice with a fork before serving.

261

Turkey sloppy Joe

Turkey sloppy Joe

Makes 4 servings *Prep* 5 minutes *Cook* 17 minutes

Traditionally made with ground beef, the sloppy Joe is updated here with ground turkey. What could be better than a side helping of coleslaw?

Per serving
432 calories, 27 g protein, 16 g fat, 44 g carbohydrate, 991 mg sodium, 59 mg cholesterol.

1 pound ground turkey
2 teaspoons olive oil
1 large red onion, coarsely chopped
1 sweet green pepper, cored, seeded and coarsely chopped
1 teaspoon dried oregano, crumbled

1 teaspoon ground cumin
1 teaspoon chili powder
1 can (8 ounces) tomato sauce
½ cup bottled barbecue sauce
¼ cup chopped stuffed green olives (optional)
4 hard rolls, split

1. Heat a medium-size nonstick skillet over medium heat. Add turkey; cook, breaking up meat with a wooden spoon, until no longer pink, about 6 minutes. Remove turkey from skillet with a slotted spoon; discard any liquid. Wipe skillet clean with paper toweling.

2. Heat oil in skillet over medium heat. Add onion, green pepper, oregano, cumin and chili powder; cook, covered, 6 minutes or until softened, stirring occasionally. Add turkey, tomato sauce, barbecue sauce and olives if using. Bring to simmering; cook 5 minutes. Serve on rolls.

Make-ahead tip: This recipe can be made 2 days ahead and refrigerated, or frozen for up to 1 month.

Turkey enchiladas

Makes 5 servings *Prep* 30 minutes *Cook* 20 minutes *Bake* at 375° for 30 minutes

This recipe works as well with ground beef and you can vary the amount of jalapeño depending on your "heat" tolerance. Round out your dinner plate with a salad of avocado and romaine lettuce.

Per serving
382 calories, 24 g protein, 16 g fat, 38 g carbohydrate, 1,052 mg sodium, 89 mg cholesterol.

1 pound ground turkey
1 tablespoon olive oil
1 large onion, chopped
1 jalapeño chile, seeded and chopped
1½ teaspoons ground cumin
1½ teaspoons dried oregano
¼ teaspoon ground cinnamon
¾ teaspoon salt
4 tablespoons tomato paste

⅓ cup chopped pitted green olives
2 tablespoons olive brine
1 can (8 ounces) reduced-sodium tomato sauce
½ cup water
10 corn tortillas (6-inch)
½ cup shredded cheddar cheese (2 ounces)
Reduced-fat sour cream (optional)

1. Coat a medium-size skillet with nonstick cooking spray. Heat skillet over medium-high heat. Add turkey; cook, breaking up with a wooden spoon, 6 to 8 minutes or until no longer pink. Remove turkey from skillet with a slotted spoon; discard any liquid. Wipe skillet clean with paper toweling.

2. Heat oil in skillet over medium heat. Add onion and jalapeño; sauté 8 minutes. Stir in cumin, oregano, cinnamon and salt; cook 2 minutes. Remove skillet from heat. Stir in 3 tablespoons tomato paste, olives, olive brine and cooked turkey.

3. Heat oven to 375°. Coat a 13 x 9 x 2-inch baking dish with nonstick cooking spray.

4. Combine remaining 1 tablespoon tomato paste, tomato sauce and water in a small skillet. Heat over medium heat just until simmering, 1 to 2 minutes.

5. Dip 1 tortilla in tomato sauce to soften. Place on a plate. Spoon ⅓ cup of turkey mixture down center of tortilla. Roll up and place, seam side down, in prepared pan. Repeat with remaining tortillas and filling. Spoon remaining tomato sauce over top. Sprinkle with cheese. Cover loosely with aluminum foil.

6. Bake in heated 375° oven 30 minutes or until heated through. Serve with sour cream if you wish.

POULTRY

Orange-herbed roast turkey

Makes 24 servings   *Prep* 20 minutes   *Cook* gravy 5 minutes   *Bake* at 350° for 3½ hours

No part of the orange is wasted in this recipe. The rind, the juice and the juiced halves themselves—they all get used.

Per serving
397 calories, 52 g protein, 18 g fat, 3 g carbohydrate, 218 mg sodium, 151 mg cholesterol.

1 orange
1 tablespoon light-brown sugar
1½ teaspoons poultry seasoning
1 teaspoon salt
1 bunch green onions
1 cup chopped fresh parsley (reserve stems)

1 turkey (about 17 pounds)

Gravy
½ cup milk
6 tablespoons all-purpose flour
¾ teaspoon salt
½ teaspoon poultry seasoning

1. Heat oven to 350°.

2. Remove rind from orange with a vegetable peeler, avoiding bitter white pith. Finely chop rind. Cut orange in half; juice orange halves. Reserve juice for making gravy; reserve orange halves.

3. Combine rind, brown sugar, poultry seasoning and salt in a small bowl. Finely chop white part of green onions; reserve green part. Add chopped green onions and chopped parsley to rind mixture.

4. Remove neck and giblets from turkey cavity. With your fingers, carefully loosen skin around turkey breast and legs. Spread rind mixture under skin. Place parsley stems, green onion ends and orange halves in turkey cavity.

5. Place turkey on a rack in a large roasting pan. Place neck and gizzards in bottom of pan. Loosely tent turkey with aluminum foil. Roast in heated 350° oven 3½ hours or until an instant-read thermometer registers an internal temperature of 180° in innermost part of thigh and 170° in breast.

6. Remove turkey to a platter. Discard neck and gizzard. Cover loosely with foil; let stand 20 minutes.

7. Meanwhile, prepare gravy: Scrape pan drippings into a 1-quart liquid measuring cup. Skim off fat. Add water to equal 4 cups. Pour into a medium-size saucepan along with reserved orange juice. Bring to simmering.

8. Whisk together milk, flour, salt and poultry seasoning in a small bowl until smooth. Stir into saucepan. Simmer over medium-high heat, stirring, 4 minutes or until gravy is thickened. Serve with carved turkey.

Jules's stuffing

Makes 10 servings   *Prep* 15 minutes   *Cook* 22 minutes

Bake chestnuts at 350° for 20 to 25 minutes; stuffing at 350° for 1 hour 10 minutes

Here's a full-flavored stuffing. Once you've tried it, you'll never go back to the plain old version.

Per serving
280 calories, 10 g protein,
10 g fat, 35 g carbohydrate,
633 mg sodium,
23 mg cholesterol.

Love stuffing?
For fans who can't get enough stuffing, consider doubling the recipe—bake an extra amount in a separate pan or spoon it underneath the skin of the bird. And remember, never stuff a bird ahead of time. Stuffing should reach an internal temperature of 165°. Remove stuffing immediately from bird after roasting.

1 pound fresh chestnuts or 2 cans (10 ounces each) water-packed whole chestnuts, drained
3 slices lean bacon, chopped
1 large red onion, chopped
1 pound mushrooms, coarsely chopped
1 pound sweet Italian sausage, casings removed
10 cups fresh white bread cubes
½ cup cognac or brandy
1 teaspoon dried thyme
1 teaspoon dried sage
½ teaspoon dried rosemary, crumbled
¼ teaspoon ground nutmeg
1 can (13¾ ounces) chicken broth

1. Heat oven to 350°. Coat a 13 x 9 x 2-inch baking dish with nonstick cooking spray.

2. If using fresh chestnuts, cut an X on the flat side of each. Place on a baking sheet. Bake in heated 350° oven 20 to 25 minutes or until shell curls back. Cool. Peel off shell and dark membrane.

3. Coarsely chop fresh or canned chestnuts. Place in a large bowl.

4. Cook bacon and onion in a large nonstick skillet over medium heat 6 minutes. Add mushrooms; cook 6 minutes or until mushrooms are tender. Add to chestnuts.

5. Cook sausage in same skillet, breaking up with a wooden spoon, until cooked through, about 10 minutes. Remove with a slotted spoon to chestnut mixture.

6. Add bread cubes to chestnut mixture. Mix in cognac, thyme, sage, rosemary, nutmeg and broth.

7. Spoon stuffing into prepared baking dish. Cover dish with aluminum foil. If not baking immediately, refrigerate up to 4 hours and then let stand at room temperature 1 hour before baking. (Or use to stuff a 12- to 15-pound turkey; do not stuff in advance.)

8. Bake in heated 350° oven 45 minutes. Remove foil and bake another 25 minutes or until browned on top.

Holiday roast turkey
with savory gravy
Mushroom stuffing
opposite

Holiday roast turkey with savory gravy

Makes 12 servings plus leftovers   *Prep* 10 minutes   *Roast* at 425° for 30 minutes; 325° for 3 to 3½ hours

Tuck half an onion, a lemon half and some fresh parsley inside the turkey for extra flavor.

Per serving
285 calories, 34 g protein,
13 g fat, 5 g carbohydrate,
262 mg sodium,
97 mg cholesterol.

1 turkey (14 pounds)
1 tablespoon vegetable oil
4 cups coarsely chopped onion
1 cup chicken broth

Gravy
2 tablespoons butter
¼ cup all-purpose flour
2 cups chicken broth
½ cup dry white wine
1 teaspoon salt

1. Position oven rack in lowest third of oven. Heat oven to 425°.

2. Remove neck and giblets from turkey cavity. Rub turkey with oil. Spread onion in roasting pan. Place turkey on top.

266

3. Roast in heated 425° oven 30 minutes. Add 1 cup broth to pan. Lower oven temperature to 325°. Loosely tent turkey with aluminum foil. Roast another 3 to 3½ hours or until an instant-read thermometer registers an internal temperature of 180° in innermost part of thigh and 170° in breast. Remove to a platter; let stand 20 minutes.

4. Meanwhile, prepare gravy: Scrape pan drippings into a small bowl. Skim off fat. Melt butter in a medium-size saucepan over low heat. Stir in flour. Whisk in 2 cups strained pan juices and broth. Add wine and salt; simmer over medium-high heat, stirring, until gravy is thickened, 2 to 3 minutes. Serve with carved turkey.

Mushroom stuffing

Makes 12 servings   *Prep* 25 minutes   *Cook* 15 minutes   *Bake* at 325° for 45 minutes

P O U L T R Y

The advantage of this stuffing is that it cooks on its own in a baking dish, without a turkey if you like. Excellent with a pork roast too.

Per serving
241 calories, 9 g protein, 7 g fat, 35 g carbohydrate, 723 mg sodium, 77 mg cholesterol.

4 slices bacon, chopped
3 cups chopped onion
2 cups chopped celery
1 pound mixed mushrooms (white, cremini, portabella), diced or coarsely chopped
1 teaspoon dried sage
½ teaspoon salt
¼ teaspoon black pepper
1 package (16 ounces) unseasoned corn-bread stuffing mix
½ cup chopped fresh parsley
½ cup chopped celery leaves (optional)
4 eggs
½ cup dry white wine
2 cups chicken broth
1 tablespoon butter

1. Heat oven to 325°. Lightly grease a 13 x 9 x 2-inch baking pan.

2. Cook bacon in a large, deep skillet until crisp and golden brown. Remove all but 1 to 2 tablespoons fat.

3. Add onion and celery; sauté until softened and lightly browned, about 5 minutes. Add mushrooms; cook 5 minutes. Add sage, salt and pepper; stir and cook 1 minute.

4. Add stuffing mix, parsley and celery leaves if using. Transfer mixture to a large bowl.

5. In a small bowl, whisk eggs and wine. Add to stuffing. Drizzle with half of broth; toss gently. Drizzle with remaining broth; toss. Turn into prepared baking pan. Dot with butter. Cover with aluminum foil. (Or use to stuff a 12- to 15-pound turkey; do not stuff in advance.)

6. Bake in heated 325° oven 45 minutes. Uncover; let stand 10 minutes.

Citrus hens with roasted potatoes

Makes 8 servings   *Prep* 30 minutes   *Refrigerate* overnight   *Bake* at 400° for 40 minutes

Look closely—this recipe uses both red potatoes and sweet potatoes. Splitting the hens in half lets the marinade more thoroughly flavor the meat, and it also results in more even cooking.

Per serving
573 calories, 45 g protein, 26 g fat, 40 g carbohydrate, 951 mg sodium, 134 mg cholesterol.

4 Cornish hens (1¼ pounds each)
¼ cup frozen orange juice concentrate
¼ cup fresh lemon juice
3 tablespoons chili sauce
2 tablespoons Worcestershire sauce
2 tablespoons honey or sugar
2 tablespoons chopped fresh thyme or 1½ teaspoons dried thyme

Potatoes
1 pound red boiling potatoes, unpeeled, cut into large cubes
1¼ pounds sweet potatoes, unpeeled, cut into large cubes

¾ pound shallots, peeled
3 tablespoons olive oil
¼ cup fresh thyme sprigs or 1 tablespoon dried thyme
1 teaspoon coarse kosher salt or regular salt
1¼ teaspoons black pepper

Sauce and garnishes
¼ teaspoon salt
2 tablespoons cornstarch, dissolved in 2 tablespoons cold water
Fresh thyme sprigs
Lemon and orange slices

1. Split hens down center. Place hens, skin side down, in two 13 x 9 x 2-inch baking dishes.

2. To make marinade, combine orange juice concentrate, lemon juice, chili sauce, Worcestershire sauce and honey in a medium-size bowl. Pour evenly over hens in baking dishes. Cover hens and refrigerate up to 1 day, turning occasionally.

3. Remove hens from refrigerator ½ hour before cooking. Turn hens in dishes; brush with marinade. Sprinkle with thyme.

4. Heat oven to 400°. Line a large roasting pan with aluminum foil.

5. Prepare potatoes: Toss red and sweet potatoes, shallots, oil, thyme, salt and pepper in a large bowl. Place in prepared pan.

6. Place potatoes on top rack in oven, hens on center rack. Bake hens and potatoes 40 minutes or until vegetables are fork-tender and internal temperature of thigh registers 180° on an instant-read thermometer. Stir potatoes and baste hens with pan juces halfway through cooking. Transfer hens and potatoes to a platter; cover and keep warm.

7. Prepare sauce: Strain pan juices into a 1-quart glass measuring cup; skim off fat. You should have 1 cup juices; add water or chicken broth to equal 2 cups. Place in a medium-size saucepan with remaining ¼ teaspoon salt. Bring to boiling. Stir in dissolved cornstarch mixture. Boil, stirring, until sauce is thickened, 1 minute.

8. Garnish hens with thyme sprigs and lemon and orange slices. Serve with sauce.

Rosemary Cornish hens

Makes 12 servings *Prep* 25 minutes *Bake* at 400° for 45 minutes

Need to feed a crowd? It doesn't get much easier than this. Assemble in the baking pans earlier in the day and refrigerate, then move on to other tasks.

Per serving
344 calories, 32 g protein, 21 g fat, 5 g carbohydrate, 579 mg sodium, 99 mg cholesterol.

6 Cornish hens (1½ pounds each)
½ cup dry white wine

Rosemary shallot baste
3 shallots, finely chopped
3 tablespoons finely chopped fresh rosemary or 1 teaspoon dried, crumbled

1¼ teaspoons salt
¼ teaspoon black pepper
⅓ cup olive oil

2 sweet red peppers
2 sweet green peppers
2 sweet yellow peppers

1. Split hens lengthwise in half; remove backbones. Place hens, skin side up, on racks in 2 large broiler pans. Pour wine into pans.

2. Heat oven to 400°.

3. Prepare baste: Combine shallots, rosemary, salt, pepper and oil in a small bowl.

4. Core and seed peppers. Cut into 3-inch pieces; place in a medium-size bowl. Toss peppers with one-third of baste. Arrange around hens on racks. Brush hens with remaining baste.

5. Bake in heated 400° oven 45 minutes or until internal temperature of thigh registers 180° on an instant-read thermometer and the peppers are just tender.

Pineapple-cranberry sauce

Makes 12 servings *Prep* 5 minutes *Cook* 10 minutes

Jazz up the usual cranberry sauce with a little pineapple. Equally appealing with Cornish hens, chicken and turkey—even a hamburger.

Per serving
94 calories, 0 g protein, 0 g fat, 24 g carbohydrate, 2 mg sodium, 0 mg cholesterol.

1 bag (12 ounces) fresh or thawed frozen cranberries
1 can (8 ounces) juice-packed crushed pineapple or chunks

1 cup sugar
¼ cup fresh orange juice
1 teaspoon grated orange rind
2 teaspoons vanilla

1. Place cranberries, pineapple with juice, ¾ cup sugar and orange juice in a food processor or blender. Pulse to coarsely chop.

2. Turn mixture into a medium-size nonaluminum saucepan. Bring to boiling over medium heat. Lower heat; simmer, stirring occasionally, until thickened, 10 to 12 minutes. Add remaining ¼ cup sugar. Remove from heat. Stir in rind and vanilla. Transfer to a small nonaluminum container; cool to room temperature. Refrigerate to chill.

Strip steak with rosemary
red wine sauce *page 273*

Smoked ham with tropical salsa *page 305*

meat

NO MATTER how our culinary horizons broaden, sometimes the new and exotic just won't do. Many of us still get a craving for a perfectly cooked piece of meat, be it a juicy steak or burger or a robust roast beef. Happily, staples like these can take to different spins for even better flavors.

The recipes in this chapter will delight meat lovers from coast to coast . . . and might even corral a few converts. The Mustard-Ginger-Glazed Beef Roast is rich with unexpected flavors and Strip Steak with Rosemary Red Wine Sauce packs a tangy punch. To go a little lighter, turn to lower-calorie options that use just enough meat to satisfy. Case in point: a beef and green bean stir-fry that includes sweet

Sometimes there's nothing like a much-loved standby to satisfy your appetite.

red pepper and pineapple chunks. And for the non-beef crowd, Stuffed Pork Roast and Spiral-Cut Ham with Honey Glaze are sure to appeal, while Moussaka with Lamb and Potatoes relies on spuds to satisfy. And through it all, easy preparation is the order of the night. What could be better?

271

Grilled T-bone steak

Makes 6 servings   *Prep* 5 minutes   *Marinate* 30 minutes   *Broil or grill* 10 to 15 minutes

If you haven't had a T-bone steak in a while, this is an easy recipe to use to get reacquainted. Grilled peppers or a salad of tossed greens would make a fine accompaniment.

Per serving
249 calories, 29 g protein, 14 g fat, 0 g carbohydrate, 68 mg sodium, 82 mg cholesterol.

2 cloves garlic
1 tablespoon fresh rosemary leaves
¼ teaspoon red-pepper flakes
⅓ cup extra-virgin olive oil
2 tablespoons fresh lemon juice

2 T-bone steaks (3 pounds total), each 1 inch thick
Slivered oil-packed sun-dried tomatoes for garnish
Fresh rosemary sprigs for garnish

1. Combine garlic, rosemary, red-pepper flakes, oil and lemon juice in a blender or food processor. Whirl until marinade is blended.

2. Place steak in a heavy-duty plastic food-storage bag. Add marinade; push out air and seal. Turn bag over to coat meat. Marinate at least 30 minutes; if marinating longer, refrigerate.

3. Heat broiler, or prepare a charcoal grill with medium-hot coals, or heat gas grill to medium-high. Position broiler rack or grill rack 4 inches from source of heat.

4. Broil or grill steaks 5 to 6 minutes per side for medium-rare to medium (until an instant-read thermometer registers an internal temperature of 145° to 160°) or longer for well-done (until thermometer registers 170°). Garnish steaks with sun-dried tomatoes and rosemary sprigs.

Fennel and balsamic marinated sirloin

Makes 4 servings   *Prep* 10 minutes   *Refrigerate* 1 to 4 hours

Grill 10 to 12 minutes *or broil* 6 minutes

Make the balsamic vinegar marinade not only to flavor beef but also pork or chicken.

Per serving
525 calories, 69 g protein, 25 g fat, 202 g carbohydrate, 151 mg sodium, 2 mg cholesterol.

2 teaspoons fennel seeds, crushed
2 tablespoons balsamic vinegar
2 tablespoons olive oil
1 teaspoon dried thyme

½ teaspoon ground allspice
1 sirloin steak (2 pounds), cut into 4 pieces

1. Combine fennel seeds, vinegar, oil, thyme and allspice in a plastic food-storage bag. Add steaks; push out air and seal. Refrigerate 1 to 4 hours.

2. Prepare a charcoal grill with hot coals, or heat gas grill to high, or heat broiler. Lightly coat broiler-pan rack with nonstick cooking spray. Position grill rack or broiler rack 4 inches from source of heat.

3. Grill steaks 5 to 6 minutes per side for medium-rare (145° on an instant-read thermometer), or broil 3 minutes per side.

Strip steak with rosemary red wine sauce

Makes 4 servings   *Prep* 15 minutes   *Cook* 27 to 31 minutes

Rosemary has a pinelike flavor and intense aroma. It's wonderful with strong-flavored foods like this steak.
Shown on page 270.

Per serving
610 calories, 62 g protein, 30 g fat, 5 g carbohydrate, 831 mg sodium, 159 mg cholesterol.

4 strip steaks (3 pounds total), each 1 inch thick
½ teaspoon salt
1 tablespoon cracked black pepper
3 tablespoons olive oil
¼ cup chopped onion

2 tablespoons fresh rosemary leaves
2 cloves garlic, finely chopped
1½ cups dry red wine
1 cup canned condensed beef broth
½ teaspoon dark-brown sugar

1. Season steaks with salt. Press pepper onto surfaces of steaks.

2. Heat oil in a large heavy skillet over high heat until smoking. Add steaks. Lower heat to medium. Cook steaks to desired doneness, turning once, about 6 minutes per side for medium-rare (145° on an instant-read thermometer) or 8 minutes per side for medium (160°). Remove steaks to a warmed platter and keep warm.

3. Add onion to skillet. Cook, stirring often, until browned, about 2 minutes. Add half of rosemary and half of garlic; cook, stirring, 20 seconds. Add wine. Increase heat to high; boil vigorously 2 minutes.

4. Add broth, brown sugar and any juices that have collected on steak platter. Boil about 10 minutes more or until liquid is reduced by half, to about 1 cup. Add remaining rosemary and garlic. Pour over steaks and serve.

MEAT

Blue cheese club steaks

Makes 4 servings   *Prep* 10 minutes   *Cook* 14 minutes

Club steak is cut from the short loin next to the rib. It has a bone along one side, is quite tender and cooks very quickly.

Per serving
472 calories, 41 g protein, 32 g fat, 4 g carbohydrate, 707 mg sodium, 108 mg cholesterol.

1 tablespoon olive oil
4 club steaks (1½ pounds total)
1 cup finely chopped red onion
2 cloves garlic, chopped

½ cup beef broth
½ cup bottled chunky blue cheese dressing
2 ounces blue cheese

1. Heat oil in a large nonstick skillet over medium-high heat. Add steaks and cook about 4 minutes per side for medium-rare (145° on an instant-read thermometer). Remove steaks from skillet; keep warm.

2. Add onion and garlic to skillet; sauté 3 minutes over medium heat. Add ½ cup broth; cook 1½ minutes to reduce. Remove from heat. Stir in blue cheese dressing. Spoon equal amount of sauce, about ¼ cup, over each steak. Top with crumbled blue cheese.

Herb-pepper-crusted beef fillet

Makes 8 servings   *Prep* 5 minutes   *Bake* at 450° for 40 minutes

For the starring role on your buffet table, serve the peppery fillet at room temperature or chilled, with two sauces on the side.

Per serving
272 calories, 36 g protein,
13 g fat, 1 g carbohydrate,
347 mg sodium,
106 mg cholesterol.

1 beef fillet (3 pounds), trimmed
½ teaspoon dried thyme
1½ tablespoons dried rosemary
2 tablespoons whole black peppercorns

1 teaspoon salt
Herbed Mustard Sauce or Tomato-Orange Chutney (recipes follow)

1. Heat oven to 450°.

2. Pat fillet dry with paper toweling. Place thyme, rosemary, peppercorns and salt in a small food processor or blender. Whirl to crush. Place mixture on waxed paper. Roll fillet in mixture until entirely coated. Place on a rack in a roasting pan. Sprinkle remaining herb mixture over top of fillet.

3. Roast fillet in heated 450° oven 40 minutes or until an instant-read thermometer registers an internal temperature of 145° for medium-rare. Remove from oven. Let rest 10 to 15 minutes before carving. If serving cold, cool to room temperature and then refrigerate. Serve with Herbed Mustard Sauce or Tomato-Orange Chutney.

Herbed mustard sauce

Per tablespoon
52 calories, 0 g protein,
5 g fat, 1 g carbohydrate,
87 mg sodium,
1 mg cholesterol.

Chill ¼ cup evaporated milk in freezer for 10 minutes. Combine ¼ cup tarragon vinegar and 2 tablespoons grainy Dijon mustard in a blender. Pour in chilled milk. With blender on, add ½ cup oil in a slow, steady stream until well blended. Add 2 tablespoons chopped fresh tarragon, 1 finely chopped shallot, ½ teaspoon salt and ¼ teaspoon black pepper. Blend to combine. Makes 1¼ cups.

Tomato-orange chutney

Per tablespoon
16 calories, 0 g protein,
1 g fat, 2 g carbohydrate,
63 mg sodium,
0 mg cholesterol.

Seed 1½ pounds tomatoes and then chop into ½-inch pieces. Heat 1 tablespoon oil in a large skillet. Add 2 teaspoons ground cumin and the tomatoes and cook over medium heat 5 minutes. Remove three-fourths of mixture from skillet and place in a food processor or blender. Add 3 oil-packed sun-dried tomatoes, ½ teaspoon salt and 1 teaspoon finely grated fresh ginger. Process until pureed. Place in a small bowl. Chop half a peeled orange and add to bowl along with remaining tomato mixture from skillet. Stir to combine. Refrigerate at least 1 hour to blend flavors. Makes 1¼ cups.

Greek-style steak salad

Greek-style steak salad

Makes 6 servings   *Prep* 15 minutes   *Marinate* 20 minutes   *Grill or broil* 20 minutes

A salad that's a meal. Serve chilled or at room temperature with a loaf of crusty semolina bread.

Per serving
513 calories, 38 g protein,
26 g fat, 31 g carbohydrate,
841 mg sodium,
104 mg cholesterol.

¼ cup red-wine vinegar
2 teaspoons Dijon mustard
½ teaspoon bottled horseradish
3 cloves garlic, crushed
1 teaspoon dried oregano
½ teaspoon salt
½ teaspoon black pepper

¼ cup olive oil
1 sirloin steak (1½ pounds)
¾ cup feta cheese, crumbled
1¼ cups orzo
2 cups spinach leaves
½ cup Kalamata olives,
   pitted and quartered

1. Prepare a charcoal grill with medium-hot coals, or heat a gas grill to medium high, or heat broiler. Position grill rack or broiler rack 5 inches from source of heat.

2. Combine vinegar, mustard, horseradish, garlic, oregano, salt and pepper in a food processor. With machine running, slowly add oil. Remove ½ cup and add to steak in resealable plastic food-storage bag. Reserve remaining dressing. Marinate meat 20 minutes.

3. Grill or broil steak 7 to 10 minutes per side for medium-rare. After turning steak, sprinkle with 2 tablespoons feta cheese, spreading evenly.

4. Meanwhile, cook orzo in a large pot of lightly salted boiling water until al dente, firm but tender. For the last 2 minutes of cooking, add spinach. Drain; transfer to a serving bowl. Toss with remaining feta and olives. Drizzle with reserved dressing. Serve salad warm or chilled with sliced steak.

Fennel-crusted standing rib roast

Makes 16 servings *Prep* 10 minutes *Cook* sauce about 5 minutes

Roast at 450° for 15 minutes; then at 350° for about 2 hours

Since this cut is roasted upright, resting on the ribs, the layer of fat on top self-bastes the meat as it cooks. A garlic-thyme-fennel crust makes this roast very special.

Per serving
442 calories, 48 g protein, 25 g fat, 2 g carbohydrate, 396 mg sodium, 139 mg cholesterol.

The cutting edge
The key to carving a roast is a sharp knife. Maintaining an edge is easy enough if you follow these tips before each use.
1. Hold a steel securely in one hand. In the other, grip the knife carefully and hold the edge of the blade nearly vertical at a 20° angle to the steel.
2. Applying light, steady pressure, pass the blade edge along the entire length of the steel 3 times. Repeat on the other side of the blade.

1 beef rib roast with 4 ribs (9 pounds), trimmed
2 cloves garlic, chopped
1 teaspoon salt
1 tablespoon fennel seeds, crushed
2 teaspoons dried thyme
2 teaspoons black pepper
2 teaspoons olive oil

Shallot wine sauce
1 can (13¾ ounces) beef broth
½ cup dry red wine
2 tablespoons finely chopped shallot
2 tablespoons all-purpose flour
½ teaspoon dried thyme
¼ teaspoon salt
1 tablespoon browning and seasoning sauce (optional)

1. Heat oven to 450°. Place roast in a large flameproof roasting pan.

2. Carefully mash together garlic and ½ teaspoon salt with side of a knife to make a paste; place in a small bowl. Stir in fennel seeds, thyme, pepper, oil and remaining salt. Spread over top of roast.

3. Roast beef in heated 450° oven 15 minutes. Lower oven temperature to 350°. Roast until internal temperature of thickest part registers 135° on an instant-read thermometer, about another 2 hours. Let roast stand 20 minutes. Before slicing, check to make sure temperature has risen to 145° for medium-rare.

4. Prepare shallot wine sauce: Pour pan drippings into a 2-cup measuring cup. Set roasting pan aside. Skim 2 tablespoons fat from drippings and place in a 2-quart saucepan. Skim any remaining fat from drippings and discard. Add broth and wine to roasting pan. Place pan over medium-high heat; stir up any browned bits from bottom of pan with a wooden spoon; add to drippings in measuring cup.

5. Add shallots to fat in saucepan; cook until softened, 3 minutes. Stir in flour, thyme and salt until smooth. Gradually whisk in drippings. Cook, stirring, until sauce boils and thickens. Remove from heat. Stir in browning sauce if using.

6. Carve roast. Serve with sauce.

Short-rib supper

Makes 6 servings   *Prep* 20 minutes   *Cook* 1 hour 25 minutes

There's plenty of good things in this supper— potatoes, carrots, onions—and all accented with tangy Horseradish Cream.

Per serving
411 calories, 30 g protein, 17 g fat, 33 g carbohydrate, 634 mg sodium, 73 mg cholesterol.

1 tablespoon oil
6 beef short ribs (4 pounds total)
1 cup chopped onion
2 cloves garlic, finely chopped
1 can (13¾ ounces) beef broth
½ cup Worcestershire sauce
½ cup plus 3 tablespoons water
1 bay leaf

1¾ pounds red new potatoes, unpeeled, each cut in half
1 pound whole baby carrots
3 tablespoons all-purpose flour
1 tablespoon browning and seasoning sauce (optional)
1 tablespoon chopped fresh parsley
Horseradish Cream (recipe follows)

1. Heat oil in a large Dutch oven. Working in batches, add ribs and brown. Remove ribs to a platter as they brown.

2. Pour off all but 1 tablespoon drippings from pan. Add onion and garlic; sauté over medium-low heat until onion is very tender, about 8 minutes. Return ribs to pan. Add broth, Worcestershire sauce, ½ cup water and bay leaf. Cover; simmer 40 minutes. Add potatoes and carrots; simmer, covered, 20 minutes or until vegetables are tender. Remove meat and vegetables to a large platter; keep warm. Remove and discard bay leaf.

3. Skim fat from sauce. Mix flour, remaining 3 tablespoons water and browning sauce if using in a small bowl. Stir into sauce; boil until thickened, 5 minutes. Spoon sauce over meat and vegetables. Sprinkle with parsley. Serve with Horseradish Cream.

Horseradish cream

Per tablespoon
19 calories, 1 g protein, 1 g fat, 1 g carbohydrate, 85 mg sodium, 0 mg cholesterol.

Whisk together ½ cup reduced-fat sour cream, 2 tablespoons bottled horseradish, 1 tablespoon Dijon mustard and ¼ teaspoon salt in a small bowl until well blended. Makes ⅔ cup.

MEAT

Mexican pot roast

Makes 8 servings *Prep* 25 minutes *Cook* 2½ hours

The bottom round cut of beef is from the hind leg. Since it tends to be tough, it requires long, moist cooking. Here the roast and gravy are wonderfully flavored with beer and chili powder.

Per serving
371 calories, 26 g protein, 16 g fat, 30 g carbohydrate, 455 mg sodium, 67 mg cholesterol.

2 teaspoons olive oil
1 bottom round beef roast (2½ pounds)
1 large onion, chopped
2 cloves garlic, finely chopped
4 teaspoons chili powder
1 teaspoon dried oregano
1 bottle (12 ounces) beer
1 can (8 ounces) tomato sauce
¾ teaspoon salt
¼ teaspoon black pepper
1¼ pounds all-purpose potatoes
1½ pounds zucchini
1 package (10 ounces) frozen corn kernels

1. Heat 1 teaspoon oil in a nonstick Dutch oven. Add meat and brown over medium-high heat. Remove from pan. Add remaining oil to pan and sauté onion and garlic until lightly browned. Stir in chili powder and oregano; cook 30 seconds. Add beer and tomato sauce. Return meat to pan; sprinkle with salt and pepper. Cover and simmer 2 hours or until almost tender.

2. Peel potatoes; halve or quarter, depending on size. Halve zucchini lengthwise; cut into 1-inch pieces.

3. Add potatoes to Dutch oven. Cover and cook 10 minutes. Add zucchini, pushing pieces down into sauce. Cover and cook 10 minutes. Add corn. Cover and cook 3 minutes or until meat and vegetables are tender.

4. Remove meat; let stand 5 minutes. Slice. Serve with potatoes, zucchini and corn. Pass gravy.

Mustard-ginger-glazed beef roast

Makes 10 servings *Prep* 45 minutes *Stand* 30 minutes *Roast* at 400° for 50 to 60 minutes

A bottom round roast—sometimes called a rump roast—makes a delicious meal for a crowd.

Per serving
243 calories, 26 g protein, 14 g fat, 1 g carbohydrate, 197 mg sodium, 86 mg cholesterol.

¼ cup Dijon mustard
1 tablespoon ground ginger
1 bottom round beef roast (3 pounds)

Pan gravy
1 cup plus ½ cup water
1 cube low-sodium beef bouillon
2 tablespoons all-purpose flour
½ teaspoon salt
¼ teaspoon black pepper

1. Combine mustard and ginger in a small bowl. Rub all over meat. Let stand at room temperature 30 minutes.

2. Heat oven to 400°. Place beef on a rack in a flameproof roasting pan.

3. Roast in heated 400° oven 50 to 60 minutes or until an instant-read thermometer registers an internal temperature of 145° for medium-rare or 160° for medium. Let beef stand 10 minutes. Carve into very thin slices; start at pointed end first, but turn meat to make sure you are slicing against grain.

4. Meanwhile, prepare pan gravy: Bring 1 cup water to boiling in a small saucepan and dissolve beef bouillon cube in it. Pour into roasting pan, scraping up any browned bits from the bottom of pan. Stir flour into remaining ½ cup cold water until smooth. Pour into roasting pan. Add salt and pepper. Place roasting pan over medium heat; cook, stirring, until mixture bubbles and thickens, 3 to 4 minutes.

Mustard-ginger-glazed beef roast *opposite*

Southwest burger with corn-bean salsa

Makes 4 servings   *Prep* 5 minutes   *Refrigerate* 30 minutes   *Grill or broil* 5 to 6 minutes

A classic burger—plain or with a slice of cheddar—is just fine, but a zippy salsa makes dinner a fiesta.

Per serving
423 calories, 30 g protein,
17 g fat, 36 g carbohydrate,
759 mg sodium,
76 mg cholesterol.

1 can (10 ounces) black beans, drained and rinsed
½ cup frozen corn kernels
½ cup medium-hot salsa
¼ cup sweet red pepper, cored, seeded and finely chopped

1 tablespoon finely chopped fresh cilantro
2 teaspoons fresh lime juice
1 pound ground beef
1 tablespoon chili powder
4 hamburger buns, toasted

1. Combine black beans, corn, salsa, sweet red pepper, cilantro and lime juice in a medium-size bowl. Refrigerate at least 30 minutes to blend flavors.

2. Prepare a charcoal grill with medium-hot coals, or heat a gas grill to medium-high, or heat broiler. Place grill rack 6 inches from source of heat or broiler pan 2 inches from source of heat.

3. Mix beef and chili powder and shape into four ¾-inch-thick patties. Grill on covered grill or broil, turning once, 5 to 6 minutes or until an instant-read thermometer registers an internal temperature of 160°. Serve on buns, topped with salsa.

Tex-Mex bake

Makes 4 servings   *Prep* 30 minutes   *Bake* at 400° for 50 to 55 minutes

A packaged corn muffin mix makes the golden crust a snap to fix.

Per serving
509 calories, 22 g protein,
22 g fat, 59 g carbohydrate,
669 mg sodium,
57 mg cholesterol.

1 pound lean ground beef
1 package (10 ounces) frozen corn kernels, thawed and drained
1 cup frozen chopped onion, thawed and drained
1 cup finely chopped sweet green pepper

1 cup mild salsa
1 teaspoon ground cumin
½ teaspoon salt
1 package (8 ounces) corn muffin mix

1. Heat oven to 400°.

2. Combine beef, corn, onion, green pepper, salsa, cumin and salt in 9 x 9 x 2-inch baking dish. Cover with foil. Bake in heated 400° oven 30 minutes.

3. Meanwhile, prepare muffin mix according to package directions. When 30 minutes baking time has elapsed, carefully spread batter over beef mixture, making sure entire surface is covered.

4. Bake another 20 to 25 minutes or until golden brown and a wooden pick inserted in center of topping comes out clean.

Cajun meat loaf

Makes 8 servings   *Prep* 20 minutes   *Cook* 8 minutes   *Bake* at 350° for 1 hour

Spoon some of the Sweet Pepper Sauce over the Spicy Mashed Potatoes. Hot-pepper sauce drizzled into the meat loaf mixture provides the Cajun fire.

Per serving
246 calories, 14 g protein, 13 g fat, 20 g carbohydrate, 491 mg sodium, 65 mg cholesterol.

1 tablespoon vegetable oil
1 cup finely chopped sweet red pepper
½ cup finely chopped sweet green pepper
½ cup finely chopped onion
½ teaspoon salt
4 slices white bread, torn
½ cup milk

1 pound ground beef
½ cup dry plain bread crumbs
½ cup ketchup
1 egg
1 teaspoon hot-pepper sauce
 Sweet Pepper Sauce
 (recipe follows)
 Spicy Mashed Potatoes
 (recipe, page 128)

1. Heat oil in a large skillet over medium-high heat. Add red pepper, green pepper, onion and salt; cover and cook over low heat until very tender, about 8 minutes. Remove from heat and cool slightly.

2. Heat oven to 350°. Grease a 9 x 5 x 3-inch loaf pan.

3. Combine bread and milk in a large bowl; let stand 5 minutes to soften. Add beef, bread crumbs, ketchup, egg, hot-pepper sauce and sweet pepper mixture; toss gently to mix. Spoon and pat into prepared loaf pan.

4. Bake loaf in heated 350° oven 1 hour or until internal temperature registers 160° on an instant-read thermometer. Let stand 15 minutes before serving. Top each serving with a dollop of Sweet Pepper Sauce and serve with Spicy Mashed Potatoes.

Sweet pepper sauce

Per 2 tablespoons
46 calories, 0 g protein, 2 g fat, 7 g carbohydrate, 136 mg sodium, 0 mg cholesterol.

Heat 1 tablespoon oil in a large skillet over medium-high heat. Add 1 cup diced sweet red pepper, ½ cup finely chopped onion, ¼ cup water and ½ teaspoon salt; cook, stirring occasionally, over medium heat until very tender, about 8 minutes. Stir in ¼ cup cider vinegar, ¼ cup packed light-brown sugar and 1 teaspoon whole mustard seeds; cook over medium-high heat until most of liquid has evaporated and sauce is thickened, about 8 minutes. Makes about 1½ cups.

MEAT

Blue-ribbon meat loaf

Makes 8 servings   *Prep* 25 minutes   *Bake* at 350° for 60 to 70 minutes

Not just your ordinary meat loaf. A combination of ground beef and pork plus grated potato makes this loaf memorable.

Per serving
357 calories, 22 g protein, 25 g fat, 9 g carbohydrate, 331 mg sodium, 95 mg cholesterol.

2 eggs
⅓ cup ketchup
1 tablespoon Worcestershire sauce
1 teaspoon dried basil
½ teaspoon salt
½ teaspoon black pepper

1 large potato, peeled and grated
1 onion, grated
1 sweet red pepper, cored, seeded and finely chopped
1 pound ground beef
1 pound ground pork or beef

1. Heat oven to 350°. Line a 13 x 9 x 3-inch pan with aluminum foil.

2. Stir together eggs, ketchup, Worcestershire sauce, basil, salt and pepper in a large bowl. Stir in potato, onion and sweet red pepper. Add beef and pork, stirring lightly with a fork just until mixed.

3. Spoon meat mixture down center of prepared pan, shaping mixture into a 12 x 4-inch loaf, mounding loaf in the center.

4. Bake loaf in heated 350° oven 60 to 70 minutes or until internal temperature registers 160° on an instant-read thermometer.

Meat-filled blintzes
opposite

Meat-filled blintzes

Makes 6 servings *Prep* 60 minutes *Cook* 40 minutes *Bake* at 400° for 16 to 18 minutes

Like crepes, the blintzes themselves can be made ahead and refrigerated or frozen. For a flavor boost, sprinkle a little nutmeg into the meat filling.

Per serving
347 calories, 23 g protein, 17 g fat, 25 g carbohydrate, 627 mg sodium, 202 mg cholesterol.

Blintzes
1 cup all-purpose flour
2 teaspoons sugar
½ teaspoon salt
4 eggs
⅔ cup milk
⅓ cup water
1 tablespoon butter, melted

Meat filling
1 teaspoon vegetable oil
3 medium onions, finely chopped (1½ cups)
1 pound ground beef, pork or veal
2 tablespoons all-purpose flour
1 teaspoon salt
¼ teaspoon black pepper
¼ teaspoon paprika
Sour cream (optional)

1. Prepare blintzes: Combine flour, sugar, salt, eggs, milk, water and 2 teaspoons melted butter in a blender or food processor. Whirl 1 minute or until smooth.

2. Heat remaining melted butter in an 8-inch skillet (for 6-inch blintzes) over medium heat just until bubbly. Pour about 2 tablespoons batter into hot skillet, tilting skillet until batter covers bottom. Cook until blintz is golden brown on bottom, 1 to 2 minutes. Top should look cooked through and not wet. Turn out onto waxed paper. Repeat with remaining batter, stacking the blintzes with a sheet of waxed paper between each. When done, you should have 12.

3. Prepare meat filling: Heat oil in a large skillet over medium heat. Add onions; sauté 5 to 8 minutes or until softened. Add beef; sauté, breaking up with a wooden spoon, 3 to 5 minutes or until no longer pink. Stir in flour, salt, pepper and paprika; cook, stirring, 1 to 2 minutes. Cool slightly before filling blintzes.

4. Heat oven to 400°. Lightly grease a 15 x 10 x 1-inch jelly-roll pan.

5. Spoon 2 tablespoons filling onto center of browned side of each blintz. Fold 2 sides of blintz over filling. Fold in open ends. Place blintzes, seam side down, on prepared pan.

6. Bake in heated 400° oven 8 to 10 minutes or until lightly browned. Turn over. Bake another 8 minutes or until lightly browned. Serve immediately with sour cream if desired.

MEAT

Anytime meatballs

Makes 6 servings (3 meatballs each)   *Prep* 10 minutes   *Cook* 10 minutes   *Bake* at 325° for 40 minutes

Double, triple or even quadruple the amount of meatballs and freeze the extra to have anytime.

Per serving

339 calories, 27 g protein, 18 g fat, 17 g carbohydrate, 965 mg sodium, 132 mg cholesterol.

How long will it keep?

• Set your refrigerator at 40° and store fresh meat 3 to 5 days; 1 to 2 days if ground. Refrigerate cooked meat 3 to 4 days.
• Set your freezer at 0° and store fresh meat 4 to 12 months; 3 to 4 months if ground. Freeze cooked meat 2 to 3 months.

1 tablespoon olive oil
¾ cup finely chopped onion
2 pounds lean ground beef
½ cup dry seasoned bread crumbs
2 eggs
½ cup milk
1½ teaspoons dried oregano
1½ teaspoons dried basil
1½ teaspoons garlic salt
1 teaspoon seasoning salt
1 teaspoon Worcestershire sauce
½ teaspoon black pepper

Sauce
⅓ cup ketchup
⅓ cup barbecue sauce
¼ cup packed light-brown sugar
1½ teaspoons distilled white vinegar
Pinch garlic salt

1. Heat oven to 325°.

2. Heat oil in a medium-size skillet. Add onion; sauté 10 minutes or until very tender.

3. Combine beef, bread crumbs, eggs, milk, oregano, basil, garlic salt, seasoning salt, Worcestershire sauce, pepper and sautéed onion in a bowl; lightly mix with a wooden spoon or your hands until combined but not overmixed.

4. Shape beef mixture into 2-inch meatballs. Arrange in a single layer, not touching each other, in a 15 x 10 x 1-inch jelly-roll pan.

5. Bake, uncovered, in heated 325° oven 20 minutes.

6. Meanwhile, prepare sauce: Combine ketchup, barbecue sauce, brown sugar, vinegar and garlic salt in a small saucepan. Heat over medium heat just until simmering.

7. Remove meatballs from pan to paper toweling to drain. Wipe out baking pan. Return meatballs to pan; cover with sauce. Cover pan tightly with aluminum foil.

8. Return baking pan to 325° oven and bake another 20 minutes or until meatballs are no longer pink in center.

Stuffed cabbage

Makes 6 servings   *Prep* 20 minutes   *Cook* 1 hour

Stuff and roll up the cabbage leaves up to one day ahead and refrigerate. Slip into the tomato sauce about an hour before serving.

Per serving
452 calories, 26 g protein, 23 g fat, 38 g carbohydrate, 1,429 mg sodium, 167 mg cholesterol.

1 large cabbage (3 pounds)
1 large onion, finely chopped
2 ribs celery, finely chopped
5 thick slices bacon, sliced crosswise into ¼-inch-wide pieces
1 pound ground beef
2 tablespoons chopped fresh rosemary or 2 teaspoons dried
2 teaspoons dried marjoram
1 cup cooked white rice

3 eggs, lightly beaten
1½ teaspoon salt
½ teaspoon black pepper
2 cans (8 ounces each) tomato sauce
1 can (14½ ounces) diced tomatoes, drained
¼ cup packed light-brown sugar
2 tablespoons fresh lemon juice

1. Bring a large pot of water to boiling. Core cabbage with a sharp knife. Discard any coarse outer leaves. Place cabbage, stem end down, in boiling water. Cook 6 minutes. Carefully remove cabbage. When cool enough to handle, remove 16 leaves from head. Reserve remaining cabbage for other uses.

2. Heat a large nonstick skillet over medium heat. Add onion, celery and bacon; cook 6 minutes or until vegetables are softened. Add beef, rosemary and marjoram; cook, breaking up meat with a wooden spoon, 8 minutes or until meat is no longer pink. Drain excess liquid from skillet. Remove from heat.

3. Coat a large nonstick skillet or Dutch oven with nonstick cooking spray. Stir rice, eggs, salt and pepper into meat mixture. Spoon ⅓ cup mixture in middle of each cabbage leaf. Fold thick end over filling; fold sides over and roll up, envelope style. Place rolls, seam side down, in a single layer in prepared skillet or Dutch oven.

4. Combine tomato sauce, tomatoes, brown sugar and lemon juice in a medium-size bowl. Spoon over cabbage rolls.

5. Cover skillet. Gently simmer 40 minutes or until cabbage is knife-tender. Serve cabbage rolls with sauce.

MEAT

Triple bean and beef casserole

Makes 8 servings   *Prep* 15 minutes   *Bake* at 350° for 1½ hours

This hearty casserole combines ground beef with three different kinds of beans and a big handful of shredded cheddar cheese. And it has the taste of Morocco: cinnamon, allspice and cloves.

Per serving
470 calories, 26 g protein, 18 g fat, 50 g carbohydrate, 875 mg sodium, 68 mg cholesterol.

1 can (19 ounces) chick-peas, drained and rinsed
1 can (19 ounces) white beans, drained and rinsed
1 can (19 ounces) red kidney beans, drained and rinsed
1 pound ground beef
2 teaspoons sugar
1½ teaspoons salt
1½ teaspoons ground cinnamon
½ teaspoon ground allspice
⅛ teaspoon black pepper
¼ teaspoon ground cloves
4 sweet potatoes (about 2 pounds), peeled and cut into thin slices
2 cups shredded cheddar cheese (½ pound)

1. Heat oven to 350°. Coat a 4-quart casserole with nonstick cooking spray.

2. Combine chick-peas, white beans, kidney beans, beef, sugar, salt, cinnamon, allspice, pepper and ground cloves in a large bowl.

3. Layer one-third of sweet potato slices in bottom of casserole. Spread half of bean mixture over top. Sprinkle with one-third of cheese. Repeat layering. Place remaining third of sweet potato slices on top. Cover top with foil.

4. Bake in heated 350° oven 1 hour. Sprinkle remaining cheese on top. Bake, uncovered, another 30 minutes or until potatoes are tender. Let stand 10 minutes before serving.

Pacific Rim beef kabobs

Makes 4 servings   *Prep* 12 minutes   *Refrigerate* overnight   *Grill* 4 minutes *or broil* 6 to 8 minutes

Pacific Rim cooking combines American ingredients with Thai, Vietnamese and Chinese seasonings, such as garlic, citrus, cilantro and dark Asian sesame oil.

Per serving
225 calories, 24 g protein, 11 g fat, 5 g carbohydrate, 589 mg sodium, 82 mg cholesterol.

1 cup packed fresh cilantro leaves
½ cup fresh orange juice
1 clove garlic, chopped
1 teaspoon dark Asian sesame oil
1 teaspoon honey
1 tablespoon grated orange rind
1 teaspoon salt
1 chuck steak (1 pound), cut into matchstick strips

1. Combine all ingredients except meat in a small bowl. Thread strips of meat in a ribbonlike fashion on 10-inch metal skewers. Place in a shallow dish. Cover with marinade. Refrigerate, covered, overnight, turning once.

2. Prepare a charcoal grill with medium-hot coals, or heat a gas grill to medium-high, or heat broiler. Place grill rack or broiler rack 6 inches from source of heat.

3. Brush kabobs with marinade. Grill 4 minutes, turning once, or broil 6 to 8 minutes, turning once. Discard any remaining marinade.

Pineapple beef stir-fry

Pineapple beef stir-fry

Makes 4 servings *Prep* 10 minutes *Refrigerate* 30 minutes *Cook* 12 minutes

As with many stir-fries, a reduced amount of meat is extended with other ingredients. Here we add pineapple chunks, green beans and sweet red pepper.

Per serving
184 calories, 15 g protein,
8 g fat, 15 g carbohydrate,
269 mg sodium,
38 mg cholesterol.

1 can (20 ounces) juice-packed pineapple chunks
1 tablespoon grated fresh ginger
1 tablespoon soy sauce
¼ cup chopped fresh cilantro
¾ pound round steak, cut into thin diagonal slices
1 teaspoon vegetable oil
1 clove garlic, finely chopped
½ teaspoon cornstarch
½ cup fresh green beans, trimmed
1 sweet red pepper, cored, seeded and thinly sliced
1 tablespoon chopped canned green chiles
2 green onions, chopped

1. Drain pineapple, reserving 1 cup chunks and ½ cup juice. Refrigerate remaining chunks and juice for use in other recipes.

2. Combine ½ cup pineapple juice, ginger, soy sauce, cilantro and meat in a medium-size bowl. Cover bowl and marinate in refrigerator 30 minutes.

3. Heat oil in a large nonstick skillet over medium heat. Add garlic and sauté 30 seconds or until fragrant. Remove meat from marinade and add to skillet; stir-fry 5 minutes or until meat is just cooked through. Remove meat; keep warm.

4. Mix together remaining marinade and cornstarch.

5. Add green beans, sweet red pepper, green chiles and marinade mixture to skillet. Stir-fry over medium heat 5 minutes or until vegetables are crisp-tender and mixture is thickened.

6. Stir in pineapple chunks, green onions and meat. Gently heat mixture through.

Flank steak rolls

Makes 8 servings   *Prep* 35 minutes   *Refrigerate* 1 hour   *Bake* 10 to 13 minutes at 400°

Be sure to use dry-packed sun-dried tomatoes in the stuffing—those packed in oil will only add more fat.

Per serving
319 calories, 26 g protein, 19 g fat, 16 g carbohydrate, 231 mg sodium, 52 mg cholesterol.

1 flank steak (1¾ pounds)
¼ cup olive oil
¼ cup red-wine vinegar
2 cloves garlic, chopped

Stuffing
¾ cup dry-packed sun-dried tomatoes
2 egg whites
3 tablespoons grated Parmesan cheese
¾ cup chopped sweet yellow or green pepper
2 green onions (white part only), thinly sliced
¼ cup pine nuts or chopped walnuts
½ cup unsalted dry seasoned bread crumbs

1. Cut flank steak in half horizontally. Flatten with a meat mallet. Combine oil, vinegar, garlic and steak in a plastic food-storage bag; seal. Marinate in refrigerator at least 1 hour.

2. Soak tomatoes in boiling water to soften, 15 minutes. Drain and chop.

3. Beat egg whites in a medium-size bowl until frothy. Add tomatoes, Parmesan, sweet pepper, green onions, nuts and bread crumbs.

4. Heat oven to 400°. Line a jelly-roll pan with aluminum foil.

5. Place 1 flank steak on waxed paper. Spread half of stuffing over meat, leaving a 1-inch border; press to compact. Starting from a long side, roll up meat. Tie with kitchen string at 1¼-inch intervals. Repeat with remaining meat and stuffing. Slice meat crosswise at 1¼-inch intervals. Arrange slices, cut side up, on foil-lined pan.

6. Bake in heated 400° oven 10 to 13 minutes for medium-rare (until internal temperature of meat registers 145° on an instant-read thermometer).

Cook to the safe degree

Cook meat thoroughly. Use an instant-read thermometer to ascertain the following temperatures, making sure the thermometer does not touch a bone when inserted.

	BEEF, VEAL, LAMB	PORK
Ground	160°	160°
Roasts, steaks and chops	Medium-rare: 145° Medium: 160° Well-done: 170°	Medium: 160° Well-done: 170°

Beef and vegetable fajitas

Makes 4 servings   *Prep* 25 minutes   *Refrigerate* 2 hours   *Broil* 12 minutes

A mess of vegetables makes the half pound of meat seem like much more. Use fat-free flour tortillas and you're even further ahead in the nutrition game.

Per serving
514 calories, 25 g protein, 14 g fat, 72 g carbohydrate, 920 mg sodium, 36 mg cholesterol.

¼ cup fresh lime juice
2 teaspoons vegetable oil
2 cloves garlic, finely chopped
½ teaspoon dried oregano
¼ teaspoon ground cumin
¼ teaspoon hot-pepper sauce
⅛ teaspoon salt
2 sweet green peppers, cored, seeded and sliced
1 large red onion, halved lengthwise, then sliced crosswise
1 medium zucchini, halved lengthwise, then sliced crosswise
1 top round steak or flank steak (½ pound)
⅛ teaspoon black pepper
8 flour tortillas (10-inch)
1 cup thin radish slices
2 tablespoons chopped fresh cilantro
1 cup favorite salsa (recipes, pages 39–41)

1. Combine lime juice, oil, garlic, oregano, cumin, hot-pepper sauce and salt in a large shallow dish. Add green peppers, onion and zucchini. Move vegetables to side of dish. Add steak; turn to coat. Cover and refrigerate 2 hours.

2. Heat broiler.

3. Transfer marinade liquid to a small saucepan. Bring to boiling and boil 5 minutes.

4. Broil meat 4 inches from heat 4 to 6 minutes or until browned. Turn meat over. Arrange vegetables around meat. Brush meat with marinade. Broil for 4 to 6 minutes or until meat is cooked to desired doneness (until an instant-read thermometer registers an internal temperature of 145° for medium-rare or 160° for medium) and vegetables are crisp-tender.

5. Remove vegetables to a plate and meat to cutting board. Sprinkle meat with pepper and let stand 5 minutes.

6. Meanwhile, wrap tortillas in damp paper toweling. Microwave on 100% power 1 to 2 minutes or until steaming and very pliable.

7. Cut meat across the grain into very thin slices. Divide meat and vegetables among tortillas. Sprinkle filling with radish slices and cilantro. Top each with 2 tablespoons salsa. Fold tortillas over filling. Serve at once.

MEAT

Mexican ropa vieja

Makes 8 servings   *Prep* 15 minutes   *Cook* about 2½ hours

The recipe title translates as "old clothes," which probably refers to the meat being torn apart into shreds.

Per serving
499 calories, 32 g protein, 17 g fat, 52 g carbohydrate, 654 mg sodium, 59 mg cholesterol.

2 tablespoons peanut oil
1 medium onion, chopped (about ¾ cup)
1 small sweet red pepper, cored, seeded and chopped (about ¾ cup)
1 small sweet green pepper, cored, seeded and chopped (about ¾ cup)
5 cloves garlic, chopped
1 teaspoon ground cumin
½ teaspoon dried oregano
1 can (14½ ounces) stewed tomatoes

½ cup beef broth
1 flank steak (2 pounds)
½ teaspoon salt
½ teaspoon black pepper
2 cans (4 ounces each) whole mild green chiles, drained and coarsely chopped
1 package (10 ounces) frozen corn kernels
16 flour tortillas (8-inch)
1 fresh jalapeño chile, seeded and chopped
2 tablespoons chopped fresh cilantro

1. Heat oil in a large flameproof casserole or Dutch oven over medium heat. Add onion, sweet peppers and garlic; cook until onion is translucent and peppers are softened, about 8 minutes. Stir in cumin and oregano; cook 1 minute more. Add tomatoes and broth.

2. Season steak with salt and pepper. Add steak to casserole; cover and bring to simmering. Simmer about 2 hours or until meat is very tender, turning meat occasionally.

3. Remove meat; cool briefly. Cut across grain into 2-inch-thick slices. Using 2 forks, pull slices apart into shreds.

4. Heat tomato sauce remaining in casserole to boiling. Continue to boil, stirring occasionally, until thickened, 10 to 15 minutes. Add green chiles and corn. Heat to boiling; cook 5 minutes more.

5. Meanwhile, wrap tortillas in damp paper toweling. Microwave on 100% power 1 to 2 minutes or until steaming and very pliable.

6. Add shredded beef, jalapeño and cilantro to tomato sauce mixture. Heat to boiling. Serve with warmed tortillas.

Hungarian goulash

Makes 8 servings   *Prep* 15 minutes   *Cook* 1 hour 5 minutes

For a flavor switch, replace the caraway seeds with a quarter cup or so of chopped fresh dill.

Per serving
285 calories, 21 g protein, 9 g fat, 30 g carbohydrate, 467 mg sodium, 81 mg cholesterol.

2 strips bacon, diced
1 onion, sliced, slices quartered
1 clove garlic, thinly sliced
1 pound top round beef, cut into 2 x ½ x ¼-inch strips
1 teaspoon caraway seeds
1 tablespoon paprika
1 teaspoon salt
¼ teaspoon black pepper
½ cup beef broth
2 tablespoons red-wine vinegar
¾ pound broad egg noodles
1 tablespoon butter
¼ cup chopped fresh parsley
½ cup reduced-fat sour cream

1. Cook bacon in a large Dutch oven or skillet over medium heat 3 to 4 minutes. Add onion; sauté 5 minutes or until softened. Add garlic; sauté 1 minute. Add beef; sauté 4 minutes or until browned. Reduce heat to low. Stir in caraway seeds, paprika, salt, pepper and ¼ cup broth. Cover and cook, stirring occasionally, 30 minutes, adding a little water if needed to prevent sticking. Add vinegar; cook 20 minutes more.

2. Meanwhile, cook noodles in a large pot of salted boiling water 6 to 8 minutes or until tender. Drain; toss with butter and parsley in a large serving platter.

3. Stir together sour cream and remaining ¼ cup broth in a small bowl. Stir into beef mixture in skillet. Gently heat through. Spoon beef mixture over noodles.

Mexican ropa vieja
opposite

Hungarian goulash

Tangy beef stroganoff

Makes 6 servings   *Prep* 30 minutes   *Refrigerate* 2 hours   *Cook* 20 minutes

1 pound beef round or sirloin, cut into 2 x ½ x ¼-inch strips
2 tablespoons fresh lemon juice
1 tablespoon Worcestershire sauce
¼ teaspoon salt
¼ teaspoon black pepper
2 tablespoons vegetable oil
2 large onions, diced (2 cups)
½ pound mushrooms, sliced
½ cup beef broth
2 tablespoons all-purpose flour
2 tablespoons tomato paste
1 container (8 ounces) reduced-fat sour cream
4 cups hot cooked noodles
12 pimiento-stuffed green olives

1. Combine beef, lemon juice, Worcestershire sauce, salt and pepper in heavy-duty food-storage bag; seal. Refrigerate 2 hours.

2. Heat 1 tablespoon oil in a large skillet over medium-high heat. Add onions; sauté until golden brown, 3 to 5 minutes. Add mushrooms; sauté until softened, 3 to 5 minutes. Remove to a medium-size bowl; keep warm. Increase heat to high; heat remaining oil in same skillet. Remove meat from marinade; add to skillet and sauté 2 minutes. Reduce heat to low; stir in onions and mushrooms.

3. Whisk broth, flour and tomato paste in a small bowl until smooth. Stir into skillet. Cook, stirring, until slightly thickened and bubbly, 2 minutes. Stir in sour cream; don't boil. Serve over noodles; top with olives.

Corned beef hash

Makes 6 servings   *Prep* 15 minutes   *Cook* 25 minutes

1 tablespoon olive oil
1 medium red onion, diced
1 large clove garlic, finely chopped
2 tablespoons butter
1 pound all-purpose potatoes, cooked, peeled and diced
1 piece cooked corned beef (10 ounces), diced
2 teaspoons Worcestershire sauce
½ teaspoon hot-pepper sauce
¼ teaspoon black pepper
1 tablespoon chopped fresh parsley

Heat oil in a large skillet over medium-high heat. Add onion and garlic and sauté 5 minutes. Add butter and potatoes and cook 12 minutes, stirring occasionally, until browned. Add corned beef, Worcestershire sauce and hot-pepper sauce and cook 5 to 6 minutes. Sprinkle with black pepper and parsley. Toss to combine.

Veal bundles

Makes 4 servings   *Prep* 15 minutes   *Cook* 35 minutes

Gnocchi or spaetzle is the ideal accompaniment for soaking up the tomato sauce.

Per serving
443 calories, 32 g protein, 25 g fat, 23 g carbohydrate, 736 mg sodium, 109 mg cholesterol.

2 tablespoons olive oil
1 clove garlic
¼ pound mushrooms, sliced
½ cup chopped fresh parsley
¼ cup golden raisins
3 tablespoons grated Parmesan cheese

¼ cup dry plain bread crumbs
4 veal scaloppine (1 pound total)
1 cup chicken broth
1 carrot, chopped
1 can (14½ ounces) stewed tomatoes

1. Heat 1 teaspoon oil in a large nonstick skillet over medium heat. Add garlic; sauté 30 seconds. Add mushrooms; sauté 3 minutes. Transfer mixture to a small bowl. Stir in parsley, raisins, Parmesan and bread crumbs.

2. Lay scaloppine flat. Top each with stuffing, dividing equally. Roll up scaloppine and secure each with a wooden pick. Wipe out skillet.

3. Heat remaining oil in skillet. Add rolled veal and sauté 5 minutes or until browned. Add broth and carrot; simmer 15 minutes. Remove veal rolls to a plate; remove picks and keep warm. Stir tomatoes into skillet; boil 5 minutes or until slightly thickened. Add veal rolls; heat through.

Veal kabobs

Makes 4 servings   *Prep* 30 minutes   *Refrigerate* up to 1 hour   *Cook* 20 minutes   *Broil* 20 minutes

The wine-marinated veal skewered with vegetables can be assembled earlier in the day and refrigerated.

Per serving
407 calories, 34 g protein, 13 g fat, 38 g carbohydrate, 227 mg sodium, 125 mg cholesterol.

¼ cup dry white wine
1 clove garlic, finely chopped
1 teaspoon dried basil
1 teaspoon dried oregano
¼ teaspoon salt
1 tablespoon olive oil

1 pound veal stew meat, cut into 1-inch cubes
1 pound new potatoes
1 pound zucchini, cut into 16 chunks
1 red onion, cut into 8 wedges
16 cherry tomatoes

1. Combine wine, garlic, basil, oregano, salt and oil in a medium-size bowl. Stir in veal. Refrigerate 45 minutes to 1 hour.

2. Boil potatoes until almost tender, 20 minutes. Drain. Cut into quarters.

3. Heat broiler. Remove meat from marinade. Alternately thread veal, potatoes, zucchini, onions and tomatoes on eight 10-inch metal skewers. Place on a rack in a roasting pan. Drizzle with half of marinade. Broil kabobs 6 inches from heat 10 minutes.

4. Meanwhile, bring remaining marinade to boiling in a small saucepan. Turn kabobs; drizzle with hot marinade and broil 10 minutes more.

Roast pork with sweet and white potatoes

Makes 8 servings   *Prep* 10 minutes   *Refrigerate* 1 hour   *Roast* at 400° for 1 hour

Many vegetables can be roasted with great success. The high heat brings out the natural sweetness.

Per serving
416 calories, 40 g protein,
20 g fat, 16 g carbohydrate,
125 mg sodium,
119 mg cholesterol.

1 boneless pork loin roast (3½ pounds)
1 large clove garlic, cut into slivers
Fresh thyme leaves or 1 teaspoon dried
2 tablespoons reduced-sodium soy sauce

1 teaspoon Worcestershire sauce
½ teaspoon freshly ground black pepper
2 baking potatoes
2 sweet potatoes

1. Cut tiny slits into surface of pork. Insert slivers of garlic and thyme leaves. Place pork in a plastic food-storage bag. Add soy sauce and Worcestershire sauce. Seal bag. Refrigerate to marinate pork 1 hour or overnight.

2. Heat oven to 400°. For the potatoes, lightly coat a small baking pan with nonstick cooking spray.

3. Remove pork from bag. Place pork on a rack in a roasting pan. Discard leftover marinade. Sprinkle pork with pepper. Pour ½ inch hot water into pan.

4. Roast in heated 400° oven 1 hour or until internal temperature registers 160° on an instant-read thermometer. Let rest 10 minutes before slicing.

5. Meanwhile, cut potatoes in half lengthwise and lightly oil. Place, cut side down, in prepared baking pan. Add to oven for last 25 minutes of pork roasting time. Remove from oven when pork is ready to serve.

Preparing flavorful pork

1. With the tip of a small knife, cut ½-inch-deep slits all over the surface of the pork.

2. To infuse the pork with flavor, tuck garlic slivers and thyme leaves into slits.

3. To marinate neatly, combine marinade ingredients and pork in a plastic food-storage bag.

Roast pork with sweet and white potatoes *opposite*

Maple-glazed pork and potatoes

Makes 4 servings   *Prep* 10 minutes   *Bake* at 400° for 50 to 60 minutes   *Cook* 10 to 12 minutes

Serve with steamed green beans tossed with a pat of butter and grated lemon rind.

Per serving

635 calories, 44 g protein, 22 g fat, 65 g carbohydrate, 114 mg sodium, 129 mg cholesterol.

1 boneless pork loin roast
  (1½ pounds)
4 cloves garlic, peeled
1¼ pounds new potatoes, quartered
1 tablespoon olive oil
  Salt and black pepper to taste
1 lemon
½ cup maple syrup

1. Heat oven to 400°.

2. Place roast in a small baking dish. Slice 2 cloves garlic. Place potatoes, sliced garlic, oil and salt and pepper in another small baking dish; toss to coat potatoes.

3. Bake both dishes in heated 400° oven 50 to 60 minutes or until internal temperature of pork registers 160° on an instant-read thermometer; potatoes should be tender.

4. Meanwhile, grate and then juice lemon; place in a small saucepan. Chop remaining 2 cloves garlic; add to saucepan along with maple syrup. Bring to simmering; cook 10 to 12 minutes or until syrupy. Set aside.

5. Brush pork roast with maple glaze every 10 minutes during last 30 minutes of cooking. Let roast stand 10 minutes before slicing. Serve pork with potatoes and defatted pan juices.

Stuffed pork roast

Makes 12 servings   *Prep* 25 minutes   *Roast* at 375° for 1 hour 15 minutes   *Cook* gravy 10 minutes

Figs and shallots tucked into the lean pork loin add flavor and moisture—but no extra fat.

Per serving

369 calories, 43 g protein, 15 g fat, 11 g carbohydrate, 152 mg sodium, 120 mg cholesterol.

1 boneless pork loin roast
  (4 pounds)
10 shallots, peeled, left whole
10 fresh figs, stems removed
1 teaspoon dried thyme
1 tablespoon olive oil
½ cup water
¼ cup brandy
1 tablespoon currant jam
1 cup reduced-sodium beef broth
¼ teaspoon salt
⅛ teaspoon black pepper

1. Heat oven to 350°.

2. Butterfly roast by cutting pork from one end to the other about three-quarters of the way through. Open roast like a book and place shallots and figs, side by side, down length. Close and tie at intervals with string. Rub roast with thyme.

3. Heat oil in a flameproof roasting pan over medium-high heat. Add roast and brown on all sides.

4. Roast pork in heated 375° oven 1 hour 15 minutes or until internal temperature registers 160° on an instant-read thermometer. Remove roast to a platter; keep warm.

5. Pour water into roasting pan; heat to simmering scraping up any browned bits from pan. Pour into a small saucepan. Skim off fat. Add brandy; boil 2 minutes. Stir in jam, broth, salt and pepper. Simmer 3 minutes. Remove string from pork roast; slice and serve with gravy.

Pork chops with aïoli

Makes 8 servings *Prep* 15 minutes *Broil* 10 minutes

This garlicky sauce native to France is also delicious with chicken. For another option, go Tex-Mex.

Per serving
224 calories, 22 g protein, 14 g fat, 0 g carbohydrate, 304 mg sodium, 60 mg cholesterol.

8 rib pork chops (3 pounds total)
1 teaspoon salt
½ teaspoon black pepper
1 tablespoon olive oil

1 teaspoon dried sage
Aïoli Sauce or Tex-Mex Chili Sauce (recipes follow)

1. Heat broiler.

2. Season chops with salt and pepper. Whisk oil and sage in a small bowl; brush over chops.

3. Place chops on a broiler pan; broil 6 inches from heat, turning once, 10 minutes or until no longer pink in center and internal temperature registers 160° on an instant-read thermometer. Serve with Aïoli Sauce or Tex-Mex Chili Sauce.

Aïoli sauce

per tablespoon
80 calories, 0 g protein, 9 g fat, 53 g carbohydrate, 63 mg sodium, 7 mg cholesterol.

In a small bowl, whisk together 1 cup mayonnaise, 2 tablespoons fresh orange juice, 1 teaspoon white-wine vinegar, 1 teaspoon dried sage and 1 clove garlic, crushed. Refrigerate until ready to serve. Makes about 1¼ cups.

Tex-Mex chili sauce

per tablespoon
38 calories, 0 g protein, 4 g fat, 2 g carbohydrate, 59 mg sodium, 0 mg cholesterol.

In a small bowl, stir together ¼ cup oil, 2 tablespoons fresh lime juice, 1 clove finely chopped garlic, 2 teaspoons chili powder ½ teaspoon ground cumin, ¼ teaspoon salt and pinch ground red pepper (cayenne). Add 1 large tomato, cored and chopped; 1 small green pepper, cored, seeded and chopped; ¼ cup sliced black olives and 2 tablespoons finely chopped onion. Mix well and let stand 30 minutes to blend flavors. Makes about 1 cup.

Pork medallions with apple

Makes 4 servings   *Prep* 10 minutes   *Cook* 25 minutes

Apple and fresh sage are the flavor partners with the pork tenderloin.

Per serving
502 calories, 37 g protein, 26 g fat, 30 g carbohydrate, 816 mg sodium, 116 mg cholesterol.

Tenderloin tips
Although pork tenderloin may seem expensive at first glance, it really isn't. It's boneless, with almost no fat, so there is no waste. A 3-ounce portion has 4.1 grams of fat and 139 calories. You can roast, grill, stir-fry or braise it.

2 tablespoons butter
3 tablespoons vegetable oil
4 green and red apples, such as Golden Delicious and Staymans, cored and sliced into ½-inch-thick rounds
2 pork tenderloins (about 1½ pounds total), cut into 1-inch-thick slices
¾ teaspoon salt
½ teaspoon black pepper
1 small onion, finely chopped
2 tablespoons chopped fresh sage
¾ cup apple cider
¼ cup cider vinegar
   Fresh sage leaves for garnish

1. Heat 1 tablespoon each butter and oil in a large skillet. Add apples, working in batches if necessary, adding more oil and butter as needed; cook 4 minutes or until light golden and speckled. Remove with a spatula to a large roasting pan or baking sheet with sides; spread in a single layer; place in oven.

2. Heat an additional 1 teaspoon each butter and oil in skillet. Sprinkle pork with ½ teaspoon salt and ¼ teaspoon pepper. Add to skillet; cook 2 to 3 minutes per side or until browned. Place each medallion on an apple slice; there will be more apple slices than pork.

3. Add remaining butter and oil to skillet. Add onion and chopped sage; cook 6 minutes or until softened. Add cider and vinegar. Cook, stirring up browned bits, 4 minutes or until reduced and slightly thickened. Add remaining ¼ teaspoon salt and ¼ teaspoon pepper.

4. Arrange pork with apple slices on plates. Pour sauce over. Garnish each plate with a fresh sage leaf.

Pork medallions with apple

Mustardy pork tenderloin

Makes 6 servings   *Prep* 10 minutes   *Roast* at 425° for 20 minutes

Stir the mustard-dill sauce into your egg or tuna salad for a zesty note.

Per serving
322 calories, 34 g protein, 20 g fat, 1 g carbohydrate, 149 mg sodium, 98 mg cholesterol.

Mustard-dill sauce
½ cup mayonnaise
½ cup sour cream
2 tablespoons Dijon mustard
⅓ cup chopped fresh dill
    Salt and pepper to taste

2 or 3 pork tenderloins
    (2 pounds total)
1 tablespoon olive oil
    Salt and black pepper to taste

1. Prepare mustard-dill sauce: Stir together mayonnaise, sour cream, mustard, dill and salt and pepper in a small bowl. Refrigerate, covered, up to 6 hours.

2. Heat oven to 425°.

3. Trim any bits of fat from tenderloins and remove silver skin. Rub with oil; season with salt and pepper. Place in a roasting pan.

4. Roast in heated 425° oven 20 minutes or until internal temperature registers 160° on an instant-read thermometer; meat will be slightly pink. Let stand 5 minutes before slicing. Serve with mustard-dill sauce.

MEAT

Curried pork chops

Makes 4 servings   *Prep* 15 minutes   *Cook* 8 minutes

No one will ever guess your secret ingredient is ricotta cheese.

Per serving
305 calories, 27 g protein, 16 g fat, 12 g carbohydrate, 229 mg sodium, 69 mg cholesterol.

⅔ cup water
½ cup part-skim ricotta cheese
2 tablespoons all-purpose flour
2 tablespoons chutney
1 teaspoon curry powder

¼ teaspoon salt
4 rib pork chops (1½ pounds total)
1 teaspoon olive oil
2 tablespoons golden raisins

1. Place water, ricotta cheese, 1 tablespoon flour, chutney, curry powder and salt in a food processor or blender. Whirl until smooth.

2. Place remaining flour on waxed paper. Lightly coat chops on both sides in flour, shaking off excess. Heat oil in a medium-size nonstick skillet over medium heat. Add chops; cook 4 to 6 minutes or until no longer pink in center and internal temperature registers 160° on an instant-read thermometer. Remove to a serving platter and keep warm.

3. Discard fat in skillet. Add ricotta mixture and raisins. Bring to boiling and cook, stirring, 2 minutes. Serve over chops.

Pork and squash burritos

Makes 6 servings   *Prep* 15 minutes   *Cook* 15 minutes

Since the filling can be prepared ahead, this is a good party food that's fun for kids of all ages.

Per serving
452 calories, 28 g protein, 18 g fat, 46 g carbohydrate, 788 mg sodium, 64 mg cholesterol.

½ medium butternut squash, peeled and cut into 2 x ½ x ½-inch sticks
1 tablespoon olive oil
1 red onion, halved lengthwise, then sliced crosswise
1 pork loin (1 pound), trimmed and cut into matchstick strips
1 medium zucchini, cut into 2 x ½ x ½-inch sticks
1 teaspoon chili powder
1 teaspoon ground cumin
1 teaspoon salt
⅛ teaspoon ground cinnamon
¼ cup fresh orange juice
6 flour tortillas (10-inch)
1 cup shredded pepper-Jack cheese

1. Bring ½ inch water to boiling in a large nonstick skillet. Add squash; cook 3 to 5 minutes or until tender. Drain.

2. Heat oil in skillet over medium heat. Add onion; cook 6 minutes or until softened. Increase heat to medium-high. Add the pork, zucchini, chili powder, cumin, salt and cinnamon. Cook, stirring frequently, 6 to 8 minutes or until pork is cooked through and vegetables are tender.

3. Stir in orange juice and reserved squash; cook 2 minutes or until heated through.

4. Meanwhile, wrap tortillas in damp paper toweling. Microwave on 100% power 1 to 2 minutes or until steaming and very pliable.

5. Spoon squash filling over warmed tortillas, dividing equally. Sprinkle with cheese. Fold up each tortilla, envelope style.

Pork schnitzel

Makes 6 servings   *Prep* 10 minutes   *Cook* 12 minutes

In this German-style dish, a thin cutlet of meat is dipped in egg, breaded and then fried.

Per serving
294 calories, 28 g protein, 16 g fat, 9 g carbohydrate, 283 mg sodium, 110 mg cholesterol.

6 pork cutlets (1½ pounds total), trimmed
½ teaspoon salt
⅓ cup all-purpose flour
¼ cup dry plain bread crumbs
1 egg
¼ cup milk
3 tablespoons oil

1. Place pork cutlets between sheets of plastic wrap. Lightly pound until paper-thin. Sprinkle both sides with salt.

2. Measure flour and bread crumbs onto separate sheets of waxed paper. Whisk together egg and milk in small bowl. Lightly coat cutlets in flour, shaking off excess; dip in egg mixture, then into bread crumbs, pressing crumbs to coat.

3. Heat oil in a large nonstick skillet over medium-high heat. Working in batches, add cutlets to skillet; cook, turning once, until golden brown, about 3 minutes per side. Remove cutlets to a warmed platter. Serve immediately.

Wild rice and pork cutlets

Makes 4 servings   *Prep* 20 minutes   *Cook* 1½ hours

Wild rice is not really rice but the seed of an aquatic grass. It has a chewy texture, cooks in 50 to 60 minutes and can be mixed deliciously with white or brown rice.

Per serving
524 calories, 36 g protein, 12 g fat, 72 g carbohydrate, 740 mg sodium, 73 mg cholesterol.

2½ cups water
1 cup wild rice
3 teaspoons curry powder
1¼ teaspoons salt
1 tablespoon vegetable oil
4 boneless pork cutlets (1 pound total)
¼ teaspoon black pepper
2 large green onions, cut into 1-inch pieces (about 1 cup)
1 can (11 ounces) Mandarin oranges, drained (reserve juice)
Orange juice, as needed
1 tablespoon cornstarch
1 package (8 ounces) frozen sugar snap peas
½ cup golden raisins

1. Bring water, wild rice, 1½ teaspoons curry powder and 1 teaspoon salt to boiling in a large skillet over high heat. Reduce heat to low; cover and simmer 50 to 60 minutes or until rice is tender and liquid is absorbed. Remove to a medium-size bowl and keep warm.

2. Heat oil in same skillet over medium-high heat. Sprinkle pork cutlets with remaining ¼ teaspoon salt and pepper. Add to skillet; sauté 4 minutes per side or until golden. Remove to bowl with rice.

3. Reduce heat to medium. Add green onions and remaining 1½ teaspoons curry powder; sauté 4 minutes or until onions are limp.

4. Set drained orange sections aside. Add enough orange juice to reserved Mandarin orange liquid to equal 1 cup. Whisk juice mixture and cornstarch in a small bowl until well blended. Add to skillet. Bring to boiling; cook, stirring constantly, 2 to 3 minutes or until clear and thickened.

5. Add sugar snap peas and raisins to skillet. Return to boiling; cook 4 minutes.

6. Return pork and rice to skillet along with orange sections. Heat through.

MEAT

301

Pork cutlets Mexicano

Makes 4 servings *Prep* 10 minutes *Cook* 10 minutes

Boneless pork chops cook with their own spicy salsa sauce. Serve with a heaping bowl of rice.

Per serving
258 calories, 27 g protein, 12 g fat, 8 g carbohydrate, 872 mg sodium, 94 mg cholesterol.

2 tablespoons butter
⅓ cup finely chopped red onion
1½ teaspoons finely chopped garlic
2 tablespoons all-purpose flour
4 boneless pork cutlets (1¼ pounds total), slightly flattened
¼ teaspoon ground cumin
½ cup chicken broth
½ teaspoon red-wine vinegar
1 cup salsa

1. Melt butter in a large nonstick skillet over medium-high heat. Add onion and garlic; sauté, stirring occasionally, 2 minutes or until softened.

2. Meanwhile, place flour on waxed paper. Lightly coat cutlets in flour, shaking off excess. Add cutlets to skillet; sauté 2 minutes per side or until golden brown. Add cumin, broth, vinegar and salsa; cook about 4 minutes or until the meat is cooked through.

Adobo pork skewers

Makes 4 servings *Prep* 10 minutes *Refrigerate* 20 minutes *Broil* 15 minutes

Accompany with rice and steamed broccoli, and for a finish, linger over slices of watermelon.

Per serving
295 calories, 37 g protein, 5 g fat, 9 g carbohydrate, 312 mg sodium, 68 mg cholesterol.

1 can (8 ounces) reduced-sodium tomato sauce
1 teaspoon chili powder
¾ teaspoon ground cumin
⅛ teaspoon ground red pepper (cayenne)
¼ cup pitted green olives
1 pickled jalapeño chile, seeded and stemmed
1 clove garlic
1¼ pounds cubed pork butt
2 sweet green peppers, cored, seeded and cut into 1-inch pieces
1 Spanish onion, cut into 1-inch pieces

1. Place tomato sauce, chili powder, cumin, ground red pepper, olives, jalapeño and garlic in a blender or small food processor. Process until smooth. Scrape half of sauce into a plastic food-storage bag. Reserve remaining sauce in a small bowl. Add pork to bag. Turn bag over until pork is well coated. Refrigerate 20 minutes.

2. Heat broiler. Drain pork. Thread pork with peppers and onion onto metal skewers. Brush with some of the reserved sauce.

3. Broil skewers 5 inches from heat 15 minutes, turning skewers over halfway during cooking and brushing with sauce.

Kansas City barbecued ribs

Makes 10 servings *Prep* 15 minutes *Bake* at 425° for 45 minutes; then at 350° for 1½ hours

Cook sauce 20 minutes

Just the way they do it in Kansas City—a tempting combination of sweet and sour glazes the ribs.

Per serving
686 calories, 45 g protein, 46 g fat, 24 g carbohydrate, 839 mg sodium, 181 mg cholesterol.

2 racks spare ribs (7 pounds total)

Sauce
1 bottle (14 ounces) ketchup
½ cup apricot or peach preserves
⅓ cup fresh orange juice

⅓ cup fresh lemon juice
2 tablespoons soy sauce
1 tablespoon hot-pepper sauce
1 tablespoon paprika
1 tablespoon chili powder

1. Heat oven to 425°. Line 2 baking sheets with sides with aluminum foil.

2. Place ribs on prepared baking sheets. Bake, uncovered, in heated 425° oven 45 minutes. Pour off juices.

3. Meanwhile, prepare sauce: Stir ketchup, preserves, orange juice, lemon juice, soy sauce, hot-pepper sauce, paprika and chili powder in a saucepan. Simmer, stirring occasionally, 20 minutes. Reserve half for serving.

4. Lower oven temperature to 350°. Cover ribs; bake another 1½ hours or until tender. During last 30 minutes, cook uncovered, brushing ribs with sauce every 10 minutes. Serve with reserved sauce for dipping.

Note: Ask your butcher to crack the ribs for easy serving.

MEAT

Pork cutlets Mexicano *opposite*

Kansas City barbecued ribs

303

Sweet 'n' spicy barbecued ribs

Makes 8 servings   *Prep* 20 minutes   *Cook* 15 minutes

Bake at 325° for 1 hour   *Broil* 16 to 18 minutes

These meaty ribs are slow-baked with a spice rub, then broiled with a sweet and tangy beer-based barbecue sauce: Worcestershire sauce, soy sauce and hot-pepper sauce make it tangy, and molasses and brown sugar contribute the sweet.

Per serving
571 calories, 34 g protein,
39 g fat, 20 g carbohydrate,
765 mg sodium,
153 mg cholesterol.

How many servings?
The number of servings per pound varies depending on the cut and cooking method. But in general, you can expect:
• 3 to 4 servings per pound for boneless chops and roasts.
• 2 to 3 servings per pound for bone-in chops and roasts.
• 1 to 1½ servings per pound for ribs and spareribs.

Spice rub
- 3 tablespoons paprika
- 1 teaspoon salt
- 1 teaspoon dried thyme
- 1 teaspoon garlic powder
- ¾ teaspoon onion powder
- ½ teaspoon celery seeds
- ¼ teaspoon ground red pepper (cayenne)

- 5 pounds country-style pork ribs

Barbecue sauce
- 1 cup (6 ounces) tomato paste
- 1 cup beer
- ¼ cup molasses
- ¼ cup firmly packed dark-brown sugar
- 2 tablespoons reduced-sodium soy sauce
- 2 tablespoons Worcestershire sauce
- ½ teaspoon ground ginger
- 3 drops hot-pepper sauce
- 1 small onion, chopped

1. Heat oven to 325°.

2. Prepare spice rub: Mix paprika, salt, thyme, garlic powder, onion powder, celery seeds and ground red pepper in a small bowl. Rub ribs with spice mixture. Place ribs in a single layer on racks of 2 broiler or roasting pans.

3. Bake in heated 325° oven 1 hour. Remove from oven.

4. Meanwhile, prepare sauce: Stir together tomato paste, beer, molasses, brown sugar, soy sauce, Worcestershire sauce, ginger, hot-pepper sauce and onion in a medium-size saucepan. Cook sauce, stirring occasionally, over medium heat until thickened, about 15 minutes. Divide sauce in half: one half for basting and one for serving.

5. Brush both sides of ribs with most of basting sauce. Return to oven.

6. Increase oven temperature to broil. Broil ribs 4 to 6 inches from heat 8 minutes. Turn ribs over; baste with remaining basting sauce. Broil 8 to 10 minutes. Serve with reserved sauce.

Smoked ham with tropical salsa

Makes 18 servings *Prep* 30 minutes *Bake* at 325° for 2½ hours *Stand* 15 minutes

Who says salsa has to have tomatoes? Our tropical version features pineapple, orange and kiwi for a sweet yet refreshing counterpoint to ham.
Shown on page 271.

Per serving
158 calories, 21 g protein,
5 g fat, 6 g carbohydrate,
1,132 mg sodium,
47 mg cholesterol.

1 smoked ham shank (6 pounds)
½ cup currant jelly
¼ cup orange juice
⅛ teaspoon ground allspice
⅛ teaspoon ground cloves
  Whole cloves
  Tropical Salsa (recipe follows)

1. Heat oven to 325°.

2. Remove any skin from ham. Trim fat evenly to ½-inch thickness. Place ham on a rack in a roasting pan. Bake ham in heated 325° oven 1½ hours.

3. Meanwhile, combine jelly, orange juice, allspice and ground cloves in a small saucepan; bring to boiling, stirring, until jelly is melted and mixture is smooth.

4. After 1½ hours baking, brush ham with jelly mixture. Bake another 45 minutes, basting every 15 minutes.

5. Remove ham from oven. Carefully score fat into a 1-inch crisscross pattern, cutting ⅛ inch deep. Stud fat with whole cloves. Brush with remaining jelly mixture.

6. Bake ham 15 minutes more or until internal temperature registers 140° on an instant-read thermometer. Let ham stand 15 minutes. Serve with Tropical Salsa.

Tropical salsa

Per serving
29 calories, 0 g protein,
0 g fat, 7 g carbohydrate,
1 mg sodium,
0 mg cholesterol.

Combine 2 tablespoons honey, 2 tablespoons thawed frozen orange juice concentrate, 1 tablespoon Grand Marnier and ¼ teaspoon ground mace in a medium-size bowl. Add 1 cup finely chopped fresh pineapple; 1 large navel orange, peeled and finely chopped (1½ cups); 3 kiwi, peeled and finely chopped (1 cup), and ½ cup finely chopped red onion.

Spiral-cut ham with honey glaze

Makes 16 servings   *Prep* 15 minutes   *Bake* at 375° for 1¼ hours

A presliced spiral-cut ham eliminates all that carving—a welcome shortcut when the guests are waiting.

Per serving
236 calories, 29 g protein, 6 g fat, 15 g carbohydrate, 1,507 mg sodium, 62 mg cholesterol.

½ spiral-cut smoked ham (about 7 pounds)
½ cup pear nectar
½ cup fresh orange juice

½ cup firmly packed light-brown sugar
½ cup honey

1. Heat oven to 375°. Place ham, cut end down, in a baking pan.

2. Mix together pear nectar and orange juice in a small bowl. Bake ham in heated 375° oven 15 minutes, basting twice with juice mixture.

3. Mix together brown sugar and honey in a small bowl. Brush mixture over ham. Bake about 1 hour more or until internal temperature of ham registers 140° on an instant-read meat thermometer. Serve immediately.

Ham and cheese strata

Makes 6 servings   *Prep* 10 minutes   *Stand* 30 minutes   *Bake* at 350° for 45 minutes

This make-ahead brunch or supper dish makes good use of leftover ham.

Per serving
325 calories, 21 g protein, 14 g fat, 28 g carbohydrate, 648 mg sodium, 150 mg cholesterol.

8 slices slightly firm white bread
¼ cup chopped fresh parsley
1 green onion, thinly sliced
1 cup chopped cooked ham
1 cup shredded low-sodium Swiss cheese (4 ounces)

3 eggs
2 cups milk
1 teaspoon Dijon mustard
⅛ teaspoon black pepper
⅛ teaspoon hot-pepper sauce

1. Coat a shallow 2-quart baking dish with nonstick cooking spray. Arrange half of bread in a single layer in dish, cutting to fit. Cover with half each of parsley, green onion, ham and cheese. Repeat layers.

2. Combine eggs, milk, mustard, black pepper and hot-pepper sauce in a small bowl. Pour over casserole. Cover; let stand 30 minutes.

3. Heat oven to 350°.

4. Bake, uncovered, in heated 350° oven 45 minutes or until strata is puffed and browned.

Broiled marinated leg of lamb

Broiled marinated leg of lamb

Makes 12 servings *Prep* 15 minutes *Refrigerate* 6 to 24 hours *Broil* 40 to 45 minutes

Most butchers will be happy to butterfly a leg of lamb for you. If doing the job at home, cover the meat with waxed paper after you've butterflied it, and whack it into an even thickness with a meat mallet or heavy skillet.

Per serving
264 calories, 32 g protein,
8 g fat, 14 g carbohydrate,
388 mg sodium,
89 mg cholesterol.

⅓ cup olive oil
⅓ cup fresh lemon juice
1 tablespoon Dijon mustard
4 cloves garlic, finely chopped
1 teaspoon dried oregano

½ teaspoon freshly ground
 black pepper
1 boneless leg of lamb (4 pounds),
 butterflied

1. Combine oil, lemon juice, mustard, garlic, oregano and pepper in a plastic food-storage bag; Place lamb in bag, seal and refrigerate 6 to 24 hours.

2. Heat broiler. Drain lamb, reserving any marinade. Place lamb on a rack in a roasting pan.

3. Broil 6 inches from heat, 15 minutes on each side. Baste meat once or twice with reserved marinade. Tent foil over lamb and continue cooking 10 to 15 minutes more or until an instant-read thermometer registers an internal temperature of 145° for medium-rare or 160° for medium. Remove lamb; let stand, covered with foil, 10 minutes before slicing.

To grill lamb: Prepare a charcoal grill with hot coals, or heat a gas grill to high. Place lamb on grill rack and sear, turning once, until well browned on both sides, about 10 minutes total. Lower heat to medium or move lamb to cooler edge of grill; cook 15 to 20 minutes longer or to desired doneness. Baste meat once or twice with reserved marinade. Remove lamb; let stand, covered with foil, 10 minutes before slicing.

Marinated leg of lamb with pan-roasted potatoes

Makes 16 servings   *Prep* 15 minutes   *Refrigerate* overnight

Roast 15 minutes at 450°; then 1½ to 1¾ hours at 350°

Rosemary, tarragon, garlic and mustard are time-honored seasonings for lamb. Experiment with different flavored mustards.

Per serving
264 calories, 32 g protein, 3 g fat, 13 g carbohydrate, 4 mg sodium, 89 mg cholesterol.

4 cloves garlic, finely chopped
2 tablespoons prepared mustard
1 tablespoon dried rosemary
2 teaspoons dried tarragon
1 teaspoon grated lemon rind
  Juice of 1 lemon rind
1 leg of lamb (7½ pounds)
2 teaspoons salt
½ teaspoon black pepper
3 pounds red new potatoes, cut in half

Gravy
2 cans (13¾ ounces each) reduced-sodium beef broth
¼ cup all-purpose flour
1 tablespoon prepared mustard

1. Combine garlic, mustard, rosemary, tarragon, lemon rind and lemon juice in a small bowl. Place lamb in a large roasting pan; brush with marinade. Cover; refrigerate overnight.

2. Heat oven to 450°.

3. Uncover lamb. Sprinkle with salt and pepper. Place, fat side up, on a rack in roasting pan. Roast in heated 450° oven 15 minutes. Lower oven temperature to 350°. Roast lamb 14 to 16 minutes per pound (or until internal temperature registers 145° to 160° on an instant-read thermometer), 1½ to 1¾ hours more.

4. Meanwhile, about 45 minutes after lamb has begun roasting, add potatoes to roasting pan; toss to coat with drippings and return pan to oven. Turn potatoes occasionally until lightly golden and tender. Remove roast and potatoes to a warmed platter. Let stand 20 minutes.

5. Meanwhile, prepare gravy: Drain drippings from roasting pan; reserve. Add 1 can broth to pan. Heat to simmering, scraping up any browned bits from pan. Pour into a small bowl. Return ¼ cup drippings (if not enough drippings to make ¼ cup, add olive oil) to pan and heat. Whisk in flour until smooth. Whisk in reserved broth plus remaining can of broth and mustard. Cook, stirring, until thickened; boil 1 minute. Keep warm.

6. Slice lamb. Serve with potatoes and gravy.

Easy shepherd's pie

Makes 4 servings   *Prep* 10 minutes   *Cook* 13 minutes   *Bake* at 375° for 30 minutes

Packaged refrigerated mashed potatoes are what make this pie easy—one whole cooking procedure skipped. Of course, you could use homemade mashed potatoes and fresh carrots and peas.

Per serving
501 calories, 30 g protein, 22 g fat, 52 g carbohydrate, 1,458 mg sodium, 138 mg cholesterol.

1 pound ground lamb
2 cups sliced mushrooms
1 clove garlic, finely chopped
4 green onions (both green and white parts), thinly sliced
1 teaspoon dried thyme
1 teaspoon dried sage
1 package (10 ounces) frozen carrots and peas
1 jar (15 ounces) fat-free beef gravy
3 tablespoons steak sauce or Worcestershire sauce
½ teaspoon salt
¼ teaspoon black pepper
1 package (1 pound 4 ounces) refrigerated prepared mashed potatoes
3 tablespoons finely chopped fresh chives
1 egg, lightly beaten

1. Heat oven to 375°.

2. Heat a large nonstick skillet over medium-high heat. Add lamb, mushrooms and garlic; cook, breaking up lamb with a wooden spoon, 8 minutes or until the lamb is no longer pink. Carefully drain excess liquid from skillet.

3. Stir in green onions, thyme, sage and carrots and peas into lamb mixture; cook, stirring occasionally, over medium-high heat 5 minutes. Remove from heat. Stir in gravy, steak sauce, salt and pepper. Spoon evenly into a 1½-quart casserole.

4. Mix together mashed potatoes, chives and about half of lightly beaten egg in a medium-size bowl. Spoon potato mixture over top of casserole, spreading evenly with back of a spoon. Score potatoes in a cross-hatch with a fork. Brush top of potatoes with remaining beaten egg.

5. Bake in heated 375° oven 30 minutes or until filling is bubbly and top is golden. Remove casserole to a wire rack and let stand 10 to 15 minutes.

MEAT

Moussaka with lamb and potatoes

Makes 8 servings   *Prep* 20 minutes   *Cook* 25 minutes

Bake potatoes at 400° for 13 minutes; moussaka at 375° for 45 to 55 minutes

Instead of using the usual sliced eggplant, we've layered slices of potato with lamb.

Per serving
481 calories, 25 g protein, 16 g fat, 60 g carbohydrate, 781 mg sodium, 99 mg cholesterol.

2½ pounds new potatoes, unpeeled, scrubbed and sliced ¼ inch thick
1½ tablespoons olive oil
1½ teaspoons salt
2 large onions, finely chopped
2 cloves garlic, finely chopped
¾ pound lean ground lamb or beef
½ teaspoon ground cinnamon
½ teaspoon dried oregano
½ teaspoon dried thyme
¼ teaspoon black pepper
2 cans (16 ounces each) no-salt-added tomatoes, drained and chopped
4 cups low-fat (1%) milk
⅔ cup all-purpose flour
¼ teaspoon ground nutmeg
2 eggs
1 cup grated Parmesan cheese
3 tablespoons dry plain bread crumbs

1. Heat oven to 400°.

2. Toss potatoes with 1 tablespoon oil and ½ teaspoon salt in a large bowl until well coated. Arrange in a single layer on large baking sheets or jelly-roll pans.

3. Bake in heated 400° oven 8 minutes. Turn potatoes over. Bake 5 minutes more or until just tender. Remove from oven; set aside. Lower oven temperature to 375°.

4. Meanwhile, heat remaining oil in a large nonstick skillet over medium heat. Add onions and sauté 3 minutes. Add garlic; sauté 1 minute. Stir in lamb, breaking up clumps with a wooden spoon; cook 4 to 6 minutes or until no longer pink. Stir in cinnamon, oregano, thyme, ½ teaspoon salt and pepper. Add tomatoes. Bring to boiling. Lower heat; cover and simmer 10 minutes.

5. Gradually whisk milk into flour in a medium-size saucepan. Cook over medium heat, stirring, 5 to 7 minutes or until slightly thickened. Stir in ½ teaspoon salt and nutmeg.

6. Whisk eggs in a small bowl. Slowly whisk in 1 cup of milk mixture. Whisk egg mixture into milk mixture in pan. Stir in all but ¼ cup Parmesan.

7. Lightly grease a 13 x 9 x 2-inch baking pan. Sprinkle bottom with bread crumbs. Arrange potatoes in pan in about 2 layers. Top with meat mixture; pour in milk mixture. Sprinkle with remaining Parmesan cheese. Place on a baking sheet.

8. Bake in heated 375° oven 45 to 55 minutes or until moussaka is golden brown and puffy. Let stand 15 minutes before serving.

Moussaka with lamb and potatoes *opposite*

Glazed lamb kabobs

Makes 8 servings *Prep* 30 minutes *Bake* at 375° for 40 minutes

A sweet and tangy variation on classic kabobs.

Per serving
129 calories, 12 g protein, 3 g fat, 14 g carbohydrate, 442 mg sodium, 34 mg cholesterol.

1½ pounds cubed lamb
1 sweet green pepper, cored, seeded and cut into 1-inch pieces
1 sweet red pepper, cored, seeded and cut into 1-inch pieces
1 large onion, cut in to 1-inch pieces
⅓ cup apricot preserves
¼ cup reduced-sodium soy sauce
½ cup plus 2 tablespoons chicken broth
1 tablespoon prepared mustard
1 tablespoon cornstarch

1. Heat oven to 375°.

2. Alternately thread lamb cubes, pepper pieces and onion pieces onto 8 metal skewers or wooden skewers soaked in water 30 minutes.

3. Combine preserves, soy sauce, ½ cup broth and mustard in a small saucepan; heat to simmering. Stir together remaining broth and cornstarch in a small bowl. Stir into saucepan; simmer, stirring, 1 minute or until lightly thickened. Reserve ½ cup sauce for serving.

4. Place kabobs on a large baking dish. Brush with sauce. Bake in heated 375° oven 40 minutes or until lamb is cooked through, turning occasionally and brushing with sauce. Heat reserved sauce in a small saucepan over low heat and serve with kabobs.

Apple-sage sausage patties

Makes 4 servings *Prep* 20 minutes *Cook* 10 minutes

A special treat for a weekend brunch, made from scratch. Melt a thin slice of Muenster cheese on top for a rich addition.

Per serving
258 calories, 13 g protein, 20 g fat, 7 g carbohydrate, 896 mg sodium, 48 mg cholesterol.

1 teaspoon olive oil
2 tablespoons finely chopped onion
1 Granny Smith apple, peeled, cored and finely diced
3 cloves garlic, finely chopped
½ teaspoon dried thyme, crumbled
½ teaspoon ground ginger
1 tablespoon finely chopped fresh sage or 1 teaspoon dried, crumbled
¼ teaspoon salt
¼ teaspoon black pepper
1 pound fresh pork sausage
1 egg white
Savory Biscuit Wedges (recipe, page 348) (optional)
Coarse-ground mustard (optional)

1. Heat oil in a large nonstick skillet. Add onion and apple; sauté over medium heat, stirring occasionally, until softened, about 3 minutes. Stir in garlic, thyme, ginger and sage. Remove skillet from heat. Stir in salt and pepper. Let mixture cool to room temperature.

2. Mix together apple mixture, sausage and egg white in a large bowl. Shape mixture into 12 equal patties.

3. Wipe out skillet with paper toweling. Working in batches if necessary, add patties to skillet. Cook over medium heat until browned and internal temperature registers 160° on an instant-read thermometer, 3 to 4 minutes per side. Serve patties on biscuits with a little coarse-ground mustard on the side if you wish.

Creole sausage and peppers

Makes 6 servings *Prep* 15 minutes *Cook* 55 minutes

Spoon over basmati or Texas pecan rice, or for a poor boy sandwich, pack into a hero roll.

Per serving
443 calories, 19 g protein, 24 g fat, 37 g carbohydrate, 1,332 mg sodium, 59 mg cholesterol.

3 onions, sliced
3 sweet green peppers, cored, seeded and sliced
4 cloves garlic, chopped
1 tablespoon olive oil
1 teaspoon salt
¼ teaspoon ground red pepper (cayenne)
1 teaspoon chili powder
½ teaspoon dried thyme
⅛ teaspoon ground cloves
2 tablespoons heavy cream
1 teaspoon ketchup
6 hot Italian sausages (1 pound total)

1. Combine onions and green peppers in a large bowl. Combine garlic, oil, salt, ground red pepper, chili powder, thyme, cloves, cream and ketchup in a small bowl. Pour over onions and peppers.

2. In a large skillet, cook onion-pepper mixture over medium heat 25 minutes, stirring occasionally. Move vegetables to one side. Add sausages to skillet. Spoon vegetables over sausages.

3. Cook 30 minutes more or until sausages are cooked through.

Little Italy peppers variation

Per serving
582 calories, 20 g protein,
39 g fat, 37 g carbohydrate,
1,094 mg sodium,
78 mg cholesterol.

Heat oven to 400°. Combine 3 onions, sliced; 3 sweet green peppers, sliced; 4 cloves garlic, chopped; 2 tablespoons balsamic vinegar and ⅛ teaspoon black pepper in a large roasting pan. Bake in heated 400° oven 30 minutes; add 6 hot Italian sausages and bake 25 minutes more. Serve on toasted French rolls.

Kielbasa and sweet-sour red cabbage

Makes 4 servings *Prep* 10 minutes *Cook* 1 hour

The perfect cold-weather go-with: creamy buttery mashed potatoes.

Per serving
448 calories, 17 g protein,
35 g fat, 18 g carbohydrate,
1,551 mg sodium,
76 mg cholesterol.

1 tablespoon olive oil
1 cup chopped onion
3 tablespoons beef broth
3 whole cloves
1 bay leaf
½ teaspoon caraway seeds
2 tablespoons light-brown sugar
2 tablespoon red-wine vinegar

½ teaspoon salt
2 packages (10 ounces each) shredded red cabbage (about 5 cups total)
1 pound kielbasa, cut into ½-inch-thick slices
1 Granny Smith apple, peeled, cored and sliced

1. Heat oil in a Dutch oven. Add onion; sauté 4 minutes or until tender. Add broth, cloves, bay leaf and caraway seeds. Bring to boiling. Lower heat; simmer, uncovered, 15 minutes.

2. Add brown sugar, vinegar and salt, stirring until sugar dissolves.

3. Add half of cabbage. In order, top with kielbasa, apple slices and remaining cabbage. Cover; simmer 30 minutes or until cabbage is tender.

4. Uncover; cook 10 minutes more or until most of liquid is evaporated. Remove bay leaf.

Assorted breads

Cinnamon bunny bread
page 324

NOVICE AND EXPERT bakers agree—making homemade loaves soothes body and soul. Maybe it's the physical, rhythmic action of kneading; maybe it's the first fragrant whiffs that escape from the oven. Probably it's a bit of both. Although the rising of dough seems like magic, there's no real mystery to it. Our recipes are designed to be foolproof and produce loaf after satisfying loaf.

Try your hand at everything from Honey White and Multi-Grain Wheat to Maple Oat and Pumpernickel Raisin, not to mention charming Cinnamon Bunny Bread and

When the aroma of bread fills the air, a house becomes a home.

an assortment of muffins, biscuits and buns. Waffles and pancakes are on the list too, just right for special breakfasts. In the mood for sandwiches? Go beyond the typical two-slicer to a zingy southwestern-style grilled cheese. Or experiment with fillings in purchased pitas or tortillas. They're even better than the ones Mom used to trim the crusts off. Honest.

Honey white bread

Makes 2 loaves (16 slices each)   *Prep* 30 minutes   *Rise* 2 to 3 hours   *Bake* at 350° for 30 minutes

This bread is absolutely amazing for sandwiches, especially chicken salad and sliced turkey.

Per slice
92 calories, 2 g protein,
1 g fat, 17 g carbohydrate,
112 mg sodium,
10 mg cholesterol.

1¼ cups plus 3 tablespoons warm
  (105° to 115°) water
¼ cup plus 1 teaspoon honey
1 envelope active dry yeast
5 cups all-purpose flour

1½ teaspoons salt
3 tablespoons butter, melted
  and cooled
1 egg

1. Mix 3 tablespoons warm water and 1 teaspoon honey in a small bowl. Sprinkle yeast on top; mix gently. Let stand 10 minutes or until foamy.

2. Combine flour and salt in a large bowl. Pour yeast mixture into flour. Add butter, 1¼ cups warm water, egg and remaining ¼ cup honey. Stir to form a ball.

3. Turn out dough onto a lightly floured surface. Knead until smooth and elastic, about 10 minutes.

4. Place dough in a greased large bowl, turning to coat. Cover bowl with a clean towel or plastic wrap. Let dough rise in a warm place until doubled in volume, 1½ to 2 hours. To test, stick a finger in dough; dent should remain when finger is removed.

5. Grease two 8 x 4 x 3-inch loaf pans. Punch down dough; divide in half. Knead each half a few turns. Place each half in a prepared pan. Cover with a towel or plastic wrap. Let rise 45 minutes to 1 hour or until doubled in volume.

6. Heat oven to 350°. Slash loaves down center lengthwise with a single-edge razor blade.

7. Bake in heated 350° oven 30 minutes or until loaves sound hollow when tapped. Remove bread from pans. Cool on a rack 30 minutes.

Preparing dough

1. Sprinkle yeast over warm water, about 105°. Wait 10 minutes; then combine with flour, salt and other ingredients in a large bowl.

2. Shape into a ball; remove to a floured surface. Press in heel of hand to knead, stretching dough away. Add flour if dough is sticking.

3. Fold dough back over itself. Rotate a quarter turn; knead again. Repeat until dough is smooth and elastic, about 10 minutes.

4. Place dough in a lightly greased bowl; cover and let rise. To test if dough is risen, press a finger lightly into top; it will leave an indentation.

Semolina bread

Makes 2 loaves (12 slices each)   *Prep* 30 minutes   *Rise* about 2½ hours

Bake at 425° for 25 to 30 minutes

This recipe makes two loaves—one for now and one to freeze.

Per slice
108 calories, 3 g protein, 0 g fat, 22 g carbohydrate, 178 mg sodium, 0 mg cholesterol.

1¾ cups warm (105° to 115°) water
1 envelope active dry yeast
3 teaspoons sugar

3 cups all-purpose flour
2 cups semolina flour
2 teaspoons salt

1. Mix ¼ cup warm water and 1 teaspoon sugar in a small bowl. Sprinkle yeast on top; gently mix to moisten yeast. Let stand 10 minutes to soften; mixture will be foamy.

2. Stir together flours, salt and remaining 2 teaspoons sugar in a large bowl. Pour yeast mixture into flour. Add remaining 1½ cups warm water; stir to form a ball.

3. Turn out dough onto a lightly floured surface. Knead until smooth and elastic, about 10 minutes.

4. Place dough in a greased large bowl, turning to coat. Cover bowl with a clean towel or plastic wrap. Let dough rise in a warm place until doubled in volume, 1½ to 2 hours. To test, stick a finger in dough; dent should remain when finger is removed.

5. Lightly grease a baking sheet. Punch down dough; divide in half. Knead each half a few turns on a lightly floured surface. Shape each half into a 16-inch baguette. Place on prepared baking sheet. Cover with plastic wrap. Let rise 45 minutes or until doubled in volume.

6. Heat oven to 425°. Slash tops of loaves diagonally lengthwise with a single-edge razor blade.

7. Bake in heated 425° oven 25 to 30 minutes or until loaves are golden and sound hollow when tapped. Remove bread from baking sheet. Cool on a rack at least 30 minutes.

Fresh test
• Check the expiration date on the yeast envelope—you can't rely on it after the use-by date.
• As a further check, proof (activate) the yeast by dissolving it in warm (105° to 115°) water with a small amount of sugar as directed in your recipe. Stir and let stand for 5 to 10 minutes. If the liquid swells and foams, the yeast is active.
• If you know your yeast is fresh, you can add it dry to the other dry ingredients, but be sure to heat your liquids to 120° to 125° because some of the heat will be dissipated by the dry ingredients.

Walnut-raisin baguettes

Walnut-raisin baguettes

Makes 4 baguettes (12 slices each) *Prep* 30 minutes *Rise* 30 minutes *Bake* at 425° for 20 minutes

Made with both whole-wheat flour and bread flour, this rich bread holds its own with roasted meats.

per slice
78 calories, 2 g protein,
2 g fat, 15 g carbohydrate,
68 mg sodium,
0 mg cholesterol.

4 cups whole-wheat flour
2½ cups plus 3 tablespoons
   bread flour
2 envelopes fast-rising dry yeast
1½ teaspoons salt

2 cups water
½ cup honey
1 cup golden raisins, chopped
1 cup walnuts, chopped
¼ cup yellow cornmeal

1. Combine 2 cups whole-wheat flour, 1 cup bread flour, yeast and salt in a large bowl. Heat water and honey in a small saucepan until very warm (125° to 130°). Gradually beat into flour mixture at low speed. Stir in remaining whole-wheat flour and 1 cup bread flour with a wooden spoon, ½ cup at a time, to make a soft dough. Stir in raisins and walnuts.

2. Knead dough on a floured surface until smooth and elastic, about 10 minutes, working in ½ cup bread flour as needed to prevent sticking. Shape into a ball. Cover with plastic wrap; let rest 10 minutes.

3. Divide dough into 4 equal pieces. Roll each piece on a floured surface into a 14-inch-long log. Place 2 tablespoons cornmeal on waxed paper; roll logs in cornmeal.

4. Sprinkle each of 2 large baking sheets with 1 tablespoon cornmeal. Place 2 baguettes on each sheet. Cover; let rise in a warm place until doubled in volume, about 30 minutes.

5. Heat oven to 425°.

6. Place remaining 3 tablespoons bread flour in a sieve; sprinkle over loaves. Cut four ½-inch slashes into top of each loaf. Bake in heated 425° oven 20 minutes or until hollow-sounding when tapped. Remove to a rack to cool.

Maple oat bread

Makes 1 large loaf (16 slices)   *Prep* 30 minutes   *Rise* 2¼ to 3 hours   *Bake* at 350° for 30 to 35 minutes

Maple syrup adds a mysterious hint of sweetness to the nutty flavor of oats.

Per slice

185 calories, 4 g protein, 3 g fat, 35 g carbohydrate, 202 mg sodium, 2 mg cholesterol.

Did you know?
• The date stamped on the yeast package indicates the end of its active life. If you're planning to use yeast before this date, store it in a cool dry place—the refrigerator is ideal.
• To extend yeast's dated life by several months, freeze it; defrost at room temperature before using.

1 cup plus 2 tablespoons old-fashioned rolled oats	1 envelope active dry yeast
1 cup boiling water	4 cups all-purpose flour
⅓ cup warm (105° to 115°) water	1½ teaspoons salt
½ cup maple syrup	2 tablespoons vegetable oil
	1 egg white, lightly beaten

1. Combine 1 cup oats and boiling water in a medium-size bowl. Let stand 10 minutes.

2. Combine warm water and 1 tablespoon maple syrup in a small bowl. Sprinkle yeast on top and mix gently. Let stand 10 minutes or until foamy.

3. Combine flour and salt in a large bowl. Break up soaked oats into small pieces and add to flour mixture. Add oil, yeast mixture and remaining maple syrup. If too dry, add another tablespoon water.

4. Turn out dough onto a lightly floured surface. Knead until smooth and elastic, about 10 minutes.

5. Place dough in a greased large bowl, turning to coat. Cover bowl with a clean towel or plastic wrap. Let dough rise in a warm place until doubled in volume, 1½ to 2 hours. To test, stick a finger in dough; dent should remain when finger is removed.

6. Punch down dough; knead a few turns on a lightly floured surface. Grease a 1½-quart soufflé dish or 10-inch round cake pan. Place dough in prepared dish, pressing level to fill dish. Cover with greased plastic wrap. Let rise 45 minutes to 1 hour or until doubled in volume.

7. Heat oven to 350°. For topping, brush top of bread with egg white and sprinkle with remaining 2 tablespoons oats.

8. Bake in heated 350° oven 30 to 35 minutes or until loaf is golden brown and sounds hollow when tapped. Remove bread from dish. Cool on a rack at least 30 minutes.

Multi-grain wheat bread

Makes 2 loaves (12 slices each)   *Prep* 30 minutes   *Rise* about 2 hours

Bake at 375° for 25 to 35 minutes

Serve up slices of this bread with a crock of sweet butter alongside stews and hearty soups.

Per slice

121 calories, 3 g protein, 3 g fat, 20 g carbohydrate, 183 mg sodium, 0 mg cholesterol.

Labor saver

A bread machine is a terrific helpmate for anyone who loves breadmaking. But the procedures for using different brands vary, especially on the order in which the ingredients should be added, so be sure to read your manual for methods and tips.

½ cup old-fashioned rolled oats
¼ cup boiling water
1 envelope active dry yeast
2 tablespoons sugar
1¼ cups warm (105° to 115°) water
2 cups all-purpose flour
1 cup rye flour
1 cup whole-wheat flour
2 teaspoons salt
3 tablespoons vegetable oil
½ cup hulled sunflower seeds, toasted
2 tablespoons sesame seeds, toasted

1. Combine oats and boiling water in a small bowl. Let stand 10 minutes.

2. Mix ¼ cup warm water and 1 teaspoon sugar in a small bowl. Sprinkle yeast on top; gently mix to moisten yeast. Let stand 10 minutes to soften; mixture will be foamy.

3. Stir together flours, salt, remaining 1 tablespoon plus 2 teaspoons sugar, oil, yeast mixture, soaked oats and 1 cup warm water in a large bowl. Stir to form a ball. If too dry, add a little more water; if too wet, add a little more all-purpose flour.

4. Turn out dough onto a lightly floured surface. Knead until smooth and elastic, about 10 minutes.

5. Pat dough to ½-inch thickness. Sprinkle with sunflower and sesame seeds; roll up dough. Knead a few turns to distribute seeds. Place in a large greased bowl, turning to coat. Cover loosely with plastic wrap. Let dough rise in a warm place or until doubled in volume, 1 to 1¼ hours.

6. Grease a baking sheet. Punch down dough; knead a few turns. Divide dough in half; shape each half into an 8-inch oval loaf. Place on greased baking sheet. Cover with greased plastic wrap. Place on a rack over hot water in a saucepan; cover with a towel. Let rise 45 minutes or until doubled in volume.

7. Heat oven to 375°. Slash tops of loaves with a single-edge razor blade.

8. Bake in heated 375° oven 25 to 35 minutes or until loaves sound hollow when tapped. Cool on a rack 30 minutes.

Pumpernickel raisin bread

Makes 1 large loaf (16 slices)   *Prep* 30 minutes   *Rise* 2½ to 3 hours

Bake at 350° for 25 to 30 minutes

Toast thick slices and spread with cream cheese for a wonderful breakfast treat.

Per slice

159 calories, 4 g protein, 1 g fat, 37 g carbohydrate, 272 mg sodium, 0 mg cholesterol.

Easier does it

Kitchen machinery can cut kneading time substantially.

• To use a heavy-duty food processor: Place dry ingredients in machine work bowl; pulse to combine. With machine running, pour liquid ingredients through feed tube. Process until a ball forms and clears sides of work bowl. Process for another 1 to 2 minutes to knead.

• To use a heavy-duty mixer: Follow recipe directions on mixing. Then knead with a dough hook about half the time specified in the recipe. Remove dough to a work surface and knead a few turns more by hand.

1¼ cups warm (105° to 115°) water
3 tablespoons plus 1 teaspoon molasses
2 envelopes active dry yeast
2 cups all-purpose flour
1 cup rye flour
½ cup whole-wheat flour
2 tablespoons unsweetened cocoa powder

2 teaspoons salt
2 teaspoons caraway seeds
1½ cups golden raisins

Glaze
1 tablespoon molasses
1 tablespoon water
2 teaspoons caraway seeds

1. Mix ¼ cup warm water and 1 teaspoon molasses in a small bowl; gently mix to moisten yeast. Let stand 10 minutes to soften; mixture will be foamy.

2. Stir together flours, cocoa powder, salt and caraway seeds in a large bowl. Combine remaining 2 tablespoons plus 2 teaspoons molasses and 1 cup warm water in small a bowl. Add to flour mixture. Stir to form a ball.

3. Turn out dough onto a lightly floured surface. Knead until smooth and elastic, about 10 minutes.

4. Place dough in a greased large bowl, turning to coat. Cover bowl with a clean towel or plastic wrap. Let dough rise in a warm place until doubled in volume, 1½ to 2 hours. To test, stick a finger in dough; dent should remain when finger is removed.

5. Grease a baking sheet. Punch down dough; knead a few turns on a lightly floured surface. Flatten to ½-inch thickness. Sprinkle with raisins; roll up dough. Knead a few turns to distribute raisins. Shape into an 8-inch round. Place on greased baking sheet. Place on a rack over hot water in a saucepan; cover with a towel. Let rise 1 to 1¼ hours or until doubled.

6. Heat oven to 350°.

7. Meanwhile, prepare glaze: Mix molasses and water in a small bowl. Brush over dough. Sprinkle with caraway seeds.

8. Bake in heated 350° oven 25 to 30 minutes or until loaf sounds hollow when tapped. Cool on a rack 30 minutes.

Basic white bread

Our basic recipe can be turned into a classic loaf ideal for sandwiches or two French-style baguettes or even a dozen dinner rolls (see Assorted Hard Rolls, page 329).

Per slice
87 calories, 3 g protein,
0 g fat, 18 g carbohydrate,
294 mg sodium,
0 mg cholesterol.

1   envelope active dry yeast
1¼ cups warm (about 105°) water

3   to 3½ cups bleached all-purpose
    flour
2½ teaspoons coarse kosher salt

1. Sprinkle yeast over ¼ cup warm water in a measuring cup; gently mix to moisten yeast. Let stand 10 minutes to soften; mixture will be foamy.

2. Stir together 3 cups flour and salt in a large bowl. Pour yeast mixture into flour. Add remaining 1 cup warm water; stir to form a ball. If too dry, add a little more water; if too wet, add a little more flour.

3. Turn out dough onto a lightly floured surface. Knead until smooth and elastic, about 10 minutes.

4. Place dough in a greased large bowl, turning to coat. Cover bowl with a clean towel or plastic wrap. Let dough rise in a warm place until doubled in volume, 1½ to 2 hours. To test, stick a finger in dough; dent should remain when finger is removed. Punch down dough.

5. Grease an 8½ x 4½ x 2⅝-inch loaf pan. Roll dough out to a 20 x 8-inch rectangle on a lightly floured surface. Roll up from a short side. Press ends to seal; fold ends under loaf. Place, seam side down, in prepared pan. Cover; let rise until doubled in volume, about 1 hour.

6. Heat oven to 400°. Bake 25 to 30 minutes or until loaf sounds hollow when tapped. Remove from pan to a rack to cool.

Garden loaf

The flavors of fresh parsley and green onion make this loaf distinctive. Use for making chicken salad sandwiches.

Per slice
100 calories, 3 g protein,
2 g fat, 18 g carbohydrate,
295 mg sodium,
4 mg cholesterol.

1 Basic White Bread recipe
   (above)
2 tablespoons butter

½ cup sliced green onion
2 tablespoons chopped fresh parsley

1. Prepare bread through step 4.

2. Melt butter in a small skillet. Add green onion and parsley; cook 2 minutes or until softened.

3. After punching down dough in step 4, roll out to a 20 x 8-inch rectangle on a floured surface. Spread green onion mixture over dough. Roll up from a short side. Place in pan, let rise and bake as directed in steps 5 and 6.

Everything braid

Makes 2 loaves (8 slices each)   *Prep* 45 minutes   *Rise* 2½ to 3 hours

Bake at 400° for 25 to 30 minutes

Here's a takeoff on an "everything" bagel with seeds, salt and onion. Kosher salt is coarse grained and has a more intense flavor than regular salt. You'll find it alongside all the other salts in the supermarket.

per slice

94 calories, 3 g protein,
1 g fat, 18 g carbohydrate,
416 mg sodium,
13 mg cholesterol.

1 Basic White Bread recipe (opposite)
1 egg mixed with 1 tablespoon water
1 teaspoon sesame seeds
1 teaspoon poppy seeds
1 teaspoon coarse kosher salt
1 teaspoon dried rosemary
1 teaspoon dried toasted onion

1. Prepare bread through step 4. Grease 2 baking sheets.

2. After punching down dough in step 4, roll out dough to a 12 x 8-inch rectangle on a lightly floured surface. Cut lengthwise into 6 equal strips. Braid 3 strips together to make a braided loaf. Place on a greased baking sheet. Repeat with remaining strips of dough to make another loaf.

3. Brush each loaf with egg mixture. Cover with plastic wrap; let rise in a warm place until doubled in volume, about 1 hour. Remove plastic wrap. Sprinkle with remaining ingredients.

4. Heat oven to 400°. Bake 25 to 30 minutes or until loaves are golden brown and sound hollow when tapped. Remove to a rack to cool completely.

Everything braid

Cinnamon bunny bread

Makes 12 small bunnies (2 servings each) or 6 large bunnies (4 servings each)   *Prep* 2 to 2½ hours

Rise 1½ to 2½ hours   *Bake* at 350°, small bunnies, 15 minutes; large bunnies, 20 minutes

Inspire lots of happy smiles at Easter time— or for that matter, anytime—with these whimsical breads. You can make small bunnies or large ones, depending on the size of your toddlers.

Shown on page 315.

Per serving

202 calories, 5 g protein, 6 g fat, 33 g carbohydrate, 111 mg sodium, 56 mg cholesterol.

1 cup milk
½ cup (1 stick) unsalted butter, sliced
½ cup warm (105° to 115°) water
¾ cup sugar
2 envelopes active dry yeast
5 to 6 cups all-purpose flour
1 tablespoon ground cinnamon

1 teaspoon salt
5 eggs, at room temperature (reserve 1 for glaze)
1 tablespoon cold water
Decorator Frosting (recipe follows)
Liquid food coloring
Small round candies or jelly beans

1. Combine milk and butter in a small saucepan. Place pan over low heat until butter melts, stirring occasionally. Remove pan from heat and let milk cool to lukewarm (110°).

2. Stir together warm water and 1 tablespoon sugar in a small bowl. Sprinkle yeast over surface; let stand until softened, about 1 minute. Stir to dissolve yeast. Let stand until mixture is foamy, about 5 minutes.

3. Combine 4 cups flour, remaining sugar, cinnamon and salt in a large bowl. Add 4 eggs, yeast mixture and warm milk mixture; stir with a wooden spoon until well blended. Stir in enough remaining flour to make a soft but not sticky dough.

4. Knead dough by hand on a lightly floured surface or with an electric mixer with a dough hook until smooth and elastic, 8 to 10 minutes. Place dough in a lightly greased bowl, turning to coat. Cover and let rise in a warm place until doubled in volume, 1 to 1½ hours.

5. Punch down dough; knead briefly. Cover; let rest 10 minutes. Grease 2 large baking sheets.

6. For small bunnies: Cut dough into 12 equal parts. Use one part for each bunny. If your kitchen is warm, cover and refrigerate unused portions of dough.

7. Using one piece of dough, pinch off about ¼ cup for bunny body and roll into a ball, slightly elongating it into shape of an egg. Place on a prepared baking sheet. Pinch off about 2 tablespoons dough and roll into a ball to form a head, elongating one end to a point. Dip point in water and tuck under body ball on baking sheet to attach.

8. Pinch off a tiny piece from dough for a nose. Roll into a ball, dip bottom in water and place in center of face. Divide remaining piece of dough into 6 equal pieces. Roll 4 pieces into balls for paws, making them slightly pointed and elongated at one end. Dip points into water; tuck points under body on 4

Wrap home-baked yeast breads tightly in plastic wrap or aluminum foil and refrigerate to keep them from drying out.
• To freeze, wrap cooled loaves tightly in plastic wrap and then in foil. Freeze up to 6 months. Thaw in wrapping at room temperature.
• If the recipe has a glaze or frosting, freeze bread without it and then glaze or frost when it is fully thawed.
• To reheat, wrap thawed loaves in foil and heat in 300° to 350° oven 20 to 30 minutes.

places to attach paws. Roll remaining 2 pieces into logs for ears, making a point on one end and flattening other end of each log. Dip flattened ends into water and tuck under head for ears.

9. Repeat with remaining 11 pieces of dough to make 11 more bunnies. Place bunnies about 3 inches apart on baking sheets. Cover with plastic wrap; let rise in a warm place, away from drafts, until doubled in volume, 30 minutes to 1 hour.

10. Heat oven to 350°.

11. Whisk together reserved egg and 1 tablespoon cold water in a small bowl to make an egg wash. Uncover bunny breads; brush with egg wash. Brush each a second time.

12. Bake in heated 350° oven 15 minutes or until bread is golden and sounds hollow when tapped. Remove to a rack to cool completely before decorating.

13. For large bunnies: Divide dough into 6 equal parts. Assemble as directed for small bunnies in steps 6, 7, 8 and 9, doubling amounts of dough for body and head. Brush with egg wash as in step 11.

14. Bake in heated 350° oven 20 minutes or until bread is golden and sounds hollow when tapped. Remove to a rack to cool completely.

15. Tint batches of frosting with colorings. Spoon into pastry bags with small writing tips; decorate as pictured on page 315.

Decorator frosting

Combine 2 teaspoons powdered egg whites with 2 tablespoons warm water in a small bowl. Whisk 2 minutes to dissolve. Stir in ⅛ teaspoon cream of tartar. Beat with electric mixer until frothy. Add 1½ cups sifted confectioners' sugar and beat until fluffy and stiff, about 5 minutes. If frosting is too stiff, beat in a few drops of water until frosting is proper consistency. Keep covered with a damp cloth at all times or frosting will harden. Makes 1¾ cups.

Cinnamon swirl bread

Makes 1 loaf (16 slices)   *Prep* 35 minutes   *Rise* 2½ to 3 hours   *Bake* at 400° for 25 to 30 minutes

This bread makes great breakfast toast. For an extra kick, sprinkle a little finely chopped candied ginger over the cinnamon.

Per slice
107 calories, 3 g protein, 1 g fat, 22 g carbohydrate, 295 mg sodium, 2 mg cholesterol.

1 Basic White Bread recipe (page 322)
3 tablespoons granulated sugar

1 tablespoon butter, melted
2 tablespoons brown sugar
1 tablespoon ground cinnamon

1. Prepare Basic White Bread through step 1. Add granulated sugar to flour and salt in step 2. Continue with recipe through step 4.

2. Grease an 8½ x 4½ x 2⅝-inch loaf pan. Roll dough out to a 20 x 8-inch rectangle on a lightly floured surface. Brush surface with melted butter. Sprinkle evenly with brown sugar and cinnamon. Roll up from a short side. Press ends to seal; fold ends under loaf. Place, seam side down, in prepared pan. Cover; let rise until doubled in volume, about 1 hour.

3. Heat oven to 400°. Bake 25 to 30 minutes or until loaf sounds hollow when tapped. Remove from pan to a rack to cool.

Christmas morning breakfast buns *opposite*

Christmas morning breakfast buns

Makes 24 buns　*Prep* 1 hour　*Refrigerate and rise* 4¾ hours　*Bake* at 350° for 20 to 25 minutes

Bake a batch for any Sunday brunch and watch everyone grin.

Per serving
203 calories, 3 g protein,
10 g fat, 26 g carbohydrate,
75 mg sodium,
21 mg cholesterol.

Baker's tip
For best results, bring the ingredients to room temperature; take butter and eggs out of the refrigerator an hour ahead or for a shorter time if your kitchen seems especially warm.

⅓ cup warm (105° to 115°) water
¼ cup sugar
1 envelope active dry yeast
¼ cup (½ stick) unsalted butter or margarine, melted
½ cup sour cream
1 egg
1 teaspoon vanilla
¾ teaspoon salt
3 cups all-purpose flour

Cinnamon-nut filling
1 cup packed light-brown sugar
1½ cups chopped pecans
¼ cup (½ stick) butter or margarine, melted
2 teaspoons ground cinnamon

Glaze
1 cup confectioners' sugar
4 to 6 teaspoons water
½ teaspoon vanilla

1. Mix warm water and 1 tablespoon sugar in a small bowl. Sprinkle yeast on top; mix gently. Let stand 10 minutes or until foamy.

2. Combine melted butter, sour cream, egg, vanilla, salt and remaining sugar in a large bowl. Beat until well blended. Add 1 cup flour; beat on low speed until well mixed. Add yeast mixture and another 1 cup flour; beat on medium speed 2 minutes, scraping down sides of bowl occasionally. Gradually stir in remaining 1 cup flour to make a medium-soft dough (dough should be softer than bread dough).

3. Turn out dough on a lightly floured surface. Knead until smooth, about 5 minutes, adding more flour if needed. Shape dough into a ball. Place in a lightly greased bowl, turning to coat. Cover bowl loosely with plastic wrap. Refrigerate 4 hours or up to 2 days.

4. Place dough on a lightly floured surface; punch down. Knead briefly. Cover dough; let rest up to 20 minutes.

5. Meanwhile, prepare cinnamon-nut filling: Mix brown sugar, pecans, butter and cinnamon in a small bowl.

6. Lightly grease two 8-inch round pans. Divide dough in half. Roll one half into a 12 x 8-inch rectangle. Sprinkle evenly with half of filling. Roll up from a long side, jelly-roll fashion. Pinch ends to seal. Cut roll crosswise into 12 equal pieces. Place buns, cut side up and touching, in a greased pan. Repeat with remaining dough, filling and pan.

7. Cover pans; let rise in a warm place, away from drafts, 45 minutes or until doubled in volume.

8. Heat oven to 350°. Bake 20 to 25 minutes or until buns are golden brown. Remove pans to a rack to cool slightly.

9. Meanwhile, prepare glaze: Combine confectioners' sugar, water and vanilla in a small bowl; whisk to a smooth drizzling consistency. Drizzle glaze over tops of warm buns. Separate into individual buns and serve immediately.

Aunt Mary's potica

Makes 3 loaves (18 slices each)   *Prep* 1½ hours   *Rise* 3¼ to 4½ hours   *Bake* at 350° for 45 minutes

This walnut-filled Eastern European bread is especially welcome at holiday time. The recipe came from *Family Circle* food director Peggy Katalinich's Croatian Aunt Mary, and since it ran in the magazine, we have received many, many requests for it.

Per slice

224 calories, 6 g protein, 15 g fat, 18 g carbohydrate, 50 mg sodium, 55 mg cholesterol.

Let rise in a warm spot

If you have one, a gas oven with a pilot light is the ideal place for letting yeast dough rise. Or some bakers swear by sticking the dough in a microwave oven. Be sure to resist pushing the start button.

2 envelopes active dry yeast
¼ cup warm (105° to 115°) milk
5 cups plus 3 tablespoons all-purpose flour
¼ cup plus 1 tablespoon sugar
1 cup (2 sticks) butter, at room temperature
6 egg yolks
⅔ cup heavy cream

⅔ cup milk
1 teaspoon salt

Walnut filling

3 eggs
1½ cups sugar
⅔ cup heavy cream
1½ pounds walnuts, finely chopped (6 cups)

1. Sprinkle yeast over warm milk in a glass measuring cup. Stir in 3 tablespoons flour and 1 tablespoon sugar. Let stand until foamy, about 10 minutes.

2. Beat butter and remaining ¼ cup sugar in a large bowl until creamy. Add egg yolks, one at a time, beating well after each. Stir in yeast mixture.

3. Combine cream and milk in a small bowl. Combine 3 cups flour and salt in another bowl. On low speed, beat flour mixture into butter mixture alternately with cream mixture, in 2 or 3 batches, beating well after each. With a wooden spoon, stir in remaining 2 cups flour; dough will be very soft.

4. Turn out dough onto a lightly floured surface. Knead 12 to 15 minutes or until smooth and elastic, adding more flour as needed (about ¼ cup total) to prevent sticking. Place dough in a greased large bowl, turning to coat. Cover with greased waxed paper and a clean towel. Let rise in a warm place until almost doubled in volume, about 2 hours. To test, stick a finger in dough; dent should remain when finger is removed.

5. Prepare filling: Beat eggs, sugar and cream in a large bowl. Stir in walnuts.

6. Punch dough down. On a floured work surface, divide dough into thirds. Cover 2 pieces with greased waxed paper and a kitchen towel. Grease 3 baking sheets.

7. Roll remaining piece of dough into an 18 x 14-inch rectangle. Spread with one-third of filling, leaving a ½-inch border all around. Beginning from a short side, roll up tightly, jelly-roll fashion. Place, seam side down, on a greased baking sheet. Pinch ends to seal; tuck under loaf. Cover with lightly greased waxed paper and a clean towel. Repeat with remaining pieces of dough and filling. Let rise in a warm place until doubled in volume, 1¼ to 2½ hours depending upon the kitchen temperature.

8. Heat oven to 350°. Bake 45 minutes or until golden brown. Transfer to racks. Serve warm. Or cool, wrap in aluminum foil and freeze up to 2 months.

Assorted hard rolls

Makes 12 rolls   *Prep* 35 minutes   *Rise* about 2½ hours   *Bake* at 400° for 15 minutes

per roll
122 calories, 4 g protein,
1 g fat, 24 g carbohydrate,
398 mg sodium,
18 mg cholesterol.

1 Basic White Bread recipe (page 322)
1 egg mixed with 1 tablespoon water

1 teaspoon poppy seeds (optional)
1 teaspoon sesame seeds (optional)

1. Prepare Basic White Bread through step 4. After punching down dough, divide dough in half. Lightly grease 2 baking sheets.

2. On a lightly floured surface, roll half of dough into a 12-inch-long rope. Cut into six 2-inch lengths. Repeat with other half of dough.

3. Cup your hand over one piece of dough; roll dough into a smooth ball on a lightly floured surface. Repeat with remaining dough to form a total of 12 rolls.

4. Place rolls on prepared baking sheets. If desired, cut a cross into top of each roll with a single-edge razor blade or sharp thin knife. Cover; let rise in a warm place until doubled in volume, 20 to 30 minutes.

5. Heat oven to 400°. Brush egg mixture over rolls. Sprinkle with poppy seeds or sesame seeds or leave rolls plain.

6. Bake in heated 400° oven 15 minutes or until rolls are golden brown and crusty. Remove with a spatula to a rack to cool briefly.

Onion rolls

per roll
141 calories, 4 g protein,
3 g fat, 25 g carbohydrate,
240 mg sodium,
23 mg cholesterol.

Prepare Assorted Hard Rolls through step 4 above. While rolls are rising, melt 2 tablespoons butter in a small skillet. Add 1 onion, quartered and sliced, to skillet; sauté until softened and slightly browned, about 15 minutes. Brush tops of rolls with egg mixture. Top with onions. Bake in heated 400° oven 15 minutes or until lightly golden.

Yeast corn rolls

Makes 18 rolls   *Prep* 35 minutes   *Rise* 2 hours   *Bake* at 375° for 15 minutes

Here's the perfect go-with for a baked ham or a pot of your favorite chili.

Per roll

128 calories, 3 g protein, 4 g fat, 21 g carbohydrate, 245 mg sodium, 12 mg cholesterol.

To sift or not?

For most recipes it isn't necessary to sift flour. However, if a recipe specifies sifting, be sure to do so because sifting changes the volume slightly.
• To sift: Measure slightly more flour than called for. Sift onto waxed paper. Spoon sifted flour into a measuring cup; brush off excess with flat edge of knife. Return any extra flour to canister.

½ cup cornmeal
¾ cup boiling water
¼ cup solid vegetable shortening
2 teaspoons salt
¼ cup warm (105° to 115°) water
¼ cup light molasses or honey
1 envelope active dry yeast

2¾ cups sifted all-purpose flour
1 egg

Topping (optional)
2 teaspoons cornmeal
½ teaspoon salt

1 teaspoon butter, melted

1. Place cornmeal in a large heatproof bowl. Pour boiling water over; stir in shortening and salt.

2. Combine warm water and molasses in a 1-cup liquid measuring cup. Sprinkle yeast on top; mix gently. Let stand until foamy, 5 to 10 minutes.

3. Add yeast mixture and half of flour to cornmeal mixture. Beat on medium speed 2 minutes. Add egg and remaining flour; beat 1 minute (dough will be very sticky).

4. Cover dough with greased waxed paper. Let rise in a warm place until doubled in volume, about 1 hour.

5. Grease two 8-inch round cake pans. With floured hands, punch down dough. Roll dough into an 18-inch-long rope on a floured board. With a floured knife, cut dough into 18 equal pieces. Shape each into a ball. Arrange half of balls in each prepared pan.

6. If a topping is desired, mix together 2 teaspoons cornmeal and ½ teaspoon salt. Sprinkle over rolls.

7. Cover each pan with greased waxed paper. Let rise in warm place until doubled in volume, about 1 hour.

8. Heat oven to 375°.

9. Bake rolls in heated 375° oven 15 minutes or until golden brown. Lightly brush tops with melted butter.

Make-ahead rolls

Makes 3 dozen rolls   *Prep* 30 minutes   *Refrigerator rise* 2 hours   *Stand* 2 hours

Rise 30 to 45 minutes   *Bake* at 375° for 15 to 20 minutes

Flavored with grated Parmesan cheese and onion, these rolls go with practically any main dish. The dough can be refrigerated for up to three days; you can bake it all at once or bake a dozen rolls each day.

Per roll
151 calories, 3 g protein, 6 g fat, 23 g carbohydrate, 107 mg sodium, 18 mg cholesterol.

2 envelopes active dry yeast
1¾ cups warm (105° to 115°) water
½ cup sugar
1 teaspoon salt
1 egg, slightly beaten
¼ cup (½ stick) butter, at room temperature

5½ cups all-purpose flour
½ cup grated Parmesan cheese
2 tablespoons dried minced onion
⅛ teaspoon ground red pepper (cayenne)
1 tablespoon butter, melted (optional)

1. Sprinkle yeast over warm water in a large bowl. Add sugar and salt. Stir to dissolve. Add egg, butter and 3 cups flour. Beat on high speed 2 minutes. Add Parmesan, dried onion and red pepper. Stir in another 1 cup flour.

2. Turn out dough onto lightly floured surface. Knead until smooth and elastic, working in flour as needed. Place in a large bowl. Brush top with melted butter. Cover with plastic wrap. Let rise in refrigerator until doubled in volume, 2 hours.

3. Punch down dough. Refrigerate 1 to 3 days; punch down each day.

4. For each dozen rolls: Grease an 8- or 9-inch round cake pan. Remove one-third of dough from refrigerator; let stand at room temperature 2 hours. On a floured surface, roll into a 12-inch rope; cut into 12 pieces. Shape each piece into a ball; tuck underneath to make a smooth top. Place in prepared pan. Cover with a clean towel; let rise in a warm place until doubled in volume, 30 to 45 minutes.

5. Heat oven to 375°. Bake 15 to 20 minutes or until rolls are golden brown. Brush with melted butter if desired.

BREADS AND SANDWICHES

Make-ahead rolls

Multi-grain buttermilk rolls

Makes 20 rolls *Prep* 25 minutes *Rise* about 2 hours *Refrigerate* 6 hours or overnight

Bake at 375° for 20 minutes

Mixing whole-wheat flour with all-purpose introduces the nutty taste of whole wheat but keeps the texture of the rolls light; all whole-wheat makes for a denser, heavier roll.

Per roll
112 calories, 3 g protein, 2 g fat, 20 g carbohydrate, 145 mg sodium, 5 mg cholesterol.

1 cup quick oats
¾ cup buttermilk or 2 tablespoons dry buttermilk powder mixed with ¾ cup water
½ cup warm (105° to 115°) water
2 tablespoons sugar
1 envelope active dry yeast
2 cups all-purpose flour
1 cup whole-wheat flour
1¼ teaspoons salt
3 tablespoons butter, melted
2 tablespoons molasses
Melted butter for brushing
Oats, sesame seeds or poppy seeds for sprinkling (optional)

1. Place oats and buttermilk in a 12-cup food processor. Let stand 10 minutes.

2. Combine warm water, 1 teaspoon sugar and yeast in a small bowl. Let stand until foamy, about 5 minutes.

3. Add flours, remaining 1 tablespoon plus 2 teaspoons sugar, salt and butter to processor. Add molasses to yeast mixture. With machine running, slowly add yeast mixture to processor. When a ball forms, process 1 minute. (If dough doesn't clear sides, add all-purpose flour, 2 tablespoons at a time. If too dry, add water, 1 tablespoon at a time.)

4. Place dough in a greased large bowl; turn to coat. Cover loosely with plastic wrap. Let rise in a warm place until doubled in volume, about 1½ hours.

5. Grease a baking sheet. Punch down dough. Divide in half. Roll each half into a 10-inch log. Cut each into 10 equal pieces. Shape into rolls. Place on greased baking sheet. Brush with melted butter. Cover with plastic wrap. Let rise at room temperature 30 minutes. Refrigerate 6 hours or overnight.

6. Heat oven to 375°. If you wish, sprinkle rolls with oats, sesame seeds or poppy seeds.

7. Bake in heated 375° oven 20 minutes or until rolls are golden and sound hollow when tapped. Cool on a wire rack. Serve warm or at room temperature.

Cheesy corn bread

Makes 9 squares   *Prep* 15 minutes   *Bake* at 425° for 15 to 20 minutes

Fresh corn kernels add texture, and hot-pepper sauce and a fresh jalapeño chile raise the heat quotient. Spread with a chive-flavored butter (see page 110).

Per square

206 calories, 7 g protein, 6 g fat, 32 g carbohydrate, 508 mg sodium, 55 mg cholesterol.

1¼ cups cornmeal
1 cup all-purpose flour
2 tablespoons sugar
1 teaspoon salt
1 teaspoon baking powder
½ teaspoon baking soda
2 eggs, lightly beaten
1 tablespoon corn or vegetable oil
¼ teaspoon hot-pepper sauce

1 cup buttermilk
½ cup shredded cheddar cheese (2 ounces)
½ sweet green pepper, cored, seeded and diced
1 jalapeño chile, cored, seeded, and finely chopped
1 cup fresh corn kernels

1. Heat oven to 425° Lightly grease a 9 x 9 x 2-inch baking pan.

2. Whisk together cornmeal, flour, sugar, salt, baking powder and baking soda in a medium-size bowl.

3. Stir together eggs, oil, hot-pepper sauce, buttermilk, cheese, green pepper, jalapeño and corn in a small bowl. Stir into cornmeal mixture just until dry ingredients are evenly moistened. Pour into prepared pan.

4. Bake in heated 425° oven 15 to 20 minutes or until a wooden pick inserted in center comes out slightly moist with crumbs attached. Cool corn bread in pan on a rack. Cut into squares.

Jalapeño corn bread

Makes 12 servings   *Prep* 15 minutes   *Bake* at 450° for 15 minutes

To add interest to plain old tomato soup, serve up a skillet of this zesty corn bread.

Per serving

167 calories, 5 g protein, 5 g fat, 24 g carbohydrate, 591 mg sodium, 41 mg cholesterol.

3 tablespoons bacon fat or vegetable oil
2 cups cornmeal
½ cup all-purpose flour
2 teaspoons salt

1½ teaspoons baking soda
2 eggs, lightly beaten
2¼ cups buttermilk
3 small jalapeño chiles, seeded and finely chopped

1. Place fat in a large cast-iron skillet. Place in oven and heat oven to 450°.

2. Combine cornmeal, flour, salt and baking soda in a large bowl. Stir in eggs, buttermilk and jalapeños just until blended.

3. Remove skillet from oven. Pour fat into batter, stirring just until combined. Pour batter into skillet; stir. Return to oven.

4. Bake in heated 450° oven 15 minutes or until a wooden pick inserted in center comes out clean. Serve hot.

Onion and olive bread

Makes 1 round loaf (12 slices) *Prep* 15 minutes *Cook* 10 minutes *Bake* at 400° for 50 minutes

Per slice

269 calories, 6 g protein, 15 g fat, 29 g carbohydrate, 389 mg sodium, 35 mg cholesterol.

Olive guide

• California ripe: black with crisp texture; mild flavor; ideal for salads and cooked dishes.
• Sicilian: pale greenish brown with meaty flesh; assertive taste; a must for antipasto.
• Kalamata: dark purple-green; strong olive aftertaste; good with baked fish.
• Greek black: soft pulp; winy taste; enlivens chicken dishes.

1 tablespoon olive oil
1 onion, chopped
½ cup chopped Kalamata olives
1 clove garlic, finely chopped
2 cups whole-wheat flour
1¼ cups all-purpose flour
1 tablespoon sugar
2 teaspoons baking powder
1 teaspoon salt
½ teaspoon baking soda
¾ cup (1½ sticks) cold butter or margarine, cut into 12 pieces
1½ cups milk
2 tablespoons chopped fresh rosemary or 2 teaspoons dried
1 teaspoon coarse black pepper
1 tablespoon all-purpose flour for dusting

1. Heat oven to 400°. Grease a 9-inch round cake pan.

2. Heat oil in a small skillet over medium heat. Add onion and sauté until very tender, 8 minutes (if onion browns too quickly, add a tablespoon of water). Stir in olives and garlic; sauté 2 minutes. Remove from heat.

3. Combine flours, sugar, baking powder, salt and baking soda in a large bowl. With a pastry blender or 2 knives used scissor fashion, cut in butter until mixture resembles coarse crumbs. Stir in milk, rosemary, pepper and onion mixture until flour mixture is just evenly moistened.

4. Turn out dough onto a lightly floured surface. With floured hands, shape into a ball. Place in prepared pan. In center of ball, cut a cross ¼ inch deep across top. Sprinkle top with flour.

5. Bake in heated 400° oven 50 minutes or until a wooden pick inserted in center comes out clean. Cool loaf in pan on a rack 10 minutes. Turn loaf out onto rack to cool completely.

To make muffins: Grease an oversize 6-muffin pan. Divide half of dough evenly among muffin cups. Bake in heated 350° oven 25 minutes or until a wooden pick inserted in centers comes out clean. Repeat with remaining dough for a total of 12 muffins.

Carrot soda bread

Carrot soda bread

Makes 16 servings   *Prep* 15 minutes   *Bake* at 375° for 45 minutes

Grated carrots make this soda bread extra special.

Per serving
204 calories, 4 g protein, 5 g fat, 35 g carbohydrate, 362 mg sodium, 1 mg cholesterol.

1¾ cups buttermilk
⅓ cup vegetable oil
⅓ cup sugar
2 teaspoons grated lemon rind
1¼ teaspoons salt

6 medium carrots, shredded (2 cups)
¾ cup dried currants
2 teaspoons baking soda
4 cups all-purpose flour

1. Heat oven to 375°. Coat a baking sheet with nonstick cooking spray.

2. Stir together buttermilk, oil, sugar, lemon rind and salt in a very large mixing bowl. Stir in carrots, currants and baking soda. Add flour and quickly stir until just combined.

3. Form dough into a ball in bowl. Turn out onto prepared baking sheet. Flatten into an 8-inch round. Using a sharp knife, cut a ½-inch-deep "X" in center of bread.

4. Bake in heated 375° oven 45 minutes or until a wooden pick inserted in center comes out clean. Slide bread onto a rack and cool 30 minutes before slicing.

Herbed quick bread

Makes 1 loaf (12 slices)   *Prep* 20 minutes   *Bake* at 350° for 50 minutes

Excellent with simple pasta dishes, this bread also makes a truly inspired ham sandwich.

Per slice

245 calories, 9 g protein, 12 g fat, 28 g carbohydrate, 423 mg sodium, 22 mg cholesterol.

3 cups all-purpose flour
½ cup grated Parmesan cheese
½ cup pine nuts
2 teaspoons baking powder
1 teaspoon baking soda
1 teaspoon dried basil, crumbled
1 teaspoon dried rosemary, crumbled

1 teaspoon dried thyme, crumbled
½ teaspoon salt
½ teaspoon freshly ground black pepper
1½ cups buttermilk
3 tablespoons tomato paste
¼ cup vegetable oil
1 egg

1. Heat oven to 350°. Grease a 9 x 5 x 3-inch loaf pan. Sprinkle with flour; tap out any excess.

2. Combine flour, Parmesan, pine nuts, baking powder, baking soda, basil, rosemary, thyme, salt and pepper in a large bowl.

3. Whisk together buttermilk, tomato paste, oil and egg in a medium-size bowl. Add to flour mixture; stir until no traces of flour remain. Spoon batter into prepared pan.

4. Bake in heated 350° oven 50 minutes or until a wooden pick inserted in center comes out clean. Cool loaf in pan on a rack 10 minutes. Turn loaf out onto rack to cool completely.

Caraway-rye batter bread

Makes 2 loaves (12 slices each) or 24 rolls   *Prep* 15 minutes   *Rise* 1¾ hours

Bake at 350° for 35 minutes for loaves, or 25 minutes for rolls

Yogurt adds a tangy accent and makes for a tender crumb in this no-knead yeast loaf— no hard work, just a little stirring.

Per slice

130 calories, 4 g protein, 5 g fat, 18 g carbohydrate, 246 mg sodium, 29 mg cholesterol.

2 envelopes active dry yeast
½ cup warm (105° to 115°) water
½ teaspoon sugar
3 cups all-purpose flour
1½ cups rye flour
2 teaspoons salt
¼ teaspoon baking soda
2 tablespoons caraway seeds

1 container (8 ounces) plain low-fat yogurt
½ cup (1 stick) butter or margarine, melted
2 eggs
1 egg white mixed with 1 tablespoon water
Additional caraway seeds for topping

1. Grease two 1-quart casseroles or soufflé dishes or two standard 12-muffin pans (or 1 casserole and 1 muffin pan). Sprinkle yeast over warm water and sugar in a large bowl. Let stand 5 minutes for yeast to soften.

2. Stir together 1½ cups all-purpose flour, rye flour, salt, baking soda and caraway seeds in a medium-size bowl.

3. Beat yogurt, butter and eggs into yeast mixture until blended. Add flour mixture. Beat on medium-high speed 1 minute. Add remaining 1½ cups all-purpose flour; beat until well blended. Cover and let rise in a warm place until doubled in volume, about 1 hour.

4. Punch down dough. Divide dough evenly between prepared casseroles or muffin cups. Cover; let rise in a warm place until doubled, about 45 minutes.

5. Heat oven to 350°. Brush tops of rolls or loaves with egg white mixture. Sprinkle with seeds.

6. Bake in heated 350° oven 35 minutes for loaves, 25 minutes for rolls, or until golden brown and hollow-sounding when tapped. Turn out onto racks to cool.

Cranberry-nut bread

Makes 4 small loaves (6 slices each)   *Prep* 20 minutes   *Bake* at 350° for 50 minutes

Wrap these small loaves in colored foil, tie with a pretty ribbon, and give as holiday gifts or a hostess thank-you.

Per slice
151 calories, 3 g protein, 6 g fat, 23 g carbohydrate, 107 mg sodium, 18 mg cholesterol.

2 cups all-purpose flour
1½ teaspoons baking powder
1 teaspoon ground cinnamon
½ teaspoon baking soda
½ teaspoon salt
1½ cups sugar
1 cup fresh orange juice
¼ cup vegetable oil

2 eggs
1 cup fresh cranberries
1 cup chopped walnuts or pecans
1 tablespoon grated orange rind

Glaze (optional)
1 cup confectioners' sugar
1 tablespoon milk

1. Heat oven to 350°. Grease 4 miniature loaf pans, 5¾ x 3½ x 2 inches; sprinkle inside of pans evenly with flour; tap out any excess.

2. Combine flour, baking powder, cinnamon, baking soda and salt in a large bowl. Combine sugar, orange juice, oil and eggs in another bowl. Stir into flour mixture, along with cranberries, nuts and orange rind, until no traces of flour remain. Pour into prepared pans.

3. Bake in heated 350° oven 50 minutes or until a wooden pick inserted in center comes out clean (if tops brown too quickly, cover with aluminum foil). Cool loaves in pans on racks 10 minutes. Turn loaves out onto racks to cool completely.

4. Prepare glaze if using: Combine confectioners' sugar and milk in a small bowl until a good drizzling consistency. Drizzle over tops of loaves.

Make-ahead tip: Baked loaves can be left in pans, covered with foil and frozen. Thaw and reheat, covered with foil, in oven.

Banana crunch bread

Makes 1 loaf (12 slices)   *Prep* 10 minutes   *Bake* at 350° for 1 hour 10 minutes

A healthy dose of candied ginger in the batter wakes up the senses. And the crunch? A streusel-style topping.

Per slice

386 calories, 7 g protein, 19 g fat, 51 g carbohydrate, 350 mg sodium, 67 mg cholesterol.

Ginger types

• Candied: fresh ginger that has been boiled in a sugar solution; has a sweet-tart flavor. Keeps indefinitely at room temperature if tightly sealed.
• Fresh: firm and plump. To store, wrap in a paper towel, place in loosely closed plastic bag and refrigerate up to 1 month.
• Powdered: ground from dried fresh ginger. Its flavor fades, so discard after 6 months.

2 cups all-purpose flour
1 cup sugar
2 teaspoons baking powder
1 teaspoon salt
½ cup (1 stick) cold butter or margarine, cut into pieces
2 large ripe bananas, mashed (1 cup)
1 cup coarsely chopped walnuts
¼ cup finely chopped candied ginger

2 eggs
1 teaspoon vanilla

Crunch topping
½ cup all-purpose flour
¼ cup granulated sugar
¼ cup (½ stick) butter or margarine, melted
¾ teaspoon ground cinnamon

2 tablespoons confectioners' sugar

1. Heat oven to 350°. Grease a 9 x 5 x 3-inch loaf pan.

2. Combine flour, sugar, baking powder and salt in a large bowl. With a pastry blender or 2 knives used scissor fashion, cut in butter until mixture resembles coarse crumbs. Stir in bananas, walnuts, ginger, eggs and vanilla until mixture is just moistened. Spoon batter evenly into prepared pan.

3. Prepare crunch topping: Combine flour, granulated sugar, butter and cinnamon in a small bowl. Sprinkle evenly over batter.

4. Bake in heated 350° oven 1 hour 10 minutes or until a wooden pick inserted in center comes out clean. If loaf begins to brown too quickly, cover loosely with foil. Cool loaf in pan 10 minutes. Turn loaf out onto a rack to cool completely. Sprinkle cooled bread with confectioners' sugar.

To make muffins: Grease an oversize 6-muffin pan. Divide half of dough evenly among muffin cups. Bake in heated 350° oven 25 minutes or until a wooden pick inserted in centers comes out clean. Repeat with remaining dough for a total of 12 muffins.

Raisin-date-nut bread

Makes 2 loaves (10 slices each) *Prep* 12 minutes *Bake* at 350° for 1 hour

Vanilla adds an elusive background note to this quick bread. Be sure to use real vanilla extract, not the imitation kind. The extra pennies are worth it.

per slice

262 calories, 4 g protein, 12 g fat, 36 g carbohydrate, 189 mg sodium, 42 mg cholesterol.

3 cups all-purpose flour
1 cup sugar
1 tablespoon baking powder
1 teaspoon salt
¾ cup (1½ sticks) cold butter or margarine, cut into 12 pieces

1 cup chopped pecans
1 cup chopped dates
½ cup raisins
2 eggs
1¼ cups milk
1 teaspoon vanilla

1. Heat oven to 350°. Grease two 8½ x 4½ x 2⅝-inch loaf pans.

2. Combine flour, sugar, baking powder and salt in a large bowl. With a pastry blender or 2 knives used scissor fashion, cut in butter until mixture resembles coarse crumbs. Stir in pecans, dates and raisins.

3. Combine eggs, milk and vanilla in a small bowl. Stir into flour mixture until just moistened. Spoon batter into prepared pans, dividing equally.

4. Bake loaves in heated 350° oven 1 hour or until a wooden pick inserted in center comes out clean. Cool in pans on racks 10 minutes. Turn loaves out onto racks to cool completely.

Best zucchini bread

Makes 1 loaf (16 slices) *Prep* 15 minutes *Bake* at 375° for 45 to 50 minutes

Not your usual zucchini quick bread—ginger, nutmeg, walnuts and orange rind set this one apart.

per slice

211 calories, 3 g protein, 12 g fat, 23 g carbohydrate, 156 mg sodium, 27 mg cholesterol.

1½ cups all-purpose flour
2 teaspoons baking powder
½ teaspoon baking soda
½ teaspoon salt
¼ teaspoon ground ginger
⅛ teaspoon ground nutmeg
1 cup chopped walnuts

1 cup sugar
½ cup vegetable oil
2 eggs
2 tablespoons grated orange rind
1 cup grated unpeeled zucchini
Confectioners' sugar for topping

1. Heat oven to 375°. Grease an 8½ x 4½ x 2⅝-inch loaf pan.

2. Combine flour, baking powder, baking soda, salt, ginger, nutmeg and walnuts in a small bowl.

3. Beat sugar, oil, eggs and orange rind in a large bowl 1 minute. Stir in zucchini. Add dry ingredients; stir just to blend. Scrape into prepared pan.

4. Bake in heated 375° oven 45 to 50 minutes; cover with foil during last 10 minutes if browning too quickly. Cool loaf in pan on a rack 15 minutes. Turn out onto rack to cool completely. Sprinkle with confectioners' sugar.

Pepper-Jack muffins

Makes 15 muffins *Prep* 10 minutes *Cook* 8 minutes *Bake* at 400° for 15 to 20 minutes

Bake these in cactus molds and you'll just have to make a pot of chili for the go-with. Want to double the heat? Use pepper-Jack cheese instead of the plain.

Per muffin
169 calories, 5 g protein, 3 g fat, 20 g carbohydrate, 236 mg sodium, 24 mg cholesterol.

1 tablespoon vegetable oil
½ sweet red pepper, finely diced
¼ cup finely chopped green onion
2 jalapeño chiles, cored, seeded and finely chopped
1¼ cups all-purpose flour
1 cup yellow cornmeal
3 tablespoons packed light-brown sugar
2½ teaspoons baking powder
1 teaspoon coarse black pepper
¾ teaspoon salt
¼ cup cold solid vegetable shortening
1¼ cups milk
1 egg
1 cup shredded Monterey Jack cheese (4 ounces)

1. Heat oven to 400°. Grease three 5-stick cactus molds or a standard 12-muffin pan.

2. Heat oil in a small skillet over medium-high heat. Add sweet red pepper, green onion and jalapeño. Reduce heat to medium-low; cook until vegetables are very tender, about 8 minutes. Remove from heat.

3. Combine flour, cornmeal, brown sugar, baking powder, black pepper and salt in a large bowl. With a pastry blender or 2 knives used scissor fashion, cut in shortening until mixture resembles coarse crumbs. Beat milk and egg in a small bowl until blended. Stir milk mixture, vegetables and cheese into flour mixture just until blended. Dividing batter equally, spoon into cactus molds or muffin pan.

4. Bake in heated 400° oven 15 to 20 minutes or until a wooden pick inserted in centers comes out clean. Cool in molds on a rack 10 minutes. Remove from molds and serve warm.

Mix and match pans

RECIPES SPECIFY pan size. To swap, pick a pan with similar volume or two pans with similar total volume. When baking, check early for doneness. To find volume, fill pans with water poured from a large measuring cup.

Loaf pans have a volume of 6 to 8 cups.

8-inch square pan has a volume of about 8½ cups.

Standard muffin pan (12 muffin cups) has a volume of about 4½ cups.

Oversize muffin pan (6 muffin cups) has a volume of about 5¼ cups.

Zucchini-basil muffins

Makes 12 muffins   *Prep* 10 minutes   *Bake* at 400° for 22 to 24 minutes

If you can't locate a fine crop of fresh basil, toss in 1 teaspoon of dried.

Per muffin
134 calories, 4 g protein,
6 g fat, 16 g carbohydrate,
195 mg sodium,
21 mg cholesterol.

1¾ cups all-purpose flour
3 tablespoons grated Parmesan cheese
1 tablespoon sugar
2 teaspoons baking powder
½ teaspoon salt

1 egg, lightly beaten
¾ cup milk
¼ cup olive oil
1 zucchini, shredded (1 cup)
1 tablespoon finely chopped fresh basil

1. Heat oven to 400°. Lightly grease bottom of each cup in a standard 12-muffin pan.

2. Combine flour, Parmesan, sugar, baking powder and salt in a large bowl.

3. Mix egg, milk, oil, zucchini and basil in a small bowl. Add to flour mixture all at once; stir with a fork until ingredients are just combined. Spoon batter evenly into prepared muffin pan.

4. Bake in heated 400° oven until tops are lightly browned and a wooden pick inserted in centers comes out clean, 22 to 24 minutes. Run a small knife around edge of muffins; remove from pan. Cool on a wire rack 6 minutes. Serve warm.

Irish soda muffins

Makes 12 muffins   *Prep* 8 minutes   *Bake* at 375° for 25 minutes

Imagine—Irish soda bread, transformed into muffins with a touch of caraway. Yummy with a boiled corned beef dinner.

Per muffin
214 calories, 4 g protein,
6 fat, 35 g carbohydrate,
415 mg sodium,
16 mg cholesterol.

3 cups all-purpose flour
¼ cup sugar
1 tablespoon baking powder
1½ teaspoons baking soda
¾ teaspoon salt
6 tablespoons cold butter or margarine, cut into 6 pieces

½ cup dark raisins
1 tablespoon caraway seeds
1¼ cups buttermilk
   All-purpose flour for dusting muffin tops

1. Heat oven to 375°. Grease a standard 12-muffin pan.

2. Combine flour, sugar, baking powder, baking soda and salt in a large bowl. With a pastry blender or 2 knives used scissor fashion, cut in butter until mixture resembles coarse crumbs. Stir in raisins and caraway seeds. Gently stir in buttermilk until just blended. Spoon batter evenly into prepared muffin pan. Sprinkle tops lightly with flour, about ½ teaspoon per muffin.

3. Bake in heated 375° oven 25 minutes or until a wooden pick inserted in centers comes out clean. Remove from pan to a wire rack. Serve warm.

St. Patrick's Day scones

Makes 12 scones   *Prep* 10 minutes   *Bake* at 350° for 20 to 23 minutes

This recipe came from Susan Ungaro, the Editor of *Family Circle* magazine—actually, from her Aunt Kathleen, who left Swinford, County Mayo, 40 years ago for New York City.

Per scone
218 calories, 4 g protein,
9 g fat, 33 g carbohydrate,
199 mg sodium,
37 mg cholesterol.

2 cups all-purpose flour
½ cup sugar
¼ teaspoon salt
2 teaspoons baking powder
¾ cup raisins

1 stick (½ cup) margarine, cut into small pieces
2 eggs
½ cup plus 1 tablespoon milk

1. Heat oven to 350°.

2. Whisk together flour, sugar, salt and baking powder in a medium-size bowl. Gradually mix in raisins so they are evenly distributed. Add margarine and mix in with your fingers or a pastry blender until evenly blended.

3. Whisk together 1 egg and ½ cup milk in a small bowl. Gradually stir into flour mixture until a dough forms; work dough with hands if necessary, but do not overwork.

4. Drop ¼-cup mounds of dough onto an ungreased baking sheet.

5. For egg wash, beat together remaining egg and 1 tablespoon milk in a small bowl. Lightly brush each scone with wash.

6. Bake scones in heated 350° oven 20 to 23 minutes or until lightly golden.

Lemon-blueberry muffins *opposite*

Lemon-blueberry muffins

Makes 12 muffins   *Prep* 10 minutes   *Bake* at 400° for 20 minutes

Leave the lumps
The trick to well-textured muffins without unsightly tunnels is to avoid overmixing the batter. Muffin batter should look lumpy.

2 cups all-purpose flour
1 cup sugar
1 tablespoon baking powder
1 teaspoon salt
6 tablespoons cold butter or margarine, cut into 6 pieces
1 egg
⅔ cup milk
1 tablespoon fresh lemon juice
1 teaspoon grated lemon rind
1 teaspoon vanilla
1 cup fresh or frozen blueberries (do not thaw)

Topping
2 tablespoons all-purpose flour
2 tablespoons sugar
2 tablespoons butter or margarine, melted
½ teaspoon ground cinnamon

1. Heat oven to 400°. Grease a standard 12-muffin pan, greasing pan top around cups as well.

2. Mix flour, sugar, baking powder and salt in a large bowl. With a pastry blender or 2 knives used scissor fashion, cut in butter until mixture resembles fine crumbs.

3. Lightly beat together egg, milk, lemon juice, lemon rind and vanilla in a small bowl until blended. Stir egg mixture into flour mixture until just blended. Fold blueberries into batter. Spoon batter evenly into prepared muffin pan.

4. Prepare topping: Combine flour, sugar, butter and cinnamon in a small bowl until well blended. Sprinkle mixture evenly over tops of muffin batter.

5. Bake in heated 400° oven 20 minutes or until golden and a wooden pick inserted in centers comes out clean. Remove muffins from pan to a rack. Serve warm.

To make a loaf: Grease a 9 x 5 x 3-inch loaf pan. Bake in a heated 350° oven 1 hour or until a wooden pick inserted in center comes out clean.

Orange-honey sticky bun muffins

Makes 12 muffins *Prep* 20 minutes *Bake* at 375° for 22 minutes

A sunny way to start the day: a plate of orange slices, sticky muffins and a fruity yogurt shake.

Per muffin
219 calories, 4 g protein,
8 g fat, 34 g carbohydrate,
234 mg sodium,
31 mg cholesterol.

½ cup walnuts
⅓ cup packed light-brown sugar
2 tablespoons butter, melted
2 tablespoons honey
½ teaspoon ground cinnamon

Batter
2 cups all-purpose flour
2 teaspoons baking powder
½ teaspoon salt

3 tablespoons butter, melted
¼ cup honey
2 teaspoons grated orange rind
1 egg
⅔ cup milk
1 tablespoon granulated sugar
½ teaspoon ground cinnamon
¼ cup chopped raisins

1. Heat oven to 375°. Line a baking sheet with foil. Coat a standard 12-muffin pan with nonstick cooking spray. Divide walnuts evenly among cups of muffin pan. Combine brown sugar, butter, honey and cinnamon in a small bowl. Spoon 1 rounded teaspoonful into each muffin cup.

2. Prepare batter: Combine flour, baking powder and salt in a medium-size bowl. Blend butter, honey, orange rind and egg in another medium-size bowl. Beat in milk. Stir flour mixture into milk mixture just until combined. Spoon half of batter into muffin cups.

3. Combine sugar, cinnamon and raisins in a small bowl. Sprinkle over muffins. Top with remaining batter. Place pan on foil-lined baking sheet.

4. Bake in heated 375° oven 22 minutes or until a wooden pick inserted in centers comes out clean. Cool pan on rack 5 minutes. Invert muffins onto waxed-paper-lined tray. Spoon any sticky mixture left in pan over muffins.

Cranberry-corn mini muffins

Makes 24 muffins *Prep* 10 minutes *Bake* at 425° for 15 minutes

Pack these up with a thermos of steaming chicken noodle soup for a hot lunch that travels.

Per muffin
116 calories, 2 g protein,
4 g fat, 20 g carbohydrate,
145 mg sodium,
17 mg cholesterol.

1¼ cups all-purpose flour
1¼ cups yellow cornmeal
¾ cup sugar
1½ tablespoons baking powder
¾ teaspoon salt
1 egg

½ cup fresh orange juice
⅓ cup milk
6 tablespoons unsalted butter or
  margarine, melted
1 tablespoon grated orange rind
¾ cup dried cranberries

1. Heat oven to 425°. Grease two 12-mini-muffin pans.

2. Combine flour, cornmeal, sugar, baking powder and salt in a medium-size bowl.

3. Combine egg, orange juice, milk, butter and orange rind in a small bowl until blended. Stir in cranberries. Stir into flour mixture until just moistened. Spoon batter evenly into prepared muffin pans, about 2 slightly rounded tablespoons per muffin.

4. Bake in heated 425° oven 15 minutes or until a wooden pick inserted in centers comes out clean. Remove muffins from pans to a rack. Serve warm. Or cool on a rack to serve later; reheat if desired.

To make a loaf: Grease an 8 x 8 x 2-inch square baking pan. Bake in heated 400° oven 45 minutes or until a wooden pick inserted in center comes out clean. Cover with foil if loaf browns too quickly.

Chocolate cookie muffins

Makes 6 muffin tops or 12 muffins   *Prep* 15 minutes

Bake muffin tops at 375° for 20 to 25 minutes, or muffins at 400° for 12 minutes

This is how to turn a muffin into dessert. The recipe screams out for a bowl of vanilla ice cream.

Per muffin top
603 calories, 8 g protein, 30 g fat, 76 g carbohydrate, 589 mg sodium, 100 mg cholesterol.

2 cups all-purpose flour
¾ cup sugar
2 teaspoons baking powder
¾ teaspoon salt
¾ cup (1½ sticks) cold butter or margarine, cut into 12 pieces

1 egg
½ cup milk
1 teaspoon vanilla
14 chocolate sandwich cookies, coarsely broken

1. Grease a 6-muffin-top pan or a standard 12-muffin pan. Heat oven to 375° for muffin-top pan or 400° for muffin pan.

2. Combine flour, sugar, baking powder and salt in a large bowl. With a pastry blender or 2 knives used scissor fashion, cut in butter until mixture resembles coarse crumbs.

3. Combine egg, milk and vanilla in a small bowl. Stir into flour mixture until just blended.

4. Stir broken cookies gently into batter. Spoon batter evenly into prepared muffin-top pan or muffin pan.

5. Bake muffin-top pan in heated 375° oven 20 to 25 minutes, or bake standard muffin pan in heated 400° oven 12 minutes or until a wooden pick inserted in centers comes out clean. Remove muffins from pans to wire racks to cool.

To make a loaf: Grease an 8½ x 4½ x 2⅝-inch loaf pan. Bake in a heated 350° oven 65 minutes or until a wooden pick inserted in center comes out clean. Cover with foil if loaf browns too quickly.

Marble streusel muffins

Makes 12 muffins *Prep* 20 minutes *Bake* at 350° for 22 to 25 minutes

Looking for a really decadent chocolate muffin for afternoon tea? Here it is!

Per muffin
274 calories, 5 g protein, 12 g fat, 38 g carbohydrate, 235 mg sodium, 46 mg cholesterol.

No-stick trick
Spritz nonstick muffin pans with a little nonstick cooking spray and muffins will pop out cleanly every time—guaranteed!

Streusel
⅓ cup packed light-brown sugar
¼ cup all-purpose flour
¼ teaspoon ground cinnamon
2 tablespoons butter, softened
¼ cup chocolate chips

Batter
2 cups all-purpose flour
¾ cup granulated sugar

1 teaspoon baking soda
½ teaspoon salt
3 tablespoons unsweetened cocoa powder
4 ounces reduced-fat cream cheese
2 eggs
½ cup water
⅓ cup vegetable oil
1 teaspoon vanilla

1. Coat a standard 12-muffin pan with nonstick cooking spray.

2. Prepare streusel: Combine brown sugar, flour and cinnamon. Work in butter until mixture is crumbly. Stir in chocolate chips.

3. Prepare muffins: Combine flour, sugar, baking soda and salt in a medium-size bowl. Remove ½ cup; set aside. Add cocoa powder to remaining flour mixture.

4. Beat cream cheese and 1 egg in a small bowl until smooth. Stir in reserved ½ cup flour mixture.

5. Heat oven to 350°.

6. Beat remaining egg, water, oil and vanilla in a large bowl. Add cocoa mixture.

7. Using two-thirds of cocoa batter, fill each muffin cup halfway. Using remaining cocoa batter and cream cheese batter, spoon batters side by side in each cup. Sprinkle with streusel.

8. Bake in heated 350° oven 22 to 25 minutes or until a wooden pick inserted in centers comes out clean. Cool pan on a rack 5 minutes. Turn muffins out. Serve warm.

Tomato-herb drop biscuits

Makes about 16 biscuits *Prep* 15 minutes *Cook* 8 minutes *Bake* at 425° for 10 to 12 minutes

Drop biscuits have an appetizing rustic quality, and this particular variety would be a perfect match with a grilled flank steak coated with crushed black peppercorns.

per biscuit
112 calories, 2 g protein, 6 g fat, 13 g carbohydrate, 211 mg sodium, 1 mg cholesterol.

1 tablespoon olive oil
1 small onion, finely chopped
1 medium tomato, finely diced (¾ cup)
¼ cup chopped fresh basil
½ teaspoon dried oregano
2 cups all-purpose flour

1 tablespoon baking powder
1 teaspoon salt
¼ to ½ teaspoon coarsely ground black pepper
⅓ cup solid vegetable shortening
⅔ cup milk

1. Heat oven to 425°.

2. Heat oil in a small skillet over medium heat. Add onion and sauté until tender, about 7 minutes. Add tomato; cook 1 minute longer. Remove from heat. Stir in basil and oregano. Cool slightly.

3. Mix flour, baking powder, salt and pepper in a large bowl. With 2 knives used scissor fashion, cut in shortening until mixture resembles coarse crumbs. Stir in milk and tomato mixture just until dough comes together. Drop by heaping tablespoons, 2 inches apart, onto an ungreased baking sheet.

4. Bake in heated 425° oven 10 to 12 minutes or until biscuits are golden. Remove to a wire rack to cool.

Tomato-herb drop biscuits

Sweet potato biscuits

Makes 20 biscuits Prep 15 minutes Bake at 425° for 8 to 10 minutes

A basket of these with a roast loin of pork would be welcome on any dinner table. If you prefer, cook and mash a large sweet potato instead of using canned (you'll need 1 cup mashed).

Per biscuit
103 calories, 2 g protein, 4 g fat, 15 g carbohydrate, 223 mg sodium, 1 mg cholesterol.

2½ cups all-purpose flour
1 tablespoon baking powder
1½ teaspoons salt
⅓ cup cold solid vegetable shortening

1 can (15 ounces) sweet potatoes, drained and mashed
¾ to 1 cup cold milk

1. Heat oven to 425°.

2. Sift together flour, baking powder and salt in a large bowl. Cut in shortening with 2 knives used scissor fashion until mixture resembles coarse crumbs. Whisk together sweet potatoes and ¾ cup milk in a small bowl until blended. With a fork, gradually stir sweet potato mixture into flour mixture until blended; do not overmix. If dough is too dry, add remaining milk, 1 tablespoon at a time, until dough sticks together.

3. Place dough on a floured surface; knead 8 to 10 times. Roll or pat dough into a 13 x 8-inch rectangle, about ½ inch thick. Cut out biscuits with a floured 2-inch cutter or cut into 2-inch squares with a knife. Gather scraps, pat out and cut. You should have 20 biscuits. Place on an ungreased baking sheet.

4. Bake in heated 425° oven 8 to 10 minutes or until golden. Serve warm.

Savory biscuit wedges

Makes 8 wedges Prep 15 minutes Bake at 375° for 30 to 35 minutes

These are better than a spoon for soaking up the last drops in the bottom of the soup bowl.

Per wedge
199 calories, 4 g protein, 9 g fat, 25 g carbohydrate, 269 mg sodium, 4 mg cholesterol.

2 cups all-purpose flour
1 tablespoon baking powder
½ teaspoon salt
⅓ cup solid vegetable shortening

⅓ cup finely chopped green onion
2 dashes hot pepper sauce
¾ cup milk

1. Heat oven to 375°. Lightly grease a baking sheet.

2. Combine flour, baking powder and salt in a large bowl. Cut in shortening with 2 knives used scissor fashion until mixture resembles coarse crumbs. Stir in green onion.

3. Combine hot-pepper sauce and milk. Pour about ⅔ cup milk mixture into flour mixture. Stir just until dough comes together. If too dry, add remaining milk. Knead dough on a lightly floured work surface 1 minute.

4. Pat into a 1-inch-thick round. Place on prepared baking sheet. Bake in heated 375° oven 30 to 35 minutes or until lightly browned. Cool briefly on a wire rack. Cut into 8 equal wedges.

Fluffy buttermilk pancakes

Makes 4 servings (twenty-four 4-inch pancakes) *Prep* 30 minutes *Cook* 3 minutes per batch

You have your choice of topping—go for the blueberries or try the rich taste of brown sugar and vanilla.

Per serving (without syrup)
451 calories, 16 g protein, 18 g fat, 55 g carbohydrate, 930 mg sodium, 248 mg cholesterol.

Perfect pancakes
Cook pancakes on an electric skillet or a well-seasoned cast-iron skillet—both provide even heat.

1¾ cups all-purpose flour
2 tablespoons sugar
1½ teaspoons baking soda
1 teaspoon cream of tartar
½ teaspoon salt
2 cups buttermilk
4 eggs, separated

¼ cup (½ stick) butter or margarine, melted
Vegetable oil
Blueberry Syrup (recipe follows)
Brown Sugar Syrup (recipe follows)

1. Sift together flour, sugar, baking soda, cream of tartar and salt onto a sheet of waxed paper.

2. Whisk together buttermilk and egg yolks in a large bowl. Beat flour mixture into buttermilk mixture along with melted butter.

3. Beat egg whites in a medium-size bowl until stiff, but not dry, peaks form. Fold into pancake batter.

4. Heat oven to 225°.

5. Heat a large skillet or griddle over medium-high heat. Lightly brush with vegetable oil. Working in batches, ladle in a scant ⅓ cup batter for each pancake; cook until set and bubbly on top, 2 minutes. Turn pancakes over; cook 1 minute or until cooked through. Keep warm in heated 225° oven. Serve with your choice of warm syrup.

Blueberry syrup

Per tablespoon
15 calories, 0 g protein, 0 g fat, 4 g carbohydrate, 1 mg sodium, 0 mg cholesterol.

Combine 2 cups fresh or thawed frozen blueberries, ¼ cup sugar, ¼ cup water and ½ teaspoon ground nutmeg in a small saucepan. Bring to boiling over medium heat. Reduce heat to low; simmer about 7 minutes or until syrup is thickened. Makes about 1½ cups.

Brown sugar syrup

Per tablespoon
41 calories, 0 g protein, 0 g fat, 11 g carbohydrate, 4 mg sodium, 0 mg cholesterol.

Combine 2 cups packed dark-brown sugar and 1 cup water in a medium-size saucepan. Bring to boiling; stir to dissolve sugar. Lower heat; boil gently until syrupy, about 15 minutes. Stir in 1 teaspoon vanilla. Makes about 1⅔ cups.

Puffed apple pancake

Makes 6 servings   Prep 15 minutes   Cook 15 to 20 minutes

Bake at 425° for 20 minutes; at 350° for 10 to 15 minutes

For pancake lovers, here's one you can serve for dessert or a celebratory brunch.

Per serving
251 calories, 7 g protein, 6 g fat, 44 g carbohydrate, 149 mg sodium, 82 mg cholesterol.

6 Golden Delicious apples (2 pounds total)
1 tablespoon butter or margarine
3 tablespoons granulated sugar
1 teaspoon vanilla
⅛ teaspoon ground cinnamon

1 cup milk
2 eggs
2 egg whites
¼ teaspoon salt
1 cup all-purpose flour
Confectioners' sugar

1. Peel, core and thinly slice apples into wedges. Heat oven to 425°.

2. Melt butter in a large ovenproof skillet. Add apples and 2 tablespoons sugar; cook, stirring, 15 to 20 minutes or until apples are tender and liquid has evaporated. Stir in vanilla and cinnamon. Remove from heat.

3. Beat together milk, eggs, egg whites, remaining 1 tablespoon sugar and salt in a medium-size bowl. Gradually whisk in flour until well blended and smooth. Pour batter over hot apples. Bake in heated 425° oven 20 minutes. Reduce heat to 350°; bake 10 to 15 minutes more or until puffed and browned. Sprinkle with confectioners' sugar. Cut into wedges.

Dutch bacon pancakes

Makes 5 servings (10 pancakes)   Prep 15 minutes   Cook bacon 10 minutes; pancakes about 4 minutes each

These would be very yummy for a Sunday night supper.

Per serving
594 calories, 20 g protein, 25 g fat, 72 g carbohydrate, 744 mg sodium, 131 mg cholesterol.

Keep them warm
Place a growing stack of pancakes on an ovenproof plate in a 225° oven until ready to serve.

20 strips bacon
2 cups all-purpose flour
½ teaspoon salt

2 eggs
3 cups milk
10 tablespoons maple syrup

1. Fry bacon in batches in a large skillet over medium-high heat until browned and crisp, about 10 minutes total. Remove with a slotted spoon to paper toweling to drain; carefully pour off bacon fat and reserve.

2. Stir together flour and salt in a large bowl. Beat together eggs and milk in a large glass measuring cup. Gradually add egg mixture to flour mixture, whisking constantly to keep lumps from forming.

3. Heat oven to 225°. For each pancake, place 2 strips cooked bacon in center of skillet along with ½ teaspoon bacon fat; heat. Pour ½ cup batter into skillet. Cook over medium-low heat 1 to 2 minutes or until bottom begins to brown. Turn over. Cook other side 1 to 2 minutes or until lightly browned. Stack pancakes between sheets of waxed paper on a baking sheet and keep warm in heated 225° oven. Serve with syrup.

Puffed apple pancake *opposite*

351

Baked French toast

Makes 6 servings   *Prep* 10 minutes   *Bake* at 475° for 15 minutes

Egg-rich challah bread makes for fluffy French toast, and you have a choice of three toppings: strawberry-citrus sauce, maple-walnut butter and caramel-apple cream.

Per serving (without toppings)
204 calories, 7 g protein, 12 g fat, 17 g carbohydrate, 233 mg sodium, 142 mg cholesterol.

3 tablespoons butter, melted
1½ cups milk
3 eggs
2 tablespoons confectioners' sugar
1 teaspoon vanilla
½ teaspoon ground cinnamon
⅛ teaspoon ground nutmeg

6 slices egg bread (challah), cut into 1-inch-thick slices
Caramel-Apple Cream (recipe follows)
Strawberry-Citrus Sauce (recipe follows)
Maple-Walnut Butter (recipe follows)

1. Heat oven to 475°. Drizzle butter onto a baking pan large enough to hold bread slices in one layer.

2. Whisk together milk, eggs, confectioners' sugar, vanilla, cinnamon and nutmeg in a large bowl. Dip both sides of bread into milk mixture; place on prepared pan. Pour any remaining milk mixture over bread. Let stand 20 minutes, turning bread over a couple of times.

3. Bake in heated 475° oven, turning once, until puffed and golden, about 15 minutes. Serve with your choice of topping.

Caramel-apple cream

Per 2 tablespoons
31 calories, 0 g protein, 2 g fat, 3 g carbohydrate, 21 mg sodium, 6 mg cholesterol.

Heat ¼ cup (½ stick) butter in a 12-inch skillet over medium heat. Add 2 medium Golden Delicious apples, peeled, cored and thinly sliced; cook until slices are softened slightly. Add ¼ cup firmly packed light-brown sugar, 3 tablespoons half-and-half and ⅛ teaspoon ground allspice; cook, stirring occasionally, about 2 minutes. Makes 2¼ cups.

Strawberry-citrus sauce

Per 2 tablespoons
23 calories, 0 g protein, 0 g fat, 6 g carbohydrate, 0 mg sodium, 0 mg cholesterol.

Wash and hull 1 pint strawberries. Coarsely chop ½ cup; quarter remaining berries lengthwise. Combine berries, 3 tablespoons sugar and 2 tablespoons orange liqueur or orange juice in a bowl. Let stand 15 minutes. Makes 1½ cups.

Maple-walnut butter

Per 2 tablespoons
162 calories, 0 g protein, 13 g fat, 12 g carbohydrate, 3 mg sodium, 25 mg cholesterol.

Stir together ½ cup (1 stick) butter at room temperature, ½ cup finely chopped walnuts and ¼ cup maple syrup in a small bowl until well blended. Refrigerate until ready to use. To soften, remove from refrigerator 15 minutes before using. Makes 1¼ cups.

Ginger-spice waffles

Makes 6 servings (six 8-inch waffles)   *Prep* 15 minutes   *Cook* 5 minutes per waffle

The topping of yogurt and fresh fruit goes well with the ginger, cinnamon and nutmeg flavors in the batter. Come spring, substitute fresh strawberries and raspberries for the oranges.

Per serving
562 calories, 14 g protein, 27 g fat, 70 g carbohydrate, 641 mg sodium, 139 mg cholesterol.

1 cup all-purpose flour
1 cup whole-wheat flour
2 tablespoons unsweetened cocoa powder
1 tablespoon ground ginger
1½ teaspoons baking soda
1½ teaspoons ground cinnamon
1 teaspoon ground nutmeg
½ teaspoon salt
2 eggs

1¾ cups buttermilk
¾ cups (1½ sticks) butter or margarine, melted
⅓ cup molasses

Topping
1½ cups vanilla low-fat yogurt
3 cups fruit, such as blueberries, chopped kiwi and mandarin oranges

1. Heat a waffle iron. Heat oven to 225°.

2. Sift together all-purpose flour, whole-wheat flour, cocoa powder, ginger, baking soda, cinnamon, nutmeg and salt into a large bowl.

3. Beat eggs slightly in a medium-size bowl. Beat in buttermilk and melted butter until well blended. Make a well in center of dry ingredients. Add buttermilk mixture and molasses to well; stir just until ingredients are combined and dry ingredients are moistened.

4. Make waffles in waffle maker following manufacturer's directions. Stack between sheets of waxed paper on a large baking sheet and keep warm in heated 225° oven. Serve waffles topped with vanilla yogurt and fruit.

Wonderful waffles

WAFFLES NEED a fairly high proportion of butter, oil or other shortening to keep them from sticking to the iron, and the batter should be quite thick, even cakelike.

Season a new waffle iron according to the manufacturer's directions. Then you won't need to wash it between uses but will be able to just brush any crumbs away.

Don't peek after adding batter to the iron. Wait 3 or 4 minutes and then take a look; if the waffle is not as brown as you like, bake a minute or 2 longer.

Pecan whole-wheat waffles

Makes 5 waffles (7-inch) and 2 cups sauce *Prep* 25 minutes *Cook* 4 minutes per waffle

Here's a perfect pairing—the nutty taste of the waffles and the maple-cherry flavor of the sauce.

per waffle (without sauce)
390 calories, 11 g protein,
16 g fat, 53 g carbohydrate,
410 mg sodium,
100 mg cholesterol.

1½ cups all-purpose flour
½ cup whole-wheat flour
½ cup finely chopped toasted
  pecans
2 teaspoons baking powder
¼ teaspoon ground nutmeg
¼ teaspoon salt
2 tablespoons butter, melted
⅓ cup packed light-brown sugar
2 eggs
1¼ cups milk
  Cherry Sauce (recipe follows)

1. Heat waffle iron. Heat oven to 225°.

2. Combine flours, pecans, baking powder, nutmeg and salt in a large bowl. Make a well in center.

3. Whisk butter and brown sugar in a medium-size bowl until blended. Whisk in eggs and milk. Add to well; stir to blend. Let stand 5 minutes.

4. Coat waffle iron lightly with nonstick cooking spray. Spoon batter onto iron. Cover and cook 4 minutes or until browned. Remove waffles. Stack between sheets of waxed paper on a baking sheet and keep warm in heated 225° oven. Repeat with remaining batter. Serve with sauce.

Cherry sauce

per 2 tablespoons
32 calories, 0 g protein,
0 g fat, 8 g carbohydrate,
1 mg sodium,
0 mg cholesterol.

Combine 2 cups pitted dark sweet cherries (or one 12-ounce package frozen dry-pack cherries), ½ cup maple syrup and ¼ cup honey (or ¼ cup cherry jam) in a small saucepan. Bring to simmering. Dissolve 1 tablespoon cornstarch in 1 tablespoon water and stir into cherry mixture. Cook, stirring, 1 minute or until thickened. Remove from heat. Makes 2½ cups.

Whole-grain honeyed waffles

Makes 6 servings (six 8-inch waffles)   *Prep* 20 minutes   *Cook* waffles about 4 minutes each

Top these with thinly shaved slices of country ham and you'll have a memorable brunch dish.

*Per serving
(without butter
and syrup)*
399 calories, 11 g protein,
19 g fat, 48 g carbohydrate,
493 mg sodium,
114 mg cholesterol.

1 cup natural wheat-and-barley cereal or oatmeal
2 tablespoons toasted wheat germ
½ cup (1 stick) butter or margarine, melted
2 eggs, slightly beaten
¼ cup honey
1 cup all-purpose flour

½ cup whole-wheat flour or rye flour
1 teaspoon baking soda
½ teaspoon salt
1½ cups buttermilk
Butter for serving (optional)
Syrup for serving (optional)

1. Heat waffle iron. Heat oven to 225°.

2. Mix cereal and wheat germ in a large bowl. Beat butter, eggs and honey in a second bowl. Add to cereal. Mix flours, baking soda and salt in a third bowl. Add flour mixture alternately with buttermilk to cereal, stirring; batter will be very stiff.

3. Make a total of 6 waffles in waffle maker following manufacturer's directions. Stack between sheets of waxed paper on a baking sheet and keep warm in heated 225° oven. Serve waffles with butter and syrup if desired.

355

Southwestern grilled-cheese sandwiches

Makes 4 servings *Prep* 45 minutes *Cook* 10 minutes

If you can't find arugula in your supermarket, you can use pieces of romaine lettuce for greening up the sandwich.

Per serving
528 calories, 26 g protein, 28 g fat, 54 g carbohydrate, 818 mg sodium, 48 mg cholesterol.

1 can (15 ounces) black beans, drained and rinsed
1½ cups shredded pepper-Jack cheese (6 ounces)
1¼ teaspoons ground cumin
8 slices whole-wheat bread

1 large avocado, halved, pitted, peeled and thinly sliced
2 tablespoons fresh lemon juice
12 large arugula leaves
4 teaspoons butter or margarine

1. Blot beans dry with paper toweling. Combine beans, cheese and cumin in a medium-size bowl. Spread half of mixture over 4 slices of bread.

2. Brush avocado slices with lemon juice and place on bean-topped bread slices, dividing equally. Top each bread slice with 3 arugula leaves. Spread remaining bean-cheese mixture over arugula and top sandwiches with remaining bread slices.

3. Melt 2 teaspoons butter in a large nonstick skillet over medium-low heat. Place 2 sandwiches in skillet and cook 2 to 3 minutes or until browned. Using a wide metal spatula, carefully turn sandwiches over and cook, pressing down slightly on top of each sandwich, 2 to 3 minutes or until browned. Remove sandwiches from skillet and keep warm. Repeat with remaining butter and sandwiches.

Antipasto hero

Makes 4 servings *Prep* 45 minutes *Bake* at 350° for 15 minutes

For a zingy hit, squeeze a dab of anchovy paste from a tube onto the bottom half of the hero and spread evenly.

Per serving
531 calories, 20 g protein, 13 g fat, 84 g carbohydrate, 1,200 mg sodium, 15 mg cholesterol.

4 Italian-style hero rolls
1 jar (6 ounces) marinated artichoke hearts, drained and sliced (reserve marinade)
3 tablespoons chopped fresh basil

¼ teaspoon black pepper
2 jars (7 ounces each) roasted red peppers, drained
8 thin slices provolone cheese
4 plum tomatoes, thinly sliced

1. Heat oven to 350°.

2. Slice rolls in half horizontally. Whisk together reserved artichoke marinade, basil and black pepper. Brush over cut sides of rolls. On bottom of rolls, layer half of roasted peppers and 4 slices of cheese. Top with tomatoes and artichokes. Cover with remaining roasted peppers and cheese.

3. Replace tops of rolls; wrap each roll in aluminum foil. Bake in heated 350° oven 15 minutes or until warm and cheese is melted.

Flank steak sandwiches

Makes 6 servings   *Prep* 20 minutes   *Refrigerate* 2 to 24 hours   *Grill or broil* 6 to 8 minutes

Turn the sandwiches into dinner by offering mixed-vegetable couscous and steamed broccoli with pine nuts.

Per serving
473 calories, 30 g protein, 23 g fat, 32 g carbohydrate, 977 mg sodium, 67 mg cholesterol.

1 flank steak (about 1½ pounds)
1 cup light or dark beer
¼ cup olive oil
¼ cup reduced-sodium soy sauce
¼ cup fresh lemon juice
1 tablespoon Worcestershire sauce
1 teaspoon brown sugar
1 teaspoon prepared mustard
⅛ teaspoon black pepper
⅛ teaspoon hot-pepper sauce

Horseradish dressing
½ cup reduced-fat mayonnaise
½ cup low-fat yogurt or reduced-fat sour cream
2 to 3 tablespoons drained bottled horseradish

6 Kaiser rolls, sliced in half

1. Score a diamond pattern ¼ inch deep on both sides of steak.

2. Combine beer, oil, soy sauce, lemon juice, Worcestershire sauce, brown sugar, mustard, black pepper and hot-pepper sauce in a plastic food-storage bag. Add steak; push out all air and seal. Refrigerate 2 to 24 hours, turning bag occasionally.

3. Prepare a charcoal grill with hot coals, or heat a gas grill to high, or heat broiler. Oil grill rack and place 5 inches above heat. Or oil broiler-pan rack and set broiler shelf so rack sits 4 inches from heat.

4. Grill or broil steak 6 to 8 minutes for medium-rare (until internal temperature registers 145° on an instant-read thermometer), turning halfway through and basting with marinade. Let stand 10 minutes.

5. Meanwhile, prepare horseradish dressing: Combine mayonnaise, yogurt and horseradish in a small bowl.

6. Cut steak diagonally across grain into thin slices. Spread dressing on rolls. Sandwich an equal amount of steak in each roll.

Stuffed pockets

Makes 4 servings   *Prep* 15 minutes   *Bake* at 400° for 15 minutes

Purchased bread dough makes this version of Italy's classic calzone easy to fix. For a no-fuss accompaniment, toss a prepackaged Caesar salad into a serving bowl.

Per serving
435 calories, 22 g protein, 12 g fat, 59 g carbohydrate, 905 mg sodium, 27 mg cholesterol.

1 pound fresh or thawed frozen bread dough
½ cup frozen chopped broccoli, thawed
½ cup part-skim ricotta cheese
½ cup reduced-fat mozzarella cheese
¼ cup grated Parmesan cheese
¼ teaspoon hot-pepper sauce
½ cup diced Canadian bacon (scant 2 ounces)

1. Heat oven to 400°. Coat 2 baking sheets with nonstick cooking spray.

2. Cut dough into 4 equal pieces. Roll or pat each piece on a floured surface into 8 x 6-inch ovals. If dough is too hard to work, let rest 5 minutes.

3. Squeeze out excess liquid from broccoli. Place in a medium-size bowl, along with ricotta, mozzarella, Parmesan, hot-pepper sauce and Canadian bacon; stir to combine.

4. Spoon filling lengthwise down center of each piece of dough. Fold dough over to cover filling, pressing edges together to seal. Place on prepared baking sheets. Cut 2 slits in top of each to vent steam.

5. Bake in heated 400° oven 15 minutes or until golden brown.

Mexican chicken tacos

Makes 6 servings   *Prep* 20 minutes   *Cook* 10 minutes   *Heat* taco shells at 350° for 5 minutes

For a wrap, roll the chicken salad mixture up in a flavored flour tortilla.

Per serving
282 calories, 8 g protein, 14 g fat, 33 g carbohydrate, 200 mg sodium, 10 mg cholesterol.

2 small boneless, skinless chicken breast halves (½ pound total)
1 sweet red pepper, cored, seeded and diced
1 sweet yellow pepper, cored, seeded and diced
4 green onions, sliced (about ⅓ cup)
1 cup cooked white rice
¼ cup cider vinegar
1 teaspoon chili powder
½ teaspoon salt
¼ teaspoon ground cumin
⅛ teaspoon black pepper
2 dashes hot-pepper sauce
Juice of 1 lime (about 3 tablespoons)
¼ cup vegetable oil
1 avocado, peeled, pitted and cut into chunks
12 prepared taco shells

1. Bring 3 cups water to boiling in a medium-size shallow skillet or saucepan. Reduce heat to medium; add chicken breasts. Poach chicken at a gentle simmer 10 minutes or until no longer pink in center. Remove skillet from heat. Let chicken cool slightly in poaching liquid before removing to a cutting board.

2. Once chicken has cooled completely, shred with a fork. Transfer to a medium-size bowl. Add sweet peppers, green onions and rice.

3. Whisk together vinegar, chili powder, salt, cumin, black pepper, hot-pepper sauce and lime juice in a measuring cup or bowl. Whisk in oil in a thin stream until well blended.

4. Add dressing to salad in bowl; toss to mix. Add avocado; stir gently to combine, being careful not to mash avocado.

5. Heat oven to 350°. Heat taco shells on baking sheet 5 minutes or until warmed. Divide filling among taco shells.

Mexican chicken tacos
opposite

Veggi chili wraps

Makes 10 servings *Prep* 10 minutes *Cook* 30 to 35 minutes *Microwave* tortillas 1 to 2 minutes

Not only a good match with flavored tortillas, the chili is also at home in omelets and taco shells.

Per serving
290 calories, 13 g protein, 9 g fat, 49 g carbohydrate, 949 mg sodium, 0 mg cholesterol.

Tortilla tip
If desired, you can warm tortillas in an oven. Simply wrap them in aluminum foil and heat at 300° for 12 to 15 minutes.

2 tablespoons vegetable oil
1 medium onion, chopped
1 sweet red pepper, cored, seeded and diced
1 sweet green pepper, cored, seeded and diced
1 jalapeño chile, seeded and chopped
2 medium zucchini, diced (about 2 cups)
2 tablespoons chili powder
½ teaspoon ground cumin
½ teaspoon salt
¼ teaspoon black pepper
1 can (14½ ounces) stewed tomatoes
1 can (19 ounces) black beans, drained and rinsed
1 cup corn kernels
½ cup canned vegetable broth
10 chile-flavored or plain flour tortillas (12-inch)

1. Heat oil in a large saucepan or Dutch oven over medium heat. Add onion, sweet peppers, and jalapeño; sauté 5 minutes. Add zucchini; cook until onion is translucent and softened, about 4 minutes. Add chili powder, cumin, salt and black pepper.

2. Stir in tomatoes, beans, corn and broth; simmer 20 to 25 minutes or until most of liquid is evaporated.

3. Wrap tortillas in damp paper toweling. Microwave on 100% power 1 to 2 minutes or until steaming and very pliable. Spread ½ cup filling over a tortilla and roll up. Repeat with remaining filling and tortillas.

Tortilla options

WRAPS ARE the latest use for the versatile tortilla. Here are some other ways we like to prepare this delicious flatbread.

Burrito: A heated flour tortilla filled with rice, beans and sometimes meat; folded envelope style or left open on one end. If fried, they're called **chimichangas**.

Enchilada: A softened corn or flour tortilla filled with cheese, meat or poultry, then rolled, topped with sauce and baked in a casserole.

Flauta: A tightly rolled corn tortilla, usually stuffed with chicken or beef and then fried.

Quesadilla: A flour or corn tortilla folded in half and filled or topped with cheese. Quesadillas can be pan-fried, oven-baked or grilled until cheese is melted.

Taco: A warmed soft or crisp-fried corn tortilla folded in half and stuffed.

Tostada: A corn tortilla fried crisp and flat or formed into a basket; topped or filled with various ingredients.

Chinese pork roll-ups

Makes 8 servings   *Prep* 15 minutes   *Cook* 15 minutes   *Microwave* tortillas 1 to 2 minutes

Chinese five-spice powder is usually a mixture of cinnamon, cloves, fennel seed, star anise and Szechwan peppercorns. For a change of pace, use it to season grilled chicken or steaks or hearty stews.

Per serving
268 calories, 13 g protein,
9 g fat, 34 g carbohydrate,
989 mg sodium,
21 mg cholesterol.

3 boneless pork chops (¾ pound total), sliced into thin strips
¼ teaspoon salt
¼ teaspoon black pepper
½ teaspoon Chinese five-spice powder (optional)
1 tablespoon vegetable oil
3 cups shredded red cabbage
1 can (8 ounce) sliced water chestnuts, drained
¼ pound mushrooms, sliced
1 cup beef broth
1 tablespoon cornstarch
2 tablespoons hoisin sauce
2 tablespoons soy sauce
8 flour tortillas (12-inch)

1. Toss pork with salt, pepper and five-spice powder in a medium-size bowl.

2. Heat oil in a large skillet over high heat. Add cabbage; sauté 3 minutes. Add pork; sauté 3 minutes. Add water chestnuts and mushrooms; cook 3 to 5 minutes or until mushrooms are softened.

3. Whisk together broth and cornstarch in a small bowl until smooth. Add to pork mixture in skillet; cook until thickened and clear, about 2 minutes. Remove from heat. Stir in hoisin and soy sauce.

4. Wrap tortillas in damp paper toweling. Microwave on 100% power 1 to 2 minutes or until steaming and very pliable. Spread ½ cup filling over a tortilla and roll up. Repeat with remaining filling and tortillas.

Curried egg salad in pita pockets

Makes 6 servings   *Prep* 25 minutes

You can also stuff cherry tomatoes with this egg salad to make a colorful appetizer.

Per serving
348 calories, 12 g protein,
21 g fat, 30 g carbohydrate,
503 mg sodium,
223 mg cholesterol.

6 eggs
½ cup sliced red onion
½ cup mayonnaise
½ teaspoon curry powder
1 carrot, shredded
¼ teaspoon salt
¼ teaspoon black pepper
6 pita pockets
1 small tomato, sliced
1 cup shredded lettuce

1. Place eggs in a single layer in a medium-size saucepan; add cold water to a depth of 1½ inches. Partially cover pan and bring to a rolling boil. Reduce heat to low, cover pan and let stand on heat 30 seconds. Then let stand off heat 15 minutes. Drain and rinse eggs under cold water.

2. Shell eggs and chop. Place in a medium-size bowl. Add onion, mayonnaise, curry powder, carrot, salt and pepper. Mix well and divide among pita pockets. Add tomato and lettuce.

Strawberry-banana Napoleon *page 364*

Peach cobbler *page 380*

REMEMBER WHEN you were little and thought a meal was merely the necessary prelude to dessert? At this point you've learned to appreciate the main event, but that doesn't mean you've stopped wondering about what's to come.

The possibilities are more delectable than you can imagine. The final fillip might be a generous helping of goes-down-easy Butterscotch or Rice Pudding, or maybe homemade Old-Fashioned Vanilla Ice Cream. A comforting crisp or cobbler bursting with fruit is sure to please, but for something a bit fancier, Strawberry-

When nothing but a sweet reward will do, these indulgences will hit the spot.

Banana Napoleon layered with pastry cream could be the answer. And there's always the chance of a cocoa extravaganza with delights like Chocolate Cream Pie or Chocolate-Raspberry Truffle Tart. All the important food groups—pudding, pie, ice cream, fruit and chocolate—are irresistibly accounted for. Dessert, anyone? Do you even have to ask?

Strawberry-banana Napoleon# Strawberry-banana Napoleon

Makes 8 servings   *Prep* 45 minutes   *Bake* at 400° for 15 to 17 minutes

The filling and pastry can be prepared separately ahead of time: Keep the filling refrigerated and the puff pastry at room temperature in an airtight container. Allow about 15 minutes for assembling when it's dessert time.

Shown on back cover and page 362.

Per serving
382 calories, 7 g protein, 22 g fat, 41 g carbohydrate, 178 mg sodium, 102 mg cholesterol.

1 sheet (half of 17¼-ounce package) frozen puff pastry, thawed according to package directions
¼ cup sugar
3 tablespoons all-purpose flour
1 envelope unflavored gelatin
¼ teaspoon salt
1½ cups low-fat (1%) milk
3 egg yolks
1 teaspoon vanilla
1 teaspoon coconut extract
½ cup heavy cream, whipped
¼ cup confectioners' sugar
2 squares (1 ounce each) semisweet chocolate, melted
1 cup sliced, hulled strawberries
2 medium bananas, thinly sliced
Strawberries and mint sprigs for garnish

1. Heat oven to 400°.

2. Unfold thawed pastry on a floured surface. Cut lengthwise into three 3-inch-wide strips. Place on an ungreased baking sheet.

3. Bake in heated 400° oven 15 to 17 minutes or until puffed and golden. Cool pastry on a wire rack.

4. Stir together sugar, flour, gelatin and salt in a medium-size saucepan. Whisk together milk and egg yolks in a medium-size bowl. Stir milk mixture into sugar mixture. Cook over low heat, stirring constantly, until mixture thickens and coats back of a spoon, about 15 minutes; do not boil or custard will curdle. Remove saucepan from heat.

5. Stir vanilla and coconut extract into custard. Spoon custard into a small bowl. Place in a larger bowl filled halfway with ice and water. Cover and refrigerate until custard is chilled and set, about 15 minutes. Remove from larger bowl. Fold in whipped cream until blended.

6. To assemble, split pastries in half horizontally, as you would an English muffin. Sprinkle 2 of the top layers with confectioners' sugar; set aside. Spread each remaining layer with melted chocolate, ½ cup custard, ¼ cup sliced strawberries and one-quarter of banana slices.

7. Stack one prepared pastry on top of a second prepared pastry. Top with a confectioners' sugar-dusted layer, making a three-layered Napoleon. Repeat with remaining 3 layers for a second Napoleon.

8. At serving time, with a serrated knife, gently cut each Napoleon crosswise into 4 pieces, using a sawing motion, for a total of 8 servings. Garnish each serving with strawberries and mint sprigs.

Phyllo purses

Makes 12 servings *Prep* 20 minutes *Bake* at 350° for 15 minutes

Tucked away inside these flaky pastry purses is a surprising treat: a chocolate-covered caramel, a chocolate-coconut candy or banana slices.

Per serving
176 calories, 2 g protein,
11 g fat, 19 g carbohydrate,
197 mg sodium,
21 mg cholesterol.

12 sheets (about half of 1-pound package) frozen phyllo dough, thawed according to package directions
½ cup (1 stick) butter, melted

12 vanilla cookie wafers
12 chocolate-covered caramels or chocolate-coconut bar halves and/or banana slices
Confectioners' sugar

1. Heat oven to 350°.

2. Unfold 12 sheets of phyllo. Remove top sheet to a clean, dry surface. Keep unused sheets covered with damp paper toweling to prevent phyllo from drying out.

3. Cut the one sheet of phyllo into four 6-inch squares. Lightly brush one square with melted butter. Top with a second phyllo square, placed at angle; brush with melted butter. Repeat layering with 2 more sheets, angling sheets (4 layers total). Place a cookie in center of square; top with a piece of candy and/or a banana slice. Bring up corners; pinch and twist together at top to secure, forming a little bundle or purse. Place on an ungreased baking sheet. Cover with damp paper toweling while making remaining purses.

4. Bake in heated 350° oven 15 minutes or until golden and crisp. Remove baking sheet to a wire rack to cool slightly. Sprinkle purses with the confectioners' sugar.

Make-ahead tip: To prepare phyllo purses in advance, proceed through step 3. Then cover entire baking sheet of purses with several layers of damp (not wet) paper toweling; overwrap whole baking sheet with plastic wrap and freeze. To bake, unwrap baking sheet, remove toweling, place baking sheet in heated 350° oven straight from freezer and bake 20 to 25 minutes.

Cranberry-pear jalousie

Makes 2 pastries (8 servings each)   *Prep* 20 minutes   *Cook* 8 minutes   *Bake* at 350° for 45 minutes

These free-form rectangular tarts resemble the louvers in jalousie windows.

Per serving
248 calories, 3 g protein, 12 g fat, 32 g carbohydrate, 83 mg sodium, 13 mg cholesterol.

1 cup sugar
2 tablespoons cornstarch
2 cups (8 ounces) fresh or frozen cranberries
2 pears, peeled, cored, cubed
2 teaspoons grated fresh ginger
1 tablespoon fresh lime juice

¼ teaspoon ground allspice
1 package (17½ ounces) frozen puff pastry, thawed
1 egg, lightly beaten
Sweetened whipped cream for serving (optional)

1. Stir together sugar and cornstarch in a medium-size saucepan until blended. Stir in cranberries, pears, ginger, lime juice and allspice. Bring to simmering over medium heat, stirring occasionally; simmer 8 minutes or until fruits are tender. Set aside to cool.

2. Heat oven to 350°.

3. Cover one sheet of thawed pastry with a damp cloth. Cut second sheet of pastry in half crosswise. Roll out each half with a lightly floured rolling pin on a lightly floured surface, one piece into a 15 x 7-inch rectangle and the other into a 14 x 6-inch rectangle. Fold larger rectangle lengthwise in half. Along folded edge, cut parallel slits, ½ inch apart and about 1½ inches long.

4. Place smaller rectangle on an ungreased baking sheet. Spread half of cranberry filling lengthwise down center in a 3-inch-wide strip, leaving a 1½-inch border at each short end of pastry.

5. Brush edges of pastry around filling with egg. Unfold slashed pastry and lay over filling. Brush top lightly with egg. Trim edges even with a sharp knife.

6. Repeat with remaining sheet of pastry and filling.

7. Bake in heated 350° oven 45 minutes or until golden brown. Cool to room temperature before cutting into serving pieces. Serve with sweetened whipped cream if you wish.

Make-ahead tip: Pastries can be assembled through step 5, tightly wrapped, and frozen up to 1 month. Thaw overnight in refrigerator before baking.

Cranberry-pear jalousie
opposite

367

Cannoli mousse

Makes 6 servings *Prep* 10 minutes *Refrigerate* 1 hour

If you love cannoli, this will be a hit! It's the traditional ricotta filling, studded with pieces of chocolate, raisins and walnuts and flavored with orange, but without the cannoli "wrapping."

Per serving

311 calories, 10 g protein, 16 g fat, 32 g carbohydrate, 91 mg sodium, 22 mg cholesterol.

1 container (15 ounces) part-skim ricotta cheese
3 tablespoons sugar
1 teaspoon vanilla
1 tablespoon grated orange rind
¼ cup golden raisins
½ cup mini semisweet chocolate chips
½ cup walnuts, finely chopped
1 pint strawberries, raspberries or blueberries, stemmed
2 tablespoons orange-flavored liqueur

1. Process ricotta in a food processor until smooth. Add sugar and vanilla; process to blend. Transfer to a medium-size bowl.

2. Stir in orange rind, raisins, chocolate chips and walnuts. Cover and refrigerate, or scoop into 6 small ramekins or dessert dishes, cover and refrigerate.

3. Quarter strawberries (leave raspberries or blueberries whole); toss with liqueur in a bowl. Refrigerate up to 1 hour. Garnish mousse with berries.

White chocolate mousse cups

Makes 12 servings *Prep* 20 minutes *Refrigerate* 2 hours

The contrast of white chocolate mousse in phyllo cups that are rimmed with dark chocolate only enhances the flavors of both. If you can't find phyllo cups on your supermarket shelves, don't despair, the mousse is delicious served in bowls.

Per serving

390 calories, 4 g protein, 28 g fat, 32 g carbohydrate, 125 mg sodium, 65 mg cholesterol.

8 squares (1 ounce each) white baking chocolate
2¼ cups heavy cream
1 teaspoon vanilla
6 squares (1 ounce each) semisweet chocolate
2 packages (6 cups each) prepared large phyllo cups

1. Coarsely chop white chocolate. Heat chopped chocolate and cream in a small heavy saucepan over very low heat, stirring constantly, until chocolate is melted and mixture is smooth. Stir in vanilla. Pour into a large bowl; cover with plastic wrap. Refrigerate, stirring occasionally, 2 hours or until mixture is very cold.

2. Melt semisweet chocolate and place in a shallow dish. Dip top of each phyllo cup into melted chocolate to a depth of about ½ inch along rim. Place cups upright on a rack to let chocolate harden. Repeat with remaining chocolate and phyllo cups. If necessary, refrigerate to harden.

3. Beat white chocolate mixture on high speed until stiff peaks form. Spoon into prepared phyllo cups. Drizzle any remaining semisweet chocolate over filled cups. Serve immediately or chill.

Quick chocolate mousse

Makes 8 servings   *Prep* 10 minutes   *Refrigerate* 3 to 4 hours

Got a blender or food processor? Plug it in to assemble the mousse in about 10 minutes; after 3 hours of chilling, it's ready to eat.

Per serving
338 calories, 5 g protein, 24 g fat, 32 g carbohydrate, 42 mg sodium, 41 mg cholesterol.

½ cup strong brewed coffee
1 package (12 ounces) chocolate chips
¼ cup packed dark-brown sugar
½ cup cholesterol-free egg replacement
2 teaspoons vanilla
1 cup heavy cream

1. Heat coffee in a glass measuring cup in microwave oven or in a small saucepan just until beginning to simmer.

2. Place chocolate chips and sugar in a blender or food processor. With machine running, pour in hot coffee in a steady stream; process 1 minute or until smooth. Add egg replacement and vanilla. Whirl to combine. Scrape into a medium-size bowl; refrigerate 2 hours or until mixture begins to mound. Do not clean blender or processor. Refrigerate work bowl until ready to whip cream.

3. Once chocolate is thickened, pour cream into blender or processor. Whirl to whip, 45 seconds; do not overprocess. Fold cream into chocolate. Refrigerate 1 to 2 hours.

Strawberry mousse

Makes 6 servings   *Prep* 10 minutes   *Refrigerate* 3 hours

Other berries for the mousse: blueberries, raspberries and blackberries. You may need to adjust the amount of sugar depending on the tartness of the berries.

Per serving
199 calories, 2 g protein, 15 g fat, 16 g carbohydrate, 18 mg sodium, 54 mg cholesterol.

1 envelope unflavored gelatin
¼ cup cold water
2 cups hulled, sliced strawberries
¼ cup granulated sugar
1 cup heavy cream, chilled
3 tablespoons confectioners' sugar
Whole strawberries for garnish

1. Sprinkle gelatin over cold water in a small saucepan; let stand 1 minute to soften. Stir over low heat until gelatin is dissolved, about 1 minute. Remove from heat.

2. Place strawberries, granulated sugar and gelatin mixture in a food processor or blender. Whirl to puree. Pour into a bowl. Chill until mixture mounds when dropped from a spoon, 1 hour.

3. Beat cream and confectioners' sugar in a chilled bowl until soft peaks form. Stir one-quarter of cream into strawberry puree to lighten mixture. Fold in remaining cream.

4. Spoon into 6 stemmed glasses or dessert bowls, dividing equally. Chill 2 hours. Or, after lightening puree with cream, layer remaining whipped cream with strawberry puree in stemmed glasses. Garnish with whole berries.

Jelly-roll trifle

Makes 12 servings   *Prep* 30 minutes   *Bake* at 375° for 10 minutes   *Cook* 10 minutes

Refrigerate filling 1 hour; trifle 2 hours or overnight

A spectacular finale for any dinner party, one that no one will be able to refuse. Make the day before and then present it at the table to ooohs and aaahs.

Per serving
436 calories, 8 g protein, 20 g fat, 58 g carbohydrate, 249 mg sodium, 190 mg cholesterol.

Jelly roll
1 cup all-purpose flour
1 teaspoon baking powder
¼ teaspoon salt
4 eggs
¾ cup granulated sugar
¼ cup orange juice
1 teaspoon vanilla
  Confectioners' sugar

Custard
⅔ cup granulated sugar
¼ cup cornstarch
¼ teaspoon salt

4 cups milk
¼ cup dry sherry
4 egg yolks
¼ cup (½ stick) butter, at room temperature
1 tablespoon vanilla

¾ cup seedless raspberry preserves
1½ pints raspberries
1 cup heavy cream
2 tablespoons confectioners' sugar
1 teaspoon vanilla
½ cup sliced almonds, toasted

1. Heat oven to 375°. Grease a 15½ x 10½ x 1-inch jelly-roll pan. Line pan with waxed paper; grease paper.

2. Prepare jelly roll: Combine flour, baking powder and salt in a small bowl. Beat eggs in a large bowl on medium speed until thickened slightly, 2 minutes. Add sugar, a tablespoon at a time; continue beating until mixture is very thick and lemon colored, 5 minutes. Beat in orange juice and vanilla. Beat in flour mixture until just mixed. Spread evenly in prepared pan.

3. Bake in heated 375° oven 10 minutes or until top of cake springs back when lightly touched in center.

4. Sprinkle a large towel with confectioners' sugar. When cake is done, immediately loosen edges. Invert cake onto towel. Starting from a short side, roll up cake with towel, jelly-roll fashion. Place cake, seam side down, on a rack to cool.

5. Prepare custard: Mix sugar, cornstarch and salt in a medium-size saucepan. Gradually stir in milk and sherry. Bring to boiling over medium heat, stirring constantly, until thickened. Boil 1 minute. Reduce heat to low.

6. Whisk yolks slightly in a small bowl. Beat in ¼ cup hot milk mixture to warm yolks. Slowly pour yolk mixture into milk mixture in saucepan over low heat, stirring quickly and constantly to keep lumps from forming. Heat, stirring, until custard thickens and coats back of a spoon.

7. Remove saucepan from heat. Stir in butter and vanilla. Cover surface with plastic wrap; refrigerate until custard is well chilled, about 1 hour.

Jelly-roll trifle

8. Unroll cooled cake. Spread with preserves. Roll up cake without towel. Cut into ½-inch-thick slices. Line sides of a 14-cup glass bowl with half of slices. Cut remaining slices into quarters; layer alternately in center with custard and raspberries. Cover; refrigerate 2 hours or overnight.

9. To serve, beat heavy cream, confectioners' sugar and vanilla in a bowl until soft peaks form. Spoon over top of trifle. Sprinkle with almonds.

Chocolate tiramisu

Makes 16 servings   *Prep* 45 minutes   *Bake* at 350° for 17 minutes   *Refrigerate* overnight or up to 2 days

The Italian word *tiramisu* means "carry me up." After you take a taste, you'll think you've been transported to heaven—it's that good. The layers of liqueur-soaked cake and mascarpone cheese, or in this case ricotta, along with grated chocolate are truly ethereal.

Per serving
358 calories, 8 g protein,
18 g fat, 41 g carbohydrate,
147 mg sodium,
114 mg cholesterol.

Chocolate cake

- 1½ cups all-purpose flour
- ½ cup unsweetened cocoa powder
- 1 teaspoon baking soda
- ½ teaspoon baking powder
- ¼ teaspoon salt
- ½ cup (1 stick) unsalted butter, at room temperature
- 1 cup sugar
- 2 eggs
- 1 teaspoon vanilla
- 1¼ cups milk

Filling

- 3 egg yolks
- ½ cup sugar
- ⅓ cup milk
- 1 container (15 ounces) part-skim ricotta cheese, pureed
- 1 cup heavy cream, whipped
- ½ cup coffee liqueur
- 4 ounces (4 squares) semisweet chocolate, chopped

1. Heat oven to 350°. Line a 15¼ x 10¼ x 1-inch jelly-roll pan with aluminum foil. Coat foil with nonstick cooking spray.

2. Combine flour, cocoa powder, baking soda, baking powder and salt in a medium-size bowl.

3. Beat butter, sugar, eggs and vanilla in a large bowl until light and fluffy, about 3 minutes. On low speed, alternately beat flour mixture and milk into butter mixture. Spread batter in prepared pan.

4. Bake in heated 350° oven 17 minutes or until cake springs back when lightly touched in center. Cool cake in pan on a wire rack 10 minutes. Invert cake onto rack; cool completely.

5. Meanwhile, prepare filling: Whisk together egg yolks, sugar and milk in a medium-size saucepan. Bring to simmering over medium heat, whisking constantly. Do not boil. Remove saucepan from heat and let cool. Fold in ricotta cheese and whipped cream.

6. Cut cake lengthwise into thirds and crosswise into tenths, making 30 pieces. Arrange half of cake pieces in bottom of a large serving dish, about 14 x 8 inches. Drizzle cake with half of liqueur. Spoon on half of cream mixture. Sprinkle with half of chopped chocolate. Repeat layering with remaining ingredients.

7. Cover and refrigerate overnight or up to 2 days. Serve cold.

Make-ahead tip: Cake can be made up to 1 month ahead, wrapped securely and frozen. Thaw at room temperature before using.

Tiramisu squares

Makes 15 squares   *Prep* 25 minutes   *Refrigerate* 3 hours

Taking advantage of purchased pound cake and a few other convenience products really reduces the prep time for this blissful dessert.

Per square

356 calories, 8 g protein, 22 g fat, 34 g carbohydrate, 203 mg sodium, 67 mg cholesterol.

1 envelope unflavored gelatin
¼ cup cold water
1 prepared marble or chocolate pound cake (14 ounces)
3 tablespoons coffee liqueur
2 packages (8 ounces each) cream cheese
1 container (15 ounces) ricotta cheese

1½ cups confectioners' sugar
3 tablespoons unsweetened cocoa powder
1 package (6 ounces) mini chocolate chips (1 cup)
Unsweetened cocoa powder for dusting

1. Sprinkle gelatin over cold water in a small saucepan; let stand 1 minute to soften. Stir over low heat until gelatin is dissolved, about 1 minute. Remove from heat.

2. Cut cake into scant ½-inch-thick slices. Fit slices in bottom of a 13 x 9 x 2-inch baking pan in a single layer, cutting and adding scraps to fit snugly. Drizzle liqueur over cake.

3. Process cream cheese, ricotta, confectioners' sugar and cocoa powder in a food processor or blender until smooth. Add gelatin mixture, processing to blend. Add chocolate chips; process just to combine. Scrape into cake-lined pan, spreading to cover cake. Cover pan with plastic wrap. Chill 3 hours or until set. Dust with cocoa powder; cut into squares.

Rich chocolate pudding

Makes 4 servings   *Prep* 10 minutes   *Cook* 6 to 10 minutes   *Refrigerate* 2 hours

Mascarpone is a fresh, thick, Italian sweet cheese, available in supermarket refrigerator cases. It gives this creamy pudding an out-of-this-world texture.

Per serving

477 calories, 9 g protein, 43 g fat, 19 g carbohydrate, 84 mg sodium, 326 mg cholesterol.

4 egg yolks
¼ cup sugar
6 tablespoons unsweetened cocoa powder

1 teaspoon vanilla
Pinch salt
½ pound mascarpone cheese
½ cup heavy cream

1. Whisk yolks and sugar in top of a double boiler over (not in) hot (not boiling) water until light, about 3 minutes. Continue whisking until mixture falls in ribbons when whisk is lifted above pan.

2. Whisk cocoa powder, vanilla, salt and mascarpone into egg mixture. Remove top of double boiler from hot water. Press waxed paper directly against surface of pudding. Refrigerate 2 hours.

3. Beat cream until stiff peaks form. Remove waxed paper from pudding and fold cream into pudding. Cover and keep chilled until ready to serve.

Butterscotch pudding

Makes 8 servings   *Prep* 10 minutes   *Cook* 5 minutes   *Refrigerate* 2 hours

A luscious classic.

Per serving
283 calories, 7 g protein,
11 g fat, 40 g carbohydrate,
90 mg sodium,
135 mg cholesterol.

Tempering yolks
To keep egg yolks from curdling when they're added to hot liquid, first heat them gradually by whisking a little of the hot liquid into them.

1½ cups packed light-brown sugar
½ cup all-purpose flour
2¼ cups evaporated milk
¾ cup water
4 egg yolks

2 tablespoons butter
2 teaspoons vanilla
  Whipped cream for garnish
  (optional)

1. Mix brown sugar and flour in a medium-size saucepan. Rub with fingers to blend. Whisk in evaporated milk and water. Bring to boiling; cook, stirring, until mixture is thick, 3 minutes. Remove from heat.

2. Place yolks in a medium-size bowl. Stir in ½ cup hot milk mixture. Stir yolk mixture into milk mixture in saucepan. Simmer over medium-low heat 1 to 2 minutes; do not boil. Remove from heat. Stir in butter and vanilla. Spoon into a clean bowl. Place in a larger bowl filled halfway with ice and water; cool about 5 minutes.

3. Spoon into 8 dessert glasses; cover with plastic wrap and refrigerate 2 hours. Garnish with whipped cream if desired.

Eggnog-mocha mugs

Makes 8 servings   *Prep* 10 minutes   *Cook* 12 minutes   *Refrigerate* about 2¾ hours

For the holidays or any time, turn party-favorite eggnog into a rich custard dessert.

Per serving
269 calories, 6 g protein,
19 g fat, 19 g carbohydrate,
58 mg sodium,
87 mg cholesterol.

2½ cups prepared eggnog
2 tablespoons sugar
1 envelope plus 1 teaspoon gelatin
½ teaspoon rum extract
2 squares (1 ounce each) semisweet chocolate, coarsely chopped

2 teaspoons unsweetened cocoa powder, sifted
1½ teaspoons instant coffee powder
1 teaspoon vanilla
1 cup heavy cream
  Cinnamon sticks, for garnish
  (optional)

1. Combine eggnog and sugar in a small saucepan. Sprinkle gelatin over eggnog; let stand 1 minute to soften. Stir over low heat until gelatin is dissolved, about 1 minute. Remove 1 cup mixture to a small bowl; stir in rum extract.

2. Add chocolate, cocoa powder and coffee powder to mixture in saucepan. Cook over low heat, stirring, until chocolate melts, 7 to 8 minutes. Add vanilla. Remove to a second small bowl.

3. Chill mixtures separately until they mound when stirred, 40 to 60 minutes; watch carefully and don't overchill or they will become lumpy.

4. Beat cream in a chilled bowl until stiff peaks form. Fold one-third of whipped cream into plain eggnog mixture and remaining two-thirds into chocolate mixture.

5. Divide chocolate mixture among eight 4- to 5-ounce glasses or cups. Top with plain mixture. Cover and refrigerate until set, about 2 hours.

Chocolate-walnut bread pudding

Makes 12 servings   *Prep* 25 minutes   *Bake* at 350° for 35 to 40 minutes

White chocolate adds a luxurious note to the sauce, but it can be temperamental to work with. Avoid subjecting it to high heat or it may separate.

Per serving
415 calories, 10 g protein,
28 g fat, 34 g carbohydrate,
193 mg sodium,
117 mg cholesterol.

6 cups cubed stale Italian bread
1 cup chopped walnuts, toasted
4 cups milk
3 tablespoons unsalted butter
¾ cup packed light-brown sugar
⅛ teaspoon salt
4 squares (1 ounce each) semisweet chocolate
1 square (1 ounce) unsweetened chocolate
4 eggs
2 teaspoons vanilla

White chocolate sauce
1 cup heavy cream
2 tablespoons granulated sugar
⅛ teaspoon salt
2 teaspoons cornstarch, dissolved in 1 tablespoon cold water
3 squares (1 ounce each) white baking chocolate
¼ teaspoon vanilla

1. Heat oven to 350°. Grease a shallow 2-quart baking dish with butter. Combine bread and walnuts in dish.

2. Combine 2 cups milk, butter, brown sugar and salt in a medium-size saucepan. Bring to simmering; stir until butter is melted. Remove from heat. Add semisweet and unsweetened chocolate; let stand 5 minutes. Whisk until smooth.

3. Whisk eggs, vanilla and remaining milk in a medium-size bowl. Whisk into chocolate mixture; pour over bread.

4. Bake in heated 350° oven 35 to 40 minutes or until set in center.

5. Prepare white chocolate sauce: Bring cream, sugar and salt to simmering in a small saucepan. Stir in cornstarch mixture; simmer, stirring, until cream is thickened, about 1 minute. Remove from heat. Stir in white chocolate and vanilla until smooth. Serve with warm or room-temperature pudding.

Rum-raisin bread pudding

Makes 12 servings *Prep* 20 minutes *Bake* at 325° for 1¼ hours

Low-fat milk and a fat-free egg substitute reshape this traditional comfort food into a dessert more nutritionally reasonable than the standard.

Per serving
221 calories, 7 g protein,
6 g fat, 36 g carbohydrate,
256 mg sodium,
12 mg cholesterol.

2 cups low-fat (1%) milk
1 cup whole milk
3 tablespoons unsalted butter
1 pound raisin bread, in pieces
1 tablespoon all-purpose flour
¼ teaspoon salt
¼ teaspoon ground cloves
¼ teaspoon ground nutmeg
1 container (8 ounces) cholesterol-free egg replacement
¾ cup sugar
⅓ cup rum
1 teaspoon vanilla

1. Heat oven to 325°. Coat a 13 x 9 x 2-inch baking dish with nonstick cooking spray.

2. Bring both milks and butter almost to boiling in a medium-size saucepan. Place bread in a large bowl. Pour milk over bread. Stir in flour, salt, cloves and nutmeg.

3. Mix together egg replacement, sugar, rum and vanilla in a small bowl. Add to bread mixture; stir until well mixed. Pour into prepared baking dish.

4. Bake in heated 325° oven 1 hour 15 minutes.

Rice pudding

Makes 4 servings *Prep* 5 minutes *Cook* 40 minutes *Cool* 30 minutes

To go easy on the pocketbook, purchase dried cranberries or cherries in bulk from a health food store or specialty herb shop. Keep a supply of either or both on hand—they're great for snacking.

Per serving
295 calories, 7 g protein,
2 g fat, 61 g carbohydrate,
96 mg sodium,
7 mg cholesterol.

3 cups low-fat (1%) milk
½ cup short-grain rice
½ cup maple syrup
¼ to ½ teaspoon ground cinnamon
¼ teaspoon ground nutmeg
½ cup dried cranberries or dried cherries
½ teaspoon vanilla

1. Bring milk to boiling in a covered large saucepan. Stir in rice. Lower heat; simmer, uncovered, stirring frequently, until rice is tender, about 25 minutes. Add a little more milk if rice starts to dry out. Stir in maple syrup, cinnamon and nutmeg. Cook, uncovered, 15 minutes longer.

2. Meanwhile, place cranberries in a small heatproof bowl. Add boiling water to cover; let stand 10 minutes or until cranberries are plumped. Drain.

3. Stir cranberries into hot rice. Cool mixture 30 minutes at room temperature. Stir in vanilla. Serving pudding warm or chilled.

Cherry and cheese Danish

Makes 16 Danish   *Prep* 15 minutes   *Bake* at 375° for 15 to 18 minutes

Pot cheese is fresh, similar to cottage cheese. Ready-to-use crescent-roll dough and canned cherry pie filling make this an easy-fix Danish you can whip up almost on the spur of the moment.

Per Danish
200 calories, 5 g protein, 9 g fat, 24 g carbohydrate, 267 mg sodium, 17 mg cholesterol.

1 package (8 ounces) pot cheese or cream cheese, at room temperature
¼ cup sugar
2 tablespoons all-purpose flour
2 teaspoons grated lemon rind
1 tablespoon fresh lemon juice
1 teaspoon vanilla

2 packages (8 ounces each) refrigerated crescent-roll dough
¾ can (21-ounce can) cherry pie filling
1 egg, lightly beaten with 1 tablespoon water
¼ cup sliced almonds

1. Combine pot cheese, sugar, flour, lemon rind, lemon juice and vanilla in a medium-size bowl. Stir with a wooden spoon until well blended and smooth.

2. Heat oven to 375°.

3. Unroll 1 package of dough and separate dough into 4 rectangles. On a lightly floured work surface, cut each rectangle crosswise in half to make 2 squares from each rectangle. Pinch together any perforations or holes in dough. Then stretch 2 opposite corners of each square slightly to lengthen dough and form flaps that will enclose filling. Transfer to an ungreased baking sheet.

4. Spoon 1 tablespoon cheese filling diagonally onto center of each square, at a right angle to stretched corners. Top with about 1 tablespoon cherry pie filling. Fold one of the flaps across mixture. Fold other flap across, overlapping first flap. Brush each Danish with egg and water mixture. Sprinkle with some of the almonds. Continue making more Danish with remaining crescent-roll dough, cheese filling and cherry pie filling, including second package of dough.

5. Bake in heated 375° oven until golden, 15 to 18 minutes. Cool on a wire rack.

Note: You can find pot cheese in the dairy section of some supermarkets and in specialty food shops.

Cherry clafouti

Makes 8 servings   *Prep* 10 minutes   *Bake* at 375° for 35 to 40 minutes

In this French country sweet, the cherries bake right in the batter, resulting in a cakelike dessert bursting with fruit.

Per serving
212 calories, 4 g protein,
6 g fat, 37 g carbohydrate,
25 mg sodium,
63 mg cholesterol.

4 cups pitted fresh cherries or
  2 bags (12 ounces each) frozen
  cherries, thawed and drained
½ cup milk
½ cup sugar
2 tablespoons all-purpose flour

2 eggs
2 tablespoons butter, melted
½ teaspoon almond extract
¼ cup sliced almonds
3 tablespoons confectioners' sugar

1. Heat oven to 375°. Grease a 10 x 1½-inch round baking dish or other shallow 1½-quart baking dish. Spoon cherries into dish.

2. Combine milk, sugar, flour, eggs, butter and almond extract in a food processor or blender. Whirl until pureed. Pour batter over cherries. Sprinkle with almonds.

3. Bake, uncovered, in heated 375° oven until top is golden and center is set, 35 to 40 minutes. Tent loosely with foil if top begins to brown too quickly. Cool to room temperature. Spoon confectioners' sugar into a small sieve; sprinkle over top. Serve warm or chilled.

Cherry clafouti

Citus soufflé

Plan your dinner so the soufflé emerges from the oven just when you're ready for dessert. A soufflé waits for no one!

Per serving
293 calories, 6 g protein,
5 g fat, 56 g carbohydrate,
153 mg sodium,
213 mg cholesterol.

¾ cup sugar, plus extra for coating
6 eggs
¼ teaspoon salt
1 tablespoon fresh lemon juice
¼ cup orange marmalade
1 tablespoon fresh lime juice
1 tablespoon orange liqueur
1 teaspoon grated lime rind
1 cup Marmalade Sauce (recipe follows)
Candied flowers for garnish (optional)

1. Heat oven to 350°.

2. Lightly coat a 6-cup soufflé dish or six 1-cup soufflé dishes with nonstick cooking spray. Add sugar to dish(es), shaking to coat sides and bottom evenly; tap out excess sugar.

3. Separate eggs and place whites in a medium-size bowl with salt and lemon juice. Place yolks in a second medium-size bowl.

4. Beat egg yolks until light in color, about 3 minutes. Beat in ½ cup sugar, marmalade, lime juice, orange liqueur and lime rind until light and fluffy, about 2 minutes.

5. With clean beaters, beat egg whites until foamy. Gradually beat in remaining ¼ cup sugar and beat until soft peaks form. Fold whites into yolk mixture just until combined. Scrape into prepared soufflé dish(es). If using a large soufflé dish, place in a shallow roasting pan; pour enough boiling water into roasting pan to reach a depth of 2 inches. (Small soufflé dishes can be baked directly on a baking sheet in oven, without a water bath.)

6. Bake in heated 350° oven until puffed and lightly browned, 40 to 50 minutes for large soufflé, 20 to 25 minutes for small soufflés.

7. Dust top of soufflé(s) with confectioners' sugar. Serve immediately with Marmalade Sauce. Garnish with candied flowers if you wish.

Marmalade sauce

Whisk together ½ cup orange marmalade, ½ cup apricot nectar, and 1 tablespoon orange liqueur in a small saucepan. Bring to simmering. Stir together 1 tablespoon water and 1 teaspoon cornstarch in a small bowl. Stir into saucepan; cook, stirring occasionally, 2 minutes or until sauce is thickened. Cover saucepan and set aside. Makes 1 cup.

Peach cobbler

Makes 4 servings *Prep* 15 minutes *Bake* at 400° for 20 minutes

Craving the taste of this cobbler during the winter months? Frozen sliced peaches make it possible. A splash of vanilla is as tasty as the almond extract. Shown on page 363.

Per serving
336 calories, 5 g protein, 7 g fat, 65 g carbohydrate, 553 mg sodium, 1 mg cholesterol.

1 pound peaches, peeled, pitted and cut into chunks
½ cup sugar
¼ teaspoon almond extract
½ teaspoon ground ginger
¼ teaspoon ground cinnamon
¼ teaspoon ground nutmeg
¼ teaspoon salt

Biscuit topping
1 cup all-purpose flour
1½ teaspoons baking powder
½ teaspoon salt
2 tablespoons solid vegetable shortening
⅓ cup low-fat (1%) milk
4 teaspoons sugar

1. Heat oven to 400°. Butter four 6-ounce custard cups.

2. Combine peaches, sugar, almond extract, ginger, cinnamon, nutmeg and salt in large bowl. Spoon mixture into custard cups.

3. Prepare biscuit topping: Stir together flour, baking powder and salt in a medium-size bowl. Cut in shortening with a pastry blender or 2 knives used scissor fashion until mixture resembles coarse crumbs. Stir in milk until mixture comes together, adding more milk, a tablespoon at a time, if necessary. Spoon topping evenly over peach filling. Sprinkle topping with sugar. Place custard cups on a baking sheet.

4. Bake in heated 400° oven until filling is bubbly and crust is golden, about 20 minutes. Tent with aluminum foil if tops begin to brown too quickly. Serve warm or at room temperature.

Apple-raspberry cobbler

Makes 8 servings *Prep* 25 minutes *Refrigerate* 30 minutes *Bake* at 375° for 40 minutes

This is a cobbler in disguise with a lattice top. Serve drizzled with a little heavy cream or top with a scoop of vanilla ice cream.

Per serving
342 calories, 4 g protein, 14 g fat, 52 g carbohydrate, 236 mg sodium, 63 mg cholesterol.

1¼ cups all-purpose flour
¾ cup sugar
2 teaspoons baking powder
Pinch salt
6 tablespoons cream cheese, chilled
6 tablespoons cold butter, cut into small pieces
3 tablespoons milk

1 egg yolk
1 teaspoon vanilla
3 Golden Delicious apples (1½ pounds total), peeled, cored and cut into ¼-inch-thick slices
1 package (12 ounces) frozen raspberries (about 3 cups)
4 teaspoons cornstarch

1. Combine 1 cup flour, ¼ cup sugar, baking powder and salt in a medium-size bowl. Cut in cream cheese and butter with a pastry blender or 2 knives used scissor fashion until mixture resembles coarse crumbs.

2. Combine milk, egg yolk and vanilla in a small bowl. Pour into flour mixture; stir just until mixed. If mixture is too wet, stir in remaining ¼ cup flour. Shape into a ball; cover with plastic wrap. Refrigerate 30 minutes.

3. Heat oven to 375°.

4. Combine apples, raspberries, remaining sugar and cornstarch in a large bowl. Transfer to an 8 x 8 x 2-inch baking pan; press filling down.

5. Roll out dough on a floured surface into a 12 x 10-inch rectangle. Trim to a 10 x 8-inch rectangle. Cut into eight 8 x 1¼-inch strips. Weave strips over top of fruit, 4 strips in each direction.

6. Bake in heated 375° oven 40 minutes or until browned and bubbly. Serve warm.

Winter fruit crisp

Makes 8 servings   *Prep* 35 minutes   *Bake* at 375° for 1 hour 10 minutes

Crisps have been around almost since the Pilgrims. Cut-up fruit mixed with sugar and flour is dumped into a baking dish and topped, in this case, with a mixture of bread cubes, butter and sugar that crisps during baking.

Per serving

343 calories, 2 g protein, 8 g fat, 71 g carbohydrate, 50 mg sodium, 16 mg cholesterol.

1 cup sugar
3 tablespoons all-purpose flour
3 large Golden Delicious apples (1½ pounds total), peeled, cored and sliced
2 large pears (1 pound total), peeled, cored and sliced
1½ cups fresh or thawed frozen cranberries
2 tablespoons fresh lemon juice

Topping
4 slices cinnamon-raisin bread, cubed
¼ cup (½ stick) unsalted butter, melted
½ cup sugar
½ teaspoon ground cloves
2 tablespoons sliced almonds

Vanilla ice cream (optional)

1. Heat oven to 375°.

2. Toss together sugar and flour in a large bowl until combined. Add apples, pears, cranberries and lemon juice, tossing until combined. Spoon into a 13 x 9 x 2-inch baking dish.

3. Prepare topping: Combine bread, butter, sugar, cloves and almonds in a large bowl. Sprinkle topping over fruit, leaving a 1-inch border of fruit showing around edge of dish. Tent loosely with aluminum foil. Place on a baking sheet.

4. Bake in heated 375° oven until bubbly and fruit in center of dish is tender when pierced with a fork, about 1 hour 10 minutes. Remove foil during last 30 minutes of baking. Cool until warm. Serve with vanilla ice cream if you wish.

Plum tart

Makes 8 servings   *Prep* 25 minutes

Bake tart shell at 400° for 15 minutes; then tart at 350° for 45 minutes

Although the lattice crust appetizingly frames the plum filling, you can leave the top crust solid, cutting a few steam vents in a circular pattern.

Per serving
478 calories, 7 g protein, 27 g fat, 56 g carbohydrate, 140 mg sodium, 47 mg cholesterol.

Almond Pastry (recipe follows)
6 medium plums (about 1½ pounds), pitted and sliced
½ cup plus 2 tablespoons sugar
2 teaspoons fresh lemon juice
1 teaspoon ground cinnamon
1 teaspoon ground ginger
¼ teaspoon salt
2 tablespoons milk

1. Heat oven to 400°.

2. Divide pastry dough in half; return one half to refrigerator. Roll out remaining half on a lightly floured surface into a 12-inch round; press over bottom and up sides of a 9-inch tart pan with removable bottom. Place pastry-lined tart pan in freezer 15 minutes.

3. Remove pan from freezer; line with aluminum foil. Fill with dried beans or weights. Bake in heated 400° oven 15 minutes. Remove foil and beans. Cool on wire rack. Lower oven temperature to 350°.

4. Combine plums, ½ cup sugar, lemon juice, cinnamon, ginger and salt in a medium-size bowl. Spoon into tart shell.

5. Roll out remaining dough into a 9-inch round. Cut dough into fourteen ¾-inch-wide strips. Place 7 strips, about ½ inch apart, over plum filling. Place other 7 strips at a right angle and weave together to make a lattice top. Trim ends of strips almost even with tart pan; press ends of strips to inside edge of tart shell to seal. Brush pastry strips with milk; sprinkle with remaining 2 tablespoons sugar.

6. Bake in heated 350° oven 45 minutes or until pastry is golden and filling is bubbly. Tent with foil if tart begins to brown too quickly. Cool on a wire rack 30 minutes. Remove sides of pan. Serve warm or at room temperature.

Almond pastry

Combine 2 cups all-purpose flour, 1 cup finely ground almonds, ¼ cup sugar and ¼ teaspoon salt in a medium-size bowl. Cut in ¾ cup (1½ sticks) unsalted butter with a pastry blender or 2 knives used scissor fashion until mixture resembles coarse meal. Sprinkle with 3 to 4 tablespoons cold water, a tablespoon at a time, mixing with a fork just until pastry holds together. Cover with plastic wrap and refrigerate until ready to use, at least 30 minutes; let warm slightly before rolling out.

Blueberry tartlets

Makes 6 tartlets   *Prep* 20 minutes   *Bake* at 400° for 40 minutes

Blueberry filling is wonderfully aromatic with a tumble of spices. If you're playing beat the clock, use prepared tartlet shells.

Per serving
276 calories, 3 g protein,
11 g fat, 44 g carbohydrate,
264 mg sodium,
0 mg cholesterol.

Single-Crust Pie Pastry (recipe, page 384)
3 cups blueberries
½ cup sugar
2 tablespoons all-purpose flour
1 tablespoon fresh lemon juice
2 teaspoons grated lemon rind
1 teaspoon ground ginger
½ teaspoon ground cinnamon
¼ teaspoon ground nutmeg
¼ teaspoon salt

1. Heat oven to 400°.

2. Roll out dough on a floured surface with a floured rolling pin. Cut dough into six 5-inch rounds. Fit dough into six 4-inch tartlet shells with removable bottoms. Refrigerate tartlet shells while preparing filling.

3. Combine blueberries, sugar, flour, lemon juice, lemon rind, ginger, cinnamon, nutmeg and salt in a large bowl. Spoon into tartlet shells. Place aluminum foil on bottom of oven to catch drips.

4. Bake in heated 400° oven until filling is bubbly and pastry is golden, about 40 minutes. Tent with foil if pastry browns too quickly.

Blueberry tartlets

Single-crust pie pastry

Makes one 9-inch crust   *Prep* 20 minutes   *Refrigerate* 30 minutes

Preparing a single-crust pie is a good way to get the great taste of pastry with fewer calories than in a double-crust pie.

1¼ cups all-purpose flour
½ teaspoon salt
¼ cup (½ stick) cold unsalted butter, cut into small pieces
¼ cup solid vegetable shortening, chilled and cut into small pieces
3 to 4 tablespoons cold water

1. Mix flour and salt in a medium-size bowl.

2. Cut in butter and shortening with a pastry blender or 2 knives used scissor fashion until mixture resembles coarse meal.

3. Sprinkle cold water, 1 tablespoon at a time, over mixture, mixing lightly with a fork after each addition, until pastry is just moist enough to hold together.

4. Shape and flatten dough into a disc. Cover with plastic wrap. Refrigerate until well chilled, about 30 minutes. To blind-bake, see box (opposite).

Preparing pie pastry

1. With a pastry blender, cut butter and shortening into flour. Continue cutting until texture resembles coarse meal.

2. Slowly add ice water, a bit at a time, to flour mix. Combine with a fork.

3. Shape dough into 1 or 2 balls as directed in recipe, then press each ball into a disc. Wrap; chill 30 minutes.

4. On a lightly floured surface, roll chilled dough into a round 3 inches bigger than the top of your pie plate.

5. Carefully roll pastry around rolling pin so you can lift and transfer to pie plate without tearing.

6. Place rolled pastry over pie plate; gently unroll. Press pastry into plate without stretching.

To flute edge: Using both hands, pinch stand-up edge of pastry between thumbs and index fingers.

To scallop edge: Press stand-up edge of pastry with back of a spoon.

Pie crust savvy

To make pie crust in a food processor

COMBINE FLOUR and salt in a food processor fitted with the steel blade. Pulse just to mix. Add butter and shortening. Whirl until mixture has texture of coarse meal, about 30 seconds. With machine running, add cold water in a slow and steady stream just until mixture begins to form a ball. Proceed with step 4 of Double- or Single-Crust Pie Pastry recipe.

To blind-bake a pie shell

HEAT OVEN to 400°. Roll out chilled pastry into a 12-inch round on a floured surface. Fit into a 9-inch pie plate. Fold excess dough under to form a stand-up edge; flute edge. Prick bottom with a fork. Line inside with aluminum foil. Fill with pie weights.

Bake in lower third of heated 400° oven 15 minutes. Carefully remove foil and weights. Return to oven 10 to 15 minutes or until light golden brown.

Remove pie shell from oven. Cool completely on a wire rack before filling.

Double-crust pie pastry

Makes two 9-inch crusts *Prep* 20 minutes *Refrigerate* 30 minutes

This crust recipe is simply the best—half butter for flavor and half vegetable shortening for flakiness.

2½ cups all-purpose flour
1 teaspoon salt
½ cup (1 stick) cold unsalted butter, cut into small pieces
½ cup solid vegetable shortening, chilled and cut into small pieces
6 to 7 tablespoons cold water

1. Mix flour and salt in a medium-size bowl.

2. Cut in butter and shortening with a pastry blender or 2 knives used scissor fashion until mixture resembles coarse meal.

3. Sprinkle cold water, 1 tablespoon at a time, over mixture, mixing lightly with a fork after each addition, until pastry is just moist enough to hold together.

4. Divide pastry in half; shape each half into a disc. Cover with plastic wrap. Refrigerate until well chilled, about 30 minutes.

Sour cherry pie

Makes 12 servings   *Prep* 30 minutes   *Refrigerate* 30 minutes   *Cook* 5 minutes

Bake at 400° for 40 to 50 minutes

¾ cup sugar
5 tablespoons cornstarch
3 cans (16 ounces each) water-packed pitted tart red cherries, drained (reserve ½ cup liquid)

1 teaspoon almond extract
Double-Crust Pie Pastry (recipe, page 385)

1. Combine sugar and cornstarch in a medium-size saucepan. Stir in reserved ½ cup cherry liquid. Bring to boiling, stirring constantly; cook 3 to 5 minutes or until thickened. Remove from heat; stir in almond extract and cherries. Cool.

2. Heat oven to 400°.

3. For bottom crust, roll out one disc of dough on a floured surface into a 12-inch round. Fit into a 9-inch pie plate. Trim off excess dough. Spoon cherry mixture into prepared crust.

4. For lattice, roll out second disc of dough until ⅛ inch thick; cut into eight ¾-inch-wide strips. Place 4 strips parallel to one another over pie. Fold every other strip back halfway from center. Place fifth strip over pie, slightly off center and perpendicular to others. Flip back folded pieces over crosspiece. Fold alternate strips back; place second crosspiece over top. Flip folded strips back over crosspiece. Rotate pie; continue to weave 2 more strips into pattern. Press ends to inside of bottom crust to seal. Flute edge.

5. Bake in heated 400° oven until crust is golden and filling is bubbly, 40 to 50 minutes. If crust browns too quickly, cover edge with strips of aluminum foil for last 20 minutes of baking. Cool on a wire rack.

Berry basics

FRESH BERRIES may be the sweetest treat of summer; make the best of them.

Purchase: Strawberries that are deep crimson with fresh green caps. Raspberries, blueberries and blackberries should be plump, firm and unblemished.

Store: Discard blemished fruit, then store berries, loosely wrapped and unwashed, in the refrigerator for a few days. For longer storage, arrange unwashed berries in a single layer on a baking sheet; freeze 2 hours until solid. Place in a plastic food-storage bag; press out excess air and seal. Use within 2 months.

Strawberry-rhubarb pie

Makes 10 servings   *Prep* 15 minutes   *Stand* 20 minutes   *Bake* at 375° for 1 hour

One slice and you'll instantly remember why this spring combination is so terrific: tart rhubarb melds perfectly with sweet strawberries.

Per serving
348 calories, 3 g protein, 17 g fat, 47 g carbohydrate, 216 mg sodium, 3 mg cholesterol.

4 cups strawberries, hulled and halved
1 pound rhubarb (without tops), cut into ½-inch pieces, or 2 cups frozen rhubarb, thawed
1 cup sugar
3 tablespoons quick-cook tapioca
2 teaspoons chopped crystallized ginger
½ teaspoon ground cinnamon
¼ teaspoon salt
  Double-Crust Pie Pastry (recipe, page 385)
1 tablespoon butter or margarine

1. Combine strawberries, rhubarb, sugar, tapioca, ginger, cinnamon and salt in a large bowl. Let stand 20 minutes.

2. Heat oven to 375°. Line a baking sheet with aluminum foil.

3. Roll out one disc of dough on a well-floured surface into an 11-inch round. Fit into a 9-inch pie plate. Trim pastry even with edge of pan. Spoon filling into pie crust. Dot with butter.

4. Roll out second disc of dough into an 11-inch round. Place over filling. Make a decorative edge. Cut vents in top. Place on baking sheet.

5. Bake in heated 375° oven 1 hour or until crust is golden. Tent with foil if browning too quickly. Remove to a wire rack to cool.

Sour cherry pie
opposite

Peach crumble pie

Makes 8 servings   *Prep* 20 minutes   *Refrigerate* 30 minutes   *Cook* 10 minutes

Bake at 450° for 10 minutes; then at 350° for 45 minutes

Use the sinfully rich cream cheese crust for other fruit-filled pies. Dried and frozen fruit can be used, so this pie can be made year-round.

Per serving
565 calories, 7 g protein, 36 g fat, 57 g carbohydrate, 314 mg sodium, 86 mg cholesterol.

3 ounces dried peaches or dried apricots, chopped
2 tablespoons peach nectar or apple cider
5 ripe peaches (2 pounds total), peeled, pitted and sliced, or 1 package (20 ounces) frozen peach slices, completely thawed
¼ cup packed brown sugar
¼ cup all-purpose flour
¼ cup (½ stick) butter, melted
2 tablespoons fresh lemon juice

½ teaspoon ground cinnamon
Cream Cheese Pastry (recipe follows)

Topping
1 cup all-purpose flour
½ cup finely chopped walnuts
½ cup packed brown sugar
½ teaspoon ground cinnamon
Pinch salt
6 tablespoons cold butter, cut into small pieces

1. Combine chopped dried peaches and peach nectar in a medium-size saucepan. Simmer over medium-low heat 10 minutes or until peaches are softened. Set aside to cool. Combine fresh peaches, brown sugar, flour, butter, lemon juice and cinnamon in a large bowl. Add cooled dried peaches. Set aside.

2. Heat oven to 450°.

3. Roll out dough into a 12-inch round. Fit into a 9-inch pie plate. Fold excess dough under to form a stand-up edge; flute edge. Refrigerate while preparing topping.

4. Prepare topping: Combine flour, walnuts, brown sugar, cinnamon and salt in a medium-size bowl. Work in butter with your fingertips until mixture is crumbly and large pieces of butter are no longer visible. (Or chop walnuts in a food processor. Add flour, brown sugar, cinnamon and salt; pulse. Add butter and pulse until mixture is crumbly.)

5. Spoon peach mixture into prepared pie shell. Sprinkle topping over all.

6. Bake pie on a baking sheet in heated 450° oven 10 minutes. Lower oven temperature to 350°. Bake 45 minutes more or until filling is bubbly and topping is golden brown. Remove pie to a wire rack to cool slightly.

Cream cheese pastry

Beat 4 ounces cream cheese and ½ cup (1 stick) butter in a medium-size bowl on medium speed until smooth and creamy. On low speed, beat in 1 cup flour until mixture comes together. Pat dough into a disc; cover with plastic wrap. Refrigerate 30 minutes.

Classic apple pie

Makes 8 servings   *Prep* 25 minutes   *Cook* 10 minutes

Bake at 450° for 10 minutes; then at 350° for 45 to 55 minutes

When you want a taste of Americana, bake up this classic—it's a guaranteed winner.

Per serving

550 calories, 5 g protein, 27 g fat, 74 g carbohydrate, 277 mg sodium, 62 mg cholesterol.

Apple types

• McIntosh are tender, juicy, aromatic and sweet. They're great for snacks or good mixed with other types in baked desserts.
• Granny Smiths are crisp and tart. They're a wonderful all-purpose apple.
• Golden Delicious are crisp, mild and sweet. Use them fresh or cooked.
• Empire are a cross between Red Delicious and McIntosh. Choose them for cooking or snacking.
• Jonagold are crisp, juicy, sweet-tart. They're best baked in pies or other desserts.
• Rome are crisp and somewhat tart. They hold up well for baking or cooking.

Double-Crust Pie Pastry (recipe, page 385)
⅔ cup sugar
2 tablespoons cornstarch
½ teaspoon ground cinnamon
Pinch ground nutmeg
Pinch ground cloves

6 assorted McIntosh, Golden Delicious and Granny Smith apples (3 pounds total)
1 tablespoon fresh lemon juice
1 tablespoon unsalted butter
1 egg, slightly beaten

1. Heat oven to 450°.

2. For bottom crust, roll out one disc of dough on a well-floured surface into a 12-inch round, ⅛ inch thick. Fit into a 9-inch pie plate. Refrigerate while preparing filling.

3. Combine sugar, cornstarch, cinnamon, nutmeg and cloves in a small bowl.

4. Keeping McIntosh apples separate, peel, core and slice apples ⅛ inch thick. Place McIntosh apples in one bowl, the remaining apples in a second bowl. Drizzle lemon juice over both bowls of apples.

5. Toss McIntosh apples with ¼ cup of sugar mixture; set aside. Toss Granny Smith and Golden Delicious apples with remaining sugar mixture.

6. Melt butter in a large skillet. Scrape Golden Delicious–Granny Smith mixture into skillet; sauté 10 minutes or until softened. Cool to room temperature.

7. Once the sautéed apples are cooled, combine with raw McIntosh apples. Arrange apple mixture in dough-lined pan, packing apples as tightly as possible. Brush edge of dough with beaten egg.

8. For top crust, roll out second disc of dough on a well-floured surface into an 11-inch round. Cut out a 1-inch hole in center of dough. Center dough over apple mixture. Trim dough to a ¼-inch overhang. Crimp top and bottom edges together. Brush top crust with beaten egg.

9. Bake on bottom rack in heated 450° oven 10 minutes. Lower oven temperature to 350°. Bake 45 to 55 minutes more. If crust begins to brown too quickly, cover loosely with aluminum foil for last 10 minutes of baking. Serve warm from oven or cool pie on a wire rack to room temperature. If you wish, reheat briefly at 350° to serve warm.

Apple galette

Our galette is nothing more than a rustic open-faced tart. Peaches, pears, plums and nectarines are other filling choices.

Per serving
157 calories, 2 g protein,
7 g fat, 22 g carbohydrate,
92 mg sodium,
18 mg cholesterol.

3 Golden Delicious apples (1½ pounds total), peeled, cored and thinly sliced
1 tablespoon fresh lemon juice
¼ cup plus 1 tablespoon sugar
1 tablespoon all-purpose flour
1 teaspoon ground cinnamon

Single-Crust Pie Pastry (recipe, page 384)
1 tablespoon unsalted butter
1 tablespoon milk
1 tablespoon chopped walnuts
1 tablespoon apricot preserves

1. Combine apples with lemon juice in a medium-size bowl. Stir in ¼ cup sugar, flour and cinnamon.

2. Roll out dough on a lightly floured surface into a 14-inch round. Roll dough back onto rolling pin; unroll onto an ungreased large baking sheet.

3. Heat oven to 400°.

4. Mound filling onto dough, leaving a 2½-inch border. Cut butter into pieces and dot over filling. Fold border up over filling, working all the way around. Brush edge with milk. Sprinkle with 1 teaspoon sugar and nuts.

5. Bake in heated 400° oven until filling is hot and crust is golden, about 40 minutes.

6. Meanwhile, heat apricot preserves over low heat in a small saucepan just until melted. Brush top of galette evenly with preserves.

Apple galette

Cappuccino mousse pie

Makes 8 servings   *Prep* 25 minutes   *Refrigerate* 3 hours or overnight

Per serving
461 calories, 5 g protein,
30 g fat, 42 g carbohydrate,
166 mg sodium,
138 mg cholesterol.

Lump-free gelatin
**Always first soften
gelatin in water or
other liquid. Then
dissolve it over very
low heat, stirring.
You'll be guaranteed of
thoroughly dissolved
gelatin without lumps.**

1 envelope unflavored gelatin
¾ cup double-strength brewed
 coffee, cooled
1 teaspoon espresso powder or 2
 teaspoons instant coffee powder
½ cup sugar
2 egg yolks
⅓ cup coffee liqueur
¼ cup egg white powder (see Note,
 below)
¼ cup cold water
1½ cups heavy cream
 Chocolate Cookie Crust, baked
 and cooled (recipe follows)
 Chocolate-covered espresso beans
 and unsweetened cocoa powder
 for garnish

1. Sprinkle gelatin over ¼ cup coffee in a small bowl. Let stand about 5 minutes to soften.

2. Heat remaining ½ cup coffee, espresso powder and sugar in a small saucepan to barely simmering; stir in gelatin mixture to dissolve. Remove from heat. Whisk in egg yolks. Cook over low heat just until thickened; do not boil.

3. Remove from heat. Stir in liqueur. Spoon into a clean bowl. Place in a larger bowl filled halfway with ice and water; cool, stirring occasionally, until mixture is consistency of raw egg whites.

4. Meanwhile, beat egg white powder and water in a small bowl until peaks form. Beat cream in a medium-size bowl until stiff peaks form.

5. Fold beaten egg white mixture into coffee mixture. Fold in 1 cup whipped cream; reserve remaining whipped cream for garnish. Scrape mixture into cooled baked pie shell, spreading evenly. Chill at least 3 hours or overnight.

6. To serve, garnish with remaining whipped cream and espresso beans. Dust with cocoa powder.

Note: Egg white powder is available in select supermarkets, gourmet shops, and health-food stores. Because of health concerns about eating raw eggs, it's our choice for this uncooked filling.

Chocolate cookie crust

Crumble 30 chocolate wafer cookies; you should have 1½ cups crumbs. Combine crumbs and ¼ cup sugar in a small bowl. Melt 6 tablespoons (¾ stick) butter; stir into crumb mixture until blended. Coat a 9-inch pie plate with nonstick cooking spray. Scrape crumb mixture into pie plate; pat in an even layer over bottom and up sides of plate. Bake in heated 350° oven 7 minutes. Transfer to a wire rack to cool.

Banana cream pie

Makes 8 servings   *Prep* 20 minutes   *Cook* 10 minutes   *Refrigerate* 4 hours

Shout "Banana cream pie" in a crowded room and watch the reaction! The custard filling is all egg yolks for incredible richness, with banana puree stirred into the filling and sliced banana on top.

Per serving
452 calories, 7 g protein, 26 g fat, 49 g carbohydrate, 324 mg sodium, 193 mg cholesterol.

¾ cup sugar
⅓ cup cornstarch
2½ cups milk
5 egg yolks
1 tablespoon butter
1 tablespoon vanilla
3 large ripe bananas
  Single-Crust Pastry, blind-baked and cooled (recipe, page 384)
1½ cups heavy cream

1. Mix ½ cup sugar and cornstarch in a medium-size heavy saucepan. Add milk; cook, stirring, over medium heat until thickened, 5 minutes. Remove saucepan from heat.

2. Stir egg yolks lightly in a small bowl. Slowly stir 1 cup hot mixture into yolks. Slowly whisk yolk mixture into saucepan. Return to medium heat. Bring to boiling, stirring constantly. Cook, stirring, 3 to 5 minutes or until very thick. Remove from heat. Stir in butter and 2 teaspoons vanilla. Place plastic wrap directly on surface. Cool 15 minutes.

3. Slice 1 banana; arrange slices in a single layer over bottom of pie shell. Mash second banana in a bowl; stir into custard filling. Pour into crust. Place plastic wrap directly on filling. Refrigerate 4 hours or until firm.

4. Beat cream and remaining ¼ cup sugar and 1 teaspoon vanilla in a large bowl until stiff peaks form. Uncover pie. Top with whipped cream. Slice third banana and garnish pie with slices.

Chocolate cream pie

Makes 12 servings   *Prep* 20 minutes   *Refrigerate* 2 hours

You could use a packaged chocolate pudding mix for the filling, but our old-fashioned homemade version makes all the difference in the world.

Per serving
356 calories, 6 g protein, 23 g fat, 31 g carbohydrate, 165 mg sodium, 114 mg cholesterol.

½ cup sugar
2 tablespoons cornstarch
1 envelope unflavored gelatin
¼ teaspoon salt
2 cups milk
4 egg yolks
1 teaspoon vanilla
6 squares (1 ounce each) semisweet chocolate, chopped
  Single-Crust-Pastry, blind-baked and cooled (recipe, page 384)

Topping
1 cup heavy cream
2 tablespoons confectioners' sugar
1 teaspoon vanilla
  Chocolate curls (optional)

1. Combine sugar, cornstarch, gelatin and salt in a medium-size heavy saucepan. Stir in milk. Cook, stirring constantly, over medium heat until mixture is thickened. Remove saucepan from heat.

2. Stir egg yolks lightly in a small bowl. Stir in ½ cup hot mixture. Slowly pour yolk mixture back into saucepan, stirring with a wire whisk to keep lumps from forming. Return saucepan to heat. Cook over low heat, stirring constantly, about 2 minutes or until mixture is very thick; do not boil. Remove saucepan from heat. Add chocolate and stir until chocolate is melted.

3. Pour filling into pie shell. Place plastic wrap directly on surface of filling. Refrigerate 2 hours or until filling is thoroughly chilled.

4. Prepare topping: Combine cream, confectioners' sugar and vanilla in a medium-size bowl. Beat on medium speed until soft peaks form. Spoon on top of pie. Scatter chocolate curls over top of pie if desired.

Strawberry black-bottom pie

Makes 8 servings *Prep* 30 minutes *Refrigerate* 5 hours or up to 1 day

Hiding under the cheese filling is a thin layer of melted chocolate on top of a vanilla cookie crust— that's the black bottom.

Per serving

423 calories, 7 g protein, 22 g fat, 55 g carbohydrate, 191 mg sodium, 34 mg cholesterol.

8 ounces milk-chocolate chips (1¼ cups)
3 tablespoons milk
2 teaspoons vanilla
1 prepared vanilla cookie crumb crust or Shortbread Cookie Crust (recipe, page 397)
12 ounces light cream cheese, at room temperature

½ cup confectioners' sugar
1½ pint baskets strawberries (4¾ cups), hulled
⅓ cup seedless raspberry jam
Whipped cream for garnish (optional)
Melted semisweet chocolate for garnish (optional)

1. Melt together chocolate chips and milk in a small saucepan over very low heat, stirring occasionally, until smooth. Remove from heat. Stir in 1 teaspoon vanilla. Pour chocolate mixture into prepared crust, spreading until level. Refrigerate until chocolate is firm to the touch.

2. Blend together cream cheese, confectioners' sugar and remaining 1 teaspoon vanilla until smooth. Spread evenly over chocolate layer in crust. Arrange strawberries on top of cheese layer, pointed ends up.

3. Melt jam in a small skillet over low heat until smooth. Brush melted jam over strawberries. Spoon on remaining jam to cover cheese layer. Refrigerate, covered, 5 hours or up to 1 day. Serve with whipped cream and drizzle with melted chocolate if you wish.

Caramel pumpkin pie

Makes 12 servings   *Prep* 15 minutes   *Cook* caramel about 5 minutes

Bake crust at 425° for 13 to 15 minutes; pie at 425° for 10 minutes, then at 325° for 45 minutes

Be sure to use solid-pack pumpkin puree, not pie filling, which can have additives, including sugar.

Per serving
335 calories, 3 g protein, 19 g fat, 39 g carbohydrate, 281 mg sodium, 91 mg cholesterol.

Double-Crust Pie Pastry (recipe, page 385)
½ cup evaporated milk
¼ cup granulated sugar
1 cup heavy or light cream
¾ cup packed dark-brown sugar
2 tablespoons honey
2 cups canned pumpkin puree (not pie filling)
1 tablespoon cornstarch
1 teaspoon ground cinnamon
½ teaspoon ground nutmeg
⅛ teaspoon ground cloves
¼ teaspoon salt
3 eggs, at room temperature
2 teaspoons vanilla
Whipped cream for garnish (optional)

1. Position rack in bottom third of oven. Heat oven to 425°.

2. Roll out one disc of dough on a well-floured surface into an 11-inch round. Fit into a 9-inch pie plate. Cut out leaf shapes from other disc of dough. Line pie shell with aluminum foil; fill with dried beans or rice. Place on a baking sheet with leaf cutouts.

3. Bake in heated 425° oven 8 to 10 minutes or until light brown. Remove foil with beans; remove leaves to a wire rack to cool. Return pie shell to oven. Bake until bottom sets, pricking with a fork any places that bubble up, about 5 minutes. Remove to a rack to cool. Leave oven on.

4. In a small saucepan, heat evaporated milk until small bubbles appear around edge of pan. Remove from heat.

5. Prepare caramel: Place granulated sugar in a large heavy saucepan. Heat over medium heat, without stirring, until sugar begins to melt. Tilt pan all around and continue melting until syrup is medium brown, 1 to 2 minutes. Remove from heat. Carefully add hot milk all at once; mixture will bubble up, then subside. Stir in cream, brown sugar and honey; stir to dissolve sugar. If clumps do not dissolve, simmer briefly, stirring, 2 minutes. Cool to room temperature.

6. Place pumpkin puree in a large bowl. Sprinkle with cornstarch, cinnamon, nutmeg, cloves and salt; stir to blend. Whisk in eggs, one at a time. Stir in caramel and vanilla. Turn filling into pie shell. Place on baking sheet.

7. Bake in heated 425° oven 10 minutes. Lower oven temperature to 325°. Continue to bake about 45 minutes or until center of filling is set. Turn oven off. Leave pie in oven with door partially open. Let cool completely, 2 hours. Garnish top with pastry leaves. Serve with whipped cream if you wish.

Pecan pie

Makes 8 servings   *Prep* 10 minutes   *Bake* at 350° for 45 to 50 minutes

Looks like any other pecan pie, but wait— there are butterscotch chips all melty on top of the crust.

Per serving
542 calories, 6 g protein,
37 g fat, 52 g carbohydrate,
216 mg sodium,
69 mg cholesterol.

Single-Crust Pie Pastry (recipe, page 384)
½ cup butterscotch chips
2 cups pecan pieces

¼ cup (½ stick) unsalted butter, melted
½ cup sugar
½ cup light corn syrup
2 eggs

1. Heat oven to 350°.

2. Roll out one disc of dough on a well-floured surface into an 11-inch round. Fit into a 9-inch pie plate. Crimp edges. Scatter butterscotch chips and pecan pieces in pie shell.

3. Beat together butter, sugar, corn syrup and eggs in a medium-size bowl. Pour over nuts and butterscotch chips.

4. Bake in heated 350° oven 45 to 50 minutes or until golden brown. If pie browns too quickly, cover with aluminum foil after 20 minutes. Cool pie completely on a wire rack.

Caramel pumpkin pie
opposite

Lemon meringue pie

Makes 8 servings   *Prep* 15 minutes   *Cook* 10 minutes   *Bake* at 350° for 15 minutes

Refrigerate 4 hours

Twice the usual amount of airy meringue makes this pie extraordinary.

Per serving
343 calories, 4 g protein, 13 g fat, 54 g carbohydrate, 153 mg sodium, 88 mg cholesterol.

Meringue magic
The key to any successful meringue pie is to make sure the meringue touches the crust all around the edge, sealing the top. Otherwise, the meringue will shrink during baking.

1 cup sugar
¼ cup cornstarch
1½ teaspoons grated lemon rind
¼ cup fresh lemon juice
1⅔ cups water
2 tablespoons unsalted butter, cut into pieces
3 egg yolks

Single-Crust Pie Pastry, blind-baked and cooled (recipe, page 384)

Meringue
4 egg whites
¼ teaspoon cream of tartar
½ cup plus 1 tablespoon sugar

1. Heat oven to 350°.

2. Stir together sugar and cornstarch in a medium-size saucepan until well blended. Gradually stir in lemon rind and juice until smooth. Mix in water and butter; cook over medium heat, stirring constantly, until mixture is thickened and then boils for 1 minute. Remove saucepan from heat.

3. Stir egg yolks lightly in a small bowl. Stir in about half of hot mixture. Slowly pour yolk mixture into saucepan, stirring with a wire whisk to keep lumps from forming. Return saucepan to heat. Cook over medium-low heat, stirring constantly, 1 to 2 minutes or until mixture thickens slightly and temperature registers 160° on an instant-read thermometer. Pour mixture into pie shell.

4. Prepare meringue: Combine egg whites and cream of tartar in a medium-size bowl. Beat on medium speed until soft peaks form. Then gradually beat in sugar, 1 tablespoon at a time, and continue to beat until stiff peaks form.

5. Spread meringue over hot filling so it touches pie crust all around edge.

6. Bake in heated 350° oven until meringue is lightly browned and temperature in center of meringue registers 160° on an instant-read thermometer, about 15 minutes. Remove to a wire rack and cool to room temperature. Refrigerate until chilled, 4 hours or overnight. Serve cold.

Lemon tart with berries

Makes 12 servings   *Prep* 20 minutes   *Cook* 6 to 10 minutes   *Stand* 45 minutes   *Refrigerate* 2 hours

The filling for this tart is a lemon curd, which is a cooked concoction of lemon juice, sugar, butter and egg yolks, although here we add whole eggs as well. Cook slowly over very low heat, stirring constantly, or you'll have a saucepan of sweetened scrambled eggs.

Per serving

327 calories, 3 g protein, 24 g fat, 28 g carbohydrate, 99 mg sodium, 142 mg cholesterol.

2 eggs
3 egg yolks
¾ cup sugar
½ cup fresh lemon juice
1 tablespoon grated lemon rind
½ cup (1 stick) cold unsalted butter, cut into pieces

Shortbread Cookie Crust (recipe follows)

Garnish
½ cup heavy cream, whipped
   Fresh raspberries and blackberries
   Fresh mint sprigs (optional)

1. Stir together eggs, egg yolks, sugar, lemon juice and lemon rind in a medium-size heavy saucepan. Cook over low heat 6 to 10 minutes, stirring constantly, until thickened and just beginning to simmer; do not boil. Do not overstir or stir too vigorously, or mixture will separate. Place pan in a large bowl of cold water. Stir in butter until blended. Place plastic wrap directly on surface of pudding. Cool 45 minutes.

2. Pour filling into cookie crust. Refrigerate to chill thoroughly, about 2 hours.

3. To serve, spoon whipped cream into a pastry bag fitted with star tip. Pipe cream onto tart. Arrange berries on top. Garnish with fresh mint sprigs if desired.

Shortbread cookie crust

Place 30 square shortbread cookies in a food processor. Whirl until finely crumbed; you should have about 2 cups of cookie crumbs. Add 6 tablespoons unsalted butter and ¼ cup confectioners' sugar. Whirl until combined. Scrape into a 9-inch tart pan with removable bottom, pressing evenly over bottom and up sides. Refrigerate until firm.

Chocolate-raspberry truffle tart

Makes 12 servings   *Prep* 30 minutes   *Refrigerate* 4 hours

A no-bake tart with a double chocolate whammy! The crust is made with chocolate wafer cookies, but where's the chocolate truffle? The melted chocolate and heavy cream filling hiding under the raspberry topping.

Per serving
312 calories, 3 g protein, 20 g fat, 32 g carbohydrate, 86 mg sodium, 40 mg cholesterol.

25 chocolate wafer cookies
5 tablespoons unsalted butter, at room temperature
½ cup seedless raspberry jam

8 squares (1 ounce each) semisweet chocolate, chopped
1 cup heavy cream
2 cups raspberries

1. Place cookies in a food processor. Whirl until finely ground. Or place cookies in a large plastic food-storage bag; crush with a rolling pin until finely ground. Mix together crumbs and butter in a medium-size bowl. Press over bottom and up sides of a 9-inch tart pan with removable bottom.

2. Heat jam in a small saucepan over low heat just until melted. Pour over bottom of tart shell. Place in freezer for 15 minutes.

3. Meanwhile, heat chocolate and cream in a small saucepan over low heat until chocolate is melted and smooth. Pour into tart shell. Refrigerate until chocolate is set, about 4 hours.

4. Arrange berries on top. Refrigerate until ready to serve.

Chocolate-raspberry truffle tart

Berry-topped ice cream pie

Makes 8 servings *Prep* 20 minutes *Bake* crust at 350° for 20 to 35 minutes *Freeze* 3 hours

14 round buttery crisp crackers, finely crushed (about ½ cup)
⅔ cup walnuts, finely chopped
3 egg whites
⅛ teaspoon salt
½ cup sugar
1½ pints vanilla ice cream or vanilla frozen yogurt (3 cups), softened
½ pint blueberries (about 1¼ cups)
½ pint raspberries (about 1¼ cups)
1 cup strawberries, hulled and quartered
¼ cup currant jelly, melted
2 squares (1 ounce each) semisweet chocolate, melted
Fresh mint sprigs for garnish (optional)

1. Heat oven to 350°. Coat a 9-inch pie plate with nonstick cooking spray. Combine crackers and walnuts in a small bowl. Dust pie plate with 2 tablespoons cracker mixture.

2. Place egg whites in a large bowl; beat on medium-high speed until foamy. Add salt; beat until soft peaks form. Gradually beat in sugar until stiff peaks form. Gently fold in remaining cracker mixture until just blended. Spoon meringue into pie plate; form a crust by spreading meringue from center to edges to cover pie plate completely.

3. Bake in heated 350° oven 20 to 25 minutes or until meringue is golden brown. Transfer to a wire rack to cool completely.

4. Spoon softened ice cream into cooled meringue-cracker crust. Cover with plastic wrap and freeze 3 hours or until ice cream is firm.

5. Meanwhile, combine blueberries, raspberries, strawberries and melted jelly in a large bowl; gently toss to coat completely.

6. To serve, spoon berry mixture over top of pie, mounding berries in the center. Drizzle with melted chocolate. Garnish with mint sprigs if you wish.

DESSERTS AND CANDY

Old-fashioned vanilla ice cream

Makes 5 cups *Prep* 5 minutes *Cook* 5 to 8 minutes *Refrigerate* 3 hours *Freeze* 1 hour

No additives, just the basics: milk, sugar, egg yolks, heavy cream and, of course, a splash of vanilla. This is what vanilla ice cream should be about—plainly rich and unadorned.

Per ½ cup
316 calories, 4 g protein, 21 g fat, 29 g carbohydrate, 45 mg sodium, 157 mg cholesterol.

2 cups milk
1¼ cups sugar
4 egg yolks

2 cups heavy cream
1¼ teaspoons vanilla

1. Stir together milk, sugar and egg yolks in a medium-size heavy saucepan. Heat over low heat, stirring constantly with a wooden spoon until mixture registers 180° on instant-read thermometer, 5 to 8 minutes; do not boil. Mixture will thicken slightly but will not coat a spoon.

2. Strain mixture through a sieve into a bowl. Cover; refrigerate until well chilled, 3 hours. Stir in cream and vanilla.

3. Freeze mixture in an ice cream maker according to manufacturer's directions. Transfer to a bowl, cover and place in freezer at least 1 hour.

Strawberry ice cream

Per ½ cup
203 calories, 2 g protein, 13 g fat, 19 g carbohydrate, 28 mg sodium, 98 mg cholesterol.

Prepare Old-Fashioned Vanilla Ice Cream through step 2. Coarsely chop 1 cup hulled strawberries. Puree another 1 cup hulled strawberries in a food processor. Stir chopped strawberries and berry puree into cream mixture. Freeze mixture in an ice cream maker according to manufacturer's directions. Transfer to a bowl, cover and place in freezer at least 1 hour. Makes 7 cups.

Choco-cookie ice cream

Per ½ cup
321 calories, 4 g protein, 20 g fat, 32 g carbohydrate, 116 mg sodium, 131 mg cholesterol.

Prepare Old-Fashioned Vanilla Ice Cream through step 2. Pulse 10 cream-filled chocolate sandwich cookies in a food processor until broken into small pieces. Stir cookies into cream mixture. Freeze mixture in an ice cream maker according to manufacturer's directions. Transfer to a bowl, cover and place in freezer at least 1 hour. Makes 6 cups.

Lorene Smith's peach ice cream

Makes 8 servings *Prep* 45 minutes *Freeze* 1 hour

The real thing, with old-fashioned rich taste: heavy cream and egg yolks. Nectarines are an appealing substitute.

Per serving

399 calories, 6 g protein, 18 g fat, 59 g carbohydrate, 326 mg sodium, 159 mg cholesterol.

4 egg yolks
1¾ cups sugar
¼ cup all-purpose flour
1 teaspoon salt

3 cups milk
1 cup heavy cream
3 cups peeled, sliced ripe peaches

1. Combine egg yolks, 1½ cups sugar, flour and salt in large saucepan. Add ¼ cup milk, stirring to form a paste. Gradually add remaining milk; cook over low heat, stirring frequently, until mixture is pudding-like in consistency. Pour into canister of an ice cream maker. Press waxed paper on top of custard. Cool in refrigerator.

2. Remove waxed paper and add cream to cooled custard. Freeze in ice cream maker according to manufacturer's directions.

3. Meanwhile, gently mash peaches with ¼ cup sugar. When ice cream begins to stiffen, add peaches. Process until ice cream is difficult to turn. Transfer to a bowl, cover and place in freezer at least 1 hour.

Hot fudge sauce

Makes 1½ cups *Prep* 5 minutes *Cook* 10 minutes

Make a batch, maybe even a double batch, and store in the refrigerator for those midnight ice cream attacks.

Per 2 tablespoons

136 calories, 1 g protein, 8 g fat, 16 g carbohydrate, 6 mg sodium, 21 mg cholesterol.

½ cup heavy cream
¼ cup (½ stick) unsalted butter
½ cup granulated sugar
½ cup packed light-brown sugar

½ cup unsweetened cocoa powder
2 squares (1 ounce each) semisweet chocolate, chopped
1 teaspoon vanilla

1. Heat cream, butter, sugars, cocoa powder and chocolate in a medium-size saucepan over medium-low heat, stirring, until smooth and sugars are melted, 10 minutes. Remove from heat. Stir in vanilla.

2. Serve warm. Store, tightly covered, in refrigerator up to several days. To warm, place over hot water and stir.

Rocky road ice cream extravaganza

While this layered ice cream bombe takes some time to assemble, most of it is unattended as layers set up in the freezer. And the results? Guests will be screaming for just one more bite.

Per serving
253 calories, 4 g protein, 10 g fat, 39 g carbohydrate, 106 mg sodium, 27 mg cholesterol.

2 pints vanilla ice cream
¾ cup chocolate wafer crumbs (about 12 wafers)
¾ cup chocolate syrup
½ cup mini marshmallows
¼ cup dry-roasted peanuts, chopped
1 cup maraschino cherries, drained, stemmed, cut in half and patted dry

1 pint chocolate ice cream
Hot Fudge Sauce (recipe, page 401)
Fresh mint sprigs for garnish (optional)
Maraschino cherries for garnish (optional)

1. Place 1 pint vanilla ice cream in refrigerator to soften. Line a 2-quart mixing bowl with plastic wrap.

2. Combine ½ cup wafer crumbs and ½ cup syrup in a small bowl. Combine remaining ¼ cup crumbs, ¼ cup syrup and the mini marshmallows and peanuts in another small bowl.

3. Transfer softened vanilla ice cream to a medium-size bowl. Stir in maraschino cherries. Spoon into prepared bowl, smoothing top. Spoon wafer-syrup mixture over top, smoothing until level. Cover and place in freezer until firm, at least 1 hour.

4. Transfer remaining 1 pint vanilla and 1 pint chocolate ice cream to refrigerator to soften.

5. When ice cream in bowl is firm, spread softened chocolate ice cream over top, smoothing until level. Sprinkle with marshmallow-peanut mixture. Spread remaining vanilla ice cream over top. Cover and freeze at least 6 hours or overnight.

6. To serve, quickly dunk bowl halfway into warm water to loosen dessert. Invert onto a chilled serving plate; remove bowl. Peel off plastic wrap. Top with Hot Fudge Sauce. Garnish with mint sprigs and maraschino cherries if desired.

**Rocky road ice cream
extravaganza**
opposite

Peanut-butter-swirl ice cream cake

Makes 16 servings   *Prep* 25 minutes   *Freeze* 6 hours or overnight

This is such a show-stopper! As if the ice cream-cookie-peanut-butter filling weren't enough—the chocolate-dipped wafer cookies around the sides move it into a whole new realm of dessert delight.

Per serving
496 calories, 8 g protein,
29 g fat, 54 g carbohydrate,
269 mg sodium,
40 mg cholesterol.

½ gallon vanilla ice cream
24 cream-filled chocolate sandwich cookies
5 tablespoons butter, melted
29 chocolate-dipped wafer cookies

⅔ cup peanut butter (not reduced-fat)
¼ cup honey
2 tablespoons vegetable oil
½ cup bottled or homemade Hot Fudge Sauce (recipe, page 401)

1. Remove ice cream from freezer 30 minutes before using. Place chocolate sandwich cookies in a food processor. Whirl until crumbed. Add butter. Whirl until combined.

2. Stand wafer cookies around inside edge of a 9-inch springform pan. Reserve ¾ cup chocolate crumb mixture. Spoon remaining crumb mixture into pan; press evenly over bottom.

3. Stir peanut butter, honey and oil in a small bowl until blended. Place softened ice cream in a large bowl. Drizzle about half of peanut butter mixture onto ice cream; fold together to swirl.

4. Spoon half of ice cream mixture into prepared pan; spread until level. Sprinkle evenly with reserved chocolate crumb mixture, pressing mixture down with back of spoon.

5. Spoon on remaining ice cream; spread until level. Place cake on a baking sheet and place in freezer. Freeze until cake is solid, at least 6 hours or overnight.

6. To serve, stir fudge sauce in a glass measuring cup to loosen, but do not warm. Spoon remaining peanut butter in blobs over top of cake along with blobs of fudge sauce. Swirl together with tip of a knife. Let stand 10 minutes.

7. Remove sides of springform pan and slice cake into wedges.

Pineapple-mango ice

Here's a basic recipe for an ice that will accommodate practically any fruit.

Per ½ cup
108 calories, trace protein, trace fat, 28 g carbohydrate, 19 mg sodium, 0 mg cholesterol.

2 cups cubed pineapple (fresh or juice-packed canned)
1 cup cubed mango
½ cup water
¼ cup light corn syrup
¼ cup honey
1 tablespoon fresh lemon juice
2 to 3 tablespoons sugar (optional; to taste)

1. Blend pineapple, mango, water, corn syrup, honey and lemon juice in a food processor or blender until smooth. Taste; add sugar by tablespoonfuls if needed. Pour into a 9 x 9 x 2-inch baking pan. Freeze 2 hours or until firm.

2. Cut frozen mixture into cubes. Place in processor or blender. Whirl until smooth, scraping down bowl as needed. Place in chilled airtight freezer container. Freeze up to 2 months.

Blueberry-blackberry ice

Per ½ cup
123 calories, trace protein, trace fat, 27 g carbohydrate, 24 mg sodium, 0 mg cholesterol.

Substitute 2 cups blueberries for the pineapple and 1 cup blackberries for the mango in basic recipe above. Blend, freeze and puree in the same way. Makes 3 cups.

Honeydew-kiwi ice

Per ½ cup
103 calories, trace protein, trace fat, 27 g carbohydrate, 24 mg sodium, 0 mg cholesterol.

Substitute 2 cups cubed honeydew for the pineapple and 1 cup cubed, peeled kiwi for the mango in basic recipe above. Blend, freeze and puree in the same way. Makes 3½ cups.

Watermelon-strawberry ice

Per ½ cup
92 calories, trace protein, trace fat, 23 g carbohydrate, 19 mg sodium, 0 mg cholesterol.

Substitute 2 cups cubed, pitted watermelon for the pineapple and 1 cup sliced strawberries (scant pint) for the mango in basic recipe above. Blend, freeze and puree in the same way. Makes 3½ cups.

DESSERTS AND CANDY

Festive fruit-ice mold

Makes 12 servings   *Prep* 15 minutes   *Freeze* each of 3 layers for 3 hours

A grand production that can be the centerpiece of a summer party. And there's no fat. If you don't have a kugelhopf pan, a bundt pan or ring mold will do nicely.

Per serving
110 calories, trace protein, trace fat, 28 g carbohydrate, 21 mg sodium, 0 mg cholesterol.

3 cups Blueberry-Blackberry Ice (recipe, page 405), softened
3 cups Pineapple-Mango Ice (recipe, page 405), softened

2 cups Watermelon-Strawberry Ice (recipe, page 405), softened
Strawberries, raspberries, kiwi slices, peach slices and mint leaves for garnish

1. Spoon Blueberry-Blackberry Ice into an 8-cup kugelhopf pan. Spread in an even thickness around tube in center of pan. Freeze at least 3 hours or until firm.

2. Spoon Pineapple-Mango Ice into mold, packing well to remove any air spaces; spread top until level. Freeze at least 3 hours or until firm.

3. Spoon Watermelon-Strawberry Ice into mold, packing well to remove any air space; spread top until level. Freeze at least 3 hours or until firm.

4. To unmold, fill with cool water a pan large enough to hold kugelhopf pan. Dip kugelhopf pan in the cool water about 30 seconds. Run a thin knife around sides of pan. Invert onto a serving dish, giving pan a good shake to release the ice. If necessary, repeat process. Garnish with fruit and mint leaves. To serve, slice with a thin knife.

Summer fruit salad

Makes 10 cups   *Prep* 10 minutes

Berries, berries, berries! That's what this salad is about. And it's easily transportable too.

Per serving
118 calories, 1 g protein, 1 g fat, 29 g carbohydrate, 5 mg sodium, 0 mg cholesterol.

2 pints strawberries, hulled, halved if large
1 pint blueberries
1 pint raspberries
1 pint blackberries

2 kiwis, peeled and cut into 1-inch chunks
⅔ cup maple syrup
⅓ cup fresh orange juice
1 tablespoon chopped fresh mint

1. Combine strawberries, blueberries, raspberries, blackberries and kiwis in a large bowl.

2. Whisk maple syrup, orange juice and mint in a small bowl. Pour over berries; toss gently to coat.

Roasted pears with maple-orange sauce

Makes 6 servings   *Prep* 10 minutes   *Cook* 10 minutes   *Roast* at 425° for 40 minutes

For complete decadence, spoon the sauce on its own over bowls of vanilla ice cream or slices of pound cake.

Per serving
331 calories, 1 g protein,
14 g fat, 54 g carbohydrate,
70 mg sodium,
43 mg cholesterol.

6 Bosc pears
3 tablespoons butter, melted
2 tablespoons sugar

Maple-orange sauce
¾ cup pure maple syrup
2 tablespoons Grand Marnier or other orange-flavored liqueur
½ cup heavy cream

1. Heat oven to 425°.

2. Peel pears; cut in half lengthwise. Using a melon baller or small spoon, scoop out core. Place each pear half, cut side down, in a metal roasting pan or on a baking sheet with sides. Brush pears with half of melted butter. Sprinkle with sugar. Brush again with melted butter.

3. Roast pears in heated 425° oven 15 minutes. Brush pears again with melted butter or with any juices that have collected in roasting pan. Roast another 15 minutes. Flip pears over so cut side is face up. Baste again. Roast another 10 minutes.

4. Meanwhile, prepare sauce: Combine maple syrup and Grand Marnier in a small saucepan. Bring to simmering over medium-low heat. Cook until reduced to ½ cup, about 10 minutes. Remove saucepan from heat. Stir in heavy cream.

5. To serve, arrange 2 pear halves on each plate. Pour some sauce over each plate.

Roasted pears with maple-orange sauce

Nut chocolate bark

Makes 12 servings   *Prep* 25 minutes

For chocolate lovers, this is about as good as it gets—nuts and chocolate. For a handsome gift, package the bark in a wooden box.

Per serving
142 calories, 2 g protein, 10 g fat, 12 g carbohydrate, 16 mg sodium, 4 mg cholesterol.

8 ounces milk chocolate, bittersweet chocolate or white chocolate, chopped

¾ teaspoon vegetable oil (for use with white chocolate only)
¾ cup pecans, almonds or pistachios, toasted and chopped

1. Coat a baking sheet evenly and lightly with nonstick cooking spray.

2. Place chocolate in a microwave-safe bowl; if using white chocolate, add oil. Microwave at 100% power, checking every 30 seconds, until melted. Stir until smooth. (Or melt chocolate in top of a double boiler over barely simmering, not boiling, water, stirring until smooth.) Stir in nuts. Scrape onto prepared baking sheet; spread in an even layer, 8 to 9 inches square, distributing nuts evenly through the chocolate.

3. Let bark stand until completely cooled. Break or cut into pieces. Store bark pieces in an airtight container in a cool, dry place up to 1 month.

Milk chocolate crunch

Makes 4½ dozen squares (1-inch)   *Prep* 10 minutes   *Microwave* 2 minutes   *Refrigerate* 2 hours

We all grew up with those famous crisp rice cereal confections. Here's a version with chocolate and raisins.

Per square
52 calories, 1 g protein, 2 g fat, 7 g carbohydrate, 11 mg sodium, 2 mg cholesterol.

2 milk chocolate bars (7 ounces each), chopped

1½ cups crisp rice cereal
1 cup dark raisins

1. Line bottom of an 8 x 8 x 2-inch pan with aluminum foil; smooth out wrinkles.

2. Place chocolate in a microwave-safe bowl. Microwave at 100% power, checking every 30 seconds, until melted. Stir chocolate until smooth.

3. Stir cereal and raisins into chocolate until well combined. Spread mixture evenly in prepared pan. Refrigerate about 2 hours or until mixture is firm.

4. Invert pan onto a work surface; remove pan and peel off aluminum foil. Cut into squares and serve. Squares can be stored in an airtight container in refrigerator up to 2 weeks.

About chocolate

CHOCOLATE starts as a bean from the tropical cacao tree. When roasted and ground, the beans become chocolate liquor (a paste); when cooled, this becomes baking chocolate. Chocolate liquor is also processed into cocoa butter and cocoa powder.

Unsweetened (baking) chocolate: Bitter, dark and brittle. You wouldn't want to eat it on its own, but used in baked goods, it delivers lots of rich flavor.

Cocoa powder: Unsweetened chocolate with about 75% of the fat removed. In Dutch-process cocoa, the chocolate is treated with a mild alkali, which causes the cocoa to become less intense, darker and more easily mixed into liquid. (3 tablespoons cocoa powder + 1 tablespoon vegetable shortening = 1 square baking chocolate)

Bittersweet and semisweet chocolate: Partially sweetened blends of chocolate liquor, cocoa butter and sugar; tend to vary in flavor and sweetness (and name) depending upon the manufacturer. Excellent for eating or cooking.

Sweet chocolate: Dark, fully sweetened blend of chocolate liquor, cocoa butter and sugar. Excellent for eating or cooking.

Milk chocolate: Fully sweetened blend of chocolate liquor, cocoa butter and sugar plus milk or cream and vanilla. Excellent for eating or cooking.

White chocolate: Blend of cocoa butter, milk, sugar and flavoring, without any chocolate liquor. Very mild and sweet flavored, but difficult to melt—watch carefully and be sure not to overheat.

Melting chocolate

CHOCOLATE SHOULD BE melted carefully to keep it from curdling, separating or scorching; take particular care to avoid getting any water in chocolate or it will seize. Here are failsafe techniques.

To melt on the stovetop: Place chocolate squares in a heavy saucepan over the lowest heat or in the top of a double boiler over (not in) simmering water. With a wooden spoon or spatula, stir constantly until chocolate is just melted.

To melt in the microwave: Place chocolate squares in a microwave-safe bowl; do not cover. Microwave on 100% power for 30 seconds. Remove and stir; if only partially melted, repeat microwaving.

- When preparing a recipe, use the melting technique specified if there is one; otherwise, use either technique.
- When you want to melt chocolate completely, begin with squares. When heated, chips become gooey inside but retain their shape—save them for cookies and cakes.

White and dark chocolate apricots

Makes 24 candies *Prep* 1 hour *Toast* hazelnuts at 350° for 10 minutes

Microwave 2 minutes *Refrigerate* 3 hours

These are unbelievably good! Dried apricots stuffed with a hazelnut or pistachio and then coated with dark or white chocolate. Keep these out of your own reach or no one else may have a chance to enjoy.

Per piece
68 calories, 1 g protein,
4 g fat, 8 g carbohydrate,
5 mg sodium,
1 mg cholesterol.

Storage fact
When refrigerated, chocolate may develop a little "bloom"—a white or gray discoloration—on the surface, but this in no way affects the flavor.

12 hazelnuts
24 dried whole apricots
12 pistachio nuts, shelled

4 squares (1 ounce each) semisweet chocolate, chopped
4 squares (1 ounce each) white baking chocolate, chopped

1. Heat oven to 350°. Line a baking sheet with aluminum foil or waxed paper.

2. Spread hazelnuts on a jelly-roll pan and toast in oven about 10 minutes or until lightly golden. When hazelnuts are cool enough to handle but still warm, rub lightly between paper toweling to remove skins; discard skins.

3. Place apricots on prepared baking sheet. Gently loosen open edge; insert a hazelnut or pistachio in center of each apricot. Press edges together to seal. Keep hazelnut- and pistachio-stuffed apricots separate.

4. Place 3 squares semisweet chocolate in a small microwave-safe bowl. Cover with plastic wrap. Microwave at 100% power 1 minute. Stir until smooth. Stir in remaining semisweet chocolate until well blended and smooth.

5. Using a fork, spear a hazelnut-stuffed apricot; dip into melted semisweet chocolate, turning to coat completely; shake off excess chocolate by gently tapping fork on edge of bowl. Return to baking sheet. Repeat with remaining hazelnut-stuffed apricots. Set aside remaining semisweet chocolate.

6. Repeat steps 4 and 5, substituting white chocolate and the pistachio-stuffed apricots.

7. Refrigerate coated apricots 3 hours or until chocolate is firm.

8. Microwave remaining semisweet chocolate at 50% power 30 seconds or until drizzling consistency. Drizzle over white-chocolate-coated apricots. Refrigerate on baking sheets to harden. Repeat with reserved white chocolate; drizzle over semisweet-coated apricots. Store in an airtight container in a cool, dry place up to 1 week.

Chocolate peanut-butter balls

Makes 3½ dozen   *Prep* 20 minutes   *Microwave* 1 minute   *Refrigerate* 2 hours   *Stand* 2 hours

Pop one of these candies into your mouth and encounter the lushness of peanut butter. When melting chocolate in the microwave, check frequently because the chocolate may appear solid even after it's softened.

Per piece
82 calories, 2 g protein, 5 g fat, 9 g carbohydrate, 44 mg sodium, 1 mg cholesterol.

1 cup chunky peanut butter
½ cup dark corn syrup
1 cup crisp rice cereal

8 ounces milk chocolate, broken into pieces
¼ cup finely chopped peanuts

1. Beat peanut butter and corn syrup in a medium-size bowl until well blended. Stir in cereal until well mixed.

2. Using rounded teaspoon, shape mixture into balls. Place on a large baking sheet lined with aluminum foil. Chill several hours or until firm.

3. Place 6 ounces of chocolate in a medium-size microwave-safe bowl. Cover with plastic wrap. Microwave at 100% power 1 minute. Stir chocolate until melted and smooth. Add remaining chocolate and continue stirring until smooth and well blended.

4. Using a fork, spear a peanut-butter ball; dip into chocolate, turning to coat completely; shake off excess chocolate by gently tapping fork on edge of bowl. Return to baking sheet. Repeat with remaining balls. If chocolate thickens too much, microwave at 50% power 30 seconds or until soft.

5. Let stand about 2 hours or until chocolate is almost firm. Sprinkle tops with finely chopped peanuts. Let stand until hardened.

Chocolate peanut-butter balls

White and dark chocolate apricots *opposite*

Cognac-laced truffles

Makes 3½ dozen truffles *Prep* 25 minutes *Freeze* 30 minutes

The chocolate candy center is made with three chocolates: semisweet, unsweetened and white. What else is there to say? Refrigerate in an airtight container for up to 1 month. But serve at room temperature for best flavor.

Per truffle
76 calories, 1 g protein,
5 g fat, 8 g carbohydrate,
3 mg sodium,
4 mg cholesterol.

¼ cup cognac
½ cup heavy cream
11 squares (1 ounce each) semisweet chocolate, chopped
3 squares (1 ounce each) white baking chocolate, chopped
1 square (1 ounce) unsweetened chocolate, chopped

¾ cup confectioners' sugar

Coating
2 tablespoons unsweetened cocoa powder
2 tablespoons confectioners' sugar

1. Line 2 baking sheets with waxed paper. Heat cognac in a small saucepan just to simmering. Remove from heat. Add cream. Bring to simmering.

2. Place all the chocolate and ¾ cup confectioners' sugar in a food processor and whirl 1 to 2 minutes or until finely chopped. With machine running, add cream mixture in a steady stream. Process until smooth. Scrape into a medium-size bowl. Refrigerate just until thick enough to hold shape, about 1 hour.

3. Drop by rounded teaspoonfuls onto prepared baking sheets. With your hands, quickly shape into balls. (Refrigerate to firm while working if necessary.) Place in freezer 30 minutes.

4. Prepare coating: Sift cocoa powder and confectioners' sugar into a small bowl. Add truffles, 3 at a time; toss to coat. Refrigerate in airtight containers up to 1 month. Serve at room temperature.

Cashew brittle

Makes 1½ pounds *Prep* 10 minutes *Cook* 30 minutes

Witness huge smiles when guests bite into this treat.

Per 1-ounce serving
137 calories, 2 g protein,
5 g fat, 23 g carbohydrate,
116 mg sodium,
0 mg cholesterol.

1 cup sugar
1 cup water
1 cup light corn syrup

2 cups cashews
1 teaspoon vanilla
½ teaspoon baking soda

1. Grease a 17 x 11 x 1 inch jelly-roll pan

2. Combine sugar, water and corn syrup in a large heavy saucepan. Cook, stirring occasionally, over medium-high heat until temperature registers 275° or soft-crack stage on a candy thermometer, about 20 minutes (mixture will form pliable strands when drizzled from a metal spoon).

3. Stir in cashews. Continue cooking, stirring occasionally to keep nuts from scorching, until temperature reaches 305° (hard-crack stage), 5 to 7 minutes longer (mixture will be amber-colored and, when dropped into ice water and removed and bent, will snap). Remove saucepan from heat. Quickly stir in vanilla and baking soda.

Quick as can be
The trick to making brittle is to work fast—very fast. You need to stretch the brittle thin before it hardens.

3. Stir in cashews. Continue cooking, stirring occasionally to keep nuts from scorching, until temperature reaches 305° (hard-crack stage), 5 to 7 minutes longer (mixture will be amber-colored and, when dropped into ice water and removed and bent, will snap). Remove saucepan from heat. Quickly stir in vanilla and baking soda.

4. Pour onto prepared pan, pushing brittle to edges with back of a wooden spoon. As candy cools, stretch it out until thin by lifting and pulling from edges, using 2 forks. When brittle is completely cooled, loosen from pan; break into pieces.

5. Store in an airtight container at room temperature up to 1 month.

Spiced brownie brittle

Makes 24 pieces   *Prep* 15 minutes   *Bake* at 375° for 10 minutes

Top broken pieces with a scoop of vanilla ice cream, a drizzle of chocolate sauce, a puff of whipped cream, a dusting of grated chocolate, and a maraschino cherry for a dessert that will please anyone.

Per piece
79 calories, 1 g protein, 6 g fat, 6 g carbohydrate, 3 mg sodium, 19 mg cholesterol.

½ cup (1 stick) unsalted butter
1 square (1 ounce) unsweetened chocolate, broken into pieces
½ teaspoon ground ginger
½ teaspoon ground cinnamon
¼ teaspoon black pepper
½ cup sugar
¼ teaspoon vanilla
1 egg
⅓ cup all-purpose flour
½ cup ground pecans, almonds or walnuts

1. Heat oven to 375°.

2. Melt butter in a large saucepan over medium heat. Add chocolate, ginger, cinnamon and pepper. Remove from heat; stir until chocolate is melted.

3. Stir in sugar, vanilla and egg until smooth. Stir in flour and mix well.

4. Pour batter into a 15 x 10 x 1-inch jelly-roll pan. Tilt pan back and forth, allowing batter to flow into a thin, even layer across bottom of pan. Use a spatula to spread if necessary. Scatter nuts over top.

5. Bake in 375° oven 10 minutes or until cake is just set. Remove to a wire rack to cool 20 minutes.

6. Cut or break into 24 rough-shaped pieces as you would a nut brittle. Use a spatula if necessary to remove from pan. Store in airtight container at room temperature up to 1 month.

Boston cream pie *page 417*

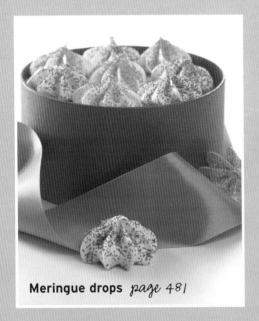
Meringue drops *page 481*

MORE OFTEN than not, cakes are a testament to the skill and patience of their maker. The quest for the tenderest of layers, the most delectable of flavors, the just-so swirls of frosting spurs the showman in now-and-then and avid bakers alike.

Why not a Sacher Torte to satisfy your sophisticated side or a whimsical Carousel Cake to bring out the kid in you? Or give in to that craving for chocolate with a luscious Marble Fudge Cake or the divine Chocolate Intensity. There are plenty of spectacular possibilities for special days too: Valentine's Day, Easter, the

Besides flour, butter, sugar and eggs, the most important ingredient is love

Fourth of July and, of course, Christmas. But for those times when you just can't wait for everyone else before indulging, cookies are the obvious solution. Oatmeal Apricot Thumbprints, Best-Ever Chocolate Chips, Peaches and Cream Bars, whatever your pleasure. Rest assured no one will notice if the batch is short is a cookie or two.

cakes and cookies

Double chocolate cake

Makes 15 servings *Prep* 25 minutes *Bake* at 375° for 35 to 40 minutes

This is a pull-out-all-the-stops layer cake. There's chocolate in the buttermilk batter as well as chocolate in the cream cheese frosting.

Per serving
404 calories, 7 g protein,
21 g fat, 52 g carbohydrate,
326 mg sodium,
75 mg cholesterol.

2 cups sifted all-purpose flour
2 teaspoons baking soda
¼ teaspoon salt
½ cup (1 stick) unsalted butter or margarine, softened
¾ cup granulated sugar
¾ cup firmly packed light-brown sugar
3 eggs

3 squares (1 ounce each) unsweetened chocolate, melted
½ cup buttermilk
1 cup boiling water
1 tablespoon vanilla
Chocolate Cream Cheese Frosting (recipe follows)
Fresh strawberries and white chocolate, for garnish (optional)

1. Heat oven to 375°. Grease and flour two 9-inch round cake pans.

2. Sift together flour, baking soda and salt onto a sheet of waxed paper.

3. Beat together butter and sugars in a large bowl until light and fluffy. Add eggs, one at a time, beating well after each addition. Beat in chocolate.

4. Add dry ingredients to butter mixture alternately with buttermilk in 3 additions. Add boiling water and vanilla; mix until smooth (batter will be thin). Pour into pans, dividing evenly.

5. Bake in heated 375° oven 35 to 40 minutes or until a wooden pick inserted in center comes out clean. Cool layers in pans on wire racks 15 minutes. Loosen cake layers around edges with a small spatula; turn out onto wire racks to cool completely.

6. Fill and frost cooled layers with Chocolate Cream Cheese Frosting. If you wish, garnish cake with strawberries dipped in white chocolate that has been melted over hot (not boiling) water.

Chocolate cream cheese frosting

Beat together 1½ packages (8 ounces each) light cream cheese, 6 squares (1 ounce each) melted unsweetened chocolate, 1 teaspoon vanilla and ⅛ teaspoon salt in a medium-size bowl until creamy and smooth. Gradually beat in 3 cups sifted confectioners' sugar alternately with 2 to 3 tablespoons milk until blended and a good spreading consistency. Makes 4 cups.

Boston cream pie

Makes 10 servings   *Prep* 30 minutes   *Bake* at 350° for 25 minutes   *Cook* 5 minutes

Refrigerate 4 hours

Looks like a pie, sort of, but it's really layers of spongy cake filled with vanilla custard and extravagantly topped with a rich chocolate glaze.

Shown on page 414.

Per serving

325 calories, 6 g protein, 10 g fat, 56 g carbohydrate, 244 mg sodium, 98 mg cholesterol.

Sponge cake

1½ cups sifted cake flour
1½ teaspoons baking powder
½ teaspoon salt
3 eggs, separated
1 cup sugar
⅓ cup water
1 teaspoon vanilla

Filling

⅓ cup sugar
¼ cup all-purpose flour
⅛ teaspoon salt
1 cup milk
1 egg
1 teaspoon vanilla

Chocolate Glaze (recipe follows)

1. Prepare cake: Heat oven to 350°. Line bottom of two 8-inch round cake pans with waxed paper.

2. Sift flour, baking powder and salt onto a sheet of waxed paper.

3. Beat egg whites in a medium-size bowl until soft peaks form. Beat in ½ cup sugar 1 to 2 minutes or until stiff peaks form.

4. Beat egg yolks and remaining ½ cup sugar in a large bowl until thickened and light in color. Beat in water and vanilla. Fold in egg whites. Fold in flour mixture in 2 additions. Scrape into pans.

5. Bake in heated 350° oven 25 minutes or until tops spring back when lightly touched. Cool pans on wire racks 20 minutes. Turn cakes out onto racks to cool completely. Peel off waxed paper.

6. Prepare filling: Mix sugar, flour and salt in a medium-size saucepan. Stir in ¾ cup milk. Heat over medium heat, whisking constantly, until mixture boils; cook 2 minutes. Remove from heat. Whisk together remaining milk and egg. Whisk mixture into saucepan. Return to heat. Cook, stirring, 1 minute. Stir in vanilla. Cover with plastic wrap, pressing on surface to prevent a film. Refrigerate 3 hours.

7. To assemble, invert a cake layer onto a serving plate. Stir cooled filling; spread over layer. Invert second cake layer on top. Spoon Chocolate Glaze on top of cake; spread until level, allowing some of glaze to flow over edge. Refrigerate 1 hour.

Chocolate glaze

Melt 3 tablespoons unsalted butter and 2 ounces unsweetened chocolate in a small saucepan over low heat, stirring occasionally. Stir in 1 tablespoon corn syrup and 2 tablespoons water until blended. Stir in 1 cup confectioners' sugar until smooth. Makes 1 cup.

Chocolate intensity

A flourless recipe that makes a very rich, candylike dessert. How much caffeine in chocolate? One cup brewed coffee, 125 mg; 1 cup tea, about 40 mg; 1 ounce chocolate, about 17 mg.

Per serving

285 calories, 4 g protein, 23 g fat, 19 g carbohydrate, 13 mg sodium, 139 mg cholesterol.

1 cup milk
16 squares (1 ounce each) semisweet chocolate, finely chopped
1 cup (2 sticks) butter or margarine
2 tablespoons brandy

1 tablespoon vanilla
8 egg yolks
Whipped cream for garnish
Fresh raspberries for garnish
Pureed sweetened raspberries, strained, for serving (optional)

1. Heat oven to 350°. Coat a 9-inch springform pan with nonstick cooking spray.

2. Heat milk in a large heavy saucepan over low heat until tiny bubbles form around edge of pan. Add chocolate; heat, stirring occasionally, until chocolate is melted and smooth. Stir in butter, brandy and vanilla and heat until butter is melted. Remove saucepan from heat.

3. Whisk egg yolks lightly to mix in a small bowl. Whisk a small amount of hot mixture into egg yolks. Slowly pour yolk mixture into saucepan, whisking to keep lumps from forming. Pour mixture into prepared pan.

4. Bake in heated 350° oven 20 minutes or until just set in center. Remove to a wire rack to cool completely. Cover and refrigerate.

5. To serve, loosen sides of pan and remove. Garnish with whipped cream and raspberries and serve with pureed raspberries for a sauce if desired.

Chocolate intensity

Chocolate pudding cake

Chocolate pudding cake

Makes 8 servings   *Prep* 20 minutes   *Bake* at 350° for 35 minutes   *Stand* 20 minutes

The best of two popular desserts: cake and pudding married in a gooey treat. Unsweetened cocoa powder has had most of the cocoa butter removed; as a result, it has the lowest fat content of any chocolate product.

Per serving
283 calories, 4 g protein, 11 g fat, 45 g carbohydrate, 247 mg sodium, 11 mg cholesterol.

1 cup all-purpose flour
¾ cup sugar
1½ tablespoons unsweetened cocoa powder
2 teaspoons baking powder
½ teaspoon salt
¾ cup chopped walnuts (about 3 ounces)

¾ cup milk
2 tablespoons butter, melted
1 teaspoon vanilla
1 cup hot water
½ cup chocolate syrup
Whipped cream or vanilla ice milk or ice cream

1. Heat oven to 350°. Coat an 8 x 8 x 2-inch square baking pan with nonstick cooking spray.

2. Mix together flour, sugar, cocoa powder, baking powder, salt and walnuts in a large bowl. Stir in milk, butter and vanilla until blended. Scrape batter into prepared pan.

3. Stir together hot water and syrup in a small bowl. Pour over cake batter.

4. Bake in heated 350° oven 35 minutes until cake is done and pudding bubbles up on sides. Cool pudding cake in its pan on a wire rack 20 minutes. Cut into squares. Serve warm or at room temperature. Spoon extra syrup over cake and serve with whipped cream, ice milk or ice cream.

Sacher torte with chocolate ganache

Makes 12 servings   *Prep* 45 minutes   *Refrigerate* 4 hours   *Bake* at 350° for 30 to 35 minutes

Ganache is a cooked mixture of heavy cream and chocolate, which thickens to a good spreading consistency. It makes an incredibly rich cake frosting or filling or even chocolate truffles.

Per serving
371 calories, 6 g protein, 22 g fat, 38 g carbohydrate, 159 mg sodium, 116 mg cholesterol.

Chocolate ganache
1 cup heavy cream
8 squares (1 ounce each) semisweet chocolate, chopped
1 teaspoon vanilla

Cake
6 squares (1 ounce each) semisweet chocolate, chopped
1 cup unsifted cake flour

1½ teaspoons baking powder
¼ teaspoon salt
5 eggs, separated
¼ cup water
½ cup sugar
1½ teaspoons vanilla

¼ cup orange marmalade
2 tablespoons orange liqueur

1. Prepare chocolate ganache: Bring cream to boiling in a medium-size saucepan over medium-high heat. Remove from heat. Add chocolate and stir until melted and smooth. Stir in vanilla. Pour half into a small bowl; refrigerate until a good spreading consistency, 2 hours. Cover remaining half; let stand at room temperature to use as a glaze.

2. Prepare cake: Heat oven to 350°. Grease bottom of a 9-inch springform pan. Line bottom with waxed paper.

3. Melt chocolate in a small bowl set over hot (not boiling) water or in a small heavy saucepan over very low heat. Cool.

4. Sift flour, baking powder and salt onto a piece of waxed paper.

5. Add water to egg yolks in a large bowl and beat until foamy. Gradually beat in sugar and vanilla; beat until thickened and light in color. Fold in flour mixture just until incorporated. Fold in cooled chocolate.

6. Using clean beaters, beat whites on high speed in a large bowl until soft peaks form. Gently fold into yolk mixture just until no streaks of white remain. Pour into prepared pan.

7. Bake in heated 350° oven 30 to 35 minutes or until a wooden pick inserted in center comes out clean. Cool in pan 10 minutes. Loosen edge with a knife; remove sides of pan. Cool on a wire rack. Peel off waxed paper.

8. Bring marmalade to simmering in a small saucepan. Press through a fine sieve; discard solids. Stir in liqueur.

9. Trim cake to level top. Cut in half horizontally. Place top layer, cut side up, on a platter. Brush top with marmalade. Place second layer on top, cut side down. Spread refrigerated chocolate ganache over sides and top of cake, smoothing with a long metal spatula to coat top and sides. Chill 1 hour.

10. Pour room-temperature chocolate ganache over top. (If ganache is too thick to pour, gently stir in 1 to 2 tablespoons cream.) Smooth carefully with spatula to coat top and sides of cake. Refrigerate 1 hour or until firm.

Cookies 'n' cream cupcakes

Makes 12 cupcakes   *Prep* 15 minutes   *Bake* at 375° for 14 minutes

Take a bite of one of these cupcakes, and you'll crunch into cookie pieces. Yum!

Per cupcake
254 calories, 4 g protein, 11 g fat, 36 g carbohydrate, 218 mg sodium, 47 mg cholesterol.

1¾ cups all-purpose flour
2 teaspoons baking powder
½ teaspoon salt
⅓ cup unsalted butter or margarine, at room temperature
¾ cup sugar
1 egg
¾ cup milk

1 tablespoon grated orange rind
1 teaspoon vanilla
5 cream-filled chocolate sandwich cookies, coarsely broken
Creamy Chocolate Frosting (recipe follows)
Broken chocolate sandwich cookies for garnish (optional)

1. Place an oven rack in lower third of oven. Heat oven to 375°. Coat cups of a standard 12-muffin pan with nonstick cooking spray or insert a paper liner in each.

2. Mix flour, baking powder and salt on a sheet of waxed paper.

3. Beat butter and sugar in a large bowl until creamy. Add egg; beat well. Beat flour mixture alternately with milk into butter mixture, beginning and ending with flour. Beat in orange rind and vanilla. Stir in cookies.

4. Spoon batter into prepared cups, filling each about two-thirds full.

5. Bake in lower third of heated 375° oven 14 minutes or until a wooden pick inserted in centers comes out clean and tops spring back when lightly touched. Cool in pan on a wire rack 5 minutes. Gently loosen cupcakes from pan; remove to rack to cool.

6. Spread Creamy Chocolate Frosting over top of cupcakes. Garnish with broken cookies if desired.

Creamy chocolate frosting

Beat together ½ cup heavy cream and ¼ cup presweetened chocolate drink mix in a small bowl until soft peaks form. Makes about 1 cup.

Uncle Jim's marble fudge cake

Makes 16 servings *Prep* 60 minutes *Bake* at 350° for 30 to 35 minutes

FAMILY CIRCLE ALL-TIME FAVORITE RECIPES

Uncle Jim is Jim Fobel, who has captured the spirit of American cooking in several of his cookbooks. This marble cake slathered with a fudgy frosting is Jim at his best.

Per serving
386 calories, 6 g protein, 18 g fat, 55 g carbohydrate, 148 mg sodium, 49 mg cholesterol.

1 square (1 ounce) unsweetened chocolate, coarsely chopped
2¼ cups all-purpose flour
1½ teaspoons baking powder
¼ teaspoon salt
¼ cup (½ stick) butter or margarine, at room temperature
¼ cup solid vegetable shortening
1¼ cups plus 1 tablespoon sugar

2 eggs
1 cup milk
1 teaspoon vanilla
¼ teaspoon almond extract
1 tablespoon strong brewed coffee or water
½ teaspoon ground cinnamon
¼ teaspoon baking soda
  Fudge Frosting (recipe follows)

1. Heat oven to 350°. Grease and flour two 8-inch round cake pans.

2. Melt chocolate in top of a double boiler over hot (not boiling) water, stirring until smooth. Cool slightly.

3. Combine flour, baking powder and salt on a sheet of waxed paper.

4. Beat butter and shortening in a large bowl until smooth and creamy. Gradually add 1¼ cups sugar, beating until light and fluffy. Beat in eggs, one at a time.

5. Beat flour mixture alternately with milk into butter mixture, beginning and ending with flour mixture. Beat in the vanilla and almond extract.

6. Spoon 1 cup batter into a small bowl. Stir in melted chocolate, remaining 1 tablespoon sugar, coffee, cinnamon and baking soda.

7. Spoon chocolate and vanilla batters in equal amounts in alternating blobs on each prepared pan. Using a knife or thin metal spatula, cut through batter to marbleize.

8. Bake in heated 350° oven 30 to 35 minutes or until a wooden pick inserted in center comes out clean. Cool in pans on racks 10 minutes. Turn cakes out; invert top side up; cool completely.

9. Place a cake layer, top side down, on a platter. Spread ½ cup Fudge Frosting over layer. Place remaining layer, top side up, on top. Spread a thin layer of frosting over sides and top of cake. Spread any remaining frosting over cake.

Fudge frosting

Combine 1½ cups sugar and 1 cup evaporated milk in a large heavy saucepan. Bring to boiling over medium heat, stirring occasionally. Simmer 10 minutes, occasionally brushing down sides of pan with a brush dipped in cold water. Coarsely chop 6 squares (1 ounce each) unsweetened chocolate. Combine with ¼ cup (½ stick) butter or margarine, 2 teaspoons vanilla and 1 teaspoon ground cinnamon in a large bowl. Pour hot milk mixture over chocolate, stirring until chocolate is melted and smooth. Cool to room temperature, stirring occasionally. Cool in refrigerator until frosting is a good spreading consistency. Makes 2 cups.

Uncle Jim's marble fudge cake
opposite

Whoopie pies

Makes 15 pies *Prep* 35 minutes *Bake* at 375° for 11 to 14 minutes

**Why the name?
Take a bite of the
cream-filled cookie-
cake sandwiches, and
you'll know why.
Whoopie!**

Per pie

453 calories, 4 g protein,
19 g fat, 69 g carbohydrate,
336 mg sodium,
78 mg cholesterol.

2 cups all-purpose flour
2 teaspoons baking powder
2 teaspoons baking soda
½ teaspoon salt
½ cup (1 stick) unsalted butter,
  at room temperature
1 cup packed light-brown sugar
1 teaspoon vanilla
2 eggs

⅓ cup unsweetened cocoa powder
¾ cup milk

Cream filling
6 cups confectioners' sugar
¾ cup (1½ sticks) butter, at room
  temperature
1 package (3 ounces) cream cheese,
  at room temperature
2 tablespoons vanilla

1. Heat oven to 375°. Line 2 large baking sheets with aluminum foil; coat with nonstick cooking spray.

2. Mix flour, baking powder, baking soda and salt in a large bowl.

3. Beat butter and brown sugar on medium speed in a medium-size bowl until creamy, about 1 minute. Add vanilla and eggs; beat 30 seconds. On low speed, beat in cocoa powder. Beat in flour mixture alternately with milk in 3 additions.

4. Place a 2¼-inch cookie cutter on a prepared baking sheet. Spoon 2 tablespoons mixture into cutter and smooth. Lift cutter and place back on sheet, about 3 inches from first cake. Make 6 cakes on each baking sheet.

5. Bake in heated 375° oven 11 to 14 minutes or until cakes spring back when lightly touched in center. Cool on sheets 5 minutes. Remove to a wire rack to cool completely. Repeat steps 4 and 5 to make a total of 30 cakes.

6. Prepare filling: Beat together confectioners' sugar, butter, cream cheese and vanilla in a large bowl on medium-high speed at least 5 minutes or until mixture is very creamy. Scrape bowl down often.

7. Place ¼ cup filling on flat side of a cake; top with flat side of a second cake and press together until filling begins to show around edges. Store between sheets of waxed paper in airtight containers in refrigerator up to 3 days or in freezer up to 1 month.

Banana cake with peanut butter frosting

Makes 12 servings *Prep* 45 minutes *Bake* at 375° for 25 minutes

2 cups sifted all-purpose flour
1 teaspoon baking soda
1 teaspoon baking powder
½ teaspoon salt
¾ cup (1½ sticks) unsalted butter or
  margarine, at room temperature
1½ cups sugar
2 eggs
2 to 3 medium bananas, mashed
  (1 cup)

1 tablespoon vanilla
½ cup buttermilk
½ cup finely chopped pecans
  Peanut Butter Frosting
  (recipe follows)

Decorations
  Sliced bananas
  Lemon juice
  Chopped pecans

1. Heat oven to 375°. Coat two 9-inch round cake pans with nonstick cooking spray. Line bottoms with waxed paper. Coat paper.

2. Sift together flour, baking soda, baking powder and salt onto a sheet of waxed paper.

3. Beat butter and sugar in a large bowl on medium speed until light and fluffy. Beat in eggs, mashed bananas and vanilla; beat 2 minutes. On low speed, beat in flour mixture alternately with buttermilk, beating after each addition. Fold in pecans. Spread batter in prepared pans.

4. Bake in heated 375° oven 25 minutes or until a wooden pick inserted in centers comes out clean. Cool cakes in pans on wire racks 10 minutes. Invert cakes onto racks to cool completely.

5. Remove waxed paper. Stack layers, spreading Peanut Butter Frosting between layers and over top and sides of cake.

6. To decorate, dip banana slices in lemon juice and place on top of cake. Sprinkle with chopped pecans.

Peanut butter frosting

Beat 4 ounces room-temperature cream cheese, ¼ cup (½ stick) room-temperature butter and 2 tablespoons milk in a large bowl until smooth. Gradually beat in 1 box (1 pound) confectioners' sugar until creamy and smooth. Fold in ½ cup peanut butter. Stir in 1 tablespoon vanilla and, if needed, 1 tablespoon milk until smooth. Makes 2⅔ cups.

Sweet-cream cake
with cherries

Sweet-cream cake with cherries

Makes 16 servings   *Prep* 35 minutes   *Bake* at 350° for 25 to 30 minutes

This beauty appears bakery-made, but the homemade taste is unmistakable. The confectioners' sugar, which is actually a mixture of cornstarch and sugar, helps to stiffen and stabilize the whipped cream so it stands up as a frosting.

Per serving
339 calories, 4 g protein,
18 g fat, 43 g carbohydrate,
180 mg sodium,
101 mg cholesterol.

2 cups all-purpose flour
1 tablespoon baking powder
½ teaspoon salt
1¼ cups sugar
3 eggs
1½ teaspoon vanilla

1½ cups heavy cream, whipped
1 jar (10 ounces) cherry jam
   Whipped-Cream Frosting (recipe follows)
¼ pound fresh cherries for garnish
   Fresh mint sprigs for garnish

1. Heat oven to 350°. Grease two 8 x 8 x 2-inch square baking pans. Line bottoms with waxed paper. Grease paper; flour paper and sides of pans.

2. Sift flour, baking powder, salt and ¾ cup sugar onto waxed paper. Beat eggs, vanilla and remaining sugar in a medium-size bowl. Beat in flour mixture just until combined. Fold in whipped cream. Scrape into prepared pans.

3. Bake in heated 350° oven 25 to 30 minutes or until tops of cakes spring back when lightly pressed. Cool cakes in pans on wire racks 10 minutes. Turn cakes out onto racks to cool completely.

4. Split cakes in half horizontally with a serrated knife, using wooden picks as a guide to mark center of layer. Place one layer, cut side up, on a serving plate. Spread with one-third of jam. Repeat with remaining layers and jam, leaving top plain. Frost sides and top with Whipped-Cream Frosting. Garnish with fresh cherries and mint sprigs.

Whipped-cream frosting

Beat 1½ cups heavy cream and 3 tablespoons confectioners' sugar in a medium-size bowl until soft peaks form. Makes 3 cups.

Lemon-curd coconut cake

Makes 14 servings   *Prep* 45 minutes   *Cook* 7 minutes   *Bake* at 350° for 20 to 25 minutes

Cake flour has less toughening gluten in it than regular all-purpose flour, so the resulting cake crumb is very tender.

Per serving
367 calories, 4 g protein,
15 g fat, 58 g carbohydrate,
299 mg sodium,
21 mg cholesterol.

2½ cups unsifted cake flour
2½ teaspoons baking powder
½ teaspoon salt
1 cup milk
¼ cup cold water
1½ teaspoons vanilla
4 egg whites
1½ cups sugar

½ cup (1 stick) butter or margarine, at room temperature
¼ cup lemon curd
3 cups Vanilla Buttercream (recipe page 443)
2 cups unsweetened flake coconut or shaved fresh coconut

1. Heat oven to 350°. Grease two 9-inch round cake pans; dust with flour; tap out excess flour.

2. Sift together cake flour, baking powder and salt onto a sheet of waxed paper.

3. Combine milk, water and vanilla in a small bowl.

4. Beat egg whites in a medium-size bowl until frothy. Gradually beat in ½ cup sugar until soft peaks form.

5. Beat butter and remaining 1 cup sugar in a large bowl until fluffy and light colored, 2 minutes. Beat in flour mixture alternately with milk mixture. Fold in beaten egg whites, half at a time. Scrape into prepared pans.

6. Bake in heated 350° oven 20 to 25 minutes, or until edges start to pull away from sides of pans. Cool cakes in pans on wire racks 10 minutes. Turn cakes out onto racks to cool completely.

7. Place a cake layer on a serving plate. Spread with lemon curd. Top with second layer. Spread top and sides with Vanilla Buttercream Frosting. Press coconut onto top and sides.

Chocolate angel food cake

Makes 10 servings   *Prep* 20 minutes   *Bake* at 350° for 40 minutes

There are two options for this ethereal cake—marbled or all-chocolate. You choose.

Per serving
194 calories, 6 g protein,
1 g fat, 44 g carbohydrate,
67 mg sodium,
0 mg cholesterol.

1 cup cake flour
   Pinch ground nutmeg
1½ cups egg whites (about 12 whites)

1½ teaspoons cream of tartar
1⅓ cups superfine sugar
¼ cup unsweetened cocoa powder

1. Position an oven rack in lower third of oven. Heat oven to 350°.

2. Sift cake flour and nutmeg together into a medium-size bowl.

3. Beat egg whites and cream of tartar in a large bowl until frothy. Beat in sugar, 2 tablespoons at a time, until stiff, glossy peaks form, 5 to 7 minutes.

4. Fold half of flour mixture into egg whites until incorporated; repeat with remaining flour mixture. Transfer half of batter to a clean bowl and fold cocoa powder into it.

5. For marbled cake: Alternately spoon white batter, then chocolate batter, into an ungreased 10-inch tube pan. Swirl with a sharp knife to create a marbled pattern. For all-chocolate cake: Gently fold chocolate batter into white batter; blend until no white streaks remain. Gently pour into an ungreased 10-inch tube pan.

6. Bake in heated 350° oven 40 minutes or until springy when touched and a wooden pick inserted in center of cake comes out clean. Invert pan onto its legs to cool completely. If pan has no legs extending above rim, invert onto a wine or similar weighted bottle, placing center of tube over neck of bottle.

Preparing chocolate angel food cake

1. Beat egg whites until frothy. Add sugar, 2 tablespoons at a time; whip to form stiff peaks.

2. Sprinkle half of flour mixture over beaten whites. Fold in; repeat to fold in remaining flour.

3. Place half of batter in a clean bowl. Gently fold in cocoa powder until uniform in color.

4. For all-chocolate cake, fold chocolate batter into white batter, blending gently.

Strawberry and white chocolate cake

Makes 12 servings   *Prep* 35 minutes   *Bake* at 350° for 25 minutes   *Refrigerate* 1½ hours

Cake

2 cups all-purpose flour
1 tablespoon baking powder
1 teaspoon salt
1 cup granulated sugar
½ cup (1 stick) butter or margarine, at room temperature
2 eggs
3 squares (1 ounce each) white baking chocolate, melted (see box, page 409)
¾ cup milk
1 teaspoon almond extract

Filling

5 squares (1 ounce each) white baking chocolate, coarsely chopped
⅓ cup heavy cream
⅔ cup sifted confectioners' sugar
¼ cup strawberry jelly

White Chocolate Frosting (recipe follows)
½ cup sliced almonds for garnish
1 pint strawberries for garnish

1. Heat oven to 350°. Grease a 15½ x 10½ x 1-inch jelly-roll pan. Line pan with waxed paper. Grease paper.

2. Prepare cake: Combine flour, baking powder and salt in a small bowl. Beat sugar and butter in a medium-size bowl until creamy. Add eggs, then melted chocolate, beating well after each addition. Beat in flour mixture alternately with milk. Stir in almond extract. Spread batter in prepared pan.

3. Bake in heated 350° oven 25 minutes or until a wooden pick inserted in center comes out clean. Place pan on a rack to cool completely. Cut crosswise into 3 equal rectangles. Invert cake onto a work surface. Peel off paper.

4. Prepare filling: Combine chocolate and cream in top of a double boiler over hot (not boiling) water. Stir until smooth. Beat in confectioners' sugar. Spread top of one cake layer with half of chocolate filling. Spread top of second layer with half of jelly. Place second layer, jelly side down, on first layer. Spread remaining filling over top of second layer. Spread remaining jelly over top of third layer; place layer, jelly side down, on second layer. Refrigerate 60 minutes. Trim edges even with a knife.

5. Spread frosting over sides and top of cake. Refrigerate at least 30 minutes, then garnish with almonds and strawberries before slicing.

White chocolate frosting

Melt 6 squares (1 ounce each) white baking chocolate in top of a double boiler, stirring, over simmering (not boiling) water. Beat 8 ounces room-temperature cream cheese and 1 tablespoon unsalted butter in a medium-size bowl until smooth. Add melted chocolate and 1½ cups sifted confectioners' sugar and beat until smooth. Makes 3 cups.

Chocolate raspberry-cream roll

Makes 10 servings *Prep* 25 minutes *Bake* at 375° for 15 to 20 minutes *Stand* 45 minutes

Who can resist a gorgeous chocolate dessert? Certainly no one we know! The white chocolate filling can be accented with any berry-flavored liqueur or even an orange liqueur.

Per serving

270 calories, 5 g protein, 16 g fat, 29 g carbohydrate, 163 mg sodium, 47 mg cholesterol.

Cake
2½ squares (1 ounce each) unsweetened chocolate
½ cup sifted all-purpose flour
½ teaspoon baking powder
¼ teaspoon salt
4 eggs
⅔ cup plus 1 tablespoon sugar
2 tablespoons raspberry-flavored liqueur
¼ teaspoon baking soda

3 tablespoons water
¼ cup unsweetened cocoa powder

Raspberry-cream filling
1½ squares (1 ounce each) white baking chocolate
1 tablespoon raspberry-flavored liqueur
¾ cup heavy cream

Decoration (optional)
Chocolate curls
Confectioners' sugar
Fresh raspberries

1. Heat oven to 375°. Spray a 15 x 10 x 1-inch jelly-roll pan with nonstick cooking spray. Line bottom with waxed paper; do not let paper come up sides of pan.

2. Prepare cake roll: Melt chocolate in top of a double a boiler over hot (not boiling) water.

3. Sift together flour, baking powder and salt onto a sheet of waxed paper. Beat together eggs and ⅔ cup sugar in a medium-size bowl on high speed 3 to 5 minutes or until thickened and pale yellow. Gradually fold in flour mixture and 2 tablespoons raspberry liqueur.

4. Add 1 tablespoon sugar, baking soda and water to melted chocolate; stir until thick. Using a wire whisk, quickly fold chocolate mixture into batter, whisking until well blended (there will be tiny flecks of chocolate). Turn into prepared pan, spreading evenly. Bake in heated 375° oven 15 to 20 minutes or until cake springs back when lightly pressed with a fingertip.

5. Loosen cake around edge with a knife. Sift cocoa powder over surface of cake. Invert pan onto clean paper toweling. Remove pan. Carefully peel off waxed paper. Trim ¼ inch from long edges of cake. Starting at a short end, roll up cake and toweling together. Place on a wire rack; cool 45 minutes.

6. Prepare raspberry-cream filling: Heat chocolate and raspberry liqueur in top of a double boiler set over hot (not boiling) water, stirring occasionally, until melted and smooth. Beat heavy cream in a small bowl until stiff peaks form. Gradually fold cream into melted chocolate mixture.

7. When cake is cool, unroll carefully. Spread roll evenly with raspberry-cream filling, leaving 1-inch border on all sides. Reroll cake from a short end, removing toweling as you roll. Place roll, seam side down, on a serving plate. Garnish top and sides of cake with chocolate curls, confectioners' sugar and fresh raspberries if desired.

Lemon pound cake

Makes 24 servings   *Prep* 20 minutes   *Bake* at 350° for 30 minutes; at 300° for 50 minutes

You could call this a pound cake plus, since there is more than a pound of butter in this tube version. If you wish, lightly dust the top with confectioners' sugar.

Shown on page 3.

Per serving
215 calories, 3 g protein, 13 g fat, 22 g carbohydrate, 72 mg sodium, 84 mg cholesterol.

2¼ cups (4½ sticks) unsalted butter
2¼ cups sugar
9 eggs, at room temperature
1 tablespoon lemon extract
1½ teaspoons grated lemon rind

3 cups all-purpose flour
1 tablespoon baking powder
½ teaspoon salt
1 quart strawberries, hulled and sliced

1. Heat oven to 350°. Butter and flour a 10-inch tube pan. Tap out excess flour.

2. Beat butter in a large bowl until creamy. Gradually beat in sugar until light and fluffy. Add eggs, one at a time. Beat in lemon extract and rind.

3. Combine flour, baking powder and salt in a small bowl. Gradually beat into butter mixture; beat on medium speed 3 minutes or until thick and creamy. Pour into prepared pan.

4. Bake in heated 350° oven 30 minutes. Lower oven temperature to 300°. Bake 50 minutes more or until a wooden pick inserted in center comes out clean. Let cake cool in pan on a wire rack 15 minutes. Turn cake out onto rack to cool completely. Serve with strawberries.

Chocolate raspberry-cream roll *opposite*

Chocolate strawberry shortcake

Makes 8 servings   *Prep* 30 minutes   *Bake* at 425° for 12 minutes

How much more fun can strawberry shortcake be? Wait until you see this luscious chocolate version. It's stacked so high, each serving is for two.

Per serving
433 calories, 6 g protein, 21 g fat, 58 g carbohydrate, 298 mg sodium, 66 mg cholesterol.

1 pint strawberries, hulled and sliced
½ pint raspberries
1 cup sugar
2 cups all-purpose flour
½ cup unsweetened cocoa powder
1 tablespoon baking powder
½ teaspoon salt

6 tablespoons (¾ stick) cold unsalted butter, cut into bits
½ cup milk
1 teaspoon vanilla
1 cup heavy cream, whipped
Fresh mint sprigs for garnish
Hot Fudge Sauce (recipe, page 401) (optional)

1. Place strawberries and raspberries in a medium-size bowl. Gently stir in ¼ cup sugar; toss to coat. Let stand 20 minutes, stirring occasionally.

2. Meanwhile, prepare chocolate shortcake: Combine flour, cocoa powder, remaining ¾ cup sugar, baking powder and salt in a large bowl. With a pastry blender or 2 knives used scissor fashion, cut in butter until mixture resembles fine crumbs. Slowly add milk and vanilla, stirring with a fork until mixture just comes together.

3. Heat oven to 425°.

4. Turn dough out onto a lightly floured surface. Knead lightly about 10 times. Pat or roll dough to a ¾-inch thickness. Cut out 4-inch rounds with a fluted cookie cutter. Place on an ungreased baking sheet, about 1 inch apart. Reroll scraps and cut out more shortcakes, for a total of 4.

5. Bake in heated 425° oven 12 minutes or until a wooden pick inserted in centers comes out clean. Remove shortcakes to a wire rack to cool completely.

6. Cut each shortcake in half horizontally. Place bottom halves on plates. Spoon some juice from strawberry mixture over bottoms. Spoon strawberry mixture on each bottom half, reserving a few berries for garnish. Spoon about ½ cup whipped cream over each. Cover with top half. Garnish with fruit and mint. Drizzle with Hot Fudge Sauce if desired. Cut each in half to make 2 servings.

Double peach shortcake

Makes 12 servings   *Prep* 20 minutes   *Bake* at 400° for 12 to 15 minutes

Of course you expect sliced peaches with this shortcake, but there's diced peach in the shortcakes too.

Per serving
457 calories, 7 g protein, 24 g fat, 57 g carbohydrate, 289 mg sodium, 89 mg cholesterol.

7 large ripe peaches (about 3½ pounds total)
¾ cup plus 2 tablespoons granulated sugar
3 cups all-purpose flour
1½ teaspoons baking soda
¾ teaspoon cream of tartar
½ teaspoon salt
2 cups sour cream
1 egg
2 cups heavy cream
¼ cup packed light-brown sugar
2 teaspoons vanilla
1 tablespoon unsalted butter, at room temperature (optional)

1. Peel, pit and dice 1 peach; reserve for shortcake batter. Peel, pit and thinly slice remaining peaches and place in a large bowl. Toss with ½ cup granulated sugar; let stand.

2. Heat oven to 400°. Lightly coat 2 baking sheets with nonstick cooking spray.

3. Sift flour, baking soda, cream of tartar, salt and ¼ cup granulated sugar into a large bowl.

4. Beat together sour cream and egg in a medium-size bowl. Stir in reserved diced peach.

5. Stir sour cream mixture into flour mixture just until blended; knead about 5 times in bowl if necessary to blend. Drop dough by scant ½ cups in 12 mounds onto prepared baking sheets, spacing 2 to 3 inches apart. Sprinkle tops with remaining 2 tablespoons granulated sugar.

6. Bake in heated 400° oven 12 to 15 minutes or until golden and a wooden pick inserted in centers comes out clean. Cool on wire racks slightly.

7. Meanwhile, beat cream in a large bowl until soft peaks form. Beat in brown sugar and vanilla; beat until stiff peaks form.

8. Split warm shortcakes in half. Spread each lightly with softened butter if you wish.

9. To serve, place bottom of shortcake, buttered side up, on a serving plate. Reserving 12 peach slices, spoon ⅓ cup sliced peaches on each shortcake bottom; top with a dollop of cream. Place shortcake top, buttered side down, on top; dollop with more cream. Garnish each with a reserved peach slice.

Fresh gingerbread cake

Makes 14 servings   *Prep* 20 minutes   *Bake* at 375° for 25 to 30 minutes

A splash of balsamic vinegar in the batter adds an elusive accent. For a special touch, garnish the cake with sprigs of fresh herbs, such as marjoram or thyme.

Per serving
583 calories, 5 g protein,
22 g fat, 94 g carbohydrate,
212 mg sodium,
102 mg cholesterol.

3¼ cups all-purpose flour
1 teaspoon ground cinnamon
½ teaspoon salt
⅛ teaspoon ground cloves
¾ cup (1½ sticks) unsalted butter, at room temperature
1 cup sugar
3 eggs
1 cup molasses
⅓ cup grated peeled fresh ginger (about 3 ounces)
4 teaspoons grated lemon rind
1 tablespoon balsamic vinegar
1 teaspoon baking soda
1 cup milk
3 cups Lemon Buttercream Frosting (recipe follows)

1. Heat oven to 375°. Grease two 9 x 2-inch round cake pans. Line bottoms with waxed paper rounds.

2. Combine flour, cinnamon, salt and cloves on a sheet of waxed paper.

3. Beat butter and sugar in a large bowl until light and fluffy. Add eggs, one at a time, beating well after each addition. Beat in molasses, ginger and lemon rind.

4. Mix together vinegar and baking soda in a small bowl. Beat into butter mixture. Beat in flour mixture alternately with milk, beginning and ending with flour mixture. Spread in prepared pans.

5. Bake in heated 375° oven 25 to 30 minutes or until a wooden pick inserted in centers comes out clean. Cool cakes in pans on wire racks 10 minutes. Turn cakes out onto racks to cool completely.

6. Place one cake layer on a serving platter. Spread top with about ¾ cup Lemon Buttercream. Place second layer on top; spread top and sides with remaining frosting.

Lemon buttercream frosting

Beat together ¾ cup (1½ sticks) room-temperature unsalted butter or margarine, 1 tablespoon grated lemon rind and a pinch of salt in a medium-size bowl until light and fluffy. Stir in 5 cups (1 pound plus 1 cup) confectioners' sugar and about ¼ cup milk until frosting is a good spreading consistency. Makes about 3 cups.

Apple cornmeal cake

Makes 8 servings   *Prep* 15 minutes   *Cook* 20 minutes   *Bake* at 400° for 15 to 20 minutes

Cornmeal is the surprising ingredient here. It adds texture and a wonderful subtle sweetness. A versatile cake you can serve for dessert or brunch or as a late afternoon picker-upper with a cup of coffee or tea.

Per serving
332 calories, 3 g protein,
11 g fat, 57 g carbohydrate,
164 mg sodium,
48 mg cholesterol.

5 Granny Smith or other cooking apples (2½ pounds total)
⅓ cup packed dark-brown sugar
¼ cup (½ stick) unsalted butter
1 cup yellow cornmeal
½ cup granulated sugar
½ cup all-purpose flour
½ teaspoon baking powder
½ teaspoon baking soda
¼ teaspoon ground ginger
½ cup buttermilk
¼ cup molasses
1 egg
2 tablespoons vegetable oil

1. Peel and core apples. Quarter apples lengthwise and cut each quarter into 3 wedges.

2. Heat brown sugar and butter in an ovenproof 10-inch nonstick skillet until sugar is melted. Add apple wedges. Cook, stirring occasionally, 10 minutes or until lightly browned. Cook 5 minutes more while carefully arranging apple slices in concentric circles, using small tongs.

3. Heat oven to 400°.

4. Whisk together cornmeal, granulated sugar, flour, baking powder, baking soda and ginger in a large bowl.

5. Whisk together buttermilk, molasses, egg and oil in a small bowl. Whisk buttermilk mixture into cornmeal mixture until well blended. Spoon batter over the apples, spreading out evenly with the back of a spoon. Batter will spread more as it bakes.

6. Bake in heated 400° oven 15 to 20 minutes or until cake springs back when lightly touched in center. Invert cake onto a heatproof serving plate. Serve warm.

CAKES AND COOKIES

Apple cornmeal cake

435

Classic carrot cake

Makes 16 servings *Prep* 25 minutes *Bake* at 350° for 45 to 50 minutes

2 cups all-purpose flour
2 teaspoons baking powder
1 teaspoon baking soda
½ teaspoon salt
2 teaspoons ground cinnamon
¾ teaspoon ground ginger
½ teaspoon ground allspice
1 cup vegetable oil or light olive oil

4 eggs
1 cup granulated sugar
¾ cup packed dark-brown sugar
½ cup fresh orange juice
1 teaspoon vanilla
2 cups shredded carrots
2 cup chopped walnuts, toasted
 Cream Cheese Icing (recipe follows)

1. Heat oven to 350°. Grease and flour a 13 x 9 x 2-inch baking pan.

2. Sift flour, baking powder, baking soda, salt, cinnamon, ginger and allspice onto a sheet of waxed paper.

3. Beat oil, eggs, granulated sugar and brown sugar in a large bowl on medium speed 2 minutes or until well blended. Stir in orange juice and vanilla.

4. Beat in flour mixture on lowest speed just until blended. Stir in carrots and walnuts until combined. Scrape into prepared pan.

5. Bake in heated 350° oven 45 to 50 minutes or until a wooden pick inserted in center comes out clean.

6. Cool completely in pan on a wire rack. Spread with Cream Cheese Icing. Cut into 16 squares and serve.

Cream cheese icing

Beat 6 ounces room-temperature cream cheese, 2 tablespoons room-temperature butter, 1½ cups confectioners' sugar and 1 teaspoon grated lemon rind in a medium-size bowl until mixture is blended and smooth. Makes about 1⅓ cups.

Crunchy toffee coffee cake

Makes 10 servings   *Prep* 30 minutes   *Bake* at 375° for 40 to 50 minutes

This sour cream coffee cake with its toffee-streusel topping makes an excellent dessert—just warm up in a low oven and garnish with a dollop of billowy whipped cream.

Per serving
406 calories, 7 g protein, 19 g fat, 54 g carbohydrate, 224 mg sodium, 77 mg cholesterol.

Streusel topping
½ cup all-purpose flour
½ cup firmly packed
   light-brown sugar
½ teaspoon ground cinnamon
3 tablespoons unsalted butter
½ cup chopped walnuts
   (about 2 ounces)
2 chocolate-covered toffee candy
   bars (about 1.4 ounces each),
   chopped (⅔ cup)

Coffee cake
2 cups all-purpose flour
1 teaspoon baking powder
½ teaspoon baking soda
½ teaspoon salt
2 eggs
⅓ cup granulated sugar
½ cup sour cream
⅓ cup butter, melted
½ cup maple syrup
½ teaspoon vanilla
   Sugar Icing (recipe follows)
   (optional)

1. Prepare streusel topping: Stir together flour, brown sugar and cinnamon in a medium-size bowl. With a pastry blender or 2 knives used scissor fashion, cut in butter until mixture resembles coarse meal. Stir in walnuts and toffee.

2. Prepare coffee cake: Heat oven to 375°. Coat a 9-inch springform pan or other baking pan with removable bottom with nonstick cooking spray.

3. Stir together flour, baking powder, baking soda and salt in a medium-size bowl.

4. Beat together eggs, sugar, sour cream, butter, maple syrup and vanilla in a large bowl. Stir in flour mixture just until blended. Scrape into prepared pan. Sprinkle with streusel topping.

5. Bake in heated 375° oven 40 to 50 minutes or until a wooden pick inserted in center comes out clean. Cool pan on a wire rack 10 minutes. Remove cake from pan. Cool cake on rack 10 minutes more. Drizzle with Sugar Icing if you wish.

Sugar icing

Stir together ½ cup confectioners' sugar and 3 to 4 teaspoons milk in a small bowl to make an icing of good drizzling consistency. Spoon into a small plastic bag; press icing to one corner. Snip off corner; pipe over top of coffee cake. Makes about ½ cup.

Blueberry crumb coffee cake

Makes 12 servings   *Prep* 25 minutes   *Bake* at 350° for 50 to 55 minutes

Like many coffee cakes, this is welcome for dessert, breakfast or snack time. Raspberries would be scrumptious in this recipe too.

Per serving
234 calories, 3 g protein, 12 g fat, 29 g carbohydrate, 143 mg sodium, 50 mg cholesterol.

Crumb topping
½ cup all-purpose flour
½ cup firmly packed light-brown sugar
¼ cup (½ stick) cold unsalted butter, cut into 1-inch pieces
½ cup chopped walnuts
½ teaspoon ground cinnamon
¼ teaspoon ground cardamom

Coffee cake
1¼ cups all-purpose flour
1½ teaspoons baking powder
¼ teaspoon baking soda
¼ teaspoon salt
½ teaspoon ground cardamom
½ cup (1 stick) unsalted butter, at room temperature
¾ cup granulated sugar
1 egg
1 teaspoon vanilla
⅓ cup milk
1 cup blueberries

1. Heat oven to 350°. Line a 9 x 9 x 2-inch square baking pan with aluminum foil, with foil overhanging pan on 2 opposite sides. Coat foil with nonstick cooking spray.

2. Prepare crumb topping: Combine flour and brown sugar in a small bowl. With a pastry blender or your fingertips, mix butter into flour and sugar until mixture resembles coarse meal. Stir in walnuts, cinnamon and cardamom until combined.

3. Prepare coffee cake: Stir together flour, baking powder, baking soda, salt and cardamom in a medium-size bowl.

4. Beat together butter and granulated sugar in a large bowl on medium speed until mixture is smooth and creamy, about 2 minutes. Add egg and vanilla, beating until smooth. On low speed, alternately beat in dry ingredients and milk, beginning and ending with dry ingredients. Mix just until all ingredients are blended.

5. Spread batter evenly in prepared pan. Sprinkle blueberries over batter in an even layer. Sprinkle crumb topping evenly over blueberries.

6. Bake in heated 350° oven 50 to 55 minutes or until a wooden pick inserted in center comes out clean. Remove pan to a wire rack to cool coffee cake slightly. Carefully grasp foil edges and lift coffee cake from pan. Cut cake into squares; remove from foil. Serve warm.

New York cheesecake

Makes 16 servings   *Prep* 15 minutes   *Bake* at 350° for 50 minutes   *Refrigerate* 12 hours or overnight

New York style cheesecake is densely textured, and this one has a hint of lemon in the filling. For a less outrageous crust, use plain graham crackers. To add a tasty flourish, top with whole strawberries and fresh mint sprigs.

Per serving
402 calories, 7 g protein,
31 g fat, 27 g carbohydrate,
220 mg sodium,
127 mg cholesterol.

Chocolate pecan crust
10 whole chocolate graham crackers, finely crushed (1½ cups)
¾ cup ground pecans
3 tablespoons sugar
½ teaspoon ground cinnamon
6 tablespoons unsalted butter, at room temperature

Filling
4 packages (8 ounces each) cream cheese, at room temperature
1¼ cups sugar
4 eggs
1 tablespoon fresh lemon juice
1 teaspoon vanilla

1. Prepare crust: Place graham cracker crumbs in a medium-size bowl. Add pecans, sugar and cinnamon; stir to mix well. Add butter; mix until well blended. Scatter crumb mixture over bottom of a 9-inch springform pan. Press mixture evenly over bottom and up sides of pan. Refrigerate pan until ready to use.

2. Heat oven to 350°.

3. Prepare filling: Beat cream cheese in a large bowl until smooth. Gradually beat in sugar until well blended. Add eggs, one at a time, beating well after each addition. Add lemon juice and vanilla; beat until blended. Pour cheese filling evenly into crust.

4. Bake cheesecake in heated 350° oven 50 minutes or until center is just set. Remove pan to a wire rack to cool completely. Refrigerate at least 12 hours. To serve, remove sides of pan. Cut cake into wedges.

New York cheesecake

Key lime cheesecake

Makes 16 servings   *Prep* 30 minutes   *Refrigerate* about 5 hours

For authentic Key lime flavor, use Key limes, which are more aromatic and citrusy than the commonly available, larger Persian limes.

Per serving
474 calories, 7 g protein,
30 g fat, 47 g carbohydrate,
247 mg sodium,
144 mg cholesterol.

Crust
3 cups graham cracker crumbs
⅔ cup sugar
⅔ cup butter, melted

Filling
1 cup fresh lime juice
¼ cup water
2 envelopes unflavored gelatin
1½ cups sugar
5 eggs, slightly beaten

2 teaspoons grated lime rind
½ cup (1 stick) butter, at room temperature
2 packages (8 ounces each) cream cheese, at room temperature
½ cup heavy cream, chilled

Whipped cream for garnish (optional)
Lime slices for garnish (optional)

1. Prepare crust: Stir crumbs, sugar and melted butter in a medium-size bowl. Press over bottom and up sides of a 9-inch springform pan.

2. Prepare filling: Combine lime juice and water in a small saucepan; sprinkle gelatin over top. Let stand 5 minutes to soften. Stir sugar, eggs and lime rind into pan. Cook, stirring, over medium heat until almost boiling, about 7 minutes or until instant-read thermometer registers 160°; do not boil. Remove from heat.

3. Beat butter and cream cheese in a large bowl until well mixed, about 1 minute. Gradually beat in lime mixture until well blended. Refrigerate, stirring occasionally, until mixture thickens enough to mound slightly when dropped from a spoon, about 45 minutes.

4. Beat chilled cream in a small chilled bowl until stiff peaks form. Fold into lime mixture. Pour into prepared crust. Cover; refrigerate until firm, 3 to 4 hours.

5. Run a thin knife around inside of pan to loosen sides; remove sides of pan. Garnish with whipped cream and lime slices if desired. Store in refrigerator.

Black-and-white cheesecake

Makes 16 servings   *Prep* 35 minutes   *Bake* at 350° for 1 hour, then stand in turned-off oven for 1 hour

Stand 4 hours   *Refrigerate* overnight

There's a double hit of chocolate here: semisweet chocolate and unsweetened cocoa powder. Garnish with strawberries, sliced and fanned out.

Per serving
434 calories, 8 g protein, 36 g fat, 24 g carbohydrate, 266 mg sodium, 157 mg cholesterol.

Foolproof cheesecake

Follow these tips for no-mess cheesecake.
• Wrap aluminum foil around base of the springform pan to prevent leaks. Pour in filling.
• When baked, remove foil and set springform pan on wire rack to cool 30 minutes, then chill in refrigerator.

¼ cup vanilla wafer crumbs
4 packages (8 ounces each) cream cheese, at room temperature
16 ounces sour cream
1 cup plus 2 tablespoons sugar
½ cup (1 stick) butter, at room temperature

2 tablespoons cornstarch
2 teaspoons vanilla
5 eggs
4 squares (1 ounce each) semisweet chocolate
¼ cup unsweetened cocoa powder, sifted

1. Heat oven to 350°. Grease a 9-inch springform pan; sprinkle with cookie crumbs, tapping out any excess. Refrigerate while preparing filling.

2. Beat together cream cheese, sour cream, 1 cup sugar, butter, cornstarch and vanilla in a large bowl on low speed until mixed. Add eggs, one at a time, beating after each addition just until combined. Do not overbeat.

3. Melt the chocolate in a small heavy saucepan over very low heat; stir in remaining 2 tablespoons sugar. Remove 2 cups of batter to a clean small bowl; stir in melted chocolate and cocoa powder; mixture will be thick.

4. Pour half of plain cheesecake batter into prepared pan. Spoon half of chocolate batter in dollops over top of plain batter. Repeat with remaining batters. Run knife through batter in a figure-8 pattern to create a marble effect.

5. Bake in heated 350° oven 1 hour; center should still be soft. After first 30 minutes, cover cheesecake with aluminum foil to prevent further browning. Turn oven off. Let cheesecake stand in oven, with door closed, 1 hour. Remove pan to a wire rack, away from drafts, to cool, about 4 hours. Remove sides of pan and refrigerate overnight.

Carousel cake
opposite

442

Carousel cake

Makes 12 servings   *Prep* 30 minutes   *Bake* cake at 350° for 25 to 30 minutes

Pan picks
You can use any of the following pans for this cake, but note that baking times are approximate. Test for doneness by inserting a wooden pick in the center of the cake; when it comes out clean, the cake is done.
• Two 9 x 2-inch round pans: bake in 350° oven 25 to 30 minutes.
• Two 8 x 2-inch round pans: bake in 350° oven 30 to 35 minutes.
• One 13 x 9 x 2-inch pan: bake in 350° oven 45 to 50 minutes.

3 cups all-purpose flour
2 teaspoons baking powder
¾ teaspoon salt
1 cup (2 sticks) unsalted butter, softened
1⅔ cups granulated sugar
3 eggs, at room temperature
1 teaspoon vanilla
1½ cups milk
3 cups Vanilla Buttercream Frosting (recipe follows)
Star and Animal Cookies (recipe page 444)
1 swirl lollipop stick
5 peppermint sticks (6-inch)
Ribbons and flags

1. Heat oven to 350°. Grease two 9 x 2-inch round cake pans. Line with waxed paper; grease paper.

2. Stir together flour, baking powder and salt in a medium-size bowl.

3. Beat together butter and sugar in a large bowl until pale and fluffy, about 5 minutes, scraping down sides of bowl with a rubber spatula as needed. Beat in eggs, one at a time, until blended. Beat in vanilla. Stir in flour mixture alternately with milk, beginning and ending with flour, until just mixed. Pour batter into prepared pans, dividing equally.

4. Bake in 350° oven 25 to 30 minutes or until a wooden pick inserted in center comes out clean. Cool cakes in pans on wire racks 5 minues. Turn out cakes onto racks to cool completely.

5. Place one cake, flat side up, on a serving plate. Slide waxed paper strips under bottom edges of cake. Spread a scant cup buttercream over top. Top with second layer, flat side down. Frost cake. Place star cookies around sides. Remove waxed paper strips.

6. Insert lollipop into top center of cake. Arrange peppermint sticks evenly around inside edge of cake. Arrange animal cookies, flags and ribbons as shown opposite.

Vanilla buttercream frosting

Beat together 1 box (16 ounces) confectioners' sugar, 1 cup (2 sticks) room-temperature unsalted butter, ⅓ cup heavy cream and 1½ teaspoons vanilla in a large bowl until smooth. Keep covered with plastic wrap until ready to use. Makes about 3 cups.

Star and animal cookies

Makes about 1 dozen 3-inch animal cookies and about 3 dozen small stars (Serve extras separately.)

Prep 25 minutes   *Refrigerate* 2 hours   *Bake* at 350° for 10 to 12 minutes

Designed for the Carousel Cake on the preceding page, these fun shaped cookies will also brighten the day if tucked into a lunchbox.

Per 3-inch cookie
311 calories, 4 g protein,
16 g fat, 39 g carbohydrate,
121 mg sodium,
59 mg cholesterol.

2¾ cups all-purpose flour
½ teaspoon baking powder
½ teaspoon salt
1 cup (2 sticks) unsalted butter, at room temperature
1 cup sugar

1 egg
1 teaspoon lemon extract
    Royal Icing (recipe follows)
    Paste food colors
    Assorted colored sugars

1. Combine flour, baking powder and salt in a medium-size bowl.

2. Beat butter, sugar, egg and lemon extract in a large bowl until light and fluffy, about 3 minutes. Stir in flour mixture. Divide dough in half. Flatten each half into a 6-inch disc. Cover with plastic wrap; chill at least 2 hours.

3. Heat oven to 350°. Coat baking sheets with nonstick cooking spray.

4. Lightly flour dough. Roll one disc of dough between sheets of waxed paper until ¼ inch thick. Using cookie cutters, cut out animals and small stars. Reroll scraps; cut out. Place cookies, 1 inch apart, on baking sheets. Repeat with remaining dough.

5. Bake in heated 350° oven 10 to 12 minutes or until lightly golden around edges. Cool cookies on baking sheet on a wire rack 5 minutes. Remove cookies to rack to cool completely.

6. Stir extra water into Royal Icing, drop by drop, to create a good flowing consistency. Divide into batches; tint with different colors. Spread over cookies. Dip into colored sugars. Let stand until dry and hardened.

Royal icing

In a medium-size bowl, stir together 3 tablespoons meringue powder or egg white powder and 6 tablespoons water. Beat in 4 cups confectioners' sugar (a 1-pound box); continue beating until peaks form, about 10 minutes. Press plastic wrap directly onto surface of icing and keep covered until ready to use. Makes 3 cups.

Note: Meringue powder and egg white powder are available in select supermarkets, gourmet shops, and health-food stores. Because of health concerns about eating raw eggs, be sure to use either meringue powder or egg white powder for this uncooked icing.

Valentine heart cakes

Makes 11 cakes *Prep* 45 minutes *Bake* at 350° for 25 minutes

2 cups all-purpose flour
1½ teaspoons baking powder
½ teaspoon baking soda
¾ teaspoon salt
¾ cup (1½ sticks) unsalted butter, at room temperature
2½ cups confectioners' sugar
2 egg whites
½ teaspoon vanilla

1 cup buttermilk
⅔ cup seedless raspberry jam
2 tablespoons water
   Chocolate Buttercream Frosting (recipe follows)
   Royal Icing (recipe opposite) or purchased edible sugar decorations

1. Heat oven to 350°. Line a 15 x 10 x 1-inch jelly-roll pan with waxed paper. Lightly coat with nonstick cooking spray and dust with flour.

2. Combine flour, baking powder, baking soda and salt on waxed paper.

3. Beat together butter and confectioners' sugar in a medium-size bowl until smooth and creamy. Add egg whites and vanilla; beat until fluffy. Beat in flour mixture alternately with buttermilk in 3 additions. Spread evenly in prepared pan.

4. Bake in heated 350° oven 25 minutes or until cake springs back in center when lightly pressed with a finger. Remove cake from pan to a wire rack to cool 15 minutes; carefully peel off waxed paper. Trim off sides of cake. Using 2¾-inch heart-shaped cookie cutter, cut out 22 hearts.

5. Heat raspberry jam and water in a small saucepan over low heat until jam is melted. Remove from heat and cool slightly.

6. Using a pastry brush, paint each heart with a thin coating of raspberry jam. Place on a large baking sheet lined with waxed paper. Let stand at room temperature for several hours or until almost dry (cakes will remain a little sticky).

7. Stack one heart cake on top of a second. Frost with Chocolate Buttercream Frosting. Decorate as desired with Royal Icing.

Chocolate buttercream frosting

Melt 6 squares (1 ounce each) semisweet chocolate, chopped, in a small heavy saucepan over low heat, stirring occasionally, until melted and smooth. Cool slightly. Beat ¼ cup (½ stick) room-temperature unsalted butter or margarine, 7 tablespoons milk, 1 teaspoon vanilla, ½ teaspoon salt and 1 cup sifted confectioners' sugar until creamy. Add chocolate and blend until smooth. Gradually beat in 3 cups sifted confectioners' sugar until a good spreading consistency. Add 2 to 3 tablespoons milk if too thick. Makes about 2¾ cups.

Fourth of July cake

Makes 12 servings *Prep* 45 minutes *Bake* at 350° for 30 minutes

Want to make an even bigger patriotic splash? Bake the layers in two 6-cup star pans, and then decorate the top in a free-form stars-and-stripes pattern.

Per serving
(without decoration)
470 calories, 5 g protein,
29 g fat, 48 g carbohydrate,
153 mg sodium,
154 mg cholesterol.

3 cups cake flour
2½ teaspoons baking powder
¼ teaspoon salt
1 cup (2 sticks) unsalted butter or margarine, at room temperature
1¼ cups sugar
4 eggs
2 tablespoons poppy seeds
1 tablespoon grated lemon rind

¼ cup milk
¼ cup fresh lemon juice
   Lemon Whipped-Cream Frosting (recipe follows)

Decoration
   Red fruit leather
1 pint raspberries
1 pint blueberries

1. Heat oven to 350°. Coat two 9-inch round cake pans with nonstick cooking spray.

2. Sift together flour, baking powder and salt on waxed paper.

3. Beat butter and sugar in a large bowl until light and fluffy. Beat in eggs, one at a time. Beat in poppy seeds and lemon rind. Add flour mixture alternately with milk and lemon juice, beating well after each addition. Spread batter evenly in prepared pans.

4. Bake in heated 350° oven 30 minutes or until a wooden pick inserted in centers comes out clean. Cool cakes in pans on wire racks 10 minutes. Turn out cakes onto racks to cool completely.

5. Place one cake layer on a plate. Spread top with frosting. Top with second layer. Frost top and sides of cake. Cut fruit leather into strips 2 inches wide and as long as the cake is high. Make vertical stripes around cake by pressing fruit leather strips into frosting, leaving about 2 inches of frosting between strips. Decorate edge of cake top with a ring of raspberries. Place a ring of blueberries inside raspberry ring and a second raspberry ring inside blueberries.

Lemon whipped-cream frosting

Beat 1½ cups heavy cream, ⅓ cup sifted confectioners' sugar, 1¼ teaspoons grated rind and 1 teaspoon lemon juice in a large bowl just until stiff peaks form. Makes about 3 cups.

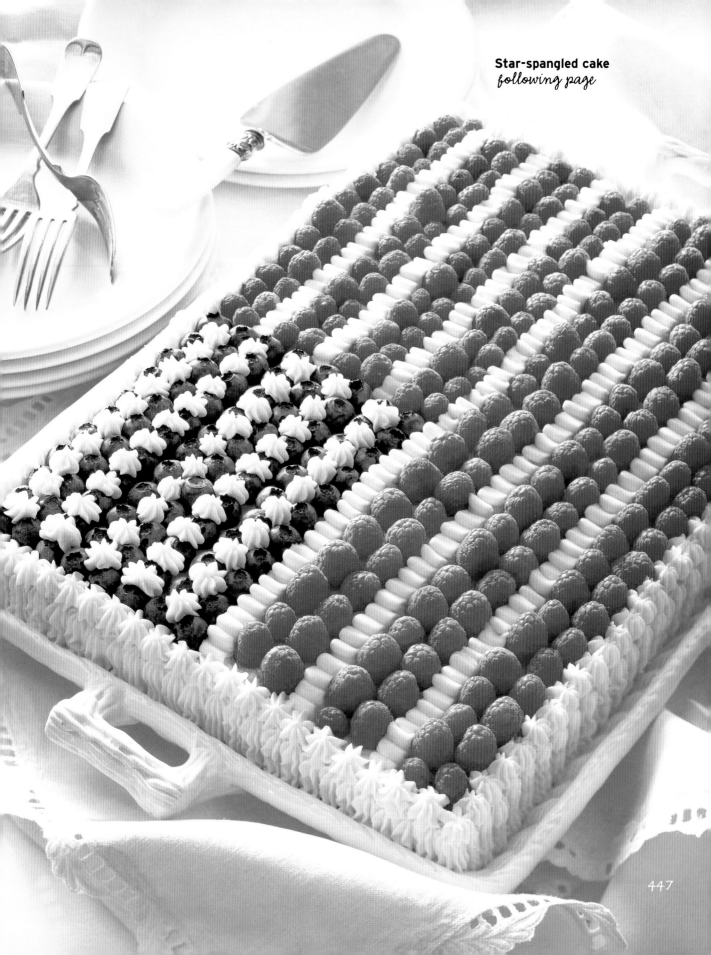

Star-spangled cake
following page

447

Star-spangled cake

Makes 35 servings *Prep* 20 minutes *Bake* at 350° for 20 minutes *Decorate* 30 minutes

A tribute to Old Glory, this cake will inspire pride when displayed on your party table. Shown on preceding page.

Per serving
318 calories, 3 g protein, 19 g fat, 35 g carbohydrate, 109 mg sodium, 85 mg cholesterol.

Lemon cake
3 cups sifted cake flour
4 teaspoons baking powder
½ teaspoon salt
5 eggs
2 cups sugar
  Grated rind of 2 lemons
¼ cup lemon juice (2 lemons)
1 tablespoon vanilla
2 cups heavy cream

½ cup raspberry jam

Cooked frosting
2 cups sugar
½ cup water
6 egg whites
¼ teaspoon cream of tartar
⅛ teaspoon salt
2½ cups (5 sticks) unsalted butter, at room temperature
1 tablespoon vanilla

Decoration
2 cups fresh raspberries
¾ cup fresh blueberries

1. Heat oven to 350°. Grease two 15½ x 10½ x 1-inch jelly-roll pans. Line bottoms of pans with waxed paper; grease and flour paper.

2. Stir together flour, baking powder and salt in a medium-size bowl.

3. Beat eggs in a large bowl until thick and lemon colored. Gradually beat in sugar, lemon rind, lemon juice and vanilla. Stir in flour mixture alternately with cream, beginning and ending with flour mixture. Spread batter evenly in prepared pans; smooth tops.

4. Bake in heated 350° oven 20 minutes or until a wooden pick inserted in centers comes out clean. Cool in pans on wire racks 10 minutes. Place a large wire rack over each cake layer. Carefully invert layers and racks. Remove pans, then carefully remove waxed paper. Handle cake layers very carefully–they will be very thin. Cool to room temperature.

5. Spread jam in a thin layer over top of one layer. Place another layer on top; place entire cake on a tray.

6. Meanwhile, prepare frosting: Combine sugar and water in a small heavy saucepan. Bring to boiling without stirring. Cover and boil 2 minutes or until no sugar crystals remain. Uncover pan; continue boiling until syrup registers 240° on a candy thermometer, the soft-ball stage (syrup will form a rapidly flattening ball when dribbled into cold water).

7. While sugar syrup is cooking, beat egg whites, cream of tartar and salt in a medium-size bowl until stiff, but not dry, peaks form.

8. At moment syrup reaches soft-ball stage, pour into egg whites in a fine, thin stream, beating constantly with a mixer. When all the syrup has been added, continue to beat egg whites at high speed until cool, about 5 minutes.

9. In a separate small bowl, beat butter until fluffy. Beat butter into cooled egg white mixture, 1 tablespoon at a time, until frosting is thick and creamy. Beat in vanilla. Use frosting immediately, or cover and store in a cool place 1 to 2 hours. (Do not refrigerate.) If frosting is too soft and thin, stir briefly over a bowl of ice water to stiffen.

10. Frost top and sides of cake, saving some frosting for decorating. Spoon reserved frosting into a pastry bag fitted with a decorative tip. Pipe a design on sides of cake. Pipe a fancy border around top and bottom edges of cake.

11. Prepare flag design: Mark off star field with wooden picks to measure 6 inches across top and 4½ inches down (this point will also mark continuing line of center red stripe). Outline star field with a piped frosting border.

12. Along bottom edge of cake top, place 2 rows of raspberries. Along top edge of cake top, place 2 rows of raspberries from star field to right edge of cake. On short sides of cake, measure another 5 evenly spaced rows for stripes (for a total of 7), and mark with wooden picks. Using wooden picks as guides, arrange raspberries in rows for remaining stripes. Using pastry bag fitted with a broad, flat decorating tip, fill in spaces between rows with a thick piping of frosting.

13. Tightly fill in star field with blueberries. Using a star tip, pipe 50 frosting stars in blueberry field, staggering as on the American flag.

14. Refrigerate cake until frosting sets. Then cover loosely with waxed paper or aluminum foil and keep refrigerated until serving time.

15. To serve, cut cake into 5 equal pieces across width of flag. Then cut from top to bottom into 7 equal sections.

Making cooked frosting

1. Drizzle a bit of hot sugar syrup into cold water. It should form a rapidly flattening ball.

2. Whip egg whites, salt and cream of tartar. Lift turned-off beaters to check for stiff peaks.

3. As soon as syrup is done, add to beaten whites in a thin stream. Whip 5 minutes more.

4. In small amounts, beat whipped butter into whites until blended. Then add vanilla.

Cakey fruitcake

Makes 2 cakes   *Prep* 20 minutes   *Bake* at 325° for 1 hour for tube pans, 65 to 70 minutes for loaves

Remember the chewy versions that always showed up at holiday office parties? Prepare this one for fellow workers, and you'll be the talk of the water-cooler crowd. Its cakey texture is light and delectable.

Per serving
378 calories, 4 g protein, 15 g fat, 60 g carbohydrate, 216 mg sodium, 22 mg cholesterol.

2 cups candied red and green cherries, chopped
2 cups walnuts, chopped
1 cup chopped dates
½ cup chopped citron
1½ cups packed light-brown sugar
1 cup (2 sticks) butter or margarine, softened
½ cup light molasses
1 teaspoon salt
1 teaspoon ground cinnamon
½ teaspoon ground nutmeg
½ teaspoon ground cloves
2 cups boiling water
4 cups all-purpose flour
2 teaspoons baking soda
Bourbon Glaze (recipe follows)
Assorted berries and grapes for garnish

1. Heat oven to 325°. Generously coat two 6-cup fluted tube pans or two 9 x 5 x 3-inch loaf pans with nonstick cooking spray.

2. Combine cherries, walnuts, dates, citron, brown sugar, butter, molasses, salt, cinnamon, nutmeg and cloves in a large bowl. Pour 2 cups boiling water over mixture; stir until butter is melted. Stir in flour and baking soda until well mixed. Scrape into prepared pans, dividing equally.

3. Bake in heated 325° oven 1 hour for tube pans, 65 to 70 minutes for loaf pans. Cool cakes in pans on wire racks 15 minutes. Unmold cakes onto racks. Cool completely.

4. When cakes are cooled, drizzle with Bourbon Glaze. Let stand until glaze hardens. Decorate with berries and grapes.

Bourbon glaze

Whisk together 1 cup confectioners' sugar, 1 tablespoon bourbon and 1 tablespoon room-temperature butter or margarine in a small bowl until smooth. Gradually stir in 1 to 2 tablespoons hot water to make a good drizzling consistency. Cover; set aside. Makes about ½ cup.

Mini fruitcakes with cream cheese frosting

Makes 6 fruitcakes (2 servings each)   *Prep* 30 minutes   *Bake* at 350° for 35 to 40 minutes

Cool 1 hour

These mini holiday fruitcakes will win everyone over, even those a little hesitant about the doorstop versions. Prettily wrapped, these two-serving loaves will be welcome in any household.

Per serving
527 calories, 9 g protein,
26 g fat, 68 g carbohydrate,
213 mg sodium,
104 mg cholesterol.

1¾ cups all-purpose flour
2 teaspoons baking powder
¼ teaspoon salt
1 package (8 ounces) cream cheese, at room temperature
1 cup sugar
½ cup (1 stick) unsalted butter, at room temperature
2 teaspoons vanilla

3 eggs
1 cup dried pineapple, finely chopped
1 cup dried apricots, finely chopped
1 cup dried cranberries, coarsely chopped
1 cup chopped pecans
Cream Cheese Frosting (recipe follows)

1. Heat oven to 350°. Grease and flour 6 mini bundt or loaf pans or six 6-ounce glass custard cups.

2. Combine flour, baking powder, and salt in a small bowl.

3. Beat together cream cheese, sugar, butter and vanilla in a medium-size bowl until blended and smooth. Beat in eggs, one at a time, until well mixed. Gradually add flour mixture to egg mixture until blended.

4. Reserve 1 tablespoon each of dried pineapple, apricots, cranberries and pecans for garnish. Stir remaining dried fruit and nuts into batter until blended. Divide batter evenly among prepared pans. Run a knife through batter to remove any air pockets.

5. Bake in heated 350° oven 35 to 40 minutes or until a wooden pick inserted in centers comes out clean. Cool cakes in pans on wire racks 10 minutes. Turn cakes out on racks to cool completely.

6. Drizzle frosting evenly over cakes. Sprinkle with reserved dried fruit and nuts.

Cream cheese frosting

Beat together 2 tablespoons softened cream cheese and 1 tablespoon fresh lemon juice in a medium-size bowl until smooth. Sift in ⅔ cup confectioners' sugar; beat to combine. Beat in ¼ cup heavy cream and 1 teaspoon vanilla until blended and smooth. If too thick, add 1 tablespoon milk to thin. Makes about 1 cup.

Pumpkin and cream cheese jelly roll

Makes 12 servings *Prep* 15 minutes *Stand* 1 hour *Bake* at 375° for 10 to 12 minutes
Refrigerate 4 hours

The pumpkin is in the roll, and the cream cheese in the filling. But that's not all that's inside—how about chocolate chips and slivered almonds? Be sure to cool the cake rolled up to avoid cracking.

Per serving
310 calories, 6 g protein, 14 g fat, 42 g carbohydrate, 233 mg sodium, 102 mg cholesterol.

Cake

- 1 cup all-purpose flour
- 1½ teaspoons baking powder
- ½ teaspoon ground cinnamon
- ½ teaspoon ground nutmeg
- ¼ teaspoon salt
- 4 eggs, at room temperature
- ¾ cup sugar
- ¾ cup canned pumpkin pie filling
  Confectioners' sugar

Cream cheese filling

- 12 ounces cream cheese, at room temperature
- ⅔ cup sugar
- 1 teaspoon vanilla
- ¼ cup mini semisweet chocolate chips
- ¼ cup blanched slivered almonds, toasted and coarsely chopped

1. Heat oven to 375°. Line a 15½ x 10½ x 1-inch jelly-roll pan with waxed paper. Coat paper with nonstick cooking spray.

2. Prepare roll: Combine flour, baking powder, cinnamon, nutmeg and salt in a small bowl.

3. Beat eggs in a large bowl on medium speed 2 minutes or until slightly thickened. Beat in sugar, a tablespoon at a time; continue beating until very thick and lemon colored, 5 to 7 minutes. On lowest speed, beat in pumpkin pie filling just until blended. With a rubber spatula, fold in flour mixture in 2 batches. Spread evenly in prepared pan.

4. Bake in heated 375° oven 10 to 12 minutes or until top of cake springs back when lightly touched in center. Generously sieve confectioners' sugar over a clean kitchen towel. When cake is done, immediately loosen edges; invert onto towel. Remove waxed paper. Sprinkle cake with additional confectioners' sugar. From a short end, roll up cake with towel, jelly-roll fashion. Cool on a wire rack 1 hour.

5. Meanwhile, prepare filling: Beat cream cheese, sugar and vanilla in a medium-size bowl 5 to 8 minutes or until creamy. Stir in chocolate and almonds.

6. Unroll cake. Spread with filling. Reroll without towel. Cover and refrigerate at least 4 hours or overnight.

453

Traditional Yule log

Makes 16 servings   *Prep* 20 minutes   *Bake* at 350° for 10 minutes

Refrigerate ganache 20 to 30 minutes   *Assembly* 35 minutes

Cake
10 eggs
1 cup all-purpose flour
¼ teaspoon ground nutmeg
1 cup sugar
2 teaspoons vanilla
1 teaspoon rum extract
  Unsweetened cocoa powder

Chocolate cream filling
½ cup heavy cream
2 cups cold milk
2 packages (3.9 ounces each) chocolate pudding-and-pie filling
1 teaspoon vanilla

Chocolate Ganache
6 squares (1 ounce each) semisweet chocolate, chopped
1 cup heavy cream

1. Prepare cake: Separate eggs, placing yolks and whites in 2 separate large bowls. Let eggs come to room temperature for no more than 1 hour.

2. Heat oven to 350°. Grease two 15 x 10 x 1-inch jelly-roll pans. Line pans with waxed paper.

3. Combine flour and nutmeg on a sheet of waxed paper.

4. Beat egg whites until frothy. Gradually beat in ½ cup sugar. Beat until stiff peaks form.

5. Beat yolks with remaining ½ cup sugar until thick and lemon colored, 5 minutes. Beat in vanilla and rum extract. Fold in flour mixture.

6. Gently fold yolk mixture into whites until no white streaks remain. Spread batter evenly in prepared pans.

7. Bake in heated 350° oven 10 minutes or until cake springs back when gently pressed in center with a fingertip.

8. Meanwhile, sprinkle cocoa powder over a clean dish towel long enough to hold both cakes. Turn cakes out onto cocoa-covered towel, slightly overlapping 2 long sides. Carefully peel off waxed paper. Beginning at one end and rolling across the seam, roll up cakes with towel. Place, seam side down, on a wire rack to cool.

9. Meanwhile, prepare chocolate cream filling: Whip cream in a medium-size bowl until stiff peaks form; you should have 1 cup. Pour milk into another medium-size bowl. Stir in chocolate pudding-and-pie filling. Whisk until thickened, 2 minutes. Fold in whipped cream and vanilla.

10. Prepare chocolate ganache: Melt chocolate in a bowl over hot (not simmering) water, stirring occasionally. Remove from heat. Pour cream into chocolate, stirring with a rubber spatula until smooth. Refrigerate, stirring occasionally, until of spreading consistency, 20 to 30 minutes.

11. Unroll cake and towel. Spread cake evenly with chocolate cream filling. Reroll cake without towel.

12. Cut each end off cake, using parallel diagonal cuts. Reserve ends to use as the tree knots. Lift the cake, seam side down, onto a serving plate. Place a knot on each side of log, with diagonally cut side facing log. Spread ganache over log and knots, leaving all spiral ends exposed. For bark effect, run fork gently over frosting. Garnish as desired.

Traditional Yule log

Cranberry cake wreath

Makes 12 servings   *Prep* 30 minutes   *Bake* at 350° for 45 to 50 minutes

3 cups all-purpose flour
1¼ cups sugar
2 teaspoons baking powder
½ teaspoon baking soda
¾ teaspoon salt
3 eggs
¾ cup fresh orange juice
½ cup (1 stick) unsalted butter, melted
1 cup fresh or thawed frozen cranberries
1 cup coarsely chopped walnuts (4 ounces)
2 cups Confectioners' Sugar Glaze (recipe follows)

Decorations
Cinnamon red candies or fresh cranberries
Red ribbon bow (optional)

1. Heat oven to 350°. Grease and flour a 12-cup tube pan or Bundt pan.

2. Combine flour, sugar, baking powder, baking soda and salt in a large bowl. Make a well in center. Add eggs, orange juice and butter to well; stir liquid ingredients just until blended.

3. Add cranberries and walnuts to well. Stir all ingredients together just until combined. Spread batter in prepared pan.

4. Bake in heated 350° oven 45 to 50 minutes or until a wooden pick inserted in center comes out clean. Cool cake in pan on a wire rack 10 minutes. Remove from pan and cool completely.

5. Pour 1 cup glaze over top of cake and let it flow down sides. Tint remaining 1 cup glaze with green paste food coloring. If glaze is too thin for piping, stir in a little more confectioners' sugar. Spoon tinted glaze into a pastry bag fitted with a small round tip. Pipe on green leafy designs to resemble a wreath of pine branches. Decorate with candies or cranberries and a red bow if you wish.

Confectioners' sugar glaze

Gradually stir 3 to 4 teaspoons milk into 2 cup confectioners' sugar in a small bowl until smooth and a good glazing consistency. Makes about 2 cups.

Snowman cake

Makes 24 servings   *Prep* 20 minutes   *Bake* at 350° for 20 to 45 minutes, following recipe directions

Our adorable stand-up snowman is unbeatable in terms of kiddie appeal. You'll need to prepare and bake the recipe twice in order to have the right components. But don't just double the recipe; from a production standpoint, it is much better to make it twice. Since cake freezes well, you can bake one batch at a time and freeze until ready to assemble.

Per serving
(without decoration)
342 calories, 2 g protein,
15 g fat, 50 g carbohydrate,
194 mg sodium,
11 mg cholesterol.

Chill out

Cakes are easier to frost when they've been chilled. Cover with plastic wrap and freeze, or refrigerate for 3 hours or overnight; then frost and decorate.

2 cups all-purpose flour
1 tablespoon baking powder
½ teaspoon salt
¼ teaspoon baking soda
½ cup (1 stick) unsalted butter, at room temperature
1½ cups sugar
1½ teaspoons vanilla
¾ cup milk
4 egg whites

2 cans (16 ounces each) creamy vanilla frosting or 3 cups Vanilla Buttercream (recipe, page 443)
1 bag (14 ounces) sweetened flake coconut
Black food coloring
Large gumdrops, chocolate-flavored red and black licorice, red fruit leather and pretzels, for decorations

1. Heat oven to 350°. Position an oven rack in center of oven. Grease and flour one 1½-quart ovenproof glass bowl, one 1-quart ovenproof glass bowl and one 1½-cup soufflé dish.

2. Stir together flour, baking powder, salt and baking soda in a medium-size bowl. Beat together butter and 1 cup sugar in a large bowl until light and fluffy. Beat in vanilla. Beat in flour mixture alternately with milk, beginning and ending with flour.

3. Beat egg whites in a medium-size bowl until foamy. Gradually add remaining ½ cup sugar, beating until stiff, but not dry, peaks form. Gently fold beaten egg whites into batter. Spoon about 3 cups batter into 1½-quart bowl, 1½ cups into 1-quart bowl, and ½ cup into soufflé dish.

4. Bake in heated 350° oven: 20 minutes for soufflé dish; 33 minutes for 1-quart bowl, 40 to 45 minutes for 1½-quart bowl or until a wooden pick inserted in center of cakes comes out clean. Cool in bowls on a wire rack 10 minutes. Unmold onto rack to cool completly.

5. Make recipe again, baking 3¼ cups batter in larger bowl, 1¾ cups in smaller bowl and none in soufflé dish; test with a wooden pick for doneness.

6. Trim tops of bowl cakes to make level. Place one larger cake, flat side up, on a plate. Spread a small amount of frosting in middle. Top with other large cake, flat side down. Spread frosting on top. Place one small cake, rounded end down, on top. Spread with frosting; top with other small cake, flat side down. Push 3 or 4 long wooden skewers down center of snowman.

7. Reserve ½ cup frosting for hat. Frost cake with remaining frosting. Press coconut onto cake. Refrigerate until set, 30 minutes.

8. Cut a 5-inch cardboard circle for hat brim. Tint reserved ½ cup frosting black. Frost brim; place on "head." Place soufflé cake on top for crown; frost. Use a skewer to hold hat in place if needed. Refrigerate until set. Decorate with candy and pretzel details.

Super-chunk peanut butter cookies

Makes 3½ dozen cookies   *Prep* 15 minutes   *Bake* at 350° for 10 minutes

To turn these into monster cookies, use 2 or 3 tablespoons of dough per cookie and allow a little extra baking time.

Per cookie
150 calories, 3 g protein, 9 g fat, 16 g carbohydrate, 92 mg sodium, 16 mg cholesterol.

½ cup (1 stick) unsalted butter, at room temperature
¾ cup creamy peanut butter
⅓ cup granulated sugar
⅓ cup light-brown sugar
2 eggs
1 teaspoon vanilla

2¼ cups all-purpose flour
1 teaspoon baking soda
½ teaspoon salt
¾ cup peanut butter chips
1 package (12 ounces) semisweet chocolate chips (2 cups)
½ cup chopped unsalted peanuts

1. Heat oven to 350°.

2. In a large bowl, beat butter and peanut butter until smooth. Add granulated sugar and brown sugar and beat until smooth. Add eggs, one at a time, and beat until light and fluffy. Beat in vanilla.

3. Sift together flour, baking soda and salt on a sheet of waxed paper. Slowly beat into peanut butter mixture until well combined. Fold in peanut butter chips, chocolate chips and peanuts.

4. Scoop about 1 heaping tablespoonful of batter into your hands. Carefully flatten into a 2-inch round. Place on an ungreased baking sheet. Continue with remaining batter.

5. Bake in heated 350° oven 10 minutes or until lightly golden and firm. Cool 2 minutes on sheet, then transfer to a wire rack to cool.

Super-chunk peanut butter cookies

Chocolate-peanut pinwheels

Makes 5½ dozen cookies   *Prep* 30 minutes   *Refrigerate* 2 hours   *Bake* at 350° for 8 to 10 minutes

If you have seen these in bakery shops and wondered how they were made, this recipe explains it all. Any similar soft cookie dough will do, and for a flash of frivolity, color the doughs with food paste colors.

Per cookie
65 calories, 1 g protein, 3 g fat, 9 g carbohydrate, 48 mg sodium, 11 mg cholesterol.

Chocolate dough

1½ cups all-purpose flour
2 tablespoons unsweetened cocoa powder
½ teaspoon baking soda
¼ teaspoon salt
6 tablespoons (¾ stick) unsalted butter, at room temperature
¾ cup sugar
1 egg
1 teaspoon vanilla

Peanut dough

1 cup all-purpose flour
½ teaspoon baking soda
¼ teaspoon salt
¼ cup (½ stick) unsalted butter, at room temperature
½ cup creamy peanut butter
¾ cup sugar
1 egg
½ teaspoon vanilla

1. Prepare chocolate dough: Combine flour, cocoa powder, baking soda and salt in a medium-size bowl. Beat butter, sugar, egg and vanilla in a large bowl until combined. Beat in flour mixture. Pat dough into a 1-inch-thick disc, wrap and chill until firm, about 1 hour.

2. Prepare peanut dough: Combine flour, baking soda and salt in a medium-size bowl. Beat butter, peanut butter, sugar, egg and vanilla in a second medium-size bowl until well blended. Beat in flour mixture. Pat dough into a 1-inch-thick disc, wrap and chill until firm, about 1 hour.

3. Divide chocolate dough and peanut dough in half. On floured waxed paper, using a floured rolling pin, roll out each piece of dough into a 12 x 6-inch rectangle. Invert one rectangle of peanut butter dough onto a rectangle of chocolate dough. Remove waxed paper. Starting from a long side, roll up dough, jelly-roll fashion. Repeat with remaining dough. Wrap rolls in waxed paper; chill until firm, about 1 hour.

4. Heat oven to 350°. Coat baking sheets with nonstick cooking spray.

5. Slice dough into ¼-inch-thick cookies. Place on baking sheets. Bake in heated 350° oven until lightly browned, 8 to 10 minutes. Transfer cookies to wire racks to cool.

Note: If dough becomes too soft at any time, place in refrigerator and chill 5 to 10 minutes.

Best-ever chocolate chip cookies

Makes 3½ dozen cookies   *Prep* 15 minutes   *Bake* at 375° for 9 minutes

As if chocolate chips and walnuts weren't enough, we've tossed in white chocolate chips for the best-ever cookie treats. Cool briefly on the baking sheet to ensure easy removal.

Per cookie
179 calories, 2 g protein, 11 g fat, 18 g carbohydrate, 64 mg sodium, 23 mg cholesterol.

2¼ cups all-purpose flour
1 teaspoon baking soda
½ teaspoon salt
1 cup (2 sticks) unsalted butter, softened
¾ cup granulated sugar
¾ cup light-brown sugar

2 eggs
2 teaspoon vanilla
1 package (12 ounces) extra-large or regular semisweet chocolate chips (2 cups)
1 cup white chocolate chips
1½ cups chopped walnuts

1. Heat oven to 375°.

2. In a small bowl, sift together flour, baking soda, and salt.

3. In a large bowl, cream butter until smooth. Add granulated sugar and brown sugar and beat until light and fluffy. Add eggs, one at a time, until batter is smooth and creamy. Beat in vanilla.

4. Beat in sifted flour mixture until well combined. Fold in semisweet chocolate chips, white chocolate chips and walnuts. With a spoon or small ice cream scoop, spoon 2 tablespoonfuls of batter per cookie onto ungreased baking sheets.

5. Bake in heated 375° oven 9 minutes or until lightly golden. Cool on sheet 2 minutes. Remove to a wire rack. Serve warm or at room temperature.

Soft, chewy or crisp?

THERE'S CHEMISTRY IN COOKIES. Here are some tricks for getting different textures.

Soft: Choose recipes with a low amount of butter and a relatively high proportion of liquid. Use cake flour. Substitute brown sugar or molasses for some or all of the sugar. Add an egg. Form large, thick cookies. Bake on parchment-lined baking sheets, and underbake slightly. Cool on a wire rack.

Chewy: Select high-fat recipes that call for shortening or half shortening, half butter. Include moist extras such as coconut or dried fruit. Chill dough before baking. Set oven temperature a bit higher and underbake slightly. Cool on a wire rack.

Crisp: Select high-fat recipes with a lower proportion of liquid. Use all-purpose flour and granulated sugar. Grease heavy baking sheets with vegetable shortening or nonstick cooking spray. Form small cookies with room-temperature dough. Set oven temperature a bit lower and bake a little longer. Cool on baking sheet.

Everything cookies

Makes 3 dozen cookies   *Prep* 20 minutes   *Bake* at 375° for 12 to 15 minutes

Everything but the kitchen sink—that's what these cookies contain. Some of our favorite ingredients: chocolate chips, walnuts, peanut butter chips, raisins and granola.

Per cookie
179 calories, 3 g protein, 10 g fat, 22 g carbohydrate, 98 mg sodium, 26 mg cholesterol.

1½ cups low-fat granola
1 cup golden raisins
1 cup old-fashioned rolled oats
1 cup chocolate chips
2 cups walnut halves
½ cup peanut butter chips
1⅔ cups all-purpose flour
1 teaspoon baking soda
1 teaspoon baking powder
½ teaspoon salt
½ cup packed dark-brown sugar
½ cup granulated sugar
1 cup (2 sticks) unsalted butter, cut into small pieces
2 eggs
1 teaspoon vanilla

1. Heat oven to 375°.

2. Toss together granola, raisins, oats, chocolate chips, walnut halves and peanut butter chips in a large bowl until well combined.

3. Sift flour, baking soda, baking powder and salt into a small bowl; stir with a whisk to combine ingredients well.

4. Place brown sugar and granulated sugar in a food processor (or use a large bowl and an electric mixer). Whirl to combine. With processor running, add butter, a few pieces at a time, whirling until smooth and creamy. Add eggs and vanilla. Whirl until incorporated, scraping down sides of work bowl as needed. Add flour mixture. Pulse with on-and-off motions until just combined.

5. Scrape mixture from food processor into bowl with chocolate chip mixture; stir to combine ingredients well.

6. Shape dough into 2-inch balls; place balls 2 inches apart on ungreased baking sheets.

7. Bake in heated 375° oven 12 to 15 minutes or until light brown.

8. Cool cookies on baking sheets on a wire rack until firm enough to lift with a spatula. Remove cookies to rack to cool completely.

Oatmeal chocolate chip cookies

Makes 4 dozen cookies   *Prep* 20 minutes   *Bake* at 350° for 10 to 12 minutes

Dried fruit—apricots, raisins and glacé cherries—make these delightfully chewy.

Per cookie
106 calories, 2 g protein,
5 g fat, 16 g carbohydrate,
45 mg sodium,
10 mg cholesterol.

½ cup (1 stick) unsalted butter, at room temperature
¼ cup shortening
¾ cup light-brown sugar
½ cup granulated sugar
1 egg
1 teaspoon vanilla
¼ cup water
3 cups old-fashioned rolled oats
1 cup all-purpose flour

1 teaspoon ground cinnamon
½ teaspoon baking soda
¼ teaspoon salt
1 cup milk chocolate chips
¾ cup chopped dried apricots (4 to 5 ounces)
½ cup golden raisins
½ cup chopped glacé cherries (3-ounce container)

1. Heat oven to 350°.

2. Beat together butter, shortening, brown sugar and granulated sugar in a large bowl until fluffy. Add egg, vanilla and water and beat until smooth and light in color.

3. Combine oats, flour, cinnamon, baking soda and salt in a medium-size bowl. Beat into butter mixture. Fold in chocolate chips, apricots, raisins and cherries until evenly distributed.

4. Drop dough by heaping tablespoonfuls onto ungreased baking sheets. Bake 10 to 12 minutes or until evenly browned. Cool slightly on baking sheets to firm, then remove to a wire rack to cool completely.

Hazelnut biscotti

Makes 3 to 4 dozen biscotti   *Prep* 15 minutes

Bake at 350° for 25 minutes; bake second time at 350° for 12 to 15 minutes

The word *biscotti* actually means twice baked. First you bake a loaf, and then you cut the loaf into slices and bake again.

Per biscotti
105 calories, 2 g protein,
6 g fat, 12 g carbohydrate,
38 mg sodium,
19 mg cholesterol.

1 cup hazelnuts
½ cup (1 stick) unsalted butter, at room temperature
¾ cup sugar
2 eggs

1 teaspoon vanilla
2 cups all-purpose flour
1½ teaspoons baking powder
¼ teaspoon salt
⅔ cup mini white chocolate chips

1. Heat oven to 350°. Grease a baking sheet.

2. Toast hazelnuts in a dry large skillet over medium-low heat until golden and fragrant, 3 to 4 minutes. Rub nuts in a clean dish towel to remove skins. Coarsely chop.

3. Beat together butter and sugar in a large bowl until light and fluffy. Beat in eggs, one at a time. Stir in vanilla.

4. Combine flour, baking powder and salt in a medium-size bowl; toss with a fork. Add to butter mixture along with hazelnuts and chocolate chips; mix well.

5. Divide dough in half. Place one half on prepared baking sheet. Pat into a 12-inch-long log. Repeat with second half, placing on baking sheet 2 inches from first.

6. Bake in heated 350° oven until lightly browned, about 25 minutes. Remove from oven; leave oven on. Cool logs 10 minutes.

7. Place logs on a cutting board. Cut diagonally into ½-inch-thick slices. Place slices, cut side down, on baking sheet. Bake 12 to 15 minutes. Remove to a wire rack to cool.

Oatmeal chocolate chip cookies *opposite*

Hazelnut biscotti

Chocolate-dipped cappuccino biscotti

Makes 28 biscotti   *Prep* 20 minutes   *Bake* at 350° for 40 to 45 minutes   *Refrigerate* 30 minutes

When melting chocolate, mixing in a little solid vegetable shortening makes for a smooth chocolate coating that will harden.
Why cappuccino? Espresso powder flavors the biscotti.

Per biscotti
131 calories, 2 g protein,
7 g fat, 16 g carbohydrate,
69 mg sodium,
20 mg cholesterol.

Biscotti-making basics

1. Grease hands lightly and divide dough in half. On baking sheet, pat each half into a log.

2. After first bake, when the logs are cool enough to handle, cut into slices on the diagonal.

1 cup hazelnuts
1¾ cups all-purpose flour
¾ cup sugar
1 tablespoon instant espresso coffee powder
1 tablespoon ground cinnamon
½ teaspoon baking powder
½ teaspoon salt
¼ cup (½ stick) unsalted butter or margarine, cut in small pieces
2 eggs
6 squares (1 ounce each) semisweet chocolate
1 teaspoon solid vegetable shortening

1. Heat oven to 350°. Grease a large baking sheet.

2. Toast hazelnuts in a dry large skillet over medium-low heat until golden and fragrant, 3 to 4 minutes. Rub nuts in a clean dish towel to remove skins. Coarsely chop.

3. Combine flour, sugar, espresso powder, cinnamon, baking powder and salt in a medium-size bowl. With a pastry blender or 2 knives used scissor fashion, cut in butter until mixture resembles coarse crumbs. Stir in hazelnuts and eggs. Divide dough in half.

4. On a floured surface, with floured hands, roll each half into a 12-inch-long log. Flatten to a 2½-inch width. Place logs, about 4 inches apart, on prepared baking sheet.

5. Bake in heated 350° oven 30 minutes or until logs are slightly firm to the touch. With 2 spatulas, remove logs to a wire rack and cool 20 minutes. Leave oven on.

6. With a serrated knife, cut logs diagonally into ¾-inch-thick slices. Return biscotti to baking sheet. Bake 10 to 15 minutes or until crisp and firm to the touch. Transfer to rack to cool.

7. Line a baking sheet with waxed paper. Melt chocolate, stirring occasionally, in a small saucepan over low heat. Remove from heat. Stir in shortening until well blended. Dip one flat side of biscotti in chocolate. Dip one end and half of other flat side into chocolate. Place biscotti on waxed-paper-lined baking sheet. Repeat with remaining biscotti. Refrigerate biscotti until chocolate hardens completely, 30 minutes.

Note: Store unfrosted biscotti in an airtight container up to 2 weeks. Frost up to 2 days before using or giving and then store in an airtight container.

Spicy molasses cookies

Makes 2½ dozen cookies   *Prep* 20 minutes   *Bake* at 375° for 8 to 10 minutes

Gotta have a tall glass of milk with these—they're great dunkers. These also freeze very well, so double or triple the recipe to have a supply just a freezer door away.

Per cookie
72 calories, 1 g protein, 2 g fat, 12 g carbohydrate, 73 mg sodium, 11 mg cholesterol.

2¼ cups unsifted all-purpose flour
1½ teaspoons baking soda
1 teaspoon baking powder
1 teaspoon ground cinnamon
½ teaspoon ground nutmeg
¼ teaspoon ground allspice
¼ teaspoon salt

½ cup (1 stick) unsalted butter, at room temperature
¾ cup packed dark-brown sugar
¾ cup dark molasses
1 egg
⅓ cup milk
Clear, large-crystal decorating sugar

1. Heat oven to 375°. Coat a baking sheet with nonstick cooking spray.

2. Combine flour, baking soda, baking powder, cinnamon, nutmeg, allspice and salt in a small bowl.

3. Beat butter and brown sugar in a large bowl until smooth and creamy. Beat in molasses and egg. Beat in flour mixture alternately with milk, beginning and ending with flour mixture.

4. Drop dough by rounded tablespoonfuls 2 inches apart onto prepared baking sheet.

5. Bake in heated 375° oven 8 to 10 minutes or until soft-firm to the touch. Transfer sheet to a wire rack for 1 to 2 minutes. Remove cookies to rack. Sprinkle with sugar. Cool completely.

6. If not serving right after baking, freeze in layers, separated by waxed paper, in a sealed plastic container. To serve, bring to room temperature.

Store them right

CHANCES ARE they'll be eaten long before they get stale. But to keep cookies at their best, follow any specific storage guidelines given with the recipe. If there are none, follow these tricks.

Soft cookies: Store at room temperature in a container with a tight-fitting lid.

Crisp cookies: Store at room temperature in a container with a loose-fitting lid.

Bars: Store tightly covered in the baking pan. Refrigerate fudgy varieties; store others at room temperature.

To each its own: Don't store different types of cookies in the same container; the flavors might merge and lose their distinct characters. Cookies with fruit can cause crisp cookies to soften.

Banana ginger cookies

Makes 2½ dozen cookies   *Prep* 20 minutes   *Bake* at 375° for 8 to 10 minutes

Fresh ginger makes all the flavor difference in this cakey cookie. When grating rind from citrus, be sure to avoid the bitter white pith that lies directly under the colored peel.

Per cookie
123 calories, 1 g protein, 5 g fat, 20 g carbohydrate, 76 mg sodium, 13 mg cholesterol.

Here's the scoop
Use a small ice cream scoop to drop cookie dough onto baking sheets—it's exactly the right size.

2 cups unsifted all-purpose flour
¾ teaspoon salt
¼ teaspoon baking soda
¾ cup (1½ sticks) unsalted butter, at room temperature
1 cup packed light-brown sugar

2 ripe bananas, mashed (1 cup)
2 tablespoons grated fresh ginger
1 teaspoon vanilla
   Lemon Glaze
   (recipe follows)
   Grated lemon rind

1. Heat oven to 375°. Coat a baking sheet with nonstick cooking spray.

2. Mix flour, salt and baking soda in a medium-size bowl.

3. Beat butter and brown sugar in a large bowl until smooth and creamy. Beat in banana, ginger and vanilla. Gradually beat in flour mixture.

4. Drop mixture by rounded tablespoonfuls about 2 inches apart onto prepared baking sheet.

5. Bake in heated 375° oven 8 to 10 minutes or until lightly browned and soft-firm to the touch. Let stand on sheet on a wire rack 1 to 2 minutes. Remove cookies to rack to cool completely.

6. When cookies are completely cooled, frost with Lemon Glaze. Sprinkle with lemon rind. If not serving these cookies right after baking, leave unfrosted, pack in a tightly sealed plastic container with waxed paper between layers and freeze. To serve, bring to room temperature. Frost and sprinkle with rind.

Lemon glaze

Whisk 2 cups confectioners' sugar, 2 tablespoons milk, 2 teaspoons grated lemon rind, 1½ teaspoons lemon juice and ⅛ teaspoon salt in a small bowl until well blended. If too thick, stir in more milk, drop by drop. Makes about 1½ cups.

Bear paws

Makes 1½ dozen cookies   *Prep* 20 minutes   *Refrigerate* 1 hour   *Bake* at 350° for 10 to 12 minutes

You'll need a madeleine pan for this recipe. It's a baking pan with a series of scallop shell indentations. Look for one in a better kitchenware store or mail-order catalog.

Per cookie
127 calories, 2 g protein, 10 g fat, 8 g carbohydrate, 18 mg sodium, 26 mg cholesterol.

1 cup hazelnuts
¾ cup all-purpose flour
½ cup confectioners' sugar
1 teaspoon unsweetened cocoa powder
¼ teaspoon ground cinnamon
⅛ teaspoon salt
Pinch ground cloves
½ cup (1 stick) unsalted butter, cut into small pieces
1 egg yolk
1 teaspoon grated lemon rind
Confectioners' sugar for dusting

1. Toast hazelnuts in a dry large skillet over medium-low heat until golden and fragrant, 3 to 4 minutes. Rub nuts in a clean dish towel to remove skins. Coarsely chop. Whirl in food processor until finely ground.

2. Add flour, confectioners' sugar, cocoa powder, cinnamon, salt, cloves, butter, egg yolk and lemon rind to processor. Whirl until a ball forms. Wrap; chill 1 hour.

3. Heat oven to 350°. Grease individual depressions in a madeleine pan; dust with flour.

4. Press a scant tablespoon of dough into each depression in pan. Bake in heated 350° oven 10 to 12 minutes or until light golden. Cool pan on a wire rack 3 minutes. Cover with a baking sheet. Invert; tap pan to loosen. Cool completely. Just before serving, dust with confectioners' sugar.

Banana ginger cookies
opposite

Shortbread

Makes 16 pieces *Prep* 15 minutes *Bake* 325° for 40 minutes

Shortbread borrows its traditional round shape from the Scottish bannock, or griddle cake. Notches around the edge of the bannock symbolize the sun's rays. Like the bannock, the shortbread is divided into wedges.

Per piece
183 calories, 2 g protein, 12 g fat, 18 g carbohydrate, 69 mg sodium, 31 mg cholesterol.

2 cups all-purpose flour
½ cup sugar
½ teaspoon salt

1 cup (2 sticks) unsalted butter, at room temperature, 1 cut into 16 pieces

1. Position an oven rack in lower third of oven. Heat oven to 325°.

2. Place flour, sugar and salt in a food processor. Whirl 5 seconds. Scatter butter pieces over mixture. Whirl until dough forms a ball, 1 to 2 minutes. (Or in a medium-size bowl, cut in butter with a pastry blender or fingertips.) Divide dough in half. Press each half evenly into a 9-inch pie plate. Score each plate of dough into 8 equal pie-shaped wedges.

3. Bake in lower third of heated 325° oven 40 minutes. Cool pans on wire racks 5 minutes. Cut through scored marks. Cool completely before removing from pan.

Chocolate chip shortbread

Per piece
97 calories, 1 g protein, 6 g fat, 11 g carbohydrate, 68 mg sodium, 14 mg cholesterol.

Add ¼ cup unsweetened cocoa powder to dry ingredients in recipe above. Increase sugar to ⅔ cup. After dough forms a ball, remove to a bowl. Mix in ½ cup mini chocolate chips. Press mixture into a 9 x 9 x 2-inch square baking pan. Score into 36 pieces. Bake in lower third of heated 325° oven 45 minutes. Cut through score marks as above. Makes 35 pieces.

Macadamia white-chocolate shortbread

Per piece
181 calories, 2 g protein, 13 g fat, 16 g carbohydrate, 18 mg sodium, 22 mg cholesterol.

Coarsely chop 4 squares (1 ounce each) white baking chocolate and 4 ounces macadamia nuts; reserve. Prepare dough as above but omit salt. When dough forms a ball, remove to a bowl. Mix in chocolate and nuts. Press into an 11 x 7 x 2-inch baking pan. Score into 24 pieces. Bake in lower third of heated 325° oven 45 minutes. Cut through score marks as above. Makes 24 pieces.

Lemon bars

Makes 35 bars   *Prep* 20 minutes   *Bake* crust at 350° for 20 minutes; bars at 350° for 20 minutes

Everyone has a recipe for these favorites, and here's another to add to your collection. Other citrusy variations are equally as good: Substitute orange juice and rind or lime juice and rind.

per bar
106 calories, 1 g protein, 4 g fat, 15 g carbohydrate, 44 mg sodium, 29 mg cholesterol.

Crust
2 cups all-purpose flour
¾ cup (1½ sticks) cold unsalted butter, cut into pats
½ cup confectioners' sugar
½ teaspoon salt

Filling
1⅓ cups granulated sugar
3 tablespoons all-purpose flour
½ teaspoon baking powder
⅓ cup fresh lemon juice
3 eggs
2 teaspoons grated lemon rind
Confectioners' sugar for dusting

1. Heat oven to 350°. Line a 13 x 9 x 2-inch baking pan with aluminum foil so foil overhangs short ends. Lightly coat with nonstick cooking spray.

2. Prepare crust: Combine flour, butter, confectioners' sugar and salt in a food processor. Whirl with on-and-off pulses until mixture resembles coarse meal. (Or in a medium-size bowl, cut butter into flour mixture with a pastry blender or 2 knives used scissor fashion.)

3. Scrape crust into prepared pan; spread until level and pat down to compact evenly. Bake crust in heated 350° oven 20 minutes or until lightly colored. Leave oven on.

4. Meanwhile, prepare filling: Combine sugar, flour, baking powder, lemon juice, eggs and lemon rind in a food processor. Whirl until well blended. Pour mixture over hot crust.

5. Bake in 350° oven 20 minutes or just until set in the center. Transfer pan to a wire rack to cool completely. Carefully lift foil to remove whole Lemon Bar. Cut into squares. Dust with confectioners' sugar and remove from foil. Bars can be refrigerated in an airtight container up to 1 week.

Successful bar cookies

Plan ahead: Line the pan with aluminum foil, allowing sufficient overhang on opposite edges to make lifting bars out later a breeze.

Avoid sticky mess: Cover your hand with plastic wrap; press dough into pan and smooth surface.

Match baking time to your pan: If you use a pan larger than the one specified in the recipe, the bars will cook more quickly; check often. If you use a smaller pan, extra time will be needed. If you use a glass pan, lower the oven temperature by 25°.

Prevent crumbs: For clean edges, let bars cool completely before cutting.

Rugelach

Rugelach

Makes 6 dozen cookies *Prep* 35 minutes *Refrigerate* 6 hours or overnight

Bake at 375° for 20 to 25 minutes

A traditional Jewish cookie, the rugelach is filled with a fruit mixture and the pastry is made with cream cheese. Refrigerate for up to 1 month.

Per cookie
58 calories, 1 g protein, 4 g fat, 5 g carbohydrate, 11 mg sodium, 10 mg cholesterol.

1 cup (2 sticks) unsalted butter, at room temperature
1 package (8 ounces) cream cheese, at room temperature
2 cups all-purpose flour
2 tablespoons sugar
1 teaspoon ground cinnamon
6 tablespoons raspberry, apricot or strawberry jam
6 tablespoons finely chopped walnuts
6 tablespoons dried currants

1. Beat butter and cream cheese in a large bowl until blended. Stir in flour until smooth. Divide dough into 6 equal portions; flatten into discs. Cover each with plastic wrap; refrigerate at least 6 hours or overnight.

2. Heat oven to 375°. Lightly coat baking sheets with nonstick cooking spray.

3. Stir sugar and cinnamon together in a small bowl. Roll out one disc of dough on a lightly floured surface into an 8-inch round. Spread 1 tablespoon jam in a 1-inch-deep band around outer edge of round, leaving a ½-inch border. Sprinkle 1 teaspoon cinnamon sugar over center of dough. Sprinkle 1 tablespoon each of nuts and currants over jam. With a pizza cutter or sharp knife, cut into 12 wedges. Roll each wedge up toward narrow point; bend ends to shape into crescents. Place on baking sheets, ½ inch apart. Repeat with remaining dough and ingredients.

4. Bake in heated 375° oven 20 to 25 minutes or until golden brown. Remove cookies from pans to wire racks to cool. Store in an airtight container, refrigerated, up to 1 month, or freeze up to 3 months.

Oatmeal apricot thumbprints

Makes 3 dozen cookies   *Prep* 20 minutes   *Bake* at 350° for 8 to 10 minutes

A tiny pool of preserves delivers a sweet spark to these classic thumbprints.

Per cookie
149 calories, 2 g protein, 6 g fat, 23 g carbohydrate, 78 mg sodium, 13 mg cholesterol.

2½ cups all-purpose flour
 1 teaspoon baking soda
 ½ teaspoon baking powder
 ½ teaspoon salt
 ½ cup (1 stick) unsalted butter, at room temperature
 ½ cup solid vegetable shortening

1½ cups packed light-brown sugar
 ¾ cup apricot preserves
 1 egg
 1 tablespoon grated orange rind
2½ cups old-fashioned rolled oats
 ½ cup golden raisins

1. Heat oven to 350°. Coat 2 baking sheets with nonstick cooking spray.

2. Combine flour, baking soda, baking powder and salt in a small bowl.

3. Beat butter, shortening and brown sugar in a large bowl until smooth and creamy. Beat in ½ cup preserves, egg and orange rind. Gradually beat in flour mixture. Stir in oats and raisins.

4. Drop mixture by rounded tablespoonfuls, 2 inches apart, onto prepared baking sheets.

5. Using a thumb or handle end of a wooden spoon dipped in flour, press a slight indentation in middle of each cookie, not pressing through bottom of cookie. Spoon ¼ teaspoon apricot jam into each indentation.

6. Bake in 350° oven 8 to 10 minutes or until lightly browned. Let stand on sheets on a wire rack 1 to 2 minutes. Remove to rack to cool. Store at room temperature in a sealed plastic container with sheets of waxed paper or foil between layers.

Oatmeal apricot thumbprints

Peanut butter bars

Makes 2 dozen bars   *Prep* 15 minutes   *Bake* at 350° for 20 to 25 minutes   *Cook* 2 minutes

Peanut lovers alert! Not one, not two, but three different peanut hits: peanut butter, unsalted peanuts and peanut butter cups.

Per bar

193 calories, 4 g protein, 10 g fat, 23 g carbohydrate, 83 mg sodium, 29 mg cholesterol.

1½ cups all-purpose flour
1 teaspoon baking powder
¼ teaspoon salt
1 cup packed light-brown sugar
½ cup granulated sugar
½ cup (1 stick) unsalted butter, at room temperature
¼ cup creamy peanut butter

2 eggs
1 teaspoon vanilla extract
½ cup chopped unsalted peanuts
24 mini peanut butter cups

Topping
¼ cup semisweet chocolate chips
1 teaspoon butter

1. Heat oven to 350°. Coat a 13 x 9 x 2-inch baking pan with nonstick cooking spray.

2. Stir together flour, baking powder and salt in a small bowl.

3. Beat together brown sugar, granulated sugar, butter and peanut butter in a large bowl until smooth. Add eggs, one at a time, beating well after each addition. Beat in vanilla. Stir in flour mixture until blended. Fold in peanuts.

4. Spread dough in prepared pan. Quarter peanut butter cups and press slightly into dough.

5. Bake in heated 350° oven 20 to 25 minutes. Cool in pan on a wire rack.

6. Prepare topping: Melt chocolate chips and butter in top of a double boiler over simmering water, stirring until smooth. Drizzle chocolate mixture over bar in pan. Cool. Cut into bars.

Pack 'em up

SOFT DROP, BAR AND FRUIT COOKIES are among the best travelers; choose them to mail off to far-flung family and friends.

Use a metal container or decorative tin: Line the container with waxed paper or aluminum foil.

Wrap airtight: Wrap 2 drop cookies back to back, wrap bar cookies individually in aluminum foil.

Nest securely: Pack cookies close together to minimize shifting. Use crumpled foil, tissue paper or waxed paper as filler. The container should be so full that you have to use a little pressure to tape it shut. Place the container in a sturdy shipping box, cushioning it so it fits tightly.

Strawberry streusels

Makes 12 bars   *Prep* 10 minutes   *Bake* at 375° for 40 minutes

Lemon streusel on the bottom, lemon streusel on the top and strawberry jelly in the center. Mmm!

per bar
277 calories, 2 g protein, 12 g fat, 42 g carbohydrate, 59 mg sodium, 31 mg cholesterol.

2 cups all-purpose flour
½ cup packed light-brown sugar
1 teaspoon grated lemon rind
¼ teaspoon ground nutmeg

¼ teaspoon salt
¾ cup (1½ sticks) unsalted butter
1 jar (12 ounces) strawberry jelly

1. Heat oven to 375°. Grease a 9 x 9 x 2-inch square baking pan.

2. Combine flour, brown sugar, lemon rind, nutmeg and salt in a large bowl. Cut in butter with a pastry blender or 2 knives used scissor fashion until mixture is crumbly. Set aside 1 cup. Pat remaining mixture into prepared pan.

3. Spread jelly evenly over top of dough in pan, leaving a ¼-inch border all around edges. Sprinkle with reserved 1 cup flour mixture.

4. Bake in heated 375° oven 40 minutes or until lightly browned. Cool in pan on a wire rack. Cut into bars.

Dalmatian bars

Makes 2 dozen bars   *Prep* 10 minutes   *Cook* 5 minutes   *Bake* at 350° for 20 to 25 minutes

When you see these bars spotted with white chocolate chips and chopped macadamia nuts, you'll understand how they got their name.

per bar
273 calories, 3 g protein, 17 g fat, 30 g carbohydrate, 63 mg sodium, 54 mg cholesterol.

4 squares (1 ounce each) unsweetened chocolate
¾ cup (1½ sticks) unsalted butter
1¼ cups all-purpose flour
1 teaspoon baking powder
¼ teaspoon salt

1¾ cups sugar
4 eggs
2 teaspoons vanilla
1 jar (3½ ounces) macadamia nuts, coarsely chopped
1½ cups mini white chocolate chips

1. Heat oven to 350°. Coat a 13 x 9 x 2-inch baking pan with nonstick cooking spray.

2. Melt unsweetened chocolate and butter in top of a double boiler over simmering water, stirring until smooth.

3. Mix together flour, baking powder and salt in a small bowl.

4. Beat sugar, eggs and chocolate mixture in a medium-size bowl. Mix in vanilla, then flour mixture until combined. Stir in nuts and half of white chocolate chips. Spread evenly in prepared pan. Sprinkle remaining chocolate chips on top.

5. Bake in 350° oven 20 to 25 minutes or until firm and chocolate chips are lightly colored. Cool in pan. Cut into bars.

Super-chunk brownies

Makes 2 dozen brownies   Prep 15 minutes   Bake at 350° for 30 to 35 minutes

Chunks of walnuts and chocolate are responsible for making this bar cookie incredibly good. Taste carefully and see if you can detect the tartness from the dried cherries.

Per brownie
210 calories, 3 g protein, 13 g fat, 24 g carbohydrate, 53 mg sodium, 51 mg cholesterol.

6 squares (1 ounce each) semisweet chocolate
¾ cup (1½ sticks) unsalted butter
1 cup all-purpose flour
1 teaspoon baking powder
¼ teaspoon salt
4 eggs
1½ cups sugar
1 teaspoon vanilla
½ cup chopped walnuts
½ cup dried cherries or cranberries
½ cup large semisweet chocolate chips or chocolate chunks

1. Heat oven to 350°. Coat a 12 x 7½ x 2-inch glass baking dish with nonstick cooking spray.

2. Melt chocolate squares and butter in top of a double boiler over simmering water, stirring until smooth.

3. Stir together flour, baking powder and salt in a large bowl.

4. Beat eggs and sugar in a second large bowl until blended, 3 to 5 minutes. Stir in chocolate mixture and vanilla until blended. Beat in flour mixture.

5. Reserve 2 tablespoons nuts. Add remaining nuts, dried cherries and chocolate chips to batter. Scrape into pan. Sprinkle reserved nuts over top.

6. Bake in heated 350° oven 30 to 35 minutes or until firm on top. Cool completely in pan on a wire rack. Cut into bars.

Frosted brownies

Makes 3 dozen brownies   Prep 15 minutes   Cook 3 minutes   Bake at 350° for 15 to 20 minutes

The cooked chocolate frosting is a wonderful topping for this brownie, but you can also spread it over a sheet cake, layer cake or store-bought pound cake.

Per brownie
209 calories, 2 g protein, 12 g fat, 28 g carbohydrate, 38 mg sodium, 42 mg cholesterol.

6 squares (1 ounce each) unsweetened chocolate, coarsely chopped
¾ cup (1½ sticks) unsalted butter
1¼ cups all-purpose flour
1 teaspoon baking powder
¼ teaspoon salt
1¾ cups sugar
4 eggs
2 teaspoons vanilla
Chocolate Frosting (recipe follows)

1. Heat oven to 350°. Coat a 15 x 10 x 1-inch jelly-roll pan with nonstick cooking spray.

2. Melt chocolate and butter in top of a double boiler over simmering water, stirring until smooth.

3. Stir together flour, baking powder and salt in a small bowl.

4. Stir together sugar, eggs, vanilla and chocolate mixture in a medium-size bowl. Beat in flour mixture. Spread in prepared pan.

5. Bake in heated 350° oven 15 to 20 minutes or until dry-looking on top and firm to the touch.

6. Cool in pan on a wire rack. Spread evenly with Chocolate Frosting. Let stand until set, about 30 minutes. Cut into bars.

Chocolate frosting

Combine 2 cups sugar; ⅔ cup milk; ½ cup (1 stick) unsalted butter at room temperature, cut into pieces; 4 squares (1 ounce each) unsweetened chocolate, chopped, and 2 tablespoons light corn syrup in a medium-size saucepan. Bring to boiling over medium-high heat; cook 1 minute. Remove from heat. Stir in 1½ teaspoons vanilla extract. Cool to room temperature. Beat with a mixer until a spreading consistency, 4 to 6 minutes. Makes about 2½ cups.

Super-chunk brownies
opposite

Frosted brownies
opposite

Dalmation bars
page 473

Toffee blondies

Blondies are brownies but without the chocolate. The toffee bits can be replaced quite successfully with chocolate chips or butterscotch chips.

Per blondie

200 calories, 2 g protein, 11 g fat, 24 g carbohydrate, 111 mg sodium, 45 mg cholesterol.

1½ cups all-purpose flour
1 teaspoon baking powder
¼ teaspoon salt
½ cup (1 stick) unsalted butter, at room temperature
¾ cup packed light-brown sugar
¼ cup granulated sugar
2 eggs
2 teaspoons vanilla
¼ cup plus 2 tablespoons coarsely chopped pecans
½ cup toffee bits

1. Heat oven to 350°. Coat a 13 x 9 x 2-inch baking pan with nonstick cooking spray.

2. Stir together flour, baking powder and salt in a small bowl.

3. Beat butter with both sugars in a medium-size bowl until fluffy. Add eggs, one at a time, beating well after each addition. Beat in vanilla, then flour mixture. Fold in ¼ cup pecans and toffee bits. Scrape into pan, spreading evenly. Sprinkle with remaining chopped pecans.

4. Bake in heated 350° oven 25 to 30 minutes or until a wooden pick inserted in center comes out clean. Cool in pan on a wire rack. Cut into bars.

Chewy granola bars

Ideal as the dessert to go with a portable lunch, as a super-energizing snack or a fast breakfast, this has all the good stuff: coconut, raisins, chocolate, almonds and honey.

Per bar

98 calories, 1 g protein, 4 g fat, 17 g carbohydrate, 20 mg sodium, 3 mg cholesterol.

½ cup plus 2 tablespoons packed light-brown sugar
¼ cup plus 2 tablespoons honey
1 teaspoon vanilla
¼ cup (½ stick) unsalted butter
3 cups low-fat granola mix (not cereal)
½ cup sweetened flake coconut
½ cup golden raisins
¾ cup mini semisweet chocolate chips
½ cup slivered almonds

1. Combine brown sugar, honey, vanilla and butter in a medium-size saucepan. Bring to boiling over medium heat. Lower heat; simmer 2 minutes or until sugar is dissolved. Cool.

2. Meanwhile, combine granola, coconut, raisins, ½ cup chocolate chips and almonds in a large bowl.

3. Stir brown sugar mixture into granola mixture. Spread in a 13 x 9 x 2-inch baking pan. Press remaining chocolate chips into top.

4. Refrigerate 2 hours or until completely cooled. Cut into bars.

Peaches and cream bars

Makes 2 dozen bars *Prep* 20 minutes *Bake* at 350° for 40 minutes

A graham cracker crust, a cream cheese filling with a peach preserves glaze, and an almond streusel topping. Better make an extra batch since the first will probably vanish quickly.

Per bar
219 calories, 3 g protein, 12 g fat, 26 g carbohydrate, 107 mg sodium, 44 mg cholesterol.

30 graham cracker squares
  (15 whole graham crackers)
⅓ cup plus ½ cup granulated sugar
½ cup sliced almonds
6 tablespoons unsalted butter
  (¾ stick), melted
12 ounces cream cheese,
  at room temperature
2 eggs
1 teaspoon vanilla

Topping
2 tablespoons cold unsalted butter,
  cut into pieces
¼ cup packed light-brown sugar
½ cup sliced almonds
2 tablespoons all-purpose flour

1 jar (13 ounces) peach preserves

1. Heat oven to 350°. Coat a 13 x 9 x 2-inch baking pan with nonstick cooking spray.

2. Combine graham crackers, ⅓ cup granulated sugar and almonds in a food processor or blender. Process until well combined. Pour in melted butter. Process until crumbs hold together. Press over bottom of prepared pan.

3. Bake in heated 350° oven 10 minutes or until lightly colored.

4. Meanwhile, beat together cream cheese and ½ cup granulated sugar in a large bowl until smooth. Add eggs, one at a time, beating well after each addition. Beat in vanilla.

5. Remove crust from oven. Pour in cream cheese mixture; spread evenly. Return to oven. Bake 15 minutes or until slightly puffed. Leave oven on.

6. Prepare topping: Crumble together cold butter, brown sugar, sliced almonds and flour in a bowl.

7. Remove pan from oven. Stir preserves to break up clumps. Gently spread peach preserves over top of creem cheese filling. Sprinkle with topping. Bake another 15 minutes or until hot and bubbly. Cool completely in pan on a wire rack. For firmer bars, chill in refrigerator. Cut into bars.

Candy cane puffs

Makes 4 dozen cookies   *Prep* 10 minutes   *Refrigerate* 1 hour   *Bake* at 375° for 10 to 12 minutes

White chocolate and candy canes are a magical combination.

Per cookie
83 calories, 1 g protein, 4 g fat, 11 g carbohydrate, 19 mg sodium, 10 mg cholesterol.

2½ cups all-purpose flour
¼ teaspoon salt
½ cup (1 stick) unsalted butter, at room temperature
1 cup confectioners' sugar
1 egg

½ teaspoon peppermint extract
½ teaspoon vanilla
8 squares (1 ounce each) white chocolate, melted
½ cup finely crushed candy canes

1. Stir together flour and salt in a medium-size bowl.

2. Beat butter and confectioners' sugar in a large bowl until smooth and creamy. Beat in egg. Mix in peppermint extract and vanilla.

3. Beat in flour mixture. Cover dough with plastic wrap; refrigerate 1 hour.

4. Heat oven to 375°.

5. Shape dough into 1-inch balls; place on lightly greased baking sheets.

6. Bake in heated 375° oven 10 to 12 minutes or until bottoms are lightly browned. Remove cookies to wire racks to cool completely.

7. To coat, brush each cookie with melted white chocolate; dip lightly in crushed candy canes. Place on waxed paper to harden.

Candy cane puffs

Lebkuchen
opposite

Lebkuchen

Makes 3½ dozen cookies   *Prep* 20 minutes   *Refrigerate* 1 to 2 hours   *Bake* at 400° for 7 to 9 minutes

These famous German cakelike cookies are seasoned with a blend of aromatic spices and sweetened with honey and molasses.

Per cookie
103 calories, 1 g protein, 2 g fat, 20 g carbohydrate, 43 mg sodium, 8 mg cholesterol.

½ cup honey
½ cup molasses
¾ cup packed light-brown sugar
¼ cup (½ stick) unsalted butter
½ cup candied orange rind pieces
½ cup sliced almonds
1 tablespoon grated lemon rind
1 egg, lightly beaten
2½ cups all-purpose flour
1 teaspoon baking powder
½ teaspoon baking soda
¼ teaspoon salt
1 teaspoon ground cinnamon
1 teaspoon ground nutmeg
1 teaspoon ground ginger
½ teaspoon ground cloves
½ teaspoon ground allspice
42 whole blanched almonds
    Simple Sugar Glaze (recipe follows)

1. Combine honey, molasses, brown sugar and butter in a medium-size saucepan. Cook over medium heat until sugar is melted and mixture almost comes to a boil. Stir in candied orange rind, sliced almonds and lemon rind. Cool slightly. Stir in egg.

2. Stir together flour, baking powder, baking soda, salt, cinnamon, nutmeg, ginger, cloves and allspice in a medium-size bowl. Stir into honey mixture. Cover dough with plastic wrap; refrigerate 1 to 2 hours.

3. Heat oven to 400°.

4. Shape dough into 1-inch balls. Place on lightly greased baking sheets, 3 inches apart. Using a fingertip, press each lightly to make an indent ¼ inch deep. (If dough is sticky, wet fingers.) Place an almond in center of each cookie.

5. Bake in heated 400° oven until firm in center and a wooden pick inserted in a cookie comes out not quite clean, 7 to 9 minutes.

6. Spread Simple Sugar Glaze on warm cookies. Place on wire racks to cool.

Simple sugar glaze

Stir together 1 cup confectioners' sugar, ½ teaspoon lemon extract and 2 tablespoons water in a small bowl until a good spreading consistency, adding more water if needed. Makes 1 cup.

Cherry drops

Makes 3 dozen cookies   *Prep* 20 minutes   *Bake* at 350° for 10 to 12 minutes

Candied fruit lovers, sit up and take notice! These bite-size cookies are a luscious treat, full of glacé cherries and pineapple as well as shredded coconut.

Per cookie
64 calories, 1 g protein, 3 g fat, 10 g carbohydrate, 41 mg sodium, 8 mg cholesterol.

1¼ cups all-purpose flour
½ teaspoon baking powder
¼ teaspoon salt
3 tablespoons unsalted butter
3 tablespoons margarine
½ cup sugar

1 egg
½ teaspoon rum extract
¼ cup chopped glacé pineapple
½ cup sweetened flake coconut
36 glacé cherry halves

1. Stir together flour, baking powder and salt on a sheet of waxed paper.

2. Beat together butter, margarine and sugar in a medium-size bowl until creamy. Beat in egg and rum extract until well blended. Stir in flour mixture, glacé pineapple and coconut. Shape into a disc; cover with plastic wrap. Refrigerate several hours or overnight.

3. Heat oven to 350°.

4. For each cookie, drop a rounded teaspoon of dough onto an ungreased baking sheet. Top each cookie with a glacé cherry half.

5. Bake in heated 350° oven 10 to 12 minutes. Remove cookies to a wire rack to cool.

Coconut snowballs

Makes 2 dozen cookies   *Prep* 10 minutes   *Bake* at 325° for 20 to 25 minutes

Not for tossing! Crunchy balls of meringue filled with flaky coconut.

Per cookie
73 calories, 1 g protein, 3 g fat, 11 g carbohydrate, 57 mg sodium, 0 mg cholesterol.

4 egg whites
¼ teaspoon salt
⅔ cup sugar
1 teaspoon vanilla

¼ cup all-purpose flour
3 cups lightly packed sweetened flake coconut

1. Heat oven to 325°. Coat 2 baking sheets with nonstick cooking spray.

2. Beat egg whites in a large bowl until stiff, but not dry, peaks form. Beat in salt, sugar, vanilla and flour. Stir in coconut. Drop dough by rounded teaspoonfuls, 1 inch apart, on prepared baking sheets.

3. Bake in heated 325° oven 20 to 25 minutes or until lightly browned. Let cookies cool briefly on baking sheets. Remove to wire racks to cool.

Almond squares

Makes 32 squares   *Prep* 10 minutes   *Bake* at 325° for 35 to 40 minutes

A luscious almond cookie crust topped with a firm almond-flavored custard means you can't eat just one. Nuts that have been blanched means the dark, papery, bitter-tasting skin has been removed.

Per square
144 calories, 3 g protein, 7 g fat, 17 g carbohydrate, 60 mg sodium, 41 mg cholesterol.

Cookie base
1¾ cups all-purpose flour
¾ cup confectioners' sugar
½ teaspoon salt
½ cup (1 stick) cold unsalted butter, cut into pieces
1 egg
8 ounces sliced blanched almonds

Cookie topping
4 eggs
¾ cup dark corn syrup
⅓ cup firmly packed light-brown sugar
⅓ cup amaretto liqueur

1. Heat oven to 325°. Grease a 13 x 9 x 2-inch baking pan.

2. Combine flour, confectioners' sugar and salt in a large bowl. Cut in butter with a pastry blender or 2 knives used scissor fashion until coarse crumbs form. Stir in egg until mixture sticks together. Knead slightly in bowl until a ball forms. Press mixture evenly in prepared pan; sprinkle with almonds.

3. In same bowl, beat eggs, corn syrup, brown sugar and liqueur until well blended. Pour over cookie base.

4. Bake in heated 325° oven 35 to 40 minutes or until a knife inserted in center comes out clean. Remove pan to a wire rack and cool completely before cutting into squares or diamonds.

Meringue drops

Makes 2 dozen cookies   *Prep* 10 minutes   *Bake* at 250° for 55 to 60 minutes

Heavenly! That's the only way to describe miniature crunchy meringues that melt in your mouth.
Shown on page 415.

Per cookie
35 calories, 1 g protein, 0 g fat, 8 g carbohydrate, 33 mg sodium, 0 mg cholesterol.

4 egg whites
¼ teaspoon salt
¼ teaspoon cream of tartar

1 cup granulated sugar
Red decorating sugar
Green decorating sugar

1. Heat oven to 250°. Butter and flour 2 baking sheets.

2. Beat egg whites in a medium-size bowl until frothy. Add salt and cream of tartar; beat until soft peaks form. Continue beating, gradually adding granulated sugar, until meringue is stiff and glossy.

3. Spoon meringue into a pastry bag fitted with a large star tip. Pipe out stars, 1 inch apart, onto prepared baking sheets. Sprinkle with decorating sugar.

4. Bake in heated 250° oven 55 to 60 minutes or until firm but not browned. Remove cookies to wire racks to cool.

Chocolate chewies

Makes 4½ dozen   *Prep* 15 minutes   *Bake* at 375° for 8 to 11 minutes

Colorful candies dot these chewy cookies like confetti.

Per cookie

387 calories, 4 g protein, 7 g fat, 55 g carbohydrate, 427 mg sodium, 58 mg cholesterol.

2½ cups all-purpose flour
¾ cup unsweetened cocoa powder
1 teaspoon baking powder
¼ teaspoon salt
1 cup (2 sticks) unsalted butter, at room temperature
¾ cup packed light-brown sugar
¾ cup granulated sugar
2 eggs
2 teaspoons vanilla
¼ cup hot brewed coffee
1 cup red and green candy-coated chocolate pieces
½ cup toasted pine nuts

1. Heat oven to 375°.

2. Sift together flour, cocoa powder, baking powder and salt in a medium-size bowl.

3. Beat butter in a large bowl until creamy. Beat in brown and granulated sugars until light and fluffy. Beat in eggs, one at a time, then vanilla.

4. Beat flour mixture into butter mixture. Stir in hot coffee. Fold in chocolate pieces and pine nuts.

5. Drop dough by heaping tablespoonfuls onto ungreased baking sheets. Bake in heated 375° oven 8 to 11 minutes or until set. Let cool slightly on baking sheet. Transfer cookies to wire racks to cool completely.

Ginger cookie pops

Makes 18 cookies   *Prep* 15 minutes   *Freeze* 30 minutes   *Bake* at 350° for 10 minutes

Let the whole family and even the neighbors join together in this decorating party. They look like lollipops, but they're really molassey ginger cookies, decorated as far as your imagination will take you.

Per cookie

234 calories, 3 g protein, 11 g fat, 32 g carbohydrate, 213 mg sodium, 39 mg cholesterol.

3 cups all-purpose flour
1½ teaspoons baking soda
¾ teaspoon salt
1 cup (2 sticks) unsalted butter, at room temperature
⅔ cup packed light-brown sugar
⅔ cup light molasses
2 teaspoons ground cinnamon
2 teaspoons ground ginger
1 teaspoon ground cloves
1 egg
18 lollipop sticks (8 inches long)
   Royal Icing (recipe, page 444)
   Paste food colors

1. Combine flour, baking soda and salt in a medium-size bowl.

2. Beat butter, brown sugar, molasses, cinnamon, ginger, cloves and egg in a large bowl until fluffy. Stir in flour mixture. Divide dough in half and shape each half into a disc. Cover with plastic wrap; freeze 30 minutes.

3. Heat oven to 350°. Coat 2 baking sheets with nonstick cooking spray. Place lollipop sticks, 3 inches apart, on prepared baking sheets.

For best results, follow these tips.

• Paste food colors will tint icing the richest, deepest hues. Use a clean wooden pick to dip into color, then into icing. Stir to mix.

• When glazing and piping, divide the icing. To make a glaze suitable for a base coat, thin one portion slightly with water, a drop at a time, until its consistency is that of sour cream. For piping, leave the other portion thicker so it holds a line or shape.

• Use a fine-tipped paintbrush to apply a base coat of the thinner icing. Let it dry thoroughly. Then, to decorate, use a pastry bag fitted with a writing tip to pipe on the thicker icing.

4. On a floured surface, with a floured rolling pin, roll out dough until ¼ inch thick. Cut out rounds with a 4-inch cutter or 1-pound coffee can. Reroll scraps. Press cookies onto top third of sticks, like a lollipop.

5. Bake in heated 350° oven 10 minutes or until lightly browned around edges. Cool cookies on baking sheets on wire racks 5 minutes. Remove cookies to racks to cool completely.

6. Stir extra water into icing, drop by drop, to create a good flowing consistency. Divide into batches; tint with different colors. Decorate cookies as shown or as desired. Let dry.

Ginger cookie pops
opposite

Meltaways

Makes 4½ dozen cookies   *Prep* 15 minutes   *Refrigerate* 1 to 2 hours   *Bake* at 325° for 19 to 20 minutes

The recipe title says it all. Buttery pecan cookies are everybody's favorite. Careful—you can easily eat more than one.

Per cookie
67 calories, 1 g protein, 5 g fat, 6 g carbohydrate, 1 mg sodium, 9 mg cholesterol.

1 cup (2 sticks) unsalted butter, at room temperature
1 cup confectioners' sugar
2 teaspoons vanilla

2 cups all-purpose flour
1 cup finely ground pecans
Confectioners' sugar for dusting

1. Beat together butter and confectioners' sugar in a medium-size bowl until smooth and creamy. Add vanilla. Beat in flour and nuts. Cover dough with plastic wrap; refrigerate until firm, 1 to 2 hours.

2. Heat oven to 325°.

3. Pinch off pieces of dough in rounded teaspoonfuls. Roll into logs. Taper ends; bend into crescents. Place on an ungreased baking sheet.

4. Bake in heated 325° oven 19 to 20 minutes or until lightly browned.

5. Remove cookies to a wire rack. Sprinkle with a heavy layer of confectioners' sugar. Cool completely. Sprinkle again with confectioners' sugar.

Mexican wedding cakes

Makes 2 dozen cookies   *Prep* 20 minutes   *Bake* at 375° for 13 to 14 minutes

Crumbly and delicate. These cookies are very "short," which means they have a high ratio of fat, in this case butter, to flour.

Per cookie
115 calories, 1 g protein, 8 g fat, 10 g carbohydrate, 50 mg sodium, 21 mg cholesterol.

1 cup (2 sticks) unsalted butter, at room temperature
½ cup confectioners' sugar
2¼ cups all-purpose flour

½ teaspoon salt
1 teaspoon vanilla
Confectioners' sugar for rolling

1. Heat oven to 375°.

2. Beat butter with a wooden spoon in a medium-size bowl until creamy. Gradually beat in confectioners' sugar until smooth. Beat in flour, salt and vanilla; mixture will be stiff.

3. Pinch off small pieces of dough with moistened fingers; roll into 1-inch balls. Place, 2 inches apart, on ungreased baking sheets.

4. Bake in heated 375° oven 13 to 14 minutes or until bottoms are golden. Do not let tops brown. Remove to a wire rack to cool slightly, then roll in confectioners' sugar. Return to rack to cool completely.

Venetians

Makes 6 dozen cookies   *Prep* 30 minutes   *Bake* at 350° for 15 minutes   *Assembly* 20 minutes

Refrigerate overnight

The layers of color take their inspiration from the beautiful handblown glass made in Venice. You can decorate the top of each cookie with a simple tube frosting or tinted homemade frosting piped into a design.

Per cookie

98 calories, 1 g protein, 6 g fat, 11 g carbohydrate, 14 mg sodium, 22 mg cholesterol.

1 can (8 ounces) almond paste
1½ cups (3 sticks) unsalted butter, at room temperature
1 cup sugar
4 eggs, separated
1 teaspoon almond extract
2 cups sifted all-purpose flour

¼ teaspoon salt
10 drops green food coloring
8 drops red food coloring
1 jar (12 ounces) apricot preserves
5 squares (1 ounce each) semisweet chocolate

1. Heat oven to 350°. Grease three 13 x 9 x 2-inch baking pans; line with waxed paper; grease paper.

2. Break up almond paste in a large bowl with a fork. Add butter, sugar, egg yolks and almond extract. Beat until fluffy, 5 minutes. Beat in flour and salt.

3. Beat egg whites in a large bowl until stiff peaks form. Stir into almond mixture with a wooden spoon, using a turning motion similar to folding.

4. Remove 1½ cups batter; spread evenly in one prepared pan. Remove another 1½ cups batter to a small bowl; tint green with food coloring. Spread in second pan. Tint remaining 1½ cups batter pink. Spread in remaining pan.

5. Bake in heated 350° oven 15 minutes or until edges are lightly golden; layers will each be ¼ inch thick. Immediately turn layers out onto large wire racks. Carefully peel off waxed paper. Cool.

6. Place pink layer on an inverted jelly-roll pan. Heat and strain preserves. Spread half of strained preserves over pink layer. Top with yellow layer. Spread with remaining preserves. Cover with green layer, top side up.

7. Cover with plastic wrap. Weight down with a large wooden cutting board, heavy flat tray or large book. Refrigerate overnight.

8. Melt chocolate in a bowl over simmering water in a saucepan. Trim edges of stacked layers even. Cut crosswise into 1-inch-wide strips. Frost pink layer of one strip with chocolate. Frost green layer of second strip. Continue frosting alternating pink and green layers. Let chocolate dry; then cut into 1-inch pieces.

Cappuccino blossoms

Makes 2 dozen cookies *Prep* 20 minutes *Refrigerate* several hours *Bake* at 350° for 10 to 12 minutes

Great with coffee—or better yet, cappuccino!

Per cookie

86 calories, 1 g protein, 4 g fat, 12 g carbohydrate, 54 mg sodium, 13 mg cholesterol.

1¼ cups all-purpose flour
½ teaspoons baking powder
¼ teaspoon salt
2 teaspoons instant espresso coffee powder
¼ teaspoon ground cinnamon
3 tablespoons unsalted butter

3 tablespoons margarine
½ cup sugar
1 egg
½ teaspoon vanilla
   Vanilla Buttercream Frosting (recipe, page 443)
   Chocolate-covered espresso beans

1. Stir together flour, baking powder, salt, espresso powder and cinnamon on a sheet of waxed paper.

2. Beat together butter, margarine and sugar in a large bowl until creamy. Beat in egg and vanilla until well blended. Stir in flour mixture. Shape into a disc; cover with plastic wrap. Refrigerate several hours or overnight.

3. Heat oven to 350°.

4. Place dough in a cookie gun fitted with a flower template or a pastry bag fitted with a large star tip. Press out or pipe dough onto ungreased baking sheets. Bake in heated 350° oven 10 to 12 minutes.

5. Remove cookies to wire racks to cool completely. Spoon a small dab of frosting on each cookie and top with a chocolate-covered espresso bean.

Chocolate sandwich cookies

Makes 3 dozen cookies *Prep* 15 minutes *Refrigerate* 3 to 4 hours *Bake* at 375° for 8 to 10 minutes

Even without the filling, just on their own, these cookies are so-o-o good.

Per cookie

115 calories, 1 g protein, 5 g fat, 16 g carbohydrate, 46 mg sodium, 20 mg cholesterol.

1¼ cups all-purpose flour
½ cup unsweetened cocoa powder
¾ teaspoon baking soda
¼ teaspoon salt
1 cup granulated sugar
½ cup (1 stick) unsalted butter, at room temperature
1 egg
½ teaspoon vanilla
¼ teaspoon mint extract

Filling

2½ cups sifted confectioners' sugar
½ cup (1 stick) unsalted butter, at room temperature
2 tablespoons milk
½ teaspoon mint extract
   Red food coloring
   Green food coloring

1. Sift together flour, cocoa powder, baking soda and salt into a medium-size bowl; set aside. In a large bowl, beat together sugar and butter until smooth and creamy. Beat in egg, then vanilla and mint extract.

2. Beat flour mixture into butter mixture. Divide dough in half; shape each into a log about 1½ inches in diameter. Cover with plastic wrap; refrigerate 3 to 4 hours.

3. Heat oven to 375°. Cut each log into 3/16-inch-thick slices; place on ungreased baking sheets.

4. Bake in heated 375° oven 8 to 10 minutes or until almost firm. Remove cookies to a wire rack to cool.

5. Prepare filling: Beat together confectioners' sugar, butter, milk and mint extract in a medium-size bowl until a good spreading consistency. Divide filling in half; tint half with red food coloring, and other half with green food coloring.

6. Spread flat side of one-quarter of the cookies with red filling and one-quarter with green filling. Top each with a plain cookie. Chill until set.

Chocolate sandwich cookies

Party-planning time line

Whether you're entertaining a few friends or a crowd, good planning makes the party go smoothly.

4 weeks ahead

- Decide what kind of party you want. Make a guest list.
- Write a to-do list with dates and times.
- Book a caterer and arrange for rentals if necessary. (During holidays, contact the caterer at least a month ahead; six weeks is even better.)

3 weeks ahead

- Invite your guests. Allow one week for the invitations to arrive by mail. During the busy winter holiday season, invite guests extra early.

2 weeks ahead

- Finalize your menu. Draft a shopping list of everything you'll need, from food to candles to bathroom tissue. Confirm the caterer if applicable.
- Purchase the groceries for make-ahead recipes. Prepare and freeze whatever possible.

1 week ahead

- Buy nonperishables, including liquor, wine, soda, mixers, flour, sugar, canned goods, aluminum foil, plastic cups, and paper towels.

1 to 3 days ahead

- Clean and decorate the house; polish the silver; press the tablecloth.
- Buy perishable food and any nonperishables you forgot to buy earlier.
- Make extra room in your refrigerator.
- Prepare any recipes that can be made fully or partially this far in advance.
- Confirm again with the caterer and rental company.

1 day ahead

- Cook all food that can possibly be prepared now.
- Remove all prepared food from the freezer; thaw overnight in the refrigerator.
- Double-check your list to make sure you have everything you need.
- If displaying flowers, buy and arrange them now.

2 to 8 hours ahead

- Set the table. Position the centerpiece. Set all serving pieces nearby.
- Prepare any dishes that don't require a lot of last-minute attention.
- Arrange any platters of food that will be served cold.

30 minutes to 2 hours ahead

- Empty the dishwasher and then get dressed and rest.
- Quickly survey the table arrangements, beverages, and food; make any last-minute adjustments as needed. Add any needed garnishes to food.
- Put out any foods that are to be served at room temperature.
- Line up appropriate musical selections so they're ready to play.

Table decorating ideas

Inspiration for terrific tablesettings lurks everywhere—in your garden, at the market, even in the attic.

• Be sure to keep flowers or other centerpieces low enough so that guests can easily see each other. Ditto for candles.

• Accent floral arrangements with touches of the season, such as dried leaves and berries.

• For a holiday centerpiece, fill an attractive bowl with multicolored glass ornaments or a combination of fruit, nuts and pinecones.

• Place a small potted herb at each place. Tie each container with a pretty ribbon. Offer the plants as party favors.

• For a buffet, roll flatware in large cloth napkins, tie with decorative cord, and stack in a big basket.

• Go for drama by sticking to all one color for flowers—all white or all red, for example.

Selecting a dinner menu

No matter what the style of the dinner, welcome your guests with a light nibble to set the stage and take the edge off their hunger. This can be as simple as chips and dip or as fancy as smoked salmon canapés.

For a formal sit-down dinner plan on serving a minimum of three courses—an appetizer, a main course and a dessert. The rule of thumb is if the main course is substantial, such as a roast with lots of vegetable accompaniments, the appetizer and desserts should be relatively light. On the other hand, if you have your heart set on serving a triple-rich chocolate fudge cake, start with a generous appetizer, then serve a light main course such as broiled fish or chicken. Afterward, with a clear conscience, present your extravagant finale.

For a casual buffet everything that goes on the buffet table should generally go together since everything is served at one time. Try to avoid foods with lots of sauce—they tend to make a guest's plate a gloppy mess. The best foods for buffets are roasts, salads, baked pasta and any food that can be served in individual pieces, such as shrimp or chicken.

For a cocktail party everyone will be holding a drink, so whatever you serve must be easy to eat with the remaining hand. Don't make it bigger than one or two bites. Salty and spicy foods tend to complement drinks best, which is why chips and dip are naturals. Skip juicy nibbles that will wind up dripping down a sleeve. Ham, smoked fish, cheese and hors d'oeuvres spiked with soy sauce are good choices.

Entertaining do's and don'ts

Do ask invited guests about any dietary restrictions.

Don't ask people to BYOB, unless you still live with college roommates.

Do have someone behind the table to serve at a large buffet. Otherwise, before long the food display will look like the day after a huge white sale.

Don't depend on people to bring wine—they may decide to treat you to their latest "discovery."

Do expect the unexpected; have extra food and place settings ready in case someone brings a surprise guest.

Don't set up the bar and buffet next to each other, or you'll need to call in a traffic cop to keep the crowd moving.

Do use your best china and silver for formal dinners. Isn't that what it's for?

Don't use scented candles; they'll detract from the flavor of the food.

Do keep the room cool before guests arrive—a crowded party will quickly generate more than enough heat.

Don't experiment on your guests by making dishes that you've never made before. That's what family is for.

Do clear away plates, glasses and utensils at a buffet as soon as people are done using them.

Don't delay dinner for latecomers—it's not fair to your other guests, not to mention the effect on the food. Instead, let them feast on what's left.

Do wait to clear the table at a sit-down dinner until everyone is done.

Don't apologize for your food, even if it hasn't come out quite right.

Spice	Meat/Poultry	Sauces/Soups	Vegetables	Breads/Desserts
Allspice Flavor reminiscent of cloves, cinnamon and nutmeg. Available ground or as dried berries to grind.	Use sparingly as an accent on roast beef or pork and in stuffing.	Shake a little into orange juice; sprinkle on fruit salad.	Bake winter squash with a pinch on top; add to glazed carrots.	Whisk a bit into applesauce or waffle or pancake batter; sprinkle in fruit or pumpkin pie fillings.
Cinnamon Sweet, warm, nutty, pleasantly scented. Available in sticks or ground.	Stir into moussaka and other Middle Eastern lamb dishes; good as a rub on pork ribs or on chicken in Indian fare.	Add a pinch to pureed fruit soups, chutneys or white sauce for lamb or pork.	Add a pinch to melted butter, then toss with cooked Hubbard or acorn squash, carrots, peas, spinach or onions.	Mix with sugar and sprinkle on toast; add to pies; use sticks to stir creamy drinks.
Cloves Medicinal, pungent. Available ground or whole.	Pierce onions with whole cloves to flavor stews.	Add ground to homemade fruit chutneys or use to flavor prepared varieties.	Add a pinch to mashed sweet potatoes along with butter or cream and some brown sugar.	Blend ground into smoothies, puddings and cakes, especially gingerbread.
Cumin Strong, hot, slightly bitter. Available ground or as whole seeds.	Grind and add to chili, fajitas, taco filling; add a small amount to chicken salad.	Sauté ground with garlic and ginger; add to sauce of pan juices.	Add ground to stir-fry of onions, string beans and carrots; mash into black beans.	Add crunch to homemade bread by sprinkling seeds on the crust before baking.
Fennel seed Warm, sweet, licorice-like. Seeds can be used whole, crushed or ground.	Crush and rub onto steaks or fish before grilling; stir whole into homemade sausage.	Heat whole seeds along with onion and garlic for base of pasta sauce; also good in minestrone.	Give tomato relish or cabbage dishes a spark with whole seeds.	Scatter seeds on rolls before baking; crush or grind and add to cake or scone batter.
Ginger Spicy-sweet, hot. Available fresh, in crystallized chunks or dried and ground.	Mince fresh for chicken, beef or pork stir-fries.	Use a pinch to bring up flavor of gravy for roast pork, veal or beef, or to highlight chicken broth.	Sweeten carrots or winter squash with brown sugar and grated fresh or ground ginger.	Mince crystallized and beat into cookie dough; add ground or fresh to cake batter, rice pudding or whipped cream.
Nutmeg Sweet, warm. Available whole or ground.	Grate whole to add to cheese filling in lasagna, or use in ground-meat dishes.	Grate whole to add to simmering white béchamel sauce.	Add a dusting to steamed broccoli or spinach.	Grate and add to pancake batter or eggnog; stir into spiced fruit.
Paprika Rich, earthy flavor. Available ground in hot, mild and sweet varieties.	Add to sautéing sliced onions for traditional goulash or chicken paprikash.	Prepare dressing for egg salad or deviled eggs with a pinch of hot version.	Top homemade or store-bought potato salad with a sprinkling.	
Black peppercorns Hot, biting; best when freshly ground.	Press coarsely ground onto steaks or roasts.	Work ground pepper into soft butter, then freeze; grind over cream soups.	Mix ground pepper with lemon juice for Brussels sprouts or green beans.	Use whole to stud top of bread before baking; add ground to ginger or spice cookie doughs.
Red pepper flakes Spicy, warm; may be mild or intense; also may be called crushed red pepper.	Combine with cumin, salt and pepper as a rub for grilled or broiled steaks and chicken breasts.	Add to tomato-based pasta sauces, with a generous hand for spicy arrabbiata.	Toss with cooked spinach or broccoli.	Place on top of focaccia or pizza.

490

Herb	Meat	Poultry	Seafood	Miscellaneous
Basil Flavor hints of mint, cloves, anise; fresh is very fragrant; dried is more pungent.	Wrap leaves around beef kabobs; add to homemade sausage or stew.	Slide leaves under skin with butter; stir chopped into stir-fries and sauces just before serving.	Toss chopped fresh into seafood salad; slice into thin strips and roll up inside fillets.	Grows easily in garden; use for pesto; garnish pizza and soup; layer fresh mozzarella with leaves.
Bay leaf Slightly bitter, aromatic; intensifies when dried.	Tuck into stews, pot roasts or casseroles; good with game such as venison.	Simmer wine-based stews with 1 or 2 leaves; add to chicken potpies.	Skewer with scallops; stir into seafood-tomato stews.	Add at beginning of cooking; always remove before serving.
Dill Light, mild, lemony; fresh offers more punch than dried.	Mix with sour cream and use to season beef.	Stir into mustard and spread on chicken breasts; also good in cream sauces for poultry.	Arrange fresh over cold salmon; add to tuna salad; place sprigs in whole fish before roasting.	Add to pickling mixtures; stir into yogurt or sour cream sauces for potato or cucumber salads.
Mint Cool, refreshing; significantly more flavorful when fresh.	Use fresh as an accent for grilled beef or lamb or mix into ground lamb.	Mix with garlic and basil and use to season chicken breasts before grilling.	Mix fresh with a touch of lemon and wine to season whole fish.	Toss fresh into fruit salad or couscous with chopped tomatoes; chew on a small bit to cleanse palate.
Oregano Strong, peppery; stronger dried than fresh. Usually used in conjunction with other seasonings.	Work dried into meatball mixture or any dish that includes sausage; sprinkle over roasts.	Mix dried with lemon and garlic, add to chicken parts to bake with a Greek flair.	Place fresh on fish fillets before grilling; use sparingly in fish or scallop casseroles.	Add to simmering tomato sauce; sprinkle on pizza or sliced tomatoes; stir into salad dressings.
Parsley Grassy, aromatic. Fresh available with curly or flat leaves; flat-leaf is more flavorful than curly; both more so than dried.	Scatter chopped fresh over grilled or sautéed steak.	Cut up fresh and mash with butter; spread under skin. Slip bundle into stock or whole bird.	Chop fresh and toss into kettle of fish chowder; mix with mayonnaise to spread on fish fillets.	Rely on as a flavorful, but not overwhelming, garnish for almost any dish.
Rosemary Piney, bittersweet; equally good dried or fresh.	Crush leaves with garlic and spread on lamb before cooking; insert sprigs into slits cut in pork, then roast.	Lay on top of chicken, then roast or bake; stir into chicken à la king or other saucy dishes.	Insert fresh sprigs in whole fish, then grill or bake.	Use to season roasted vegetables, bean soups, stuffings.
Sage Smoky, woodsy, vaguely bitter; taste strengthens when dried.	Scatter over pork or veal chops before baking; layer with cheese in beef roll-ups.	Layer under chicken skin; use sparingly in chicken soups, salads and chicken-melt sandwiches.	Stir just a little into fish chowders; place whole leaves inside strongly flavored whole fish, then grill.	Blend into buttery pasta or ravioli sauces, baked rice dishes and stuffings for poultry or pork.
Tarragon Sharp with a hint of vanilla, licorice-like; fresh more flavorful than dried.	Combine with minced garlic, then press over leg of lamb; add dried to burgers.	Sauté dried or fresh with chicken cutlets.	Mix into scallop dishes; pair with lemon butter to season all kinds of fish.	Whisk into omelets and other egg dishes, cream sauces and salad dressings; add to potato salad.
Thyme Sweet, lemony-minty; fresh more pungent, but dried retains flavor well.	Stir into beef or lamb stew; add dried to sausages and meat loaf.	Use to season chicken breasts, duck or other game birds before grilling.	Sprinkle over flounder fillets, clam chowder, gumbo and jambalaya; place sprigs inside whole fish before cooking.	Use fresh or dried to season soups, sautéed or baked vegetables, and fresh tomatoes.

491

Mom was right when she told us to wash our hands. It's a simple habit that can prevent a lot trouble. Here are tips to help you shop wisely, keep your kitchen clean and store food properly.

Takeout tactics

Fast foods are great backups when you don't have time to cook. If you don't eat them right away, the same safe-handling rules apply to them as to food you prepare yourself.

• Refrigerate cold food immediately.

• Eat hot food within two hours. If you're going to wait longer, be sure to keep it hot, no cooler than 140°.

• If reheating, be sure food reaches at least 165°.

Supermarket smarts

- Buy only food that's in the best condition, fresh and properly packaged.
- Make sure eggs are not cracked before adding them to your cart.
- Make sure that frozen foods are rock solid, that milk and cheese feel cold to the touch and that canned goods don't have any cracks or dents.
- Add perishables to your shopping cart just before you check out. Bag them together and stow in the back seat of your car, not in the trunk.

Cleaning clues

- Wooden and plastic cutting boards should be sanitized occasionally with a solution of 1 teaspoon liquid chlorine bleach per quart of water. Flood the surface with the solution, let stand several minutes, rinse and then let air dry or pat with paper toweling.
- Wash sponges with hot soapy water, rinse well, squeeze, and let dry. Discard after several weeks of use.
- Wash dishrags in the washing machine with warm water and bleach.

Germ warfare

- Wash your hands before you start to cook. Scrub with warm water and soap for 20 seconds, rinse well, towel dry and use the towel to turn off the faucet.
- Always use an instant-read thermometer to verify that food has reached the correct internal temperature.
- If you defrost meat or poultry in the microwave, cook it right away. The food may have partially cooked while it thawed.
- To cook food safely in the microwave, always cover dishes with plastic wrap that is vented to let out steam. Stir food occasionally, rotate the plate, and let stand to finish cooking as your recipe directs.
- If you sample cooking food with the stirring spoon, be sure to wash the spoon well before putting it back into the pot.

Fridge and freezer do's and don'ts

- DO check the temperature often, with a thermometer that stays in the refrigerator. Set the freezer 0° and the fridge at 40°.
- DON'T overstuff the freezer; air should circulate around the packages.
- DO refrigerate raw meat and poultry in plastic bags so they're never in contact with other foods.
- DO freeze meat and poultry if you don't plan to use it within a few days.
- DON'T thaw frozen foods on the counter. Thaw them in the refrigerator, it takes longer, but it's much safer.
- DON'T store eggs in the refrigerator door. They should be kept in their carton in the coldest part of the refrigerator.

Leftover logic

- Refrigerate or freeze all leftovers no more than two hours after cooking.
- Always use shallow food storage containers to cool food down quickly.
- Before freezing a large cut of meat carve it into serving portions and package them individually.
- Always take the stuffing out of turkey and store it separately.
- Discard food left out at room temperature for more than two hours.

How to know what you need

Making a shopping list based on a recipe can be tricky when some of the ingredients are listed as cut, grated or otherwise transformed. Here are equivalents for some common ingredients.

When the recipe calls for	You need
4 cups shredded cabbage	1 small cabbage
1 cup grated raw carrot	1 large raw carrot
2½ cups sliced carrots	1 pound raw carrots
4 cups cooked cut fresh green beans	1 pound fresh green beans
1 cup chopped onion	1 large onion
4 cups sliced raw potatoes	4 medium potatoes
1 cup chopped sweet pepper	1 large sweet pepper
1 cup chopped tomato	1 large tomato
2 cups canned tomatoes	16 ounce can
4 cups sliced apples	4 medium apples
1 cup mashed banana	3 medium bananas
1 teaspoon grated lemon rind	1 medium lemon
2 tablespoons lemon juice	1 medium lemon
4 teaspoons grated orange rind	1 medium orange
1 cup orange juice	3 medium oranges
4 cups sliced peaches	8 medium peaches
2 cups sliced strawberries	1 pint strawberries
1 cup fresh breadcrumbs	2 slices fresh bread
1 cup bread cubes	2 slices fresh bread
2 cups shredded Swiss or cheddar cheese	8 ounces cheese
4 cups chopped walnuts or pecans	1 pound shelled nuts
3 cups cooked white rice	1 cup raw white rice
2 cups granulated sugar	1 pound granulated sugar
1 cup graham cracker crumbs	7 whole graham crackers
2 cups whipped cream	1 cup heavy cream
1 cup egg whites	6 or 7 large eggs
1 egg white	2 teaspoons egg white powder plus 2 tablespoons water

In a pinch substitutions

It can happen to the best of us: halfway through a recipe, you find you're completely out of a key ingredient. Here's what to do.

When the recipe calls for	You may substitute
1 square unsweetened chocolate	3 tablespoons unsweetened cocoa powder plus 1 tablespoon butter
2 tablespoons flour (for thickening)	1 tablespoon cornstarch
1 cup corn syrup	1 cup sugar plus additional ¼ cup liquid used in recipe
1 cup milk	½ cup evaporated milk plus ½ cup water
1 cup buttermilk or sour milk	1 tablespoon vinegar or lemon juice plus enough milk to make 1 cup
1 cup sour cream (for baking)	1 cup plain yogurt
1 cup firmly packed brown sugar	1 cup sugar plus 2 tablespoons molasses
1 teaspoon lemon juice	¼ teaspoon vinegar (not balsamic)
¼ cup chopped onion	1 tablespoon instant minced onion
1 clove garlic	¼ teaspoon garlic powder
2 cups tomato sauce	¾ cup tomato paste plus 1 cup water
1 tablespoon prepared mustard	1 teaspoon dry mustard plus 1 tablespoon water

Numerals set in bold type indicate photographs.

494

THE EDITORS OF FAMILY CIRCLE would like to thank the entire food team for producing the fabulous recipes that have become the essence of this book: Diane Mogelever, Julie Miltenberger, Patricia Hoffman, Keisha Davis, Robert Yamarone, Michael Tyrell, Patty Santelli, JoAnn Brett and Lauren Huber. Also thanks to frequent contributors Jean Anderson, Marie Bianco, Sylvia Carter, Bea Cihak, Jim Fobel, Libby Hillman, Michael Krondl and Andrew Schloss. More kudos to the writers, editors and designers who bring the recipes to life: David Ricketts, Jonna Gallo and Diane Lamphron. Thanks to Tammy Palazzo for all her encouragement and Eileen Lamadore for her cheery perseverance. And grateful thanks to the entire team at Roundtable Press, without whom there would be no book: Carol Spier, Marsha Melnick, Susan Meyer, Julie Merberg and John Glenn.

PHOTOGRAPHY CREDITS

Melanie Acevedo: pages 175 and 291 (right).

Antonis Achilleos: pages 467, 471 and 490–91.

Steve Cohen: pages 6 (left, right), 10, 59, 97 (all), 98, 103, 122, 127, 147, 194, 203, 220 (all), 275, 298, 316 (all), 323, 384 (all), 390, 407, 415, 418, 435, 449 (all), 464 (all), 478 and 487.

Kari Haavisto: pages 94, 130, 335 and 342.

Brian Hagiwara: pages 2, 7 (right), 54 (left), 70, 79, 83, 87, 91, 142, 159, 166, 174, 182, 186, 215, 235, 242, 247, 303 (left), 411, 414, 426–28 and 439.

Kit Latham: pages 266 and 395.

Steven Mark Needham: pages 25, 51 (all), 80 (all), 118, 121 (all), 189 (all), 294 (all) and 387.

Dean Powell: pages 50, 82, 136 (all), 160 (all), 428 (all) and page 483.

Alan Richardson: pages 3, 6 (middle), 7 (left, middle), 11, 15, 18, 23, 31, 34, 42, 54 (right), 63, 66, 70, 74, 86, 95, 103, 111, 115, 135, 139, 151, 154–55, 162, 171, 179, 198, 207, 211, 219, 223, 226–27, 230, 239, 250, 255, 259, 262, 270–71, 279, 282, 287, 291 (left), 295, 303 (right), 307, 311, 314–5, 318, 326, 331, 347, 351, 355, 362–63, 367, 371, 378, 383, 398, 403, 419, 423, 442, 447, 451, 455, 463, 470 and 475.

Carin Riley: pages 195 and 431.

Mark Thomas: pages 107, 108, 191, 359, 458 and 463.